Management

An introduction

Liz Herring.

Management
An introduction

David Boddy
Robert Paton

FINANCIAL TIMES
Prentice Hall

An imprint of **Pearson Education**

Harlow, England · London · New York · Reading, Massachusetts · San Francisco
Toronto · Don Mills, Ontario · Sydney · Tokyo · Singapore · Hong Kong · Seoul
Taipei · Cape Town · Madrid · Mexico City · Amsterdam · Munich · Paris · Milan

Pearson Education Limited
Edinburgh Gate
Harlow
Essex CM20 2JE
England

and Associated Companies throughout the world

Visit us on the World Wide Web at:
http://www.pearsoneduc.com

Typeset in 9.5/12pt Stone serif
by Goodfellow & Egan, Cambridge

Printed and bound in Great Britain by
Ashford Colour Press Ltd, Gosport, Hampshire

Library of Congress Cataloging-in-Publication Data

Boddy, David
    Management: an introduction / David Boddy, Robert Paton.
        p.   cm.
    Includes bibliographical references and index.
    ISBN 0-13-257098-X (alk. paper)
        1. Management.   I. Paton, Rob.   II. Title.
HD31.B583   1998
658–dc21   97-32792
                                                        CIP

British Library Cataloging in Publication Data

A catalogue record for this book is available from the British
Library
ISBN 0-13-257098-X

10 9 8 7 6 5 4 3
04 03 02 01 00

Contents

Preface

This book is intended for readers who are undertaking their first systematic exposure to the study of management. Most will be first-year undergraduates following courses leading to a qualification in management or business. Some will also be taking an introductory course in management as an element of other qualifications, for example in engineering, accountancy, law, information technology, science, nursing or social work. The book should also be useful to readers with a first degree or equivalent qualification in a non-management subject who are taking further studies leading to Certificate, Diploma or MBA qualifications.

The book has three main objectives:

▶ To provide newcomers to the formal study of management with an introduction to the topic.
▶ To show that ideas on management can apply to most areas of human activity, not just to commercial enterprises.
▶ To make the topic attractive to students from many backgrounds and with diverse career intentions.

Most research and reflection on management has focused on commercial organisations. However, there are now many people working in the public sector and in not-for-profit organisations (charities, pressure groups, voluntary organisations and so on) which have begun to adapt management ideas to their own areas of work. This text reflects this wider interest and practice – it should be as useful to those who plan to enter public or not-for-profit work as to those entering the commercial sector.

European perspective

We present the ideas from a European perspective. While many management concepts have developed in the United States, the text encourages readers to consider how their particular context shapes management practice. There are significant cultural differences between countries and organisations and we aim to alert the reader to these – not only as part of an increasingly integrated Europe but also as part of a wider international management community. Hence the text recognises European experience and research in management. The case studies and other material build an awareness of cultural diversity and the implications of this for working in organisations with different managerial styles and backgrounds.

Integrated perspective

To help the reader to see management as a coherent whole, the material is presented within an integrative model of management and demonstrates the relationships between the many academic perspectives. The intention is to help the reader to see management as an integrating activity relating to the organisation as a whole, rather than as something confined to any one disciplinary or functional perspective.

While the text aims to introduce readers to the traditional mainstream perspectives on management which form the basis of each chapter, it also recognises that there is a newer body of ideas which looks at developments such as the weakening of national boundaries and the spread of information technology. Since they will affect the organisations in which readers will spend their working lives, these newer perspectives are introduced where appropriate. The text also recognises the more critical perspectives which some writers now take towards management and organisational activities. These are part of the intellectual world in which management takes place and have important practical implications for the way that people interpret their role within organisations. These perspectives are introduced at several points within the text.

Relating to personal experience

The text assumes that many readers will have little if any experience of managing in conventional organisations, and equally little prior knowledge of relevant evidence and theory. However, all will have experience of being managed and of managing activities in their domestic and social lives. Wherever possible the book encourages readers to use and share such experiences from everyday life in order to explore the ideas presented. In this way we try to show that management is not just a remote activity performed by others, but a process in which all are engaged in some way.

Most readers' careers are likely to be more fragmented and uncertain than was once the case, and many will be working for medium and smaller enterprises. They will probably be working close to customers and in organisations that incorporate diverse cultures, values and interests. The text therefore provides many opportunities for readers to develop skills of gathering data, comparing evidence, reflecting and generally enhancing self-awareness. It not only transmits knowledge but also aims to support the development of transferable skills through individual activities in the text and through linked tutorial work. The many cases and data collection activities are designed to develop generic skills such as communicating, teamwork, problem solving, and organising – while at the same time acquiring relevant knowledge.

How to use this book

The book encourages an active approach to learning, introducing many real-world case examples illustrating how real people have tackled the issue under discussion. The cases are widely representative – European and international as well as UK; private, public and not-for-profit; manufacturing and service. All the cases are original in this form (though some draw on other published material) and describe real situations – some of which were unresolved at the time of writing. Some have to be anonymous, but most are clearly identified so that readers can follow later developments in the company. As well as adding interest to individual study, they are also suitable for group-work in tutorials.

The book has a clear structure throughout and is divided into five Parts. A *Part Case* case study begins each part, illustrating aspects of management which will be covered in the part. Relevant aspects of the case are referred to throughout. *Part Case Questions* end each chapter by relating one or more of the issues in the chapter to the larger case.

---

p a r t   o n e

Setting the scene

Introduction

This part considers why management exists and what it contributes to human wealth and well-being. Management as a universal human activity is distinguished from management as a distinct occupation. All of us manage in the first sense, as we organise our lives and deal with family and other relationships. We are all affected by the activities of those who manage in the second sense, as employees and customers. As business becomes more international so does the work of those managing businesses. The geographical scope changes, and in some respects so does the nature of the work as it is influenced by different national cultures and institutions.

Chapter 1, then, clarifies the nature and emergence of management and the different ways in which the role has been described. It argues that management is not a neutral, technical activity: it inevitably involves some degree of controversy as the manager balances the expectations of stakeholders and interest groups. They have different views of what counts as success. The chapter concludes with some discussion and ideas about managing your study of the topic. You are likely to benefit most by actively linking your work on this book to events in real organisations, and the chapter includes some ideas on that.

Chapter 2 sets out the main theortical perspectives on management and shows how these can complement each other despite apparently competing underlying values about the nature of the management task. You are again encouraged to be active in relating these theoretical perspectives to real events to understand and test the theory. Chapter 3 then examines the international aspects of organisations and their management, and finally, Chapter 4 compares alternative theories of the role of management and different types of manager.

The Part Case is The Body Shop, a leading retailer with extensive international operations. It is an organisation with two missions: to produce personal care products for a profit, and to create a vehicle for environmental education and practical social activism. It has also developed a controversial, yet evidently successful, approach to management that contrasts sharply with that of conventional businesses.

The Body Shop International

Anita Roddick opened the first Body Shop in 1976. 'My main motivation for going into the cosmetics business was irritation: I was annoyed that you couldn't buy small sizes of everyday cosmetics ... I also recognised that a lot of the money I was paying for a product was being spent on fancy packaging which I didn't want. So I opened a small shop to sell a small range of cosmetics made from natural ingredients in ... the cheapest possible plastic containers' (Roddick, 1991, p.19). The company has grown rapidly and in 1997 had over 1,500 outlets around the world and in Europe.

What is wonderful about The Body Shop is that we still don't know the rules. Instead we have a basic understanding that to run this business you don't have to know anything. Skill is not the answer, neither is money. What you need is optimism, humanism, enthusiasm, intuition, curiosity, love, humour, magic and fun and that secret ingredient – euphoria. The status quo says that the business of business is to make profits. We have always challenged that. For us the business of business is to keep the company alive and breathlessly excited, to protect the workforce, to be a force for good in society and then, after all that, to think of the speculators. I have never kow-towed to the speculators or considered them to be my first responsibility. They play the market without much concern for the company or its values.

Social and environmental issues are woven into the fabric of the company itself. They are neither first or last among our objectives, but an ongoing part of what we do. Not a single decision is ever taken in Body Shop without considering environmental and social issues. We have an Environmental Projects Department which monitors the comany's practices and products to ensure they are environmentally sound and up to date. We have a simple credo. You can run a business differently from the way most businesses are run: you can share your prosperity with your employees and empower them without being in fear of them: you can rewrite the book of how a company interacts with the community: you can rewrite the book on third world trade and on global responsibility and on the role of educating the company, customers and shareholders. You can do all this and still play the game according to the City, still raise money, delight the institutions and give shareholders a wondrous return on their money. (p.24)

The Body Shop's mission – 'Our reason for being' – is 'To dedicate our business to the pursuit of social and environmental change'. The mission statement is followed by five objectives intended to support it:

▸ To creatively balance the financial and human needs of our stakeholders: employees, customers, franchisees, suppliers and shareholders.
▸ To courageously ensure that our business is ecologically sustainable, meeting the needs of the present without compromising the future.
▸ To meaningfully contribute to local, national and international communities in which we trade, by adopting a code of conduct which ensures care, honesty, fairness and respect.
▸ To passionately campaign for the protection of the environment and human and civil rights, and against animal testing within the cosmetics and toiletries industry.
▸ To tirelessly work to narrow the gap between principle and practice, while making fun, passion and care part of our daily lives.

These values clearly stem from Anita Roddick's personal principles that have guided her in building up The Body Shop. She and her husband Gordon believe fervently

Each chapter opens with a two-page spread high-lighting the *aim* of the chapter, its *objectives* and *topics* to be introduced in the chapter and a one-page chapter *Case Study*.

CHAPTER 1

Management and organisation

CONTENTS

Introduction

Management as a general human activity

Management as a specialist occupation

An integrative framework: content, process and control agendas

The contexts of management: levels and time

Management and managers

Management institutionalised in organisations

Gender in organisations

Conventional and critical perspectives on management

Studying management

Recap

Review questions

AIM

To introduce a framework which you can use to integrate your study of management.

OBJECTIVES

By the end of your work on this chapter you should be able to outline the concepts below in your own terms and:

1 Compare views of management as a universal activity and as a specialised function

2 Recognise the differences between functional, general, line and staff management

3 Analyse management work using an integrative framework

4 Explain how management work is affected by its context

5 Explain the meaning of the term 'management'

6 Describe the main functions of organisations

7 Give examples of how gender affects management and organisational activity

8 Compare conventional and critical views of management

9 Begin your active study of the topic by identifying sources of ideas

Global Instruments Corporation

A group of entrepreneurs created Global Instruments in 1990. One member had invented a component which was highly valued by a rapidly growing segment of the consumer electronics industry. The company manufactured and sold that product. To satisfy demand as cheaply as possible, it based its manufacturing in China. Demand in Europe grew strongly, but service to customers was sometimes disrupted by transport delays. In response, the company established a plant in the UK in 1994. This received product in bulk from China, repackaged it and delivered it to the European customers. The UK plant also carried out some advanced manufacturing operations that the Chinese plant could not do. Late in 1995 it became clear that a technical innovation by another company was going to destroy the need for the main product supplied from the newly opened plant. This put at risk the 120 manufacturing jobs which had so recently been created.

Staff at corporate headquarters did the design and marketing work. The main shareholders also exercised tight control over the expenditures and many other activities of the UK plant. The local management team believed that they were rapidly learning the distinctive features of the European market, and were better able to manage it than was HQ. They claimed they had lost opportunities for new business because global companies in the industry were expected to deal with company HQ. However, the managers there were not fully aware of their plant's capabilities. It received investment incentives from the EU, the UK government and the local authority. All wanted to support a new local manufacturing business. They were keen to encourage it to carry out more manufacture locally rather than bring products from China, and also to develop design capability.

A respected entrepreneur led the local management team. His task in early 1996 was to ensure the survival of the plant. One of the four members of his management team, Carol Harvey, said:

The loss of our main market made Bob think about how we needed to change the organisation to meet the need to get new products. We obviously couldn't continue with the original structure which focused on manufacturing. We needed to put the focus on sales and developing new products. The priority had to move to developing and designing product here, suitable for manufacture for European markets. Bob's a very good visionary, very good at strategically related matters, and he could see that the product wasn't going to last for ever, and was concentrating on getting new business. So in the reorganisation the focus was put even more on sales. As a gap-filler, we've got some subcontract work, while Mike is working on new designs.

CASE QUESTIONS

▶ What different types of manager are referred to in the case?

▶ In what ways are they adding value or creating wealth?

▶ What has happened to make their task even more difficult than it was a year previously?

These subjects are reflected in the *Review Questions* at the end of each chapter, which are intended to help readers to check their understanding of the material. *Case Questions* are included throughout the chapter to encourage the practical application of the concepts and issues being discussed and to allow comparisons between cases.

A short *Recap* section relates the material of the chapter to the integrative framework described. There is also a guide to *Further Reading* at the end of each chapter for those who want to study aspects of the topic more deeply. Relevant *Website Addresses* are included for the organisations featured in the chapter.

Several short *Case Examples* are featured in most chapters to illustrate particular aspects of the topic.

228 Management: an introduction

notebook 7.4

Think of a task you have done with a group of people where you created a small organisation to do something. It could be a voluntary or charity project, or a group assignment as part of your course. How did you communicate with each other? List all the methods used, and any advantages or disadvantages they had.

As the organisation continues to grow, the informal system is likely to experience strains. There are more people, probably concentrating on particular aspects of the overall task. They work in different places, so that the state of affairs is not immediately obvious to everyone. People will be there at different times. Because it has grown, there will simply be more things happening. A change in one area has effects on others, which people inevitably begin to forget to take into account.

CASE QUESTIONS 7.3

▶ How has the balance shifted between verbal and electronic communication in the ambulance service?

▶ Identify where in the whole system each form has increased or decreased. What are the likely advantages and disadvantages from that change in pattern?

Communication failure in a small Dutch company

The company was founded in 1881 and the present owner is one of the fourth generation of the family. The company trades and manufactures packaging machines and employs sixteen people. Someone who has recently joined the company said:

1997 was a difficult year. Five people left the company and took with them much knowledge and experience. The company really consists of one person – the owner. He does not delegate much and there is little communication between him and the rest of the organisation. The only part of the company that interests him is the game of selling machines. He describes the rest of his tasks as annoying. The result is that, for example:

1 When we sell a machine, Operations do not know exactly what Sales has promised a customer. The customer expects the machine they specified, but do not always get it.

2 There is lack of internal communication – people in the company do not know their precise responsibilities or who is responsible for which tasks.

3 There is no time planning for ordered machines. No one knows the delivery date that we have promised a customer.

4 There is no budget system for a machine project. When we sell a machine we do not know if we will make a profit or a loss.

All together, the company faces serious problems because of a lack of policy, management, information and communication.

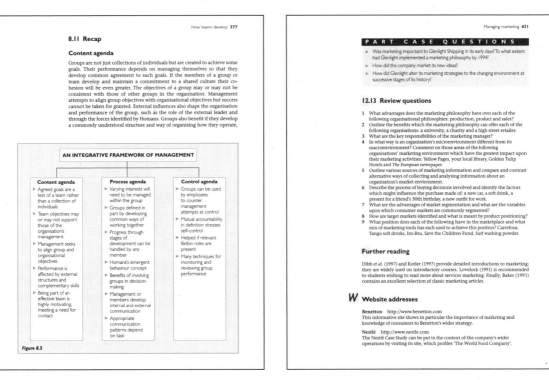

8.11 Recap

Content agenda

Groups are not just collections of individuals but are created to achieve some goals. Their performance depends on managing themselves so that they develop common agreement to such goals. If the members of a group or team develop and maintain a commitment to a shared culture their co-hesion will be even greater. The objectives of a group may or may not be consistent with those of other groups in the organisation. Management attempts to align group objectives with organisational objectives but success cannot be taken for granted. External influences also shape the organisation and performance of the group, such as the role of the external leader and through the forces identified by Homans. Groups also benefit if they develop a commonly understood structure and way of organising how they operate,

AN INTEGRATIVE FRAMEWORK OF MANAGEMENT

Content agenda	Process agenda	Control agenda
▶ Agreed goals are a test of a team rather than a collection of individuals	▶ Varying interests will need to be managed within the group	▶ Groups can be used by employees to counter management attempts at control
▶ Team objectives may or may not support those of the organisation's management	▶ Groups defined in part by developing common ways of working together	▶ Mutual accountability in definition stresses self-control
▶ Management seeks to align group and organisational objectives	▶ Progress through stages of development can be handled by any member	▶ Helped if relevant Belbin roles are present
▶ Performance is affected by external structures and complementary skills	▶ Homans's emergent behaviour concept	▶ Many techniques for monitoring and reviewing group performance
▶ Being part of an effective team is highly motivating, meeting a need for contact	▶ Benefits of involving groups in decision-making	
	▶ Management or members develop internal and external communication	
	▶ Appropriate communication patterns depend on task	

Figure 8.5

P A R T   C A S E   Q U E S T I O N S

▶ Was marketing important to Glenlight Shipping in its early days? To what extent had Glenlight implemented a marketing philosophy by 1994?

▶ How did the company market its new ideas?

▶ How did Glenlight alter its marketing strategies to the changing environment at successive stages of its history?

12.13 Review questions

1 What advantages does the marketing philosophy have over each of the following organisational philosophies: production, product and sales?
2 Outline the benefits which the marketing philosophy can offer each of the following organisations: a university, a charity and a high street retailer.
3 What are the key responsibilities of the marketing manager?
4 In what way is an organisation's microenvironment different from its macroenvironment? Comment on those areas of the following organisations' marketing environment which have the greatest impact upon their marketing activities: Yellow Pages, your local library, Golden Tulip Hotels and *The European* newspaper.
5 Outline various sources of marketing information and compare and contrast alternative ways of collecting and analysing information about an organisation's market situation.
6 Describe the process of buying decisions involved and identify the factors which might influence the purchase made of: a new car, a soft drink, a present for a friend's 30th birthday, a new outfit for work.
7 What are the advantages of market segmentation and what are the variables upon which consumer markets are commonly segmented?
8 How are target markets identified and what is meant by product positioning?
9 What position does each of the following have in the marketplace and what mix of marketing tools has each used to achieve this position? Carrefour, Tango soft drinks, Irn-Bru, Save the Children Fund, Surf washing powder.

Further reading

Dibb *et al.* (1997) and Kotler (1997) provide detailed introductions to marketing; they are widely used on introductory courses. Lovelock (1991) is recommended to students wishing to read more about services marketing. Finally, Baker (1991) contains an excellent selection of classic marketing articles.

W ▶ **Website addresses**

Benetton http://www.benetton.com
This informative site shows in particular the importance of marketing and knowledge of consumers to Benetton's wider strategy.

Nestlé http://www.nestle.com
The Nestlé Case Study can be put in the context of the company's wider operations by visiting its site, which profiles 'The World Food Company'.

Active learning is also encouraged by two key features included in each chapter. *Noticeboards* contain summaries of major theories or empirical studies. *Notebooks* pose questions, encourage data collection, prompt reflection and comparison between the topic and the reader's interests and experience. Many can be developed by the teacher into group and tutorial activities.

The definitions of key terms are highlighted in the margins of the text and are reproduced in the *Glossary* at the end of the book.

The chapters are self-contained and do not have to be read in a particular order. There are obviously links between them, but teachers can use the material in the order which best suits their teaching plan, supporting their lectures and tutorials with the case and Notebook material.

Lecturer support

An integrated Teacher's Manual has been prepared to accompany the text. This provides additional material to support the case and Notebook features. Microsoft® PowerPoint® electronic transparencies are also available.

NOTICEBOARD Features of an organisation with a strong commitment to HRM

▶ The firm competes on the basis of product quality and differentiation as well as price.
▶ Human resource considerations weigh heavily in corporate strategic decision-making and governance processes. Employee interests are represented through the voice of human resource staff professionals and/or employee representatives consult and participate with senior executives in either case, employees are treated as legitimate stakeholders in the organisation.
▶ Investments in new hardware or physical technology are combined with the investments in human resources and changes in organisational practices required to realise the full potential benefits of these investments.
▶ The firm sustains a high level of investment in training, skill development and education, and personnel practices are designed to capture and utilise these skills fully.
▶ Compensation and reward systems are internally equitable, competitive and linked to the long-term performance of the firm.
▶ Employment continuity and security are important priorities and values to be considered in all corporate decisions and policies.
▶ Workplace relations encourage flexibility in the organisation of work, empowerment of employees to solve problems, and high levels of trust among workers, supervisors and managers.
▶ Workers' rights to representation are acknowledged and respected. Union or other employee representatives are treated as joint partners in designing and overseeing innovations in labour and human resource practices.

Source: Kochan (1992)

notebook 15.2

An organisation has decided to pursue a quality-enhancement strategy in which teamworking arrangements will be a central feature. It recognises the need to enhance its level of workforce training and to replace its individual performance-related pay arrangements. Are there any other changes in the HRM area that it needs to consider? (Use Table 15.1 to assist your answer.)

Within the broad HRM approach some commentators draw attention to differing emphases. One particularly popular distinction here is betweer the 'hard' and 'soft' emphases of human resource management (Storey, 1992, pp.26–8; Legge, 1995, pp.66–7). The former emphasises the resource notion, rational planning activities and a strategic, business-led perspective. The latter puts more weight on people as valuable assets whose motivation, involvement and development should receive a relatively high priority.

However, the literature emphasises that, for HRM to have the desired effect on performance, management needs to balance two key themes: external and internal fit (Beer and Spector, 1985).

External fit

External fit refers to the link between wider stratgey and HRM strategy. Ideally management tries to establish a close and consistent link between

Acknowledgements

This book has benefited from the comments, criticisms and suggestions of many colleagues and reviewers of earlier versions. It also reflects the reactions and comments of students who have used sections of the material and earlier versions of some of the case material. Their advice and feedback has been of immense help.

Most of the chapters were written by the authors who have also edited the text throughout. We are grateful to these colleagues who contributed specific chapters: Alison More, Chapters 10 and 11; Dr Eleanor Shaw, Chapter 12; Ian Fraser and Alison Price, Chapter 13; Professor Phil Beaumont, Chapter 15; Douglas Briggs, Chapter 18; Professor Douglas Macbeth, Chapter 19, and Dr Albert Boonstra, Chapter 20. We are also grateful to Alex Fawcett for the Glenlight Shipping case; to Linda Adamson for the Benefits Agency case; to Elizabeth Foster for the Save the Children Fund case, and to Dr Niki Panteli for the material on gender and management in Chapter 1. Janey Ferguson, the Business School librarian, has willingly and efficiently searched for appropriate and unusual European sources to complement the more standard material. The errors and omissions in the text are our responsibility alone.

Every effort has been made to locate and acknowledge sources and holders of copyright material in this book, but if any have been inadvertently overlooked the publisher will be pleased to make the necessary arrangements at the first opportunity.

David Boddy
University of Glasgow Business School
January 1998

1

Setting the scene

Introduction

This part considers why management exists and what it contributes to human wealth and well-being. Management as a universal human activity is distinguished from management as a distinct occupation. All of us manage in the first sense, as we organise our lives and deal with family and other relationships. We are all affected by the activities of those who manage in the second sense, as employees and customers. As business becomes more international so does the work of those managing businesses. The geographical scope changes, and in some respects so does the nature of the work as it is influenced by different national cultures and institutions.

Chapter 1, then, clarifies the nature and emergence of management and the different ways in which the role has been described. It argues that management is not a neutral, technical activity: it inevitably involves some degree of controversy as the manager balances the expectations of stakeholders and interest groups. They have different views of what counts as success. The chapter concludes with some

discussion and ideas about managing your study of the topic. You are likely to benefit most by actively linking your work on this book to events in real organisations, and the chapter includes some ideas on that.

Chapter 2 sets out the main theortical perspectives on management and shows how these can complement each other despite apparently competing underlying values about the nature of the management task. You are again encouraged to be active in relating these theoretical perspectives to real events to understand and test the theory. Chapter 3 then examines the international aspects of organisations and their management, and finally, Chapter 4 compares alternative theories of the role of management and different types of manager.

The Part Case is The Body Shop, a leading retailer with extensive international operations. It is an organisation with two missions: to produce personal care products for a profit, and to create a vehicle for environmental education and practical social activism. It has also developed a controversial, yet evidently successful, approach to management that contrasts sharply with that of conventional businesses.

The Body Shop International

Anita Roddick opened the first Body Shop in 1976. 'My main motivation for going into the cosmetics business was irritation: I was annoyed that you couldn't buy small sizes of everyday cosmetics ... I also recognised that a lot of the money I was paying for a product was being spent on fancy packaging which I didn't want. So I opened a small shop to sell a small range of cosmetics made from natural ingredients in ... the cheapest possible plastic containers' (Roddick, 1991, p.19). The company has grown rapidly and in 1997 had over 1,500 outlets around the world and in Europe.

> What is wonderful about The Body Shop is that we still don't know the rules. Instead we have a basic understanding that to run this business you don't have to know anything. Skill is not the answer, neither is money. What you need is optimism, humanism, enthusiasm, intuition, curiosity, love, humour, magic and fun and that secret ingredient – euphoria. The status quo says that the business of business is to make profits. We have always challenged that. For us the business of business is to keep the company alive and breathlessly excited, to protect the workforce, to be a force for good in society and then, after all that, to think of the speculators. I have never kow-towed to the speculators or considered them to be my first responsibility. They play the market without much concern for the company or its values.
>
> Social and environmental issues are woven into the fabric of the company itself. They are neither first or last among our objectives, but an ongoing part of what we do. Not a single decision is ever taken in Body Shop without considering environmental and social issues. We have an Environmental Projects Department which monitors the comany's practices and products to ensure they are environmentally sound and up to date. We have a simple credo. You can run a business differently from the way most businesses are run: you can share your prosperity with your employees and empower them without being in fear of them: you can rewrite the book of how a company interacts with the community: you can rewrite the book on third world trade and on global responsibility and on the role of educating the company, customers and shareholders. You can do all this and still play the game according to the City, still raise money, delight the institutions and give shareholders a wondrous return on their money. (p.24)

The Body Shop's mission – 'Our reason for being' – is 'To dedicate our business to the pursuit of social and environmental change'. The mission statement is followed by five objectives intended to support it:

- ▶ To creatively balance the financial and human needs of our stakeholders: employees, customers, franchisees, suppliers and shareholders.
- ▶ To courageously ensure that our business is ecologically sustainable, meeting the needs of the present without compromising the future.
- ▶ To meaningfully contribute to local, national and international communities in which we trade, by adopting a code of conduct which ensures care, honesty, fairness and respect.
- ▶ To passionately campaign for the protection of the environment and human and civil rights, and against animal testing within the cosmetics and toiletries industry.
- ▶ To tirelesssly work to narrow the gap between principle and practice, while making fun, passion and care part of our daily lives.

These values clearly stem from Anita Roddick's personal principles that have guided her in building up The Body Shop. She and her husband Gordon believe fervently that business must be a force for social and environmental change. Business organisations are not just for profit – their resources can be used to promote wider purposes. This inspiration and the set of values associated guide the trading principles of Body Shop management, which are:

> We aim to ensure that human and civil rights, as set out in the Universal Declaration of Human Rights, are respected throughout our business activities.
>
> We will support long term, sustainable relationships with communities in need.
>
> We will use environmentally sustainable resources wherever technically and economically viable.
>
> We will promote animal protection throughout our business activities and in many ways.
>
> We will institute appropriate monitoring, auditing and disclosure mechanisms to ensure our accountability and demonstrate our compliance with these principles.

The products are sold in refillable containers as part of the company's commitment to reducing packaging and waste. Environmental campaigns are promoted through the shops, with posters and information sheets designed to promote customer awareness of current threats and campaigns. Customers are encouraged to use the recycling service which entitles them to a discount. To help balance the energy used on the company's properties, management has invested in a wind-power development in Wales. The project had the support of the local community and was done in association with National Power, an electricity generating company.

In the past, the cosmetics industry routinely tested new products on animals. The Body Shop campaigned vigorously against this. It raised public awareness of the issue through its campaigns, and its Ethical Audit Department monitors the ingredients used to ensure that the suppliers have not tested them on animals.

Many of its ingredients come from suppliers in poor countries. The company uses its resources not just to buy the products but also to help the communities from whom it buys to achieve sustainable economic independence. It buys directly from the small producers (rather than through intermediate trading companies). It also supplies technical assistance to them to ensure sustainable and good quality supplies, as well as supporting the wider aspects of a community's development. Dismayed by the economic conditions in a deprived part of Glasgow, the company set up a plant in the area to make most of its soap.

The structure of the company is shown in Figure 1. About three-quarters of the shops are owned by franchisees. These are businesspeople who provide the capital for a shop and the stocks, and then run the shop. They do this under strict Body Shop guidelines which ensure that the brand image is projected consistently. The Body Shop provides advice and support in setting up and running the outlet but the franchisee is responsible for recruiting and managing staff and for making the shop a success.

Franchisees are carefully selected to ensure that they are fully committed to Anita Roddick's vision of the business. The company's culture values people who are able to work enthusiatically as a team to promote the mission. Specific financial or retailing experience is less important as this can be learned. The values are maintained and spread by many personal visits to the stores by the Roddicks. They also send a weekly video to all stores keeping staff up to date with developments elsewhere in the business and with news of the company's current environmental campaigns.

The mission statement itself is an attempt to institutionalise and systematise these values. The Roddicks hope that this will help to keep the values at the front of staff's minds even though the growth in the company means that staff are increasingly remote from the personal energy and charisma of the founder.

This charisma helped to hold the company together in the early days. As it grew and prepared to issue shares to the public in 1984 (to finance further expansion), more systematic ways of managing the business

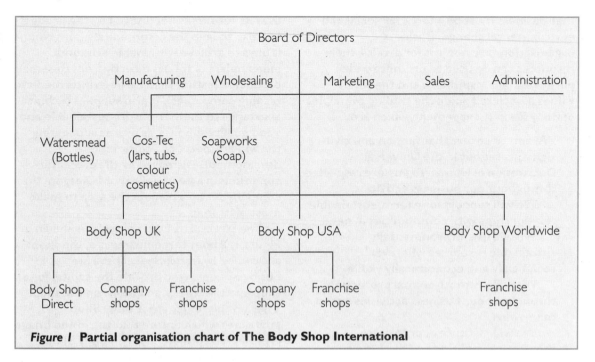

Figure 1 **Partial organisation chart of The Body Shop International**

were needed. **More professional managers were recruited at that time. There is a constant need to balance the values and the commercial needs of the business. The table summarises the company's turnover and profit for the financial years 1996 and 1997.**

	1997 (52 weeks) £m	1996 (53 weeks) £m	Change %
Retail sales	622.5	577.5	+ 8.0%
Pre-tax profit	38.2	32.7	+17.0%
Earnings per share (p)	11.4p	9.8p	+16.0%

The company has also formalised how it monitors its own ethical performance. As the business has grown there is a danger that decisions are taken that are out of line with the company's underlying values. In 1994 it completed a twelve-month study of best practice approaches to social accounting and auditing. This formed the basis of a social audit of the company which led to the production of an independently verified report on the ethical performance of the company, particularly with regard to social issues.

As part of this process, focus groups were held with interested parties. Alongside this a data gathering and benchmarking exercise was carried out. This compared the company's policies on matters such as human resource management, health and safety, fair trade, company giving and campaigning. The growing social audit process was verified by an independent foundation and a panel of independent experts on social issues.

Another issue for the company is to develop managers who can become future leaders of The Body Shop. Anita Roddick has said:

> **[We must] make sure that we don't suppress the leadership of our staff. By their nature big organizations always suppress leadership. They always do. It's their nature, their bigness. Our young people are born into a society that is very huge and impersonal going to large schools and large cities. I want to find ways of mentoring to encourage more moral leadership in our company.**

Sources: extracts from Roddick (1991); 'The Body Shop: a case study', Kellogg School, North Western University, Case No. 495-019-8; company annual reports

PART CASE QUESTIONS

▶ If you have not done so, visit a Body Shop so that you are familiar with the physical aspects of case. What campaigns is it running at the moment? You could also build up a file of press cuttings on the company's performance to update this account.

▶ How does The Body Shop compare with other companies selling similar products? Are other companies beginning to copy the Body Shop approach?

▶ What clues are there in the case about ways in which the individual founder is trying to institutionalise her ideas in this now very large company?

▶ What dilemmas are there likely to be for management in an organisation with two missions?

There will be other questions about the case in the chapters which follow.

Management and organisation

CONTENTS

AIM

To introduce a framework which you can use to integrate your study of management.

OBJECTIVES

By the end of your work on this chapter you should be able to outline the concepts below in your own terms and:

1   Compare views of management as a universal activity and as a specialised function

2   Recognise the differences between functional, general, line and staff management

3   Analyse management work using an integrative framework

4   Explain how management work is affected by its context

5   Explain the meaning of the term 'management'

6   Describe the main functions of organisations

7   Give examples of how gender affects management and organisational activity

8   Compare conventional and critical views of management

9   Begin your active study of the topic by identifying sources of ideas

Global Instruments Corporation

A group of entrepreneurs created Global Instruments in 1990. One member had invented a component which was highly valued by a rapidly growing segment of the consumer electronics industry. The company manufactured and sold that product. To satisfy demand as cheaply as possible, it based its manufacturing in China. Demand in Europe grew strongly, but service to customers was sometimes disrupted by transport delays. In response, the company established a plant in the UK in 1994. This received product in bulk from China, repackaged it and delivered it to the European customers. The UK plant also carried out some advanced manufacturing operations that the Chinese plant could not do. Late in 1995 it became clear that a technical innovation by another company was going to destroy the need for the main product supplied from the newly opened plant. This put at risk the 120 manufacturing jobs which had so recently been created.

Staff at corporate headquarters did the design and marketing work. The main shareholders also exercised tight control over the expenditures and many other activities of the UK plant. The local management team believed that they were rapidly learning the distinctive features of the European market, and were better able to manage it than was HQ. They claimed they had lost opportunities for new business because global companies in the industry were expected to deal with company HQ. However, the managers there were not fully aware of their plant's capabilities. It received investment incentives from the EU, the UK government and the local authority. All wanted to support a new local manufacturing business. They were keen to encourage it to carry out more manufacture locally rather than bring products from China, and also to develop design capability.

A respected entrepreneur led the local management team. His task in early 1996 was to ensure the survival of the plant. One of the four members of his management team, Carol Harvey, said:

> The loss of our main market made Bob think about how we needed to change the organisation to meet the need to get new products. We obviously couldn't continue with the original structure which focused on manufacturing. We needed to put the focus on sales and developing new products. The priority had to move to developing and designing product here, suitable for manufacture for European markets. Bob's a very good visionary, very good at strategically related matters, and he could see that the product wasn't going to last for ever, and was concentrating on getting new business. So in the reorganisation the focus was put even more on sales. As a gap-filler, we've got some subcontract work, while Mike is working on new designs.

CASE ?QUESTIONS

▶ What different types of manager are referred to in the case?

▶ In what ways are they adding value or creating wealth?

▶ What has happened to make their task even more difficult than it was a year previously?

1.1 Introduction

This chapter introduces the following ideas:
- ▶ Management as a general human activity
- ▶ Management as a specialist occupation
- ▶ Functional, general, line and staff managers
- ▶ Manager
- ▶ Adding value
- ▶ Efficiency and effectiveness
- ▶ Organisations
- ▶ Critical perspective

The Global Instruments case illustrates several aspects of management. A group of entrepreneurs have created an organisation to make a product which customers are willing to buy. They bring resources together from around the world, and transform them into something with greater value. The tasks which make up this enterprise are divided among different countries, functions and levels of authority. An unexpected external change suddenly challenges the company's product and its ability to survive. There is now a management problem. How can those in the European plant rearrange their resources to design and make another saleable product quickly enough to keep the plant open?

---

notebook   1.1

What is management?

Write a few notes summarising what you think 'management' means. You might find it helpful to think of instances in which you have encountered 'management' – when you have been managed, or when you have managed something. Keep the notes where you can refer to them later.

1.2 Management as a general human activity

The skills required to run an organisation efficiently are not confined to a group of people called managers. As individuals we run our own lives, and in this respect we are managing. Hales (1993) distinguishes clearly between management as a general human activity and management as a specialised occupational group. In the first sense, management is visible in social and domestic activities as well as in the business world:

> When human beings 'manage' their work, they take responsibility for its purpose, progress and outcome by exercising the quintessentially human capacity to stand back from experience and to regard it prospectively, in terms of what will happen; reflectively, in terms of what is happening; and retrospectively, in terms of what has happened. Thus management is an expression of human agency, the capacity actively to shape and direct the world, rather than simply react to it. (p.2)

He argues that this 'general human process' includes five distinct but related elements. These are, deciding what to do and planning how to do it, allocating time and effort necessary to do it, motivating or generating that effort, co-ordinating separate but related efforts, and controlling what is done to ensure that it matches what was intended. These are discussed more fully later: Hales's point is that management is an element in most human work activity.

n o t e b o o k   1.2

Is management a general human activity?

Do you agree with Hales's argument above? Test it by choosing some form of domestic or community-based work you have undertaken. Can you recognise things which you did in the elements listed by Hales?

Does your list match Hales's elements? In what ways does it differ?

Historically, work in agriculture or related industrial trades and professions was done by people working on their own or in close family units. They retained control of their time and other resources used in producing goods or delivering services. They decided what to make, how they would make it and how or when to sell it. Management and work were intertwined in the process of creating goods and service. This is still the pattern in many human activities. Self-employed craftworkers, many professionals in small practices or individuals running their one-person business combine both activities. We all do it when we work on household tasks and projects or take part in small voluntary activities.

1.3 Management as a specialist occupation

Origins

While work and management were historically combined, the 'management' element is often seen as being distinct from the actual work process. This creates a new occupational group of 'managers', who are in varying degrees separated from those doing the core work. This was not, and is not, the only way to arrange things. People have deliberately separated the roles, and on other occasions have equally deliberately brought them together. The boundary between 'management' and 'non-management' work is a human creation, and is fluid and ambiguous.

Hales (1993) explains the causes and consequences of this separation. The first step in management becoming distinct occurs if an external agency, such as a private owner of capital, or the state, gains some control of a previously unified work process. The external agents may have accumulated capital, raw materials or access to markets – the resources necessary for the work to be done – and in return for making these resources available they exact a price. Thus they take control of those parts of the work process which determine what is made and sold. This includes deciding and planning what work is to be done, obtaining materials, controlling outputs to ensure that work has been done properly, and selling the products. The agents thus take responsibility for some elements of management previously integrated with the work process itself. The functions relating to the detail of how the work itself is done, however, remain integrated within the work process.

According to Hales, a second stage in the separation of management from work occurs 'when the direction of the work process itself ... becomes the responsibility of owners and their agents' (p.5). In order to secure greater control over the production process, those who previously supplied material and/or bought finished goods from self-employed workers begin to employ workers directly. Independent workers become employees, selling their labour, rather than the results of their labour. So, as factory owners took control of the physical and financial means of production they also took control of the time, behaviour and skills of those who were now employees rather than autonomous workers. As employees, they have their own view of what they are prepared to do. They can also try to influence fellow employees to take a similar view – which may be different from that of the owner or manager. Generating action towards objectives then becomes the responsibility and problem of the new, separate, employers.

The same evolution takes place when an individual or a partnership starts an enterprise. While it is a one-or two-person operation, management and ownership functions are combined. The owner or the partners perform all the management funtions involved in the work as well as the work itself. If the business grows and employees are engaged, certain management functions become the primary province of the owners or partners, with employees having more limited roles.

C A S E   Q U E S T I O N S   1 . 1

▶ Try to trace how this process might have happened in the history of Global Instruments, from the point at which the person who invented the original product, working entirely alone, had the idea. At that point, work and management were combined.

▶ What divisions have probably taken place on the route to the present structure?

To sum up the argument so far, management in the fundamental sense is a generic human activity. It is an integral part of most work even if people do not use or recognise the term. For various reasons, and by various routes, management has become separated into a specialised function or occupation. The extent and form of this separation is not fixed or pre-ordained: indeed a common practice in modern organisations is to reintegrate some management and work activities which had been divided.

Specialisation between areas of management

Management as a specialist occupation develops when activities previously embedded in the work itself become the responsibility not of the employee but of owners or their agents.

Another theme which Hales discusses is the specialisation of the (separated) management activity. As organisations become larger, management becomes divided into more detailed elements. Different management specialisms are created, and a management hierarchy develops. A common distinction between management specialisms identifies functional, general, line and staff managers.

Functional managers are those responsible for a single common activity within the organisation, such as personnel, research, marketing or production. Most of their staff will be specialists in those areas, and typically the manager will have worked in that area too in the past.

General managers typically head a complete unit of the organisation, such as a division or a subsidiary, within which there will be several functions. The general manager is responsible for the overall performance of the unit, and therefore relies on the managers in charge of particular functions. A small organisation will have just one or two general managers, who will also manage specific functions.

Line managers are those in charge of a function which is directly involved in making or supplying products or services to customers. Depending on their level they will be in charge of a retail shop, a group of nurses, a social work department, or a manufacturing area. Their performance has a significant impact on the performance and image of the organisation, as they and their staff are in direct contact with the customers or clients.

Staff managers are in charge of support functions such as finance, personnel, purchasing or legal affairs. These functions do not earn income directly for the organisation, and their staff are not usually in direct contact with external customers. Their customers are the line departments of their own organisation, so their impact on outside customers may not be direct but it will affect the performance of the line departments. In managing their own staff, heads of such departments operate as line managers.

Functional managers are responsible for the performance of a common area of technical or professional work.

General managers are responsible for the performance of a distinct unit of the organisation.

Line managers are responsible for the performance of activities which are directly involved in meeting customers' needs.

Staff managers are responsible for the performance of functions which provide support to line managers.

CASE QUESTIONS 1.2

▶ What specialised management functions have been created at Global Instruments?

▶ What signs are there of efforts to reintegrate some of the separate functions that had been created?

▶ What problems has the present specialisation created?

notebook 1.3

Does managers' experience support these categories?

Arrange a discussion with one or more managers and ask them about the four categories of manager. Do their jobs fit into them? Do they combine parts of each? If so, what are the different demands they meet in the different categories?

How much variety is there in the way the different managers describe their jobs?

Specialisation between levels of management

As organisations grow, they usually create a hierarchy of positions. The amount of 'management' and 'non-management' work within these positions varies. The descriptions below distinguish among positions which are concerned mainly with performing direct operations, managing staff on direct operations, managing managers and managing the business.

Performing direct operations

Managers who perform direct operations do the manual and mental work to produce and deliver products or services. These include very lowly paid ancillary activities, through skilled or technical work, to highly paid professional or creative activities. The management activity may not have been completely separated from this work. Staff may plan or control some activities.

Managing staff on direct operations

Sometimes called supervisors or first-line managers, these managers ensure that staff perform the daily operations of the organisation. They also help to overcome any difficulties that arise. Examples would include the supervisor of a production team, the head chef in a hotel, a nurse in charge of other nurses in a hospital ward, or the manager of a bank branch. They will probably spend less time on direct operations than their subordinates – except in small companies where they do these as well. The example of Barings illustrates a case in which senior management failed to control a member of staff, with disastrous consequences for the company.

 Whatever happened at Barings?

On 27 February 1995, Barings, one of the UK's oldest merchant banks, collapsed following the revelation that one of its Singapore traders, Nick Leeson, had accumulated losses of over £800 million in trading financial products. The initial response by the senior management of the bank was to place all the blame for the disaster on the individual trader – who had clearly acted in an unauthorised and fraudulent way. Inquiries into the incident told a different story:

> While it is true that Leeson traded in an unauthorised fashion ... it is astonishing that the layers of controls and supervision ... failed to detect the fiasco, or to pick up warning signals ... Both official inquiries conclude that the failure at Barings was not due to the complexity of the business undertaken. The UK report states that: 'The failings ... were primarily a failure on the part of a number of individuals to do their job properly'.
>
> First, the organisation structure was ill-defined ... Leeson had confused reporting lines locally and to head office. He was left in the astonishing position of being in charge of both the front office [trading] and back office [settlements] which allowed him ... to cover up ...
>
> Second, Barings internal audit failed to act upon warnings ... that the concentration of power in Leeson's hands was a potentially explosive situation ...
>
> Third, although Barings managed risk through an Asset and Liability Committee ... vast funds were remitted to Leeson from within the group [which] were never subject to credit check.

Source: extracts from Stonham (1996)

Managing managers

Usually referred to as middle managers (a very numerous group), these managers are expected to ensure that the first-line managers work in line with broader company policies. They check whether performance targets are being met, keep in touch with what is happening and provide support or pressure as required. They also form a communication link, ensuring that information flows up and down the organisation. They tell first-line managers what they expect of them, and brief senior management about developments deep down in the business. Managers also spend time managing other managers at the same level and those above them in the hierarchy. Some have close and frequent links with managers in other organisations on whom they depend in some way.

Managing the business

Managing the business is the work of a relatively small group of people who are responsible for the overall direction and performance of the organisation. These managers establish policy and have a particular responsibility for managing relations with people and institutions in the world outside, such as shareholders, media, elected representatives. They need to be aware of the internal detail, and able to comprehend it, but spend most of their time looking to the future or dealing with external affairs. They will spend little, if any, of their time on direct operations – though again in small companies they remain directly involved.

1.4 An integrative framework: content, process and control agendas

Within the overall activity of management, three separate, though interacting, components or 'agendas' can be distinguished. The approach is similar to that suggested by Hales (1993) and also draws on research in a wide range of management situations by Boddy and Buchanan (1992).

Management is made up of three broad areas of work called the content, process and control agendas. The work takes place within a context which has both contemporary and historical dimensions, so it includes managing these links with the outside world and taking account of the past and future. Remember that the term 'management' is used here in the sense of the overall activity, without making any judgement about which individuals or specialist groups undertake the activity. This may or may not be part of a unified area of human work.

Content agenda

The content agenda refers to the substantive tasks of management. It includes shaping the broad objectives of the work – whether of the individual craftworker or sole trader, of a department, or of an organisation. It also involves identifying a range of decisions intended to support those objectives. These include most of Hales's categories (deciding what to do and planning how to do it, allocating time and effort necessary to do it, motivating and co-ordinating). It is also similar to Fayol's (1949) model which described the management functions in terms of planning, organising, directing, leading and controlling. It differs from both in that it excludes controlling, which we treat as a distinct agenda.

Developing objectives

The content agenda deals with the overall direction of the work to be done. It includes forecasting future trends, assessing actual and potential resources and developing objectives and targets for future performance. Any work activity inevitably raises choices about where to concentrate effort and resources. We can choose not to set objectives. We can take things as they come, react to problems as they arise, respond on the moment. Where few resources or other people are involved, this is a reasonable approach. It also makes sense in stable or routine activities – the effort of setting objectives can be disproportional to the benefits.

Where more people and interests are involved, or the activity uses expensive resources, failing to develop objectives can be costly. Mistakes get made, people are not clear why they are doing something, misunderstandings arise, and the uncertainty can lead to stress. A lack of objectives can also mean that people are so busy dealing with immediate issues that they neglect the bigger or longer-term picture. They ignore what is happening outside their own area, missing wider trends and events. A project manager in construction describes such a situation: 'I have found that my role has developed into that of a firefighter, and have great difficulty in allocating sufficient time to longer-term projects and strategies.' This will mean that resources are not used effectively, so that costs are higher and service quality lower than they could be. To avoid this, managers invest time and effort in developing a sense of direction for the organisation, or their part of it, and express this in a set of objectives for the activity.

Planning to achieve the objectives

This is the activity of moving abstract plans closer to reality (Hales refers to this as 'allocating time and effort'), and preparing for action. It includes defining the primary business processes required to meet the objectives, and deciding on the technologies and other facilities that will be needed. The whole needs to be organised into a structure in which work is allocated and co-ordinated. Who is to be responsible for each of the business processes? How should their work be linked with that of others? At more detailed levels it includes decisions about matters such as selecting staff, revising payment systems, or which supplier to choose.

Generating action

This, following Hales, is the activity of generating effort and commitment towards meeting objectives. It is sometimes referred to as influencing, directing or motivating, and is essential if plans are to be turned into action. It is necessary whether or not management is a unified or separate activity. In the former, the individual has to have the inner commitment to turn intention into action (such as when you have planned to meet the objective of writing an assignment at the weekend, but then have to will yourself actually to do it). When management has become separated from work, and subdivided into horizontal and vertical specialisms, the task of securing the required commitment and action from others becomes problematic. People exercise choice over what they do at work. Managers cannot assume that others will act as they would like them to. Compliance may be achieved if the balance of power is such that others have no real choice but to comply. Or others may be equally committed to the work, and willing do what is asked.

▶ Which activities can you see, or imagine, that the management at Global Instruments would be carrying out as part of its content agenda?

Process agenda

The content agenda refers to *what* management does: the process agenda refers to *how* it does it. This element of management follows directly from the separation of management from work activities, and greater specialisation within management. In situations where management and work activities are closely intertwined, process activities scarcely arise. The person who decides what to do is also deciding how he or she wants to do it. The separation of management from work, means, as Hales pointed out, that the motivation of other people becomes a responsibility of the specialist management function.

> **Carol Harvey of Global Instruments**
> ❝ I work a lot globally as well, looking at other sites. I also make a point of sitting down with each of the seven people who report directly to me, for at least an hour each week. I think it's important to give people individual time, so they feel good – not just to discuss their responsibilities and what they've achieved in the week, but also to review their training and so on. As long as I know they're on top of their job, I can get on and deal with the other things, because, obviously, the management team have a lot of discussion on where the company is going. It's easier for us now to set the priorities within the management team, whereas before the reorganisation there were eight of us, with different interests and priorities. ❞

▶ What difficulties in the process aspect of the work are hinted at in the preceding paragraph?

The starting point for considering the process agenda is likely to be the stakeholders (see below) whose support management needs. Managers must decide *how* to ensure the willing co-operation of people, and how to deal with suppliers and customers. They can manage by instruction or request, by autocratic or democratic styles of management, by taking care over communication, or being indifferent to it. This is not just a matter of how managers decide to treat subordinates. The specialisation of management functions means that managers often require the support of managers in other departments, or of those above them in the hierarchy. Some managers act entirely on their own, others work closely with others, seeking consensus at each stage. How these processes of influence are conducted is a key area of the process agenda. There are choices about communication – is information to pass freely around the organisation, or is there to be an emphasis on limiting the information that people have? How managers choose to deal with these issues has a significant effect on the attitude and behaviour of the managed. In turn that affects the extent to which managers are able to achieve the objectives and plans of the content agenda.

A power behind the throne?

Because the requirements of the management job at senior levels are so complex, it is common for senior managers in prominent positions to depend heavily on a close confidant, with deep experience of the business. X is the entrepreneur at the head of a small business in the electronics sector, which involves frequent external contact with distant and technologically demanding customers. This uses a great deal of X's time and energy.

Meanwhile the complex manufacturing and commercial aspects of the business have to run smoothly. While X has in place a formal and capable management team he also relies heavily for strategic advice on an assistant Y who has no formal management role. Y has been with the company since it started, and is acutely aware of the business issues that it faces. Y is also close to the human interactions within the plant. X makes no major decision without consulting Y. The relationship is one of equals – although X is the boss, disagreements with Y about strategy are vigorous.

n o t e b o o k   1.4

The aspect of management style or process described in the Case Example is noticeable in small firms, but is probably widespread. When you are studying an organisation do not just focus on the figurehead. Also look for a less visible presence with considerable influence behind the scenes.

It is in the way that managers handle the process agenda that we can see different cultural styles emerging. For example, teamwork is handled differently in different countries – some cultures prefer managers to adopt more distant, autocratic styles, whereas others value more democratic approaches.

Control and learning agenda

There are two distinct perspectives on management and control. The conventional approach is to see control as a relatively technical matter in which managers monitor what happens against what they expected to happen. Budgets are set for a housing department, an outpatients clinic, a marketing department; information on expenditure is collected regularly to allow managers to check that they are keeping to budget, or if not, they can decide how they bring actual costs back into line with expected costs. Managers set targets for stock level, sales, profit and many other measures of performance, reflecting decisions made in the content agenda. They can also monitor aspects of the process agenda – How good is communication? Are employees satisfied with the way they are treated by managers? This agenda includes those activities whereby the manager monitors and reviews what is going on around the operation. Are people and departments doing what was expected of them? Is the information reaching people accurate and timely enough to help them do their job? Is what is being done consistent with the objectives? If it is, they may decide to leave well alone. But what if by Wednesday the week's production schedule is clearly not going to be met, or if the level of customer complaints in March is well above the monthly average?

Global Instruments' finance director on control

❝ A critical factor will be getting totally focused on costs – because we will be bringing new products right through from design to manufacture and then on to distribution. We won't have made them before, so we'll have to be very closely focused on the costs. We've put out quotations for new business based on estimates of what we think it will take – so it's going to be absolutely critical to know if we're as good as we think we are at doing the new satellite products. So we've got a new costing group to focus on monitoring what everything costs, against what we said it was going to cost. We knew the assembly costs on the old business very well, but now we're taking a new product from a new customer, we're into the unknown. The costing group includes engineering people, product design and finance people, and will monitor exactly what we do.

The satellite product is one thing, and then there's the step beyond that, when we're making something that is our own design. We'll also need to ensure that all the costs are recovered then. The other thing is that we've built up the overhead, which has been soaked up by the high volume business; we now need to be sure that the way the factory is loaded is taking care of all that overhead – and to know that before the end of a quarter. ❞

CASE QUESTIONS 1.5

▶ Why is control difficult in Global Instruments' present position?

▶ How does the present position relate to decisions made in the content agenda?

▶ Can you identify the process agenda issue in this quotation?

Managing the control agenda enables management to know if some corrective action is needed to meet the objectives and plans. The corrective action may be very short term (authorise some overtime this evening to catch up); or it may involve taking a much longer view to solve the problem fully (review planning systems or staff development to improve performance radically). At the highest content level, an example would be the board reviewing overall financial performance against shareholder expectations, and taking corrective action if this seems to be necessary. At lower levels an example would be a department or project manager trying to control his or her area by, again, comparing performance with plans and then doing whatever is practicable to keep performance in line with expectations.

Similarly, managers can attempt to monitor and control the process agenda. If a policy decision has been taken to adopt a more consultative style of management, or to improve communication, that too can be monitored to see if what is happening is in line with expectations. Learning becomes harder with the fragmentation of management into specialisms. Much learning in organisations is of a tacit rather than explicit variety. Unless people are in close working relationships, learning does not pass readily from one part of the organisation to another. At a time of rapid change, learning and skill are crucial sources of competitive advantage, and learning is an important issue for managers to include on their collective control agenda.

These conventional perspectives on control assume a degree of agreement on goals which radical theorists (such as Thompson and McHugh, 1995) dispute. They argue that many attempts at control by management are not neutral, technical matters. They acknowledge that some degree of control is necessary to get things done in organisations with a reasonable degree of efficiency. However, most attempts at control by management reflect, in their view, fundamantel divisions in social relations at work. Control is exercised not as an end in itself, but to help convert people's capacity to work into some form of profitable service or product.

Such attempts by management to subordinate employees to its requirements are as old as organisations themselves. The controls so exercised are not necessarily tyrannical or visible. Many are seen by radicals as 'insidious'. By this they refer to controls which are relatively unobtrusive and impersonal. An example is computer-based telephone response centres in which agents' conversations with customers are tightly prescribed by the technology. Another is when managers recruit professional staff in the knowledge that their values in relation to the subject or the patient will ensure a high degree of conformity to management requirements. The other side of this is that management attempts at control may be contested by employees. This contest (both within management and between management and staff) is a recurrent theme of organisations and throughout this book.

An integrative framework – the CPC model

The content, process and control model ('the CPC model') will be used as a way of linking the discussion of management throughout the book. The elements are summarised in Figure 1.1.

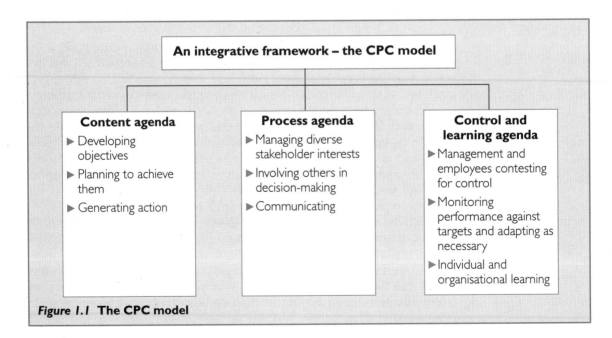

Figure 1.1 **The CPC model**

1.5   The contexts of management: levels and time

The management of the agendas takes place within organisations which are themselves part of a wider contemporary and historical context.

Levels – the contemporary context

This refers to several dimensions of the external world that are discussed more fully later. All aspects of the content agenda are influenced by the contemporary context – such as the choice of objectives being shaped by beliefs about the pattern of market demand, or about the policy at higher levels of the organisation. How well these issues are managed also influences the environment – by changing a customer's view of the organisation, for example. Equally, how the process agenda is managed will reflect the context. The prevailing distribution of power will affect whether or not trade unions take part in discussions about objectives and plans. Figure 1.2 illustrates this.

Time – the historical context

Management also takes place within a flow of historical events. This involves recognising the influence of the past, as well as balancing present and future. History exerts an influence whatever specialised functions have been created. On the day-to-day level, management involves dealing with

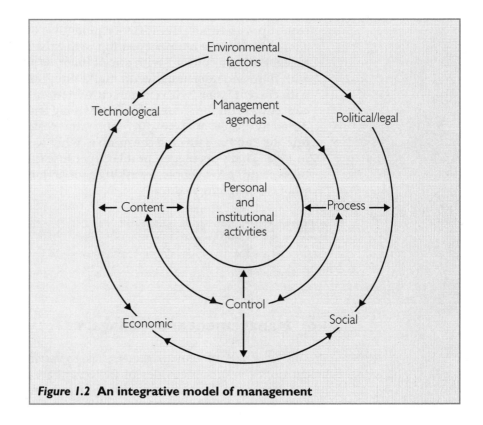

***Figure 1.2* An integrative model of management**

the present detail – bringing resources of all kinds together to achieve something, co-ordinating, ensuring that things run properly, sensing trouble, making things work. It may involve ensuring that supplies are available, undertaking technical activities with the resources or dealing with customer requirements. These are examples of the operating issues that require management.

Management also means looking to the future. However good the present situation, or the present operation, managers must look outwards, and to the future. This means questioning present systems and seeking improvements, and this involves observing how the environment is changing and considering the implications for the current activity. Does work need to be redirected towards another purpose? Are resources being used too wastefully, requiring some changes in method? What are others doing? All of these pose issues for most kinds of human activity, and they are resolved through processes of management.

Managers experience endless conflict between dealing with the day-to-day and the longer term. An example from Global Instruments is quoted below.

Lisa Scott, European account manager at Global Instruments, on the dilemma she faced in working for the plant's survival

‘There had never been a marketing function as such in the UK, so I was brought in to try to look at that. I set up the marketing function, and especially to look after our three major accounts. There was a marketing function at headquarters, but it didn't pay much attention to Europe.

We need to be able to anticipate what the customers require, and come up with innovative ideas, be proactive. But I also have to spend a lot of time at the moment dealing with existing customers. We are renegotiating a contract with one of them, so a lot of time is taken up with that, and not enough with marketing. I am still having to deal with current issues, with current customers, rather than being able to concentrate on the strategy bit. That's a big tension, because it's two different people: analysing inventory and costings, negotiating pricing; and then turning the mind to what we need to be producing in 1998. That's my biggest problem, because the short-term always takes priority. Yet people are asking a lot of questions of me, about what we are going to do.’

CASE QUESTIONS 1.6

- What are the day-to-day demands and the long-term demands that Lisa faces?
- What effects do you think these conflicting demands may have on her work?

1.6 Management and managers

The universal activity of management has, to varying degrees, become separated from the other activities of the organisation – including those of 'non-managers'. This separation of managers from managed need not be permanent, irreversible or fixed. Indeed, a common theme in modern management writing is the need to eliminate some aspects of the management hierarchy.

Some writers have taken the view that creating a distinct specialism of management is an inevitable consequence of the growth of large organisations. Writers such as Drucker (1955) take this view. They see management as a technical activity which becomes more pronounced as organisations themselves become larger and more complex. The view is often reflected in political assertions about the 'rights' of management to manage.

Others disagree. They argue that separating the management process from the work itself is not inevitable or indeed complete. Distinguished writers such as Chester Barnard (1938) in the United States and Henri Fayol (1949) in France both pointed out the fluidity of the division. Barnard observed that while what he called executive work was distinct, executives themselves would often undertake the technical work of the organisation; and Fayol made it clear that:

> Management ... is neither an exclusive privilege nor a particular responsibility of the head or senior members of a business; it is an activity spread, like all other activities, between head and members of the body corporate. (p.6)

The boundaries between managers and non-managers today are often fluid and ambiguous. Someone in charge of part of an organisation, say a production department, will usually be treated as a manager, and referred to as one. The people who operate the machines will be called something else. However, if these operators have significant responsibilities for how they plan and organise their work, they are clearly undertaking some management activities.

Relating management to those in particular positions or with a particular title is too limited a perspective. Many 'non-managers' now perform significant management tasks as part of their direct work, irrespective of their title. Practice in many of today's most innovative organisations supports the view that the boundaries between managers and non-managers are ill-defined. Many businesses are making conscious efforts to place more responsibility directly onto staff, and at the same time to reduce the number of managers – with corresponding changes in the responsibilities of the managers who remain. For a variety of reasons, management positions are being eliminated and the work reallocated to operators or other more junior staff. Staff achieve many things by their own initiative, unrelated to any formal authority.

CASE QUESTIONS 1.7

▶ What evidence is there in Global Instruments that managerial responsibilities are being reallocated throughout the company?

notebook 1.5

Try to find at least two examples in the newspapers, etc. of organisations deliberately reducing the number of managers and changing managerial responsibilities.

Hence management is not exclusive to managers – non-managers may engage in parts of the activity. Conversely, as the management activity has become specialised, individual managers not only perform just certain parts of it, but also engage in some technical work, especially in smaller organisations.

The title of 'manager', or its close relatives, is often attached to jobs with rather limited management responsibilities – branch manager, executive consultant. Conversely, many people with significant management responsibilities have titles which do not include the word – director of television, chief actuary, principal, senior partner. A definition which avoids the problems of particular titles and which is consistent with our view of the universality of the process was suggested by Rosemary Stewart (1967):

> A manager is someone who gets things done with the aid of other people.

Note that 'other people' does not refer only to subordinates. Managers usually have subordinates, but in addition will draw on the skills of people over whom they have no direct authority, in order to get things done. They may need to get suppliers or customers to work in a new way for a particular project. They often need the support of managers in other departments, or they need to influence their own boss to increase their budget or give support in some other way. Some managers have few, if any, subordinates, but are able to call on many other resources to get things done.

Different kinds of organisation need different kinds of management. Some are full of rules and regulations, laying down in great detail what staff must do. The management task will reflect this, with a lot of emphasis placed on ensuring that the rules are kept and established procedures followed. Others operate in such uncertain conditions that most rules would be quickly out of date, so the management task will be different from that in the rule-based organisation. Management is as diverse a task as the organisations in which it takes place. You will find more about the diversity of management work in Chapter 4.

1.7 Management institutionalised in organisations

A distinction needs to be drawn between management activity performed by an individual, using personal skills, and management as an institutionalised activity. Both are necessary. The key point is that organisations formalise and structure the way in which the three agendas of management and their interaction with the wider context are carried out. Organisations represent the 'institutionalisation' of management, in that they are the source of mechanisms, procedures and rules through which management activities on the content, process and control agendas are conducted. Managements create organisations which embody in their procedures and systems many of the activities which managers as individuals may also carry out: for example, job descriptions can be used to define the standards of work expected, and various forms of performance measure can be used to assess each employee's contribution. Hence, our experience is not influenced only by management as performed by individual managers, but by management as it has been given institutional support.

The organisations thus created affect us in most aspects of our lives. We live in communities, families, households, groups of friends, all of which

A manager is someone who gets things done with the aid of other people.

help to shape our experience of life as unique individuals. Those communities are part of our wider societies containing economic and political organisations which shape our world. We live in a world of managed organisations.

---

n o t e b o o k   1 . 6

Your experience of an organisation's performance

Do you agree with the previous paragraph? To test the assertions made in it, reflect on what you have done today. List the organisations with which you have come into contact, or depended on in some way. Alternatively you could list the types of organisation which have probably been involved in producing and supplying this · book.

As a second exercise, reflect on an organisation that you know well, such as a place where you have studied. Describe its main features in terms of the definition of organisation given here. Does the definition adequately describe the main elements?

Organisations consist of people trying to influence others to achieve certain objectives that create wealth or well-being through a variety of processes, technologies, structures and cultures.

The organisations you have listed in the first part of Notebook 1.6 will be of many different types. They will include domestic organisations of various kinds (family or flatmates), large public organisations (the postal service), small businesses (the newsagent), well-known private companies (which made the jar of coffee), or a voluntary group (the club where you attended a meeting). They have two things in common though: they each had an effect on you, and you will have made some judgement, perhaps unconsciously, about the encounter. Did the transaction work smoothly and was it in line with what you hoped for? Did you feel in the midst of chaos or that things could have worked better? If it was a business or public organisation, was the service good, reasonable, poor? Will you go there again?

---

n o t e b o o k   1 . 7

Voluntary bodies are organisations too. Charities and other kinds of voluntary group are big business. A recent estimate is that UK charities have an annual income of £16 billion and employ 250,000 people – and have perhaps another 1.5 million volunteer staff. All that needs managing. If you are connected with a voluntary group of any kind, reflect on how it is managed. How is it different from a business?

If you feel good about an organisation, it probably means that it is fulfilling the broad purpose often attributed to organisations, which is to create wealth or human well-being. We live with the fact that most resources – people, equipment, land, finance – are fundamentally scarce, and so people inevitably have to make choices about what to use them for, and how to use them. Nothing happens without some human intervention. Wealth or well-being is created when resources are managed in a way that *adds value* to them. By this view, the only reason that an organisation comes into being, and the only reason it survives, is that someone, or some group, believes that an organisation can do more than an individual working alone.

An organisation takes in resources of various kinds and uses them to produce and deliver a product or service that customers value. In return it receives the means to go on taking in resources as part of a continuing cycle. Gerard Egan (1993) has expressed the point like this:

> Well-run businesses create wealth for the societies in which they operate. While for-profit businesses create material wealth, not-for-profit and human service institutions create human capital or wealth. Counselling the troubled and helping them manage problems in living more effectively, creating learning opportunities for young and old alike, helping children grow and develop, healing the sick ... all these activities create human capital, human wealth. Furthermore since the best for-profit companies tend to develop [the skills and abilities of their staff] in the pursuit of financial goals, they benefit society by creating both material and human wealth. (p.9)

Thus organisations create wealth or human well-being by *providing goods and services* which people value.

If the organisation works inefficiently, or uses resources to do things that people do not require or value, it is destroying wealth. Then management is reducing value and destroying resources. It can be inefficient and wasteful, not only of material things but of other socially valued assets as well. At one level this waste is of limited significance. If the management of a motorway construction site fails to plan deliveries properly, staff will be paid for doing nothing while they await materials. So the road will be late, and cost more, than if its construction had been managed well. This will be a problem for the contracting company, perhaps for the users, but for no one else.

Some will take a more critical view. If you are opposed to a motorway being built through an area of woodland rich in wildlife, or because it will add to pollution, you will not regard the activities of the construction company as adding wealth to society. You will see it as using resources in a way that destroys some of our natural wealth. Therefore to you, even if the construction had been managed efficiently, it would still have destroyed valuable assets and placed long-term costs on society – management reduced rather than added value to society. The concept of wealth creation is not neutral – it is subjective and influenced by personal perspective.

This relates to an important distinction between efficiency and effectiveness. The former is a measure of the ratio between inputs and outputs; the latter refers to the wider objectives of an organisation. Both are needed. An organisation that is efficient but ineffective will not survive as it may be devoting resources to improving the way that it delivers things that customers do not want.

Another function of organisations – another form of intangible wealth that they create – is to provide a *sense of continuity*, a link to the past and the future. Individual members come and go, but organisations (usually) survive, as institutions with a place in their community, industry or profession. Knowledge and ideas are preserved. Organisations are also part of the institutional fabric of the society: people who neither work for an organis-

Value is added to resources when they are transformed into goods or services that are worth more than their original cost plus the cost of transformation.

Efficiency is a measure of the output produced with each unit of input. Effectiveness is a measure of the degree to which an organisation meets its objectives and the expectations of stakeholders.

ation nor use its services are yet aware of the organisation as a familiar and enduring piece of their lives. Again you can see a possible downside to this function. While some may value a sense of continuity provided by the continued existence of an instituion, others may see it as a block on progress, or as preserving outdated values and social structures.

Another form of wealth which organisations create is to *give people work, status and social contact*. They are a source of careers and training as well as immediate jobs, of contact with others, of a wider outlook, a source of structure in life. They often engender deep and distinctive loyalties amongst employees. You can see the disadvantage of this when someone is made redundant or retires. Some experience great stress, as they lose a significant part of their life. The emotional damage, especially if unexpected, often goes well beyond any economic loss.

Organisations can also *harm those who work for them*. They can take the vitality out of people by the jobs they are asked to do, or the demands they make. Those who succumb, or who become obsessed by work have little time for the other things they could do with their lives. The following extract is an example taken from an account of working life in a factory in France.

An obsession with work
❛ It was easy to find volunteers for Sundays as well. I'm sure that there were times when you could have asked them to work seven days out of seven for a whole year ... and there were people who worked after hours as well, for cash in hand, as well as their shift ... A friend said to me 'when I'm not working, I don't know what to do, I'm bored stiff ... I'm better off at work.' Your factory is your life. When you're at work, it's kind of secure, you've nothing else to do, it's all set up for you, you don't have to use your initiative ... It's real security, you have no more responsibility, its almost like going back to childhood. ❜
(Quoted in Gorz, 1989, p.117)

Organisations are also a way of *articulating and implementing ideals* – through charities, protest groups, environmental movements, or political parties. Individuals with an interest in a topic, or a passion to change something, can sometimes achieve what they want by themselves, but usually they need the tangible or moral support of others. Visible movements like Greenpeace or Oxfam started out as the vision of individuals. To achieve their worldwide operations, in both raising funds and managing their charitable and publicity activities, they have become multinational organisations.

Large organisations have access to political and economic resources far beyond those available to most individuals. Many own resources greater than those of the nations in which they operate, yet are not accountable to the people in those nations. So they can be a means of *gaining power* over others, as when entrepreneurs build great business empires. Some do so not just to create wealth but also to exercise power and to influence events. Others use them as instruments with which to dominate others – and they can *protect the interests* of particular groups. Workers created trade unions to increase their collective power relative to that of their employers. Professional associations serve a similar purpose, though they usually present their arguments in terms of the benefits their privilege will bring to the public.

Firms in a particular industry create trade organisations to protect their interests by lobbying or public relations work. Organisations can be a place where wider forces in society contend for control and influence alongside the business of delivering services to customers.

---

n o t e b o o k   *1.8*

Examples of organisational outcomes

Gather examples to illustrate each of the organisational outcomes outlined above, especially of organisations which exist to implement ideals or to defend particular interests. They will provide useful comparisons later with commercial organisations.

1.8   Gender in organisations

If organisations are mainly coalitions of interest groups, depending on a range of stakeholders for their survival, then this has implications both for assessing their performance in relation to their goals and for the meaning of the activity of management.

One particular way in which organisations can be used to protect established interests is through their effects on gender inequality. There are several perspectives on the gendered nature of work.

---

n o t e b o o k   *1.9*

Women and work in Europe

The female share of economic activity has increased in every member state of the European Union throughout the 1980s, and this increase continues in the 1990s. Between 1985 and 1990 women's employment increased at twice the rate of men's (Equal Opportunities Commission, 1992). In the UK, the number of men at work fell by 2.8 million between 1970 and 1990, while the number of women at work increased by 2 million (Incomes Data Service, May 1993). Despite this growth and the debates and campaigns about equal opportunities, women are much less likely than men to be economically active. Why do you think this is? Arrange a discussion with a woman of working age who is not in paid employment. Try to establish which, if any, of the following factors have influenced her situation: insufficient childcare arrangements; lack of flexible working hours; inequalities of access to training and education; prejudices such as 'women's place is at home'; and stereotypes such as 'men are the breadwinners' and 'women are less career-minded'.

Compare your answers with those of other students to see what conclusions you can draw.

Gendered segregation

Many tasks are predominantly male or female occupations. For example, women are much more likely than men to work as teachers, nurses or librarians than as doctors, judges or chartered accountants. They often do routine office work and shop work, but rarely do what is defined as skilled manual work. The reverse is true for men.

Gender segregation is both horizontal and vertical. Horizontal segregation occurs where men and women are associated with different types of jobs. For example, a survey on women in broadcasting occupations across the European Union found that females were over-represented in the administrative category (which includes secretarial and clerical posts), while men were over-represented in craft and technical occupations (Gallagher, 1992).

Even when male and female employees have the same job title and formal role in their organisation, they are likely to undertake different tasks and responsibilities. Podmore and Spencer (1986) studied male and female solicitors and concluded that the profession was not homogeneous:

> Men solicitors were more likely than women to be engaged in company and commercial work, one of the most prestigious areas of legal practice and in criminal and litigation work which often involves frequent court appearances. Women solicitors ... were more heavily involved than men in matrimonial work and such 'desk-bound' work such as wills and estate duty. (p.40)

Sonnentag (1994) studied female and male team leaders in software development in Swiss and German organisations. Women leading teams experienced less complex work situations than did their male colleagues. When a man was promoted to team leader he was more likely to deal with an increased amount of complexity in his work and to spend more time communicating with other people. When a woman was promoted, the complexity of the work and the pattern of communication remained much the same. Clearly the same job title does not imply equivalent responsibilities, challenge and opportunity for further advancement.

Similarly an exploratory study in the UK by Grundy (1996) showed that men get intensively involved with the 'pure', abstract computing work which is challenging and prestigious. They leave the 'messy' type of work to their female colleagues. This latter involves tasks such as merging and tidying databases and writing summary report programs. These are important tasks but are considered monotonous and unglamorous.

If women are confined to lower occupational positions and to less responsible work they will have fewer opportunities for professional growth and promotion. This in turn distances them from positions of power and the exercise of formal authority. This results in vertical segregation – men in the higher ranks of an organisation and women in the lower. To return to broadcasting, few senior management posts are held by women. Data from forty-three organisations in twelve European states in 1990 showed that women constituted at most 11 per cent of those in the top three levels of management (Gallagher, 1992). Vertical segregation occurs even in the so-called traditional women's occupations: 9 per cent of nurses are men but they occupy 45 per cent of the nurse manager jobs (Stamp and Robarts, 1986).

Gendered work and organisational processes

How are these horizontal and vertical divisions created? A major influence has been the simplification and standardisation of work, often as a result of automation. Historians on the evolution of computerisation identified that feminisation and automation of work are highly interrelated. Steiger and Reskin (1990) carried out a historical analysis of feminisation in the baking industry over the period 1950 to 1980, concluding that:

> what has changed is not the traditional sexual division of labour in baking but the baking process itself ... Technological innovation that permitted freezing and preserving dough so it could be shipped long distances ushered in bake-off bakeries and allowed schools, hospitals and restaurants to purchase ready-made or ready to bake products instead of baking them from scratch ... Rather than significantly altering the entrenched social roles of men and women in the baking industry, technical innovations gave rise to a less-skilled variant, bake-off baking, that was quickly defined as women's work. (p.269)

The supposedly masculine nature of organisational work is also identified as a barrier to the entry and advancement of women (Knights and Murray, 1994). Managers who emphasise the value of hard analytical skills above soft interpersonal skills support, perhaps unwittingly, the progression of men and discourage that of women. Stressing competitiveness, tension and long unsocial working hours has a similar effect. It drives some women away from senior positions owing to domestic responsibilities that continue to be their primary responsibility.

Gendered organisational studies

A third perspective which gives insight into gender inequality at work is the attention that researchers give to women. Research on management has focused on the male side of organisations, and remained largely blind and deaf to gender (Wilson, 1996). Studies have treated the workforce as unisex or only involved male participants in the research. See, for example, Acker and Van Houton's (1992) critique in Chapter 2 of one influential piece of research.

Even some comparative male/female studies and analyses obstruct understanding of male and female experience in organisations. Men and male behaviour become the standard against which women's experiences are evaluated (Marshall, 1984). Similarly, the idea of male as a norm may be implicitly accepted (Wilson, 1995). For instance, in a university course on management it is common to have a lecture on 'women in management' but rare to have one on 'men in management'. The presence of men is always taken for granted and their progression in organisations is not only not constrained but it is encouraged by organisational and wider social factors.

Put together, the three perspectives show that the dynamics of gender inequality at work are complex. Even research on the topic is often shaped from a male perspective, while the efforts that women themselves make to gain occupational identity and/or to change organisational practices are overlooked.

Steve Shirley, OBE, founder and life-president of FI Group Plc, a highly successful UK software company with a 50:50 gender mix across all levels, including the board, on 'putting the gender issue on the agenda'
❝With women forming more than half the working population, it certainly seems strange that so few of us get through the glass ceiling

to serve at a corporate level. I expect to be judged by the same inexorable criteria as my male colleagues: do I enable my group or organisation to achieve this task? Nowadays that is less by command and control, more by building teamwork and empowering individuals.

There are undoubted business benefits in having a work environment that is more encouraging to women. So, in the absence of quotas, what can be done to increase the quality and quantity of women's participation?

First, companies should consider introducing general management training specifically for women. I'm also a great believer in senior managers, of either sex, mentoring more junior female colleagues. Then there is 'career pathing' as a system of stepped experience towards career goals. Like men, women have to face the issue of whether they are prepared to pay the price of a vigorous career. Success is not an easy option. It requires sacrifices but also provides excitement and a sense of fulfilment.

Funnily enough, I also believe that God is in the detail. We have to get job advertisements and applications forms worded so that women who have been through career breaks to have children or to follow a husband's job move do not feel they have to break into an alien world of steady progression and unbroken continuity.

If you want to get a women on your board as a non-executive, think of the characteristics you want in any director. Then if there is a shortage in your industry extend your search to professions where women have hit the top.

On the subject of positive discrimination, there is Opportunity 2000's idea of percentages agreed with business unit heads so as to target, say, 30 per cent of all department heads of unit leaders to women. Once the middle management posts are filled, there will be competences enough for the top posts later. The main reason people give me for not appointing women to their boards is that there are no women around. By this they usually mean visible at the level below the board.

The process of managing change is an enormous challenge. But it is not always necessary to guess. Ask the women in your organisation what they think will help them fulfil their aspirations. **,**

(*Financial Times*, 10 January 1994, p.10)

1.9 Conventional and critical perspectives on management

Management takes place in a social setting in which people and institutions hold and express many different values, priorities and interests. These reflect deeper divisions in wealth, power and opportunity. Alvesson and Wilmott (1996) argue that, in capitalist societies, the development of management as an occupational group limits the risks of ownership and protects established positions. Managers act as agents of the owners and represent their interests. They are accountable to the owners of the business not to employees, consumers or wider communities.

The rise of management has institutionalised the lack of democratic control over the allocation of resources within, and by, work organisations. This lack of accountability increases the social and ecological risks for employees, customers and citizens. Once management becomes a separate social group the idea of a community of interest becomes problematical, especially when there is little or no accountability of managers to the managed. (Alvesson and Wilmott, 1996, p.12)

In consequence, management is not a neutral, professional process. It reflects existing unequal divisions within societies and within organisations. Writers such as Alvesson and Wilmott use ideas from Critical Theory to challenge institutions and practices that obstruct the search for alternative ways to manage co-operative activity. They do not see 'best practice' in terms of how best to achieve current ends (such as profitable growth or market share). Instead they ask what a practice contributes to objectives such as autonomy, responsibility, democracy and ecologically sustainable development.

They argue that Critical Theory is not 'anti-management'. Rather, their aim is to raise a broader set of questions not only about ways of accomplishing existing ends, but about whether the *existing ends routinely generate needless waste and divisiveness*' (p.3, emphasis in original). The technical and other skills of management remain highly relevant – solving technical problems is an essential activity in complex organisations. Their argument is that society will benefit more from such technical skills within a less irrational and socially divisive view of management.

> **d**
> A critical perspective is one which evaluates an institution or practice in terms of its contribution to human autonomy, responsibility, democracy and ecologically sustainable activity.

C A S E   Q U E S T I O N S   1.8

Two perspectives on Global Instruments

▶ We have set out above both a conventional and a critical view of management. With which of them do you agree? Do you need to choose? To help you reach a conclusion consider the Global Instruments case from both a conventional and a Critical Theory perspective.

▶ Alternatively, find an example of a management activity that the writer presents as a success in conventional terms (adding value, creating wealth). Then try to list the questions that you could ask about it from a Critical Theory perspective.

Managing in the hope of adding value and creating wealth is not just a logical or rational process – it cannot be so when it takes place within a human institution. Organisations have a history that shapes how people respond to events, and the political as well as rational choices they make. It is also taking place within a social and political context, where other values and influences shape what happens. Organisations do not exist in a vacuum, but in a wider economic and social structure, made up of many interest groups. It is therefore about managing both internally and externally in order to create wealth or well-being in a way that is acceptable to a wide range of stakeholders.

1.10 Studying management

Courses in management have been a rapidly growing area of European higher education in recent years as students seek courses with greater perceived relevance to their future. Do not confuse relevance in such a complex topic as management with easy examples or simple prescriptions. It is hoped that you will discover as you work through this book that many aspects of organisations are highly uncertain. There are frequently significant disagreements over both ends and means, especially over the strategic issues which determine the future direction and shape of the business. The greater this unpredictability, the more organisations become inherently beyond the ability of management to control, in the sense of doing things that lead to predictable results. Simple prescriptions and ready solutions are unlikely to work in the complex and ambiguous reality of a particular organisation.

We suggest that you take a critical perspective towards your study of management. Thomas (1993) cites the four components of critical thinking identified by Brookfield (1987). These are:

▶ a readiness to challenge assumptions,
▶ to understand management in its wider context,
▶ to be aware of alternative ways of doing things,
▶ to be generally sceptical towards what is presented.

This in no way implies a do-nothing cynicism that leads nowhere. A critical perspective helps to ensure that proposals and arguments are well founded. They are more likely to succeed than those based on inaccurate assumptions, or which ignore the context of the problem, or which do not recognise alternatives. The Noticeboard includes more details on this approach to thinking about the topic of management.

A more radical approach argues that management practice reflects wider structures of society, and may unwittingly reinforce social inequalities (Wilmott, 1984, 1987). On this view, objectivity implies analysing management practices (such as on the promotion of women or ethnic minorities) in terms

---

NOTICEBOARD **Ways of thinking critically**

1 Identifying and challenging assumptions about:
▶ the nature of management, its tasks, skills and purposes,
▶ the nature of people and why they behave as they do,
▶ the nature of organisations,
▶ learning, knowing and acting,
▶ values, goals and ends.

2 Creating contextual awareness by understanding:
▶ how management has developed historically,
▶ how management is conceived of in other societies,
▶ the implications of different industrial, organisational, economic, political and cultural contexts for management,
▶ the interrelationship between organisations and society.

3 Identifying alternatives by:
▶ becoming aware of the variety of ways in which managing and organising can be undertaken,
▶ inventing and imagining new ways of managing,
▶ specifying new goals and priorities.

4 Developing reflective scepticism by:
▶ adopting a questioning, quizzical attitude,
▶ recognising the limitations of much that passes for knowledge in the management field,
▶ knowing how to evaluate knowledge claims,
▶ developing a resistance to dogma and propaganda,
▶ being able to distinguish systematic argument and reasoned judgement from sloppy thinking, simplistic formulae and sophistry.

Source: Thomas (1993)

of their wider effects on society, rather than against measures of business performance alone. The success of a particular organisation might be at the expense of other interests in society. Thompson and McHugh (1996) urge that those studying management should pay attention to the following:

▶ **Reflexivity**   Critically reflecting on prevailing values, practice and knowledge so that they are not taken for granted, but challenged.

▶ **Embeddedness of organisations**   Stressing the insights from exploring the historical roots of current practices, and how wider social, political and economic structures affect them. Theories or prescriptions which ignore these contexts lack reality.

▶ **Multi-dimensionality**   Using several pespectives in the search for understanding. It is unlikely that any one set of theories or approaches will capture the complexity of management life.

▶ **Contradictions**   Looking for forces pulling in opposite directions, such as between management searching for control and professional staff seeking to retain autonomy.

▶ **Practical implications**   Analysing theory and practice together. Explore how the results of careful empirical work can guide practice more usefully than unsupported prescriptions.

Rigour implies being ready to look closely at the evidence behind the prescriptions and theories that writers commonly offer as ways of improving management practice. Management and organisations, perhaps because of their relative wealth, are tempting targets for those who believe that they have developed new or different solutions to the deeply complex problems of modern organisations. Activities such as total quality management, empowerment, business process re-engineering (topics introduced later) have undoubtedly helped to improve performance in some organisations. They are potentially valuable approaches, of which those studying management need to be aware. The difficulty is that they are never easy to apply, often fail, and may have loose links to subsequent improvements in performance. Too-ready acceptance of promotional success stories carries with it the severe danger of trying to apply the technique in the wrong place, or with extravagant expectations.

You are therefore encouraged to become knowledgeable, critical and reflective in your approach to the study of management. You should find out as much as you can about management: the activity is vital to modern economies and many of you will follow careers in management. You will almost certainly be better and more effective managers if your study of the subject now is objective and rigorous, rather than if you expect to acquire a portfolio of immediately relevant practices. You will acquire some, but they will be in the context of a relatively dispassionate study of the nature and functions of management.

In doing so, you will ideally be discussing their jobs with managers. In that context, some ideas from Watson (1994) are relevant:

> all humans are managers in some way. But some of them also take on the formal occupational work of being managers. They take on a role of shaping aspects of human social structure and culture in parts of our societies – those parts we call work organisations. But these managers are not supermen and women. They have all the human anxieties, inadequacies and needs for meaning to be found in those whom they are meant to 'manage'. Managers' work thus involves a double essential task: managing others at the same time as managing themselves. But the very

notion of 'managers' being separate people from the 'managed', a notion at the heart of traditional management thinking, undermines a capacity to handle this. Managers are pressured to be technical experts, devising rational and emotionally neutral systems and corporate structures to 'solve problems', 'make decisions', 'run the business'. These 'scientific' and rational-analytic practices give reassurance but can leave managers so distanced from the 'managed' that their capacity to control events is undermined. And they also tend to leave managers isolated from the essentially human community which the organisation might be. This can mean that their own emotional and security needs are not handled, with the effect that they retreat into all kinds of defensive, backbiting and ritualistic behaviour which further undermines their effectiveness as people moulding and maintaining a 'healthily' and productively cooperative organisation. (pp.12–13)

Your task of learning about management is in itself a task to be managed – and is therefore an opportunity to gain some practice in the subject. You can go through the processes of planning what you want to achieve and of organising the resources you will need. You will also experience various controls as you go through the course. Other people will impose some of these (such as your examinations), and you will create others yourself (such as creating a weekly work plan).

Your study of management is intended to develop your general mental and personal skills, as well as to develop your critical understanding of management in particular. Therefore in the course of your work on this book, you will have opportunities to improve the following skills:

▶ **Literacy**   Reading, writing and discriminating between different pieces of information.

▶ **Understanding argument**   Recognising arguments, and evaluating why particular conclusions were drawn.

▶ **Numerical operations**   Performing elementary arithmetical and numerical techniques.

▶ **Communicating**   Scanning several pieces of information, selecting those relevant to a particular task, combining them in a logical manner, and writing an informative account for a non-specialist audience.

▶ **Critical thinking**   Producing and evaluating arguments on real issues, and creatively putting forward your own reasons and explanations for some situation in a creative manner.

▶ **Problem-solving**   Using insight in approaching problems, finding information which will allow the problem to be solved, sensing the way towards a solution by combining information.

The most accessible sources of ideas and theory about management that you will have are this book, and your lectures and tutorials. There are many other ways in which you can supplement this material that should add to your interest and enrich your understanding. Such resources include the following:

▶ **Newspapers, television and radio**   The media include many stories that illustrate management themes. You can gather examples of these – often from the business pages but also from the sports section to get insights into, for example, management methods of some national team. The arts pages can give insights into the marketing and strategic plans of artistic and cultural enterprises.

- ▶ **World Wide Web**   The Internet is now a useful source of information about business and management issues. For example, you can call up the Biz-ed Website for information about many well-known companies, though access to sites can be slow and time-consuming.
- ▶ **Films and novels**   These provide examples of management issues being dealt with even when it was not the main intention. Classic examples of films are *The Magnificent Seven* and *Twelve Angry Men*, which illustrate a variety of influencing styles and decision-making processes respectively. Novels such as *The Goal* (Goldratt and Cox, 1989) or *Nice Work* (Lodge, 1989) give unusual insights into the work of managing.
- ▶ **Friends and relatives**   Some activities will invite you to conduct small surveys amongst people – possibly friends and relatives – who work in an organisation, whether or not in a management position, and to discuss the issues with them. These help you to gather information about current practices, which you can compare with that of other members of your tutorial group and with the theories in the book.
- ▶ **Direct observation**   As you go about your educational and social lives, you are experiencing organisations, and in some cases helping to manage them. Actively reflecting on these experiences will provide valuable support to your study of management.

1.11 Recap

The chapter began by showing how management and work can either be a unified activity or separated into relatively distinct functions. 'Management' work is, however, deeply embedded in most other kinds of work, and the differences between the work of managers and non-managers are often ambiguous. A definition of management was offered, and the different types of management that you are likely to meet in your studies were described. Three agendas or components of the overall management task were introduced as an integrating framework of content, process and control – the CPC model.

Content agenda

Management involves developing objectives and dealing with both short-term and long-term issues. A primary aim is to create wealth and well-being for society – though views will differ on whether they do that, and some see organisational objectives as destroying rather than adding value. The range of organisational objectives extends far beyond providing goods and services. Planning involves securing and allocating resources of many kinds (as in the Global Instruments example) in order to support the prevailing objectives. It is the primary role of management to add value to those resources. Generating action becomes more problematical with the separation of management from work. That separation leads to management that relies more on institutional and less on personal methods.

Process agenda

The process agenda refers to the way in which management seeks to achieve its content and control agendas. This agenda too becomes more important with the separation and specialisation of management. Organisations have many stakeholders, and management involves identifying them and balancing their conflicting interests. This helps to maintain an acceptable degree of external support. It also involves creating personal or institutional methods for taking account of stakeholder views. Managers are more likely to support the interests of powerful stakeholders than those of disadvantaged or weak ones. Management is not a neutral, technical activity. Important process tasks also involve creating and using internal and external communication systems.

Control agenda

The control agenda has both political and technical aspects. In the first sense it is used to describe the continuing attempts by management to control employees' behaviour. This affects the balance of power within the organisation; some claim it also affects the division of power in the wider society. In the more conventional and neutral sense, it refers to management monitoring what is happening and taking corrective action. Separate activities inevitably need co-ordination and control or they get into a mess. The measures used will need to reflect the interests of stakeholders, and leads to corrective action and learning. That information leads to a further set of content and process actions.

These points are summarised in Figure 1.3.

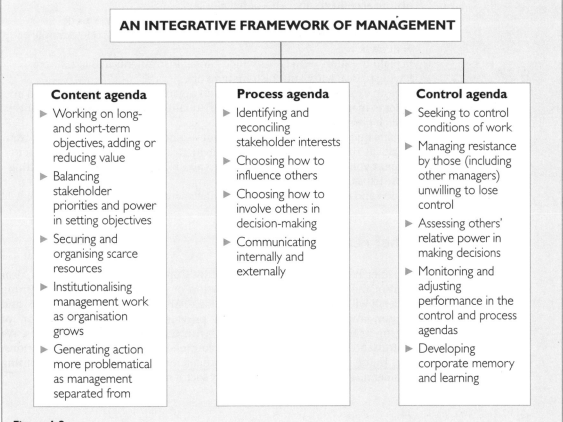

AN INTEGRATIVE FRAMEWORK OF MANAGEMENT

Content agenda
▶ Working on long- and short-term objectives, adding or reducing value
▶ Balancing stakeholder priorities and power in setting objectives
▶ Securing and organising scarce resources
▶ Institutionalising management work as organisation grows
▶ Generating action more problematical as management separated from

Process agenda
▶ Identifying and reconciling stakeholder interests
▶ Choosing how to influence others
▶ Choosing how to involve others in decision-making
▶ Communicating internally and externally

Control agenda
▶ Seeking to control conditions of work
▶ Managing resistance by those (including other managers) unwilling to lose control
▶ Assessing others' relative power in making decisions
▶ Monitoring and adjusting performance in the control and process agendas
▶ Developing corporate memory and learning

Figure 1.3

▶ Identify the issues which management at The Body Shop is likely to include on its content, process and control agendas. Use current evidence from sources such as the company's Website and the media to gather information for your answer.

▶ How do The Body Shop's agendas compare with those of Global Instruments?

▶ In what ways are managers in the two organisations adding value to the resources they use?

1.12   Review questions

1   What is the difference between management as a general human activity and management as a specialised occupation? How has this division happened, and what are some of its effects?

2   Can you illustrate both the division and the reintegration of management from current examples? What are the implications of reintegration likely to be for the people involved? Again, try to find and compare real examples.

3   Can you describe in your own words, with examples, the differences between general, functional, staff and line managers? Illustrate your answer by referring, where possible, to Global Instruments or The Body Shop.

4   Using an example of a manager's job, analyse the content, process and control agendas that he or she deals with. How do the contemporary and historical contexts affect his or her work?

5   Apart from delivering goods and services, what other functions do organisations perform? Illustrate your answer with at least one example of your own.

6   Explain the short-term issues which Global Instruments managers were having to deal with, and the long-term ones.

7   Give an example of the way in which an organisation has been managed in order to maintain or increase gender inequality? What are the consequences of such practices likely to be?

8   Prepare questions which you would put to a household name company, from a Critical Theory perspective. Gather evidence from the newspapers, etc., to support your questions or observations about how the company is handling these issues.

9   Review and revise the definition of management that you gave in Notebook 1.1.

Further reading

The chapter has clearly been influenced by Colin Hales's (1993) full and clear account of the separation and specialisation of management. Anyone wishing more detail will find that an accessible source. Alvesson and Wilmott (1996) and Thompson and McHugh (1995) both provide very detailed discussion of management from a critical perspective, with numerous further references. We have stressed that management is not confined to commercial organisations: Charles Handy (1988) provides a very valuable perspective for anyone wanting to consider management in the voluntary sector more fully.

W Website addresses

Biz/ed   http://www.bized.ac.uk
A useful site to become familiar with. This contains some files of company information and a list of other resources that may be useful to those studying business and management.

The Body Shop   http://www.the-body-shop.com
This site contains information about the company and its policies.

Critical Management   http://www.mailbase.ac.uk/lists/critical management
This site is a source of critical discussion, reflection and information.

Models of management

AIM

To present the major theoretical perspectives on management and to show how they relate to each other.

OBJECTIVES

By the end of your work on this chapter you should be able to outline the concepts below in your own terms and:

1 Explain why models are useful in studying management

2 Outline the purpose and structure of the competing values framework

3 Outline the main elements of the following approaches:
   Rational goal (Taylor, the Gilbreths and operational research)
   Internal process (Weber, Fayol)
   Human relations (Follett, Mayo)
   Open systems (sociotechnical and contingency)
   and evaluate their strengths and weaknesses

4 Outline Morgan's 'images of organisation', and show your understanding by giving your own examples

5 Illustrate how each of the earlier theories has contributed to some aspect of the management agendas

6 Compare the approaches in terms of their contribution to specific management situations

7 Explain the influence of uncertain conditions on management

8 Compare the assumptions of linear and non-linear models of management

9 Compare unitary, pluralist and critical perspectives on organisations

10 Evaluate the influence of these alternative models on practice in a specific organisation

Robert Owen – an early management innovator

Robert Owen (1771–1856) was a successful manufacturer of textiles, who ran mills both in England and, most famously, at New Lanark in Scotland, which he bought in 1801. New Lanark was an unusually large business unit for the time, requiring a range of management and production control techniques beyond the needs of the owner of a smaller enterprise. The mills were in poor shape when he took them over, and he quickly tried to improve the quality of the labour force. Most employees, at this stage of the Industrial Revolution, had little or no experience of factory work. He found 'the great majority of them were idle, intemperate, dishonest [and] devoid of truth' (quoted in Butt, 1971). He also had 'to deal with slack managers who had tolerated widespread theft and embezzlement, immorality and drunkenness' (Butt, 1971).

Owen quickly introduced new management practices. These included daily and weekly measurements of stocks, output and productivity; a system of labour costing, and measures of work-in-progress. He used a novel technique to control employees. A small four-sided piece of wood, with a different colour on each side, hung beside every worker. The colour set to the front indicated the previous day's standard of work – black indicating bad. Everyone could see this measure of the worker's performance. Overseers recorded this to check any trends in a person's work. Owen was keen on discipline, and introduced community singing 'to counteract incipient lawlessness'. The workers are reported to have been less than enthusiastic.

Owen actively managed the links between his business and the wider world. On buying the mills he quickly became part of the Glasgow business establishment, and was closely involved in the activities of the Chamber of Commerce. He took a prominent role in the social and political life of the city. He used these links in particular to argue the case for reforms in the educational and economic systems, and was critical of the effect which industrialisation was having upon working class life. Owen believed that education in useful skills would help to release working class children from poverty. He provided a nursery for workers' children over one year old, allowing both parents to continue working, and promoted the case for wider educational provision. He also developed several experiments in co-operation and community-building, though with only limited success. More broadly, he sought new ways of organising the economic system in a way that would raise wages and increase security of employment, at a time of severe business fluctuations. For example, in 1815 he persuaded allies in Parliament to propose a Bill on child labour. This would have made it illegal for children under 10 to work in mills. It would also have limited their working hours to ten a day. The measure met strong opposition from mill owners and a much weaker measure became law in 1819, to Owen's disappointment.

CASE QUESTIONS

- In what ways do the management issues in this case differ from those at Global Instruments?
- How did Owen interpret his role as manager?
- What were the main issues that he and other managers of the time had to deal with?

2.1 Introduction

This chapter introduces the following ideas:

▶ Model
▶ Models of management
▶ Feedback
▶ Metaphor
▶ Scientific management
▶ Operational research
▶ Bureaucracy
▶ Administrative management
▶ Human relations
▶ System
▶ Subsystem
▶ Open systems
▶ System boundary
▶ Sociotechnical systems
▶ Non-linear systems
▶ Environment
▶ Contingency

The brief historical sketch of Robert Owen illustrates three themes that run through this book. First, he was active in devising management systems of all kinds to improve the performance of his mills. The point that comes through most clearly is the emphasis on *control*. This remains a major pre-occupation of management and a major source of tension between manager and managed. Secondly, Owen was clearly aware of the wider social environment in which he lived – especially of a workforce unused to the factory system, and with different values from his own. He criticised the effects of industrialisation on that social system. He tried to influence local and national policy to alleviate these, and so represents an early example of business leaders trying to influence social and economic policy. His practice of providing nurseries for employees' children from the age of one year would be rare even today.

CASE QUESTIONS 2.1

Applying the integrative framework

You can start using the CPC model by analysing Owen's approach to management.

▶ What are the main items which feature on his content agenda?
▶ What process issues does the account refer to?
▶ What methods of control did Owen use?
▶ How did the wider context affect Owen's management activities?
▶ What evidence is there of the management activity being institutionalised?

Thirdly, this example from two centuries ago introduces a historical perspective to your study of management. The past as well as the present shapes management problems and practices. In Owen's time the dominant concern was the transition from an agricultural to an industrial economy.

Many of the practices he invented were directed at the conflicts between these two systems. Today the advanced industrial countries are in transition from an industrial to a post-industrial era. In the newer industrial countries of eastern Europe and Asia, the transition is again from agriculture to industry. Both are experiencing a transition to global rather than national economies. These changing contexts do not happen independently – they are the cumulative result of management actions, which sometimes generate conflicts and contradictions or sometimes exacerbate them further. Managements try to cope with these conflicts in their own particular organisations.

2.2 Why study models of management?

A model represents a more complex reality. It helps us understand that complexity, and offers alternative ways of looking at an issue. Most management problems require several perspectives. No single model offers a complete solution, so practitioners need to use models together. For example, management in a globally competitive business typically requires flexibility, quality *and* low-cost production, so it has an interest in models of the production process that show how it can be organised most efficiently from a technical perspective. Management also has an interest in models of human behaviour at work, which show the limitations of work-simplification, and how, if taken too far, it has negative effects on staff, who may become less flexible and produce lower-quality output.

Managerial action is guided by the models that managers hold, whether explicitly or implicitly. To understand these activities, we need to be conscious of the range of perspectives available, and what each can contribute to the management process.

A model represents a complex phenomenon by identifying the major elements and relationships.

Models help to understand complexity

Models help analysis by formally identifying the key variables, suggesting possible relationships and predicting the possible outcomes of change. The better the model is, the more useful it will be. Valid models represent a toolkit we can choose from to try to understand situations. They help us to cope with complexity, rather than ignoring it. Charles Handy has pointed out that theories can:

Help to *explain* the Past which
in turn
helps one to *understand* the Present
and thus
to *predict* the Future which leads
to
more *influence* over future events
and
less *disturbance* from the Unexpected.

Many people who begin to study management quickly experience a sense of frustration with the topic, especially if they have previously studied in the physical or natural sciences. The fixed laws governing the scientific phenomena under study allow people to predict the relationship between cause and effect with great accuracy within a specified range of circumstances.

Management has few such certainties. One reason is the number of variables likely to be having an impact on the situation. Figure 2.1 indicates the range of items that can influence the performance of an organisation.

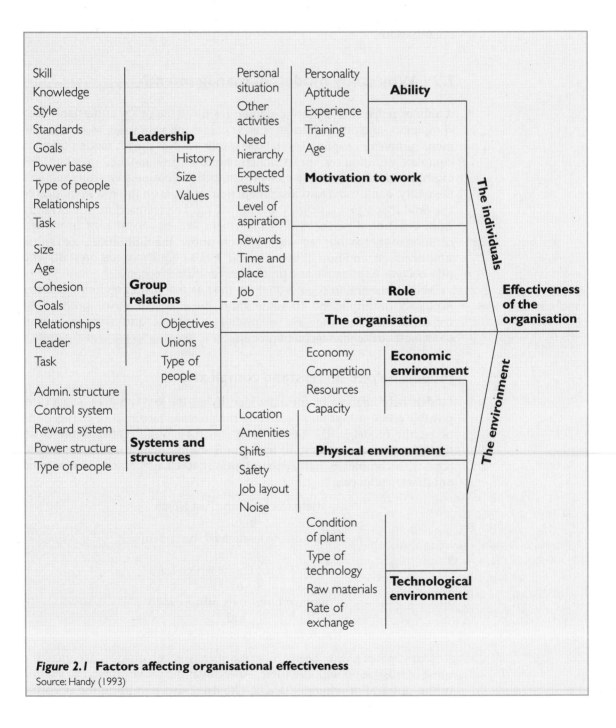

Figure 2.1 **Factors affecting organisational effectiveness**
Source: Handy (1993)

However, scientific phenomena also embody numerous variables. The difference in developing theories of management is that data are hard to collect and are often subjective. Researchers can rarely collect data with the degree of accuracy associated with physical or natural sciences. They can easily collect data on some items in Figure 2.1. Others cause more difficulty: either they are hard to obtain, or their meaning is open to dispute. People's satisfaction with their job is a good example. Does one person's response that they find their job quite satisfying mean the same as another person's identical reply? If not, how do you aggregate the data?

C A S E   Q U E S T I O N S   2.2

▶ Which of the variables in Figure 2.1 was Robert Owen attempting to influence?

▶ Which of the variables were influencing the performance of his mill?

Models offer a range of perspectives

A metaphor is an image used to signify the essential characteristics of a phenomenon.

Models also reflect different ways of looking at the phenomenon under discussion and so broaden our perspective. Some models represent organisations as machines, others as political battlegrounds, others again as career ladders. The images or metaphors which researchers use influence the problems they study and the variables they analyse.

These different metaphors are one source of the apparently inconsistent results of management research. Gareth Morgan has developed this influential idea (see the Noticeboard).

NOTICEBOARD **Gareth Morgan's images of organisation**

Since organisations are complex and contradictory creations, no single perspective or theory can explain them adequately. We need to see them from several viewpoints, each of which will illuminate one aspect or feature – while at the same time obscuring others. Gareth Morgan (1997) shows how alternative mental images and metaphors can represent organisations. Metaphors are a way of thinking about a phenomenon, attaching labels to it, which vividly indicate the image being used. We express alternative images in different theoretical constructions, focusing on different ways of looking at the problem. Images help understanding – but also obscure or distort understanding if we use the wrong image. Morgan explores eight images, which represent organisations as:

▶ **Machines** Mechanical thinking and the rise of the bureaucratic organisation.

▶ **Organisms** Recognising organisational needs, and how organisations' health is affected by the environment.

▶ **Brains** An information processing, learning and self-organising perspective.

▶ **Cultures** A perspective focusing on the underlying assumptions, beliefs and values.

▶ **Political systems** The role of interests, conflicts and power in shaping organisations.

▶ **Psychic prisons** How people can become imprisoned or confined by modes of thinking and acting which become habitual.

▶ **Flux and transformation** A focus on change and renewal, and the logic behind them.

▶ **Instruments of domination** The exploitation of members, nations, environments.

n o t e b o o k   2 . 1

At least three of these images were mentioned in the previous chapter: psychic prison, instrument of domination, and as political system. Can you identify where this was?

Look out for other examples of these images, with the aim of identifying at least one example of your own of each image.

Models reflect their context

People develop models and theories in response to circumstances, in this case to the most pressing issues facing managers at the time. In the late nineteenth century, skilled labour was scarce, unskilled labour plentiful, and management was keen to increase its control of both. The pressing problem was how to control vast numbers of people with limited experience whom factory owners had recruited to work for them. Managements wanting to increase production to meet growing demand were receptive to theories about methods of production. They sought ways of simplifying tasks so that they could make more use of less-skilled employees. Early management theories gave priority to these issues.

Today a key issue for many managements is how to organise to meet a rapidly changing market. They are interested in models which suggest ways of organising work for maximum flexibility. Current theories reflect this interest by offering ways of coping with a highly turbulent and competitive world, where flexibility, quality and low cost are often essential for survival.

2.3 Competing values framework

The range of models of management appears confusing and contradictory. Academics and practitioners have developed them independently, in different contexts and with different aims. It is not immediately obvious how the different approaches relate to each other. Robert Quinn's 'competing values' model is an attempt to show the relationship between these different models. It also highlights the contrasting values that lie behind the details – a theme that is central to an understanding of management. The competing values approach is outlined here and each model is then described in more detail.

Quinn and his colleagues argue that while the main models add to our knowledge of management, none is in itself sufficient to capture its full complexity (Quinn *et al.*, 1996). The different approaches are not mutually exclusive, but are complementary and equally essential elements in a larger whole. They argue that although models help us to see some aspects of a phenomenon, they can also blind us to other aspects that may be equally relevant.

Their framework has two axes, each of which represents a different perspective on management problems. The vertical axis contains the dimensions of control and flexibility. As already mentioned, control has been a pervasive concern of management, with some of the early theorists placing a particular emphasis on the topic. More recent approaches emphasise ways of enhancing flexibility – apparently the opposite of control. The horizontal axis distinguishes an internal focus from an external one. Some theories are primarily inward-looking, while others stress the relationship between the organisation and its external environment. Figure 2.2 shows these axes.

The human relations model, upper left in the figure, stresses the human-centred criteria of commitment, participation, openness. The open systems model, upper right in the figure, stresses criteria of innovation, adaptation, resource acquisition. The rational goal in the lower right focuses on productivity, direction, goal clarity, while, finally, the internal process model, stresses administrative efficiency, documentation, control.

The labels within the circle indicate the primary concerns of theories in that segment. The four broad models that have sought to address those

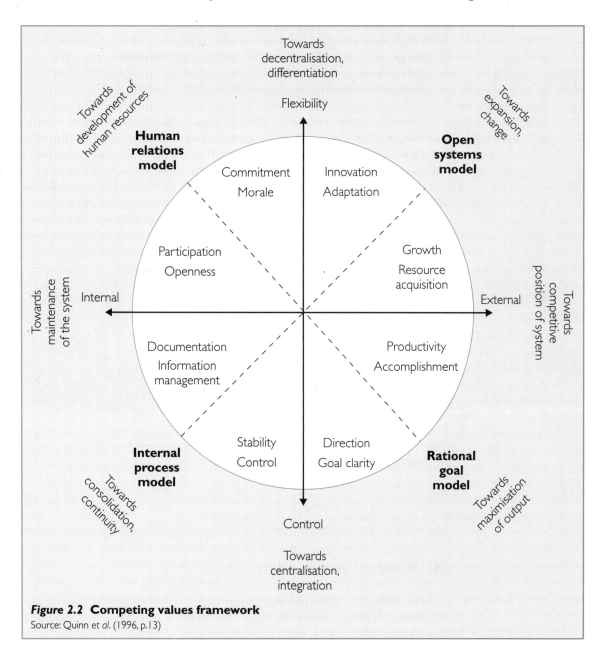

***Figure 2.2* Competing values framework**
Source: Quinn *et al.* (1996, p.13)

concerns appear around the outside. Lastly, Figure 2.2 indicates some of the general values associated with each of the models. For example, it shows that the value associated with the rational goal model is that of maximising output. The human relations model emphasises developing personnel.

Quinn uses the overall framework to locate the main models of management into a comprehensive whole. He uses the term 'competing' values, as each of the models seems at first to carry a competing message. Customers expect organisations to be adaptable and flexible, yet also to provide stability and continuity. Some players want their organisation to develop close relations with other organisations, yet at the same time others want them to have tight information management and clear lines of communication.

C A S E   Q U E S T I O N S   2 . 3

▶ Before we go into the detail, refer back to Global Instruments. In which of the models would the manager of the European plant be most interested? And the production manager?

While the values associated with these models appear competing and contradictory, they need not be so. They may be complementary in the sense that each illuminates a different aspect of the same phenomenon. The outer ring locates different general values within the framework. For example, the internal process model links with the values of consolidation and continuity. The open systems model stresses values of expansion and change.

According to Quinn, each model has a perceptual opposite: the human relations model, defined by flexibility and internal focus, is a sharp contrast to the rational goal model, defined by control and external focus. The first values people for themselves while the second values them as contributors to attaining goals. Quinn stresses that the parallels among the models are also important. Both the human relations and the open systems models share an emphasis on flexibility, while both the internal process and rational goal models share an emphasis on control.

Quinn argues that the model reflects the complexity faced in organisations, and provides a conceptual framework to help cope with that complexity. The framework allows us to appreciate both the weaknesses and the strengths of each model. It can also be used to identify the different competences needed to perform the management task implied by each model.

n o t e b o o k   2 . 2

How does Quinn's model relate to critical perspectives on management? What question does it appear to ignore?

2.4 Rational goal models

The availability of powered machinery during the Industrial Revolution transformed manufacturing and mining processes. Entrepreneurs faced the issue of how to organise their production and administrative activities to exploit these advances profitably. Although domestic and export demand for manufactured goods was high, so was the risk of business failure. Economic and social considerations probably motivated their search. Incomes were very low by today's standards, and price was a major influence on demand. Manufacturers wanted to arrange their businesses to make the best use of the new machinery to produce large volumes of cheap manufactured goods.

Adam Smith, the Scottish economist, had written enthusiastically in 1776 of the way in which pin manufacturers in Glasgow had broken a job previously done by one man into several small steps. A single worker now performed each of these steps repetitively. This greatly reduced the discretion which workers had over their work, but because each was able to specialise, output increased dramatically. Smith believed that this was one of the key ways in which the new industrial system was increasing the wealth of the country.

Charles Babbage supported and developed Smith's observations. He was an English mathematician better known as the inventor of the first calculating engine. During his work on that project he visited many workshops and factories in England and on the Continent. He then published his reflections on 'the many curious processes and interesting facts' that had come to his attention (Babbage, 1835). He believed that 'perhaps the most important principle on which the economy of a manufacture depends is the division of labour amongst the persons who perform the work' (p.169). There were several reasons why this method – in which 'each process by which any article is produced is the sole occupation of one individual' – had become so widespread. It reduced training costs, saved the time of moving between jobs, and increased the skill which people working at one task would acquire. This in turn meant that workers were able to suggest improvements to the process (pp.169–76).

Babbage also observed that employers in the mining industry had applied the idea to what he called 'mental labour'. 'Great improvements have resulted ... from the judicious distribution of duties ... amongst those responsible for the whole system of the mine and its government' (p.202). He also recommended that managers should know the precise expense of every stage in production. Factories should also be large enough to secure the economies made possible by the division of labour and the new machinery.

Thompson and McHugh (1995) have argued that technological innovation was not the only reason for the growth of the factory system. The earlier 'putting-out' system of manufacture, in which workers at home worked on materials supplied and collected by entrepreneurs, allowed workers great freedom over their hours, pace and methods of work. The system was difficult to control, and the quantity and quality of output were unpredictable. Emerging capitalist entrepreneurs concluded that they could only secure the control they required by a new approach. This was to bring all their workers together in a factory. Having all workers on a single site meant that 'coercive authority could be more easily applied, including systems of fines, supervision ... the paraphernalia of bells and clocks, and incentive payments. The employer could dictate the general conditions of work, time and space; including the division of labour, overall organisational layout and design, rules governing movement, shouting, singing and other forms of disobedience'

(Thompson and McHugh, 1995, p.25). These trends were evident across Europe as individual factory owners experimented with new forms of control.

C A S E   Q U E S T I O N S   2 . 4

▶ We have presented the 'efficiency' and 'control' theories accounting for the growth of the factory system. Review the description of Robert Owen's management practices in the light of these alternatives. From the information in the case, which theory does this example support?

Taylor's perspective

The fullest development and dissemination of these ideas came in the work of Frederick W. Taylor (1856–1915). An American mechanical engineer, Taylor focused on the relationship between the worker and the machine-based production systems which by then were in widespread use. He wrote that 'the principal object of management should be to secure the maximum prosperity for the employer (the development of every branch of the business to its highest state of excellence), coupled with the maximum prosperity for each employee' (Taylor, 1917, p.9). He believed that the way to achieve this was to ensure that workers reached their highest state of efficiency, that is when they were producing their largest daily output. This would follow from detailed control of the process, which would become the primary responsibility of management, not of the worker. Management should concentrate on understanding the production systems, and use this knowledge to specify every aspect of the operation. He advocated five basic principles designed to help managers to achieve this greater control and predictability:

▶ Use scientific methods to determine the one best way of doing a particular task, rather than rely on the older 'rule of thumb' methods.
▶ Select the best person to do the job so defined, ensuring that both physical and mental qualities were the most appropriate for the task.
▶ Train, teach and develop the worker to follow the defined procedures precisely.
▶ Provide financial incentives to ensure that all the work is done in accordance with the prescribed method.
▶ Shift all responsibility for planning and organising work from the worker to the manager.

Taylor's underlying philosophy was that scientific analysis and fact, not guesswork, should inform management. Like Smith and Babbage before him, he believed that efficiency rose if tasks were as routine and predictable as possible. He therefore advocated the use of techniques such as time and motion studies, standardised tools and individual incentives. Control would be increased if work were broken down into small, specific tasks. Specialist managerial staff, would design these, and generally plan and organise the work of manual staff:

> The work of every workman is fully planned out by the management at least one day in advance, and each man receives in most cases complete written instructions, describing in detail the task which he is to

accomplish, as well as the means to be used in doing the work ... This task specifies not only what is to be done but how it is to be done and the exact time allowed for doing it. (Taylor, 1917, p.39)

The industrialised economies adopted Taylor's ideas widely, if selectively, during the 1920s and 1930s (Thompson and McHugh, 1995). His methods allowed productivity to rise many times, and led to the replacement of skilled artisans by semi-skilled workers following set routines of work. They also encouraged the development of separate planning and administrative staffs. Henry Ford was an enthusiastic advocate of Taylor's ideas. When he introduced the assembly line in 1914 he was able to reduce the time taken to assemble a car from over 700 hours to 93 minutes. Taylor also had a great influence in the development of administrative systems to support the core operation in areas like record-keeping and stock control. Ford also developed his systems of materials flow and plant layout, making a significant contribution to the development of scientific management (Biggs, 1996; Williams, 1992).

However, the gains in worker productivity were often achieved at great human cost, as the Case Example shows.

case example Ford's Highland Park plant

Ford's new plant at Highland Park, completed in 1914, was deliberately designed on rationalised lines, in the particular sense that it introduced predictability and order 'that eliminates all questions of how work is to be done, who will do it, and when it will be done. The rational factory, then, is a factory that runs like a machine' (Biggs, 1996, p.6). Biggs provides abundant evidence of the effects of the wide application of rational production methods in the plant:

> The advances made in Ford's New Shop allowed the engineers to control work better. The most obvious and startling change in the entire factory was, of course, the constant movement, and the speed of that movement, not only the speed of the assembly line, but the speed of every moving person or object in the plant. When workers moved from one place to another, they were instructed to move fast. Laborers who moved parts were ordered to go faster. And everyone on a moving line worked as fast as the line dictated. Not only were workers expected to produce at a certain rate in order to earn a day's wages but they also had no choice but to work at the pace dictated by the machine. By 1914 the company employed supervisors called pushers (not the materials handlers) to 'push' the men to work faster.

The 1914 jobs of most Ford workers bore little resemblance to what they had been just four years earlier, and few liked the transformation of their work. Even as early as 1912, job restructuring sought an 'exceptionally specialized division of labor [to bring] the human element into condition of performing automatically with machine-like regularity and speed' (Biggs, 1996, p.132).

The trade unions in the United States believed his methods increased unemployment, and vigorously opposed them. For many people, work on an assembly line or similarly routine operation is boring and alienating, devoid of much human meaning. In extreme cases, the time taken to complete an operation before starting to repeat it – the cycle-time – is less than a minute, and makes use of a very limited range of human abilities.

The Gilbreths' perspective

Frank and Lillian Gilbreth (1868–1924 and 1878–1972) worked as a husband and wife team, and enthusiastically promoted the development of scientific management. Frank Gilbreth had originally been a bricklayer, and observed a variety of practices that made the pace of work slow and output unpredictable. He studied the movements involved with the help of film, and used this to find the most economical motions for each task. He also specified exactly what the employer should provide. This included equipment such as trestles at the right height, and materials at the right time. Supplies of mortar and bricks (arranged the right way up!) should arrive at the right time, so as not to interrupt the work. In a book published in 1909, he laid down very precise guides on the process of laying the bricks. These were intended to reduce unnecessary actions, and hence fatigue. He claimed that his methods would reduce the number of movements needed to lay a brick: the conventional method required eighteen, his method would require five. He gave equally precise guidance on how to train apprentices, to ensure that they followed the correct systems:

> These rules and charts will enable the apprentice to earn large wages immediately, because he has here a series of instructions that show each and every motion in the proper sequence. They eliminate the 'wrong' way [and] all experimenting. (Quoted in Spriegel and Myers, 1953, p.57)

Lillian Gilbreth focused more on the psychological aspects of management, and on promoting the welfare of the individual worker. She too promoted the ideas of scientific management, believing that, properly applied, they would enable individuals to reach their full human potential. Through careful development of systems, careful selection, clearly planned training, and proper equipment, workers would be able to build their self-respect and pride. In *The Psychology of Management* (1914) she argued that if workers did something well, and that was made public, workers would develop pride in their work and in themselves. To the charge that scientific management turned workers into machines, she argued that:

> under really successful scientific management, it is realised that the worker is of an inquiring mind, and that, unless this inquiring tendency is recognised, and his curiosity satisfied, he can never do his best work. Unless the man knows why he is doing the thing, his judgement will never reinforce his work … His work will not enlist his zeal unless he knows exactly why he is made to work in the particular manner prescribed. This giving of the 'why' to the worker through the system, and thus allowing his reason to follow through all the details, and his judgement to conform absolutely, should silence the objections of those who claim that the worker becomes a machine, and that he has no incentive to think. (Quoted in Spriegel and Myers, 1953, p.431)

━━━━━━━ ✒ ─→   n o t e b o o k   2.3

Which of the three agendas in the CPC model was Frederick Taylor mainly concerned with?

What assumptions did (a) Frederick Taylor and (b) Lillian Gilbreth make about the interests and abilities of industrial workers?

The Gilbreths believed that time and motion study, and indeed the whole apparatus of scientific management, would raise workers' morale. It would bring obvious physical benefits, and demonstrate that management cared about the welfare of workers. In that way, workers would be willing to follow the prescribed tasks, and to work in an orderly and predictable way.

Operational research

Another perspective that is included within the rational goal model is that of operational research. This originated during the early 1940s, when the United Kingdom War Department faced severe management problems. To solve these it formed what were called operational research (OR) teams which pooled the expertise of various scientific disciplines such as mathematics and physics. The teams produced significant results, especially when their intellectual expertise was supported by the earliest computers, which were developed in the same period.

After the war, management in both industrial and governmental organisations saw that they could apply OR to the problems of managing complex civil organisations as well as military ones. The scale and complexity of business were increasing, and required new techniques to analyse the many interrelated variables involved. Mathematical models could help and computing developments supported the increasing sophistication of the models the scientists produced. This led to the continuing growth of the 'management science approach'.

The management science approach to a problem usually begins by putting together a team from relevant disciplines to analyse the issue and propose a solution to management. The team constructs a mathematical model showing the links between all the relevant factors. By changing the values of variables in the model (such as increasing transport costs) and comparing different forms of the equations, the team can establish the quantitative effects of each change. The team can present management with apparently objective analyses of alternatives, as a guide to their decisions.

Large organisations in both the public and private sectors use the techniques of management science. The model supports planning activities within the content agenda such as production scheduling, cash flow management, and calculating how much stock is needed at different levels of production. It also contributes to the control agenda by helping to specify and measure appropriate performance levels.

One difficulty with management science is that some managers find the mathematical basis forbidding and inaccessible. A second difficulty is that it cannot take into account the human and social uncertainties of modern organisations. The assumptions built into the models may in practice be invalid, especially if they involve political interests. The technique can clearly contribute to the analysis of management problems, and probably does so best when recognised as only one, relatively technical, part of the total solution.

Evaluation

Hales (1993) identifies five general principles within the rational model of management. These are, the use of systematic work methods, detailed division of labour, centralised planning and control, a 'low-involvement' employment relationship, and a view that technical efficiency is neutral, favouring both employers and workers.

Systematic work methods and detailed division of labour echo the beliefs of Taylor and the Gilbreths that carefully observing and measuring work enables management to identify the most rational and efficient methods. Time and motion studies involve identifying and measuring the physical movements made by workers as they perform a task. Experts analyse the results and eliminate any movements that slow down production. The objective is to make a job highly routine and efficient, eliminating wasted physical effort and specifying an exact sequence of activities that minimises the amount of time, money and effort needed to make a product.

Later writers have refined the ideas and methods, but the underlying principle of searching for the best way of doing a task remains the same. Work study and process engineering departments aim to put these principles into practice in modern organisations. They develop standard methods for doing work, clear descriptions of each activity and clear job descriptions for staff.

Centralised planning and control take many forms, but the assembly line and similarly tightly defined production systems reflect the ideas most clearly. Even without assembly lines, many factories use detailed models to direct materials along the most efficient route. Many service organisations use similar procedures to set out the order in which staff are to perform activities in dealing with a patient or client. Computer systems increasingly allow management to link these different stages, with information being updated as each activity is completed. Such integrated information systems assist staff doing successive stages of the work. They also enable management to monitor and control activities much more closely than with manual systems. Management can then receive quick and detailed information on output rates, costs, wastage rates and other performance measures relevant to a particular process.

A further feature of the rational models is that they embody an explicit or implicit assumption about the motivation of workers. In essence, this is that the relationship between employee and organisation is one of low involvement. Taylor believed that the only way to gain the effort required was through financial incentives, with few other strands in the link between the two. He believed that money was the primary incentive, and that workers would be willing to follow the standard tasks and routine operations if the financial reward was worthwhile. He recommended using an individual piecework system to establish pay. If a worker achieved a predetermined production target, management would pay a standard wage rate. If workers produced more, management paid more.

A low-involvement employment relationship typically embodies performance evaluation systems that focus on short-term and precisely defined results. In extreme cases, not meeting the required targets leads to dismissal and the end of the relationship. Management has used such such systems widely for manual workers and uses similar commission-based systems for sales staff.

CASE QUESTIONS 2.5

▶ Which of the ideas in the rational model of management was Owen experimenting with at New Lanark?

▶ Would you describe Owen's approach to management as low involvement?

▶ What assumptions did he make about the motivation of workers?

Examples of rational goal approaches are easy to find today, not only in manufacturing but also in many offices and service organisations. Many call-centre staff, dealing with customer enquiries or orders, work on precisely specified tasks. They have little discretion in how they do the job, as management expects them to follow the prescribed system. Watch the staff in a bank or a travel agency dealing with a routine transaction with a customer. The chances are that they will be following very closely a set of prompts on their computer screen, keying in the answer, which then prompts the next question. This severely limits the scope for error and for any deviation from the prescribed route (Gabrial, 1988; Ritzer, 1993).

case example — A modern example of using technology to control staff

A successful travel company introduced a networked computer system linking all of its branches to head office. Many benefits were expected and achieved. One of these was that, having sold a holiday, staff should work in a more disciplined routine to complete the administrative details. The information technology director commented:

> **We are finding that paper is never a standard system – there are always different ways you can handle paper. You can always choose to fill in a form or not fill it in, choose to complete a box or not. We expect that automation will finally provide the disciplined system that people must adhere to.**

Source: Boddy and Gunson (1996)

notebook 2.4

Current examples of scientific management

There are many examples today of work being carefully planned and designed on scientific management principles. Try to find at least one example in which these principles seem to have guided the way the work was set up. There are examples in office and service areas as well as in factories. Compare your examples with those of colleagues.

2.5 Internal process models

Weber's perspective

A major contribution to the search for ways of managing organisations efficiently came from Max Weber (1864–1920). Weber was a German social historian who drew attention to the growing significance of large organisations. As societies became more complex, responsibility for core activities became concentrated in specialised units. They could only operate with systems that institutionalised the management process by creating organisations that relied heavily on rules and regulations, hierarchy, precise division of labour and detailed procedures. Weber was one of the first to write extensively about the problems of organisations and to observe that bureaucratic processes were bringing routine to office operations just as machines had to production.

Bureaucratic management is usually associated with seven characteristics, outlined in the Noticeboard below. When you have read them, you can apply them by working on Notebook 2.5.

> Bureaucracy is a system in which people are expected to follow precisely defined rules and procedures rather than to use personal judgement.

NOTICEBOARD **The characteristics of bureaucratic management**

Rules and regulations   The formal guidelines that define and control the behaviour of all employees while they are working. This formal system helps to provide the discipline that an organisation needs to exercise control and reach its goals. Adherence to rules and regulations ensures uniformity of procedures and operations, regardless of an individual manager's or employee's personal desires. Rules and regulations also enable top management to direct and co-ordinate the efforts of the middle managers and, through them, the efforts of first-line managers and employees. Managers may come and go, but rules and regulations help to maintain organisational stability.

Impersonality   Reliance on rules and regulations leads to impersonality, which protects employees from the personal whims of managers. Although the term often has negative connotations, Weber believed that impersonality ensured fairness for employees. An impersonal superior evaluates subordinates objectively on performance and expertise rather than subjectively on personal or emotional considerations. In other words, impersonality heightens a manager's objectivity and minimises discretion (or favouritism).

Division of labour   Managers and employees perform officially prescribed and assigned duties based on specialisation and expertise, with the benefits originally noted by Adam Smith. This enables management to set people to work on jobs that are relatively easy to learn and control.

Hierarchical structure   Weber advocated the use of a clear hierarchical structure in which jobs were ranked vertically by the amount of authority the holder had to make decisions. Typically, power and authority increase through each level up to the top of the hierarchy. Each lower position is under the control and direction of a higher position.

Authority structure   A system based on rules, regulations, impersonality, division of labour, and hierarchical structure is tied together by an authority structure – the right to make decisions of varying importance at different levels within the organisation.

Rationality   The last characteristic of bureaucratic management, rationality, refers to using the most efficient means to achieve the organisation's objectives. Hence managers should run their organisations logically and 'scientifically'. All decisions should lead directly to achieving the organisation's objectives.

Source: Hellriegel and Slocum (1988)

Does bureaucratic management occur in education?

Reflect on your role as a student and how rules have affected the experience. Try to identify one example of your own to add to those below or which illustrates the point specifically within your institution:

▶ Rules and regulations: the number of courses you need to pass for a degree.

▶ Impersonality: admission criteria, emphasising previous exam performance, not friendship.

▶ Division of labour: chemists not teaching management, and vice versa.

▶ Hierarchical structure: to whom your lecturer reports, whom they in turn report to.

▶ Authority structure: who decides whether to recruit an additional lecturer.

▶ Rationality: appointing new staff to departments that have the highest ratio of students to staff.

Compare your examples with those of other students and consider what are the effects of these features of bureaucracy on the institution and its students.

Weber was aware that, as well as creating bureaucratic management structures, organisations were applying scientific management techniques to the control of production systems. He approved of this development, seeing it as the ideal vehicle for imposing discipline on factory work. The two systems complemented each other. Formal structures of management enhance the centralisation of power, and hierarchical organisation aids functional specialisation. Fragmenting tasks, imposing close discipline on employees and minimising their discretion ensures controlled, predictable performance (Thompson and McHugh, 1995). Job descriptions that define the work expected and performance measures which assess each employee have the same effect.

Weber demonstrated the bureaucratic structures that support the continuity of organisations. Jobs are clearly defined through manuals and written procedures which must be followed. Individual employees are thus separated from the job in that they come and go but the organisation will remain. Moreover, the next employee can probably do the job as well as the last. This in itself presents an opportunity for management control, as employees see that they can be easily replaced. Unpredictable humans can be replaced or controlled by predictable systems and technology.

While the work organisation aspects of Weber are therefore consistent with those of scientific management, his ideas on the *employment relationship* were new. He stressed the importance of a career structure clearly linked to the position a person held in the hierarchy: this would offer them the chance to improve their personal position by moving up the hierarchy in a predictable, defined and open way. The person would then show more commitment to the organisation. By recommending job security linked to fair and predictable rewards, he was giving attention to factors that could both motivate employees and help to tie them to the organisation. Such notions were absent from Taylor's prescriptions.

Weber also emphasised that officials should work within a framework of rules. The right to give instructions was based on a person's authority derived from impersonal rules set by those higher in the organisation. This in turn reflected a rational analysis of how staff should do the work. Weber observed that this approach was an appropriate way to control large public and private organisations. Large private enterprises, as well as public bodies such as the civil service, became powerful examples of strict bureaucratic organisation.

For the worker there were both positives and negatives in the bureaucratic system. People may have objected to rules that over-specified how they should do their job, but they are likely to have welcomed those to do with selection and promotion – these brought some fairness to these processes at a time when nepotism and favouritism were still common.

n·o t e b o o k   2.6

Is bureaucracy always undesirable?

Rules and regulations often get a bad press, and we have all been frustrated at times by rules that got in the way of what we wanted to do. Are they always bad news? Think back to a job that you or a friend has held. Did the supervisors appear to operate within a framework of rules, or did they do as they wished? What were the effects?

Did clear rules guide selection and promotion procedures? What were the effects?

As a customer of an organisation, how have rules and regulations affected that experience?

Fayol's perspective

Administrative management is the use of institutions and order rather than relying on personal qualities to get things done.

Managers were also able to draw on the ideas of Henri Fayol (1841–1925), whose work carries echoes of both Taylor and Weber. While Taylor's scientific management focused on the production systems, Fayol devised management principles that would apply to the organisation as a whole. Fayol was a distinguished French mining engineer who from 1860 to 1918 worked for a major coal mining company. From 1888 until his retirement he was managing director of the Commentry–Fourchambault–Decazeville combine, turning it from an almost bankrupt business into one of the success stories of French industry. Throughout his career he maintained close contacts with French business and government. From 1918 until his death in 1925 he worked to publicise his ideas on business administration. His book *Administration, industrielle et generale* only became widely available in English in 1949 (Fayol, 1949).

Fayol credited his success as a manager to the methods he used, not to his personal qualities. He stresses here the benefits of relying on institutions, rather than on personal qualities. He believed that, to be successful, management had to apply certain management principles to the basic managerial roles (see Chapter 4). He emphasised that his use of the term 'principles' did not imply anything rigid or absolute about them:

It is all a question of proportion … allowance must be made for different changing circumstances … the principles are flexible and capable of adaptation to every need; it is a matter of knowing how to make use of them, which is a difficult art requiring intelligence, experience, decision and proportion. (Fayol, 1949, p.14)

Fayol expressed his main ideas in fourteen management principles, listed in the Noticeboard.

NOTICEBOARD Fayol's principles of management

1 **Division of work** If people specialise, the more they can concentrate on the same matters, and so acquire an ability and accuracy, which increases their output. However, 'it has its limits which experience teaches us may not be exceeded'.

2 **Authority and responsibility** The right to give orders and to exact obedience, derived from either a manager's official authority or his or her personal authority. 'Wherever authority is exercised, responsibility arises.'

3 **Discipline** 'Essential for the smooth running of business … without discipline no enterprise could prosper.'

4 **Unity of command** 'For any action whatsoever, an employee should receive orders from one superior only' – to avoid conflicting instructions and resulting confusion.

5 **Unity of direction** 'One head and one plan for a group of activities having the same objective … essential to unity of action, co-ordination of strength and focusing of effort.'

6 **Subordination of individual interest to general interest** 'The interests of one employee or group of employees should not prevail over that of the concern.'

7 **Remuneration of personnel** 'Should be fair and, as far as possible, afford satisfaction both to personnel and firm.'

8 **Centralisation** 'The question of centralisation or decentralisation is a simple question of proportion … of finding the optimum degree for the particular concern … [the] share of initiative to be left to [subordinates] depends on the character of the manager, the reliability of the subordinates and the condition of the business. The degree of centralisation must vary according to different cases.'

9 **Scalar chain** 'The chain of superiors from the ultimate authority to the lowest ranks – the route followed by all communications which start from or go to the ultimate authority … is at times disastrously lengthy in large concerns, especially governmental ones.' Fayol pointed out that many activities depend on speedy action. Then it was appropriate for people at the same level of the chain to communicate directly, as long as their immediate superiors approve of the contact. 'It provides for the usual exercise of some measure of initiative at all levels of authority.'

10 **Order** Materials should be in the right place to avoid loss, and the posts essential for the smooth running of the business filled by capable people.

11 **Equity** Managers should be both friendly and fair to their subordinates – 'equity requires much good sense, experience and good nature'.

12 **Stability of tenure of personnel** A high employee turnover is not efficient – 'Instability of tenure is at one and the same time cause and effect of bad running.'

13 **Initiative** 'The initiative of all represents a great source of strength for businesses. This is particularly apparent at difficult times; hence it is essential to encourage and develop this capacity to the full. The manager must be able to sacrifice some personal vanity in order to grant this satisfaction to subordinates … a manager able to do so is infinitely superior to one who cannot.'

14 *Esprit de corps* 'Harmony, union among the personnel of a concern is a great strength in that concern. Effort, then, should be made to establish it.' Fayol went on to suggest two ways of doing so: avoid sowing dissension amongst subordinates, and use verbal rather than written communication when it is simpler and quicker.

Source: Fayol (1949)

Evaluation

Expressing the organisation in such prescriptive terms as Fayol's is a distinctive feature of classical management theory. The focus is on the individual employees performing predictable and repetitive tasks under close supervision, whether in manufacturing or service operations. The approach has both strengths and limitations. From a purely business perspective, it works well under certain conditions. These include a straightforward task, predictable demand, few design changes and people willing to behave as planned.

Some organisations have been spectacularly successful with these methods the McDonald's hamburger chain being perhaps the most visible and widely quoted example. It has established a worldwide reputation (and many imitators) in the fast-food industry by developing a highly mechanised organisation in which all the outlets, often owned by independent operators or franchisees, deliver a uniform product. The system specifies all details of the business precisely, from production of the ingredients by suppliers, their delivery to the outlets, their storage, and their delivery to the customer. The company recruits young people, whom it judges will fit into the organisation as it is, and will follow the rules. There are, of course, dynamic and innovative activities as well, but these are largely confined to the staff at the centre.

n o t e b o o k   2.7

Does bureaucracy work for McDonald's?

Do you agree with the statement that McDonald's has been successful? What criteria can be used? Try to gather information about its performance in the following areas:

(a) in the United States,

(b) in new markets elsewhere in the world,

(c) in public relations and legal battles.

Many organisations have used the same general approach to great effect, especially when they have many geographically dispersed outlets that are expected to deliver a common and predictable service. Hotel chains, staff agencies, estate agents and banks are usually like this. They centralise design and development activities to ensure a standard product. Detailed manuals set out precisely how to deliver the product or service. They also set out standards and procedures which managers should follow in running the operation. These include how staff are to be recruited and trained and what the premises must look like. The manuals explain how to treat customers, how to conduct the transaction and the accounting procedures to follow.

The approaches also have their limitations. Academics often criticise Fayol's fourteen principles for their lack of a clear empirical source other than his own extensive experience. Clegg and Dunkerley (1980) suggest they are 'neither universally empirically applicable nor theoretically coherent'. To be fair, Fayol himself made exactly this point (see p.57). Management can use the principles (incorrectly) to justify an unquestioning bureaucracy. This can have dehumanising effects on those working in the systems, especially in the lower, structured operations. This point is examined in Chapter 6. Their fundamental danger is that the principles were designed to support management in relatively predictable and routine situations. They were not intended to help it deal with change and innovation. The more rapidly the business environment changes, the more limited their application is likely to be.

2.6 Human relations models

In the early twentieth century several writers such as Follett and Mayo recognised the limitations of the scientific management perspective as a complete answer.

Follett's perspective

Mary Parker Follett (1868–1933) graduated with distinction from Radcliffe College (now part of Harvard University) in 1898, having studied economics, law and philosophy. Rather than take up an academic career, she took up social work. She quickly acquired a reputation as an imaginative and effective professional, both in creating innovative policies and in putting them into practice. Local and national government sought her advice. As well as being a practical manager, she was also a keen observer of events. She was learning at first hand about the dynamics of group process – how people work together to develop and implement plans and tasks. She became impressed by the creativity of the group process and realised the potential it offered for truly democratic government – which people themselves would have to create.

Follett advocated replacing bureaucratic institutions by group networks in which people themselves analysed their problems and then produced and implemented their solutions. True democracy depended on tapping the potential of all members of society by enabling individuals to take part in groups organised to solve particular problems and accepting personal responsibility for the result. If the essence of democracy is creating, the technique of democracy is group life. Such ideas are finding renewed relevance today in the work of institutions such as community action and tenants' groups.

n o t e b o o k   2.8

Work with community groups

Do you agree about the renewed relevance of Follett's ideas to today's institutions? Identify a community or similar voluntary group and find out how it works. What benefits do the members say they get from involvement in this kind of activity? What insights can you draw from that evidence that are relevant to management more generally?

In the 1920s Follett became increasingly involved in the business world, investigating specific problems at the invitation of management. She again advocated the application of the self-governing principle which would facilitate the growth both of individuals and of the group to which they belonged. Conflict was essential if valuable differences of view were to be brought to bear on solving problems. The group then had to solve the conflict in a way that helped to create what she called an integrative unity amongst the people concerned. The essential point about a common belief or policy was not that people shared it, but that they had *produced* it in common, through processes aimed at integrating the differences.

Follett (1920) agreed that organisations had to optimise production, but did not accept that the strict division of labour advocated by scientific management was the right way to achieve this. The notion of individual workers performing endless repetitive tasks under close supervision devalued human creativity. The human side should not be separated from the mechanical side, as the two are bound up together. She believed that people, whether managers or workers, behave as they do because of the reciprocal response that occurs in any relationship. If managers tell people to behave as if they are extensions of the assembly line, they will do so. This implied that, to achieve effective results, managers should not manipulate their subordinates, but train them in the use of responsible power – 'managers should give workers a chance to grow capacity or power for themselves'.

Follett also wrote about leadership, pointing out that leadership shifts from one person to another, depending on the situation. The situation determines what needs to be done, but not who should do it. The person who discovers how best to deal with the situation should take over the leadership. An excellent review of her contribution is provided by Graham (1994).

Mayo's perspective

Elton Mayo was a professor at the Harvard Business School who conducted a series of research studies into aspects of industrial management. He drew attention to aspects of human behaviour that practitioners of scientific management had neglected. In terms of Morgan's images, the appropriate metaphor should not be that of the machine but of the living organism. This organism has needs that it can satisfy in interaction with the environment. Mayo's insight grew out of attempts to discover the social and psychological factors which affected performance. His team conducted a series of studies at the Hawthorne plant which was owned by the Western Electric Company. The work began in 1924 as a series of experiments to discover the effect on output of changing defined environmental factors. With the emphasis on the physical working conditions, and how they might affect productivity, the questions were similar to ones which Taylor might have asked.

The first group of experiments was into the effect of lighting. The researchers established two groups, one as a control. In the experimental group, they gradually varied the level of illumination and measured the output. As light rose, so did output. More surprisingly, as lighting fell, making it harder to see the components being assembled, productivity continued to rise. Even stranger was the fact that the output in the control group also rose, even though there had been no change in their working conditions. Clearly the physical conditions had only a small effect on the results. The team set up a more comprehensive set of experiments to identify the other factors.

They assembled a small group of workers in a separate room and altered several variables in turn. These included the working hours, the length of breaks and the provision of refreshments. The experienced workers were assembling small components into telephone equipment. A supervisor was in charge of them. There was also an observer to record the experiments and how the workers reacted. Great care was taken to prevent external factors disrupting the effects of the variables under investigation. The researchers were careful to explain what was happening and to ensure that the workers understood what they were expected to do. They also took into account the workers' views on aspects of the working situation.

The experiment began, with conditions being varied every two or three weeks and output measured regularly by the supervisor. The trend in output showed a gradual, if erratic, increase – even when the researchers returned conditions to those prevailing at an earlier stage. Figure 2.3 shows the trend.

---

n o t e b o o k   2.9

Explaining the trend

Describe in your own terms the pattern shown in Figure 2.3. Compare in particular the output in periods 7, 10 and 13. Before reading on, what explanations would you put forward for this trend?

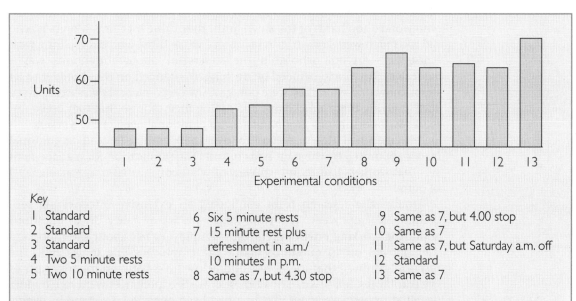

Key

1 Standard
2 Standard
3 Standard
4 Two 5 minute rests
5 Two 10 minute rests

6 Six 5 minute rests
7 15 minute rest plus
   refreshment in a.m./
   10 minutes in p.m.
8 Same as 7, but 4.30 stop

9 Same as 7, but 4.00 stop
10 Same as 7
11 Same as 7, but Saturday a.m. off
12 Standard
13 Same as 7

Figure 2.3 The relay assembly test room – average hourly output per week in experimental periods

Source: based on Roethlisberger and Dickson (1939, pp.76, 77)

During the experiments, Mayo and some associates from Harvard tried to interpret the results (Roethlisberger and Dickson, 1939; Mayo, 1949). They concluded that the increase in productivity was not related to the physical changes, but to a change in the social situation in which the group was working:

> the major experimental change was introduced when those in charge sought to hold the situation humanly steady (in the interests of critical changes to be introduced) by getting the co-operation of the workers. What actually happened was that 6 individuals became a team and the team gave itself wholeheartedly and spontaneously to co-operation in the environment. (Mayo, 1949, p.64)

The group felt they were special: managers asked for their views, were involved with them, paid attention to them and they had the chance to influence some aspects of the work.

The research team also observed another part of the factory, the bank wiring room. This revealed a different aspect of group working. Workers in this area received their wages according to a piece-rate system. As the term implies, this is a system in which management pays workers a set amount for each item, or piece, which they produce. The more they produce, the more they earn. Such schemes reflect the theory that they will encourage staff to work. Mayo's researchers were surprised to observe that employees regularly produced much less than they could have done, the reason being that they had developed their own sense of what a normal rate of output should be. They also made sure that all members of the team adhered to this rate. Any more or any less would be unacceptable to the group. The workers believed that if they produced, and earned, too much, then management would conclude that the piece-rate was too high. They would then reduce the rate, so that employees would have to work harder for the same pay. Group members therefore exercised informal sanctions against any of their colleagues who worked too hard (or too slow), until they came into line. Members who did too much were known as 'rate-busters' while those who did too little were 'chisellers'. Anyone who told the supervisor about the norms was a 'squealer'. Sanctions included being 'binged' – tapped on the shoulder to let them know that what they were doing was wrong. Practical jokes were played such as giving them a nickname and hiding their tools so that they could not work. Membership of a group satisfied an emotional need of the workers.

Managers had little or no control over these groups. Instead, an informal leader appointed by the men had control. The implication for management was that workers had their own view of what constituted a reasonable level of output.

Finally, the research team conducted an extensive interviewing programme of employees. The team began by asking fairly direct questions about the working environment, how employees felt about their job, and then moved on to questions about the employees' life in general. The responses showed that there were often close links between the two parts of the employees' life – work and domestic. Work experiences went much more deeply into people's wider life than had been expected. Conversely, events in their domestic life affected their feelings about work. The implication was that supervisors needed to pay attention to emotional needs of subordinates as well as to the narrower aspects of work.

A comparison with Taylor's prediction

How does this evidence compare with Frederick Taylor's belief that piece-rates would be an incentive to individuals to raise their performance?

Overall, these and similar observations led Mayo to introduce the idea of 'social man', in contrast to the 'economic man' who was at the centre of the earlier theories. While financial rewards would influence the latter, work-group relationships and loyalties would influence the former. These would outweigh management pressure.

Mayo on financial incentives

❢ Man's desire to be continuously associated in work with his fellows is a strong, if not the strongest, human characteristic. Any disregard of it by management or any ill-advised attempt to defeat this human impulse leads instantly to some form of defeat for management itself. In [a study] the efficiency experts had assumed the primacy of financial incentive; in this they were wrong; not until the conditions of working group formation were satisfied did the financial incentives come into operation. ❢

(Mayo, 1949, p.99)

People had social needs that they sought to satisfy – and how they did so may be either in line with management interests or in opposition to them. Mayo's study also drew attention to the informal groups existing alongside the formal organisation designed by management.

By stressing the influence of social factors in the workplace, the human relations approach added another dimension to knowledge of the management process. Scientific management stressed the technical aspects of work, and the assumption that people would be willing to fit into those requirements. The Hawthorne experiments indicated that such assumptions were incorrect. Workers' social needs, as well as individual economic incentives, influenced behaviour. The nature of people would influence what they did at work as much as the formal design of the work environment. This implied that management would need to pay close attention to the human side of the organisation. Employees would work more effectively if management showed some interest in their well-being through more humane supervisory practices.

C A S E   Q U E S T I O N S   2 . 6

▶ In what ways did Robert Owen anticipate the conclusions of the Hawthorne experiments?

▶ Which of the practices that he used took account of workers' social needs?

Evaluation

The Hawthorne studies themselves have been controversial, and the interpretations questioned. Also, the idea of social man is itself now seen as an incomplete picture of people at work. Providing good supervision and decent working environments may increase satisfaction, but not necessarily productivity. The influences on performance are certainly more complex than Taylor assumed – but are also more complex than Mayo assumed.

Other writers have followed and developed Mayo's emphasis on the human side of organisations. They have addressed the fundamental problem raised by the fragmentation of work into management and non-management roles that were discussed in Chapter 1: how can management motivate others to give the effort which management expects? The major perspectives on offer are presented in Chapter 6. The conclusion reached there is that the range of factors that will influence employees is much greater than the financial incentives which Taylor advocated, and greater than the social needs which Mayo identified. The work of writers such as Maslow, Alderfer, McGregor and Maccoby have suggested ways of integrating human needs with those of the organisation as expressed by management.

Such writers have explored how bureaucratic forms of organisation could be redesigned to take more account of human needs and capabilities. Rather than seeing workers as there to carry out management instructions, they argued that, if given the chance, most would be willing to take on additional responsibilities. This led to interest in redesigning work to encourage human capacities for self-control, creativity and personal growth. Some of this reflected a human relations concern for employees' own well-being. A much stronger influence was the changing external environments of organisations, which have become much less predictable since the time of Taylor and Mayo. The theoretical roots of these ideas are contained in open systems models.

NOTICEBOARD **Women and research**

The Hawthorne studies are often quoted as an example of theorists' failure to pay attention to the significance of gender (Acker and Van Houton, 1992; Wilson, 1996). Despite the striking differences between the findings of the relay assembly test female group and the male group in the bank wiring observation room, generalisations made were equally applicable to workers of both genders. The female group increased their output and showed increasingly co-operative attitudes towards management. The male group restricted their output, contrary to management's efforts. These observations rightly led the researchers to acknowledge the significance of group dynamics.

However, when Acker and Van Houton (1992) re-examined the Hawthorne studies they found that the researchers failed to pay attention to the possible effect of the different sex of the subjects in the two rooms. They 'also seem to have taken no notice of the possible effects of variation in research procedures and the interaction of those variations with the sex of the subjects' (p.21). The analysis of the experiments ignored the fact that the women in the relay assembly test room were individually and informally selected by the plant manager to make sure that they really wanted to participate. Further to this, when two of these women were uncooperative to managers' strenuous efforts to control, they were replaced. In contrast to the female group, in the male-based experiment the pressure to participate in the research was on the group rather than on the individuals. During this experiment, no one was replaced even though 'there was slowing down, laughing and talking'.

2.7 Open systems models

A system is a set of interrelated parts designed to achieve a purpose.
Subsystems are the separate but related parts which make up the total system.
An open system is one which interacts with its environment.
A system boundary separates the system from its environment.

The open systems approach builds on earlier work in general systems theory, and has been widely used to help understand management and organisational issues. The basic idea is to think of the organisation not just as a system, but as an open system.

An open system draws attention to the relationships among the various internal parts of the system, and the links of the whole system to the outside world. The system is sustained by flows of energy and materials, which enter it from the environment, undergo some transformation process within the system, and leave the system as goods and services. The central theme in open systems views of management is that organisations depend on the wider environment for different kinds of sustenance if they are to survive and prosper. Figure 2.4 is a simple model of the organisation as an open system.

n o t e b o o k   2.11

Taking the course you are studying as the focus, draw a systems diagram of the course in the form shown in Figure 2.4. You may want to share your conclusions with a fellow student, to see if there are other system elements that you can add.

How well do the feedback elements in the system work? Can you identify any areas that you think should be strengthened?

The perspective provides a framework that people can use to understand organisational problems. It specifies *input* and *output* processes, *conversion* processes and *feedback* loops. Above all, it emphasises the relationship between the organisation and the wider environment: the organisation must satisfy the environment well enough to be able to receive sustaining

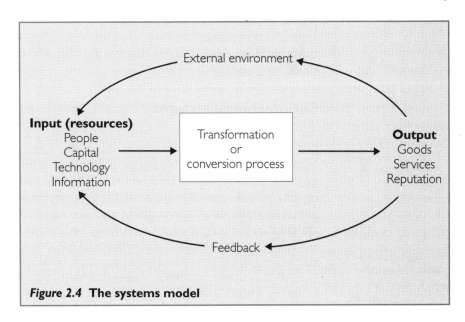

Figure 2.4 The systems model

resources from it. The management task is to sustain those links if the organisation is to thrive. Feedback refers to information about the performance of the system. It may be deliberate through customer surveys, or unplanned such as the loss of business to a competitor. Feedback enables those managing the system to take remedial action.

CASE QUESTIONS 2.7

A systems diagram of Owen's mill

▶ Draw a systems diagram detailing the main inputs, transformation and outputs of Robert Owen's mill. Which aspects of the environment probably had most influence on his management practices?

Another key idea is the idea of subsystems, or system levels. A clinic is a subsystem within a hospital, the hospital a subsystem of a local healthcare system. This in turn is part of a national health system. Within the clinic itself there will be smaller subsystems – one for admitting patients, another for managing staff, perhaps several for providing treatment. These subsystems interact with each other, and the way these interactions are conducted will affect the functioning of the organisation. Figure 2.5 illustrates this.

Besides drawing attention to the environment, the systems approach also helps to avoid the danger of oversimplification. It emphasises the links between systems, and alerts management to the possibility that a change in one will have consequences for another. In the same way, what counts as the environment depends on the level at which the analysis is being conducted. If, for example, it is a matter of hospital policy being discussed, the relevant environmental factors will be mainly outside the organisation – the policies of competing hospitals, other organisations, national policies on health care. If the discussion is about a procedure for dealing with appointments within a single clinic, then the relevant environment would include other actual or planned systems within the hospital. In either case the principle is the same: the importance of taking account of the wider systems that surround the immediate one. That implies being ready and able to scan those environments, to sense changes in them, and to take action to manage them.

Sociotechnical systems

An important variant of systems theory is the idea of the sociotechnical system. The approach developed from the work of Eric Trist and Ken Bamforth at the Tavistock Institute in London during the 1950s. Their most prominent study was of an attempt by the coal industry to mechanise the mining system. Introducing what were in essence assembly line technologies and methods at the coalface had severe consequences for the social system that the older pattern of working had encouraged. The technological system destroyed the fabric of the social system, and the solution lay in reconciling the needs of both technical and social systems.

This and similar studies in many different countries showed the benefits of seeing a work system as a combination of a material technology (tools, machinery, techniques) and a social organisation (people, relationships,

A sociotechnical system is one in which outcomes depend on the interaction of both the technical and social subsystems.

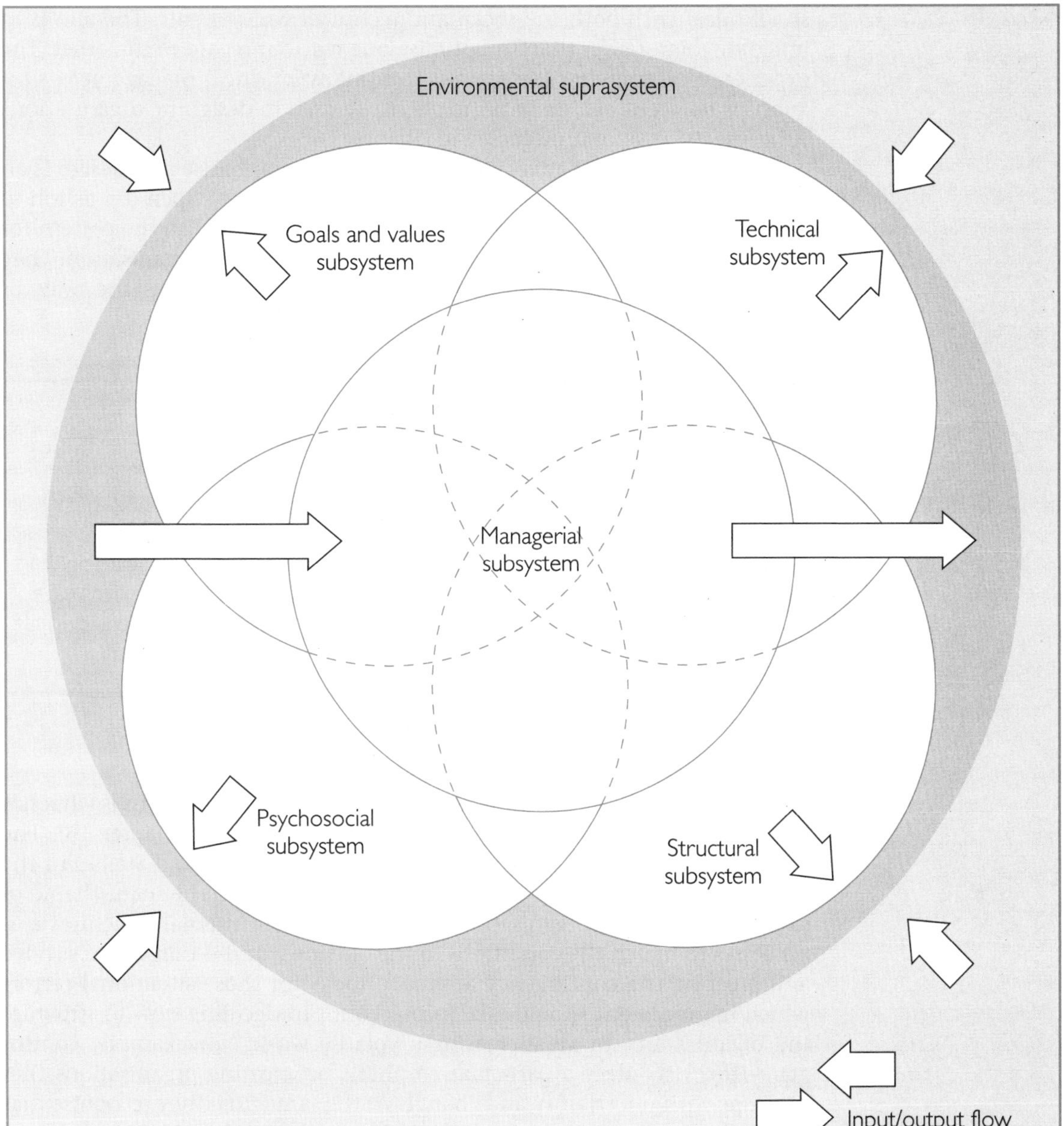
Environmental suprasystem
Goals and values subsystem
Technical subsystem
Managerial subsystem
Psychosocial subsystem
Structural subsystem
Input/output flow of materials, energy and information

***Figure 2.5* The organisational system**
Source: Kast and Rosenzweig (1973)

constitutional arrangements). In other words, there are technical and social subsystems within an organisation. The social system refers to the human side of the business; the technical system relates to the machinery, information systems and physical facilities which the organisation uses. As each affects the other, people need to manage them together, so that they work in harmony.

The general message of systems theory is that in designing any kind of system it is necessary to take account of the interdependencies between the various elements of the system. The sociotechnical view, in particular, argues that organisations are best understood as interdependent systems. Analysis should deal with both the social and technical components. The aim is to integrate them rather than to optimise one without regard to the other. The experience of applying the approach in many practical management situations is reflected in a set of principles to be used in designing organisations (Cherns, 1987), a topic discussed in Chapter 16.

For example, those advocating the approach emphasise that design is an area of conflict as it has to satisfy an array of objectives. Open discussion to resolve these conflicts is recommended, as this will establish the pattern for managing similar conflicts constructively within the new organisation. They also recommend specifying objectives clearly but leaving the way of achieving them more open.

n o t e b o o k   2.12

What are the main features of the technological system which supports the delivery of your course? What are the main features of the social system which also supports it?

How does the interaction of these two systems help or hinder your learning? For example, what effects does the location of staff rooms and teaching rooms have on staff/student contact? Are the computing facilities supported by adequate staff, available when you want to consult them?

Contingency management

A further development of the open systems view of organisations is what has become known as the contingency model (discussed in Chapter 16). The model began with the work of Woodward and of Burns and Stalker in the UK, and of Lawrence and Lorsch in the United States. The main theme of such models is that organisations must adapt their internal structures and processes to match the conditions in the outside world if they are to survive and prosper. The contingency approach looks for those situational factors which management should take into account in deciding how to structure the organisation. In an increasingly volatile world, for example, contingency theorists place a particular emphasis on creating organisations that can cope with uncertainty and change. At the same time they recognise that some functions within such organisations may need to be handled in a highly stable and predictable way, using the values of the internal process model.

A further group of ideas has developed since the publication by Peters and Waterman of their best-selling book *In Search of Excellence* (1982). As management consultants with McKinsey & Co., Peters and Waterman set out to discover the reasons for the success of what they regarded as forty-three excellently managed US companies. The eight attributes that they claimed characterised the excellent companies are summarised in the Noticeboard.

One of their conclusions was that the excellent companies had a distinctive set of philosophies about human nature and the way that people interact in organisations. They did not see people as rational beings, motivated by fear and willing to accept a low-involvement employment relation-

NOTICEBOARD Peters and Waterman's basic practices of excellently managed companies

1 A bias for action

- Project teams tend to be small, fluid, *ad hoc* and problem/action focused.
- Communications are of the essence, and there is an important commitment to learning and experimentation.
- Complex problems are tackled through a willingess to shift resources to where they are needed to encourage fluidity and action (chunking).

2 Close to the customer

- The market-driven principle of commitment to service, reliability and quality, based on an appreciation of 'nichemanship' and the ability to custom-tailor a product or service to a client's needs.

3 Autonomy and entrepreneurship

- A principle which champions innovation, decentralisation, the delegation of power and action to the level where they are needed, and a healthy tolerance of failure.

4 Productivity through people

- The principle that employees are people and a major resource, and should be

trusted, respected, inspired and made 'winners'.

- Organisational units should be small-scale to preserve and develop a people-oriented quality.

5 Hands-on, value driven

- Organisation guided by a clear sense of shared values, mission and identity, relying on inspirational leadership rather than bureaucratic control.

6 Stick to the knitting

- The principle of building on strengths and knowledge of one's niche.

7 Simple form, lean staff

- Avoid bureaucracy; build main commitments to projects or product division rather than to the dual lines of responsibility found in formal matrix organisations; use small organisational units.

8 Simultaneous loose/tight properties

- The principle that reconciles the need for overall control with a commitment to autonomy and entrepreneurship.

Source: Thomas (1993)

ship. Instead, the excellent companies regarded people as emotional, intuitive and creative social creatures who like to celebrate victories, however small, who value self-control, but who also need and want the security and meaning of achieving goals through organisations. From this, Peters and Waterman deduced some general rules for treating workers with dignity and respect. This was not out of a sense of philanthropy, but to ensure that people did quality work in an increasingly uncertain environment. In his later work, Peters (1987) continued to stress that people were not components in a rational machine, but were the main source of ideas and creativity. Only by tapping the full ingenuity of its staff could management succeed in the current business world.

In Search of Excellence has had a significant influence on management thinking and practice, especially through encouraging attention to the culture and values of organisations. In this it developed the ideas associated with the human relations school, such as those of Douglas McGregor. Equally it reflected a move away from rational goal approaches that emphasised complex and usually quantitative analytical techniques as the route to effective management. Peters and Waterman criticised management for having become over-reliant on analytical techniques at the expense of the more intuitive and human aspects of business. This, they believed, led to inflexibility and an inability to innovate through experimentation.

Watson (1994) has argued of the eight principles listed in the Notice-board, the last (simultaneous loose/tight properties) is the most significant, in providing a conceptual underpinning for the rest. The excellent organis-ation has loose controls in the sense that people are not constrained by close supervision, tightly defined roles or detailed procedures.

> Yet, in those organisations, people do not wander away from serving the key purposes of the organisation's founders or leaders. The tightness of control comes from people *choosing* to do what is required of them because they wish to serve the *values* which they share with those in charge. These values, typically focusing on quality of service to customers, are transmitted and manifested in the organisations' culture. This culture uses stories, myths and legends to keep these values alive and people tend to be happy to share these values and subscribe to the corporate legends because to do so is to find meaning in their lives. (p.16)

The empirical basis of their work has been criticised, while others have ques-tioned the conservative ideology which it expresses (Silver, 1987). However, Watson (1994) observes that these shortcomings in themselves should not obscure the importance of Peters and Waterman's underlying message. He notes with approval Thompson and McHugh's comment that:

> Creating a culture resonant with the overall goals is relevant to any organisation, whether it be trade unions, voluntary groups or producer co-operatives. Indeed, it is more important in such consensual groupings. Co-operatives, for example, can degenerate organisationally because they fail to develop adequately mechanisms for transmitting the original ideals from founders to new members and sustaining them through new shared experiences. (pp.18–19)

Evaluation

It would be wrong to assume that those writing about management in the late nineteenth and early twentieth centuries were unaware of the external world. They could observe the massive shift from an agricultural to an industrial economy, and the often severe economic fluctuations and pol-itical changes that periodically affected organisations. Yet there were also significant sources of stability. Communication systems were such that most organisations were able to operate in a local market with relatively little risk of new competition. Scientific discoveries opened up new possibilities, and threatened old businesses, but at a relatively slow pace. There was wide-spread conflict between management and labour, but the fundamental power of capitalist enterprises remained intact.

These may explain why the emphasis in the early theorists' work was on ways of perfecting the internal arrangements of business so that it could cope with, to modern eyes, a relatively stable business environment. Hence they appear to have viewed organisations as if they were closed systems, and paid relatively little attention to the external world.

An open systems perspective is different, emphasising that people need to plan with the environment of the system in mind. This not only affects the need to adjust objectives and plans more rapidly to external change but also raises the need to find new ways of motivating people to act appropriately in these new conditions.

Yet, identifying successful management practice in such conditions is hazardous. The subsequent history of the 'excellent' companies identified by Peters and Waterman demonstrates this. Richard Pascale has observed that within five years of publication only fourteen of the original forty-three companies were still regarded as excellent, and some were in serious trouble. He argued that the pursuit of excellence should not be seen as an end in itself, but as a never-ending task.

The open systems approach may undervalue the scope for human choice. Such models often appear to assume some kind of automatic transmission between the external world and internal arrangements. It is important to recall that organisations in themselves achieve nothing: any change in policy depends on the initiative and action of individuals. Open systems models draw attention to the wide, theoretically infinite, range of issues that potentially have implications for an organisation. Whether these issues are noticed, how they are interpreted, and what action is taken on them depends on the goals, interests and power of individuals. Factors such as these shape an organisation's response to uncertain conditions.

2.8　Management theories for uncertain conditions

Although theories of management develop at particular times in response to current problems, this does not mean that newer is better. While new concerns bring out new theories, old concerns usually remain. Hence, while current theories are heavily weighted towards ways of encouraging flexibility and change, management still seeks control. It does so either because the circumstances seem to require it, or from an ingrained way of thinking. Rather than thinking of theoretical development as a linear activity, it may be better to think of it as a circular or iterative process in which certain themes recur in addition to new concerns arising.

The competing values approach is useful in that way, in that it captures the main theoretical developments in one framework and shows the relationships between them. Table 2.1 summarises the model and the earlier discussion in a comparative way.

The emerging management challenges which theorists are beginning to deal with come from many sources. One is the increasingly global nature of the economic system (electronics, branded consumer products such as tobacco). Another is the deregulation of many areas of activity allowing new competitors to enter previously protected markets (airlines, financial services). Another is the closer integration between many previously separate areas of business (telecommunications, consumer electronics and entertainment). Consumer expectations are increasing and networked computer systems are developing rapidly. Some radical solutions are being sought by management thinkers – just as was done at the start of the Industrial Revolution.

Some argue that traditional notions of efficiency and asset management may not be adequate to meet the new tasks. They talk instead of *resource leverage*, signifying a search for ways of exploiting more fully the physical and especially the invisible intellectual resources of the company. They talk

Table 2.1 Summary of the models within the competing values framework

Features/model	Rational goal	Internal process	Human relations	Open systems
Main exponents	Taylor Gilbreths	Fayol Weber	Mayo Follett Barnard	Trist and Bamforth Woodward Burns and Stalker Lawrence and Lorsch Peters and Waterman
Criteria of effectiveness	Productivity, profit	Stability, continuity	Commitment, morale, cohesion	Adaptability, external support
Means/ends theory	Clear direction leads to productive outcomes	Routinisation leads to stability	Involvement leads to commitment	Continual innovation secures external support
Emphasis	Rational analysis, measurement	Defining responsibility, documentation	Participation, consensus-building	Creative problem-solving, innovation
Role of manager	Director and planner	Monitor and co-ordinator	Mentor and facilitator	Innovator and broker

also of the speed with which this has to be done, as intellectual or performance assets can be short-lived. Assets need to be fully exploited to achieve the greatest return from investment. This leads to an emphasis not on size to achieve economies of scale, but on speed and flexibility; on integration, not specialisation, and on management that encourages innovation, not control.

Another new theme in management thinking in such volatile conditions is to consider the implications of feedback. People in organisations, both as individuals and as members of a web of working relationships, can choose how they react to an event or to an attempt to influence their behaviour. That reaction in turn leads to a further response – setting off a complex feedback process. Figure 2.6 illustrates this for three individuals, X, Y and Z.

If we look at the situation in Figure 2.6 from the perspective of X, then X is in an environment made up of Y and Z. X discovers what Y and Z are doing, chooses how to respond and then acts. That action has consequences for Y and Z, which they discover. This leads them to choose a response, which has consequences that X then discovers, and acts on. This continues indefinitely. Every act X takes feeds back to have an impact on Y and Z's next action – and the same is true of Y and Z. Hence, as they interact, they make up a feedback system – and what is true of individuals as depicted in the diagram can also be used to indicate the interactions of three groups or three organisations. It can then extend to large numbers of organisations operating in their economic and social environment.

A key element in this way of thinking about organisations is to understand the difference between what are called 'linear' and 'non-linear' systems. 'Linear' describes systems in which an action leads to a predictable reaction. If you light a fire in a room, the thermostat will turn the central heating down. 'Non-linear' systems are those in which outcomes are less predictable. If a company reduces the price of a product, it will be surprised

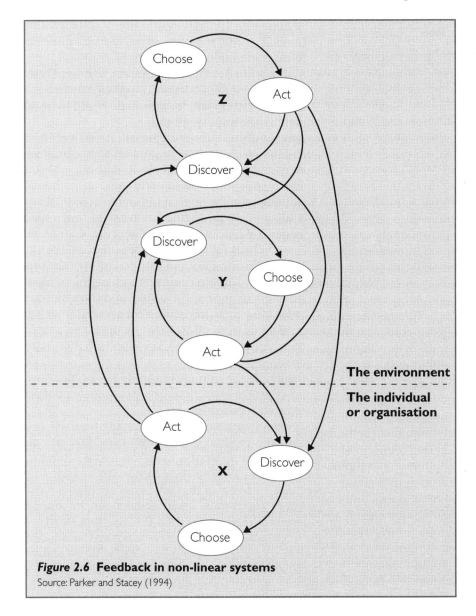

***Figure 2.6* Feedback in non-linear systems**
Source: Parker and Stacey (1994)

if sales in the following period accord exactly with expectations – the company cannot predict with certainty the reactions of competitors, of changes in taste or the appearance of completely different products which attract customer spending away from their industry.

Events happen and circumstances in the outside world change in ways which management cannot anticipate in their plans. For these reasons it is impossible to trace with certainty any clear links between actions and their long-term effects. While short-run consequences may be clear, long-run ones are not. Hence managers cannot predict accurately the long-term outcomes of what they do.

Glass (1996) argues that the modern business world corresponds much more closely to this non-linear world than to a linear one. He contrasts the assumptions of the linear and non-linear models in the following way:

▶ **Assumption 1**   The organisation is almost a simple 'closed system'. Generally, what it decides to do, will take place without too much disruption from outside events.

▶ **Assumption 2**   The operating environment is stable enough for management to understand it sufficiently well to develop a relevant detailed strategy and for that strategy still to be relevant by the time it comes to be implemented.

▶ **Assumption 3**   In an organisation, or an economy, there is a series of clear levers that can be applied to cause a known response (e.g. if you cut staff numbers, profitability should go up, or if you increase interests rates, the value of your currency will rise).

These three assumptions have been replaced by three new realities:

▶ **Reality 1**   Organisations are complex 'open systems', constantly and deeply influenced by, and influencing, their environments. Often, intended actions will be diverted off-course by external events or by the internal political and cultural processes of the organisation itself.

▶ **Reality 2**   The environment is changing so rapidly (continuously throwing up new opportunities and threats) that senior management cannot expect to have sufficient sense of what is happening to formulate detailed strategies. Moreover, by the time a strategy moves from concept to being operationalised, key aspects of the environment have often changed.

▶ **Reality 3**   The simple linear models of cause and effect have broken down and many actions can lead to quite unexpected (positive or negative) consequences.

In linear systems, negative or damping feedback is used to bring the system back to the original or preferred condition. People used to such systems think in terms of 'what actions can we take to return to the desired equilibrium?' (Glass, 1996, p.102). In non-linear systems, the complexities of the feedback loops mean that outcomes are highly sensitive to small differences in initial conditions. Small actions can be amplified through a series of actions and reactions so that the eventual effect is out of all proportion to the initial action or change. Glass argues that sudden changes in technology, taste or regulation can amplify small actions. Many of the growth industries of today have come from scientific breakthroughs which have been aggressively exploited. He goes on:

> A manager's way of thinking and acting are quite different if they see the world as being in something near stable equilibrium, than if they believe they are operating in chaos … In stable equilibrium the manager is constantly trying to bring a situation back to a pre-planned state. In chaos, managers have goals but are also looking for the kind of positive amplification that can give extraordinary, rather than just ordinary, results. (p.102)

It follows that research into management, trying to understand and explain what has happened, faces exactly the same uncertainty. For a start there may be ambiguities about the dependent variable – the state of the long-term effect being measured. Was the change a success or not? Then there may be a host of ambiguities about attributing causes to effects. It is easy to point to actions or events that preceded others – and to fall into the trap of assuming that the one caused the other. Since managers are active and busy people, they are understandably keen to have quick and straightforward explanations – and equally clear solutions. Many management books and articles attempt to meet that demand, with very readable accounts of how company A solved problem B by using technique D. The accounts may be accurate, but the true picture will almost certainly have been a great deal more complex. For a discussion of the issues in carrying out and interpreting management research see Easterby-Smith *et al.* (1991).

2.9 Unitary, pluralist and critical perspectives

Since organisations are such prominent features of society, we need to consider what kind of creation they are – what are their dominant character-istics. A useful distinction is provided by the unitary, pluralist and critical views.

Unitary perspective

The unitary perspective emphasises the common purpose of the organi-sation, and the assumption that this purpose is widely shared and accepted by all members. The latter are expected to subordinate their individual inter-ests to the good of the whole. Disagreement or dissent is a sign of disloyalty or failure, and the expectation is that all the parts will work smoothly together to achieve the accepted objectives. Analogies of sporting teams or ships ('we're all in this together') are often used, and the importance of loyalty to the leader is unquestioned.

Pluralist perspective

An alternative view is the pluralist view: that organisations are more accu-rately seen as coalitions of interest groups. Each group has its own objectives that will sometimes coincide and at other times conflict with those of other groups. Unitary theories assume that employees have the same goals as management. Yet both employees and managers, even while acting on behalf of the owners, also have their own personal goals. The pluralist perspective recognises, too, that individual members of the organisation (including managers) have competing loyalties. They have loyalties to the colleagues they work beside, to other members of their profession or to the rules of the profesional association, to the local business unit as well as to the corporation as a whole; to their family and the local community, and to particular customers or suppliers. The assumption therefore is that there will be debate and disagreement within the organisation both about goals and about how they are to be achieved.

Goals are not attributed without question to 'the organisation'. Rather they are seen as the property of particular individuals or groups who will press for their goals to be adopted as those of the organisation as a whole. There will be debate about both ends and means. Within reason, this is seen as a sign of strength rather than of weakness. Analogies are typically made with nation states, in which it is accepted that there are different and equally legitimate views which are resolved through political mechanisms and processes. Hence disagreement is not seen as a sign of inherent failure, but as an essential process in which the naturally competing interests making up the organisation reconcile their differences.

Critical perspective

The critical perspective finds weaknesses in both the unitary and pluralist views. Proponents attack the rational approaches to management for presenting the issues as if they were neutral and as if issues of politics, power and control could be taken out of consideration. They also attack the pluralists for focusing on the task of balancing conflicting interests. This implies that different interests have approximately equal power and resources, and that appropriate interpersonal or other skills will resolve conflict in a satisfactory way.

Those taking a critical perspective argue that beneath the search for a rational and efficient solution there is an underlying struggle for resources. Organisations are not just vehicles for the efficient delivery of services but are also tools for achieving personal or group interests. The rational ideology legitimises and rewards the activities of dominant groups and is supported by an assumption that members' interests are in harmony. Yet some stakeholders are more powerful than others, and it is spurious for those taking a pluralist perspective to imply that management can take account of these interests and achieve some equality of trade-offs. The critical perspective draws attention to the underlying differences of power in organisations and society.

The view also challenges the idea of rationality as a dominant point of reference in management discussion, claiming that appeals to rationality are often used to disguise underlying sectional interests. It argues that managers gain power by accumulating knowledge of the way the organisation and its processes work. This again, critical theorists argue, is not a neutral business of acquiring knowledge. Much of this 'organisational rationale' is derived by observing the way that operators work and then incorporating that knowledge in standard or computerised systems. The barcoding systems in shops are good examples of the way that knowledge possessed by staff is incorporated into a system that tightly controls employee actions.

2.10 Recap

This chapter has reviewed the main theories of management within the competing values model.

Content agenda

Many of the approaches help us to understand the issues which arise in the content agenda. The rational goal models outlined ways in which management could meet its objectives by separating management from work activities. The internal process model also stressed the need for carefully planned organisations, through which management could control activities. The open systems models pay particular attention to the external environment

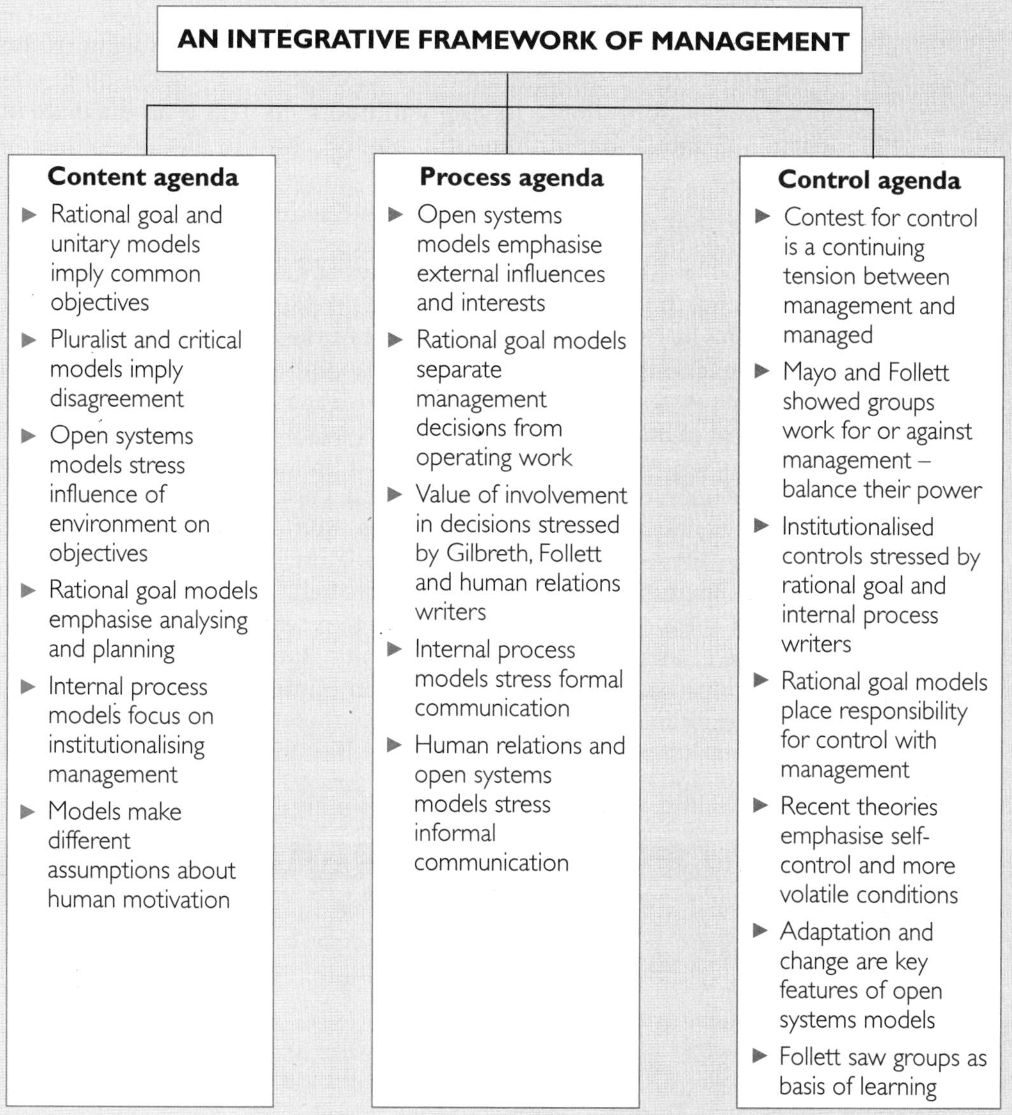

AN INTEGRATIVE FRAMEWORK OF MANAGEMENT

Content agenda

▶ Rational goal and unitary models imply common objectives

▶ Pluralist and critical models imply disagreement

▶ Open systems models stress influence of environment on objectives

▶ Rational goal models emphasise analysing and planning

▶ Internal process models focus on institutionalising management

▶ Models make different assumptions about human motivation

Process agenda

▶ Open systems models emphasise external influences and interests

▶ Rational goal models separate management decisions from operating work

▶ Value of involvement in decisions stressed by Gilbreth, Follett and human relations writers

▶ Internal process models stress formal communication

▶ Human relations and open systems models stress informal communication

Control agenda

▶ Contest for control is a continuing tension between management and managed

▶ Mayo and Follett showed groups work for or against management – balance their power

▶ Institutionalised controls stressed by rational goal and internal process writers

▶ Rational goal models place responsibility for control with management

▶ Recent theories emphasise self-control and more volatile conditions

▶ Adaptation and change are key features of open systems models

▶ Follett saw groups as basis of learning

Figure 2.7

in which management is operating. They stress the need for management to satisfy key stakeholders.

Process agenda

The human relations approaches introduced ideas relevant to the process agenda – *how* management goes about its task. Mary Parker Follett and Elton Mayo drew attention to the weaknesses of rational approaches to management. They showed the importance to individuals of social contact and argued that groups could be powerful creative forces in organisations. Members should be trained to deal with conflicts openly and constructively. These writers also emphasise trying to understand the internal processes of organisations. Follett, in particular, drew attention to the benefits of involving people in groups in decision-making, given their capacity for creative problem-solving. She, Mayo and those who followed in the human relations school emphasised the importance of establishing effective communication systems to keep staff informed. This is all the more important in a turbulent environment.

Control agenda

A recurring theme since the earliest days of management has been management's search for a better way to control people. Some theories have sought to solve this by focusing on the individual worker, with a battery of fairly direct techniques of measurement and control. Others focused on broader organisational systems that would help to institutionalise and depersonalise this aspect of management. The techniques range from Owen's bits of coloured wood to the very tight controls that can be exercised by modern computer-based work systems. The Hawthorne studies also drew attention to the way in which cohesive groups can themselves exert control over people, irrespective of management wishes. Control is not just a prerogative of management.

The increasing turbulence and unpredictably of a system as complex as that of the world economy is leading to a search for theories that help to capture at least some of that complexity. Rational goal models advocated that control should lie with management. Current models argue that greater complexity makes it impossible for distant management to exercise control. Hence the emphasis is on the scope for self-control that reintegrates this aspect of management with the work itself. Figure 2.7 summarises these points.

PART CASE QUESTIONS

▶ In what ways, if at all, are the models in the competing values framework supported by the evidence of the Body Shop case?

▶ How does the management approach of Anita Roddick compare with that of Robert Owen?

▶ How do you imagine (on the evidence) that Body Shop managers view uncertainty?

2.11 Review questions

1 Why are management theories inherently complex and uncertain?
2 Draw your own diagram showing the two axes of the competing values framework, and then place the theories outlined in this chapter in the most appropriate sector.
3 Compare examples of open and closed systems.
4 Name at least four of Morgan's organisational images.
5 List the five principles of scientific management and evaluate their use in examples of your own choice.
6 What was the particular contribution which Lillian Gilbreth made concerning how workers' mental capacities should be treated?
7 Compare Taylor's assumptions about people with those of Mayo. Evaluate the accuracy of these views by reference to an organisation of your choice.

8   What did Follett consider to be the value of groups?
9   Compare the conclusions reached by the Hawthorne experimenters in the relay assembly test room with those in the bank wiring room.
10   Outline an organisational system of your choice, paying particular attention to the feedback loops.
11   How does uncertainty affect organisations and how do non-linear perspectives help to understand this?
12   Can you give an example of a management group adopting a unitary perspective to a problem? What would it have done differently if it had taken a pluralist or critical view?

Further reading

The original works of many of the writers discussed here are short and quite readable. Taylor (1917) contains illuminating detail that brings the ideas to life, and Fayol's (1949) surviving ideas came from only two short chapters, which again are worth reading in the original. A short and clear overview of the development of production systems from the eighteenth to the early twentieth centuries, in a range of industries, is given by Biggs (1996). The contribution of Mary Parker Follett has been relatively unrecognised, perhaps overshadowed by Mayo's Hawthorne studies. Or perhaps it was because she was a woman. This point, and a wider appreciation of her work, can be found in Graham (1994). Discussions of these approaches from a critical perspective are contained in Gillespie (1991), Thompson and McHugh (1995), Morgan (1997) and Alvesson and Wilmott (1996).

The international context of management

AIM

To provide some perspectives from which to view the international aspects of management, and to compare some alternative systems.

OBJECTIVES

By the end of your work on this chapter you should be able to outline the concepts below in your own terms and:

1 Compare explanations of the fact that more business activity is now organised internationally

2 Assess the extent to which a particular organisation is likely to be affected by international issues

3 Distinguish between low- and high-context cultures and assess the implications for management

4 Outline Hofstede's research on cultural differences between nations and give examples of how these differences shape management activities within nations

5 Identify and give examples of institutional factors which affect the management of organisations and illustrate how these differ between countries

6 Compare differences in management roles and practices among different countries

7 Compare the main features of Japanese management systems with US and European models

8 Describe and illustrate how greater internationalisation of business affects the nature of management activities, such as more interaction within cross-cultural teams

9 Compare views on the controversies raised by increased globalisation of business and the dilemmas these create for management

Lufthansa and globalisation

Senior management at the German airline Lufthansa decided in 1995 to turn the airline into a truly global company. It could see that competition from other airlines was going to increase because of new EU regulations enabling free competition in Europe. Internationally, the barriers to entry are low and many governments subsidise national airlines. Lufthansa wishes to be one of the few big players and has embarked on a strategy of globalisation. Its plans include creating a global network of services by developing alliances with carriers in other regions; internationalising its costs to balance the increasing proportion of non-German revenues; developing managers willing to operate in a variety of markets and cultures; and developing a service culture which meets the expectations of increasingly diverse customers.

Lufthansa has alliances with Thai Airways in South East Asia, United Airlines in the USA and the Scandinavian airline SAS in Europe. The carriers remain financially independent but merge many of their operations. In this way, the airlines are able to offer customers similar service from ground and flight staff throughout a trip.

In 1996, about 50 per cent of the company's revenue came from Germany, compared with 65 per cent of costs and 80 per cent of staff. Employing German staff is expensive because of German statutory requirements, and management believes that if it is to compete internationally, it needs to reduce costs. One way is to transfer some administrative and support functions to cheaper overseas locations. For example, it sends aircraft to be maintained in the Republic of Ireland.

Senior management acknowledges that to implement a strategy of globalisation more of the company's managers must become 'global'. Some feel that the company should train managers to understand and respect other cultures; others that they should spend part of their career outside Germany. A further view is that a proportion of the company's managers will need to be non-German.

One of the few ways that airlines can compete is through the quality of the interaction between customers and staff, both on the ground and in the air. Now that Lufthansa is in partnership with other airlines such as Thai, it must meet the service expectations of Thai's customers as well. By 1996 the need to develop a more customer-focused service culture had become a major issue for Lufthansa. On some Asian routes over half the passengers are non-German, raising the question of whether the company should recruit more cabin staff locally.

Source: based on Gardner et al. (1996), with permission

CASE QUESTIONS

▶ What external pressures are persuading management to build a global airline?

▶ What issues do you think it will need to manage in order to achieve this?

3.1 Introduction

This chapter introduces the following ideas:
- Internationalisation
- Globalisation
- National culture
- Ethnocentrism
- Cultural relativism
- High-context and low-context cultures
- Power distance
- Uncertainty avoidance
- Individualism/collectivism
- Masculinity/femininity
- National institutional features
- Japanese, US and European management models

A major fact shaping the practice of management is the growing international dimension of business. Ever more of the world's production comes from organisations operating beyond their national boundaries. Some of the growth comes from businesses conducting more trade than before within regional trading blocs (sometimes referred to as regional integration arrangements). Examples include the European Union (EU), the Association of South East Asian Nations (ASEAN), the North American Free Trade Association (NAFTA): there are more than one hundred others (Dent, 1997). In addition, many companies now operate on a global scale. They have merged with foreign companies and now have manufacturing and selling operations in or near their major markets. They also have increasingly complex supply arrangements, alliances and joint ventures with other local or multinational companies.

These developments have considerable implications for managers. At the political level, the value of goods and services traded daily is far beyond the annual national income of many nations. The economic resources possessed by the major multinational corporations is greater than that of many of the countries in which they conduct their operations. The multinational's primary interest is likely to be that of distant shareholders, rather than that of the people of the countries in which it works.

There are also management implications in the widening geographical spread of organisations. The threat of new competition balances the promise of new markets. Meeting objectives profitably on a wider scale poses challenging organisational and co-ordination issues. Goffee and Jones (1995) suggest that these include:
- managing matrix structures where products are made and sold in several countries,
- improving the relationships between research and development, marketing and production to reduce the time taken to introduce new products,
- facilitating the transfer of knowledge around the different national components of the business,
- encouraging tactical and local flexibility while maintaining strategic coherence.

Although they were discussing the issues from the perspective of companies integrating their activities within Europe, identical considerations arise within businesses operating across the world.

Similarly, the processes of management take on a new aspect. The range of stakeholders is greater, with correspondingly more competing interests to satisfy. Reaching decisions and communicating them become more difficult when the players are physically distant. Geographical dispersion implies that control methods differ from those in physically compact organisations.

Hence the contexts in which individual managers operate become more diverse and more international. This can mean several things: working as an *expatriate manager* in another country, joining or managing an *international team* with members from several countries, or managing a *multicultural organisation* whose employees, systems and structures are truly international in that they no longer reflect its original, national base (Adams, 1996).

C A S E   Q U E S T I O N S   3 . 1

▶ What criteria would you use to decide if Lufthansa had succeeded in the aim of becoming a truly global airline?

▶ Which stakeholders is management having to satisfy while moving in that direction?

▶ What practical issues do you expect to arise if more managers and cabin staff are non-German?

In varying degrees these trends mean that employees will work with colleagues from different countries, and managers will deal with those from organisations, institutions and cultures widely different from their own. To handle this well means more than learning foreign languages, though that clearly helps. It is also necessary to be sensitive to more intangible differences in how people live, work and relate to each other. These cultural differences are deeply embedded in their particular context and may not be immediately obvious to a colleague from abroad. So the scope for misunderstanding is high.

 ## Cultural variety in the early days of the European Commission

Marcello Burattini is the head of protocol for the European Commission. On the fortieth anniversary of the Treaty of Rome, he recalled the early days of the Commission:

> At the beginning of the 1960s the rules, based on the principles of Franco-Prussian administration, were strict, formal modes of address, and ties were *de rigeur* ... Then certain political leaders decided to enlarge [the community]. Thus the British and the Irish arrived, bringing with them the English language, humour, simplicity in human relations, many original ideas – for example, pragmatism – somewhat softening the rigorous orthodoxy. The Danes taught us to be less formal, and were astonished by our way of doing things – and by the fact that secretaries made coffee for their bosses.

Source: *The European,* 27 March 1997

People perform the universal activities of management in unique and variable ways. Acceptable management practices evolve as managers act in a particular national context and culture. Cultures affect, amongst other things, how people are expected to behave and relate to each other. Employees' values, attitudes and behaviours bring aspects of the local culture into the workplace. They thus create the unique context within which management operates, and through which it learns appropriate behaviours for that location. So as business spreads, management makes contact with ever more diverse cultures, and different ways of interpreting the roles of management.

Culture also interacts with the institutions of a country – its education system, legal arrangements and the role of the state. Financial systems vary, reflecting their place and history. All combine to shape the context within which business and management operates within a country. The different institutional forms which organisations in different countries display are not usually due to chance or whim. They reflect the history and institutions within which entrepreneurs formed and developed them.

There is abundant anecdotal evidence of differences in national practice, as you will rapidly discover if you talk to someone who has worked or managed internationally. There are many studies on the cultural aspects of managing internationally. A counterview is that commentators may have overstated the management significance of cultural differences. This argues that the competences required for similar jobs have much in common irrespective of location.

This chapter introduces some models for thinking about management internationally; later chapters develop specific aspects.

3.2 Regionalism and globalisation

There has been a degree of international trade since the earliest times. Many great trading businesses were operating worldwide by the late nineteenth century. What is new at the end of the twentieth century is the much greater proportion of production which crosses national boundaries. Much of this trade is organised by businesses operating not on a national but on a regional or global scale.

Many forces drive this growth. One is the volume of private capital that is available for direct investment in a foreign country – as when Ford decided to build an engine plant in Spain. Instead of investing capital in a US plant and then exporting the product, Ford invested in another country, and exported products from there. Capital is highly mobile, and almost without exception countries compete with each other for investment. This is most visible in the publicity surrounding attempts to attract major manufacturing investments to less prosperous regions, whether of Europe, Asia or South America. Investment in services – financial, legal, design and other forms of intellectual capital – also increase world trade. One estimate is that one-third of all trade takes place within transnational companies, quite apart from external sales of foreign subsidiaries.

International trade negotiations have had to accommodate to new services. The General Agreement on Tariffs and Trade (GATT) reduces the propensity of national governments to put tariffs on physical goods to protect domestic companies, and other institutions are furthering this opening process. Thus the Uruguay trade agreement was reached by sixty-eight countries committing themselves to liberalising markets in telecommunications. The World Trade Organisation is negotiating for the removal of tariffs in information technology. Work is also being undertaken towards a world agreement on rules governing foreign investment – both to encourage it and, where thought necessary, to control it.

---

n o t e b o o k   3.1

Foreign direct investment

Identify a major example of foreign direct investment (FDI) which has recently occurred in your area. Find as much as you can about how that investment fits into the overall production system of the company. From which countries do the major components come? Where do the finished products go? How many other countries are named?

Clearly, the greater the volume of international trade, the more disputes arise. Those active in this area argue that, as within nation states, there is an urgent need for some framework of internationally agreed rules on competition policy. These would be enforced nationally, and buttressed by agreed mechanisms for settling outstanding disputes. International business, as much as nationl business, needs a viable framework of rules within which its management can operate. Does the development of supranational mechanisms and rules make it easier to control multinationals?

Supporters of more liberal world trade argue that the adverse effects of the phenomenon on some countries are not the result of globalisation, but of technological change that leads to a declining need for unskilled labour. They argue that, to ensure basic human rights, pressure should be directed towards achieving core labour standards, to ensure that the high-cost countries do not protect their own industries under the guise of not taking goods from poorer countries. Benefiting depends on ability to accept lifelong training, fluid, deregulated labour markets and a willingness to change.

Information technology (IT) has also stimulated trade. It does this both as a product and as a way of supporting widely dispersed production systems. A characteristic of IT systems is that the finished product is assembled from many small components. These have a high value-to-weight ratio, so they are cheap to transport long distances, and it pays to do so if that gives access to a cheap source of components. Much of the growth in international trade is due to the emergence of countries in Asia as sources of supply of electronic components. These flow in vast numbers every day to American, European and Japanese assembly plants.

Information technology also helps to manage the efficient flow of data on which international operations depend. The complex supply and manufacturing networks depend on computer systems to track and monitor the flow of orders, components and payments. Without information systems of the kind now common, world trade could not have grown to the present scale.

The EU is credited with being the model for many other regional trade groupings (Dent, 1997). Since the Treaty of Rome was signed in 1959 the aim has been the gradual elimination of tariffs and other restrictions which national governments use to protect domestic industries. This was broadly achieved by 1968, and led to further efforts to bring about closer economic integration between the member states. This culminated in the Single European Act of 1986 that aimed to create a single internal market by 1993. This further extended the scope for companies to operate in an integrated way across Europe. Companies were able to offer their goods and services much more widely within the EU, leading to a rapid growth in trade within the region. Much of this growth has been in intra-industry trade (Drabek and Greenaway, 1984). This is the simultaneous import and export of goods from the same industries, as when motor manufacturers set up plant in different countries to specialise in particular components or models. The companies then export products between the countries as part of a region-wide production system, leading to growth in intra-industry trade.

The other major trend affecting the management of organisations has been internationalisation and globalisation. Dicken (1992) distinguishes them as follows:

'Internationalisation is the increasing geographical dispersion of economic activities across national borders. Globalisation is a more advanced form of internationalisation which implies a degree of functional integration between internationally dispersed economic activities.

> Internationalisation is the increasing geographical dispersion of economic activities across national borders. Globalisation is a more advanced form of internationalisation which implies a degree of functional integration between internationally dispersed economic activities.

C A S E   Q U E S T I O N S   3.2

Consider Dicken's two definitions in relation to Lufthansa.

▶ From what you know about airline operations, how would a global airline differ from an international one?

▶ What are the additional management issues raised by globalisation, compared with internationalisation?

Globalisation is a process whereby transactions across national borders increase in importance relative to those within them. Another feature is that national boundaries become less significant barriers to the movement of goods and services – most clearly seen in the growing trade in electronically transmitted information products. Globalisation marks a new phase in business activity with, as Dent (1997) notes, the following characteristics:

▶ the accelerated growth of foreign direct investment,

▶ the growth of intra-firm trade in which firms buy or make components in one country and export them to their own assembly plants in another (Digital Europe, the Case Study in Chapter 5 is an example of this),

▶ the growth of complex supply arrangements amongst multinational firms as a result of mergers, joint ventures and other forms of supply-chain relationships.

Globalisation – what it means to small nations

In July 1996 the prime minister of Malaysia, Dr Mahathir Mohamad, gave a lecture in which he questioned whether globalisation would bring benefits to poorer countries. Some extracts from his speech were reported as follows.

> A globalised world is not going to be a very democratic world but will belong to powerful, dominant countries. Those countries would impose their will on the rest who will be no better off than when they were colonies of the rich. Fifty years ago, the process of decolonisation began and in about twenty years was virtually completed. But before any had become truly and fully independent, recolonisation has begun. This is what globalisation may be about. It does not contain much hope for the weak and poor. But unfortunately it is entirely possible.

He said that globalisation might bring about a utopia but nothing that had happened so far seemed to justify this dream. As interpreted by developed countries, it meant breaking down boundaries so that every country had access to others.

> The poor countries will have access to the markets of the rich, unrestricted. In return, or rather by right, the rich will have access to the markets of the poor. This sounds absolutely fair. The playing field will be level, not tilted to favour anyone. It will be a borderless world. But if there is only one global entity there cannot be nations. Everyone would be equal citizens of the globe. But will they be truly equal?

Dr Mahathir said that, after thirty years or more of 'independence', the former colonies of the West have found out the emptiness of the independence they had won. They have found that their politics, their economy, their social and behavioural systems are all under the control, directly or indirectly, of the old colonial masters and the great powers. He added that it was clear that the developed countries wished to use the World Trade Organisation to impose conditions on the developing countries. This will result not in improving human rights or labour practices or greater care for the environment but in stunting their growth and, consequently, in suffering for their people. If the developing countries were competing with the West in any way then their records were scrutinised and threats issued. The net effect is to prevent the development of these newly industrialising economies.

Dr Mahathir said globalisation would leave these countries totally exposed and unable to protect themselves, adding that true globalisation might result in increasing foreign investment in these countries. The effect would be the demise of the small companies based in the developing countries: 'Large international corporations, originating in the developed countries will take over everything.'

He said globalisation would result in all societies being exposed to the global culture, adding that this was going to become more universal because of the development of information technology. 'The unfortunate things is that the IT industry, and all that will be disseminated through it, will again be dominated by the big players – the huge corporations owned by the developed countries.'

Source: *New Straits Times*, July 1996

n o t e b o o k   3 . 2

Malaysia has attracted much foreign direct investment, especially from IT companies. It is a leading player in South East Asia with, in 1997, almost no unemployment. Yet the architect of its economic success clearly has serious doubts about the emergence of the global economy. What are his main concerns?

Can you find examples of global companies using their economic bargaining power to take advantage of the weaker countries in which they operate?

All of these developments imply much greater patterns of contact between managers in different countries. Legislative changes and treaties remove some barriers to trade, but they do not solve the management problems of making those economic activities work efficiently. Above all, they bring many managers face-to-face with the need to manage cultural differences.

3.3   Relevance of cultural differences

Managers in all companies experience in some way the cultural context of the country in which they work. In the home country they take this for granted, but it is still a powerful influence on the management processes. The extent to which managers need to be aware of other cultures depends on the importance of those cultures to the performance of their job. At one extreme, organisations deliver a service to a local community and manage the whole process from within that country, so international involvement will not arise. Others engage in a limited amount of export business, or may franchise the provision of services in other countries. Here there is rather more need for awareness of cultural differences. A very limited awareness will probably be sufficient. At the other extreme are those global businesses that deliberately operate in many countries around the world, have major foreign subsidiaries or significant joint ventures with companies based in

Table 3.1 **Company strategies and relevance of national culture**

Character of the firm	Relevance of national culture	
	Home culture	Foreign culture
Domestic, single-nation firm with no foreign interests	high	nil
Single-nation firm with import/export activities	high	low to moderate
Multinational firm with franchising and licensing activities	high	moderate to high
Multinational firm with manufacturing and/or service units abroad	high	high
Global firm with various business activities in most parts of the world	high	high

Source: Tayeb (1996)

another country. Here the issues are much greater, and the penalties for misunderstanding other systems more severe. Table 3.1 sums up the options.

Where the significance of foreign cultures is high, Tayeb suggests that management needs to deal with a range of interface and internal activities.

Interface activities

Firms deal with their external environment through a series of interface activities. These occur within a single country but take on new complexities when managing affairs across national boundaries.

Advertising

A company's advertising is its most visible aspect in many countries, and is particularly susceptible to differences about what is acceptable. Many advertising tactics that companies use widely in Europe are unacceptable in the Middle East. Chapter 12 discusses this and broader aspects of marketing in an international context.

Negotiating

Severe difficulties arise when people from different countries engage in direct interpersonal contact towards an agreement. The way they approach the interaction will reflect their respective cultures. Some will aim to get straight to the point; others will expect to spend hours, perhaps even several meetings, establishing a relationship with the other.

Internal organisational activities

An organisation with significant international activities will need to develop a management style to reflect these differences. Even the geographical spread of the activities introduces a new dimension. People have to spend more time arranging meetings and securing the agreement of different interests. There are also technical issues to do with the conditions of people working for the same company in different countries. Is pay to be common across the company, or varied to suit local conditions? Of greatest interest here is the extent to which national differences affect management processes such as the exercise of power and influence, team-building, managing change and managing between different cultures.

CASE QUESTIONS 3.3

▶ How might Lufthansa's change to 'a global firm with various business activities in most parts of the world' have affected the interface and internal activities listed in Table 3.1?

---

notebook 3.3

Identify three organisations which fall into different categories in the left-hand column of Table 3.1. Try to discuss with them their experience of working with foreign cultures, and what that has meant for their managers and staff.

A British negotiator in Paris

Mrs Brown is a senior executive of a British design company which is trying to break into the French market. She flies to France to meet a potential client, makes a snappy, clever and witty presentation, shows how much money there is to be gained by using her agency, and has a very satisfactory lunch with several French top executives of the target company. The French promise to get in touch soon and they part on the best of terms. Two months later our executive still hasn't heard anything and picks up the telephone to chase the lead. She is told that other senior people must be involved in the decision. Consequently, she flies to Paris once more, goes through the whole thing again, and has another excellent lunch. Time passes and nothing happens. She spends time on the telephone with her contacts and pushes for a trial but they explain to her that 'things are difficult' and that they'll see what they can do. A year – and several trips to Paris – down the line, nothing has happened. Our executive has more or less given up the whole thing when she gets a telephone call from Paris. Another manager would like to see her. She agrees, and is introduced to a very senior French manager – who finally discusses price for work. Taken by surprise, the executive negotiates a fairly good fee for a trial, but feels that something is 'not quite right'. Nevertheless, the trial goes well and the company is asked to do another job, then another one.

However, in the meantime a major British retailer contacts the British firm and proposes a major redesign effort that will take up all the resources of the company. Considering the size and the importance of the contract, they hastily finish all other jobs to concentrate on this unexpected opportunity. Our executive wraps up her business with France but soon starts being bothered by her French client. The job has not been well finished, things have to be redone, tempers run high, misunderstanding follows misunderstanding, and finally both parties break contact feeling disgruntled; no more contracts will ever come from that French company.

What happened? The French were surprised that the British executive only proposed rather small contracts to them, although they gave her to understand that some rather major jobs needed doing. They felt betrayed and let down when she broke the relationship, particularly since they were counting on her for all this extra work. They felt they had invested their time in somebody who just wanted a 'quick kill'.

Both sides had widely different expectations of their obligations towards each other. The British executive assumed a relationship built on a continuation of specific one-shot deals; you start with a trial, if it works you do another, then another and so on. It was natural for her to choose to pursue a much more profitable opportunity. On the other side, the French managers expected to build a relationship with the executive before they would give her a large amount of work. They had to know her, be able to trust her. Once she had been accepted, they expected her to remain within the relationship for as long as possible, regardless of outside circumstances.

Fundamentally, both parties had widely different understandings of the deal and the relationship, and as a result failed to develop a mutually beneficial partnership.

Source: Ballé and Gottschalk (1994), reproduced with permission

3.4 Contrasts in national cultures

While people have a great deal in common in the biological sense, there are many things that are unique to those from a particular nation or region. One of these is their culture. So, as business becomes more global in its operation, a central question for management is whether there are certain organisational imperatives of structure or behaviour which organisations must fill wherever they are, or whether they vary according to the culture of the country they are in (Smith, 1992).

Perspectives on culture

As a starting point, you might consider Edgar Schein's (1985) definition of corporate culture which is paraphrased here:

> ❢ Culture is the pattern of basic assumptions that a given group has invented, discovered or developed and [which is] therefore taught to new members as the correct way to perceive, think and feel in relation to [the organisation's] problems. ❢

Social groupings of all kinds develop a distinct culture, which to some degree sets them apart from other groupings. Teams, clubs, long-term work-groups, organisations and nations develop values and beliefs that guide members – how they react to events, what they regard as important. There is growing evidence of identifiable differences in the degree to which national cultures hold certain values and attitudes. For example, a study by Cranfield School of Management concluded that 'the French, although more sensitive to people, are slightly more into power/political styles of management, but less disciplined than the Germans who freely admit less sensitivity to people but a greater adherence to organisational disciplines and systems' (Kakabadse, 1993, quoted in Adams, 1996).

Social beliefs affect what managers expect from their job, how work relates to family life, and what reward they expect. Tayeb (1996) contrasts American and Japanese managers. She suggests the former typically give priority to things that are of personal importance to them. These include their long-term professional career, their individual personal development and the quality of family relationships. They come from 'an individualistic culture in which "self" takes precedence over group. For the Japanese manager the company's performance and victory ... comes first. And if this means sacrificing private leisure time so be it. [They] come from a collectivist culture, where group takes precedence over self' (p.37).

Tayeb goes on to argue that people learn their culture in the family, from religious influences and through the history of the nation, illustrating this last point with Australia:

> Australia is another example of the influence of history on people's values and attitudes. The origins of modern Australia go back to the

eighteenth century, when Britain used to send her convicted political and social offenders there. The convicts carried with them their lack of respect for authority. On the ships that took them there everyone was on an equal footing with their fellow passengers. This combination of low respect for authority and a belief in equality has over time evolved into a democratic political system which (with New Zealand) is more or less unique within their immediate neighbouring region.

Today, Australians are as law abiding as the citizens of any other nation, but they are sceptical about people in positions of power, such as politicians, police and judges. Their federal system of government reflects their belief in decentralisation and delegation of authority. (p.41)

---

notebook 3.4

Form a group from amongst your student colleagues made up of people from different countries and cultures. Identify some of the main characteristics of the respective cultures that affect management. Note them down and compare your findings with some more formal evidence presented later.

Organisations and their management operate within this cultural context. Employees, including managers, bring their prevailing values, attitudes and beliefs into the workplace as part of their cultural heritage.

Tayeb identifies further aspects of culture relevant to the work situation, namely high- and low-context cultures and attitudes to conflict.

High-context and low-context cultures

In a low-context culture, information is explicit and clear. A high-context culture is one in which information is implicit, and can only be fully understood in conjunction with shared experience, assumptions and various forms of verbal codes. High-context cultures occur when people live closely with each other, where deep mutual understandings develop, and which then provide a rich context within which specific communication takes place. Low-context cultures occur where people are typically distant from each other so that information needs to be very explicit.

> Japanese, Arabs and Mediterranean people, who have extensive information networks among family, friends, colleagues and clients and who are involved in close personal relationships, are examples of high context cultures. Low context peoples include Americans, Germans, Swiss, Scandinavians and other northern Europeans; they compartmentalise their personal relationships, their work and many aspects of day-to-day life. (Tayeb, 1996, pp.55–6)

Attitude to conflict and harmony

Disagreements and conflict arise in all societies. The management interest is in how different societies have developed different ways of handling conflict. Individualistic cultures such as those of the United States or the Netherlands see conflict as healthy, on the basis that everyone has a right to express their views. People are encouraged to bring contentious issues into the open and to discuss conflicts rather than suppress them. Other cultures place greater value on social harmony and on not disturbing the way things are.

High-context cultures are those in which information is implicit and can only be fully understood by those with shared experiences in the culture. **Low-context cultures** are those where people are more psychologically distant so that information needs to be explicit if members are to understand it.

The notion of harmony is central in almost all East Asian cultures, such as Korea, Taiwan, Singapore and Hong Kong, through their common Confucian heritage. In the context of Korea, for instance, Meek and Song … argue that the traditional implicit rules of proper behaviour provide appropriate role behaviour for individuals in the junior and subordinate roles of an interpersonal relationship. (Tayeb, 1996, p.60)

Other clear differences between nations include their view of change and their time orientation.

View of change

This varies greatly between cultures. In the West, many take a relatively proactive view of change. People believe that they can shape what happens, things do not have to be as they are, and that change is part of the nature of the world. Other cultures see change as something that is slow, inevitable and not greatly influenced by human beings. The notion that events will take their natural course and that human intervention will probably be fruitless is difficult for a western manager in a non-western culture to accept.

Time orientation

Managers in western organisations typically view time as a scarce commodity. They take courses on how to manage it better. They expect others to meet deadlines and to arrive for meetings at the appointed time. Not all cultures see time this way. Some view it as a limitless resource, unbounded by death. Time is inexhaustible, so that the widespread western concern about saving time is seen as curious.

---

n o t e b o o k   3.5

Are we overemphasising the differences?

So far only the diversity of national cultures has been emphasised. There is another view that the underlying fundamentals of management may outweigh cultural variations in detailed processes. One powerful constraint on diversity is the economic context of an essentially capitalist economic system. This places similar requirements on managers wherever they are. They have to provide acceptable returns, create a coherent organisational structure, maintain relations with stakeholders and try to keep control.

Further, if managers work in multinational organisations that have often developed their own strong and distinctive corporate culture, will corporate culture exercise more influence on behaviour than the local national culture?

Another constraint is the dramatic spread of integrated information systems across companies (and their suppliers) operating internationally. Some companies use such systems to place new and common reporting requirements on managers irrespective of their location. Such integration is often of competitive significance, and serves to tie units more closely together. This is also likely to bring convergence in the work of management.

These are unresolved questions to remember throughout this chapter. Look for evidence as you read that supports or contradicts either point of view.

3.5 Hofstede's comparison of national cultures

Geert Hofstede, a Dutch academic, provides a widely quoted insight into national cultural differences. In 1980 he had the opportunity to survey the attitudes of employees of IBM, one of the earliest global companies. He defines culture as a collective programming of people's minds, which influences how they react to events in the workplace. He defined four dimensions of culture (described below), and was able to establish how this varied amongst people in the different countries in which IBM operated.

Power distance

Power distance is the extent to which the less powerful members of organisations within a country expect and accept that power is distributed unevenly.

Power distance is defined by Hofstede as 'the extent to which the less powerful members of ... organisations within a country expect and accept that power is distributed unevenly' (1991, p.28). One of the ways in which countries differ is the way that power and authority are distributed. A related difference is the way they view any resultant inequality. In some the existence of inequality in boss/subordinate relationships is seen as problematic. Others see it as part of the natural order of things. The questionnaire allowed the researchers to calculate scores for 'power distance' (PD), countries with a high PD being those where people accepted inequality. Those with high scores included Belgium, France, Argentina, Brazil and Spain. Those with low PD scores included Sweden, Britain and Germany.

Uncertainty avoidance

Uncertainty avoidance is the extent to which members of a culture feel threatened by uncertain or unknown situations.

Uncertainty avoidance is 'the extent to which the members of a culture feel threatened by uncertain or unknown situations' (Hofstede, 1991, p.113). People in some cultures tolerate ambiguity and uncertainty quite readily – if things are not clear, they will improvise or use their initiative. Others are reluctant to move without clear rules or instructions. High scores, indicating low tolerance of uncertainty, were obtained in the Latin American, Latin European and Mediterranean countries, and for Japan and Korea. Low scores were recorded in the Asian countries other than Japan and Korea, and in most of the Anglo and Nordic countries. The UK was 47th in the list – similar to the USA, Canada and Australia. Germany ranked 29th, indicating a lower tolerance of uncertainty than Anglo-American countries.

Individualism/collectivism

Individualism pertains to societies in which the ties between individuals are loose.
Collectivism pertains to societies in which people, from birth onwards, are integrated into strong, cohesive groups.

Hofstede distinguishes between individualism and collectivism as follows: 'Individualism pertains to societies in which the ties between individuals are loose: everyone is expected to look after himself or herself and his or her immediate family. Collectivism as its opposite pertains to societies in which people, from birth onwards, are integrated into strong, cohesive in groups which throughout people's lifetime continue to protect them in exchange for unquestioning loyalty' (1991, p.51). Some people live in societies in which the power of the group prevails: there is an emphasis on collective action and mutual responsibility, and on helping each other through difficulties. Other societies emphasise the individual, and his or her responsibility for their position in life. High scores on the individualism dimension occurred in wealthy countries such as the United States, Australia, UK and Canada. Low scores occurred in poor countries such as the less developed South American and Asian countries.

Germany, the Netherlands, the Nordic countries and Japan showed medium individualism.

n o t e b o o k   3 . 6

Consider what the implications of the differences on Hofstede's first two dimensions of culture may be for management in the countries concerned. For example, what would Hofstede's conclusions lead you to predict about the method that a French or Argentinian manager would use if he or she wanted a subordinate to perform a task, and what method the subordinate would expect his or her manager to use? How would your answers differ if the manager and subordinates were Swedish?

---

n o t e b o o k   3 . 7

A manager is in charge of a team working on a project that has clear guidelines and a clear plan. It depends on specified suppliers delivering materials on time, otherwise the whole project is seriously delayed. The company will face severe financial penalties if it does not complete particular stages on time. The manager reports to a project director, who must authorise any changes to the plan.

One stage of the project is almost complete and is on schedule. The project director is called back to the distant head office for a critical meeting. He must leave at once. He therefore leaves the manager in charge of the project. Just after the director has left, the manager hears that a machine at one of the suppliers has failed and cannot resume production for at least a week. Another supplier can offer an alternative supply that would probably overcome the difficulty and avoid delaying the work. However, for technical reasons, using this supplier will require some temporary changes to other aspects of the project.

What would Hofstede's conclusions on the first two dimensions predict the reactions of the manager to be if he was (a) Brazilian, (b) Greek, (c) British, (d) German?

Masculinity/femininity

Masculinity pertains to societies in which social gender roles are clearly distinct.
Femininity pertains to societies in which social gender roles overlap.

Hofstede defines the two characteristics, as they pertain to society, as follows: 'masculinity pertains to societies in which social gender roles are clearly distinct (i.e. men are supposed to be assertive, tough and focused on material success, whereas women are supposed to be more modest, tender and concerned with the quality of life); femininity pertains to societies in which social gender roles overlap (i.e. both men and women are supposed to be modest, tender and concerned with the quality of life)' (1991, pp.82–3). Hofstede argues that societies differ in the desirability of assertive behaviour (which he labels as masculinity) and of modest behaviour (femininity). He sees a common trend in many societies that expect men to seek achievements outside the home, while women care for things within the home. Masculinity scores were not related to economic wealth: 'we find both rich and poor masculine countries, and rich and poor feminine countries' (p.84). The most feminine countries were Sweden, Norway, the Netherlands and

Denmark. Masculine countries included Japan, Austria, Germany, Italy and the United States.

The results obtained from Hofstede's work indicate the attitudes typically held by people in different national cultures to four dimensions. They have implications for understanding how people in the different areas in which a global company operates may react to particular management and organisational practices. An implication is that people operating internationally need to develop an ability to deal with the cultural contexts in which they will work. Adams (1996) examined several models attempting to identify the competences required to manage internationally. For example, Barham and Wills (1992) found that one of several competences which successful international managers possessed was the ability to act as 'intercultural mediator and change agent'. They defined this as: 'switching one's frame of reference rapidly between different cultures; being aware of one's own cultural underpinnings and of the need to be sensitive to cultural differences; managing change in different contexts and pushing the boundaries of different cultures; and balancing the need for speed and the need for sensitivity'.

Don't confuse attitudes with behaviour

Hofstede collected information on the values and attitudes of respondents. These are different from observable behaviour, which we can only infer from the attitudes expressed. It is also worth distinguishing between the details and minutiae of interpersonal behaviour across cultures and those behaviours with significant effects on business performance. Again we can only infer that there is a link. There are visible and illuminating examples (such as the visitor to France quoted earlier), but there are dangers in overgeneralising from good anecdotes.

A study by Laurent (1983) surveying successive groups of managers participating in executive development programmes at INSEAD (a leading European centre for management education and development) provides support for the view that differences in national cultures override the influence of corporate cultures.

National culture or organisational membership
❝ The managers came from many different companies and many different organisations. When their responses were analysed, it appeared that the most powerful determinant of their assumptions about the role of management was their nationality. Across 56 different items of inquiry, it was found that nationality had three times more influence on the shaping of managerial assumptions than any of the respondents' other characteristics such as age, education, function or type of company.

One of the most illustrative examples of national differences in management assumptions was reflected in the respondents' reaction to the following statement: 'It is important for a manager to have at hand precise answers to most of the questions that his subordinates may raise about their work.'

While only a minority of Northern American and Northern European managers agreed with this statement, a majority of Southern Europeans and South East Asians did. The research results

indicated that managers from different national cultures vary widely as to their basic conception of what management is all about. "

(Laurent, 1983)

Laurent found that conceptions of organisations varied widely across national cultures, as managers from Latin cultures (French and Italian) consistently perceived organisations as social systems of relationships monitored by power, authority and hierarchy to a much greater extent than their northern counterparts did. American managers held an 'instrumental' view of the organisation as a set of tasks to be achieved through a problem-solving hierarchy where positions are defined in terms of tasks and functions and where authority is functionally based. French managers held a 'social' view of the organisation as a collective of people to be managed through a formal hierarchy, where positions are defined in terms of levels of authority and status and where authority is more attached to individuals than it is to their offices or functions (Inzerilli and Laurent, 1983). Once these results were obtained, the question arose as to whether the corporate culture of multinational organisations would reduce some of the observed national differences and therefore bring some more homogeneity into the picture.

A new research study was designed to test this hypothesis. Carefully matched national groups of managers working in the affiliated companies of a large US multinational firm were surveyed with the standard questionnaire. The overall results gave no indication of convergence between national groups. Their cultural differences in management assumptions were not reduced in working for the same firm: if anything, there was slightly more divergence between the national groups within this multinational company than originally found in the INSEAD multicompany study. These findings were later replicated with national corporations.

The overall research findings led to the conclusion that deep-seated managerial assumptions are strongly shaped by national cultures and appear quite insensitive to the more transient culture of organisations.

3.6 Institutional contrasts between nations

Another way in which cultures influence management is through the national institutional arrangements that shape the fundamental structural form which companies take.

Management processes are institutionalised through organisations. Impersonal mechanisms and procedures support activities such as planning, resource allocation and motivation. What forms does that institutionalisation take? Most organisations develop initially within a single country. So we should expect the form they take, the way management is institutionalised, to reflect the cultures and institutions of those countries. We expect firms to have created organisations that match the fabric of their country of origin.

Whitley (1996) shows how national institutional features can explain differences in the characteristics of firms in different countries. He cites nine such features – cultural conventions, state structure and policies, financial systems and labour systems – which are summarised in the Noticeboard.

These nine factors shape a country's distinct structures for corporate governance. These structures are the legal requirements and culturally shaped practices for overseeing the management of enterprises at the highest level. Such institutions provide the fora within which the groups and interests that dominate an organisation's decision-making process can express their views and influence the management policies adopted. In some countries, firms are typically embedded in a network of interdependent relations with other economic actors, such as banks, state agencies, suppliers and unions. In others, these links are much weaker or do not exist at all, so that organisations work in relative isolation. Management is then able to act much more autonomously.

At one extreme are the Japanese networks of interdependent relations. Here the tradition is of mutual ownership between different but friendly business units. Companies have close financial and obligational links with other companies in other sectors. The Ministry of Industry actively supports and guides the strategic direction of major areas of business. The firms create a network of mutually dependent organisations with interlocking obligations. They decide strategy by negotiation with independent stakeholders, which are mainly other companies and financial institutions.

---

n o t e b o o k   3.8

Select an example of a major Japanese company, such as Sony or Toyota. Using your library resources, prepare a two-page summary, including diagrams, of the ownership structure of the group and the other companies with which it is financially linked. You could do this as a team activity. Good places to start would be the index of *The Economist, Financial Times, Business Week* or *Wall Street Journal*.

C A S E   Q U E S T I O N S   3.4

▶ How would Lufthansa ownership structures compare with that of the Japanese company you have chosen in Notebook 3.8?

NOTICEBOARD Whitley's elements of national institutional features

Cultural conventions
▶ Strength of institutions governing trust relations and collective loyalties

State structure and policies
▶ Extent to which state dominates economic system
▶ Level of risk-sharing with private economic actors
▶ State support for co-operation between firms
▶ Formal regulation of entry to and exit from markets

Financial system
▶ Credit-based financial system

Labour system
▶ Significance of labour in strategic decision-making
▶ Centralisation of bargaining
▶ Collaboration in training

Source: Whitley (1995, p.51)

In contrast, firms in the UK and the United States work in a more isolated way. They receive less direct support from banks, which have traditionally avoided long-term investments. Their boards rarely contain representatives of other companies, such as suppliers or major customers, which, while independent, nevertheless have long-term interests in common.

The level of dependence affects companies' attitudes towards growth and profitability. Whitley suggests that a high level of dependence on the state encourages growth but discourages concern over profit, and he cites France as an example of this. In Japan, firms seek market share and growth within their sector, but not beyond it. The network of relations between Japanese firms and their customers and suppliers restricts unrelated diversification, but there is a strong collective interest in expansion. In contrast, the more isolated UK and US firms, where owners operate as portfolio-holders, find growth goals limited by the need to meet profit targets and expectations of the capital market. Dividend pay-outs and growth in share price are more significant measures of corporate performance than growth as such. In addition, family-owned businesses may experience limited growth because of a reluctance to share control and a desire to increase family wealth rather than firm size.

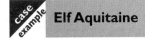

Elf Aquitaine

Elf, the largest company in France, was privatised in 1994. Before that, the state owned the company and ran it as an instrument of industrial policy. It supported the interests of the Mitterand presidency, and profit was a secondary consideration.

> **At the beginning of the 1980s the independent Atochem branch had been at the centre of the socialists' restructuring of the French chemical industry, while a decade later the investment policies ... served to create a set of interlocking shareholdings, securing crucial parts of French industry from hostile takeover. The stake in the textile company Biderman was taken to help rescue a major employer and the largest French company in the sector. The absence of any significant industrial logic behind these participations was confirmed by the reversal of the investment strategy by privatisation.**

Source: Mayer and Whittington (1996, p.102)

Relationship patterns also affect the direction of company growth. Some use a wide range of skills and capabilities, building up large, integrated organisations. Others focus what they do internally, getting the other resources they need from other organisations.

> The small specialised production units found in the Italian industrial districts clearly represent one extreme, while the highly diversified conglomerates operating in heavy industry, light industry, construction, retailing and financial services – such as some of the largest Korean *chaebol* ... are at the other end of the continuum. In between are the relatively specialised Japanese *kaish*, the vertically integrated German enterprise and the Anglo-Saxon diversified multinational. (Whitley, 1996, p.45)

Institutional influences also affect basic forms of organisational structure, which establishes where strategic decisions are made, and how activities and plans are co-ordinated. Many companies integrate activities hierarchically, in a single, strongly bounded organisation. As the scale of activities grows, the structure is adapted into multiple divisions (hence the title M-form), each with a hierarchy of management positions. The divisional hierarchy of the M-form company aims to control activities within the division, and is itself controlled by being part of a larger hierarchy of the organisation as a whole. At the apex is the board that reports on performance to the shareholders and other institutions in the capital market. This, however, is only one type of firm that has become institutionalised in Europe; there are many different ways in which managerial and entrepreneurial services can be effectively co-ordinated.

The M-form suits the prevailing institutional structures in the United States, where it first evolved. State government there has remained deliberately distant from involvement in business affairs, except to promote competition and discourage collusion amongst firms. The banks also limited their involvement in the activities of particular firms, apart from providing short-term working capital. Firms have therefore relied on the capital market for a significant proportion of their finance. Ownership is diffuse. Mayer and Whittington (1996) quote studies showing that few individuals or institutions own more than a small percentage of shares in major companies. 'Management is thoroughly professional, free of substantial family ownership interests and always conscious of the penalties for underperformance' (p.95). These diffuse owners require information on performance, especially short-term performance. An organisational structure is required which does this efficiently, and the head of the M-form organisation performs this controlling role on behalf of investors.

Other countries have created different economic institutions. Ownership and control are much more closely connected in Continental Europe. Mayer and Whittington report studies showing that, in Germany, 37 per cent of large firms were privately owned in the late 1970s, and 21 per cent were state-owned. In France at the end of the 1980s, 44 per cent of top industrial and commercial organisations were under family control and 13 per cent state-owned. In Germany and France the banks are much more closely involved in providing long-term finance for business through extended credit-based systems, and they are represented on company boards of directors. Whitley argues that, in these countries, the holding company structure is more appropriate than the M-form structure. The holding company is one in which separate companies are responsible for each of the areas of activity. Holding companies have traditionally granted their component companies greater autonomy than M-form companies grant to their divisions. He argues that the boards of holding companies provide an effective forum for discussing projects between the different business units in the company and external financial interests.

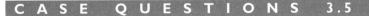

CASE QUESTIONS 3.5

▶ How would you expect these institutional arrangements to have influenced the management of Lufthansa?

3.7 Japanese management systems

Japan is a good example of the way in which features of the national culture shape the characteristics of large enterprises. Highly successful in world markets, Japanese companies have been widely studied for any lessons that they may offer to other managements. A fundamental feature of Japanese society is the belief in collectivism – in the sense that people identify strongly with the groups to which they belong. Individuals put group interests before their requirements. People try to fit in, rather than stand out. This core value has shaped many features of the Japanese *nenko* approach to business, which most large firms use. At the company level, there are strong corporate cultures emphasising achievement and harmony. Key practices are described below.

Secure employment, with emphasis on seniority

The seniority system in the large Japanese companies builds on a careful and thorough recruitment process. Management fills senior positions almost exclusively from within, so that opportunities for promotion and advancement come after long service. An employee who enters the organisation can look forward to fairly certain, but often slow, progression through the hierarchy. Performance is reviewed regularly, often by involving other members of the workgroup in the process. All employees are members of the company union, which bargains with management over a wide range of payment topics. Negotiations assume long-term unity of interest, not confrontation.

Group working

Staff typically work in groups. Employees join a multi-skilled workgroup, not a particular functional or professional discipline. They have flexible work roles within the group. The group is responsible for many tasks (such as scheduling, work-planning and some maintenance) which in other cultures have been separated and given to other people. The wider value system encourages loyalty to the group.

n o t e b o o k   3 . 9

Compare the practice of group working described here with that advocated by Frederick Taylor (see Chapter 2). What do the differences imply about the assumptions made about the abilities of staff?

Group consultation and decision-making

Management pays very close attention to employee consultation. Decision-making is a political process, in which the parties seek mutual understanding on the way to a decision. So managers and staff debate proposals for change in a highly iterative way. This typically leads to further questions and counterproposals, which they again debate. Inevitably, decision-making takes a long time, but people identify with the result to which they have contributed. Implementation, however, is swift, as people will have been able to consider these issues in the lengthy process of reaching a decision.

This process reflects a distinct underlying assumption of:

> unavoidable interdependence and, hence, the primacy of the group. This engenders an emphasis upon loyalty, obligation, conformity, respect for authority, traditionalism, co-operation and self-restraint. Being accepted by the group and avoiding anything that would bring 'shame' on it are major motivating forces. (Hales, 1993, p.200)

However, not all workgroups consist of employees with lifetime employment – there are many casual, part-time or temporary employees with much poorer working conditions.

Centralised control of recruitment and performance
Tight central control is exercised over inputs (who is hired) and performance measurement (with detailed planning and control systems administered from the centre). The manager of a division which performs poorly will be demoted. Although the operating level monitors the details of quality, the centre reinforces this by promoting 'clear and powerful corporate values relating to customer service and product quality' (Hales, 1993, p.193).

Quality through technical efficiency
Performance is supported by close attention to the technical operations. These are carefully planned for maximum efficiency and guided by detailed technical rules on the processes to use. Management and staff use the *kaizen* philosophy of looking for continuous small improvements.

High-profile managers and supervisors
Supervision is close, with much reliance on face-to-face communication. Managers work closely with their employees and show equal concern for their general well-being. Supervisors not only have line responsibility but also provide technical and problem-solving support.

---

n o t e b o o k   *3.10*

Gather your own evidence to support or modify the descriptions of Japanese management systems given here. Select a Japanese-owned company and find out what you can either from the literature or through direct contact about the local management systems. It is probably best to work as a group on this, dividing the work between you.

3.8 Contrasting management systems

Management takes place in a social context that influences its character, so we would expect that different national or continental cultures would produce different views on how management is, or should be, conducted. Keith Thurley and Hans Wirdenius (academics working in the UK and Sweden respectively) became concerned at the apparent domination of management writing and teaching by the North American experience. They believed that, while many of the ideas were powerful, they jarred with the distinctive and varied cultural experience within Europe. Was there such a thing as a European approach to management, as distinct from the prevailing American and emerging Japanese styles?

Thurley and Wirdenius summarised the distinctive features of the American and Japanese styles in this way:

American management theory is built on seven crucial ideas:
1 *Scientific management* Using a systematic approach to improve task performance.
2 *Classical management theory* Defining roles with specific job/role responsibilities and authority.
3 *Individualism* Assuming that managers are primarily individuals with their own personalities and interests and their own idea of individual self-interest.
4 *Human relations* Concern for fostering workgroup norms and relationships to serve organisational goals.
5 *Contingency theory* All organisations need to develop structures and policies that are relevant to their particular context. All organisations therefore should be different.
6 *Planned organisational change* Change requires a systematic approach to change organisational structures and culture.
7 *Strategic choice management* Organisations should try to define the basic business strategies required to achieve a satisfactory market position. This then leads to designing structures that fit this strategy.

Japanese management is essentially in contrast an argument for equality as the basis of competition and co-operation. This rejects the implicit technocratic approach of American scientific management. There are also seven crucial ideas that summarise the approach:
1 *Collective responsibility* All members of an organisation should feel responsibility for the success of that organisation.
2 *Generalist roles and job rotation* All employees work for the organisation and should be trained to perform a wide variety of roles. They do not own their jobs – they may have to do anything and need training for this.
3 *Trust of subordinates* Subordinates need to be allowed to get on with their work. They have potential that should be stimulated.
4 *Protection of all employees* All employees are vulnerable and need protection whilst working for the organisation.
5 *Life careers should be planned* Individuals need to perceive their whole potential career as an opportunity which offers a challenge for them to develop their skills and knowledge.
6 *Pragmatic adaptation and rationalism* Everything changes, so management must be flexible enough to adapt to new circumstances.
7 *Identity with the 'michi' ('the way') and personal work colleagues* The work ethic is seen as a daily personal experience and is essentially derived from constant interactions with others in the workgroup. Employees therefore need to have a clear identity with the way they live in the organisation and to show affection and loyalty to their co-workers. (Thurley and Wirdenius, 1989, pp.19–20)

Models of this sort are inevitably highly generalised summaries of diverse populations. Their value is to give some clues about broad differences in approach to management. Above all, they remind us of the variety of ways in which management is practised. This should make us sceptical towards those who offer universal solutions or prescriptions.

Thurley and Wirdenius reviewed the context and development of management in Europe. While they readily acknowledged the great diversity within that continent, they were able to put forward a *European management model*. In this,

> Six needs or values could be said to provide the major starting points for managerial action:
> 1 The need for scientific, rational thinking to guide decisions.
> 2 The need for managers to evolve specific pragmatic strategies suited to the precise situation, rather than following universalistic theories or solutions based on ideologies.
> 3 The need for emotional commitment to making a change initiative work. This implies inspiring employees to take future possibilities seriously.
> 4 The need to use managerial and technical experience – and the judgements based on this – to the fullest degree. Social capital is composed of such learnt behaviour, skills and knowledge.
> 5 The need to accept a 'pluralist' view of the enterprise which combines the necessity of achieving commitment to organisational goals and a democratic process for arriving at broadly consensual decisions.
> 6 The need for creative learning, through and with other colleagues, together with self-development, as a continuous process within organisational work life. Such learning has to be a continuation of the educational process, for all ages and for all levels.

CASE QUESTIONS 3.6

▶ Which of Thurley and Wirdenius's management models would you expect to shape management practice at Lufthansa?

▶ What examples of each approach can you find in the case study?

Other cultures are now challenging the western and Japanese models. Islamic beliefs influence management in the Arab world. Arab executives are more person-oriented than work-oriented, and more susceptible to pressures from families, friends and the wider community. These pressures influence their decisions and behaviour practices. Al-Faleh (1987) found that Arab management had the following characteristics, stemming from the prevailing value system:

▶ Organisation members are motivated by friendship and power needs, rather than by performance objectives.

▶ Social formalities are extremely important.

▶ Managers rely heavily on kinship ties to get things done.

▶ Nepotism is regarded as natural and acceptable.

▶ Punctuality and time constraints are of much less concern than in western cultures.

NOTICEBOARD **A European model?**

Bloom *et al.* summed up their conclusions by setting out what they called 'The Evolving European Management Model'. Its basic characteristics are:

Managing international diversity   Europe's political and trading history, they believe, has ensured that Europeans understand, welcome and respect diversity; they seek to integrate diversity without stifling it.

Social responsibility   European companies claimed to see themselves as part of society, which meant that they:

▶ acted in a socially responsible way,
▶ considered profits to be only one of many company goals,

▶ took a long view on decisions and investments.

Internal negotiation   European firms were seen as places where much internal negotiation took place between different levels and functions of the organisation.

An orientation towards people   Europeans believe that people ought to benefit from progress, not the reverse. This led to encouraging design work to give a high quality of working life to employees, a tolerance of differences, and a generally sympathetic approach to managing staff.

Source: based on Bloom *et al.* (1994, pp. 18–19)

▶ Subordinates act with deference and obedience to those above them in the hierarchy.

Contrast this with the opinions of a group of senior European company directors who gave their views on the distinct characteristics of a European model of management, summarised in the Noticeboard.

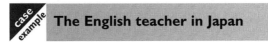

n o t e b o o k   **3.11**

The Noticeboard sets out one view of the position, painted from the inside. Can you identify where it supports the Thurley and Wirdenius model, and where it differs?

3.9   Working in other countries

There are particular hazards in cross-cultural communication. Yet in today's international business environment, being able to communicate well is becoming an essential part of being able to do a job well. Your success is likely to depend on how well you work with people from different cultures – who will see things quite differently from the way you do.

The English teacher in Japan

case example

In July 1996 I went to Japan where I was employed by a local authority as an English teacher. I knew little of the Japanese language and still less of the country's culture. I reported to a section head in the education office who in turn reported to the town's head of education.

In October of that year, I informed the head of education that I would be returning home for Christmas and planned to attend a family event on 7 January. This would mean taking an extra week of holiday than was usual in Japan. The head of education seemed surprised at what I had planned but did not comment on it directly. Later that day I booked the flight.

A few days later I received an official letter from an official in the education department. This stated that as my planned absence would fall outside of the Japanese winter holidays (27 December– 5 January), it would be impossible to be absent from work for such a long period. I would have to stay in Japan for Christmas.

The teacher was annoyed and disappointed at her plans not working out. She felt that her request was reasonable by western standards. The organisation was small and she had communicated directly with top management in order to deal with the matter quickly.

---

n o t e b o o k   3.12

From what you have read earlier about Japanese culture, why do you think this difficulty arose? What different approaches might have avoided the difficulty?

The Case Example clearly highlights the kind of cultural difference that people working in other cultures need to be aware of. Hofstede (1991) defined culture as the collective programming of the mind, and since those involved came from different cultural backgrounds with inherently different 'collective programming', disagreement was inevitable unless the teacher tried to adapt.

Some tips

▶ Take time to find out how things are done in the host country by asking general questions (in the Case Example, about holiday practices) before forming your own plan.

▶ Consider which is the right channel to take.

▶ Think through the approach (presenting the dilemma and asking for help in how to resolve it).

▶ Try to find out about other aspects of the situation (in this case it happened that a more senior teacher was also seeking time off, and had been refused).

▶ Try to learn something of the culture of a country before going there, including social structures, organisational behaviour, religion, values, language and history. This helps to create the right climate between the visiting staff and those with whom they will be communicating.

▶ Take the trouble to start learning the language and be aware of the importance of non-verbal communication (in this case what did the education chief's initial response mean?).

Ethnocentrism is the tendency to regard one's own group as the standard and all other different groups as strange and usually inferior.

These approaches may help to develop a sense of cultural relativism. This means recognising that the behaviour of members of other cultures can be understood only in the context of their own culture. It is the opposite of ethnocentrism.

3.10 Recap

More than most chapters this one has emphasised the influence that changes in the external context have on organisations and their management. Political, legal, economic and technological changes have encouraged the regionalisation and globalisation of business activity. This has affected the pattern of international contacts which many managers have. That in turn brings managers directly into contact with diverse cultures and institutions, requiring a new level of awareness of and sensitivity to these differences.

Content agenda

Increased opportunities for regional and global trade mean that the environment is bringing in new forms of competition to businesses – others can now compete in their home market. By the same token, businesses can develop their objectives towards extending their market into a wider area. Planning to achieve those objectives on a global scale raises new workflow and logistical challenges. New organisational structures are created to manage internationally, which are usually supported by developments in information technology. In shaping these changes, management and staff need to take account of the diversity of national cultures. This is particularly necessary in generating willing action and commitment from people who may have different perspectives on work.

Process agenda

Internationalisation clearly means more stakeholders, especially when companies develop complex trading networks across national boundaries. These stakeholders include the governments and communities in which they work as well as other commercial organisations.

The interests and ways of working of these players will have been shaped by local cultures and institutions. These cultural differences also affect how management can influence the behaviour of those whose support it needs – methods acceptable in one culture may not work in another. A probable consequence of globalisation is that it reduces the shared knowledge within the organisation. Communication internally assumes greater importance if the organisation is to be able to co-ordinate effectively over great distances.

Control agenda

A strategy of internationalisation or globalisation may be a way to reduce dependency on any single source. If so, it affects the relative power of stakeholders. A similar issue from a critical perspective is the way in which the power of management in multinational companies is increasing at the expense of national states. It can also be observed that national governments are keen to encourage foreign direct investment by such companies in their country on account of the access to economic power they bring. Management can use the threat (real or imagined) of increased global competition to encourage their own staff to accept change which they might otherwise have opposed.

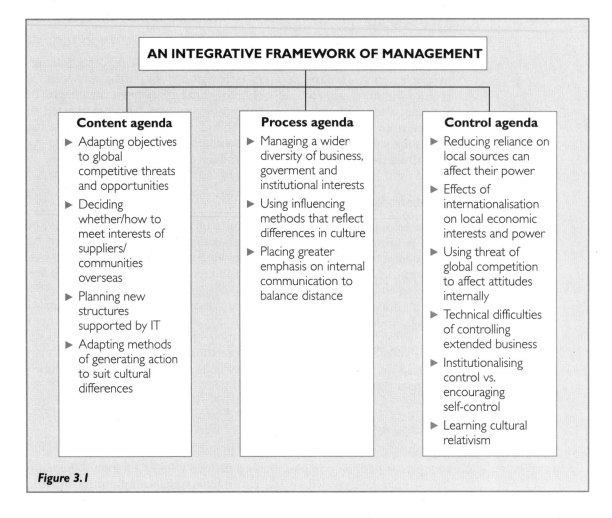

AN INTEGRATIVE FRAMEWORK OF MANAGEMENT

Content agenda
- ► Adapting objectives to global competitive threats and opportunities
- ► Deciding whether/how to meet interests of suppliers/ communities overseas
- ► Planning new structures supported by IT
- ► Adapting methods of generating action to suit cultural differences

Process agenda
- ► Managing a wider diversity of business, goverment and institutional interests
- ► Using influencing methods that reflect differences in culture
- ► Placing greater emphasis on internal communication to balance distance

Control agenda
- ► Reducing reliance on local sources can affect their power
- ► Effects of internationalisation on local economic interests and power
- ► Using threat of global competition to affect attitudes internally
- ► Technical difficulties of controlling extended business
- ► Institutionalising control vs. encouraging self-control
- ► Learning cultural relativism

Figure 3.1

The more widespread an organisation's business, the more it must rely on institutionalised forms of control. Yet they can be open to different interpretations across cultures. They may have different views on the activity of control and how it should be exercised. Some systems favour tight, centralised and supervisory controls: the current pattern in many western organisations is to emphasise the benefits of self-control in semi-autonomous teams. Different attitudes to corrective action and learning also illuminate the diversity of management practice across the globe. Managers also need to learn significant skills of cultural relativism to counter inherent perceptions. These points are summarised in Figure 3.1.

PART CASE QUESTIONS

- ► In what ways is The Body Shop operating internationally?
- ► What issues does the Lufthansa case suggest might also be on the agenda of management at The Body Shop? And vice versa?
- ► How does the Body Shop culture relate to the local cultures in which it has retail operations? Does national or company culture prevail?

3.11 Review questions

1 What factors are stimulating the growth in world trade?
2 Compare internationalisation and globalisation. Give a specific example of a company of each type about which you have obtained some information.
3 Outline the difference between a high- and a low-context culture and give an example of each from direct observation or discussion.
4 Explain accurately to another person Hofstede's four dimensions of national cultures. Evaluate his conclusions on the basis of discussions with your colleagues from any of the countries in his study.
5 Give some illustrations of your own about the way in which the history of a country has affected its culture, and how that in turn affects the management of organisations there.
6 How is the prevailing financial structure in a country likely to affect the role of management?
7 What are the distinctive features of Japanese industrial organisations? How do they differ from the prevailing western models?
8 Compare the implications of globalisation for (a) national governments, (b) their citizens, (c) the management of global companies, (d) the environment.

Further reading

Dent (1997) traces the development of a more integrated European economy and its place within wider global trends. Equally good is Bennett (1997) which includes useful summaries of relevant institutions such as the World Trade Organisation. A detailed account of the European context of business is given in Nugent and O'Donnell (1994) which includes chapters on the political, economic, legal, labour market, financial, marketing and technological environments within which European managements are operating. Excellent introductions to business in major European countries are provided by the Business Cultures in Europe series published by Heinemann, for example Gordon (1996). Ghauri and Prasad (1995) offers a good set of readings on the themes of global strategy, understanding non-western structures and ways of developing global managers. The *European Management Journal* regularly publishes case studies and accessible research with an international perspective.

W Website addresses

Cardiff Business School Japanese Management Research Unit
http://www.cf.ac.uk/carbs/japanese management
The unit conducts research into the diffusion of Japanese management practices. Information on publications, including working papers, is available on its site.

Lufthansa http://www.lufthansa.com

Interpreting the management role

CONTENTS

AIM

To show how managers have interpreted the role and to introduce some perspectives which may help to explain that diversity.

OBJECTIVES

By the end of your work on this chapter you should be able to outline the concepts below in your own terms and:

1 Define some concepts from role theory relevant to the study of management work

2 Explain and illustrate the stakeholder concept, and how it affects the management role

3 Explain and evaluate the view that management involves a significant amount of political activity

4 Compare theories of the content of management work and evaluate one theory with data from a task you need to perform

5 Summarise Rosemary Stewart's study of the characteristics of managers' work

6 List the roles identified by Henry Mintzberg, and explain with examples what they mean

7 Evaluate the traditional and Mintzberg frameworks, using some original data you have gathered

8 Summarise Luthans's study of the differences between effective and successful managers and discuss the implications for managers' roles

9 Evaluate how managers' roles are being affected by changes in the business environment

10 Explain the theory that managers themselves shape their role, and be able to use the model to analyse and compare different management jobs

British Gas

Every management job is different, so no single case can illustrate a typical management job. This example illustrates a current trend in management, in which many managers seem to be spending significantly greater amounts of time and effort in negotiating with other managers and rather less with their own subordinates.

The manager was a project engineer with British Gas. He was asked to develop a computer system to support maintenance scheduling and other work in an engineering department. The system would work from existing maintenance records to issue automatically to engineers instructions on which jobs they were to do. It would also record when the job was finished. The project had been initiated by head office, not the department in which it would operate. The manager explained:

> The director who had initiated the project was keen to use a system that had been developed in another part of the company. He has clearly defined the requirement for the system on the basis of their perception of the problem.
>
> Now that I have started work I am getting into the politics of the situation. Bear in mind that this system will open up day-to-day area performance to senior management as to how its operational management is performing. So I decided it was important to communicate with area managers, talk about the system and what the objectives are. Not really to get them on my side but to impart a fuller understanding that the system is not intended to spy on them but to help them improve their performance and also the department's performance … So a great deal of time has been spent with the area managers. I would like to think I have been successful in showing them the way we are heading, though at this stage they seem to be a little dubious.
>
> In the midst of that, the proposed system has been reviewed technically. I have been meeting with the computer professionals and am reasonably confident that it will work. So I now have to do a cost-justification of that and other systems to get a clearer picture of the options.
>
> Having appraised seven options, it was clear that the best was based around PCs linked into local networks. Interestingly, the people who were least in favour of it were the computer people. They perhaps saw a weakening of their power base. They have a vested interest in mainframes, and don't want the company to adopt a PC option … It's up to the director to decide which way to go. But I like to think that by managing this project the way I have done, the area managers are more aware of what's going on and that they have a point of view. Previously they would have just had a mainframe thrust on them from head office without discussion.

CASE QUESTIONS

- How does this manager's role differ from what you expected a manager to be doing?

- How would you describe the way he seems to have worked?

- Can you see any similarities and differences between his role and those of the managers in Global Instruments?

4.1 Introduction

This chapter introduces the following ideas:
▶ Role
▶ Role set
▶ Role behaviour
▶ Stakeholders
▶ Objectively rational action
▶ Subjectively rational action
▶ Interpersonal role
▶ Informational role
▶ Decisional role
▶ Role negotiation

Separating management from direct work creates a distinct occupational group. This chapter examines how those who take on this specialist, separate work have interpreted the role. It begins by outlining the basic idea of role and how this reflects stakeholders' interests. We introduce traditional and contemporary views of the content of the manager's role, which have set out what managers are expected to do. These are then complemented by research into how managers perform their role, looking especially at the work of Stewart, Mintzberg and Luthans. More recent research stresses the ambiguities and dilemmas in the role, and the scope which managers have to shape and negotiate rather than passively accept it. Stressed throughout is the diversity of the role: no two managers have identical roles.

---

n o t e b o o k   4 . 1

What do you think?

Before reading on, make a few notes about your present view of the manager's job. What do you think are the main characteristics of the way managers work? What do you think the job is like? Is it all calm and rational, with orderly discussions between people in suits? Is it a rush from one thing to another, desperately trying to cope with unexpected problems?

4.2 The concept of roles

It is important to be clear about the meaning of the term 'role'. We all play many roles – student, team member, club secretary, shop assistant, engineer, manager or parent. Role analysis considers how individuals meet their obligations in a social situation by interacting with others to shape those obligations. These processes also shape managers' jobs, who in turn shape those of others. To avoid ambiguity we use the established terminology of Katz and Kahn (1978):

> Role is the sum of the expectations that other people have of a person occupying a position.
> Role set is those people or institutions that have expectations of a person.

Role is the sum of the expectations that other people have of a person occupying a position. Role set is those people or institutions that have expectations of a person.

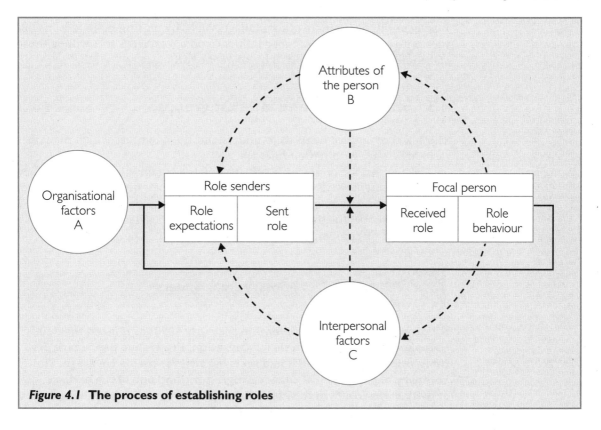

Figure 4.1 **The process of establishing roles**

Think of the person whose roles we are analysing as the focal person. He or she is at the centre of a group of other people or institutions who make up the *role set*. This in turn consists of those with whom the person has significant contact. They have expectations about the person's performance in the job. These *role senders* communicate their *role expectations* to the focal person during their interaction with him or her. Communicating these expectations produces the *sent role*. The focal person's receipt and interpretation of that communication becomes their *received role* – what they believe the role senders expect of them. *Role behaviour* is what the focal person does in response to those messages. So the role set's expectations create demands and constraints on the person; and that person's behaviour in turn provides the role set with information about the person's compliance with expectations. Figure 4.1 shows the relationship between these elements.

The expectations of the role senders provide the context in which the person works. They are also a basis for comparison between expected and actual behaviour.

In Chapter 1 a distinction was drawn between management as a set of activities to be undertaken, and the status or title of the people who perform those activities. People who are not formally part of the management structure often manage (for example, a nurse planning how to rearrange working practices to reduce waiting time in a clinic). Those who are in the management hierarchy often spend time on non-management activities (for example, a university vice-principal giving a course of lectures). The distribution of management activities around the organisation is itself the result of management actions, so there is a wide variety of practices to be found. Senior managers often eliminate other managers' jobs by putting more responsibilities onto subordinates. A major influence on a manager's role will be those stakeholders with an interest in his or her performance.

4.3   Stakeholders and interest groups

The stakeholder idea helps us to understand the dilemmas which managers need to balance within their role.

Stakeholders are both within and beyond the organisation. Wherever they are, management needs to be aware of them, and their interests, and to try to balance those interests against the demands or expectations of others. The Case Example describes the stakeholder map used by management in BP, the world's third largest oil company, to identify the interests they need to balance.

Stakeholders are those people, groups, or institutions that have an interest in, or are affected by, an organisation.

case example   BP's view of its primary stakeholders

BP experienced severe problems in the early 1990s as it faced the need to make radical changes in the organisation. Profits had been static, its share price had fallen and it had received adverse media coverage. The company began a radical change programme and one of the earliest activities was to affirm the idea of 'stakeholder symmetry'. Management recognised five primary groups of stakeholders:

Suppliers	Employees
Shareholders	
Communities	Customers

Each group had different – and conflicting – expectations of the company. Shareholders demanded additional value from the company, which at the time meant that the company would have to cut costs. This would run against employees' established expectations of job security. To prosper in the long term, the company would have to satisfy them all to an acceptable level.

There is clearly a tension between the groups and a pull between the different values. The management test is how it manages the dynamic that links them. If management tries to satisfy one stakeholder group, what will be the effect on the others?

BP management may also shift the emphasis it gives to different stakeholders. In the early stages of the change programme, around 1992, shareholders came first. The share price had fallen to 172p, and the board was under increasing attack from investors. By 1997 the share price had risen to over 700p, and investors were taking a more positive view of the company's management. The latter was now devoting more time to satisfying the community stakeholders, especially in areas like Colombia where the company owned large oil reserves. Management was also said to be devoting more effort to satisfying expectations in the areas of human rights and environmentally sustainable development.

n o t e b o o k   4.2

What will each of the five stakeholder groups expect of BP? Try to be specific.

How have specific actions of the company affected the different stakeholders? You could gather information on this by looking for items about the company in the newspapers. Try to relate stories about company policies to the different stakeholders, and the tensions these produce. As a bigger project, you could do the same for several high-profile companies and compare results.

Neglecting influential stakeholders is likely to damage an organisation. A customer goes elsewhere, a supplier gives priority to someone else, a local authority refuses planning permission for a new facility, a pressure group mounts a campaign or boycott. Traditionally, management was accountable to one group of stakeholders – the shareholders. This no longer applies. Many other stakeholders or interest groups are able to influence management. Shell's decision in 1996 not to dispose of a disused oil-rig by dumping it was a clear example of the power of well organised stakeholders – in this case Greenpeace – to alter management decisions. The general point is that management needs to identify and manage significant stakeholders and to communicate with them effectively. This is especially difficult if the interests of stakeholders are in conflict.

In public sector organisations, the absence of equity shareholders representing a controlling interest means that accountability is more complex. A local authority's stakeholders, for example, include councillors, officers, local (domestic and business) taxpayers, central government, a broad range of customers and clients (for the different services provided, such as education, social work and housing), and a variety of interest groups (for example, local conservation groups). Balancing the interests of such a wide range and number of stakeholders complicates the management task. For instance, it lengthens the time taken to reach a decision because of the need to consult widely on proposed policy changes.

n o t e b o o k   4.3

Equal opportunities in public sector housing

UK legislation requires local authorities to operate equal opportunities policies in allocating council housing. This means that they should give priority to households considered to be most in need of housing, and take no account of length of time on the waiting list or connections with the area. They must not discriminate on grounds of race, gender or sexual orientation.

Which stakeholders would have an interest in the council's allocations policy? What concerns might each express about the effects of a policy based only on need?

The idea of the stakeholder also has major implications for measuring performance. Financiers judge organisations and their management on their performance: but who else judges them, and what measures do they use? An even more difficult question is, who sets the performance goal, and whose interests do they serve?

Measuring performance is not as straightforward as it may seem. A distinction can be made between the concepts of economy, efficiency and effectiveness.

Economy means producing goods or services with the least possible input costs – the costs of staff, equipment, accommodation and so on which are required to produce the good or service.

Efficiency means 'doing things right', in other words making good use of the inputs for the outputs achieved. An engineer who redesigns a machine so that it uses less energy, or produces less scrap, has made it more efficient. An organisation that delivers more goods or services with fewer resources than a comparable one is more efficient.

Effectiveness means 'doing the right things', in other words, choosing and meeting objectives that are appropriate to the organisation at the time. Efficiency in itself does not ensure acceptable performance. An organisation may produce familiar, standard products very efficiently, but if customers do not buy them because they want new and personalised models then the organisation is not effective. Organisations that are effective, which do the right things, are more likely to prosper.

The performance of some types of organisation – particularly in the public sector – may also be judged on a fourth E, *equity*, which is related to effectiveness. This concept is concerned with the fairness of service outcomes. A principal objective of a welfare benefits system, for example, is to ensure that the recipients are those who most need them. A system which succeeded in spending its annual budget but had no regard for the distribution of benefits would be regarded as unfair and, therefore, ineffective.

Europe in the late 1990s has a great deal of spare capacity in the coal and steel industries. While some plants are old and inefficient, others are modern and highly efficient – but are they effective? This raises the next and more difficult question of what are the 'right' things, and who decides? There is no right answer. Different stakeholders will try to influence those taking the decisions to support their interests. They will judge the organisation's performance against criteria that reflect those interests. The various criteria will probably conflict with each other – few measures will suit the interests and priorities of all stakeholders equally. The owners of shares in a privatised power company will probably equate effectiveness with short-term profits. Environmental groups judge the company by its impact on air and water quality. The regulator appointed to protect consumer interests will judge the company by how well it follows the rules on prices or other customer matters.

The Body Shop view of shareholders

❝ I have said publicly, time and time again, that I did not consider speculators to be my primary responsibility, or even one of my primary responsibilities. They were way down the list, as far as I was concerned, particularly since many of them only came in for the profits and did not give a damn about what we were doing. ❞

(Roddick, 1991, p.118)

The tenants of a local authority house will judge their landlord according to how satisfied they feel with the house itself and the repairs and other services provided by the local housing office. Other stakeholders might assess the same authority on the basis of how low its running costs are. In other words, the tenant's interest is in *effectiveness* while others are concerned with *economy*. A second example occurs in the healthcare sector. While hospital managers are concerned with controlling costs, society at large hopes that patients can always benefit from available treatments. However, we now hear frequently of cases where treatment is withheld on the grounds that it is too expensive. These examples illustrate the conflict often found in public sector or not-for-profit management. This arises because social values are often just as important as financial ones but point to different courses of action. Stewart and Walsh (1994) describe this as 'the dilemma of performance management in the public domain'. Managers there are expected 'to secure effective performance when the meaning to be given to it can never be completely defined, and the criteria by which it is judged can never be finally established'.

Within an organisation, interest groups sometimes argue for policies that contradict the goals of senior management. Some parts of the organisation may develop goals of their own. These may be quite distinct from those originally intended by senior management. This happens within any type of organisation, as the Case Example illustrates.

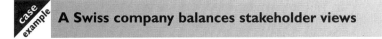

A Swiss company balances stakeholder views

In the late 1980s the Swiss-based pharmaceutical group Hoffman–La Roche decided to review the principles that should guide the business. Its chairman at the time commented:

> **Naturally we had different currents of opinion. There was the more American school which thought that we ought to state that the primary purpose of the company was to make money. Another school of thought was more science-based and said, 'we have a long tradition of research, of knowledge, of relationships with the medical profession. Thus the aim of the company is above all to make progress in science and to achieve solutions to health problems. Profits should be the results of this process, not the primary purpose.' Others felt that the company had a moral obligation to the public at large: the patients needing better drugs and services, the environmental concerns, the employees, and the communities depending on our activities.**
>
> **Ultimately – and this is quite typical of the European cultural environment – it was felt that if the company was not able to meet and combine all these *raisons d'être*, it would be missing something. Only the sharing of many deep-seated values would be worth the commitment of everyone.**

Source: quoted in Bloom *et al.* (1994)

The clear conclusion to be drawn from the Case Example is that a key concern of management is to establish an acceptable degree of integration among the goals of the different stakeholders. They all have an interest in the business and can affect its future, so management needs to work to maintain the required degree of commitment or support. This will mean balancing the trade-offs between satisfying some stakeholders and antagonising others, depending on how management satisfies competing goals. Does it earn a decent return for shareholders? Is the quality consistently high or scarcely adequate? What is its reputation in the community? Does it treat employees fairly? How good is it at keeping up with changing fashions and demands?

Many uncontrollable factors can affect an individual incident or experience, but over the long term the essential ingredient in an organisation's performance, and its acceptance by a range of stakeholders, is its management. It is management's skill, or lack of it, which balances and satisfies competing interests. This is not an inherently rational or logical process. It involves people making choices about how they build and exercise power and how they exercise control over people and resources. Management often uses the language of rationality, but other languages, such as that of equity or community, are equally legitimate.

---

n o t e b o o k   4.4

Choose an organisation with which you are familiar and gather information from annual reports, media coverage or personal contact in order to answer the following questions. What are the primary goals that senior management says it is pursuing? Do you know how it decided these, and whom it consulted? Is there any sign of other stakeholders arguing for different or contradictory goals? How does management try to balance the interests of different stakeholders?

C A S E   Q U E S T I O N S   4.1

▶ How did the British Gas project manager try to balance the interests of different stakeholders?

▶ Did he balance their interests equally or did he oppose one group?

This need to make such choices means that a manager is unlikely to be able to operate in a way that is completely rational. Given the uncertainties surrounding organisations, complete rationality is very hard to achieve. Even if that were possible, most managers do not work in organisations that have a unified and single-minded approach – a unitary type of structure. They are much more likely to work in one that contains many sectional interests, as well as those in the wider environment. In other words, they work in a pluralist situation, where they have to balance different sectional interests.

4.4   Towards a political view of management

Alan Thomas (1993) distinguishes some basic assumptions which writers on management use. These are about the means and ends of management practice. On means, some theorists assume that management is a rational activity and others that it is only partially rational. On ends, the difference arises over sectionalism. Some theorists start from the position that management is pursuing a unitary set of goals, and that these have substantial support within the organisation. They assume that the goals meet the needs of both internal and external stakeholders, including the interests of the wider community. The alternative view sees management as pursuing one-sided policies, favouring one or more particular interest groups.

Thomas uses these dichotomies to present a framework within which he places different approaches to understanding the management role (Figure 4.2). The framework shows four alternative ways of looking at management – as a rational profession, an exploitative practice as an agent of capital, a magico-religious activity, and as a political activity. In his discussion of rationality, Thomas defines actions as either objectively or subjectively rational:

> An action is objectively rational when the connection between the actions and the results can be shown to hold objectively. An action is subjectively rational when it is based on a set of beliefs about how means are related to ends.

Objectively rational actions are those most easily demonstrated when scientific procedures are applied: if done correctly, the action will produce a predictable result. Another way of putting this is to say that the link between cause and effect is clear. Subjectively rational behaviour is that which makes sense and appears reasonable, but the person cannot be sure that the action will produce the desired result. The link between cause and effect is unclear and therefore in some degree unpredictable.

Sectionality refers to assumptions about the ends which management aims to achieve. Theories making unitary assumptions see management as pursuing a set of goals that have the support of the stakeholders in the organisation. There may be several goals, but all appear legitimate to those with an interest. Management represents a neutral attempt to achieve a number of shared ends.

Writers making sectional assumptions argue that management pursues its own interests at the expense of other stakeholders. It may justify its actions as being in the interests of the organisation as a whole; the reality is more self-interested.

An action is objectively rational when the connection between the actions and the results can be shown to hold objectively.
An action is subjectively rational when it is based on a set of beliefs about how means are related to ends.

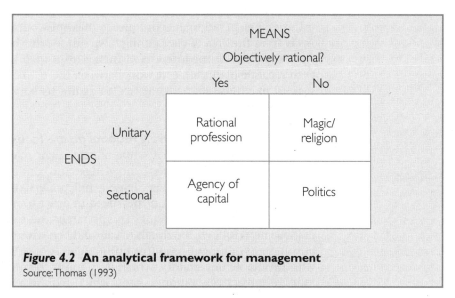

Figure 4.2 An analytical framework for management
Source: Thomas (1993)

n o t e b o o k   *4.5*

Privatisation, mutualisation and management salaries

In the UK and elsewhere, for example France, publicly owned industries have been sold to private shareholders. Financial institutions previously owned by the members have also been sold to private shareholders. Their directors encouraged members (the owners) to approve the change by offering them free shares in the new organisation. One common result of both changes in ownership has been a large increase in the salary and benefits paid to directors and senior managers in the companies.

Is this an example of management pursuing a sectional interest, or is it acting in the best interests of all stakeholders? Try to obtain the annual reports of an organisation that has recently changed its ownership structure, for a year before and after the change. What evidence is there about changes in the benefits awarded to directors?

Thomas's model then leads to four images of management derived from the different combination of assumptions.

Unitary interests, objectively rational means (cause/effect link clear)

This view is that management is the rational administration of unitary organisations. Organisations are tools designed for agreed and uncontentious purposes, and management is a largely technical activity intended to make things work. 'The manager acts as a kind of applied scientist or technician whose chief task is to take appropriate steps, in the light of established knowledge, to achieve non-controversial ends' (Thomas, 1993, p.37). This view often appears in the early writing on management, and in much mainstream management education.

Sectional interests, objectively rational means (cause/effect link clear)

The assumption here is that management acts rationally but in the interests of a particular group. Managers represent the owners of capital who expect them to achieve the best possible return from the enterprise. They do this by using a range of rational techniques to maximise output, but are not neutral. Away from the area of class conflict, we can see this happen when managers work explicitly in the interests of their part of their business. Organisations with separate plants allocate work between them. Managers in any one plant seek to maximise its performance to assure its survival at the expense of others (Lindblom, 1959).

Unitary interests, subjectively rational means (cause/effect link unclear)

The assumption here is that while management may be following unitary ends it works with limited knowledge and understanding. Rationality assumes that decision-makers have a full understanding of the situation, and have all the information they need in order to make the decisions that will lead to the desired result. This is rarely the case in practice. Even if management follows the rituals of rational behaviour, the complexity of the business environment produces unintended results. Management is coping with inevitable uncertainty, which it attempts to combat by using methods that are subjectively rational – and which require a leap of faith to believe they will work. On this view, 'management has more to do with magic and religion than it has to do with science' (Thomas, 1993, p.39).

Sectional interests, subjectively rational means (cause/effect link unclear)

Thomas argues that this is the most radical departure from conventional views of management. The emphasis is on managers facing competing sectional interest groups within and beyond the organisation. It needs to balance these different constituencies in a way that at least ensures their continued support. These ends are not always clear at the start. In a complex world, the players lack complete information on the intentions of other players or the effects of actions they may take. The outcome is a very unpredictable result of the inter-action of forces. This is in essence a political view of management, in the sense that the goals that dominate at any one time, and the ends used to achieve them, arise from political processes of bargaining, negotiation and compromise.

Building on our earlier discussions of stakeholding, this political perspective on management has a particular resonance in public service organisations. Writers in the field of public policy have argued that the rational approach to management is in essence a prescriptive model with 'centralist, technocratic connotations' (Hogwood and Gunn, 1984). The rational approach ignores political processes, above all the role played by value judgements. Lindblom (1959) described the processes of decision-taking and policy formulation in government organisations as one of mutual adjustment in which the various actors (or stakeholders) reach a compromise solution. This will meet 'a wider range of interests than could be done by one group centrally'.

CASE QUESTIONS 4.2

▶ Where in Thomas's model would the British Gas project manager's work fit?

▶ What leads you to that conclusion?

What do the interests of stakeholders have for the kind of work which managers are expected to do? The next section reviews some theories about the content of management work.

4.5 Content theories of management work

Henri Fayol (1949), whose views were discussed in Chapter 2, distinguished six groups of activities within industrial enterprises: technical, commercial, finan-cial, accounting, security and managerial. The last consisted of:

> drawing up the broad plan of operations of the business, with assembling personnel, co-ordinating and harmonising effort and activity ... [These] make up another group usually indicated by the term Management with somewhat ill-defined frontiers ... I have therefore adopted the following definition: to manage is to forecast and plan, to organise, to command, to co-ordinate and to control ... Management, thus understood, is neither an exclusive privilege nor a particular responsibility of the head or senior members of a business; it is an activity spread, like all other activities, between head and members of the body corporate. (pp.5–6)

Fayol went on to describe each of the elements in his definition, the key points being that management were to *forecast and plan*; *organise*; *command*; *co-ordinate and control*. These headings were the basis of the discussion in Chapter 2, so the detail is not repeated here. Others have put forward similar interpretations of this 'classical' view of the management role (for example, Urwick, Brech).

This is clearly a very simple way of expressing a complex process. Some other perspectives which reflect that reality more closely are discussed later. Nevertheless, managers, both junior and senior, recognise this view as at least a partial description of their main activities. As Stewart (1967) showed, managers typically switch between activities many times a day. They deal with them in an intermittent and often parallel fashion, touching on many different parts of the job at once. However, they can usually identify these elements in their job, as this manager in a housing association explains:

❝ My role involves each of these functions to some extent. Planning is an important element in that I am part of a team which is allocated a budget of £8 million to spend in pursuit of specific objectives, and to promote particular forms of housing. So planning or 'profiling' where we will spend the money is very important. Organising and leading are important too, as staff have to be clear on which projects to take forward, clear on objectives and clear on deadlines. Controlling also forms part of my role, as I have to compare the actual money spent with the planned budget and take corrective action as necessary. ❞

And a manager in a legal firm:

❝ As a manager in a professional firm, I find that each assignment involves all the elements in the list, to ensure that we carry it out properly. For example, I have to set clear objectives for the assignment, organise the necessary staff and information to perform the work, supervise staff and counsel them if necessary, and evaluate the results. However, all the roles interrelate with each other and there are no clear stages for each one. ❞

Evaluating the classical framework

There is clearly anecdotal support for the model, in that others can observe managers performing these activities within their work. The framework is also supported by empirical studies of management work. For example, Hales (1986) compared six studies of the content of management work and identified some common, though not universal, strands. He concluded that, allowing for differences in terms, the list exhibited 'striking parallels with the supposedly outdated "classical principles of management"' (p.95); Carroll and Gillen (1987) drew a similar conclusion. This evidence suggests that the traditional labels do describe some relatively common elements in management work, and perhaps in getting any task done. They are a reasonable approximation from which to consider management activities.

The model also contains weaknesses. It says little about the other activities that managers say they do. These include dealing with the interpersonal aspects of the work which later studies (notably Mintzberg, 1973) have shown to be important elements. It gives no guidance to managers about how they should perform the different elements. Not surprisingly, the earlier models pay little attention to the more dynamic and uncertain world in which managers now operate – the earlier expressions have a 'static' feel. Above all, versions of the traditional model (including that above) typically try to set out the definitive nature of management work – there is little recognition of the diversity and variation of the job. The following sections develop these points.

---

n o t e b o o k   4.6

Managing an essay

An essay or a group project is a task that you need to manage. Make notes on how you could use the classical model as a guide to completing such a task.

Gerard Egan (1993) proposes a model of the content agenda of management to match the needs of the business. He argues that to add value – which leads to satisfied customers, committed employees and good financial returns – managers need to follow six principles which he terms the 'master tasks' of management. The tasks represent the major issues facing any institution concerned about its performance, though the emphasis will vary between organisations and at different times. Figure 4.3 illustrates the master tasks.

Strategy

Formulate a strategy that provides overall focus and direction. Ideally the strategy will shape all other activities, and give a focus for work, and a way of setting priorities.

Operations

Deliver valued products and services cost-effectively to customers. Operations translate the strategy into the detail work that satisfies customers. They do this by taking extra care over quality or reliability, or speed of delivery, or any other aspect of the product. Their aim should be to deliver benefits that customers value.

> ❛ GE Plastics has created a 'customer action team' dedicated to eliminating the causes of any failure in service to their major industrial customers. Whenever a problem arises, management has authorised the team to deal with the immediate difficulty and satisfy the customer. The team then tracks to the root cause of the problem. Finally it works with the relevant management to alter systems and procedures to prevent the complaint arising again. ❜

Structure

Design the type of organisational structure needed to optimise information sharing, decision-making and workflow. As described in Chapter 16, many companies are finding that structures well suited to stable conditions no longer work. They cannot provide the speed of response or flexibility now required, so management must create new structures.

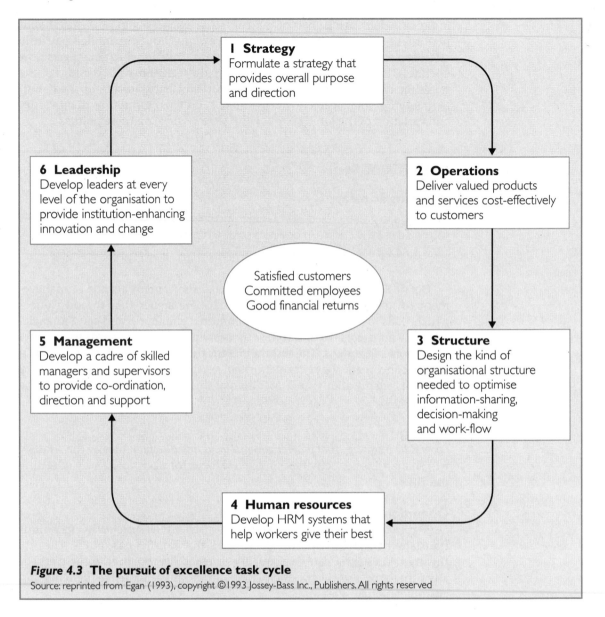

Figure 4.3 The pursuit of excellence task cycle

Human resource management systems

Develop human resource management systems that managers and supervisors can use to help workers give their best. Flexibility and responsiveness in the market-place depend on capable employees being able and willing to meet customer needs – and management needs to develop systems that encourage such behaviour.

Value-added management

Develop a cadre of skilled and enthusiastic managers and supervisors to provide co-ordination direction and support for all workers. This is to ensure that managers transmit and implement the policies and principles guiding the business throughout the organisation.

Pragmatic leadership

Develop leaders at every level of the organisation to provide institution-enhancing innovation and change. Similar to the previous one, this is to ensure that everyone understands and applies the organisation's values on leadership.

---

n o t e b o o k   4.7

To help you evaluate the accuracy of these content frameworks arrange a short interview (30 minutes will be enough) with someone with experience in a management role. Ask them to describe what they do on a typical day. If possible, ask them to indicate approximately how much time they spend on each main activity they have identified.

Write up your notes on the interview, using where possible the words they used (tape-recording the discussion will help). Then against each activity indicate the 'classical' or 'Egan' categories to which it most closely corresponds. Which activities carried out by your interviewee do these models seem to ignore?

Compare your results with those of a colleague or group, and identify similarities and contrasts. How well have the models described the role of your manager? What have they missed?

4.6 Process theories of managers' work

Rosemary Stewart's theory

What are managers' jobs like? Do they resemble an orderly, methodical process – or a constant rush from one problem to the next? One of the best-known studies was that conducted in the 1960s by Rosemary Stewart (1967), an academic at Oxford University. She persuaded 160 senior and middle managers to keep a diary for four weeks, and it remains the largest study of its kind ever conducted. The managers (from different functions and from large and small organisations) completed the diary in a way that allowed the researchers to establish how the managers spent their time.

The results showed that managers worked in a fragmented, interrupted fashion. This was measured by the number of times the manager was alone long enough to concentrate on a problem. The study also measured the number of brief contacts the manager had, and the number of separate diary entries, each signifying the start of a new activity or a continuation after an interruption. Over the four weeks, the managers had, on average, only 9 periods of 30 minutes or more alone, 12 brief contacts each day, and 13 diary entries each day. They spent 36 per cent of their time on paperwork (writing, dictating, reading, calculating) and 43 per cent in informal discussion. They spent the remainder on formal meetings, telephoning and social activities.

Stewart also found great variety between managers. For example, the proportion of time they spent on paperwork ranged from 7 to 84 per cent. The research team also analysed the data to show different profiles of management work, based not on level or function, but on how they spent their time. The Noticeboard shows the conclusions.

The Emissaries   They spent much of their time out of the organisation, meeting customers, suppliers or contractors.

The Writers   They spent most of their time alone reading and writing, and had the fewest contacts with other managers. If they had meetings they were usually with just one other person.

The Discussers   They spent most of their time with other people and with their colleagues.

The Troubleshooters   These had the most fragmented work-pattern of all, with many diary entries and many fleeting contacts, especially with their subordinates.

The Committee Members   The group with a wide range of internal contacts, and who spent much time in formal meetings. They spent half their working day in discussions with more than one other person.

Source: Stewart (1967)

Diversity among managers' jobs is the key message of Rosemary Stewart's research. The study's strength is that it used a large number of observations from a variety of organisations. Her conclusions about the fragmentation and variety of managerial work have been broadly supported by later, smaller studies (for example, Martinko and Gardner, 1990). While some would find this work-pattern highly stressful, other research has concluded that many managers prefer this way of working, as being the only way that they can keep in touch with events.

Henry Mintzberg's theory

Mintzberg (1973) developed the most widely quoted challenge to the traditional perceptions of management activities. Although he did the primary research with only five chief executives, one of its strengths lies in its use of a structured form of direct observation to establish how these managers spent their time. One of his conclusions was consistent with that of Rosemary Stewart: managers' work was varied, brief, fragmented and involved much time being spent on interpersonal activities. He also proposed that management work consists of ten roles, grouped into three categories: interpersonal, informational and decisional.

Interpersonal roles

Interpersonal roles arise directly from a manager's formal authority and status, and involve relationships with other people both in and out of the organisation.

In the *figurehead role* the manager is a symbol. The manager's status requires him or her to carry out social, inspirational, legal and ceremonial duties such as greeting a visitor, signing legal documents, presenting retirement gifts. These ceremonial duties may not seem important, but they symbolise a manager's concern for employees, customers, community.

The *leadership role* defines the manager's interpersonal relationship with subordinates, bringing together their needs and those of the organisation so that they can work effectively. The manager seeks to motivate subordinates, and takes responsibility for hiring, training and career development. Most activities involving subordinates would be examples of this, as well as broader activities like creating a vision with which staff can identify.

The *liaison role* focuses on a manager's contacts with people outside the immediate organisational unit. It refers to maintaining a network in which the manager trades information and favours for mutual benefit outside his or her unit – with clients, government officials, customers, suppliers. For some managers, particularly chief executives or sales managers, the liaison role is paramount, taking a high proportion of their time and energy.

Informational roles

Through the leader and liaison roles, the manager gains access to valued information – external and internal – and so becomes a nerve centre of the organisation. Three roles – monitor, disseminator and spokesperson – describe the informational aspects of managerial work.

The *monitor role* involves seeking out, receiving and screening information to understand the organisation and its environment. Just as a radar unit scans the environment, managers scan their environments for relevant information – reading trade magazines, reports, attending conferences and exhibitions, getting information from customers or suppliers. Much of the information received is oral (from hearsay as well as formal meetings), building on personal contacts.

In the *disseminator role* the manager shares some of this information with subordinates and other members of the team or organisation. By forwarding reports and papers, telephoning to pass on gossip, or briefing staff about impending changes, the manager is able to maintain his or her access to privileged information.

Finally, in the *spokesperson role*, the manager transmits information to people outside the organisation. This happens when the manager gives information at a conference on behalf of the organisation, speaks to the media, or gives his or her department's view at a company meeting.

Decisional role

Managers use information to make decisions about when and how to commit their organisation to new objectives and actions. As entrepreneurs, arbiters of disturbances, allocators of resources and as negotiators, managers drive the organisation's decision-making system.

In the *entrepreneurial role* the manager is responsible for initiating and designing much of the controlled change within the organisation. This involves continually searching for opportunities and problems, and creating projects to deal with them. Managers play this role when they introduce a new product, launch a survey, test a new market or enter a new business.

Managers play the *disturbance-handler role* when they deal with problems and changes that are unexpected. Examples could be when a customer changes the rate at which it wants deliveries, a supplier's equipment breaks down, or there is a dispute between two members of staff. The manager concerned will spend time fighting these fires.

The *resource-allocator* role involves choosing among competing demands for money, equipment, personnel, and other demands on a manager's time, to maintain control of the strategy-making process. How much of her budget should the housing manager quoted above spend on different types of project? What proportion of the budget should a company spend on advertising and what on improving an existing product line? Should we pay overtime to other staff to replace an absent team member, or let customer service decline temporarily?

Closely linked to the resource allocator role is the *negotiator role*. In this role managers engage in negotiations with another organisation or with individuals and groups whose support they need. They may need to agree a spending programme with head office or a funding body before it can begin. They may need to agree a change in delivery requirements by negotiation with a supplier.

Although the ten managerial roles have been presented separately, in practice managers perform them together. Mintzberg proposed that every manager's job consisted of some combination of these roles, with the relative importance of each role varying between managers at different levels or in different types of business.

CASE QUESTIONS 4.3

▶ What evidence is there of the British Gas project manager performing the roles proposed by Mintzberg?

▶ Which does he seem to be performing most frequently?

Further evidence

Later studies based on Mintzberg's categories and using similar observational methods have usually confirmed his result and classification of the content of management work. For example, Martinko and Gardner (1990) studied 41 school managers. They found that they spent 24 per cent of their time in the leader role, 28 per cent as a monitor, 13 per cent as a disseminator and 9 per cent as a spokesperson. These four roles, then, accounted for 74 per cent of the managers' time – a result broadly in line with those of other studies.

Evaluating Mintzberg's theory

Mintzberg's research clearly built on earlier empirical studies by Carlson (1951) and Stewart (1967), which he also integrated into his model. It used a clear process of structured observation to gather the data, and other studies have generally supported his conclusions. However, the size of his empirical sample was small and all were chief executives. This raises questions about how representative the findings are and how widely they represent other management levels.

Nevertheless, managers can usually identify with many of the roles, and see Mintzberg's roles as complementing rather than contradicting the traditional framework. They view the roles as emphasising the interpersonal aspects of the job, which are increasingly important in completing the traditional tasks of planning or organising. They also often highlight two roles that they feel are missing: manager as subordinate and manager as worker.

Manager as subordinate

All managers have subordinates, but, except for those at the very top, all are subordinates themselves too. So part of their role is that of advising or assisting their own senior manager. This is a role which has been referred to as that of 'managing up' (Boddy and Buchanan, 1992). Advice to managers in this area is usually about how they should try to influence their subordinates. This implies that managers base their influence on their position in the hierarchy; but there is more to it than that. A great deal of management work involves attempting to influence people over whom the manager has no formal authority. In today's fluid and fast-moving organisation, managers often cannot wait to go through the 'right' channels: in order to get things done, they need to persuade people higher up the organisation that their ideas will work, or that they need a larger budget. A project manager recalled:

> ❝ This is the second time we have been back to the management team, to pose how we wish to move forward, and to try and get the resources that are required. It is, however, worth taking the time up front to get all members fully supportive of what we are trying to do. Although it takes a bit longer we should, by pressure and by other individuals demonstrating the benefits of the system we are proposing, eventually move the [top team] forward. ❞
>
> (Boddy and Buchanan, 1992, p.78)

Manager as worker

Many managers, especially those in small organisations or those in junior positions in large ones, spend some of their time doing the work of the organisation. A manager may also be a team member, performing the same tasks as a subordinate. A director of a small property company helps with sales visits, or an engineering director helps with difficult technical problems. One successful retailer in the motor trade expects all its head office staff to spend one week each year working as a mechanic in a depot. This ensures that they keep in touch with customers and the views of front-line staff. As companies become smaller and more tightly structured, expect more of this 'hands-on' management.

The relative importance of the roles is also likely to vary depending on the other members of the team, the situation in which the manager is working, and his or her ability to exercise a particular role. For example, if the structure of the organisation impedes the information flow to and from a manager, the manager will be less confident in handling the decision-making aspects of the role. Changes in company structure also affect a manager's ability to perform a role. The Case Example below illustrates this, and shows what the company did to deal with the problem.

case example | **Strengthening interpersonal roles between distant staff**

A company restructured its regional operations, closed a sales office in Bordeaux and transferred the work to Paris. The sales manager responsible for south west France was now geographically distant from her immediate boss, and the rest of the team. This caused severe problems of communication, and loss of teamwork. She concluded that the interpersonal aspects of the role were vital as a basis for the informational and decisional roles. The decision to close the office had broken these links.

She and her boss agreed to try the following solutions:
- ▶ **A 'one-to-one' session of quality time to discuss key issues during monthly visits to head office.**
- ▶ **Daily telephone contact to ensure speed of response, and that respective communication needs were met.**
- ▶ **Use fax at home to speed up communications.**

These overcame the break in interpersonal roles caused by the location change.

4.7 Managers as networkers and politicians

Does the way in which managers interpret their role affect their performance? There was no evidence on this point in Mintzberg's study. He did not suggest that spending time on all the roles he identified would improve performance. However, work by Luthans (1988) has suggested a link between how managers divide their time between different roles and their performance.

The team studied 292 managers at different levels in a variety of organisations. They initially observed 44 members of the sample in order to generate a list of 67 behaviours. Before the main research began, the researchers combined these into 12 descriptive categories, and then into 4 groups. Trained staff observed each manager for ten minutes at random times over a two-week period, and decided which of the behaviours best described what they had observed.

The researchers also distinguished between success and effectiveness: They measured success by a 'promotion index', which measured managers' level in the organisation relative to their length of service, and effectiveness by work-unit performance and subordinates' satisfaction and commitment.

Independently of the observation process, the research team used data that they gathered from other company sources to divide the managers into high, middle and low groups on each criterion. The behavioural groups and categories were as follows:

Communicating	Exchanging information
	Paperwork
Traditional management	Planning
	Decision-making
	Controlling
Networking	Interacting with outsiders
	Socialising/politicking
Human resource management	Motivating/reinforcing
	Managing conflict
	Staffing
	Training/developing

The conclusion of the analysis of *successful* managers was that they networked much more than the less successful. The most successful managers spent considerably more time networking (socialising, politicking, interacting with outsiders) and slightly more time communicating than the less successful managers, although only networking had a statistically significant effect. Human resource management made the least contribution. For many managers, most interaction takes place with people in other companies. A degree of social skill to chat and establish comfortable relationships sets the background before a meeting begins in earnest.

For *effective* managers, the results were different. For them, communication and human resource management activities made by far the largest contribution to effectiveness, and traditional management and networking made the least. The biggest contribution to managers' effectiveness, as measured in the study, came from people-orientated activities within the firm. Networking made the least contribution.

These results, like those of the previous studies, suggest that managers should give more attention than they usually do to the political skills of management. They should not focus on rational methods alone. Managers spend much time and energy seeking to influence those over whom they have little formal authority. To do this they need to exercise not only social but also political skills to get things done. This theme is revisited in Chapter 5.

n o t e b o o k   4.8

Implications and research methods

What do Luthans's results suggest to you about the promotion policies of the companies?

You may not think much of the measures used for distinguishing successful and effective managers. How would you suggest that researchers should measure these variables?

4.8 New agendas and dilemmas

External change

How are wider developments in the business world affecting the roles of the manager? Can they continue to follow the advice of the traditional or Mintzberg perspectives, or are there new priorities that they must take into account? The management literature is full of advice to managers about the new business world and what it means for them. A widely used model for such an analysis starts from a list of environmental forces that affect organisations, commonly referred to as PEST factors (see, for example, Johnson and Scholes, 1997). Some examples of the factors usually included in such lists are:

- ▶ **Political and legal** Monopolies legislation, environmental protection, foreign trade regulations, employment law, taxation policies
- ▶ **Economic** Interest rates, trends in disposable income, energy cost, trends in economic activity in major markets, integration of global businesses
- ▶ **Sociocultural** Population trends, attitudes to work and leisure, levels of education, social mobility, consumer activism and pressure groups
- ▶ **Technological** Computing and information systems, commercial availability of products based on new scientific discoveries, government support for innovation

These factors affect the nature of organisations and the work of managing them.

---

n o t e b o o k   4.9

Gathering data

Discuss with a manager which of the PEST factors have affected his or her role, and list them to compare with other students' answers. Also ask the manager whether he or she has experienced significant changes in the role, and if so, of what kind?

The common theme arising from discussing these factors with managers is that of change. Customer expectations and competitive threats are steadily increasing, so management needs to institute regular change to keep up if the business is to prosper. Undoubtedly the world is more competitive, and the pressure on managers increasing. Remember, though, that most of those articulating the problems are also offering to sell a solution.

Research based on case studies in Denmark, France, Germany, Italy, the Netherlands and the UK confirms the changes affecting middle managers (Dopson and Stewart, 1993). The study concluded that middle management jobs had become more generalist, with increased responsibilities and a wider range of tasks. Middle managers were generally responsible for more subordinates and for a wider mix of staff. They were more accountable for performance, with sharper targets being set. Information systems made that performance more visible to senior managers.

Another approach to the future of management stresses management dilemmas. The theme here is that there are no easy prescriptions and that managers are inevitably having to balance different interests and moral dilemmas. A study sponsored by the Institute of Management (1995b) drew attention to what it called the emerging paradoxes and contradictions which managers face. The research team held discussions with a representative group of managers about the nature of the management job which is emerging. They identified the following paradoxes and contradictions within the role:

- Balancing short-term and long-term
- Internationalisation vs. local performance
- Process skills vs. technical skills
- Higher quality with fewer resources
- Teamwork vs. individual performance
- Reflection vs. action
- Thinking strategically while acting operationally

The emphasis here is on ambiguity, which contrasts with some of the earlier certainties about the job of managing.

Rosabeth Moss Kanter also stresses the complexity of the management job. By training, a sociologist, she is now an internationally recognised academic and consultant whose book sought to identify the intangible factors common amongst globally excellent companies (Kanter, 1995). The arguments are complex – reflecting the realities of the business world. She believes that good managers realise that there are no simple answers to management problems. Management, in her view, means managing an entire context, since business is now part of a much wider political, social and economic framework – she describes her book as one-third business, one-third politics and one-third community action. Ignoring any of these elements in the context will lead to ineffective management.

4.9 The diversity of management roles

The type of organisation affects a manager's role and where the manager needs to focus his or her attention. A manager in a public sector organisation is answerable to the public or to elected representatives. He or she may find it prudent to pay more attention to the liaison or disseminator roles than might a manager in a less overtly political environment. A manager in a highly centralised organisation will have a more limited role than those in ones which are more decentralised. The scope for dealing with disturbances varies. Legislation, policy or the threat of legal action means that some organisations have precise guidelines on how to deal with disputes or accidents: these constrain the way their managers work. Others leave more scope for managers to respond as they see fit.

Fondas and Stewart (1992) studied the diversity in the roles of general managers. These were defined as those in charge of an organisation or a discrete part of it, and with responsibility for more than one function. The team interviewed divisional general managers in a US conglomerate and district managers in the UK health service. While variety had always been a feature of such jobs, the researchers believed that this was increasing. Possible causes were the recent introduction of new organisational forms, including mergers, creating more autonomous units, strategic alliances and partnerships, and flatter structures. The practical implication was that if jobs became more diverse then it becomes less certain that someone who has succeeded in one setting will also succeed in another. So what are the differences in the context of general managers' jobs?

Building on Kotter's (1982) work, Fondas and Stewart concluded that the most important aspects of the jobs' context are those which 'create relatively more demanding, "bigger" jobs, such as size and performance level' (p.3). While the scope of a job – its area of formal responsibility – typically increases at successive management levels, other factors that affect the challenge and diversity of a particular job are:

▶ **Scale of responsibility** As measured by, for example, the number of subordinates or the level of turnover. The greater these are, the more complex the job becomes, and the more issues managers have to deal with.

▶ **Domain of activity** The potential activities that a manager can undertake, quite apart from the formal responsibilities. Sometimes the domain is tightly defined; but when loosely defined, general managers are given scope to extend their activities.

▶ **Independence from others** More independence readily translates into wider job scope. Jobs vary in how self-contained they are, in terms of their independence from headquarters or other units, the control the general manager has over resources, and physical distance.

▶ **Expectations of others** Sometimes expectations are clear and unambiguous, leading to a relatively prescribed job. Other general managers face a diverse group of stakeholders to satisfy, which constrains their independence.

▶ **Which tasks are important** The final source of diversity identified in the study was the scope to decide which tasks, such as business growth, consolidation or financial restructuring, have priority.

---

^{case example} **Shaping a larger role**

An example of a manager taking an initiative to extend the scope of his job occurred in a multinational electronics company. He believed the company was losing competitive position because of an inadequate system for handling a complex order-processing system. He saw the benefits clearly – but had to convince others:

> **I then began a round of presentations to plant staffs around Europe, and to our European management team, describing to them the problem and suggesting a way forward. It was in general well received, but it was also clear that people were a bit sceptical.**
>
> **So over the last year my part-time team has done a lot of work with their staffs to convince them of the need. My European functional boss has been doing work with the European management team to convince them. It's taken about fifteen months to get our corporation to move forward. Eventually I was given the job of developing the new system.**

4.10 Managers shape their role: the interaction perspective

The role perspective helps us to understand both the common and the variable elements in the management role. It focuses on the social situation in which the manager works, and shows how the role set influences his or her behaviour. However, it ignores the fact that managers themselves can shape what others expect them to do. Managers are not puppets, and can influence their role sets. Fondas and Stewart (1992) argue that the traditional use of roles in this area 'underemphasises the focal person's impact on the role expectations of him or her' (p.87). They argue instead for what they call an 'expectations enactment' view of the manager's job. This stresses the impact that a manager can have on others' expectations. Managers can deliberately create opportunities to shape expectations via their interactions with other people. This view is supported by three sets of research, and indicates that:

▶ Expectations of a newly appointed manager may be modified during the early weeks in the job (Graen and Scandura, 1987).

▶ Expectations may be modified as the manager attempts to reshape expectations so that they fit more closely his or her preferences (Goffman, 1961). This represents the view that expectations are not fixed, but vary by mutual adjustment between the manager and the role set.

▶ Managers are sometimes proactive in shaping the demands and constraints of their job. They initiate or choose projects to work on and informally extend the scope of their responsibilities. They seek to alter the content of their jobs so that they are more favourable (Kotter, 1982; Hales, 1986).

Changing roles

The two directors of a small company in property services and training concluded that they needed to spend more time on the financial management and strategic planning aspects of their role. The following steps were taken:

▶ **The directors held a meeting with each of the four managers, to discuss the problem and receive ideas on a solution.**

▶ **They agreed areas of work to be done by the managers alone, and that there would be a series of meetings that only the managers would attend, rather than a director as well. A briefing note for the director would be issued afterwards.**

▶ **Training events were planned to support managers in some areas.**

▶ **The directors recognised that their style would need to become less autocratic.**

▶ **The changed emphasis in directors' and managers' roles was communicated to the rest of the staff to avoid confusion.**

▶ **Managers would have not only more responsibility, but more control over income and expenditure budgets too. There would also be new, formal monthly meetings between directors and each manager, to balance the greater autonomy with some control.**

4.11 Competence models of management

An alternative way of looking at management roles is used in the UK by the national bodies responsible for training. Studies in the late 1980s showed that British managers were poorly trained and that most employers invested too little in management training (Mangham and Silver, 1986; Constable and McCormick, 1987; Handy, 1987). Moreover, many employers could not specify what they required their managers to do to be successful.

Management training in the mid-1980s
❝ There can be little doubt that, by comparison with the other countries in this study, Britain has neglected her managerial stock. With some notable exceptions her companies have asked too little from their would-be managers and given them too little in terms of education, training and development. ❞
(Handy, 1987)

These reports led to the creation of further studies, led by employers, to define what managers at different levels in the organisation should be able to do. They also looked for ways in which the competence of managers could be verified, defining competence as 'the ability to perform the activities within an occupation or function to the standards expected in employment' (MCI, 1991).

The outcome of the studies was a set of occupational standards for managers which were revised in 1997 (MCI, 1997). Their supporters claim that these standards provide a common language to describe what employers want their managers to be able to do. The standards state that managers need to perform four key roles:

- ▶ **Manage activities**   This role describes the manager's work in managing the operation to meet customers' requirements and to continuously improve its performance.
- ▶ **Manage resources**   This role describes the manager's work in planning and using physical resources effectively and efficiently. Physical resources include money, premises, capital equipment, energy, supplies and materials. They do not include people or information which are dealt with under separate key roles.
- ▶ **Manage people**   This role describes the work of all managers in getting the most from their teams. It does not, however, cover specialist personnel management issues. It covers recruiting, training, building the team, allocating and evaluating work, and dealing with people's problems. It also includes managing oneself and relations with others at work.
- ▶ **Manage information**   This role describes the manager's responsibility in obtaining, analysing and using information effectively to take decisions. It also covers leading and contributing to meetings.

Each of these key roles contains a substructure of units and elements, setting out in more detail the requirements of the role. The standards specify performance criteria that enable a person to demonstrate his or her competence by providing convincing evidence. This evidence can be used to gain credits towards a management qualification (National or Scottish Vocational Qualification – NVQ or SVQ) which is part of the wider system of national vocational qualifications.

How does this model compare with the earlier ideas? Some argue that it is a complete break with previous functional or role approaches, and has the in-built advantage of having been developed in consultation with employers. An alternative view stresses the points of similarity. For example, Stewart's view, quoted earlier, of the manager's job was that of 'deciding what to do and getting other people to do it' (Stewart, 1967). 'Deciding what to do' mainly involves managing resources and information. 'Getting other people to do it' mainly involves managing activities and people. Similarly, it is not difficult to see overlap with the traditional roles outlined in section 4.2.

A critical perspective on the approach is offered by Burgoyne (1993). He identifies three dimensions to the debate about management competences:

- ▶ **Micro to macro**   From how the learning needs of an individual might be defined, through to the effects at the national level of training based on a competence philosophy.
- ▶ **Theoretical to practical**   The theoretical bases of competence approaches through to issues of how to put the ideas into practice.
- ▶ **Technical to political**   From technical isues about how to development appropriate standards and assessment tools through to questions about the political inteersts that the competence movement might serve.

Burgoyne uses this framework to show that the complexity of the training and organisational world is perhaps greater than some of the competence models allow for.

Thomson *et al.* (1997) conducted a study to evaluate the current state of management development in the UK. This allowed comparisons to be made with the 1980s' reports mentioned earlier. They found that the picture had improved significantly, with a great increase in the number of people taking management qualifications and a recognition among managers of the need to take responsibility for their own development. In particular, as more senior managers have now been through a more coherent development process, they are more likely to see the potential benefits for subordinates.

Among the positive results reported by Thomson *et al.* were:

▶ Almost no large company and a minority of small companies reported no management training.
▶ Training is not reserved for high fliers but is extended to the vast majority of managers of average potential.
▶ The average amount of training meets the frequently recommended target of five days a year in larger organisations.
▶ There was evidence of extensive training in small companies.

4.12 Management in the twenty-first century

Our understanding of management inevitably reflects the world as it has been – but you will use that knowledge in the world that is now taking shape. What changes are likely to be most significant as we move into the next century? In the machine age, businesses were about making and selling physical products, and the language and practices of management reflected that. Knowledge, skill, ideas, copyrights, intellectual property – these are the intangible assets, embodied mostly in people, which are becoming ever more significant bases of economic and business life. What will management mean in organisations founded on such intangible, short-lived assets?

How will they 'get things done through other people'?
The information that often props up management positions is more widely available than before, through networked computer systems (Boddy and Gunson, 1996). Management actions are more visible and open to challenge when the relevant information is widely available. Will technically expert professional staff be willing to accept the instructions of those further from the action?

Where will the 'other people' be?
Management theory reflects the fact that organisations were usually based in one country and had varying degrees of international activity. That image will still hold for small local businesses and personal public services, but for many the basis of the organisation will become global rather than national:

> It means being a driver of economic and market integration, not a bystander ... [Some leading companies] are defining what 'global' really means: they are welding together a generation of global customers; they are linking capabilities across the globe to produce unique products and services. The most sophisticated customers may be in one country, the fastest growing market in another, key development resources in another, preferred suppliers in another, and critical alliance partners in another. (Hamel and Prahalad, 1996, p.240)

Behind such hyperbole, global enterprises will not be managed in the same ways as national or local businesses. As one example, their relationships with the political structures of the respective nation states across which they are doing business will be a significant part of the activity.

Will the organisation itself be visible?

Organisations will disperse around the globe and some will be almost invisible. Charles Handy has pointed out that:

> When intelligence is the primary asset the organization becomes more like a collection of project groups, some fairly permanent, some temporary, some in alliance with other parties. Instead of an organization being a castle, a home for life for its defenders, it will be more like a condominium, an association of temporary residents gathered together for their mutual convenience. [It] may in fact not have any physical existence, because the project groups or clusters do not have to be in the same place. This has caused some to talk of the 'virtual corporation' ... The challenge for tomorrow's leaders is to manage an organization that is not there in any sense which we are used to. (1994, p.39)

What sort of career will management offer?

While 'management' is often the group seen to be imposing unwelcome changes on others, it is not immune. Changes in the wider economic and competitive world affect management itself. Many managers have discovered that management is no longer a job for life. They often work on short-term contracts lasting one or two years, with no certainty about their long-term future.

4.13 Recap

Content agenda

The chapter presented Fayol's classical prescriptive model of what the management role was expected to contain. Much more recently, Egan has put forward a modern version of the content of management work. Both stress not only the task of developing objectives but also the planning that managers need to do to achieve them. Fayol identifies these as organising, commanding and co-ordinating; Egan identifies operations, structure and human resource management. The nature of the job is also shaped by assumptions about sectional interests and the certainty or otherwise of the link between cause and effect. Thomas's model suggests that planning to achieve chosen objectives will only in certain cases be a rational activity. Some objectives that managers pursue may serve their own sectional ends, rather than those of the organisation as a whole. The diversity and contradictions in the content of management work, as shaped by changing external circumstances, were then stressed. The planning tasks are also shaped by the disrupted processes of management work.

Process agenda

A common conclusion is that managers' work is fragmented and diverse. Stewart showed many years ago how the working day of most managers is broken up, with very little time available for continuous thought or planning. Later research has confirmed that pattern. Managers are continually interpreting and negotiating the expectations of others, especially those of powerful stakeholders. These interests are sources of conflicting and ambiguous interpretations, as stakeholders vie for the attention of the manager. This was followed by a presentation and review of work by Mintzberg who highlighted the interpersonal and decisional aspects of the role. Contrasts and similarities between Mintzberg's model and the traditional frameworks were drawn, pointing out that many now see them as complementary rather than contradictory. It is worth distinguishing between statements or articles that are normative (saying what managers ought to do) from those that are descriptive (saying what managers actually do). Luthans's work showed how some managers engage in significant internal and external activities to build their power and influence – this political aspect of management is neglected in many studies. Management increasingly involves managing with limited formal authority, so the role often involves acquiring and using political skills. Both Stewart and Mintzberg identified the great amount of time that managers spend on communication, mainly of the interpersonal variety.

Control agenda

The view that management is about balancing stakeholder interests is challenged by various 'critical' writers. They stress the uneven distribution of power in organisations as between owners and employees, and the role of management in maintaining the existing distribution. The role is often seen as a search by managers for opportunities to extend control and to fend off

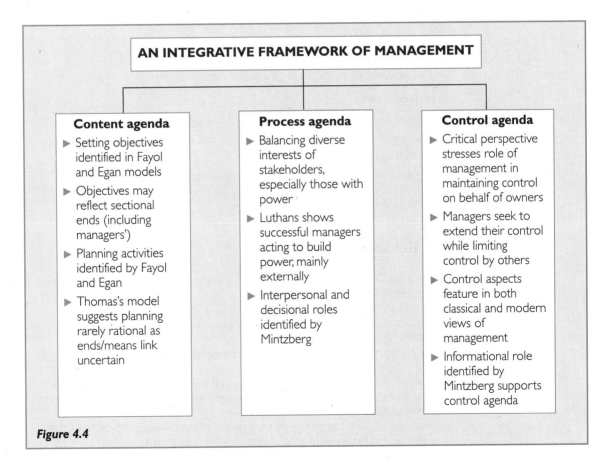

AN INTEGRATIVE FRAMEWORK OF MANAGEMENT

Content agenda
▶ Setting objectives identified in Fayol and Egan models
▶ Objectives may reflect sectional ends (including managers')
▶ Planning activities identified by Fayol and Egan
▶ Thomas's model suggests planning rarely rational as ends/means link uncertain

Process agenda
▶ Balancing diverse interests of stakeholders, especially those with power
▶ Luthans shows successful managers acting to build power, mainly externally
▶ Interpersonal and decisional roles identified by Mintzberg

Control agenda
▶ Critical perspective stresses role of management in maintaining control on behalf of owners
▶ Managers seek to extend their control while limiting control by others
▶ Control aspects feature in both classical and modern views of management
▶ Informational role identified by Mintzberg supports control agenda

Figure 4.4

attempts by others to control them. Both classical and modern models include control as part of the management activities, and the informational role identified by Mintzberg directly supports this.

Diversity, for example of national culture or industry sector, implies the need to use these ideas and the research of writers like Stewart or Mintzberg as benchmarks, or points of comparison. Their value is in providing a reasonably systematic framework by which to organise one's own observations. Ideas on role negotiation – the idea that managers do not just passively fill the role they have taken on, but actively influence its shape and scope – were also introduced. Figure 4.4 summarises these points.

PART CASE QUESTIONS

The three agendas

▶ Try to describe what Anita Roddick's objectives are for The Body Shop.

▶ What issues will managers of The Body Shop take into account in reaching those objectives?

▶ How do you think their approach affects the task of generating action with motivated staff?

▶ What clues can you get from the case about the way the process agenda is handled?

▶ How does The Body Shop monitor whether it is meeting its environmental objectives?

The stakeholders

▶ Who are the stakeholders in Body Shop International?

▶ To which does the company give most priority?

The managers

▶ What dilemmas do you think Body Shop managers might face?

▶ How might the job of the owner-manager of a retail outlet differ from Anita Roddick's?

Select another firm in a similar retailing business and make some comparisons between the two companies and how they are thinking about their dilemmas.

4.14 Review questions

1 What are the main influences on a person's role? Can you draw the main elements of Katz and Kahn's model?

2 Why is a knowledge of an organisation's stakeholders essential to an understanding of a manager's role? What can a manager do if the interests of stakeholders conflict?

3 Why are political skills becoming an important aspect of the management role?

4 Evaluate Stewart's main conclusions about the nature of managers' work by interviewing at least two managers and asking them to describe the pattern of their working day.

5 Mintzberg lists three groups of managerial roles. Compare them with the information gathered in your interviews for question 4.

6   What did Luthans conclude about the roles most likely to be carried out by successful managers?

7   Evaluate Egan's model in the light of discussions which you have had with managers.

8   Do you agree that management roles are characterised by diversity and contradictions? What evidence do you have for your conclusion?

9   Compare evidence on the environmental forces changing the role of managers whom you know.

Further reading

The standard introduction to management in the UK public sector is Flynn (1997). This traces the changes which have taken place in the public sector and how these have changed the roles of management. A complete contrast is provided by the personal accounts which high-profile entrepreneurs regularly deliver. An excellent example is Anita Roddick's (1991) account of how she created The Body Shop and of how she has interpreted the management role. Another kind of insight can be gained from Watson (1994). Watson worked alongside managers in an organisation for several months while on secondment from his business school. The result is a detailed and sympathetic insight into the dilemmas that managers face on a daily basis, and how they shape themselves as well as try to shape the organisation. Finally, any of the books by Rosemary Stewart are worth reading: these are always based on careful research clearly presented.

W Website addresses

British Petroleum   http://www.bp.com.uk
The BP site gives financial and operating performance about the company over the past five years, including the previous year's annual report and accounts and the most recent quarterly reports to the financial community. It also includes a section on the company's policies on health, safety and the environment, and details its community projects around the world.

Severn Trent Water   http://www.severn-trentco-uk
As an alternative to BP, you could visit the Severn Trent Water site, which indicates how management in the company manages environmental, community and business interests.

Managing people at work

Introduction

Generating the effort and commitment to work towards objectives is central to managing any human activity. One person working alone, be it in private life or in business, has only him or herself to motivate. As an organisation grows, management activities become, in varying degrees, separated from the core work activities. The problem of generating effort changes its nature: now one person, or one occupational group, has to secure the willing co-operation of other people and their commitment to the task. Those other people may be subordinates, peers or superiors whose support, and perhaps approval, needs to be generated and mobilised.

The quality of that commitment is as important as whether or not it is secured. Staff are often in direct contact with customers. They are aware of their unique and changing requirements, and have an immense effect on the view the customer forms of the organisation. Others are in creative roles, with a direct impact on the quality of the service delivered to the final customer, whether they are contributing to a core R&D project or a TV programme. Others need to work reliably and flexibly in order to meet changing external or internal customer needs.

Throughout a business, customers' expectations of service quality and efficiency translate into expectations of all those working in the business. Unwilling or grudging commitment damages the service offered and eventually the business itself. How does management secure the motivation it needs from others? Part Two offers several perspectives on the dilemma. In part it is a matter of exercising power and influence to ensure that others behave as expected or required by external demands. Exerting power to influence others depends on having the resources available. It also depends on understanding the needs and interests of other people, so that efforts to influence them can be designed to meet some of those needs. Chapters 5 and 6 examine these issues.

Management is conducted through both personal and institutional methods. Both require communication, which is the focus of Chapter 7. Teams are an increasingly prominent aspect of organisations, and the motivation and commitment generated within them is central to organisational performance – so these are the subject of Chapters 8 and 9.

These issues are illustrated in the Part Case, which is discussed further throughout Part Two.

W.L. Gore and Associates in Europe

W.L. Gore and Associates is a remarkable example of a business organised around team principles. Since the company has grown from being a one-person business in 1965 to one with over 6,000 employees in over 40 plants around the world, can it still be a team? It depends on the creativity of its staff, as its business is based on innovation. Growth in size usually leads to more impersonal systems and controls: can this dilemma be managed? What if separate plants begin to develop competing products? Will that waste scarce development talent or is the greater risk that talent is demotivated by wider controls on research priorities? The plants have learnt to live with a great deal of self-management and followership, rather than leader-managers or leaders in the conventional sense. Is that a viable route still, or might leaders need to be appointed to ensure resources are used profitably?

These are some of the issues facing management in the European plants of this multinational high-technology company. Some of the background is set out below.

W.L. Gore and Associates is based on an invention made by the founder, William Gore. He discovered a way to make a fabric which was at the same time porous and waterproof – moisture could pass one way, but not the other. Initially used in outdoor clothing applications such as ski-wear and walking gear, many more applications have been developed by the company's research teams. These include industry (filtration bags for air-conditioning systems), medicine (porous membranes used in skin-graft operations) and health and safety (firefighters' protective clothing). The business is at the high-technology end of any market, concentrating on inventing new uses of the basic technology. Because of their specialised nature, most of the materials are manufactured in relatively low volumes for a very specific market.

The team emphasis is reported to have originated when, in the early 1970s, Bill Gore realised that he no longer knew everyone in the plant by name. Success had led to growth – and

with it the dangers of anonymity. Believing that close and direct personal contact amongst people was essential to the success of this kind of innovative business, he immediately decided that no plant would have more than about 150 employees. Up to that number, most people would be able to know each other personally.

Accordingly, as a plant grows towards that level, promising ventures are spun off into new plants. They in turn build up, and lead to further spin-offs: hence the 40 plants with a workforce of about 6,000. There are no job titles in the company – all employees are known as 'associates'. They are expected to join the company and then to find where they can make the most contribution to the work of the plant they are in. Associates commit to a project, and work with the team developing that product or system. As it comes to completion, they are responsible for finding another project where their skills can contribute.

Traditionally, there was no formal leadership of projects, although leadership of different sorts was exercised by associates as required by the situation – some would provide technical leadership, others business leadership and so on. Pay is decided by a compensation committee made up of associates from several plants. The level of increase that an associate receives depends on a judgement of the contribution they have made to the work of their group in the previous six months. This judgement is based on the evaluations made by their colleagues in the group, on a ten-point rating scale. Each associate also has a more experienced sponsor who advises and guides them on where they may want, or be able, to make a contribution.

The company has several plants in Europe. An associate from the UK commented:

> Perhaps the concept of leadership has evolved slightly. Certainly in the UK the leader takes much more of a business focus and gives business direction, pulling together a group of individuals towards achieving a business objective. The sponsor then focuses on individual development.

So any one person would normally expect to have a leader and also a sponsor. They would select the sponsor once they're in a position to be able to select someone able to give the appropriate guidance.

Leadership probably happens in three different ways. We still have the concept of natural leaders emerging through followership. There are then some areas of the business where leaders are imposed, and we probably find that more in this plant where we have a large production operation. We do have shift leaders and production leaders. That type of leader does tend to be more imposed. You also have the other side with perhaps the sales associates where they may decide for themselves that they've been working without a leader. They identify the need to have some focal point and the need to have a leader. They will get together and decide if there's somebody within the team who can take the role.

Decisions to take on additional staff are made on a consultative basis. At the moment it's very much project-driven. So a group would be working on a specific project, and they'll look at the resources required for that project – and if they haven't got the resources, a decision will be taken to go outside. What therefore tends to happen is that people are brought into the business with a specific project in mind. Not neccessarily a job description, but a role description for that project. That would then settle that person into the business. Once that project has finished, they'll then try to seek an alternative role in the business, in another project.

We have about 140 associates in this plant. The groups that people would fall into is research and development, where we have a group of engineers; then we have administration, sales, production, and support. We also have a position called product specialist, and that person is typically someone with a technical background, who is perhaps working in sales. They develop very close links with our customers, and almost act as a lubricant between sales and manufacturing.

They work very closely with our customers on current products, but also to identify customer requirements and move with them to research and develop new products. And we have a team of them in each plant. All of them take an industry sector. Say, for example, in the fabrics plant, we have a product specialist looking after the fire industry, one looking after police, one military, one ski.

They are groups, but they don't operate as a group within their functional area. They tend to operate on a project basis. So, for example, here in industrial filtration we are working on products for office automation technology – basically photocopiers – and we then assemble a team to develop that project. There'd be some production people, engineers, admin. support, and they form a group around that project. Somebody will have seen a need, researched the product, brought together a team. They will see it through to manufacture and then, as it stabilises, it comes to a different team – the manufacturing and the ongoing sales. A distinction between R&D and steady state.

The focus is very much on R&D. The challenge we have is to get that working on a global basis, to get global teams. The challenge we have is that within our culture we don't want to create structures or processes that stifle creativity. So we don't want to say that in this area this is where you'll focus on this element of research. But it's finding ways of sharing that and stopping duplication.

Some leaders have the job of persuading people to make commitments – but done very informally, and very much on an individual persuasion basis. The sponsor would not be involved unless there was an element of personal development by joining the team, in which case the individual may have the dilemma between current and new commitment and may use the sponsor as a sounding board. The sponsor certainly wouldn't be involved in initiating it. It's done on a very *ad hoc* basis.

Freedom of choice is not total. People will be asked at some point to go on a project by the leader of the business group. So sometimes people are very forcibly asked to work on a project because they have a particular expertise. And it's expected that that skill will be used to assist the project.

Leaders of projects might be appointed by people recognised as having leadership within functions (chief chemical engineer). It also could be that each plant has an overall business leader. We have a business leader for industrial filtration and if there was a particular skill needed on a project, he may make the decision to go and say to somebody that they need to work on that project.

The pay system could back that up, in that critical projects would attract bigger rewards. There is a negative element as well, in that the way the compensation process works is that people are put onto a compensation list – chemical engineers, reserch chemists or whatever – which typically has ten people on it. Twice a year, everyone on that contribution list is asked to rank each other according to their contribution to the business. It was on a plant basis, but we are now working towards assessing the global contribution and the European contribution. The remuneration committee would collate all the information and come out with an overall ranking of the contributions within that particular group. That is used in determining the salaries. They rank each member in order of their perceived contribution to the group that six months.

However, from an HR [human resources] perspective I do have some concerns as it is open to being very subjective – what does contribution mean, and how do we determine contribution? I don't think there are any guidelines apart from the associates' contribution over the past year to the business, future potential, and their willingness to co-operate in other areas outwith their discipline. In the ideal world, if everybody is objective and thinks along the same basis then that would be a very good system, but there are flaws in it. The principle is excellent, but there's the opportunity to do some

more work to make it a more objective and robust system.

The compensation scheme could almost drive behaviour both positively and negatively because there's an element of visibility, of people being seen to be doing the right thing. It's part of the performance-related pay. If the overall salary increase is 5 per cent then the compensation committee will start off with 5 per cent and make decisions – this person 0, this 7 and so on. There are a number of associates on the committee, so the criteria tend to be applied evenly across the plant.

The balance between procedures and guidelines, and human initiative

We do have standard procedures and rules and regulations. The underpinning principle is to keep them to the minimum, and its about questioning why do we need them? If there's a business reason that that is the best way to deal with it, then we're not afraid to put in a policies and procedures, for example ISO 9000. There is a mentality that people understand the need for processes when there's something tangible. So, in manufacturing, people accept that that is required. Less so in areas like HR, where there is a reluctance to do anything that people would see as a limiting structure. So if people can readily see the need, we put in procedures; but when it's not tangible we are very questioning about whether it's required. We are very flexible in the way we introduce things. If it increases profits, protects health and safety, and if people can see the tangible results, then there really isn't too much of a problem. The buy-in is absolutely essential. Even on some fairly straightforward policies and procedures we very rarely impose anything without consulting and getting buy-in.

How do you go about getting that buy-in?

You go and speak to key people and influence people, and you make a judgement as to who is key to get this project through, trying to see where opposition might come from, and trying to deal with it before you actually impose the procedure. You don't need everyone to be fully committed – apart from those who actually have to do something. As long as they just keep quiet. Commitment in Gore is very much when you personally have to deliver something, so a commitment in Gore is when you commit to doing XYZ on a certain project. It's not in terms of 'you've got my support', it's 'I have to deliver for a certain project'. Buy-in is willingness to accept.

Balance between people and institutions

Our institutional processes are minimal. Our main focus is on people, and we try to ensure that is effective by this emphasis on commitment. So if somebody starts a project, and it's so much ingrained into our culture that if you commit to do something then it's a sin not to see it through. So part of our culture enables us to be more successful through the people route than might be the case in a more traditional structure. We really have very few institutional structures. The one I mentioned is very recent and came about from a recognition that we wanted to

start working towards global teams, and we're starting to try to create centres of excellence within plants. In order to do that we need to have some way of getting knowledge transferred between plants.

That really is a big issue for us at the moment. We just had a big international conference which looked at what sort of processes we have, and how we could introduce them without compromising the elements of our culture that have been so successful for us? For me that is a fascinating dilemma. We have massive growth plans, and our company has evolved slowly. We need to stop duplication of effort, and that's not something we've done in the past. Plants have grown because somebody's had a project which has taken off, and that team has developed the plant from that project. Given the commonality of the core technology, several plants could be developing in similar directions at the same time. At some point the duplication becomes wasteful. How do we control that in R&D without stifling people's creativity? The centre of excellence and economy of resources is raising the issue of some degree of global integration between teams as a top priority, and our growth plans – which could lead to duplication.

PART CASE QUESTIONS

▶ How does management ensure that associates are motivated to work on projects that are important to the company's future prosperity?

▶ If you were a talented research scientist, what would be the attractions and rewards of working for Gore?

▶ Why do teams seem to work so well for Gore? What benefits do you think they bring both to the business and to the individuals? What if teams compete, rather than co-operate?

Power, influence and management style

AIM

To enable readers to understand critically the variety of influencing methods used in organisations and so to be more confident in their own attempts to influence others.

OBJECTIVES

By the end of your work on this chapter you should be able to outline the concepts below in your own terms and:

1 Summarise the main sources of power available to management

2 Outline Kanter's views that power can be built by delegating it and explain why management often fails to delegate

3 Compare personal and institutional forms of power

4 Evaluate the likely effects of an influencing strategy based on securing compliance

5 Outline the trait, behavioural and contingency perspectives on leadership

6 Compare the styles identified by behavioural theorists and give examples of each

7 Compare the situational perspectives with those stressing traits and behaviour

8 List the main contingencies in Vroom and Yetton's model of decision-making styles and evaluate the suitability of each style in a particular situation

9 Compare transactional and transformational approaches to leadership and influence

Digital Europe

Digital Europe is the European manufacturing and distribution operation of Digital Equipment Corporation, one of the leading players in the world electronics industry. Digital Europe had seven plants making different products within the Digital range. The plants had a high degree of autonomy and often competed with each other for the 'charter' to make new products. At the same time they had to co-operate, as systems sold to customers were usually built with parts made by several of the European plants. Hence there is also competitive pressure to improve Europe-wide systems. A senior manager recalls one such attempt:

I was asked to attend a meeting with a group of people interested in order fulfilment. They showed me some data about how long it took our competitors to process orders and how reliable their delivery promises were. It became clear that this was a major area of opportunity for our company.

I volunteered to pull together a group of people from our other facilities who understood order scheduling and who also had a vision of what it could be like. Between August and September we had two five-day meetings and came up with some ideas which I drafted into a formal document stating the problem and giving some indication of a solution. The next problem was how to enable that plan.

I then began a round of presentations to plant staffs in Europe and to our European management team, describing the problem and suggesting a way forward. The paper was well received but people were also a bit sceptical and wary. Major pan-European redesign work had been attempted in the past and had failed miserably. Europe-wide programmes, therefore, had a bad name.

Over the last year my part-time team has done a lot of work with their own staffs to convince them of the need for investment in order fulfilment and scheduling. My European functional boss had also been working with the European management team to convince them of the need for major investment in order fulfilment systems. We agreed to do a presentation that looked at all our processes and systems in order fulfilment. The aim was to get the commitment and investment that we require from the managements of the separate plants.

We managed to gather our European staff team together in Ireland on October 6th for about six hours and we did our presentation. We clearly captured the interest, imagination and energy of the group, and very clearly they were going to try to find a way even though we have no formal budget to make a system happen. It was an excellent culmination of fifteen months' work, though in many ways it was just the beginning.

CASE QUESTIONS

- What other people was the manager at Digital Europe trying to influence?
- Which of them, if any, were his direct subordinates?
- What aspects of the company's history will affect his attempts at influence?

5.1 Introduction

This chapter introduces the following ideas:
- Influence
- Sources of power – legitimate, reward, coercive, referent and expertise
- Hales's distinction between physical, economic, knowledge and normative forms, and between personal and positional sources of power
- Organisations as political systems
- Powerlessness
- Delegation
- Leadership
- Leading
- Traits
- Skill
- Behavioural models
- Situational models

Influence is the process by which one party attempts to modify the behaviour of others by mobilising power resources.

A manager was defined earlier as someone who gets things done with the support of others. This support is gained by the manager's exerting influence on these other people. How do managers influence people? How do managers ensure that people do what they want them to do? Why do the other people react the way they do?

The issue arises as management becomes a distinct and specialised activity. Those occupying management roles have to generate effort and commitment to the task – from themselves and from other people. Some of these other people are the manager's subordinates but many are not. Managers also influence colleagues on the same organisational level, those formally above them in the hierarchy and people outside the organisation.

Organisations include people with different views and interests, each of whom brings a unique perspective to the organisation. The way that they behave will reflect those interests. The issue may be over minor matters that pass with the working day, or over major matters of policy or principle that bring prolonged conflicts. How do they resolve such tensions?

To help understand this, four perspectives are examined in this chapter: the power, influence, leadership and management style approaches. The Digital Europe Case Study shows how one manager went about this.

5.2 Using power to influence others

Sources of power

What are the bases of one person's power over another? French and Raven's (1959) widely quoted classification identifies five sources of power:
- **Legitimate** power flows from the person's formal position in the organisation, and derives from the job that he or she holds. This position gives the job-holder certain forms of power, for example to make capital expenditures, to offer overtime, to choose a supplier or to recruit staff.
- **Reward** power is the ability of someone to reward another. It is visible when one person complies with another person's request or instruction because they expect some reward in return. The reward itself can take

many forms – a pay rise, time off, or more interesting work.

▶ **Coercive** power is the ability to obtain compliance through fear of punishment. This may take the form of reprimands, demotions, loss of a job – or the threat of physical force. Aggressive language and a powerful physical presence are other forms of coercive power.

▶ **Referent** power, also called *charismatic* power, is visible when some characteristics of the manager are attractive to the subordinate. They want to identify with him or her, and this gives the manager power over them.

▶ **Expertise** power is visible when people acknowledge someone's specialised knowledge and are therefore willing to follow their suggestions. During a problem-solving activity it often becomes clear who knows most about particular aspects of the problem. The leadership of the group may temporarily move to that person.

The theory predicts that people will try to use their power sources to resolve conflicts of interest in their favour. For this to work, the person targeted has to recognise and respond to the power source.

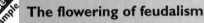

The flowering of feudalism

'Knowledge is power' has become such a managerial cliché that many at the top of big companies tend to forget that the principle can work both ways. Those lower down the management hierarchy also have an interest in husbanding information – and the power that goes with it. According to a recent survey of large European companies by the management consulting arm of KPMG, an accounting firm, the vast majority have found it impossible to establish pan-European management information systems for the simple reason that middle-ranking managers in different countries do not want those at headquarters to know what they are up to.

The European Community embarked on its ambitious project to create a single market largely at the behest of big EC firms who hoped to compete more effectively against rivals in America and Japan. While trade barriers within the EC have fallen, many firms have found national tastes vary more than they expected, as do local business practices, making economies of scale in manufacturing or marketing elusive.

In fact, few companies have even succeeded in taking the first step by collecting information on their own far-flung European operations in a uniform way. After interviewing the chief executives or financial officers of 153 large European companies, KPMG found that only 8 per cent of them had established common information systems across their European subsidiaries. And this was not because of glitches with computers. 'Technically, of course, anything is possible with information systems these days,' observed the boss of a Danish tobacco firm. 'It is not the technical aspect that we find daunting; it's the time and energy we have to spend explaining it to people and persuading them to accept it.'

The information which these companies have found it most difficult to standardise and collect is that on customers, pricing, product specifications and local personnel, says Alistair Stewart, who conducted

the survey. This is precisely the information which would be most helpful in lowering costs or responding quickly to changes in the market. When they try to introduce the computers and procedures to gather such information, reports Mr Stewart, European firms meet 'Ghandi-like' resistance from their subsidiaries.

The European bosses may inadvertently be sending mixed signals to subsidiary managers: preaching autonomy and responsibility while trying to computerise all aspects of their business so that staff at headquarters can monitor their every move. 'People are reluctant to share their information,' complained the head of one French company, which manufactures industrial equipment. 'Managers in particular seem to think it gives them extra power.' Clever chaps.

Source: *The Economist*, 27 February 1993, © The Economist, London, 1993

Hales identified some ambiguities in the French and Raven list. He offered a model that captures all the elements in the earlier list but stresses the distinction between personal and institutional sources. 'Each of these power sources [is], to varying degrees, available to managers – either as personal possessions or, more especially, by virtue of their organisational position as managers' (Hales, 1993). He distinguishes four power sources:

▶ **Physical** power resources, or the capacity to harm or restrict the actions of another, which others desire to avoid.
▶ **Economic** power resources, or scarce and desired objects or the means of acquiring them (e.g. money).
▶ **Knowledge** power resources, or scarce and desired knowledge and skills in the context of work. This knowledge and skill may be either
    (a) *administrative*, concerned with how an institution operates, or
    (b) *technical*, concerned with how tasks are performed.
▶ **Normative** power resources, or scarce and desired ideas, beliefs, values or affects. (p.22)

Table 5.1 summarises the model.

Table 5.1 **Hales's model of sources of power**

Power resource	Personal	Positional
Physical	Individual strength or possession of means of violence	Access to means of violence
Economic	Individual wealth or income	Access to or disposal of organisational resources
Knowledge		
Administrative	Individual experience	Access to or control over organisational information
Technical	Individual skill or expertise	Access to or control over technological information and technology
Normative	Individual beliefs, values, ideas, personal qualities	Access to/control over organisational values, ideas/'aura of office'

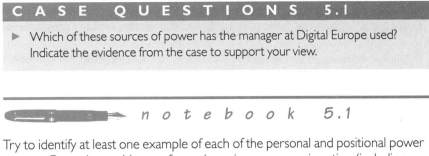

▶ Which of these sources of power has the manager at Digital Europe used?
Indicate the evidence from the case to support your view.

n o t e b o o k   5 . 1

Try to identify at least one example of each of the personal and positional power
sources. Examples could come from observing a manager in action (including
people in your university or college) or from your reading of current business affairs.

Legitimacy

A key point in understanding how power can influence behaviour is that of
legitimacy. Power is only effective if those whom a person is attempting to
influence recognise the power source as legitimate and acceptable. People
may dispute the knowledge base of the manager, or challenge the fairness of
an unequal distribution of resources that gives the manager the power to use
them to influence employees. One consequence of this is that employees
may comply with the manager's requirements, but feel coerced. This form of
grudging compliance is unlikely to lead to satisfactory performance. The
complexities of work processes often require employees to work with imagination and flexibility. In service industries, employee behaviour directly influences customer perceptions of the organisation. Competition often requires
'that employees … work responsibly and with concern for, rather than indifference towards, what they are doing. Increasingly work requires not compliance, but commitment' (Hales, 1993, p.39).

The implication is that management must establish the legitimacy of its
power sources in the eyes of those it is trying to influence. This may mean a
greater acknowledgement of mutual interdependence between manager and
managed. Developing genuinely shared goals and values towards which
both can work may be a basis for legitimacy. If so, it may enable those who
are being managed to accept willingly the use of managers' resource power.
It may also reside in greater consensus-seeking behaviour in the workplace,
rather than attempts by one party to dominate the other. In line with the
theme of this section, that implies appropriate behaviour by managers. It
may also imply the development of wider institutional frameworks that
encourage and support that behaviour within an accepted view of the political nature of organisations.

Organisations as political systems

One of Gareth Morgan's images is of the organisation as a political system.
Just as in national or international affairs, conflicts arise between people
with different interests. Political systems differ in how they resolve them. In
some the ruling power group will routinely override any challenge to its
power. In others various democratic processes make it possible to resolve
such conflicts in a more widely acceptable way.

NOTICEBOARD Organisations and methods of political rule

Organisations, like governments, employ some system of 'rule' as a means of creating and maintaining order among their members. Political analysis can thus make a valuable contribution to organisational analysis. The following are among the most common varieties of political rule found in organisations:

Autocracy A system of government in which an individual or small group holds power. They control critical resources, property or ownership rights, and draw support from tradition, charisma and other claims to personal privilege.

Bureaucracy A system in which leaders rule through the written word, which provides the basis for a rational-legal type of authority, or 'rule of law'.

Technocracy The emphasis is on ruling by knowledge and of expert power combined to solve relevant problems.

Co-determination The form of rule where opposing parties combine to manage mutual interests jointly. In coalition government or corporatism each party draws on a specific power base.

Representative democracy Where rule is exercised by electing people mandated to act on behalf of the electorate. They hold office for a specified time or so long as they command the support of the electorate. Examples include parliamentary government and forms of worker or shareholder control in business.

Direct democracy In this system everyone has an equal right to rule and be involved in all decision making. Examples are many communal organisations such as co-operatives and kibbutzim. It encourages self-organisation as a key mode of organising.

It is rare to find organisations that use just one of these different kinds of rule. While some organisations are more autocratic, more bureaucratic, or more democratic than others, they often contain elements of other systems as well. One of the tasks of political analysis is to discover which principles are in evidence, where, why and how.

Source: Morgan (1997)

There are a variety of ways in which conflicts can be resolved. They can be handled

autocratically ('We'll do it this way'),
bureaucratically ('We're supposed to do it this way'),
technocratically ('It's best to do it this way'), or
democratically ('How shall we do it?').

In each case the choice between alternative paths of action usually hinges on the power relations between the actors involved. (Morgan, 1997, p.160)

The Noticeboard outlines the options more fully.

5.3 Sharing power to increase it?

Rosabeth Moss Kanter (1979) argues that it is in managers' interests to share power more widely with subordinates. She believes that a manager's ability to influence others does not depend on interpersonal factors, such as choosing the right style for the situation. Rather it comes from managers building and using their position in the organisation to extend their power. People are more likely to follow strong and influential managers than weak and isolated ones. She identifies four organisational factors that affect a manager's power:

▶ **Rules inherent in the job**   The more of these, the less power the manager has.

▶ **Rewards for innovation**   The more the organisation rewards innovation, the more power the manager has.

▶ **External contact**   The more opportunities for this, the more power the manager has.

▶ **Senior contact**   The more opportunities for this, the more power the manager has.

These factors – the nature of the job, and the pattern of contacts that the manager can build from it – give the manager access to three lines of power:

▶ **Supply**   Money and other resources which can be used to bestow status or rewards on others in return for their support.

▶ **Information**   Being in the know, aware of what is happening, familiar with plans and opportunities which are in the making.

▶ **Support**   Able to get senior or external backing for what he or she wants to do, especially when this involves a degree of risk.

The more of these lines of power that the manager has, the more that subordinates will co-operate. They do so because they believe that the manager has the power to make things happen. Such a manager has 'clout' – weight or political influence in the organisation.

People can most easily gain power in a job that allows discretion (non-routine tasks), results in recognition (visibility and notice), and is relevant (central to major organisational problems and issues). They can also obtain it through peer networks, that is associates who provide information faster than the formal systems of communication. Subordinates who can relieve managers of some of their work and who can support the manager's plans with other employees are another source of power.

 Digital Europe – the case continues

'It is now November and a number of interesting things have happened. I have been legitimised by my own plant management team and have also been legitimised as the European Programme Manager for order scheduling. Of the seventeen part-timers that started the white paper, we now have at least ten of them committed full-time to the programme and another five individuals across the sites committed full-time to the programme. The process of engagement has begun. The full team is coming together again mid-November to compile a European paper supported by plant experts. Another major milestone.

In many ways, system and process design is going through the very same as happens to some product design in its early days. An individual or a group of individuals needs to go out on a limb with an idea and be able to articulate that idea to a wider audience before they can get any interest and therefore any support and investment to go forward. In our company, where the products and the business plan change very quickly, it is enormously difficult to get people to focus on what is important rather than on what is urgent.

There are some interesting organisational and business discussions going on in each of these plants which have a direct bearing on this programme. We have seven sites, all at different stages of development. We have in some way to make sure that each of them is positioned, in terms of resources, energy and commitment, to support an integrated European programme. It is because we have a business which is fairly complex and so diverse that we have adopted the approach that basically says, generate a common level of understanding of what needs to be done, then allow each area to specify its unique requirements within this overall framework. It also allows each individual location to move at its own pace as long as it doesn't get too far out of line.

The team member from Valbonne wrote to me two weeks ago indicating that he's now been asked to do another European programme. Therefore, because his particular group in Valbonne is very short of resources he will not be able to support this team. From my point of view as a programme manager, that is totally unacceptable as his plant is a very big part of the order-fulfilment process. So without a representative from there, any solution that we devise will only be partially successful.

I have had to speak to the individual himself, who I know well from the past is making a very clear statement around availability. I understand the circumstances in Valbonne, having worked there for some time. I have therefore agreed that we will put together a plan to augment the materials and planning resource in Valbonne. I will take that plan to the manager in Valbonne and also to the European management team to try to provide the support required so that he can support both programmes. I will also personally join the team for a week to help them with some of the technical aspects of the specification.

Christmas holidays are looming, but prior to that, next week in London I have to do an update on this programme to all my peers and my functional boss. They are obviously getting anxious about just exactly where we are. They are aware of some of the roadblocks that are causing me and the rest of team pain. So I am putting together a presentation that tries to be constructive about what is required to get the roadblocks out of the way and get us moving.

The European management team, from the conversations that I have had with them, is talking about some fairly unusual methods to drive this. For example, the concept of 'gold cards' which means that I can have the power to get whoever I want from wherever I want in Europe to drive the design for this system. Looks like we are in for a very interesting time within the first two to three weeks of January when we return to work.'

CASE QUESTIONS 5.2

▶ Which of Kanter's 'lines of supply' has the manager used?

▶ What other forms of authority has he been given?

▶ What has he done to increase his power and legitimacy in the eyes of those he is trying to influence?

Dangers of powerlessness

Kanter also argues of the dangers of powerlessness. Managers can design organisations that deny people access to resources, information and support. The effect is that those so denied will experience a sense of powerlessness. They in turn may behave in an oppressive or petty way.

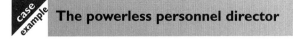

The powerless personnel director

A firm of stockbrokers had experienced severe absenteeism, with time lost from work by junior staff being well above the industry average. Senior managers expressed alarm and instructed the personnel director to do something.

His response was to introduce a new policy whereby their manager had to interview anyone who returned to work after being absent for illness or other reason. The policy assumed that staff had an inherent dislike of work and that management needed to threaten them with sanctions (the interview) if they were absent. Loyal employees who were rarely absent complained when a period of illness automatically led to an interview. They felt that Personnel was treating them as if they were one of the small number of malingerers.

Several managers questioned the policy. They disliked spending time on this new task and wondered if Personnel were wise to harass everyone. Were they treating the symptom rather than the cause?

From the perspective of a director with formal power, the easiest thing is to give an order – which is what the personnel director chose to do on this occasion. The other managers felt that it showed Personnel to be a rather weak and powerless department, displaying a despotic and oppressive management style.

Delegate to build power

Finally, Kanter argues that powerful managers are better able to influence subordinates because they have valued resources and contacts. Moreover, by sharing that power with subordinates, the manager can further increase his or her power. As subordinates carry out tasks previously done by the manager, the manager has more time to build the external and senior contacts – which further boost his or her power. By delegating not only tasks but also a degree of power, managers are able to enhance their own power.

Delegation is an essential aspect of management, as clearly no one can perform all the activities of an organisation themselves. They cannot even supervise them all directly. Hence managers at all levels routinely delegate work to their subordinates or colleagues, while remaining responsible for the work. An important point in the definition is that while managers can delegate a task and the necessary authority, they remain responsible for the area of work: he or she can still be called to account if things go wrong.

For example, a materials manager may delegate to a purchasing officer the task of informing all suppliers about the company's new requirements on delivering goods to the receiving dock. The purchasing officer now has the authority to deal with this, but the materials manager is still fully

Delegation occurs when one person gives another the authority to undertake specific activities or decisions.

responsible to her boss for implementing the new policy. She must ensure that suppliers comply with it, explain why it is or is not working, and deal with any disputes. The manager does not evade responsibility by delegating the task, but remains responsible for the actions of the person to whom the task was delegated.

Delegation therefore involves risks. Kanter argues that these should be significant. The manager should delegate significant tasks, not minor ones. Effective delegation requires managers to:

▶ recognise the ability of their subordinates,
▶ be willing to trust them,
▶ be committed to developing subordinates' skills, and
▶ get satisfaction from knowing that others can do the job as well.

What is gained by delegation?

The major benefit of delegating work to others is that it reduces the manager's own workload. Relieved of the necessity to deal with the detail of one task, the manager has more time to concentrate on major planning and creative work. More time can be spent on external matters, making contacts, keeping in touch with what is happening in the firm or the industry. This in turn can build the visibility and reputation of the manager's unit.

Another benefit is that staff who receive the delegated work use their skills more fully. This implies that managers should not delegate only the routine matters. They should also delegate tasks which allow subordinates to develop the skills and contacts for future roles. This in turn may bring benefits of greater job satisfaction and confidence. Having people trained as understudies at all levels can lead to a more effective department, better able to cope with absence or sudden changes. Finally, it can mean that people closer to the action make decisions resulting in speedier action. Subordinates lose valuable time if they have to check with their boss before they make a decision. Companies can overcome this if staff are able to deal with situations as they arise.

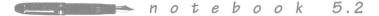

n o t e b o o k   5.2

Reflect on an experience of delegation you have had in a job. First choose an example in which you felt that your boss could have delegated more. What do you think prevented that? What effects did it have on you and on the section's performance?

Then choose an example where work was successfully delegated to you. What effects did that have on your commitment and on the section's performance?

What lessons can you draw from these contrasting experiences? How does this evidence compare with that in the text?

Obstacles to delegation

Many subordinates observe that their managers are reluctant delegators, tending to keep more things to themselves than they need to. Why are some managers reluctant to pass some of their work to their staff? They may feel that their staff are incapable of doing it, and that to train them would take too long. Or perhaps the manager is too disorganised to be able to pass on an identifiable task to a subordinate. A deeper reason could be that the manager is more comfortable with the tasks they know. Not delegating keeps him or her busy, and prevents them having to take on new roles, which they may find more challenging or risky. They may also fear that the subordinate will do the work better than they themselves can, damaging their reputation. Equally, some subordinates are content to let the manager continue to make all the decisions, limiting the stress in the subordinate's job.

Too much internal focus

A department of a local authority consisted of a director, two senior officers, three officers and fourteen staff. The director's style was to involve himself in operational matters, and he rarely found time to work with other senior managers. He normally met only with the senior officers within his department and rarely involved others in these discussions. He took the view that officers should not be involved in policy matters. He saw himself as the only competent person in the department and was comfortable in this operational role.

Staff consider themselves to be capable and professional. They expect to be involved more fully and are used to taking initiatives in both the routine and innovative aspects of the work. The fact that the director becomes involved in operational detail affects the officers in two ways. They are annoyed at the lack of trust this displays in their own abilities, and they suffer from the relatively low status of the department caused by the director not performing an active enough external role and his lack of influence outside the department.

A wider political perspective

The emphasis on political processes of influence is clearly a different perspective from that of the purely rational model. Radical writers argue that it nevertheless ignores or avoids deeper questions about the distribution of power in organisations and in the wider society.

Stakeholders are frequently mentioned in such discussions, with the manager expected to strike a balance between their conflicting demands. Critics (Thompson and McHugh, 1995; Alvesson and Wilmott, 1996) point out that some stakeholders have more power than others. They will therefore be able to shape both the institutions of conflict resolution, and the substantive issues, in their own favour. Managers have to balance the interests of different departments created by the horizontal division of labour.

Balancing the interests of those at different levels in the hierarchy is more problematic. Owners and boards of directors (the dominant coalition) normally have the greatest formal, resource and coercive power. That can raise questions about the prior distribution of that power. How do some have access to these resources while others do not? Thompson and McHugh argue that managerial power has to be considered as part of the deeper structures of economic domination. This economic power is particularly visible in the ability of intenational companies to transfer production between nation-states almost at will, in pursuit of the cheapest operating location.

5.4 Perspectives on leadership

A different and more traditional approach to the study of influence is from the perspective of leadership. As one scholar observed, 'there are almost as many definitions of leadership as there are persons who have attempted to define the concept' (Stogdill, 1974, p.259). We will not add another, but offer two existing ones. Yukl's (1994) review of the topic concluded that most definitions reflected the assumption that leadership is a social influence process:

> Leadership involves a social influence process whereby intentional influence is exerted by one person over other people to structure the activities and relationships in a group or organization. (Yukl, 1994, p.18)

This a deliberately broad definition, and you should notice four points about it. First, the process to which it refers is *not* exercised only by those at the top. People exercise social influence throughout an organisation at all levels. Anyone who wants to get something done needs to exercise leadership. If management expects people to use their initiative to get things done rather than wait to be told what to do, they will need effective leaders at all levels. Secondly, the definition does not imply that a single leader in a special role or with a particular title does all the influencing. While formally designated leaders may exercise significant leadership, there are many examples where they do not (the case of Digital Europe would be one). Groups often share the social influence process: a person who knows more about a topic than the rest of the group will usually have more influence when the group is dealing with that topic – if other members permit this.

Thirdly, the definition says nothing about the enthusiasm of the targets of the influence attempt. Some writers discuss leadership as a leader's ability to generate unusual or exceptional commitment to a vision. For example, Peter Drucker writes of leadership as being:

> the lifting of people's vision to a higher sight, the raising of their performance to a higher standard, the building of their personality beyond its normal limitations. (Drucker, 1985)

And Anita Roddick has said that:

> leadership is creating a vision to which others can aspire and energising them to work towards this vision.

'Leadership involves a social influence process whereby intentional influence is exerted by one person over other people to structure the activities and relationships in a group or organization.' (Yukl, 1994)

C A S E   Q U E S T I O N S   5.3

▶ In what ways did the actions of the manager at Digital Europe fit the definition of leadership?

▶ What role did creating a vision play in the manager's influence attempts?

▶ What lay behind the different degrees of enthusiasm that the plant managers showed for the plan?

These are important and valuable aspects of leadership and our preferred definitions do not exclude them. They offer a limited view of the topic, as leadership can also be exercised in more mundane circumstances. Leadership is effective if it influences people to do things even if they are not fired with visionary enthusiasm. This may be desirable, but is not always achieved. Fourthly, leaders sometimes use their influence for entirely selfish motives. They may have little regard for the interests of followers. Those taking the lead during a task have many motives for what they do: the way they exercise influence is a separate issue from the purposes of their influence attempt.

Is the 'social influence process' effective?

Most people studying the topic have been looking for the bases of effective leadership. A problem with this is the *unclear link between cause and effect*. Some actions that a manager takes will produce quick and direct results. Organising a training course or introducing a more efficient working system can bring quick increases in productivity. The case of the personnel director described earlier illustrates the quick (negative) results brought on by an ineffective leader. Other effects become visible, if at all, by a more indirect route, and over a longer time. A leader who initiates a change in the structure of the business or a move into a new market expects the initiatives to show significant effects on profit or some similar measure. The difficulty is that unrelated events will affect these measures over the time taken to implement the change. It is then hard to link the actions of the leader who initiated the changes with the effects observed.

Contradictory research results illustrate this. Lieberson and O'Connor (1977) studied the twenty-year performance of 167 American companies in thirteen industries. They analysed the data to show the relative effects on performance of general economic conditions, industry factors and changes of chief executive. They concluded that general economic conditions had the greatest influence on performance. The chief executive seemed to have little influence on results. 'Like corks bobbing on a choppy sea, organizations could be seen as largely driven by powerful economic currents rather than being driven masterfully against the elements by potent leaders' (Thomas, 1993, p.129). An equally major study by Weiner and Mahoney (1981) reached the opposite conclusion, showing that leaders had a substantial effect on at least some outcomes. This is consistent with the conclusion reached in Pettigrew's study of the role of Sir John Harvey-Jones in reshaping ICI.

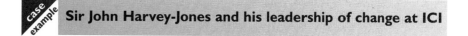

Sir John Harvey-Jones and his leadership of change at ICI

In a classic study of major change at ICI, Andrew Pettigrew paid particular attention to the link between the leadership of the company and the change process. Sir John Harvey-Jones was clearly instrumental in initiating and implementing immense and fundamental change. Pettigrew's study shows that Harvey-Jones did not achieve this by a few dramatic acts or decisions. Rather it depended heavily on actions that he took over many years to change the way that senior managers made decisions, and to make those at all levels more receptive to change.

According to Pettigrew, after Harvey-Jones arrived on the board in 1973 he spent the next several years 'orchestrating an educational process – trying to open ICI up to change. Critical to this process was a need to change the mode, style, composition and problem-solving processes of the main board. There was the crucial requirement for the visionary leader to keep one foot in the present while pushing on into the future' (p.666).

This research led to the conclusion that studies of leadership should not focus only on the actions of individuals, important though they are. Rather they should view leadership as a continuous process taking place within a particular organisational context. The leader exerts influence by actions that shape that context. These include initiating changes within the organisation that make it more adaptable: setting up management development programmes, creating new administrative mechanisms, setting up groups to work on a particular problem. These were not part of a grand design. They came as opportunities arose to build a critical mass of people behind the broad vision of the new ICI which Harvey-Jones helped his colleagues to discover and articulate. Pettigrew quotes Selznick (1957, p.70): 'A wise leader faces up to the character of his organization, although he may do so only as a prelude to designing a strategy that will alter it.'

Source: extracts from Pettigrew (1985)

---

n o t e b o o k   5.3

Before reading further, note down how you would decide whether a leader was effective or not. What criteria would you use? You may want to use the definition on page 160 as a starting point. Then read on, and review your answer considering the points below.

There is *no single measure of effectiveness*. Some researchers try to identify the effects or results of a leader's actions. There may be accurate measures such as sales performance, productivity or business growth for some of these. Other results are harder to measure, such as innovation, the ability of the group to cope with change or the group's attitude towards the leader. Researchers then rely more on subjective assessments made by the manager's boss, colleagues or subordinates.

Paradoxically, the more measures there are, the more difficult it is to judge effectiveness. Which are most important, to whom? Some measures may only become more favourable if others decline, such as higher output lowering quality. How do you assess the trade-off? There is no answer to that: it will depend on the person and the competing values that he or she holds. There may be a conflict between a manager's concern for people and his or her concern for getting the work done. There may also be conflict between using resources for employees' immediate benefit and investing them to ensure the organisation's long-term future. There can be trade-offs between meeting the wishes of shareholders and those of other stakeholders such as a local community or an environmental interest.

Constraints on a leader's influence

A further point to remember when considering how people influence others is the constraints under which they are operating (Thomas, 1993; Stewart, 1991). Since people usually exercise influence within an organisation, its features will either constrain or support attempts at influence. For instance, we would expect that the constraints on the leader's attempt to influence others would be relatively few in a small, young firm. There are few rules or procedures and few precedents to go by. As the organisation increases in size and age, more formal systems are introduced. This probably means that the leader has to exercise influence indirectly, for example by the rewards available from the performance appraisal system. The form of the organisation will also affect this. An organisation with a centralised decision-making structure will be more amenable to direction from the leader. The more it becomes decentralised, with power devolved to local levels, the more it constrains the leader seeking to exert influence: the mechanisms for doing so may simply not be there – as Sir John Harvey-Jones had realised.

C A S E   Q U E S T I O N S   5.4

▶ What measures could senior managers use to judge the project leader's effectiveness?

▶ What constraints is the project leader operating under?

There is no definitive measure by which researchers or anyone else can assess the effectiveness of leaders or managers. Accordingly, there is equal ambiguity about the effects of the different ways in which leaders have sought to exercise influence over others. The following sections review three approaches to understanding leadership. First, the traits model focuses on the personal characteristics of leaders; secondly, the behavioural model concentrates on a leader's actions, and thirdly the contingency model examines the relationship between the characteristics of a given situation and a leader's behaviour. Each approach uses a different set of factors to describe and predict effective styles of leadership.

5.5   Traits models

Traits are a variety of individual attributes, including aspects of personality, temperament, needs, motives and values. Skill refers to a person's ability to perform various types of cognitive or behavioural activity effectively.

Early studies focused on the individual leader rather than the situation in which he or she worked. They tried to identify the traits which prominent leaders possessed, on the assumption that some people had certain attributes which made it more likely that they would be effective leaders. These attributes include both traits and skills.

Traits and skills combine heredity and learning, with some being more influenced by one than the other. For example, people's experiences and what they learn from them shape their values, whereas aspects of temperament such as energy levels or personal drive are inherited. The stimulus to early researchers on leadership was the belief that they could identify the traits and skills of effective leaders. They would then be able to use this knowledge to guide the selection of future leaders. Stogdill (1974) reviewed

Table 5.2 Traits and skills found most frequently to be associated with successful leaders

Traits	Skills
Adaptable to situations	Clever (intelligent)
Alert to social environment	Conceptually skilled
Ambitious and achievement-oriented	Creative
Assertive	Diplomatic
Co-operative	Fluent in speaking
Decisive	Knowledgeable about group task
Dependable	Persuasive
Dominant (desire to influence others)	Socially skilled
Energetic	Well-organised
Persistent	
Self-confident	
Tolerant of stress	
Willing to assume responsibility	

Source: Stogdill (1974)

163 trait studies published between 1949 and 1970. Table 5.2 presents his summary of this research.

Boyatzis (1982) has also conducted research on traits and skills. His aim was to identify the competences (including traits and skills) of effective managers. The researchers interviewed a sample of 253 managers about critical incidents or events which they had had to manage. People familiar with the managers had previously rated them as low, medium or highly effective leaders. This allowed the researchers to gather information about which behaviours the managers had used, from which they inferred what traits and skills the managers possessed.

Effective managers appeared to have a strong motivation towards achievement, a concern for task objectives and high work standards. They also had a strong desire for power, were assertive and keen to influence others. They displayed self-confidence, decisiveness and a preference for initiating action, rather than waiting for things to happen. They had good interpersonal skills, especially strong presentational and communication abilities. They had developed networks of potential allies with whom they could co-operate, and were skilful in building and managing teams. They also possessed a range of conceptual skills, such as the ability to see relationships amongst apparently unconnected data, and the abilities to develop creative solutions and to detect deviations from plans.

Limitations

The major limitation of the traits model is the large number of factors which researchers have identified. Very few are consistently present across different studies, undermining the idea that some traits are essential for effective leadership. It is also clear that the lists of desirable traits look like impossible ideals, which it is hard to imagine being present in one person. There are also examples of apparently effective leaders who did not possess the traits identified to any notable degree.

One of the difficulties with this line of research is to take account of the intervening variables that are likely to affect whether a particular trait contributes to performance. Although it seems plausible that effective managers are likely to have certain skills and traits, this is hard to prove. Having certain traits is probably necessary for effective leadership, but is not in itself likely to be sufficient. The traits do not guarantee success, and their relative importance is likely to depend on other factors, including the situation in which the manager is operating.

Contributions

Despite these limitations, we should not ignore the traits model. Some of the items in Stodgill's list are probably necessary as a basis for effective management or leadership, such as reasonably high energy levels, willingness to assume responsibility, and alertness to social situations. Some management selection practices reflect this belief, and the criteria often include supposedly relevant traits. As one of the foremost scholars of leadership recently concluded, 'There is no one ideal leader personality. However, effective leaders tend to have a high need to influence others, [and] to achieve; and they tend to be bright, competent and socially adept, rather than stupid, incompetent and social disasters' (Fiedler and House, 1994).

---

n o t e b o o k   5.4

Collect some job advertisements and recruitment brochures. Make a list of the traits that the companies say they are looking for in those they recruit.

Many appraisal and development schemes also reflect traits thinking. Table 5.3 lists various traits that some major UK companies incorporated in their appraisal schemes in 1996.

Traits for future managers?

John Adair, a leading writer and consultant on leadership, recently proposed that the traits that will be needed by leaders in the twenty-first century will be different from those typical of twentieth-century leaders:

Twentieth century	*Twenty-first century*
Determination	Less reliant on rank
Clear direction	Empathy with others
Task-centred	Team-builder
Isolated	
Aggressive	Contemplative
Western	Eastern
'Masculine'	'Feminine'

5.6 Behavioural models

Although no single set of personal traits distinguishes effective leaders, another set of theories sought to identify the behaviours or styles of leadership.

Table 5.3 Traits featured in the appraisal schemes of some UK companies in 1996

Company A 'Performance domains'	Company B 'Key performance dimensions'	Company C 'Performance criteria'	Company D 'Aspects of performance'
Strategic business awareness	Commercial awareness	Strategic/business awareness	Job knowledge
Planning and organisation	Planning and evaluation skills	Implementation	
Judgement and decision-making			
Commitment and urgency	Drive	Personal delivery	General performance and overall contribution
Flexibility and creativity			Initiative and problem-solving
Communicating/ influencing	Leadership	Leadership	Communication and interpersonal skills
People management	People management		Training and development

What did effective managers do to influence subordinates that less effective managers did not? Scholars at the Universities of Michigan and Ohio State developed their models at about the same time. Their research identified two major categories of leader behaviour: one was concerned with interpersonal relations, the other with task accomplishment (structuring). Subordinates judge their leaders on these two dimensions.

Ohio State University model

Researchers at Ohio State University developed questionnaires which subordinates used to describe the behaviour of their manager. The researchers who analysed the responses concluded that subordinates viewed their managers' behaviour on two dimensions, 'consideration' and 'initiating structure'.

A *considerate* style reflects concern for subordinates' well-being, status and comfort. Considerate leaders were those who tried to build a pleasant working environment, by listening to subordinates' problems, giving encouragement, and treating subordinates with respect. Such leaders assume that subordinates want to work well and try to make it easier for them to do so. They place relatively little stress on their formal position and power. Typical behaviours of considerate leaders included:

▶ expressing appreciation for a job well done,
▶ not expecting more from subordinates than they can reasonably do,
▶ helping subordinates with their personal problems,
▶ being approachable and available for help,
▶ providing rewards for high performance.

An *initiating-structure* style is one that emphasises defining and planning work, including the activities of subordinates. Leaders with this approach focused on getting the work done, ensuring that everything was properly planned and worked out. They asked subordinates to follow the procedures laid down, and made sure that they were working to full capacity. Typical behaviours of initiating-structure leaders included:

▶ allocating subordinates to specific tasks,
▶ establishing standards of job performance,
▶ informing subordinates of the requirements of the job,
▶ scheduling work to be done by subordinates,
▶ encouraging the use of uniform procedures.

The results showed that leaders displayed distinctive patterns of scores on the two dimensions. Some were high on measures of initiating structure and low on consideration, while others were high on consideration and low on initiating structure. Some were high on both, others low on both.

Later studies tried to assess the effects of the leader's style on measures of performance. For example, Fleishman and Harris (1962) examined the behaviour of 57 production supervisors at an International Harvester Company truck plant. They measured effectiveness by the number of written grievances and the amount of labour turnover during an eleven-month period. Supervisors who were very considerate had fewer grievances and lower turnover than those who scored low on consideration. Those who adopted a pronounced initiating-structure style had more grievances and more turnover than those who scored low on this dimension.

Subsequent research in a wide range of situations has been less conclusive (see, for example, Bass, 1990). In some cases subordinates were more satisfied with a structuring leader, while others failed to find any significant relationships. It is also possible that the direction of the cause/effect relationship is unclear. It is usual to assume that the relationship is from leader behaviour to subordinate behaviour. An alternative possibility is that leaders are able to behave in a considerate style to subordinates who are performing well.

Finally, behaviour may be influenced by employees' perceptions of both aspects of the managers' behaviour. Employees' reactions to initiating-structure style may have depended on their perceptions of how considerate their manager was. If managers were considerate, employees also viewed initiating structure as effective. If managers were inconsiderate, subordinates viewed initiating structure as 'watching over employees' shoulders'.

Michigan University model

Researchers at the University of Michigan (Likert, 1961, 1967) conducted similar studies to those at Ohio at about the same time. They found that two types of behaviour distinguished effective from ineffective managers: task-oriented and relationship-oriented behaviour.

Task-oriented managers ensured that they worked on different tasks from their subordinates, concentrating especially on planning, co-ordinating and supplying a range of support activities. These were similar to the initiating-structure activities identified at Ohio.

Relationship-oriented managers combined the task-oriented behaviour with a range of relationship-centred activities. They were more considerate, helpful and friendly to subordinates than less effective managers. They tended to engage in broad supervision rather than detailed observation of all activities. These behaviours were similar to what the Ohio group referred to as consideration.

Managerial grid model

The managerial grid model identifies various combinations of concern for production (initiating structure) and people (consideration) as shown in Figure 5.1. Robert Blake and Jane Mouton developed this as an extension and application of the Ohio State model (Blake and Mouton, 1964).

The vertical scale relates to concern for people, ranging from 1 (low concern) to 9 (high concern). The horizontal scale relates to concern for production, which also ranges from 1 (low concern) to 9 (high concern). At the lower left-hand corner (1,1) is the impoverished style: low concern for both people and production. The primary objective of such managers is to stay out of trouble. They merely pass instructions to subordinates, follow the established system, and make sure that no one can blame them if something goes wrong. They do only as much as is consistent with keeping their job.

At the upper left-hand corner (1,9) is the country club style: high concern for people and low concern for production. Managers who use this style try to create a secure and comfortable family atmosphere. They assume that their subordinates will respond productively. Thoughtful attention to the need for satisfying relationships leads to a friendly atmosphere and work tempo.

High concern for production and low concern for people is found in the lower right-hand corner (9,1). This is the produce or perish style. These managers do not consider subordinates' personal needs. All that matters is the achievement of the organisation's objectives. They use their formal authority to pressure subordinates into meeting production quotas. They believe that efficiency comes from arranging the work so that employees merely have to follow instructions.

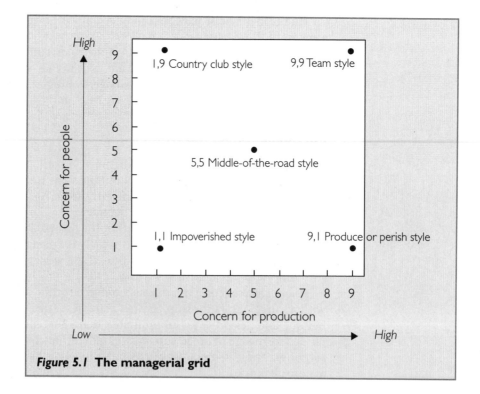

Figure 5.1 The managerial grid

In the centre (5,5) is the middle-of-the-road style. These managers seek to balance subordinates' needs and the organisation's productivity objectives. They obtain adequate performance by balancing the need to get the work done with reasonable attention to the interests of employees.

In the upper right-hand corner (9,9) is the high–high style: high concern for both people and production. According to Blake and Mouton, this leadership style is the most effective. Managers of this kind attempt to develop committed workgroups and staff, to produce both high performance and high job satisfaction. The manager fosters performance by building relationships of trust and respect. Similar work in Japan suggested that effective leaders are high in both performance behaviour and in maintenance behaviour – the 'PM' leader (Misumi, 1985).

---

n o t e b o o k   5 . 5

Reflect on two managers you have worked with, one effective and one ineffective from your point of view. Which of the positions in the Blake and Mouton grid most closely describe their style? Note specific behaviours which come to mind that typified their approach.

C A S E   Q U E S T I O N S   5 . 5

▶ On the basis of the information you have, can you decide which style best decribes the manager in the Digital Europe case?

Many trainers use the Blake and Mouton model with the aim of helping managers develop towards the '9,9' style. Implicit in the approach is the idea of flexibility. The '9,9' manager would be successful not by applying the same behaviour in every situation, but by using task- or relationship-centred behaviours in a way that was appropriate to the situation at hand.

A more basic question is whether there are situations where showing a high level of concern for both production and people may not be the best path for the leader to follow. In some situations a concern for production may be more important than concern for people. A sudden crisis may require swift action irrespective of the concerns of some staff. Situational or contingency theorists developed this perspective more fully.

5.7 Situational and contingency models

Contingency theories draw attention to the situation in determining the most appropriate leadership style. Four such approaches are outlined here.

House's path–goal model

The path–goal model attempts to explain how the way a leader works influences subordinate satisfaction or performance. The basic idea is that the leader enhances subordinates' commitment by enabling them to achieve their goals (House and Mitchell, 1974). The leader does this by establishing subordinates' goals, establishing a reward system that links effective performance to those goals, and assisting subordinates to perform effectively. The leader can do this by specific actions, such as providing support for followers, alleviating boredom and frustration, providing direction and advice and encouraging expectations that effort will lead to task accomplishment. In brief, the leader's function is to motivate and help subordinates to reach their job-related objectives by providing what is lacking in the environment, the task or in the subordinate.

The effect of a leader's behaviour on the subordinates' performance depends on the situation. In House's model, the situation consists of two variables: the characteristics of the task and environment, and the characteristics of the subordinates. The causal variable is the leader's behaviour. The third element in the model is the idea of intervening variables. These include the subordinates' expectations about the likelihood of the goals being achieved and the rewards obtained. Figure 5.2 shows the general relationship of the elements in the model:

▶ **Task characteristics** Whether tasks are routine and simple, or non-routine and complex.
▶ **Employee characteristics** Their pattern of needs: for affiliation and self-esteem, or for autonomy, responsibility and achievement.

Four types of leader behaviour were proposed:

▶ **Supportive leadership** Giving consideration to the needs of subordinates, displaying concern for their welfare and creating a friendly climate in the work unit.
▶ **Directive leadership** Letting subordinates know what the leader expects, giving specific guidance, asking subordinates to follow rules and procedures, scheduling and co-ordinating their work.
▶ **Participative leadership** Consulting subordinates and taking their opinions and suggestions into account, finding ways of overcoming blockages to performance.
▶ **Achievement-oriented leadership** Setting challenging goals, clarifying targets, seeking performance improvements, emphasising excellence in performance and showing confidence that subordinates will attain high standards.

The intervening variable was the employees' expectation about the effects of the leader's actions on their ability to perform the task. Will the leader's efforts make it more or less likely that the task will be done, and the rewards received? For example, if the task is boring and tedious, the leader may supply what is missing by supportive behaviour which builds the social relationships amongst subordinates. The leader can also assure them that he or she is aware of their difficulties. By doing so, the leader increases the subordinates' expectation that they will receive rewards that they value, and hence encourages their effort.

If the work environment lacks structure, so that subordinates face ambiguous task demands and have little guidance, a sense of direction may be missing. The leader can supply this by directive behaviour that gives guidance on how to do the task and the required standards. Such behaviour would increase the subordinates' confidence that they will be able to do the work and receive the rewards. The theory predicts that if the task is unstructured and the subordinates skilled and experienced, directive leadership may have a negative effect. In that

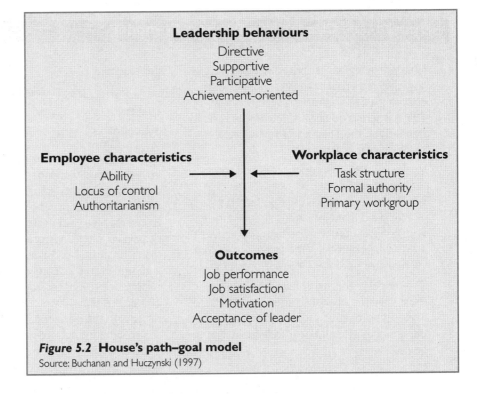

Leadership behaviours
Directive
Supportive
Participative
Achievement-oriented

Employee characteristics
Ability
Locus of control
Authoritarianism

Workplace characteristics
Task structure
Formal authority
Primary workgroup

Outcomes
Job performance
Job satisfaction
Motivation
Acceptance of leader

Figure 5.2 **House's path–goal model**
Source: Buchanan and Huczynski (1997)

case, participative or achievement-oriented leadership would be more effective.

The path–goal model does not provide a formula for the best way to lead. It suggests that effective leaders select the style most appropriate to the particular situation and the needs of subordinates. Indvik (1986) reviewed 48 empirical studies that generally supported the propositions of the theory.

The House model indicates that participative leadership styles are not always the most effective. Under some conditions the participative approach is ineffective. Participation is needed most when subordinates' acceptance of the decision is important, when the manager does not have all the information needed, and when the problem is unstructured. Directive leadership seems to work better when subordinates do not share the manager's and/or organisation's objectives, when the production schedule is critically short, and when subordinates are receptive to top-down decisions.

Vroom and Yetton's decision model

The aim of Vroom and Yetton's contingency model of decision-making is to guide managers in thinking through how fully to involve subordinates in making a decision. The model defines five leadership styles and seven characteristics of problems. The manager can use these characteristics to diagnose the situation. Users find the solution for that type of problem by answering the diagnostic questions and following the branches of a decision tree, as set out in Figure 5.3. The five leadership styles defined are:

▶ **AI (Autocratic)**   You solve the problem yourself using information available to you at that time.

▶ **AII (Information-seeking)**   You obtain the necessary information from your subordinate(s), then decide on the solution to the problem

---

NOTICEBOARD Charles Handy's best-fit model

Charles Handy has proposed what he calls a 'low definition tool of analysis' as a guide to choosing a decision-making style (Handy, 1993). There is no universally correct style. It depends on the situation facing the leader, made up of four factors:

▶ The leader – his or her preferred style of operating.
▶ The subordinates – their preferred style of being led, in the prevailing circumstances.
▶ The task – its clarity, certainty, objectives.
▶ The environment – the setting in which the manager operates – culture, predictability.

The model predicts that leadership will be most effective when the requirements of leader, subordinates and task fit together. Each dimension is assessed on a scale from tight to flexible.

For example:

	Tight	Flexible
Leader	✓	
Subordinates		✓
Task		✓

In this situation the leader prefers a tight decision-making style, but the subordinates prefer a flexible one. The task also is one that is uncertain, suggesting a flexible approach to dealing with it. Handy predicts that if the manager and subordinates are too far apart, and remain so, the team will break up or experience severe tensions. A more likely outcome is that they move towards each other, with the leader becoming a bit more flexible, and the subordinates accepting a little more control.

---

yourself. You may or may not tell your subordinates what the problem is in getting the information from them. The role played by your subordinates in making the decision is clearly one of providing the necessary information to you, rather than generating or evaluating alternative solutions.

▶ **CI (Consulting)** You share the problem with relevant subordinates individually, getting their ideas and suggestions without bringing them together as a group. Then you make the decision that may or may not reflect your subordinates' influence.

▶ **CII (Negotiating)** You share the problem with your subordinates as a group, collectively obtaining their ideas and suggestions. Then *you* make the decision that may or may not reflect your subordinates' influence.

▶ **G (Delegating)** You share the problem with your subordinates as a group. Together, you generate and evaluate alternatives and attempt to reach agreement (consensus) on a solution. Your role is much like that of a chairperson. You do not try to influence the group to adopt 'your' solution, and you are willing to accept and implement any solution that has the support of the entire group.

The idea behind the model is that no style is in itself better or more virtuous than another. Some have argued that consultative or delegating styles are inherently preferable to autocratic approaches, as being more in keeping with democratic principles. Vroom and Yetton argue otherwise. In some situations (such as when time is short, or the manager has all the information needed for a minor decision), going through the process of consultation will waste time and add little value. In other situations, where the subordinates have the relevant information, it is essential to use one of the more consultative approaches. The point of the model is to make managers more

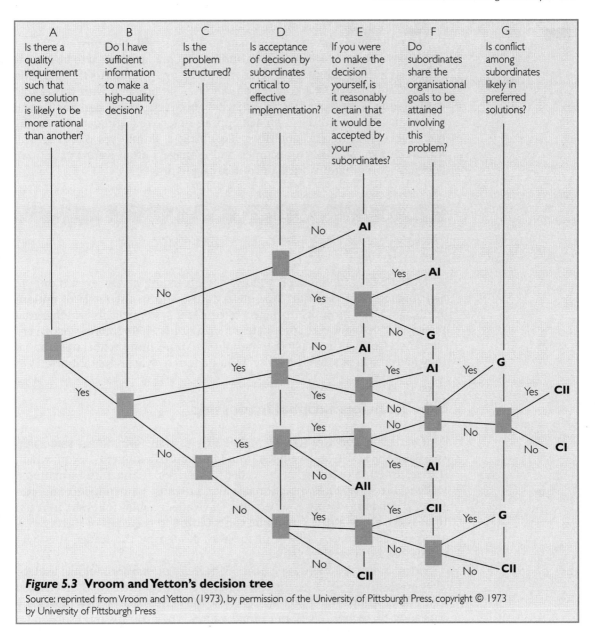

A
Is there a quality requirement such that one solution is likely to be more rational than another?

B
Do I have sufficient information to make a high-quality decision?

C
Is the problem structured?

D
Is acceptance of decision by subordinates critical to effective implementation?

E
If you were to make the decision yourself, is it reasonably certain that it would be accepted by your subordinates?

F
Do subordinates share the organisational goals to be attained involving this problem?

G
Is conflict among subordinates likely in preferred solutions?

***Figure 5.3* Vroom and Yetton's decision tree**

Source: reprinted from Vroom and Yetton (1973), by permission of the University of Pittsburgh Press, copyright © 1973 by University of Pittsburgh Press

aware of the range of factors to take into account in using a particular decision-making style.

The problem criteria are summed up in seven problem attributes, which are expressed in specific diagnostic questions:

▶ Is one solution likely to be better than another?
▶ Does the manager have enough informaton to make a high-quality decision?
▶ Is the problem structured?
▶ Is acceptance of the decision by subordinates critical to effective implementation?
▶ If the manager makes the decision alone, is it likely to be accepted by subordinates?

▶ Do subordinates share organisational goals?

▶ Is conflict likely among subordinates over preferred solutions?

The Vroom–Yetton decision model implies that managers need to be flexible in the style they adopt. The style should be appropriate to the situation rather than consistent among all situations. The problem with this is that managers may find it difficult to switch between styles, perhaps several times a day. Although the approach appears objective it still depends on the manager answering the questions. Requiring a simple yes or no answer to complex questions is too simple, and managers often want to say 'it all depends' – on other historical or contextual factors.

CASE QUESTIONS 5.6

▶ What style did the manager at Digital Europe adopt?

Nevertheless, the model is still used as a teaching device, even if only to alert managers to the style they prefer to use and to the range of options available. It also prompts managers to consider systematically whether that preferred style is always appropriate. As such, it may help improve managers' awareness, so that they may then handle situations more deliberately than if they had continued to rely only on their preferred style or their intuition.

5.8 Transformational leadership

A newer set of theories focuses on the idea of transformational leadership (see Bass, 1985). These developed from James Burns's influential work which distinguished between what he called transactional and transformational leaders (Burns, 1978). Transactional leaders are those who influence subordinates' behaviour by way of a bargain. The leader enables followers to reach their goals, while at the same time contributing to the goals of the organisation. If subordinates behave in the way desired by the leader, they will receive rewards that they value.

Burns contrasted these approaches with those of transformational leaders. They work in ways that lead subordinates to change their goals, needs and aspirations. Transformational leaders raise the consciousness of followers by appealing to higher ideals and moral values. They do this by displaying a number of identifiable behaviours, such as 'the articulation of transcendent goals, demonstration of self-confidence and confidence in others, setting a personal example for followers, showing high expectations of followers' performance, and the ability to communicate one's faith in one's goals' (Fiedler and House, 1994, p.112). Others (such as Bass, 1985) have identified behaviours aimed at generating emotional arousal (charisma), intellectual stimulation, individual support and encouragement, and inspiration. These behaviours create a positive image in the minds of followers regarding both the leader and the organisational task concerned. Followers then develop emotional responses to transformational leaders such that they are willing to perform beyond the call of duty. They display unusual degrees of trust, admiration, loyalty and confidence in the leader that motivates them to exceed expectations.

The degree to which a leader is transformational depends on the effect on his or her followers. Transformational leaders motivate staff by making them more aware of the importance of task outcomes, and induce them to transcend their self-interest for the sake of the organisation or team. Fiedler and House (1994) claim that empirical research supports the claims for the successes of charismatic leaders. Followers and superiors see them as more effective than transactional leaders.

The effects may be most visible when such leaders play their role at the top of the organisation. However, Burns stressed that people at all levels can display transforming leadership, influencing peers and superiors as well as subordinates. The behaviour refers to developing an organisation-wide process of building commitment to the organisation's objectives, and empowering employees to work towards these objectives.

5.9 Leadership and national culture

The growing internationalisation of business means that managers need to be aware of the different cultures in which they are operating. It is likely to be inappropriate to take management methods from one culture and apply them in another. Managers in different cultures are likely to have different beliefs about the leadership behaviour that is appropriate in organisations.

Suutari (1996) tested this view empirically using questionnaire data from a matched sample of 149 managers from a multinational company in the metal industry with operations in Denmark, Finland, Germany, the UK and Sweden. The questionnaire sought their beliefs about the way a manager ought to behave on fourteen dimensions of leadership derived from earlier studies. Analysis showed that on six of the factors there were statistically significant differences of belief among managers from the five countries. These were:

▶ **Decision participation**   Danish and Finnish managers tend more frequently than German and British managers to see a need to allow subordinates to participate in decision-making.

▶ **Autonomy delegation**   Same pattern as for decision participation.

▶ **Rewarding**   Danish managers tended most frequently to see a need to reward subordinates for good performance.

▶ **Role clarification**   British (and to a lesser extent German) managers tend more frequently than managers from the Nordic countries to see a need for role clarification.

▶ **Conflict management**   British and German managers tend more than Finnish and Danish managers to emphasise conflict management behaviours.

▶ **Individualism**   British and Danish managers were more likely than managers in Finland, Germany and Sweden to see a need for managers to pay personal attention to the hopes and needs of individuals.

Overall, the study supports the view that the national origin of European managers affects their beliefs about leadership. The author suggests that this has implications for the management of multinational companies, in particular that 'management methods developed in one country are applicable in other countries to only a limited extent' (Suutari, 1996, p.405).

5.10 Developing your influencing skills

Throughout life you will be trying to influence others. Here are some suggestions on how you can use the ideas in this chapter to try to influence others. You can practise at various occasions during your course.

What's in it for me?

You can increase your effectiveness in influencing others by being aware of, and answering, the key question to which they want an answer: 'what's in it for me?' People are often stirred into action by the knowledge that they will be better off choosing one behaviour rather than another. Their choices may lie between:

▶ Alternative actions
▶ Doing something or doing nothing
▶ Doing something now or later
▶ Doing it well or just adequately

Better off might mean:

▶ Fewer complaints about their work
▶ Improved relationships
▶ Feeling good about doing a good job
▶ Getting you off their back

What you need to know is the benefit to the other people of what you are proposing or asking them to do. To find this you must listen to their answers to your questions as well as to the information that they may volunteer.

You must also avoid the trap of assuming that your reasons for wanting something are shared by others. This trap shows up when someone lists the reasons for doing something without checking the other person's view.

Advice

▶ Treat each influencing conversation as an attempt to enlist the other person's help to solve a problem which you share.
▶ Ask questions, especially at the start of your conversation, to check understanding.
▶ Listen carefully to the other person to gauge his or her interest in the topic and how it might help you get the action you want.
▶ Forget your own desires and values and try to work out what will switch the other person onto your plan of action.
▶ Ask the other person at the end of your conversation to summarise what they are going to do.

Selling your ideas

▶ **Be prepared**   This refers to your material, your audience and yourself. Whatever the material and however it is to be communicated, it has to be clearly and coherently assembled. You must present it in a way that appeals to this particular audience. You will need to research the audience in advance to find out its current position, to anticipate likely objections and to pre-sell any controversial suggestions. In your own performance you need to play to your strengths and not expose your weaknesses. If a presentation involves other members of a team, make sure that everyone understands his or her role.

▶ **Be focused** Make sure you know exactly what you want to achieve and why. What is the most you can hope for, and the least that you are prepared to accept? If you are making a formal presentation, do not allow the meeting to be diverted by someone with a particular interest. Make it easy for the other side to give you what you want. Let them see that it is in their interest too. Expose the downside and show them how to cope with it. Then, when you have agreement in principle, try to convert it into action immediately. You may not be able to get them to sign the cheque then and there, or leave with a complete timetable, but you must, at the very least, aim for minuted action points and a date for the first follow-up meeting.

▶ **Be flexible** This sounds like the opposite of being focused. It is. Like so many other aspects of the manager's job, you need a preferred strategy and a fall-back position. Occasionally, things go exactly as you planned – a triumph for your focused thinking. But it is more prudent to expect the unexpected and to have plan B tucked away but ready for use.

▶ **Be convinced** Just as salespeople rarely give of their best when they lack confidence in the product they represent, so you should always try to avoid having to put a case you do not believe in. The ideal situation is selling your own ideas in your own words. Quite often you will find yourself having to sell other people's ideas, but you are never obliged to read their text, literally or metaphorically. In fact, it is always best to rework other people's ideas and material if you have to present them. If you are in the awkward position of having to sell a decision you were opposed to, it is imperative that you make your U-turn in private and arrive at the presentation ready to make the case with conviction.

▶ **Be convincing** Effective presentations sound balanced. You need to be able to give arguments against your position in order to refute them. Search for common ground with potential opponents and build on it. Exploit the idea which states that most people will agree to a reasonable request (they know it will not be long before they are asking you for a favour). Be aware that if you come on too strong you run the risk of being turned down completely. Encourage the audience to participate. The more they do, the more convinced they will be of your case.

5.11 Recap

Content agenda

Achieving objectives usually depends on the willing commitment of other people. That depends on management's ability to influence others to display such positive attitudes and behaviour. Objectives that are seen as divisive or serving one interest will undermine that commitment. Conversely, working to develop common and agreed objectives may lead to staff seeing management's use of power as legitimate and acceptable. Transformational leadership methods use higher-level objectives to gain fuller employee commitment. How management seeks to influence others affects people's reaction to being managed. Dominant use of power may ensure compliance, but is the grudging compliance that ensues likely to help achieve the objectives?

Consensus management can provide a source of legitimacy. The structures that are created to support objectives help or hinder the exercise of influence by their effect on the supply of information and resources.

Process agenda

How management seeks to influence others began with a discussion of power and its sources. Hales has developed French and Raven's model to distinguish between personal and institutional sources. Kanter's argument for building power by sharing it was discussed. This led to an examination of how delegation can increase a manager's power by freeing time to build and use external contacts.

Situational approaches offer alternative ways of reaching decisions on plans. The form of action generated depends on accepting power as legitimate, and on employees being willing to accept a particular style. The contingency or situational approaches draw attention to the context in which management influences others, such as task, subordinates and external conditions. Communication both internally and externally is clearly critical to the manager's attempt to influence others – both the end and the means must be undertsood by the target of influence.

Control agenda

Critical perspectives challenge the unequal distribution of power in the wider society that is reproduced and maintained within major organis-

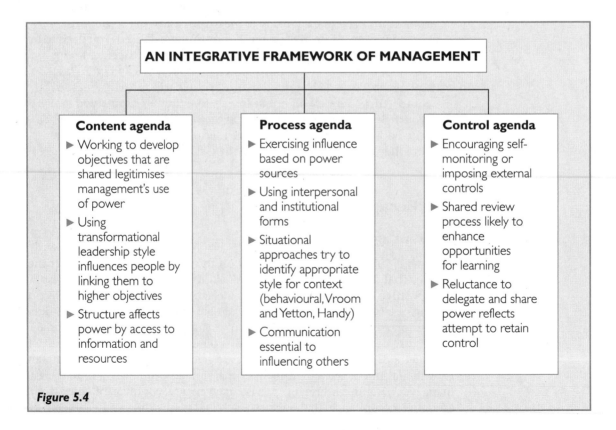

Figure 5.4

AN INTEGRATIVE FRAMEWORK OF MANAGEMENT

Content agenda
- ▶ Working to develop objectives that are shared legitimises management's use of power
- ▶ Using transformational leadership style influences people by linking them to higher objectives
- ▶ Structure affects power by access to information and resources

Process agenda
- ▶ Exercising influence based on power sources
- ▶ Using interpersonal and institutional forms
- ▶ Situational approaches try to identify appropriate style for context (behavioural, Vroom and Yetton, Handy)
- ▶ Communication essential to influencing others

Control agenda
- ▶ Encouraging self-monitoring or imposing external controls
- ▶ Shared review process likely to enhance opportunities for learning
- ▶ Reluctance to delegate and share power reflects attempt to retain control

ations. Control, like decision-making, can be imposed or consensual. The latter approaches imply more self-control and mutual agreement on the basis of measurement. A reluctance to delegate and share power reflects managers' attempts to retain control. Shared review and appraisal are likely to enhance opportunites for learning.

Figure 5.4 summarises these points.

PART CASE QUESTIONS

▶ How does W.L. Gore and Associates influence staff to work on vital projects?

▶ How do research staff influence each other? Compare the way that project managers at Gore and the project managers at Digital Europe influence other members of the company.

▶ How is W.L. Gore and Associates balancing personal and institutional sources of power and influence?

5.12 Review questions

1 Explain in your own words the main sources of power available to managers. Give examples of both personal and institutional forms of each.

2 List the lines of supply which Kanter identifies and give an example of each.

3 Explain in your own words the features that Morgan believes organisations use to maintain order amongst members.

4 Using examples of recruitment brochures from your careers service, compare the traits that employers seek in graduates.

5 What is meant by the phrase a '9,9 manager'?

6 What were the strengths and weaknesses of the behavioural approaches to leadership?

7 Discuss with someone how he or she made a particular decision. Compare this person's approach with one of the situational or contingency approaches to leadership.

8 Evaluate the situational theory in the light of the evidence acquired in question 7 and other considerations.

9 What is meant by transformational leadership, and how is it different from transactional styles?

10 What evidence is there that methods of influence vary between countries?

Further reading

An authoritative review of the leadership literature will be found in Yukl (1994). Handy (1993) includes two chapters on this topic – one on power, and the other on leadership styles. Pettigrew's (1985) account of Harvey-Jones's leadership of change at ICI is worth reading. It shows clearly how Harvey-Jones deliberately created institutional structures to support the power base of key people, rather than rely on personal expertise alone. Additional insights can be gained from reading accounts of the leadership methods used by prominent figures such as Anita Roddick (Roddick, 1991) and Richard Branson (Jackson, 1993). Another widely read source of ideas is Adair (1989).

6

Motivation

CONTENTS

AIM

To examine theories that attempt to explain the behaviour of people at work and to show how such knowledge can affect management practice.

OBJECTIVES

By the end of your work on this chapter you should be able to outline the concepts below in your own terms and:

1   Explain how managers can motivate others by rewards, rules and values

2   Compare the expectations that organisations and their employees may have of each other within the psychological contract

3   Compare behaviour modification theory with other theories of motivation

4   Compare and evaluate the theories of human need proposed by Maslow, Alderfer and McClelland

5   Compare the hygiene and motivation factors identified by Herzberg and use them to evaluate a person's job

6   Explain how self-concept theory can be compared to earlier theories of human needs

7   Evaluate the usefulness of McGregor's Theory X and Theory Y

8   Compare the assumptions believed to be held by western managers and those in other cultures

9   Explain the expectancy and equity theories of motivation

10   Summarise the implications for management of work design theories

The Benefits Agency is responsible for delivering a range of UK state benefits to the public. Most Agency staff work in a network of local offices which are organised into district management units. The 159 districts are organised into 13 area units. Each area director is accountable to the Agency's top management team.

The Benefits Agency used to form part of the Department of Social Security, the largest organisation in the UK civil service. Traditionally, the civil service provided a secure place to work. Staff usually joined straight from school and were expected to follow precisely defined rules in order to ensure equality of treatment to all citizens. The work was routine, and the service valued conformist behaviour: innovation was discouraged. The career path was predictable, jobs were secure, and a pension was guaranteed on retirement. The management structure was hierarchical; any unusual problem was referred up to the next level for decision.

In the early 1990s, government policy brought radical change: the Benefits Agency would become a separate organisation within the civil service. It would conduct the same functions on behalf of government but would be managed differently.

A chief executive was appointed in 1991 on a three-year contract (which in itself sent out signals about the previous jobs for life culture). He defined a new vision:'To provide the right money to the right person at the right time and the right place.' To deliver this more customer-centred service he gave district managers more control over their budget spending, thereby reducing control by senior managers at HQ. Management in some areas ignored the new freedoms and continued to manage in the old, hierarchical way. The area unit described in this study, however, interpreted the freedoms as a licence to do what it wanted. The Area Management Board of one such area defined the area vision as: 'To be the leading provider of Social Security services in the UK'. District managers were encouraged to give more decision-making power to staff dealing with the public, and staff were encouraged to be innovative in their approach. A critical factor in achieving this vision was to have the right number of skilled and motivated staff.

CASE QUESTIONS

▶ What attracted staff to work in the Benefits Agency before these changes?

▶ How do you expect them to react to the changes that were introduced in 1991?

6.1 Introduction

This chapter introduces the following ideas:
▶ Motivation
▶ Perception
▶ Subjective probability
▶ Self-actualisation
▶ Job enrichment
▶ Expectancy theory
▶ Valence
▶ Individual differences
▶ Self-concept

A central activity of management is to generate effort and commitment towards meeting objectives. If management has become a separate and specialised activity then the task is to persuade other people to put in the required effort and commitment. Only if they do so can plans be implemented and objectives achieved. In small-scale organisations with an owner-manager and a few employees, the relationship between manager and managed is close and direct. The manager interacts informally with employees, using a mixture of power resources and personal relationships to generate the required action. As the organisation grows, the links inevitably become less personal. Motivation increasingly depends on more formal institutional arrangements. 'What was previously management through informal, *ad hoc* face-to-face relations becomes management through formal, recurrent, impersonal routines, or management through organisation' (Hales, 1993, p.51).

This greater formalisation affects how management generates commitment by using its power resources. Hales argues that:

> [these] power resources are embodied in three modes of 'institutionalised influence', or motivational mechanisms:
> 1 Rewards, which draw upon economic resources to induce particular forms of behaviour by granting, promising, withholding, or threatening to withhold rewards.
> 2 Rules, which draw upon knowledge resources (information, skills) to induce particular behaviour by persuasion or demonstration. As organisational knowledge takes two distinct forms, so rules may be technical (relating to performance of particular work processes) or administrative (relating to behaviour towards people or events).
> 3 Rationales, or ideologies, which draw upon normative power resources (beliefs, values) to induce particular behaviour by moral force or inspiration. (p.54)

The form that these mechanisms take will vary depending in part on what resources are available. They will also depend on the assumptions that managers make about the likely response of employees to different inducements. People evaluate what management offers and exercise choice. Management cannot assume that others will act as it would wish. Since it will normally want willing and imaginative commitment rather than grudging compliance, management has shown deep interest in theories of motivation, looking to them to try to understand what inducements will bring what kind of reaction.

The term 'motivation' is used in three different ways, and this chapter examines each. One use refers to attempts to identify the needs which people possess and the goals they pursue. These are referred to as *content* theories of motivation. A second use refers to attempts to understand how people decide to take one course of action rather than another in order to achieve their goals. What decision-making routines do they follow and how do they assess the costs and rewards of alternatives? These are referred to as *process* theories. These two approaches could be summed up as 'the things we want and how we choose to obtain them'. A third perspective studies how management has used these theories to influence the behaviour of others. An example would be when a manager tries to influence her staff to improve the quality or quantity of their work: this is the *social influence* perspective on motivation.

Since management is about getting things done with the aid of other people, many managers ask what guidance motivation theories can give them. They want to know how they can ensure that others act as they would like them to. For some people, work is clearly an occasion for hard, enthusiastic and imaginative activity, and a source of rich satisfaction. For others it is something that they do grudgingly. Why such differences occur, and how they can encourage the former rather than the latter, is a pressing issue for many managements, and the stimulus for much research on people at work.

Those with a more critical perspective argue that 'workers need to be influenced to co-operate because of their essential alienation from the productive process' (Thompson and McHugh, 1995, p.304). In addition, they suggest that management typically uses motivation theories to maintain the established power relations between employer and employee. Management often imposes schemes on a relatively passive workforce to make work more interesting. The latter accept them in the absence of realistic alternatives. Staff may even express greater satisfaction with a new arrangement as a way of coming to terms with the inherent stability of the power structure. As always in management, motivation can be viewed from radically different perspectives: it is not a neutral or value-free topic.

Who are managers trying to motivate? Theories of motivation have almost always been presented from the perspective of how the manager can motivate the subordinate. Yet the management job is not just about motivating subordinates. Managers need to influence many other people: colleagues, their own senior managers, or people in other organisations. Managers also try to influence consumers to use the company's products or services – and in order to do so have utilised some of the motivational theories outlined in Chapter 12.

 The Benefits Agency – the case continues

Behaviour that had been valued was now a barrier to promotion. Staff who had hoped to gain promotion by playing to the rules now found they had little chance. Some became disillusioned but continued to deliver – but at a reduced level of productivity. Some could not adapt, and left. Others applied their efforts to a new goal – that of resisting the changes.

Another group responded in a different way. They embraced this new culture where innovation, creativity and risk-taking were valued.

Districts introduced the 'one-stop' approach, so that one member of staff (rather than several) could deal with all the benefits that a person claimed. This led to the creation of multi-function teams, and to big changes in the way staff worked. Staff responded enthusiastically to these changes, even though pay awards were still strictly controlled and promotion opportunities had become fewer.

The mid 1990s brought further changes. A new chief executive was appointed in 1995. In line with the government's policy of controlling public expenditure, the Agency's budget was reduced drastically in 1996. At the same time the National Audit Office, the body responsible for auditing public organisations, criticised the inaccuracy of benefit payments and the scope the system offered for fraud.

The new chief executive amended the Agency's vision to 'pay the right money to the right person at the right time every time'. The top management team became uneasy about the increased freedom of the area directors. Examples of a return to the older structure began to appear, such as the introduction of centrally controlled checking teams and increases in the number of mandatory management checks. Staff in the region reacted with dismay, and management again has the problem of how to create a skilled and motivated staff.

CASE QUESTIONS 6.1

- ▶ What rewards, rules and rationales did management of the Benefits Agency use when it was operating as part of the Department of Social Security?
- ▶ How were these different after the change in approach?
- ▶ How did staff react to the changes?

6.2 Some constants in motivation

There is no shortage of ideas about how to motivate people in organisations. Many theories have initially appeared attractive, but have then proved hard to use in practice or been discredited by the lack of supporting evidence. There is no single or general theory of motivation, and to expect one is a delusion, given the complexity of the organisational feedback loops. However, there are certain constants in motivation theory that apply whatever theory is being outlined, and these are looked at next.

Dependent variables

In studying people at work, we are interested both in their feelings and in their actions: what they think and what they do. The Hawthorne experimenters (see Chapter 2) believed that they had discovered that making people feel satisfied about their work would increase productivity – as seemed to have happened in the group that they studied. The link between satisfaction and productivity is uncertain, though satisfied workers are less likely to leave. We should therefore be careful to keep the two concepts – affective reactions and behavioural reactions – distinct. They appear to be influenced in different ways by other factors. Affective reactions refer to variables such as people's attitudes, their sense of satisfaction with their job, their feelings about their colleagues or about their career. Behavioural reactions are more easily observed: they include tangible, visible responses such as whether people have turned up for work, how well they perform or their willingness to take on new responsibilities.

Katz and Kahn (1978) distinguished four aspects of behaviour at work. They relate to a person's willingness:

- **To be physically available for work**   This reflects choices that people have made about whether to join the organisation and then whether to stay with it. They make further choices about whether to turn up for work rather than be absent for reasons other than sickness, and whether they turn up on time or are persistently late.
- **To perform a given, defined task**   This reflects choices that people make about whether to perform to the required standards of work in terms of quantity, cost, quality or timeliness.
- **To perform a defined new task**   The choices that people make here concern their willingness to change their method of working, to change their place or times of work, or to work more as a member of a team than as an individual.
- **To perform a range of tasks, including those not specifically defined in the role**   This refers to whether people are willing to act with initiative, imagination and responsibility in the light of the situation. Are they able and willing to help others unexpectedly and to cope with new or unexpected circumstances?

Most jobs will require some elements of each type of behaviour, although the proportion and relative importance will differ. In each case, staff will choose how enthusiastically they meet these expectations. Management practices may encourage some actions and discourage others in the list above. If they install time-recording devices and penalties for lateness, this will usually encourage people to turn up on time. What effect will it have on their willingness to use initiative and imagination?

---

n o t e b o o k   6.1

Identify a time when you were working in an organisation, or think of your work as a student. Describe what was expected of you in that job in terms of attendance, output, behaviour and use of initiative.

Which of these did the organisation see as most important aspects of your work? What specific policies or practices did the organisation use to encourage these? What were their effects?

Alternatively, ask these questions of someone who has managed other people, or consider them in a situation when you were responsible for managing others.

Purposeful behaviour

A common assumption in theories of work motivation is that behaviour has a purpose and is directed towards certain goals. People are assumed to have goals and to act in ways which they expect will help to achieve them. They make these choices in the light of their experience and their perception of the situation they are in. The assumption may be incorrect but it underlies attempts to use motivation theories in practice. Much behaviour is also fairly routine, and based on habit, precedent and unconscious scripts. Motivational theories are attempts to understand the 'precedent-setting decisions, the new decisions' rather than the routine and habitual.

Psychological contract

The psychological contract is the set of understandings people have regarding the commitments made between themselves and their organisation.

Managers have expectations of the people who work for them. At the same time, employees have expectations of managers – not just on pay, but also on such things as fairness, trust and opportunities for self-development. This set of mutual expectations makes up the psychological contract.

The psychological contract expresses the idea that each side has certain expectations of the other, regarding what they will give and what they will receive in return. Employers offer certain kinds of reward in the hope of receiving certain types and levels of performance. Employees contribute effort in the expectation of reward. Psychological contracts express what both sides expect from the employment relationship. Some elements in the contract express written agreements. Most express the outcome of a continuing process of mutual adjustment between the parties. They have no legal status, and are in essence subjective and informal. They are also dynamic, as changes in the circumstances of both parties mean that they continually adjust the contract – people fill in the blanks along the way (Rousseau, 1995). This adjustment process is both inevitable and a source of difficulty, especially if the employer changes the contract in a way that makes employees feel worse off. As Kolb *et al.* (1991) remarked, 'a company staffed by "cheated" individuals who expect far more than they get is headed for trouble'.

At a time of great change in the business world, many employees feel that their psychological contract with their employer is being broken. For example, many school-leavers joined banks expecting that if they performed adequately the bank would employ them until retirement. Technological changes and increased competition has led senior managements to make fundamental changes in their employment policies. Many staff have been made redundant years before they would otherwise have expected to leave. The job has changed for those who remain: they are under great pressure to sell a range of financial services, rather than being expected to handle customers' routine financial transactions. This point is raised again in section 6.5.

CASE QUESTIONS 6.2

▶ In the 1980s, what were the main elements of the psychological contract between the DSS and its employees? List what each was expecting of the other.

▶ How did that change in the early 1990s?

▶ How did staff respond?

▶ Are there possible links between that response and later events in the organisation?

▶ Are there any lessons which that suggests?

Perception

Perception is the active psychological process in which stimuli are selected and organised into meaningful patterns.

People's actions are influenced by their perception of reality and its meaning to them, not by some objective or factual reality.

We are subject to a stream of information beyond our capacity to absorb. We try to remain sane by the process of *selection*. We actively notice and attend to only a small fraction of the available information, filtering out what we do not need. Factors such as the strength of the signal or the reputation of the person sending it influence what we select.

Even when people observe a common piece of information they may interpret it differently, and react to it in different ways. This perceptual *organisation* allows incoming signals to be arranged into patterns which give some meaning to the information. For example, we can compare it with similar cases in our experience. We often reach conclusions about people on very limited information: we may categorise them on the basis of their profession or for whom they have worked. Others use categorisation schemes reflecting their experience, social class, education or career plans. Whatever the reason, a safe assumption is that what people do is influenced by their perception and interpretation of a situation, and these are likely to be different from those held by other people. Therefore, in trying to understand people's behaviour it is essential to try to see the situation from their point of view, and to consider how that view affects what they do.

Situational factors

The context in which people work is another influence on motivation. We cannot understand what individuals do in isolation from their current and historical context, and how they see and interpret that context. Three factors can be identified:

▶ The **job** itself, e.g. how interesting, varied, responsible it is.
▶ The **organisation**, e.g. supervision, career and promotion, pay systems.
▶ The **environment**, e.g. the chances of getting another job.

All these factors, as well as those relating to their domestic circumstances, influence the choice of behaviour. Figure 6.1 draws together the main points. Although useful, this framework contains several problems. For example:

▶ Needs and expectations can only be inferred.
▶ They may change over time, and there may be conflicts between them.
▶ What is the effect of achieving, or failing to achieve, a goal on future needs and expectations?

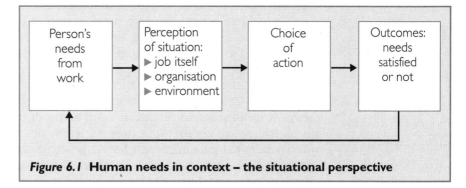

Figure 6.1 **Human needs in context – the situational perspective**

6.3 Behaviour modification

The label 'behaviour modification' refers to a range of techniques which were developed to help treat various psychological conditions such as eating disorders or heavy smoking. They have also been used in organisational settings to deal with issues such as lateness or absenteeism.

The techniques have developed from Skinner's (1971) theory that people are motivated by reinforcement. If they find that they are rewarded for doing something then they will tend to repeat that behaviour. If they experience something unpleasant as a result of a certain action then they will tend not to repeat that action.

Hence behavioural modification techniques focus on specific observable behaviours rather than on attitudes and feelings. They try to identify what leads a person to act in a particular way and what reward he or she experiences as a result of the behaviour. If the influencer sees the behaviour as undesirable, he or she may try to influence the person to change by affecting the rewards that are obtained.

To influence the person to change, the first steps help to pinpoint three relevant aspects of the situation:

▶ The specific behaviour that is undesirable (persistent lateness or carelessness, for example).
▶ The external events, or cues (perhaps Monday, or a particular type of work) which consistently precede the behaviour and appear to trigger it.
▶ The pay-off that the person gets from the behaviour and which encourages him or her to repeat it (for example, avoids unpleasant work and is not disciplined).

The focus then shifts to:

▶ Defining a desirable behaviour given the person's role and responsibilities.
▶ Deciding how to change the cues so that desirable behaviour (for example, being on time) is more likely and undesirable behaviour less so (such as by making the work more interesting and desirable, providing training).
▶ Deciding how the present pay-off can be changed to encourage desirable behaviour and discourage undesirable (such as by rewarding timely and effective performance with public recognition, increased status, promotion opportunities, and punishing the undesirable behaviour in some way).

Practitioners emphasise several principles used in the approach. The pay-offs (benefits) must be given only when the desired behaviour occurs. They must also be used as soon as possible after the behaviour, so that the link between behaviour and reward is evident. Desirable behaviour is likely to be repeated if reinforced by rewards. Reinforcement is more effective than punishment, as punishment only temporarily suppresses behaviour. Repeated reinforcement can lead to permanent change in behaviour in the desired direction.

Above all, proponents of the approach stress the need to reward desirable behaviours rather than to treat them with indifference. These rewards can result either from individual action by a manager, or through some more formal, institutionalised procedures. Advocates of the method believe that people behave to obtain what they want but do not have. It encourages management to look directly at what is likely to make a particular person act in a desirable way, and to ensure those rewards are available. For the behaviour to be sustained, the rewards must also be sustained.

Behaviour modification is a general label for attempts to change behaviour by using appropriate and timely reinforcement.

In practice, management policy can:

▶ reinforce undesirable behaviours

▶ fail to reinforce desirable behaviour

▶ reinforce desirable behaviour.

A benefit claimed of the approach is that anyone can use it to establish norms of behaviour. As these are reinforced, they become more habitual so that standards and precedents reflect a collectively understanding. The method depends on identifying rewards that the person will value (or punishments that they will try to avoid). This then indicates the kinds of reinforcement and punishment to use. Theories that attempt to understand these are known as content theories of motivation.

6.4 Content theories of motivation

Most writers on this topic have been attempting to identify and list various motivating *factors*, for example to establish what classes of needs are held by people and which are likely to influence their behaviour. For example, Frederick Taylor (see Chapter 2) clearly believed in the primacy of the individual financial incentive. Employees would follow the strictly laid down methods if management linked rewards to their output. The work of Frank Gilbreth helped to develop the systems for introducing such payment-by-results systems very widely.

---

n o t e b o o k   6.2

Was Taylor wrong?

Many managements believe that money is a powerful incentive. Find someone who works for an organisation where incentives or commissions make up a significant part of that person's pay and ask how that affects his or her behaviour, and whether there are any negative effects.

Chapter 2 described how writers such as Mary Parker Follett and Elton Mayo emphasised aspects of motivation other than money, especially the need for acceptance by other people. This can be seen in the workplace when groups develop a common understanding about the level of output that they regard as acceptable. They can then ensure that members stick to that level. If people value membership of the group more than the financial incentive, they will conform. Mayo in particular drew attention to the social motivations of people at work, and stressed that management should foster these rather than try to counter them by individual incentives.

Abraham Maslow – a hierarchy of needs

Maslow was a clinical psychologist who developed a theory of human motivation to help him understand the needs of his patients. He stressed the clinical sources of the theory and that it lacked experimental verification. He also observed that Douglas McGregor (see below) had applied the theory to industrial situations and had found it useful in ordering his data and observations.

Maslow proposed that individuals experience a range of needs, and will be motivated to fulfil whichever need is most powerful at the time (Maslow, 1970). What he termed the lower-order needs are dominant until they are at least partially satisfied. Then, Maslow predicted, normal individuals would turn their attention to satisfying the needs at the next level, and so on, so that the higher-order needs would gradually become dominant. He referred to these needs as being arranged in a hierarchy:

Self-actualisation

Esteem

Belongingness and love

Safety

Physiological

Physiological needs are the needs whose satisfaction is essential for survival – food and water particularly. Maslow proposed that if all the needs in the hierarchy are unsatisfied then the physiological needs will dominate. Capacities that are not useful for satisfying the physiological needs will remain dormant and people will concentrate on activities which enable them to obtain the necessities of life. The hierarchical nature of the theory also suggests that, until people have the basic necessities they will not respond to opportunities to satisfy the higher needs.

Maslow believed that once the physiological needs were sufficiently gratified, a new set of needs would emerge. He termed these the *safety needs* – the search for

> security; stability; dependency; protection; freedom from fear, anxiety and chaos; need for structure, order, law, limits ... and so on. (p.39)

People concentrate on satisfying these needs, to the exclusion of other considerations. For example, they may seek a stable, regular job with secure working conditions and access to insurance for ill-health and retirement. They resent sudden or random changes in job prospects. Again, Maslow implied that until people had satisfied their need for security they would not pursue higher-level needs.

Belongingness needs would follow the satisfaction of safety needs:

> [If] both the physiological and the safety needs are fairly well gratified, there will emerge the love and affection and belongingness needs ... now the person will feel keenly the absence of friends ... and will hunger for affectionate relations with people in general. (p.43)

These needs include a place in the group or family. People will also feel sharply the pangs of loneliness, rejection and rootlessness. People seeking to satisfy these needs at work want to be part of a congenial team. They may also value opportunities to feel that they are part of the wider life of the organisation, through social gatherings after work or by receiving a company newspaper. They are likely to object to any attempt to change work-patterns or locations if this would cut across an established set of working relationships. They are likely to welcome change that brings them closer to people they know and like.

Maslow then argued that most people have *esteem needs*. He identified two aspects in this evaluation: self-respect and the respect of others. Self-respect referred to a need for a sense of achievement, competence, adequacy, confidence in the face of the world, for independence and freedom. In addition, he believed that people would seek the respect of others, what he called a desire for reputation in the eyes of other people – prestige, status, recognition, attention. Satisfying the esteem needs

> leads to feelings of self-confidence, worth, adequacy ... of being useful and necessary in the world. But thwarting these needs produces feelings of inferiority, weakness and helplessness. (p.45)

In work, people may try to satisfy these needs by seeking opportunities to take on challenging or difficult tasks that will show that they are good at their job and can accomplish something worthwhile. They hope that others recognise this, and so earn status and respect.

Lastly, Maslow used the term *self-actualisation needs* to refer to the desire for self-fulfilment and for realising potential. He pointed out that the specific form this takes will vary: in one person it may take the form of the desire to be

> an ideal mother, in another it may be expressed athletically, and in still another it may be expressed in painting pictures or in inventions. At this level, individual differences are greatest. The clear emergence of these needs usually rests upon some prior satisfaction of the physiological, safety, love, and esteem needs. (pp.46–7)

This implies that people seeking to satisfy self-actualisation needs will look for personal relevance in their work. They may value new responsibilities that help them realise their potential or discover unknown talents.

To illustrate Maslow's hierarchy with a practical example, a member of staff at the Benefits Agency summarised the ways in which the organisation had traditionally satisfied the different needs (Table 6.1).

C A S E   Q U E S T I O N S   6 . 3

▶ Which needs were being met, and in what ways, under the new policy at the Benefits Agency?

Maslow did *not* claim that the hierarchy was a fixed or rigid scheme. His clinical experience suggested that most people with whom he had worked had these needs in about this order. He had also seen exceptions. There had been people for whom self-esteem was more important than love. For others, creativeness took precedence in that they did not seek self-actualisation once they had satisfied their basic needs, but in spite of these *not* being satisfied. Others had such permanently low aspirations that they experienced life at a very basic level.

He also cautioned against the impression that as people satisfy one need completely another emerges. Rather, he proposed that most normal people are at the same time partially satisfied and partially unsatisfied in their needs. This implied that a more accurate description of the hierarchy would be in terms of decreasing percentages of satisfaction at successive levels. So a person could think of himself as being, say, 85 per cent satisfied at

Table 6.1 Maslow's hierarchy of needs applied to the Benefits Agency under the traditional system

Needs	How they were met
Physiological	Good working conditions Steady incremental salary
Safety	Attractive non-contributory pension Safe working conditions 'No redundancy' policy Payment for absence due to illness
Belongingness relationships	Sports and social clubs (local and national) Office parties/outings Permission for informal activities
Esteem	Regarded in society as a good job Grade prestige Promotion
Self-actualisation	Promotion opportunities (steady and fast-track) Funding and time off for further education

the physiological level and 70 per cent at the safety level (though the percentages themselves are, of course, meaningless). Moreover, the emergence of a higher-level need was not a sudden event. Rather, a person would gradually become aware that a higher need could now be attained.

In summary, Maslow believed that people are motivated to satisfy those needs that are important to them at that point in their life, and offers a description of those needs. The strength of a particular need would depend on the extent to which needs lower in the hierarchy had been met. In particular, he stressed the importance of the physiological needs, which he believed most people would seek to satisfy first, before the others became operative. Self-actualisation was fulfilled last and least often, although he had observed exceptions.

n o t e b o o k   6.3.

Compare Maslow's theory with the ideas of Frederick Taylor and Elton Mayo. Write down where they are similar and where are they different.

To what extent do your studies and related activities on your course satisfy needs identified by Maslow? Does that reflection tend to support or contradict his theory?

What evidence can you gather from your colleagues on the relative importance to them at present of the elements in the hierarchy?

How does Maslow's approach compare with Skinner's? Skinner believed that by providing positive reinforcement (or punishment), people would be motivated to act in a particular way. The rewards they obtained would enable them to satisfy their needs. Maslow took the slightly different position that people would seek to satisfy their needs by acting in a particular way. They satisfied their needs directly by behaving in particular ways. Both theorists believe that to change behaviour it would be necessary to change the situation. Skinner emphasised that this would take the form of positive reinforcement to satisfy needs. Maslow implied that influencers should provide conditions which enable to people to satisfy their needs from the activity.

Clayton Alderfer – ERG theory

Doubtful about the empirical support for the hierarchy of motives proposed by Maslow, Alderfer developed another approach (Alderfer, 1972). His work both built on Maslow's ideas and presented an alternative to them. He developed and tested his theory in questionnaire and interview-based studies carried out in a variety of organisations with the co-operation of their managements. The settings included a manufacturing firm, a bank, two colleges and a school. He aimed to identify the primary needs – those which an organism possesses by the nature of being the type of creature it is. Satisfaction refers to the internal state of someone who has obtained what he or she is seeking. Frustration is the opposite – when someone seeks something but does not find it.

Existence needs reflect a person's requirement for material and energy exchange with his or her environment. They therefore include all the various forms of material and physiological desires – hunger and thirst represent deficiencies in existence needs. Pay and benefits of various kinds represent ways of satisfying – through the process of getting enough of – material requirements.

Relatedness needs involve relationships with significant other people – family members, colleagues, bosses, subordinates, team members, regular customers and so on. It includes groups and individuals. People satisfy their relatedness needs through processes of sharing thoughts and feelings. The essential conditions are willingness to share these as fully as possible, while trying to enable the others to do the same. Acceptance, confirmation and understanding are elements in this process of satisfying relatedness needs.

Growth needs are those which impel a person to be creative or to produce an effect on himself and his environment. People satisfy these needs by engaging with problems that call upon them to use their skills fully, or even require them to develop new ones. People experience a greater sense of completeness when they have satisfied their growth needs. That satisfaction depends on finding the opportunity to exercise talents to the full.

NOTICEBOARD **The seven major propositions of Alderfer's ERG theory**

P1 The less that existence needs are satisfied, the more they will be desired.

P2 The less that relatedness needs are satisfied, the more existence needs will be desired.

P3 The more that existence needs are satisfied, the more relatedness needs will be desired.

P4 The less that relatedness needs are satisfied, the more they will be desired.

P5 The less that growth needs are satisfied, the more relatedness needs will be desired.

P6 The more that relatedness needs are satisfied, the more growth needs will be desired.

P7 The more that growth needs are satisfied, the more they will be desired.

Source: Alderfer (1972)

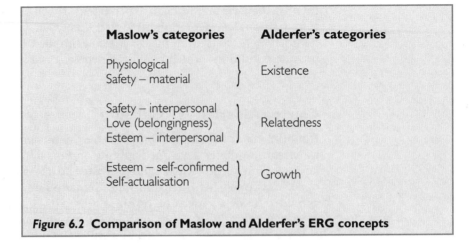

Figure 6.2 **Comparison of Maslow and Alderfer's ERG concepts**

Alderfer showed how his formulation of needs compared with that put forward by Maslow. Figure 6.2 summarises his discussion of the point.

Alderfer proposed that his three categories of need are active in everyone, although in varying degrees of strength. There is no hierarchical relationship between the needs, but there are propositions relating lower-level need satisfaction to higher-level desires, and vice versa – see the Noticeboard.

The most important difference from Maslow that Alderfer proposed was to break away from the idea that needs form a hierarchy. Alderfer's research suggested instead that if higher needs are frustrated, lower needs will become prominent again, even if they have already been satisfied. This contrasts with Maslow's view that once a need had been satisfied it ceased to be a motivator. Where Maslow saw people moving up a hierarchy of needs, Alderfer envisages people moving among the three needs as conditions change.

Both theories are hard to test empirically – at least in part because of the problem of establishing operationally whether a person has satisfied a need and how that would be known. The theories' value is in drawing together earlier theories that had postulated people being motivated by a single need, and suggesting a more varied pattern of needs which people may seek to satisfy at work.

David McClelland

McClelland (1961) and his colleagues have examined how people think and react in a wide range of situations. This work led them to identify three categories of human need, which individuals possess in different amounts:

- ▶ **Need for affiliation**   The need to develop and maintain interpersonal relationships.
- ▶ **Need for power**   The need to be able to influence and control others and to shape events.
- ▶ **Need for achievement**   The need to take personal responsibility, and to be able to show successful task results.

McClelland used the Thematic Apperception Test to assess how significant these categories were to people. People taking part in the research were shown pictures with a neutral subject and asked to write a story about the picture. The researchers then coded the stories and claimed they could then estimate the relative importance to the person of the affiliation, power and achievement motives.

You can assess your scores on these motives by completing the task in Notebook 6.4.

---

n o t e b o o k   6 . 4

From each of the four sets of statements below, choose the one which is most like you.

1 (a) I set myself difficult goals which I attempt to reach.
   (b) I am happiest when I am with a group of people who enjoy life.
   (c) I like to organise the activities of a group or team.

2 (a) I only completely enjoy relaxation after the successful completion of exacting pieces of work.
   (b) I become attached to my friends.
   (c) I argue zealously against others for my point of view.

3 (a) I work hard until I am completely satisfied with the result I achieve.
   (b) I like to mix with a group of congenial people, talking about any subject which comes up.
   (c) I tend to influence others more than they influence me.

4 (a) I enjoy working as much as I enjoy my leisure.
   (b) I go out of my way to be with my friends.
   (c) I am able to dominate a social situation.

Now add your responses as follows:

The number of (a) responses (   ) Achievement
The number of (b) responses (   ) Affiliation
The number of (c) responses (   ) Power

This simple exercise will give you an insight both into the differences between McClelland's three types of motive and into your preference. The larger your score in an area, the more likely your preference is in that area. Compare your answers with others whom you know in the class. Discuss whether the results are in line with what you would have expected, given what you already know of each other.

Source: based on Jackson (1993)

Frederick Herzberg – two-factor theory

Frederick Herzberg provided another perspective on motivation which is frequently cited (Herzberg, 1959). He developed his theory following interviews with 200 engineers and accountants about their experience of work. The interviewees were first asked to recall a time when they had felt exceptionally good about their job. Further questions probed for the events that had preceded those feelings. The respondents were then asked to recall a time when they had felt particularly bad about their work. Again the interviewers probed for the background to these negative feelings. When the team analysed the interviews they observed that when the respondents had talked about good times, five factors appeared frequently. These were:

▶ Achievement
▶ Recognition

- ▶ Work itself
- ▶ Responsibility
- ▶ Advancement

These factors appeared much less frequently when people were describing the bad times. When the team analysed the events preceding times of dissatis-faction, an entirely different set of factors emerged:

- ▶ Company policy and administration
- ▶ Supervision
- ▶ Salary
- ▶ Interpersonal relations
- ▶ Working conditions

These factors appeared much less frequently when the respondents were recalling satisfying work experiences.

Herzberg concluded that the factors associated with satisfaction seemed to describe people's relationship to what they were doing. They included factors like the nature of the task, responsibility carried or recognition received. He renamed these satisfiers 'motivators' as he believed that his evidence showed they influenced the individual to superior performance and effort. The second set, associated with dissatisfaction, seemed to relate to the circumstances surrounding the work – he labelled these the 'hygiene' or 'maintenance' factors. They served primarily to prevent dissatisfaction, rather than to foster positive attitudes. His results are illustrated in Figure 6.3.

In summary, he concluded that the factors that produce job satisfaction are separate and distinct from those which lead to job dissatisfaction, hence the term 'two-factor' theory. He suggested that, despite the terminology used, the concepts of satisfaction and dissatisfaction are not opposites, but separate dimensions. They are influenced by different factors. He drew an analogy: since vision is stimulated by light, increasing sound will have no effect on a person's vision, though it will affect hearing. Thus he argued that the factors that lead to job satisfaction (achievement, recognition, work itself, responsibility and advancement) contribute very little to job dissatis-faction. Conversely, the dissatisfiers (company policy and administration, supervision, salary, interpersonal relations and working conditions) contribute very little to job satisfaction.

Herzberg explained this by his observation that when respondents were feeling dissatisfied, their replies indicated that it was often because they felt that management had treated them unfairly. When they were satisfied, it was because they were experiencing feelings of psychological growth and gaining a sense of self-actualisation. So a 'hygienic' environment with fair policies can prevent discontent and dissatisfaction but will not in itself contribute to psychological growth and hence satisfaction. Such positive feelings could only come, he argued, from the nature of the task itself, and the opportunities for growth that it offers.

---

n o t e b o o k   6.5

Evaluate the empirical base of Herzberg's research as described here. What are the main reservations you would have about the wider applicability of the theory?

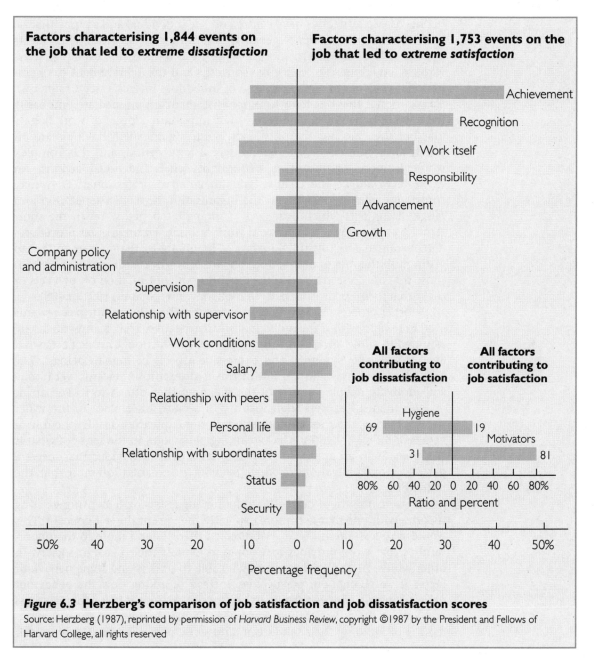

***Figure 6.3* Herzberg's comparison of job satisfaction and job dissatisfaction scores**
Source: Herzberg (1987), reprinted by permission of *Harvard Business Review*, copyright ©1987 by the President and Fellows of Harvard College, all rights reserved

Herzberg's ideas encouraged management in many organisations to redesign jobs as a way of enhancing performance. This approach is discussed in section 6.8.

Self-concept in motivation theory

Shamir (1991) has pointed out some weaknesses in traditional need theories of motivation. He argues they have an individualistic and instrumental bias. They seek to explain motivation in terms of the individual satisfying his or her needs. Most theories have centred on the individual and assume that he or she is aiming to maximise personal gain from work activities. This reflects a cultural bias in western models – Japanese models, for example, stress workers' attachment to collective concerns and the achievement of organisational goals, even at the expense of individual interests (see Chapter 3). Conventional theories tend to emphasise relatively immediate and easily measurable behaviours. These are often important aspects of work behaviour but they are not the only ones. Some significant behaviours are, in effect, an accumulation of actions over a long period, and this complex whole is more significant to performance than individual actions. An example would be the creative and imaginative professional. They may contribute valuable insights to the organisation or have a reputation and range of contacts which bring real if intangible benefits. Yet in the short term he or she may rarely arrive at work on time, ignore regular procedures and operate in a highly individual way. Shamir argues that 'it is important to distinguish theories of motivation that are concerned with specific acts from those that are concerned with the repetition or continuation of such acts or those that focus on broader patterns of behaviour' (Shamir, 1991, p.408).

Another problem is that theories that stress the value of intrinsic rewards tend to remain within the individualistic perspective. That is, individuals are assumed to value rewards for their personal satisfaction. This neglects what Shamir calls the 'symbolic and expressive aspects of human beings'. The immediate task may contain few intrinsic (or extrinsic) rewards, yet it may still motivate people because of the meaning they attach to it. Perhaps it enables them to express their identity or secures their place in the wider society. Finally, theories of motivation do not explicitly consider the role of values or moral obligations in explaining behaviour, in the sense of what is desirable. Such an approach may help to explain behaviour that meets a person's moral obligations or which benefits the organisation more than the individual.

To overcome these difficulties, Shamir suggests supplementing existing theories with one that uses more explicitly the idea of the self-concept. This would give less attention to goal-directed theories and more to the opportunities that work provides for people to express their place in society. In other words, he argues that we may be able to understand some behaviour better if we change our perspective. Instead of asking how the behaviour helps people to achieve their goals, we should ask how it helps them express or maintain their view of themselves. People may do things as away of maintaining or building their self-esteem and sense of self-worth. The approach stresses the importance of the self-concept, not so much related to individual actions, but to broad patterns of behaviour that a person consistently displays. Shamir sets out the assumptions on which such a theory rests:

Humans are not only goal-oriented but also self-expressive.
▶ People are motivated to maintain and enhance their self-esteem and self-
▶ worth.
People are also motivated to retain and increase their sense of self-
▶ consistency.
Self-concepts are composed in part of identities (which locate the self in
▶ recognisable categories within society).
Self-concept based behaviour is not always related to clear expectations
▶ or to immediate and specific goals.

NOTICEBOARD Shamir's propositions on job motivation

On the basis of his discussion, Shamir proposes that a person's general job motivation will be enhanced if:

▶ Job-related identities are a significant feature within the person's self-concept (that is, work matters to them).

▶ The job offers opportunities for enhancing self-esteem.

▶ The job offers opportunities for increased self-worth.

▶ Actions required on the job enhance or maintain the person's self-concept.

▶ Career opportunities on the job are consistent with the person's 'possible selves' (that is, the way they see themselves developing in future).

Conversely, job motivation will be lower to the extent that:

▶ The job or its context contains elements that are detrimental to the person's self-esteem.

▶ The job or its context contain elements that are detrimental to the person's self-worth.

Source: based on Shamir (1991, p.416)

Shamir stresses that a self-concept based theory would not apply to all people or to all kinds of work behaviour. It is most likely to apply to those who see work as part of an expression of their identity. It is less likely to apply to those who see work as an instrument for satisfying other needs. It is also likely to be better at explaining general work motivation – the motivation to invest effort in the work role – whatever the current job being undertaken. It will do so particularly in situations where goals are unspecified, means are unclear and rewards not clearly linked to performance.

The perspective complements earlier work on motivation. It may help to account for behaviour that benefits the group or organisation, rather than an individual's calculation of his or her self-interest. It focuses on the meaning that people attach to work in terms of the values and identities it supports. Values (such as group loyalty or commitment to the organisation) and identities (as a member of a valued service or prestigious organisation) are important to the person, who attempts to build or confirm these through his or her work behaviour. Management may thus be able to influence behaviour by creating strong values and enabling employees to express their identity through their work. Management can influence by ensuring that work provides opportunities for individuals to satisfy their self-concept through their work, noting that that self-concept is much broader than instrumental gratification of individual needs in the short run. It is also linked to transformational theories of leadership. These emphasise how the leader can enable individuals to act towards a vision beyond themselves and their immediate needs (as distinct from the transactional perspective on leadership – see Chapter 5).

C A S E   Q U E S T I O N S   6 . 4

▶ What evidence is there in the case to support Shamir's theory that some people are motivated by work that provides an opportunity to express their view of themselves and their place in society?

6.5 Management assumptions about people

Douglas McGregor

As management attempts to influence others, it must make some assumptions about how employees will react to different types of rewards, rules or norms. These assumptions will guide the organisational arrangements that they put in place to encourage the behaviour they require.

Douglas McGregor (1960) developed this idea in his book *The Human Side of Enterprise*. In this he argued that 'every managerial act rests on assumptions, generalisations and hypotheses – that is to say, on theory' (p.6). Such assumptions are often implicit and unconscious – but nevertheless shape managers' predictions that if they do *a*, then *b* will occur. The theories may or may not be adequate but it is impossible to reach a managerial decision, or take a managerial action uninfluenced by them. 'The insistence on being "practical" really means "Let's accept *my* theoretical assumptions without argument or test"' (p.7).

McGregor went on to present two contrasting sets of assumptions underlying management policy and practice. Theory X, which he called the traditional view of direction and control, expresses the following implicit assumptions:

Theory X
- ▶ The average human being has an inherent dislike of work and will avoid it if he can.
- ▶ Because of this human characteristic, most people must be coerced, controlled, directed, threatened with punishment to get them to put forth adequate effort towards the achievement of organisational objectives.
- ▶ The average human being prefers to be directed, wishes to avoid responsibility, has relatively little ambition, wants security above all.

McGregor was critical of these assumptions. He believed that they led to a management strategy towards people which ignored the full range of possible human needs. Theory X assumptions concentrated on only the lower-level needs which Maslow had by then identified. He believed that managers who accepted a Theory X view would fail to discover, let alone use, the potentialities of the average human being.

He then pointed out that accumulating knowledge about human behaviour made it possible to suggest a 'modest beginning for new theory about the management of human resources' (p.47). This he termed Theory Y – the integration of individual and organisational goals – which expressed a different set of assumptions:

Theory Y
- ▶ The expenditure of physical and mental effort in work is as natural as play or rest.
- ▶ External control and the threat of punishment are not the only means of bringing about effort towards organisational objectives. Man will exercise self-direction and self-control in the service of objectives to which he is committed.
- ▶ Commitment to objectives is a function of the rewards associated with their achievement.

- ▶ The average human being learns, under proper conditions, not only to accept, but also to seek, responsibility.
- ▶ The capacity to exercise a relatively high degree of imagination, ingenuity and creativity in the solution of organisational problems is widely, not narrowly, distributed in the population.
- ▶ Under the conditions of modern industrial life, the intellectual potentialities of the average human being are only partially utilised.

The contrasts between the two sets of assumptions are clear. Those who hold to Theory X believe that people have an inherent dislike of work, are lazy, unambitious, prefer to be directed and will avoid responsibility whenever they can. Work is of secondary importance to them, so managers must coerce them with money or other extrinsic rewards. Common practices associated with a Theory X philosophy include time-recording systems, close supervision, quality checked by someone other than the person doing the work, narrowly defined jobs and precise job descriptions. The central principle of Theory X is that of external control, by systems, procedures or supervision.

In contrast, the central principle of Theory Y is that of integration. It advocates 'the creation of conditions such that the members of the organisation can achieve their own goals *best* by directing their efforts towards the success of the enterprise' (p.49). Managers who hold to Theory Y believe that work is a natural activity which in the right conditions can provide great satisfaction – and see it as part of their job to create those conditions. They believe that people can accept responsibility, and apply imagination, ingenuity and creativity to organisational problems. McGregor argued that a problem of the modern organisation is that it does not tap the creative ability of its staff. To take advantage of these hidden assets, managers should be more willing to provide employees with scope to use their talents. They should be less prescriptive and directive. They should create the conditions that integrate individual and organisational goals.

case example   Motivating sales teams

I work as a sales manager for a medium-sized pharmaceutical company with a team of six. My role is to achieve maximum sales using the resources available. The company sets activity targets – 'more calls means more sales' is a favourite slogan. This produces a problem, as there are doctors who are readily available, but who are unlikely to produce business: others are less available but have more potential. Do we follow the company strategy or do things the way our experience tells us will work better?

Management has structured the company on Theory X assumptions. We are told what we are expected to achieve, and how we are expected to achieve them. There are few opportunities for us to express a view. We meet the senior people about twice a year. The meetings usually have a rushed agenda, and seem to be a way of telling us what will happen, rather than encouraging discussion on what should happen. They ask us to write two-monthly reports, but the points we raise seldom get a reply.

Another company in the industry is now taking a different approach. This involves each salesperson developing his or her business plan. They have considerably more autonomy to use their ideas. The trade-off is that the consequences of failure are more severe, and this will not suit everyone – it is a different psychological contract with which they are working. The curious thing is that that company had been very successful with an earlier approach, which was like ours. But the market is experiencing its biggest ever change, and shifting responsibility to salespeople who are in constant contact with customers has a considerable advantage.

---

n o t e b o o k   6.6

Write down the Theory X assumptions demonstrated in the first company, and the Theory Y ones in the second.

Make a list of management practices which you have experienced which reflect the assumptions of Theory X and Theory Y respectively. What were their effects?

Can you identify someone who behaves in a way consistent with Theory X, and someone else who behaves according to Theory Y? Did this reflect the way they themselves were managed, or some other reason?

Although McGregor expressed the view that Theory Y assumptions were the most appropriate ones for effective management, others have challenged this. They argue that Theory Y assumptions may be as inappropriate in some circumstances as Theory X assumptions are in others. Lorsch and Morse (1970) first raised this prospect following their comparative study of management practices in four companies. Two were in routine operations, at which one was successful and one was not. The other two were in highly creative businesses, and again one was successful, the other not. They concluded that the successful company in the routine business used a consistent Theory X style. The successful company in the creative business used a Theory Y style.

6.6 Individual and national differences

The patterns of needs differ significantly between people, and any attempt to understand motivation must take account of this. The relative importance of a need is likely to change over time as people's commitments and interests change. Young people or those with high-earning partners give security a low priority. People rate it more highly as they take on mortgage or family commitments. People also experience conflict between their needs. For example, a need for security because of family circumstances may challenge a need for recognition that could imply a risky job change or a move to another town.

People also vary in how they translate their needs into work behaviour. For example, one person with a high need for responsibility or advancement may satisfy it by seeking a transfer to a different department. Another may decide to move to a different type of work. How do people react when they fail to satisfy a need? Do they try harder or give up?

A final point of growing significance in the international business world is that the theories outlined were all developed in the United States. Do they apply to people working in other countries?

Hofstede (1989) articulated what he believed were the 'unspoken cultural assumptions' present in both Theory X and Theory Y. He writes:

> in a comparative study of US values versus those dominant in ASEAN countries, I found the following common assumptions on the US side and underlying both X and Y:
> 1 Work is good for people.
> 2 People's capacities should be maximally utilised.
> 3 There are 'organisational objectives' that exist apart from people.
> 4 People in organisations behave as unattached individuals.
> These assumptions reflect value positions in McGregor's US society; most of them would be accepted in other western countries as well. None of them, however, applies in ASEAN countries. Southeast Asian assumptions would rather be:
> 1 Work is a necessity but not a goal in itself.
> 2 People should find their rightful place in peace and harmony with their environment.
> 3 Absolute objectives exist only with God. In the world, persons in authority positions represent God so their objectives should be followed.
> 4 People behave as members of a family and/or group. Those who do not are rejected by society.
> Because of these different culturally determined assumptions, McGregor's Theory X and Theory Y distinction becomes irrelevant in Southeast Asia. (p.5)

Hofstede's work that was presented in Chapter 3 showed marked differences in national cultures. These are likely to influence the relative importance which people in those countries attach to the various motivational factors. McClelland found some evidence of this in a study in which he combined his work with that of Hofstede. He found that there was a correlation between the levels of achievement motivation and a combination of Hofstede's variables of 'masculinity' and 'uncertainty'.

NOTICEBOARD **Prevailing cultural norms and beliefs**

East Asia	Western
Equity	Wealth
Group	Individual
Saving	Consumption
Extended family relations	Nuclear and mobile family
Highly disciplined and motivated	Decline in work ethic and hierarchy
Protocol, rank, status	Informality and personal competence
Avoid conflict	Conflict to be managed

Source: Harris and Moran (1991)

It appears that some countries, predominantly Anglo-Saxon ones, have a relatively high need for achievement, strong masculinity scores and low uncertainty avoidance. This pattern contrasts with that shown for Spain and Portugal.

Harris and Moran (1991) also suggest that different cultures are likely to influence life goals. They distinguish broadly between East Asian and western cultures, in terms of prevailing norms and beliefs. The Noticeboard shows their conclusions. Many of the factors imply different attitudes to the motivational factors discussed earlier.

6.7 Process theories of motivation

The chapter now turns to a group of theories that try to explain why people choose one course of action towards satisfying a need, rather than another. A person may experience a need for a higher income. He or she could satisfy this need in several ways, such as moving to another company, applying for promotion, investing in some training or setting up a company. What factors will be pertinent in deciding which alternative to choose?

Expectancy theory

Victor Vroom (1964) developed one attempt to answer that question with what he termed the expectancy theory of motivation. This is based on three assumptions about how people behave in organisations:

▶ Individuals have different needs and so they value outcomes differently.
▶ They make conscious choices about which course of action to follow.
▶ They choose between alternative actions on their expectations about the likelihood of an action resulting in a desired outcome.

There are, then, three main components in expectancy theory. First, the person's expectation (or subjective probability) that effort (E) will result in some level of performance (P):

$$(E \rightarrow P)$$

This will be affected by how clear they are about their roles, the training available, whether the necessary support will be provided and similar factors. It will also be affected by the person's confidence in his or her abilities.

The second component is the person's expectation (or subjective probability) that performance will lead to a particular outcome (O):

$$(P \rightarrow O)$$

This will be affected by how confident the person is that achieving a target will produce a reward. This reflects factors such as the clarity of the organisation's appraisal and payment systems and previous experience of the predictability of the reward system.

The third component is the valence which the individual attaches to a particular outcome:

$$(V)$$

This term is best understood as the power of the outcome to motivate that individual. It introduces the belief that people differ in the value they place on different kinds of reward. So the value of V varies between individuals, reflecting their unique pattern of motivational needs (as suggested by the content theories discussed earlier). Thus a manager who values money and achievement would place a high valence on an outcome which was a promotion to a distant head office. He or she would try to work in a way which led to that. Such an outcome would be much less welcome (have a much lower valence) to a manager who values an established pattern of relationships or quality of life in the present location.

These components can be summarised as:

$$F = (E \rightarrow P) \times (P \rightarrow O) \times V$$

in which F represents the force exerted, or degree of commitment shown, by a person towards an activity. The argument is that a person's motivation will be influenced by two beliefs ('subjective probabilities' in the original model) about the likelihood of events. The first is their belief about the likelihood that putting in the effort will lead to a particular level of performance. The second is their belief about the likelihood that that level of performance will lead to an outcome (or reward) that they value. When both these beliefs are tempered by valence – the person's perception of the desirability of the outcome – a measure of motivation is gained.

The subjective probabilities which people hold will be shaped both by their own personalities, but also by specific organisational practices, as shown in Figure 6.4.

The use of the multiplication sign in the equation signifies the belief that both sets of probabilities will influence the effort someone gives to the task. For example, if a person believes that however hard they try they will be unable to perform to a required standard then they will not be motivated to do so (so $E \rightarrow P = 0$). Similarly, if a person believes that even if they meet the required standard of performance, there is little certainty that that will lead to a reward ($P \rightarrow O = 0$), that too will reduce motivation. A low score in either of these two parts of the equation or in V will lead to low effort, regardless of beliefs about the other part.

A criticism of the theory is that implies a high level of rational calculation. It implies that staff are weighing up the probabilities of various courses of action producing desired results, and planning their behaviour in a way most likely to meet their needs. Equally it implies that managers would be estimating what each of their employees values, and trying to ensure that

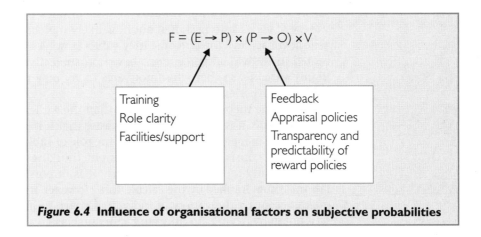

Figure 6.4 **Influence of organisational factors on subjective probabilities**

policies and practices are such as to encourage them to act in ways that meet those needs and organisational requirements. Neither of these calculations is likely to take place with that degree of rationality, raising questions about the practical value of the model.

These can be answered by suggesting that the important innovation of the model is the fact that it recognises more fully than earlier approaches the scope for individual subjective choice (Carter and Jackson, 1993). Earlier theories of motivation were usually interpreted as implying that the human needs they identified were common to most people. Although individuals' needs evidently varied, this could be explained by the assumption that they were at different stages of development in the hierarchy of needs.

Expectancy theory explicitly acknowledges that individual needs vary. Valence (V) will vary depending on the value which is placed on the outcome by the person. In addition, and more significantly, the theory incorporates the reality that people will vary in their beliefs (subjective probabilities) about the other elements in the equation. Some will be pessimistic about the chances of effort leading to performance, while others will be confident that it can be done. Some will be confident about the performance to outcome link, others will be sceptical. This will have less to do with apparently objective facts than with how individuals vary in the way they perceive and interpret the situation.

People interpret the situation facing them at work in many different ways. That in turn means that the scope for management being able to achieve what it wants by supposedly rational means is limited. What management may regard as a motivator may not be seen that way by employees. Their desired goals may be different from those offered by management, and in extreme cases will be dysfunctional for the organisation. For example, traders in the major financial markets follow highly personal career objectives. They are willing and able to move rapidly between financial institutions if their present employer is not meeting their requirements – regardless of the damage that may do.

A manager may argue that experience shows that the task is a reasonable request and the targets attainable. Staff may see it differently. A manager may claim that successful performance will bring the promised rewards, but staff may not be so sure in the light of previous promises and actions.

Expectancy theory implies that management seeking to influence employees should understand, or at least enquire about, what their employees regard as satisfying or motivating rewards. It also implies being conscious of the variety of views among staff about how likely it is that a particular course of action will achieve the outcome they value. However, these beliefs are deeply rooted in individual perceptions based on subjective experience. They are highly variable, so that what motivates today may not do so tomorrow as needs and experiences change.

While the theory is more complex than the earlier models, it is probably more realistic. It is important to emphasise that it is not within the rational tradition of management. In stressing the role of subjective interpretation of events it is consistent with much current thinking about the uncertainty and ambiguity of management. Clearly it is impossible to go through the rational ritual implied by the calculation. However, it is possible for management, accepting the variety of individual goals, to influence the effort that staff put in by paying attention to factors such as:

- ▶ establishing what types and levels of reward are valued by individuals,
- ▶ identifying performance requirements so that these can be clearly communicated,
- ▶ ensuring that the requirements are attainable with reasonable effort,
- ▶ ensuring that facilities are available to support the individual's effort,
- ▶ ensuring that the link between performance and reward is clear and understood,
- ▶ providing feedback to staff on how well they are meeting performance requirements.

The theory is thus a way of linking insights from the content theories of motivation with organisational practice.

Equity theory

Equity theory introduces the idea of fairness in comparison with others as an influence on a person's motivation (Vecchio, 1984). The argument is that people act in the light of what they regard as fair. This can be defined as a comparison of the ratio of one person's input (of effort, skill, knowledge, etc.) to rewards received, with the input-to-reward ratio of others whom they consider their equals. When people consider whether management has treated them fairly they consider what they receive for the effort they have made. They expect that these outcomes will be broadly proportional to their effort. Equity theory stresses that they will also expect management to reward others in roughly the same ratio. The formula below sums up the comparison:

$$\frac{\text{Input (A)}}{\text{Reward (A)}} : \frac{\text{Input (B)}}{\text{Reward (B)}}$$

Person A compares the ratio of her input to her reward to that of B. If the ratios are similar, she will be satisfied with the treatment received. If she believes the ratio is lower than that of other people she will feel inequitably treated and be dissatisfied.

The theory also predicts that if people feel unfairly treated they will experience tension and dissatisfaction. They will try to reduce this by:

- ▶ reducing their inputs, by putting in less effort or withholding good ideas and suggestions,
- ▶ attempting to increase their outcomes, by pressing for increased pay or other benefits, decreasing other people's outcomes, by generating conflict, withholding information or help,
- ▶ changing the basis of their comparison, by making it against someone else where the inequity is less pronounced,
- ▶ increasing their evaluation of the other person's output so the ratios are in balance.

CASE QUESTIONS 6.5

- ▶ What evidence was there at the Benefits Agency of perceived inequity?
- ▶ How did people react?

As individuals differ, so will their way of reducing inequity. Some will try to rationalise the situation, suggesting that their efforts were greater or lesser than they originally thought them to be, or that the rewards are reasonable. For example, a person denied a promotion may decide that the previously desired job would not have been so advantageous after all. Members may put pressure on other members of the team whom they feel are not pulling their weight. Some may choose to do less, so bringing their ratio into line with that of other staff.

Clearly the focus and the components of the comparisons are highly subjective, although the theory has an intuitive appeal. There is plenty of anecdotal evidence of people comparing their own effort/reward ratio with that of other people or groups.

6.8 Motivation as a form of social influence

Managers and their advisers have used both content and process theories in their attempts to influence the behaviour of others. They have drawn particularly on the ideas of higher-level needs and expectancy theory to alter employees' experience of work in the hope of increasing their satisfaction or productivity.

A key idea in such theories is the distinction between intrinsic and extrinsic rewards. Extrinsic rewards are those which are separate from the performance of the task, such as pay, security and promotion possibilities. Intrinsic rewards are those which people receive from the performance of the task itself – the use of skills, a sense of achievement, work that is in itself satisfying to do. Recall that a central element in Frederick Taylor's doctrine of scientific management was the careful design of the 'one best way' of doing a piece of manual work. This was typically arrived at by carefully analysing how people normally did the job. Experts then identified the most efficient set of tasks, usually by breaking down the task into many small parts which people could learn quickly. Jobs of this sort are boring to many people, and were often criticised for leading to dissatisfaction, absenteeism and carelessness.

As the limitations of mechanistic designs became clear, researchers began to seek ways of making jobs more interesting and challenging – in the belief that this would tap into the higher-level sources of motivation. The work of writers such as Maslow, Herzberg and McGregor prompted many experiments aimed at increasing the opportunities for people to satisfy their 'higher' needs at work. The idea was that staff would work more productively if management offered intrinsic rewards (motivators in Herzberg's terms) as well as extrinsic ones (Herzberg's hygiene factors). A series of research projects indicated the potential of this approach, and led to the development of the job enrichment model.

Job enrichment model

The job enrichment model formulated by Hackman and Oldham (1980) extended the work of earlier motivation theorists by proposing that managers could change specific job characteristics to motivate employees and promote job satisfaction. Doing so would enable staff to satisfy more of their higher-level needs and so lead to greater motivation and performance.

The model identifies three critical *psychological states* that must be present to achieve high motivation. If any are low, motivation will be low. The three states are:

▶ **Experienced meaningfulness**   The degree to which employees perceive their work as valuable and worthwhile. If workers regard a job as trivial and pointless their motivation will be low.

▶ **Experienced responsibility**   How responsible people feel for the quantity and quality of work performed.

▶ **Knowledge of results**   The amount of feedback employees receive about how well or poorly they are doing the job. Those who are given no feedback will care less about the quality of their performance.

These psychological states are influenced by five key *job characteristics* which contribute to experienced meaningfulness of work:

▶ **Skill variety**   The extent to which a job makes use of a range of skills and experience.

▶ **Task identity**   Whether a job involves a complete operation.

▶ **Task significance**   How much the job matters to others in the organisation, or to the wider society.

▶ **Autonomy**   How much freedom and independence a person has in deciding how to go about doing the work.

▶ **Feedback**   The extent to which a person receives feedback on relevant dimensions of performance.

The extent to which a job contains these elements can be calculated using a tested instrument, and then using the scores obtained to calculate the *motivating potential* score for the job. The model is presented schematically in Figure 6.5.

The model also shows how management (or staff) can increase the motivating potential of jobs by using five implementing concepts:

▶ **Combine tasks**   Rather than divide the work up into small pieces as Taylor recommended, staff can combine them so they use more skills and complete more of the whole task. For example, an order clerk could receive orders from a customer and arrange transport and invoicing, instead of having these done by different people.

▶ **Form natural workgroups**   In order to give more responsibility and enable sharing of skills, groups could be created that carry out a complete operation. For example, instead of a product passing down an assembly line, with each worker performing one operation, a group may assemble the whole product, sharing out the tasks amongst themselves.

▶ **Establish customer relations**   This would bring home to employees the expectations of the people to whom their work goes, whether inside or outside the organisation, enabling them to see how their job fits into the larger picture. Instead of people doing part of the job for all customers, they can look after all the requirements of a small group of customers. This helps them to establish closer relationships and gain a better understanding of their customers' needs.

▶ **Vertical loading**   This would involve workers taking on responsibilities traditionally taken by supervisors to solve problems and develop workable solutions, thus adding to their autonomy. For example, operators may be given responsibility for checking the quantity and quality of incoming materials, and reporting any problems. They may use more discretion over the order in which they arrange a week's work.

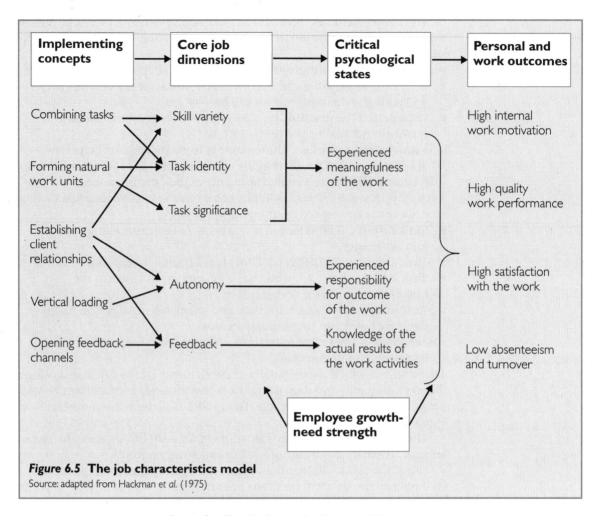

Figure 6.5 **The job characteristics model**
Source: adapted from Hackman et al. (1975)

▶ **Open feedback channels** This would ensure that people receive feedback on their performance from internal or external customers. For example, operators can be invited to attend meetings at which customers give their views on the service provided, as a basis for improving performance and building client relationships. This is not only for problem areas – public recognition of achievement contributes to a positive psychological state and improved performance and satisfaction.

The last feature of the Hackman–Oldham model is growth-need strength, that is, the extent to which an individual desires personal challenges, accomplishment and learning on the job. Some employees may want jobs that satisfy only their lower-level needs, but others want more from their job. Individuals with high needs for challenge, growth and creativity are more likely to respond positively to job enrichment programmes. If an individual's growth needs are low, attempts at job enrichment may cause resentment.

Since different individuals bring different needs to the job, they will respond to the same job in different ways. What may be a good job for one person will be a bad job for someone else. The job enrichment model demonstrates this by showing that the strength of a person's need for growth moderates the relationship of job characteristics to performance and/or satisfaction.

Many managers have changed the kind of work that they expect employees to do. They have not usually been driven by the benefits to employees of more interesting jobs, but by likely productivity benefits (Buchanan, 1987). As business conditions have changed, management has sought to improve the range of tasks employees carry out and the range of decisions they can take without referring to superiors. Sometimes they have focused on the design of individual jobs. In other cases the emphasis has been on changing how a group of staff work together. A currently fashionable approach is to alter to some degree the vertical relationships in the hierarchy, by placing more responsibility on employees lower in the hierarchy. This is usually called empowerment.

6.9 Empowerment

People use the term 'empowerment' to refer to a wide range of practices which give more responsibility to less senior staff. Clutterbuck (1994) concludes that the common features of such approaches are that they are intended to help people to:

▶ take more control of their job and working environment,
▶ enhance the contributions they make as individuals and members of a team,
▶ seize opportunities for personal growth and self-fulfilment.

Commentators have suggested several advantages for empowerment (Bowen and Lawler, 1992; Frey, 1993). These include:

▶ Quicker responses to customer queries, since answers can be given or decisions made by staff over issues that they previously had to refer to a more senior manager.
▶ Employees feel more satisfied as they are doing more responsible work and developing new skills.
▶ Employees welcome the chance to deal more intensely with customers.
▶ This in turn can encourage employees to come up with more practical ideas for service improvement than managers who are less directly involved with customers.
▶ The improved service builds customer loyalty and repeat business.

Such advantages in themselves are persuasive to managers and many have introduced programmes with the stated aim of empowering employees. In order to understand what they are trying to do, some analytical tools are necessary.

Bowen and Lawler (1992) define empowerment in terms of the degree to which four ingredients of the organisation are shared with front-line employees:

▶ Information about the organisation's performance.
▶ Rewards based on the organisation's performance.
▶ Knowledge that enables employees to understand and contribute to organisational performance.
▶ Power to make decisions that influence organisational direction and performance.

They argue that the extent to which these are present distinguishes the degree of empowerment which employees have. If they remain largely at the top of the organisation, this indicates that management still exercises fairly

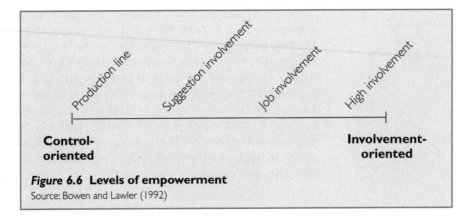

Figure 6.6 Levels of empowerment
Source: Bowen and Lawler (1992)

direct control. If they are pushed down the organisation so that front-line employees have more information and more power to make decisions, then this indicates that management is trying to adopt an empowering approach. The more that staff exercise self-control and self-direction, the more they are empowered.

Bowen and Lawler go on to suggest a model of levels of empowerment. At one extreme, management takes a control orientation towards staff, while at the other extreme it takes an involvement orientation. Figure 6.6 summarises the range of options.

Bowen and Lawler base their argument on the distinction between what they call 'control' and 'involvement' models of management. The control model is most clearly represented in the traditional production line approach, whether applied in manufacturing or service operations. In this Taylor-inspired method, tasks are simplified and clearly divided, equipment replaces employees wherever possible and those who remain make few decisions. Management designs the system, employees work to it. The alternative is the empowerment or involvement approach, in which employees have more information, knowledge and power to make decisions, and are rewarded for their contribution to organisational performance. Three forms of involvement are distinguished.

First, *suggestion involvement* represents a small shift away from control. Staff are encouraged to submit ideas to improve ways of working and are rewarded for doing so. However, control remains with management who chooses whether or not to accept an idea. Employees experience a degree of empowerment in that they have a formal outlet for their ideas, but without any change in the fundamental control-centred approach.

Secondly, *job involvement* represents a more significant change, in that employees are able to develop and use more skills, have greater autonomy and receive more feedback. Supervisors' jobs change from an emphasis on direction to an emphasis on support. Although this implies greater empowerment it is still limited, for 'it does not change higher-level strategic decisions concerning organisation structure, power, and the allocation of rewards. These remain the responsibility of senior management' (Bowen and Lawler, p.36).

For Bowen and Lawler, the third form – *high involvement* – occurs when organisations give their lowest-level employees a sense of involvement in the total organisation's performance. All of the four ingredients listed on page 211 are designed in such a way that they support empowerment: information on performance is shared, people have the skills and power to act beyond their traditional roles and are rewarded for doing so. Examples of companies with a sustained high involvement approach to empowerment are hard to find, but examples of companies which are moving in this direction are W.L. Gore and The Body Shop. Others are trying, or have tried, to move in this direction but have found the transition difficult. The overall pattern is very mixed – why should this be so? There are several explanations, ranging from rational contingency models to those which stress fundamental inertia within management.

Contingency approaches

Contingency approaches start from the premise that empowerment has disadvantages as well as advantages. These include cost of training, the dangers of variable levels of service and the dangers of incurring significant costs if empowered employees make wrong decisions. Therefore the idea is to use empowerment only in those situations where the benefits are likely to outweigh the possibly significant costs. Bowen and Lawler again provide a model of the main contingencies: Figure 6.7 illustrates these. The rational recommendation is that companies would only undertake empowerment in those circumstances to which it was suited – including a strategy to offer customised, unique service, to build long-term relationships with customers, using a complex technology in an unpredictable environment. This form of model would help explain why some types of organisation are more likely to try to empower employees than others (such as those operating in a stable and low-tech environment). This is a rational approach but is unlikely to explain the pattern. Some other evidence implies a more complex picture.

Contingency	Production line approach		Empowerment
Basic business strategy	Low cost, high volume	1 2 3 4 5	Differentiation, customised, personalised
Tie to customer	Transaction, short time period	1 2 3 4 5	Relationship, long time period
Technology	Routine, simple	1 2 3 4 5	Non-routine, complex
Business environment	Predictable, few surprises	1 2 3 4 5	Unpredictable, many surprises
Types of people	Theory X managers, employees with low growth needs, low social needs and weak interpersonal skills	1 2 3 4 5	Theory Y managers, employees with high growth needs, high social needs and strong interpersonal skills

Figure 6.7 **The contingencies of empowerment**
Source: Bowen and Lawler (1992)

Unintentional empowerment

Unintentional empowerment refers to situations where staff find they are empowered at least in part because of decisions on other matters. An example of this is the recent history of developments in nursing management within the UK National Health Service. Ward managers (previously known as sisters or charge nurses) have both clinical and managerial responsibilities. They have experienced considerable increases in the latter part of the role and have much more autonomy than used to be the case. Some of the empowerment has been the result of deliberate attempts to extend their role. Some has been the unintended by-product of changes elsewhere in the NHS. For example, the Patients Charter outlines the quality of service that a patient can expect. One aspect of this is a guarantee of the time within which a patient can expect to be admitted for non-emergency surgery. In areas of high demand the only way to achieve this is to increase the throughput of patients, and, as a result, increasing the complexity of the cases in each ward. Balancing this load has increased the responsibilities of the ward manager. Another unintended source of empowerment has been the reduction in junior doctor's working hours. This led to a policy shift to extend the range of responsibilities undertaken by individual nurses. They, and their ward managers, thus became more accountable for delivering care.

Empowerment as a tactic

There are also reported but unpublished cases where managements have introduced change in the name of empowerment when their primary aim was to cut costs. For example, a local authority made significant changes to the way it provided housing services. The most visible change was a shift from a city-wide to a neighbourhood service. This was undoubtedly intended to provide a better and more responsive service to tenants. The change also allowed the authority to rearrange work so that staff performed duties previously done by other professions. This widening of staff responsibilities meant that fewer were needed under the new arrangement. At the same time, empowering more junior staff to take more decisions meant that fewer senior staff were required. To have presented the exercise from the beginning as an exercise in cost-cutting would probably have provoked resistance. Presenting it as an exercise in tenant and staff empowerment helped to ensure acceptance.

Delays in implementation

The other reason for the variety in stages reached in attempts at empowerment is simply the difficulties which management experiences in introducing significant changes of this sort. The result is that what is observed at any time is often a partial form of empowerment, such as suggestion involvement, even though management intends, for whatever reason, to introduce more radical changes in the hope of enhancing motivation. Delays may sometimes be caused by staff who value barriers which give certainty and predictability to their working lives.

These obstacles have often arisen more amongst middle managers than they have amongst the staff who were being given additional responsibilities.

There is an understandable concern amongst management about how control will be exercised – control in the neutral sense. Clearly, there are risks in giving greater power over decisions to many different groups of staff, in that the organisation needs to remain able to monitor what staff are doing to ensure broad consistency with organisational policies. Empowerment is simply a special case of the continuing need to balance responsibility with appropriate control mechanisms (Simons, 1995; Dawson, 1992). Indeed, one of the major dilemmas that needs to be managed is how to balance greater empowerment with a redefinition of accountability and boundaries. Without these, empowerment may lead to anxiety and uncertainty rather than to commitment and performance.

Ezzamel and colleagues (1994) offer a more radical perspective. Interviews conducted in many organisations which claimed to be trying to introduce some form of empowerment, revealed that many middle managers were reluctant to extend empowerment. Much of this stemmed from managers' desire to retain control over the responsibilities and roles of others. Ezzamel *et al.* argue that this desire lies behind much of the opposition to attempts to introduce empowerment.

So empowerment is a shifting balance, reflecting a variety of forces. As the term makes clear, it is also about power and is bound to be controversial. This may imply redistributing power from an over-concentration at the centre of the organisation. Alternatively, management may remove the constraints that prevent people around the organisation using the power which they already have (e.g. power based on expertise or information).

6.10 Work and careers in a time of change

The theories described in the chapter provide points of reference, not answers, in the search for an understanding of how management influences others to act in a particular way. In part this is inherent in the limited nature of the theories themselves – the unclear concepts, limited empirical base and lack of operational variables. It has much more to do with the changing world in which management is now operating, dramatically different from that for which their originators first presented the theories. Academics ask whether rational theories can realistically try to explain behaviour in organisations when so much seems to be based on subjective interpretation of events and meaning. How are the expectations of both organisations and people changing, and what new kinds of psychological contract can we see emerging to help balance these interests?

The organisational world which McGregor and Herzberg observed was a place of large manufacturing organisations operating in relatively stable markets. Western organisations and values dominated the business world, natural resources seemed plentiful, and computers were novelties. In 1969, at least one major bank still kept customer records in handwritten books. Today the same company offers banking services on the Internet. Most employees were men, worked full-time until retirement, and expected to stay with the same employer for many years – often for most of their career. All these features have changed, and will continue to do so.

Many organisations are operating in global markets and face severe competition, not only on price but also on quality, innovation, responsiveness.

More business is in the service sector, where the quality of interpersonal interaction with the customer is an important part of the transaction. Information technology is having dramatic effects on the availability of information. This affects both organisational structures and what people delivering goods or services are expected to do. Another change is that many organisations employ other organisations to provide functions that their own staff previously performed.

Many who joined the public sector find that their organisation has been sold to the private sector. This usually requires managers and staff to work in a radically different way if they want to keep their job. Those who remain in the public sector face new pressures (Flynn, 1997). They are more likely to face conflicts with members of the public who know their entitlements and are willing to argue for them. At the same time, local and national governments require staff to work within tight budgets. They probably need to work more closely with private sector agencies who provide many services previously provided internally, and manage the shifting balance between central control and local autonomy. The psychological contract for many is very different from the ethos of public service prevailing when they joined. Then, many who joined the service may have been motivated by a sense of service to other people and of doing some good. This is quite different from being motivated by the prospect of making a profit and receiving some personal financial benefit.

Organisations are less likely to offer long-term or full-time careers. Competition is used to justify keeping staff costs low by minimising the number of regular jobs on offer and meeting extra demand by employing temporary or casual staff. Work is increasingly part-time, done at what used to be regarded as unsociable hours. Standard procedures often structure the work processes tightly to fit the requirements of information systems that link all parts of the organisation. At the same time, staff are expected to work together co-operatively in teams and build good relationships with customers. They must follow procedures, but also use their imagination and initiative as required to solve unusual problems.

People have different expectations of their organisations either because of wider social trends or in response to what organisations themselves are doing. As many women as men are in paid employment, both have to manage 'dual careers' in conjunction with family commitments, particularly the care of young children and elderly relatives. More people are setting up their own business, rather than work for an employer, although it is unclear whether this is from genuine preference or the lack of alternative. It does mean that more employment is now in small organisations.

The earlier motivational theories made strong universalist assumptions – that they were applicable to all normal people. Your work on the Notebooks and other tasks associated with this chapter will probably have confirmed that individuals differ widely in the rewards they seek from work. This feature is almost certainly becoming more pronounced. People differ in their commitment to work as a full-time career. They look for different rewards (Maccoby, 1988) and care about the kind of business for which they are willing to work.

Clearly, life is not as neat as the five categories identified by Maccoby in the Noticeboard, and most people will feel that they have elements of each in their make-up – though with some more dominant than others. The

---

NOTICEBOARD Maccoby's social character types

Michael Maccoby claims to have identified five social character types, each of which will have different expectations from work – and which management must therefore deal with in different ways.

Type	**Dominant values**
Expert	Mastery, control, autonomy, excellence in making
Helper	Relatedness, caring for people, survival, sociability
Defender	Protection, dignity, power, self-esteem
Innovator	Creating, experimenting, glory, competition
Self-developer	Balancing mastery and play, knowledge and fun

---

general point is to emphasise the diversity of values and expectations which people bring to the organisation. Identifying the kinds of reward which people seek from their work has always been a matter of intelligent guesswork and inference. It is likely to become more so, as people come to expect much more diverse rewards from fulfilling their side of the psychological contract.

Hiltrop (1995) reviews the changes taking place in the psychological contract as both organisations and people change their expectations of each other. Elements of the new contract include:

▶ Organisations are becoming more demanding places in which to work.
▶ The paternalism of earlier times, in which both sides expected a long-term career together, is gone.
▶ Roles and responsibilities are much more fluid and ambiguous.
▶ Increasingly, companies expect people to contribute their skills through specific, short-term tasks, not through long-term employment. In order to maintain their income, people need to plan their development and careers, and build their reputation.

Table 6.2 Changing psychological contracts

Characteristic	Old	New
Focus	Security	Employability
Format	Structured	Flexible
Duration	Permanent	Variable
Scope	Broad	Narrow
Underlying principle	Tradition	Market forces
Intended output	Loyalty and commitment	Value added
Employer's key responsibility	Fair pay for good work	High pay for high performance
Employee's key responsibility	Good performance in present job	Making a difference
Employer's key input	Stable income and career advancement	Opportunities for self-development
Employee's key input	Time and effort	Knowledge and skills

Source: Hiltrop (1995)

▶ Security, income and status derived from an employer are less available, implying people need to develop other sources of psychological reassurance.
▶ Opportunities to improve employability (by movement to another project) are more likely to be the reward for good work than promotion.
▶ People are increasingly paid on the basis of contribution rather than level or status.

Table 6.2 presents Hiltrop's summary of the main characteristics of the old and new psychological contracts.

Changes are taking place in the significance of work in people's life. Many do not expect self-fulfilment from their work. They seek it instead through a hobby, through social activities or perhaps by running a pressure group. Work is central for many, but not for everyone, especially as the hours of work and the length of working life decline. New generations seek different things from life and from work, and many are less committed to conventional work-patterns. These changes have implications for human resource management practices discussed in Chapter 15.

6.11 Recap

Management assumptions about other people have a fundamental effect on how they go about their role. The chapter has reviewed evidence that can guide management in the task of generating the commitment of others to behave in particular ways.

Content agenda

Early approaches to motivating people assumed that people would do what was required in return for financial or other extrinsic rewards. Later theories stressed the value of meeting people's social needs. All these needs could more or less be satisfied without reference to the objectives of the organisation. In many modern organisations, management now tries to secure people's commitment to the goals of the organisation as a way of securing their willing and flexible co-operation. They seek to integrate individual and organisational needs, so that people use their talents to benefit the organisation without constant direction by management. Until goals are genuinely shared and until organisations are seen to be serving society there will be inherent tensions between management and managed over the commitment shown.

Similar views apply to the plans made to achieve the objectives. Work design approaches advocate that management arranges a less fragmented and specialised division of work, in the interest of better meeting human needs. Several theories offer different ways of considering those needs, which also vary between cultures and individuals. Research also suggests that jobs designed in a way that meets human needs are more likely to help meet organisational objectives than jobs that ignore human needs.

Process agenda

As individual stakeholders in the organisation, employees will have different and variable needs, and can to some degree exercise choice in how they react to influence attempts. The degree of choice will, however, be constrained by the relative power of the parties. There is evidence that many employees are able and willing to contribute to management activities. Managers with Theory Y assumptions will offer employees opportunities to take part in wider roles where they can learn to exercise more responsibility. Hence, greater involvement in decisions beyond the day-to-day may foster commitment by meeting higher-level needs for autonomy and decision-taking. Unless management communicates with employees it cannot know their views and possible contributions.

Control agenda

How management deals with the control agenda reflects fundamental Theory X or Y assumptions – the former emphasising external control, the latter internal or self-control. The control process also affects the results of attempts at behaviour modification. The belief that people have in the probability of alternative outcomes as indicated by expectancy theories is also influenced by decisions by management on the control agenda. Similarly,

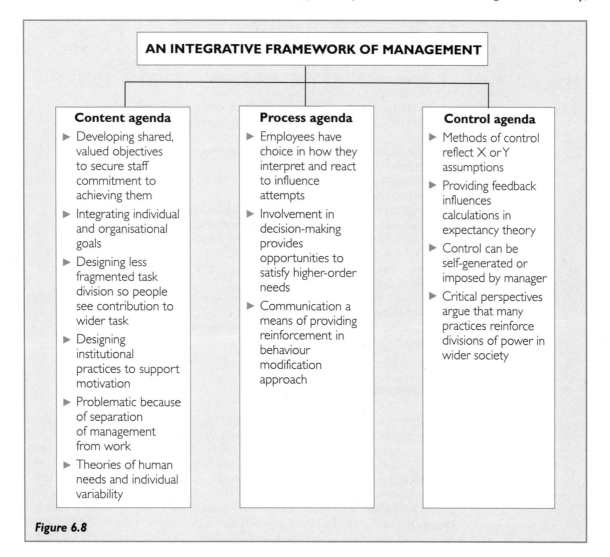

AN INTEGRATIVE FRAMEWORK OF MANAGEMENT

Content agenda
- ▶ Developing shared, valued objectives to secure staff commitment to achieving them
- ▶ Integrating individual and organisational goals
- ▶ Designing less fragmented task division so people see contribution to wider task
- ▶ Designing institutional practices to support motivation
- ▶ Problematic because of separation of management from work
- ▶ Theories of human needs and individual variability

Process agenda
- ▶ Employees have choice in how they interpret and react to influence attempts
- ▶ Involvement in decision-making provides opportunities to satisfy higher-order needs
- ▶ Communication a means of providing reinforcement in behaviour modification approach

Control agenda
- ▶ Methods of control reflect X or Y assumptions
- ▶ Providing feedback influences calculations in expectancy theory
- ▶ Control can be self-generated or imposed by manager
- ▶ Critical perspectives argue that many practices reinforce divisions of power in wider society

Figure 6.8

the opportunities for review and learning affect the testing of X or Y assumptions and are central to the behaviour modification approach.

Figure 6.8 summarises these points.

P A R T   C A S E   Q U E S T I O N S

▶ Which theories of human needs appear to be supported by the reported policies and attitudes at W.L. Gore and Associates?

▶ What similarities and contrasts are there between the motivational practices at W.L. Gore and Associates and at the Benefits Agency?

▶ In what ways are the associates at W.L. Gore empowered?

6.12 Review questions

1 What are the three ways in which management attempts to motivate people can be institutionalised in the organisation? Give an example of each.

2 Outline the idea of the psychological contract. What are you expecting (a) from a future employer in your career; (b) from an employer who provides you with part-time work while you are studying?

3 What are the three things which are pinpointed when using behaviour modification?

4 How does Maslow's theory of human needs relate to the ideas of (a) Frederick Taylor and (b) Elton Mayo and the human relations movement?

5 How does Alderfer's theory differ from Maslow's? What research lay behind the two theories?

6 How did you score on the McClelland test? How did your scores compare with those of your fellow students?

7 Explain to a colleague the difference between Herzberg's hygiene and motivating factors. Give at least three examples of each.

8 Outline the basic assumptions of Theories X and Y which Douglas McGregor used to characterise alternative ways in which managements view their workers. What management practices are associated with each set of assumptions?

9 What are the five job design elements which are expected to affect people's satisfaction with their work?

10 Can you give an example of an implementing concept associated with each?

Further reading

The original accounts of the major works that have framed our thinking about motivation are usually very readable books showing organisations and research in action. Roethlisberger and Dickson's (1939) account of the Hawthorne experiments has already been mentioned. The works by Mayo (1949), Herzberg (1959) and McGregor (1960) are short and accessible. Reading the original gives a much greater sense of the theories' evolution than the summaries offered in a textbook. Buchanan and Huczynski (1997) goes into closely related topics like perception and learning. For those interested in management in the voluntary sector and charities, Clutterbuck and Dearlove (1996) has chapters on motivation and leadership in such organisations. Finally, Brown (1997) offers a selection of papers on current trends and changes in the labour market.

W Website addresses

To examine what the changes in section 6.10 could mean for careers, you could visit some of the Websites of major companies to review their careers information. What do they appear to be offering as their side of the psychological contract? Examples include:

Commercial Union   http://www.commercial-union.co.uk
Marks & Spencer   http://marks-and-spencer.co.uk

Communication

AIM

To show how management can shape communication processes in ways that help or hinder organisational performance.

OBJECTIVES

By the end of your work on this chapter you should be able to outline the concepts below in your own terms and:

1   **Identify and illustrate each major link in the communication process**

2   **Explain why management needs to understand and manage informal and formal communication processes**

3   **Compare the advantages and disadvantages of spoken, written and non-verbal communication**

4   **Compare the suitability of different forms of interpersonal communication for different types of task**

5   **Use the concept of media richness to decide which communication medium to use for specified purposes**

6   **Compare and evaluate the main features of formal communications systems in an organisation**

7   **Describe how new technologies such as computer networks, video-conferencing and groupware are affecting organisational communication**

8   **Identify and describe the main barriers to communication in organisations**

9   **Show how those in power in organisations can use communication processes to help maintain the status quo**

10 **List several practical techniques for improving personal communication skills**

An ambulance service

This public organisation provides an accident and emergency (A&E) service at all times, and a daytime patient transfer service (PTS). This case deals with a major communication change introduced into the A&E service in 1995.

The system for handling an A&E call was typically as follows. When a member of the public dialled 999 to request an ambulance, the call was transferred by the operator to the nearest ambulance service control room. A control assistant wrote down details of the incident, especially its location and the condition of the patient, and passed these to the control officer who reviewed the status of the available ambulances and decided which one should deal with the incident. The officer spoke by radio to the crew who acknowledged the call and went to deal with the incident. The crew would usually update the control room as they arrived at and left the incident. This enabled the control officer to plan their schedule and to inform a hospital of the case being taken to them. When the crew had delivered the casualty to a hospital they informed the control room of their status and position.

The job of the control staff was very stressful as they would be dealing with several emergency calls at any time with a fixed number of available ambulances. Callers were often distressed and frustrated at any delay in an ambulance reaching the scene.

As part of the drive to save money, management decided to reduce the number of control rooms. These were expensive to operate round the clock and the plan was to use the money saved to provide additional crews and so meet the target which had been set for the time taken to respond to a call. Control staff now receive calls and despatch ambulances over a much wider area.

To make this possible, the service invested in a computerised command and control system, linked to the ambulances by a new radio. The procedure now is that a control assistant receiving a call enters the data directly into the computer system. This incorporates a geographical information system containing all the physical features of the area. As it is directly linked by radio to the ambulances, it also contains information about the present position and status of each vehicle. The system identifies immediately the most appropriate vehicle to despatch to the incident. That decision is conveyed electronically to a message box in the cab which the crew reads and acts upon. As they do the work they press codes on the message box to let the computer know the stage they have reached. Voice communication is unnecessary as the computer automatically updates the ambulance's position. Management hopes the new system will improve communication at all stages of the process, save money and enhance the service.

CASE QUESTIONS

▶ What external changes are affecting the management and staff of the service?

▶ How would you describe the existing communcations system?

▶ What questions would you have about the possible effects of the new system on communications amongst staff?

7.1 Introduction

This chapter introduces the following ideas:
- ▶ Communication
- ▶ Communication process
- ▶ Encoding
- ▶ Channel
- ▶ Receiver
- ▶ Decoding
- ▶ Communication barriers
- ▶ Feedback
- ▶ Noise

Many activities succeed or fail because of the quality of the communication process. We base our understanding of the world on information and feelings that we receive and send. Transmittting and receiving information is inherent in the management task. Managers spend most of their time communicating by spoken, written or electronic means with their supervisors, peers, subordinates or customers. They write memos and notes, send and receive e-mail messages, receive and review reports, prepare presentations. They conduct group meetings, give speeches, and communicate decisions to other people (Mintzberg, 1973).

CASE QUESTIONS 7.1

- ▶ Which aspects of communication would you want management to improve first if you were (a) a member of the public, (b) an employee, (c) a senior manager of the ambulance service?
- ▶ The case has focused on one aspect of communication within the service. What other forms of communication will also be taking place within the organisation?

As it is so central to the job, communication issues appear in every chapter of this book – whether on communication within teams, communicating marketing information to senior management, or interpreting financial data. This chapter focuses on a few generic aspects of the communication process which can inform discussion of particular communication issues as they arise. Figure 7.1 shows communication with the views of the management role that were discussed in Chapter 4.

This chapter explains the generic communication process that occurs as people try to transfer information and solve problems. It then examines particular aspects of interpersonal and organisational communication, before proceeding to outline the factors that hinder or help communication. A final section outlines some techniques that can be used to help improve your skills at communicating.

7.2 The communication process

By communicating, people co-ordinate their activities with others. Speaking and writing are in themselves relatively easy, but achieving an understanding

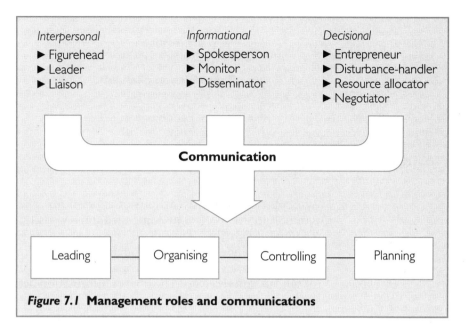

Figure 7.1 Management roles and communications

is a challenge. People each have a different background, experiences and personal needs. These affect their ability to understand messages from those with different histories. It affects the meaning that people attach to words or facial expressions. Management depends on conveying and interpreting messages clearly so that people can work together.

n o t e b o o k   7.1

The definition of communication refers to words, symbols and actions. Try to identify examples of symbols and actions which intentionally or unintentionally communicate a message to you. Some clues:

Symbols: Someone's style of dress or manner, or the appearance of the entrance to your college or university.

Actions: Someone taking time to offer directions to a visitor or looking bored during a meeting; interrupting someone.

We communicate whenever we send a message to someone and as we think about what he or she says in return. We infer meaning from both words and gestures and then from the person's reply to them. We are interpreting the person's messages and creating our own in turn. A manager and an employee have a conversation about some aspect of the work. Each listens to the other's words, looks at their gestures, reads the relevant documents, or looks over the equipment to understand what the other means. When they achieve a mutual understanding about what they will do, they have communicated effectively. In order to understand why communication problems occur we need a model of the steps that make up the process (see Figure 7.2).

The communication process requires at least two people – a sender and a receiver. The sender initiates the communication. He or she tries to transfer information expressing facts, ideas or feelings by creating a message using

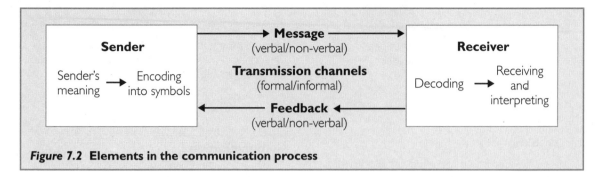

Figure 7.2 Elements in the communication process

symbols such as words, actions or expressions. The sender transmits these symbols to the receiver by some medium – visually, orally or by some other channel. From this transmitted message, the receiver attempts to recon-struct the sender's original thought. When the receiver responds to the sender, the roles are reversed. These principles apply whatever the number of senders and receivers. The flow of information between parties is continu-ous and reciprocal, each responding by giving feedback to the other. The essential purpose of the chain is to send an idea in a way that the receiver understands it as intended.

n o t e b o o k   7 . 2

Think of an example of your own where communication between two or more people failed. Note down why you think that happened.

More communication now takes place electronically: make a preliminary list of the advantages and disadvantages of that medium compared with face-to-face communication.

C A S E   Q U E S T I O N S   7 . 2

▶ Use this model to describe systematically the communication processes involved in dealing with an emergency call to the ambulance service (a) under the old system, (b) under the new system.

▶ Note on the model where the old system tended to interfere with the communication process.

Encoding

The first step in communicating is encoding. As the sender of a message, you think of an idea or sort out a problem or want to reply to a message you have received. All this takes place within your brain and is private to you. You decide you want to share that idea with the receiver, so at this point you must begin to encode the message you want to send. This means selecting symbols to relay the meaning.

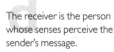

Encoding is translating information into symbols for communication.

Encoding translates internal thoughts into a form that the receiver is likely to understand. Symbols include words and numbers, pictures, facial expressions, signals, or actions. The symbols we use are sometimes ambiguous:

The receiver is the person whose senses perceive the sender's message.

NOTICEBOARD Accurate encoding

Hellriegel and Slocum (1988) suggest five principles for encoding a message accurately:

▶ **Relevancy**   Make the message relevant and significant, carefully selecting the words, symbols or gestures to be used.

▶ **Simplicity**   Put the message in the simplest possible terms, minimising the number of words, symbols and/or gestures used.

▶ **Organisation**   Organise the message into a series of points to facilitate understanding.

Complete each point in the measure before proceeding to the next.

▶ **Repetition**   State the key points of the message and repeat at least once. Repetition is particularly important in oral communication, where people may not hear or understand words clearly the first time.

▶ **Focus**   Concentrate on the essential aspects of the message. Make the message clear and avoid unnecessary detail.

other people interpret them differently especially if they are not familiar with the sender's language or culture.

Deciding how to encode the message is an important choice. It will depend in part on the purpose. Is it to convey specific and unambiguous information? Is it to raise an open and unfamiliar problem, and a request for creative ideas? Is it to pass on routine data, or to inspire people?

Selecting a channel

We can distinguish between verbal, written and non-verbal channels.

A channel is the medium of communication between a sender and a receiver.

Verbal communication

Most managers prefer to talk than to write. All studies of how managers use their time show that most of it is spent in face-to-face contact with other people. They prefer oral communication because it is quick, spontaneous and enriched by non-verbal signals. It takes place in one-to-one conversation (face-to-face or on the telephone), through meetings of several people, or when someone communicates to many people at a conference.

n o t e b o o k   7.3

What evidence did Rosemary Stewart (1967) present on the amount of time which managers spent communicating with others?

Written or electronic communication

In the one-person business, written communication is rare. Most of the information to manage the activity is within the owner-manager's head, and as they decide to do something, they do it. As the business grows and employs a few more people on the same site, this still applies. Everyone can see the state of the job, tacit understandings build up about what they need to do and they can pass information or instructions orally. Communications at this stage are still informal, even when they directly affect business operations.

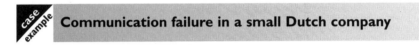

n o t e b o o k   7.4

Think of a task you have done with a group of people where you created a small organisation to do something. It could be a voluntary or charity project, or a group assignment as part of your course. How did you communicate with each other? List all the methods used, and any advantages or disadvantages they had.

As the organisation continues to grow, the informal system is likely to experience strains. There are more people, probably concentrating on particular aspects of the overall task. They work in different places, so that the state of affairs is not immediately obvious to everyone. People will be there at different times. Because it has grown, there will simply be more things happening. A change in one area has effects on others, which people inevitably begin to forget to take into account.

C A S E   Q U E S T I O N S   7.3

▶ How has the balance shifted between verbal and electronic communication in the ambulance service?

▶ Identify where in the whole system each form has increased or decreased. What are the likely advantages and disadvantages from that change in pattern?

case example   Communication failure in a small Dutch company

The company was founded in 1881 and the present owner is one of the fourth generation of the family. The company trades and manufactures packaging machines and employs sixteen people. Someone who has recently joined the company said:

> 1997 was a difficult year. Five people left the company and took with them much knowledge and experience. The company really consists of one person – the owner. He does not delegate much and there is little communication between him and the rest of the organisation. The only part of the company that interests him is the game of selling machines. He describes the rest of his tasks as annoying. The result is that, for example:
>
> 1 When we sell a machine, Operations do not know exactly what Sales has promised a customer. The customer expects the machine they specified, but do not always get it.
> 2 There is lack of internal communication – people in the company do not know their precise responsibilities or who is responsible for which tasks.
> 3 There is no time planning for ordered machines. No one knows the delivery date that we have promised a customer.
> 4 There is no budget system for a machine project. When we sell a machine we do not know if we will make a profit or a loss.
>
> All together, the company faces serious problems because of a lack of policy, management, information and communication.

The solution is to begin to develop more formal information systems. At first these are quite simple, such as a list of current orders and what stage they have reached. Then there may be a system for setting budgets for the different parts of the activity and for collecting information on what they cost. Then some rules or guidelines about passing information to other departments so that they know about changes that may affect them. These systems are the basis of the formal or institutionalised information system.

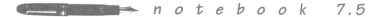

n o t e b o o k   7.5

Make a list of the different communications channels that your college has used to send you information about these aspects of your course:

▶ changes to rooms, timetables, or dates,

▶ reading lists and other study materials,

▶ ideas and information intended to stimulate your own thinking and to encourage discussion and debate,

▶ your performance so far and advice on what courses to take.

Were the methods appropriate or not? What general lessons can you draw?

Non-verbal communication

An important type of interpersonal communication is the non-verbal, which some people refer to as body language. Experts in the field claim that the actual words in a message have less impact on the sender than the accompanying non-verbal signals. These include the tone of voice, facial expression, posture and appearance, and provide most of the impact in face-to-face communication.

Decoding

Receivers try to reconstruct the sender's idea by attaching meaning to the symbols and interpreting the message as a whole. They use their experience and knowledge of the sender to help them interpret what the message is likely to mean. They also take into account the general circumstances in which the communication is taking place. One of the major requirements in communicating is that the receiver listens effectively.

Communication has only occurred when the receiver has received the message and understood it as intended by the sender. If the sender has encoded the message clearly and used an appropriate delivery medium then decoding should be routine. The receiver may still decode the symbols to mean something different from that intended by the sender. There are many obstacles to good communication. The intended receiver may not receive the message (especially if someone else had agreed to pass it on). He or she may forget to read it or read only part of it. He may be too busy to think through what it means and put it aside without understanding it. He may misunderstand what the sender intended.

A common mistake is to equate the sending of a message with its transmission. No transmission occurs unless the intended person receives it. Typical examples of transmission include passing a letter to a receiver, speaking

Decoding is the interpretation of a message into a form with meaning.

words so that the intended receiver can hear them, or enacting a gesture so that a person can see it. There is always the danger of people saying that they have understood a message when they have not.

Filtering affects reception. A filter is something that limits a person's capacity to sense or perceive stimuli. Some are physiological, such as experienced by those who are blind or deaf. Other filters are psychological – a mind-set that predisposes someone to perceive and interpret messages in a particular way. Two people may view the same speech or read the same report, yet reach different interpretations.

> ❝ Assume that communication is going to fail, and then put time and effort into preventing that. ❞

Feedback

Feedback occurs as the receiver expresses his or her reaction to the sender's message.

Some signal from the receiver to the sender completes the communication process. The same factors as influence the choice of medium also guide the appropriate form of feedback. Without some response – a nod, a question that implies understanding, a quick e-mail acknowledgement – the sender has no way of knowing how successful the communication attempt has been. Feedback occurs in many ways and takes many forms. It is a communication itself and subject to the same difficulties as other communications. What is important is that the sender must also be a receiver, and actively seek assurance of the receipt and appreciation of the original message. Communication does not occur until the target receives, understands and acknowledges the message in the form the sender intended.

Even if the receiver understands the words, he or she may not understand the concepts, and so communication has not occurred. The sender must have evidence that the message has got through – thus the importance of an active response by the receiver.

Even though communications can become complicated, the basic process remains the same: encoding the meaning, transmitting the message, and decoding and interpreting the meaning. If information is not being understood by those in the process, refer to this three-step model to find the source of the problems. Has the sender clarified and defined the message? Has he or she chosen the most effective mode of transmission? What perceptions of the receivers may be affecting how they interpret the message?

7.3 Aspects of interpersonal communication

Non-verbal communication

Sending non-verbal communications

Small changes in eye contact, such as raising eyebrows or a directed glance while making a statement, add to the meaning that the sender conveys. A stifled yawn, an eager nod, a thoughtful flicker of anxiety by the listener gives the sender a signal about how the message is being received. Gestures and body position give equally vivid messages – leaning forward attentively, moving about in the chair, hands moving nervously, pointedly gathering papers. Whether intended or not, these send a signal which the receiver may or may not notice and interpret correctly.

Receiving non-verbal communication

Like any interpersonal skill, some people are better at picking up clues from non-verbal behaviour than others. When listening to someone, especially over the telephone, the receiver will pick up more of the sender's meaning if he or she listens for what the sender does not say. This can either confirm the spoken message, or raise doubts about whether the speaker is telling the full story. The sender of a spoken message can benefit by noting the non-verbal responses to what he or she says. If they do not seem appropriate (raised eyebrows, or a hint of anxiety), the speaker should pause and take stock of the conversation, checking that the other party has received the intended message, or that he or she has not misinterpreted the message in some way.

Giving non-verbal feedback

Managers and colleagues give non-verbal feedback to others all the time, both intentionally and unintentionally. Positive non-verbal feedback can significantly build relations within a team. A smile or wave from the manager to the staff members at least acknowledges that they exist. Related to a task it indicates approval in an informal, rapid way that sustains the subordinates' confidence. Negative feedback can be correspondingly damaging. A boss who looks irritated by what the staff member sees as a reasonable enquiry is giving a negative signal. So too is one who looks bored or distracted during a presentation. This may be appropriate – but needs to be backed up quickly with clear verbal information about the problem.

Communication structure and type of task

Different tasks require different forms of interpersonal communication. Figure 7.3 illustrates this. The figure shows two types of communication pattern within a group. Information flows to and from the person or group at the centre of the web in the centralised pattern. In the other, decentralised, pattern, more of the messages pass between those away from the centre. If the task requires communication between people in a group, but is nevertheless relatively straightforward, the star pattern of communication will work adequately. An example would be to prepare next year's staff budget for the library when there are to be no major changes. The person at the centre can give and receive familiar, routine or structured information in an efficient way.

This centralised structure will obstruct performance if the task is fairly uncertain. An example would be to develop a new product rapidly in conjunction with suppliers and customers. Because of the novelty of the task, unfamiliar question or situations will arise. Group members can only deal with these by exchanging information amongst each other rapidly. That changes the situation for others who then have to change what they do in response to constantly changing circumstances. If all information has to pass through the centre, the centre will not be able to handle unexpected difficulties. That will lead to unacceptable delays while those away from the centre await a decision on their next move. So a web form of communication is more suitable, in which people communicate as required – both amongst themselves and with the centre.

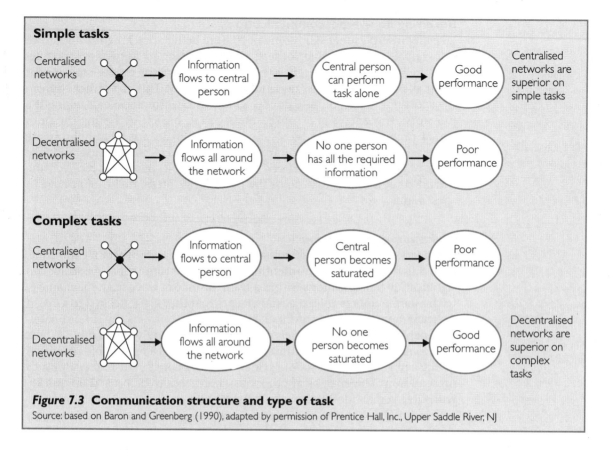

Figure 7.3 Communication structure and type of task
Source: based on Baron and Greenberg (1990), adapted by permission of Prentice Hall, Inc., Upper Saddle River, NJ

Selecting a medium

A basic question about interpersonal communication is whether it is the right medium to be using. It has advantages and disadvantages. For example, if the message is to go to many people and there is significant possibility of misunderstanding, some relatively structured written or electronic medium is likely to work best. If it is a question or problem upon which other people's opinions are needed, then a face-to-face discussion will be better, although a written note could be sent in advance to enable the others to prepare their ideas.

Lengel and Daft (1988) developed a contingency model to help make the choice of medium. It uses the idea of *media richness*. This is the capacity of a medium to convey information and promote learning. Figure 7.4 shows a range of media varying in richness from high to low.

Newsletters and routine computer reports are lean media because they provide a single cue, are impersonal and do not encourage response. Face-to-face conversation is a rich medium because it contains many cues about the message – the content itself, tone of voice, gestures. It is also personal, and response is easy.

In a study of 95 executives in a petrochemical company, Lengel and Daft found that the preferred medium depended on how routine the topic was. 'Managers used face-to-face [communication] 88 per cent of the time for non-routine communication. The reverse was true for written media.

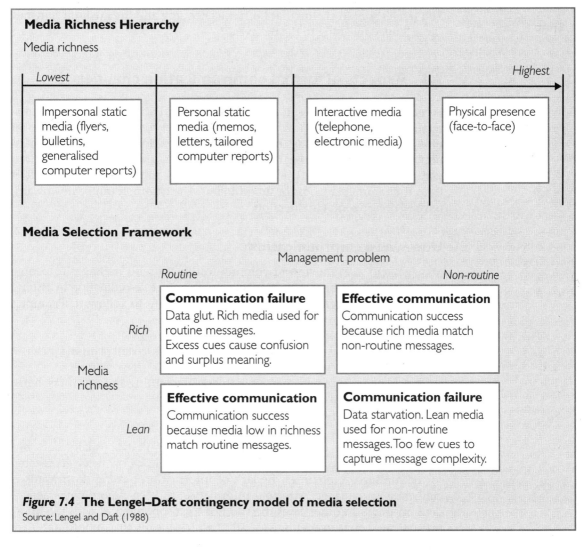

Media Richness Hierarchy

Media richness

Lowest   *Highest*

| Impersonal static media (flyers, bulletins, generalised computer reports) | Personal static media (memos, letters, tailored computer reports) | Interactive media (telephone, electronic media) | Physical presence (face-to-face) |

Media Selection Framework

Management problem

Routine   *Non-routine*

	Routine	Non-routine
Rich	**Communication failure** Data glut. Rich media used for routine messages. Excess cues cause confusion and surplus meaning.	**Effective communication** Communication success because rich media match non-routine messages.
Lean	**Effective communication** Communication success because media low in richness match routine messages.	**Communication failure** Data starvation. Lean media used for non-routine messages. Too few cues to capture message complexity.

Media richness

Figure 7.4 **The Lengel–Daft contingency model of media selection**
Source: Lengel and Daft (1988)

When they considered the topics routine and well understood, 68 per cent of the managers preferred ... written modes' (p.227).

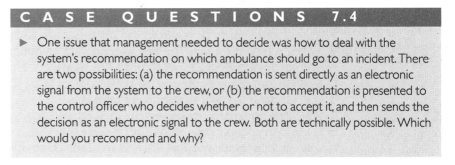

C A S E   Q U E S T I O N S   7 . 4

▶ One issue that management needed to decide was how to deal with the system's recommendation on which ambulance should go to an incident. There are two possibilities: (a) the recommendation is sent directly as an electronic signal from the system to the crew, or (b) the recommendation is presented to the control officer who decides whether or not to accept it, and then sends the decision as an electronic signal to the crew. Both are technically possible. Which would you recommend and why?

Remember also that the medium can become part of the message. A scrappy note or a badly presented essay tells the receiver a lot about the sender's intentions or attitude. The meaning of a message is not only in the encoded words or symbols: it includes the medium used to transmit them.

The sender should ensure that both the encoding and the medium transmit the intended meaning to the receiver.

7.4 Aspects of formal communication channels

Formal channels usually match the hierarchical structure of the organisation. As organisations grow, the communication channels have to cover an ever-larger area, increasing the risk of communication failure. Formal channels can also inhibit the flow of communication in the organisation, and people act without the full picture if they rely only on information from their immediate boss or subordinates. The channels can be downward, upward or horizontal in direction.

Downward communication

Management uses downward communication to send messages to people below them in the hierarchy. Managers try to ensure co-ordination by issuing a plan. They expect those lower in the hierarchy to follow it. Examples include information about:

- new policies, products or services,
- orders received, as a signal to relevant departments to start planning their part,
- budget changes or any changes in financial reporting and control systems,
- new systems and procedures,
- new appointments and reorganisations,
- job descriptions.

One problem with downward communication is that it usually does not allow for comments, so management will be unclear how receivers reacted to the message. Sometimes the lack of information passing downwards is deliberate as managers withhold information to keep subordinates dependent on them. In other cases they do not trust subordinates with the information, so keep it to themselves. All of which means that subordinates are less likely to know what is happening or what management plans. They are then less able to respond effectively.

Team briefings

Many companies use team briefings as a way of passing information rapidly and consistently throughout the organisation. Each level is briefed in turn to a standard format. The briefings provide an opportunity to communicate company issues to all staff through line managers. The opportunity to address small groups of people and use written notes bring the following benefits:

- It helps to ensure a consistent message.
- The line manager delivers the message personally.
- Many people can receive the message quickly.
- It reduces the possible distortions of the grapevine.
- Staff can ask questions.

Success or failure depends on factors such as:

- Managers must understand how the process works and why it is important.
- Every member of staff should attend a briefing session on the same day.
- Briefing sessions are short – 15 to 20 minutes.

Management needs to agree and follow the timing of a briefing session, otherwise some departments will hear before others and the grapevine will become active. Follow these steps:

Step1 What to communicate   Senior management agrees what information to communicate to staff, then draws up an approved team briefing outline.

Step 2 How it will be communicated
The senior managers agree to hold individual team briefing sessions with the managers reporting to them, on an agreed date, so that everyone hears the message on the same day.

Step 3 Delivering the message   On the appointed day, the senior managers gather their line managers, explain the purpose of the session, read through the brief and expand upon it as appropriate. The line managers receive a copy of the brief and are given time for questions and to make notes.

Step 4 Spreading the word to staff
Each line manager conducts a team briefing session – using the same briefing outline – to those reporting directly to them. This should take place within 2–4 hours. This process should continue until everyone in the organisation has attended a session.

Step 5 Feedback   Line managers should provide brief comments to their senior managers using a standard format. This highlights problems raised by staff.

▶ Briefing sessions should take place regularly or they lose impact.
▶ If a manager is unavailable they should nominate someone else to hold the session.

The Noticeboard outlines some points about the conduct of team briefings.

Upward communication

Upward communication refers to systematic methods of helping employees to pass on their views and ideas to management. Managers try to ensure co-ordination by encouraging feedback. In small organisations this is usually fairly easy. The owner-manager is likely to be in close touch with what employees are thinking. Information and ideas reach the boss quickly, and he or she can take them into account. However, it is wrong to assume that communication is necessarily good in small businesses. As the businesses grow, the layers of the hierarchy can easily break the flow. Unless they create mechanisms to allow information to move upwards, their boards too can act on incorrect information.

Employee opinion surveys

Some companies conduct regular surveys amongst their employees to gauge their attitudes and feelings towards company policy and practice. They may also seek views on current issues, or about possible changes in policy or practice. The surveys can be valuable both as a general indicator of attitudes and as a way of highlighting particular issues that need attention, such as a growing demand for childcare facilities. It is important that action follows a survey otherwise people will not take the survey seriously in future.

Suggestion schemes

These are devices by which companies encourage employees to suggest improvements to their job or other aspects of the organisation. Employees usually receive a cash reward if management accepts their idea.

n o t e b o o k   7 . 6

Gather some evidence from a company about its experience of using employee opinion surveys or suggestion schemes. What are their purposes? Who designs them and interprets the results? What have the benefits been?

Formal appeal or grievance procedures

These set out the steps to be followed when an individual or group is in dispute with the company. For example, an employee who has been penalised by a supervisor for poor time-keeping may disagree with the facts as presented or with the penalty imposed. The grievance procedure states how the employee should set about pursuing a claim for a review of the case. The procedure will usually involve the employee's trade union or staff representative.

A survey by Porter and Roberts (1983) found that two-thirds of managers' communications took place with superiors and subordinates. The accuracy of the communication increased with the similarity of outlook between the two, but diminished with status and power differences. It was also limited if there was a lack of trust between the manager and the subordinate. Subordinates are (understandably) likely to screen out problems, disagreements or complaints when they feel their superior has the power to punish them. Subordinates are likely to conceal or distort information when they do not trust the boss to be fair or if he or she is likely to use the information against them. The implication is that managers will then be unclear about the true state of the business.

Horizontal communication

Horizontal communication crosses departmental or functional boundaries, usually connecting people at broadly similar levels within the organisation. Management seeks to ensure co-ordination by encouraging lateral interaction. As different parts of the organisation co-operate on projects to introduce new products or systems, people communicate frequently. They need to pass information to each other on the current state of affairs so that each distinct unit can be ready to contribute to the project as required.

As management creates a structure for the organisation, it influences how much horizontal communication will take place. In a traditional hierarchical organisation (see Chapter 16) most information passes vertically between managers and subordinates. In the alternative organisation in which managers delegate more decisions to lower levels, there is an increase in horizontal communication. Instead of referring problems up the hierarchy to a common boss, staff in the respective departments sort out problems themselves.

Huseman and Alexander (1979) proposed that communication by plan is downward communication; feedback implies upward communication; and lateral communication implies horizontal and diagonal communication (p.331). They then link these types to what they call a *contingency model of communication* in which the manager's attention moves from one communication mode to another as the environment changes. A manager whose organisation is in a fairly stable environment should concentrate on facilitating the downward flow of information. If the business is not routine and many rapid changes and decisions are required, the manager should encourage horizontal and diagonal communication to allow those closest to the problem to apply their expertise without delay. This point is taken up in Chapter 16 when models of organisation are discussed.

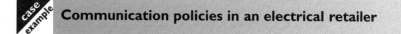

Communication policies in an electrical retailer

The company grew rapidly during the late 1980s to become a major regional retailer of electrical goods. The two joint-owners of the business were aware of the need for good communication and put in place several policies to reach high standards in this aspect of management practice. They put considerable effort into ensuring that:

- ▶ **regional managers knew about new company policies in a rapidly changing business,**
- ▶ **shop staff also knew what was expected of them,**
- ▶ **all staff knew about forthcoming advertising campaigns, so that they could respond confidently to customer queries,**
- ▶ **all staff received comments on their performance.**

They also:

- ▶ **asked all staff for their views on the way the business was run,**
- ▶ **listened to staff complaints about, for example, gaps between advertising campaigns and deliveries of advertised goods to the shops,**
- ▶ **encouraged communication across departments within head office,**
- ▶ **arranged for manufacturers to make presentations to staff on new products.**

n o t e b o o k   7 . 7

Another view is that communication patterns reflect the prevailing national culture within which management is operating, rather than universal organisational models. Refer to Hofstede's typologies of national culture in Chapter 3. Concentrate on the power distance and uncertainty avoidance dimensions. In a country with low power distance and low to medium uncertainty avoidance, would you expect companies to emphasise vertical or horizontal information flows? Why?

7.5 Developments in communication technology

Information technology is radically changing many aspects of communication within and between organisations. To give just some examples: *e-mail* makes it possible to send messages electronically and can be used for either one-to-one or one-to-many communications. *Video-conferencing* makes it possible for people who are physically remote to hold a meeting in which they can see all the others taking part. It can be used (with some difficulty) for interactive meetings of small groups, or for a presentation by one person to a large group. The *Intranet* – an internal version of the Internet – enables people within an organisation to access what is in effect an internal Website. This can be used to share company-specific information quickly and in the knowledge that everyone will receive identical information, both of which are important considerations, especially when information is changing rapidly.

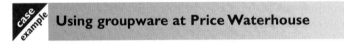

n o t e b o o k   7.8

Try to gather information on the practical use of at least one of these systems. Scan computer or professional journals for articles about the systems so that you are broadly familiar with them, then try to discuss the system with someone who has some experience of using it in a working organisation. Ask that person about matters such as:

What are the advantages and disadvantages compared with (a) traditional communication devices, (b) the options realistically available in the particular situation for which it was used?

How has it affected the way that people communicate with each other? Is it a satisfactory substitute for face-to-face spoken communication?

---

case example ## Using groupware at Price Waterhouse

Price Waterhouse is one of the world's leading accountancy and consultancy organisations; it employs almost 50,000 people in over 100 countries, including over 10,000 consultants. It has particular expertise in financial services, media, oil and gas, telecommunications and utilities. The company, founded 150 years ago, traditionally operated as a collection of national or regional groups, further divided into functions. These worked in relative isolation from colleagues, especially those in other countries.

In 1990 the company realised that clients (especially large multinationals) required it to handle bigger and more complex jobs. Staff would have to offer a wider range of experience – which was largely available in the collective but unorganised experience of the consultants. How could management gather and communicate this valuable information quickly? The solution was to install a groupware system incorporating database management, e-mail, spreadsheets and other functions.

The system is built on a document database that enables staff to share information quickly worldwide. They use their PCs to communicate and work on the same electronic files. They can access standard practice information and draw on the knowledge of colleagues either through databases or on-line bulletin boards. They can link to the network from wherever they are. Two of the main uses are knowledge-sharing and internal communication.

Knowledge-sharing
The company has invested heavily in knowledge databases. The regional offices easily held knowledge about staff and expertise when the company consisted of regional practices. Clients typically contacted the regional director and discussed the possibilities in person before deciding whether to give an assignment. Clients now are major international

companies, so management needs information very quickly about expertise anywhere in the world. 'To do that, we've built a database with all the projects we've done in particular industries and topics. So I can find out from my desk where our knowledge base is. I can have a set of case studies on our client's desk in a few hours.' Other databases contain what the company has learned from those projects. Consultants on a project use the database as a source of ideas and information.

Internal communication

The system is central to communications between offices and consultants across time zones. This is essential in a global business and the system allows much easier internal communication, irrespective of location.

A senior manager in the company reflected on their experience with the groupware product:

> The ability to manage globally in a people-business depends on good communications. Our network has helped us to move as quickly as we have. It's hard to see how we could have done so without it, though I'm not sure whether in 1990 we saw as far ahead as that. We've been able to respond to opportunities partly because we had the systems in place. Virtually everyone in the practice is now a groupware user. We communicate by e-mail through the Internet with outside clients.
>
> Physical location is much less of an issue. In our London office we have a hotel concept – if you want to go into the office you have to book the space. With the technology, people can work anywhere. They are always in touch. If I want someone to read a document, I can send it to them wherever they are. Location is less of an issue now than it used to be.
>
> It has encouraged a culture of creativity. There are some groups focused on specific things, dispersed anywhere. They have become virtual thought-leaders in particular topics. They have created a network around a specific issue. When an issue comes up with a client, they ask the network for advice. It has just grown, like an Internet noticeboard. Before, nobody ever asked you, so you never had to think 'how would I do that?' Now you are likely to be asked. Rather than borrowing a solution and trying to fit it, it has encouraged creativity and a culture of learning and sharing.

---

n o t e b o o k   7 . 9

How would a worldwide, information-dependent business such as Price Waterhouse manage without the electronic communication systems described?

What benefits does the company expect that clients will receive from the system?

How may the system affect the work of the individual consultants?

7.6 Informal communication systems

Alongside the structural and technical complexity of any company's formal systems there is the grapevine. This is the spontaneous informal system through which people pass information and gossip. It happens throughout the organisation and across all hierarchical levels. It is in action as people meet in the corridor, by the photocopier, at lunch, on the way home. The information that passes along the grapevine is usually well ahead of the information on the formal system. It is about who said what at a meeting, who has applied for another job, who has been summoned to explain their poor results to the directors or what orders the company has won.

The grapevine does not replace the formal system, but passes a different kind of information around – qualitative rather than quantitative, current ideas and proposals rather than agreed policies. As it is uncensored and reflects the views of people as a whole rather than those in charge of the formal communications media, it probably gives a truer picture of the diversity of opinions within the company than the formal policies will. Nevertheless, it should be remembered that the rumours and information on the grapevine might be wrong or incomplete. Those passing gossip and good stories of spectacular disasters in department X may also have their own interests and agendas. These may include promoting the interests of department Y. The grapevine is as likely to be a vehicle for political intrigue as any of the formal systems.

The grapevine can be a source of early information about what is happening elsewhere in the organisation. This allows those affected but not yet formally consulted to begin preparing their position. Put the other way round, someone preparing proposals or plans can be quite sure that information about them will get out onto the grapevine sooner than they expect. Sometimes it is useful to deliberately let the matter slip out and begin circulating to be able to gauge reaction before going too far with a plan.

7.7 Problems and barriers to communication

If communication were perfect, the receiver would always understand the message as the sender intended. It rarely happens that way. People interpret information from their own perspectives. Words fail to express feelings or emotions. Power games affect how people send and receive information. So we cannot assume that the message sent is the message received, because breakdowns and barriers can disrupt any link in the communication chain.

Micro-barriers to communication

Some of the barriers to communication are at the level of the interpersonal or 'micro' level. Microbarriers are in the immediate situation and include the sender's message, mutual views of sender and receiver, choice of medium, and noise.

The sender's message
The subject, and how the sender views it, is as much part of the communication process as the message itself. A communicator who has badly misjudged a situation and is trying to communicate out-of-date, inaccurate, poorly argued or poorly presented information will not convince the receiver that the message is worth receiving. There is no substitute in communicating for accurate observation, for validity, reliability and careful preparation. Similarly, the solution that the sender is proposing may not

seem very smart to the receiver, so the receiver will add his or her perspective, resulting in a muddier communication than the sender intended.

Mutual views of sender and receiver

In planning to send a message the sender has (even if only implicitly) a view of the receiver. This shapes the form, nature and content of the communication. We talk differently to different people because we make allowances for what they can understand or for their known biases. The receiver also has a view of the sender which will shape the meaning and interpretation that he or she attaches to the message. If the two people are receptive and trusting, communication will be easy. If they are antagonistic and suspicious it will be very difficult for the sender to communicate the message. The message received will be quite different from that intended by the sender – although it may be interpreted in its true light by the receiver.

Choice of medium

The medium we use greatly affects what we convey. As receivers we prefer certain media over others, so we pay more attention to some than to others. Some dislike over-formal language, while others dislike using casual terms in written documents. Putting a message in writing may help understanding, but others may see it as a sign of distrust. Some communicate readily by e-mail, others are reluctant to switch on their system.

Noise

Noise is anything that confuses, diminishes or interferes with communication.

Noise refers to anything that interferes with the intended flow of communication. Sometimes it may be physical interruptions or distractions, as when a video-conference breaks down for technical reasons. The term also includes multiple – sometimes conflicting – messages being sent and received at the same time. If our non-verbal signals or subsequent actions are inconsistent with the words we are using, the receiver may see a different meaning in our message from that which we intended.

---

n o t e b o o k   7.10

Refer to the Case Example in Chapter 3 about an English teacher in Japan. How did the mutual views of the teacher and the education chief affect their communication? Did the teacher use the right medium?

What other communication practices mentioned in this chapter might have helped avoid the trouble?

Noise also refers to the inclusion in a message of distracting or minor information that diverts attention from the main business. Communication can also suffer from interruptions which distract both parties and prevent the concentration essential to good communication. The receiver's attention may be distracted by some completely separate matters.

Macro-barriers to communication

Macro-barriers concern the environment, the larger world in which communication takes place. The main ones are discussed below.

Information overload

Most people in organisations have too much information. They are trained to search for more and better information, and so place greater burdens on already overloaded communication systems. This leads to an increasing number of communications. We receive countless messages, and we send countless messages to others. The majority of the messages beamed at us – the specific as well as the general – pass us by. There are too many of them to handle.

CASE QUESTIONS 7.5

▶ What evidence is there of micro- or macro-barriers in the ambulance service?

The variety of media

Information is communicated by so many different media that it is easy to be overwhelmed or simply to miss important items. Management is confronted by newspapers, specialist magazines, conferences, Internet communications, terrestrial, digital and satellite TV, special surveys and consultancy reports. The volume of public information becomes a barrier to its use.

Pressure of time

Time is, for most people, the scarcest resource. Our communications must fit time demands, and even when time pressure is not rigorous, we find we have developed a habit about it and make it so anyway. We cram our communications with information, whether needed or not. We compete with each other to talk. We set arbitrary deadlines and unneeded requirements. Talk is cheap, so we spend it recklessly, overloading our message systems and thereby depreciating their contents.

Departmentalisation

Organisations are typically divided into separate units, focusing on their particular part of the total task. As explained in Chapter 16, this segmentation often leads to people focusing too much on their own corner and not enough on other players. This means that departments forget that others will have an interest in what they are doing, or will be affected by it – and forget to communicate information until it is too late.

Information as currency

Information has great value. Those who possess it have something others do not have and may need or want. Sole ownership of information can also be used to boost or protect a person's status or the significance of his or her role.

As explained in Chapter 5, access to information and the means of communicating it to others is a source of power so, if it can be acquired, it can be used to influence others. It may be hoarded rather than shared, to be used at the most opportune moment. Those with access to inside information have both prestige and power.

case example **A further look at Price Waterhouse**

The manager also made the following comment which illustrates how information can be seen as 'currency', and how the company dealt with it.

We had to overcome a number of issues to encourage that because some of the consultant managers think they're competing with each other. The competition still exists in practice units. So we've 'incentivised' them to share. If they're not meeting the culture, not sharing, that's not going to help them. We have a peer recognition system and an upward appraisal system. So if a consultant thinks a manager is not applying the culture, that will show up. And the peer recognition system allows people who have been sharing and helping others to be acknowledged and rewarded. We apply peer recognition throughout the business. It also needs certain disciplines – people must see it as part of their job to maintain information and record details of their projects. It's part of how they manage a client.

7.8   Communication from a critical perspective

Information is not always neutral. People can use it to legitimise particular sets of values and to exclude discussion of others. Communication affects the distribution of power in organisations. Those with power can try to maintain it by managing what is communicated, encouraging some types of information or discussion and suppressing others. Habermas (1972) distinguished three types of knowledge that communication serves:

▶ **Prediction and control**   Communication is used to understand the links between cause and effect, making it easier to predict and control events. Rational approaches to management emphasise using this kind of knowledge to serve the goals of the organisation. For this reason writers often refer to it as *instrumental rationality*. The knowledge can be of an uncontentious technical nature, or it can be used to influence employees to support organisational goals.

▶ **Mutual understanding**   Communication enhances people's mutual understanding of each other. In organisations, it helps people to share what the organisation means to them, how they are treated and how they experience the nature and meaning of their work.

▶ **Critical reflection**   Communication enables people to reflect on the situation and challenge the goals pursued. Rather than focus on doing what is required in the name of instrumental rationality, communication provides the means of challenging what is being aimed for, questioning both means and goals.

Alvesson and Wilmott (1996) argue that most official company language is set in terms that legitimise the idea of organisations as models of rationality and especially of instrumental rationality. Management typically encourages communication that supports instrumental rationality – a concern with means not ends. They acknowledge that instrumental rationality is not in itself wrong if the goals of the activity genuinely enhance human well-being. Their criticism is that arguments presented as supporting a rational analysis or solution often hide the self-interest of those presenting the information. The emphasis is typically on communicating about the means to achieve a goal, not to challenge those goals in themselves. That is, messages are labelled as containing 'rational' data and arguments and are used to support a particular course of action. However, what is communicated as 'rational' may in fact be highly contentious or it may be highly 'irrational'. For example, a management proposal to concentrate production in smaller factories may be argued on the rational grounds of lower costs. Another view is that this ignores other costs such as extra traffic pollution or the effects on communities if plants are closed.

If these criteria are used, the decision to concentrate production may be irrational. At the root of the issue is whether communication is used instrumentally to reach particular ends (low costs to one company) or to encourage critical reflection (the possibility that company goals could include avoiding pollution and supporting smaller communities). Alvesson and Wilmott argue that the prevailing management wisdom would be to belittle as unreal idealists those who attempted to challenge fundamentally some of the goals of business organisations. 'Critical analysis subjects the rationality of such understandings and objectives to close scrutiny, arguing that the espoused rationality of conventional management theory and practice takes for granted the prevailing structure of power relations and is preoccupied with preserving the status quo' (Alvesson and Wilmott, 1996, p.51).

7.9 Improving your communication skills

Communication skills are increasingly valued by employers and colleagues at work. You will be able to practise some of them during tutorials and other study activities. The advice given here is not meant to be over-prescriptive: use it as a guideline in developing your own preferred style of communicating.

Making presentations

The first rule of making presentations is simple: do not believe people who tell you that you will be able to think on your feet. Few people can, and the consequences of standing up in front of an audience without knowing what you are going to say are serious. Not only must you know what you want to say, you should know enough about your audience to have a shrewd idea of what they expect to hear and what their reaction is likely to be. In order to make your case effectively, you must therefore:

▶ show that it is based on credible information and preparations,
▶ spell out the benefits it offers to the members of the audience.

Almost everybody is nervous about speaking in public. Remember that the learning curve for public speaking is sharper than for almost any other management activity. Most people improve dramatically over their first few presentations and everyone can benefit from practising their presentation skills. If you have prepared the subject thoroughly, keep reminding yourself that you know more about it than anyone in the audience. This reduces the two great anxieties – drying up and showing ignorance.

Here are some tips to increase your confidence as a public speaker.

▶ **Check out the room beforehand** Become familiar with the facilities and layout, and make sure you can work the technology.
▶ **Rehearse** Rehearsing with an audience (one person will do) increases your confidence, helps you get the timing right and gives you a chance to hear feedback about any irritating verbal or visual mannerisms.
▶ **Stand up** Standing gives you more authority and will force you to remember that you are performing. When standing, be careful not to

sway around to much. Keep your hands out of your pockets, and try to look as if you are in control of the situation and enjoying the event.

▶ **Start powerfully**   A strong beginning is the key to an effective presentation. Set the scene, perhaps using a graphic image to illustrate the topic or the problem you are dealing with.

▶ **Structure your talk around the central theme**   Stick to one or two central themes and signpost any essential deviations. Give interim summaries and construct an argument that leads to a positive, irresistible conclusion.

▶ **Three's enough**   Having decided on your main message, follow the Rule of Three: most people cannot absorb more than three new ideas in one sitting.

▶ **Illustrate key points**   Use real people and events to illustrate your argument. This helps the audience to build mental images which interest them now and help them remember what you have said later.

▶ **Use cards**   Cue cards are the least obtrusive way of helping you to remember the sequence of your argument. Write a couple of main points on each, three or four subheadings. Do not use complete sentences – a few words is the most you can take in at a glance. Never read from a text or sheets of notes.

▶ **Use short sentences**   Avoid going into too much detail. Be succinct.

▶ **Make eye contact**   Your eyes are an important link with your audience. Look at them, try to assess their reaction and adjust to it. Locate some friendly faces at different points in the room and return to them regularly, to make sure you seem to be addressing everyone.

▶ **End with a strong message and image**   Work out in advance the message you want to leave your listeners with. It should be as powerful as your opening thrust and must reinforce your key point. A five-point action plan will reassure them that there is a way to achieve what you are proposing – and that you know what it is.

Writing reports

A good report is easy to recognise because it leaves the reader with two positive feelings: 'there's something in this for me' and 'that report was easy to read'. Here are five suggestions to help you engender this reaction in others.

▶ **Get the story straight**   Every report has a story to tell. Make sure you tell it clearly and vigorously. Before starting, make sure you know what you want to say. It should not take more than a paragraph to write down all the main points. Refer to it frequently to make sure you are not deviating from your central message. To gain and keep the readers' attention, you need to know what they want from the report. Do they want an analysis of a problem, a source of information to refer to, or a firm recommendation?

▶ **Put the last page first**   Even when recommendations are not required, your report must have clear conclusions. Readers will turn to them first and may read no further if the conlusions do not capture their interest. The main analysis comes next, with details held back for the appendices. This may not seem the logical way to write but it is what the reader wants. A side benefit of putting the last page first is that it encourages you to keep the report brief.

▶ **When in doubt leave it out**   Short reports are easier to read and more likely to be read. Self-discipline is required, together with a rigorous adherence to priorities in order to edit out the least valuable material. Cutting marginal topics eases the readers' burden and usually detracts nothing from the report's value. Inexperienced report-writers may like to keep a record of what they eliminated from earlier drafts. They will be surprised at how much can be cut without reducing the impact of a report.

▶ **Keep the fog factor low**   The fog factor is a score derived by calculating the average number of words of more than three syllables in each sentence. The lower the fog factor, the less is demanded of the reader. If the fog factor is more than three and a half, readers will often stop reading: they have better things to do. It takes time to reduce the fog factor (most computers have grammar checks which help) but it is worse to discover that you have written a report that nobody will read.

▶ **Make the data talk**   You need to help data on its way to the readers' mind. In a well constructed table, patterns and exceptions are instantly obvious. Impact is more important than absolute accuracy, so prune numbers to the right of the decimal point ruthlessly, round up, order rows and columns by size, and summarise the key conclusion from each table. If it is hard to see a conclusion, do you need the table?

These suggestions sound obvious, but it takes real application to use them when writing because they are designed to aid the reader. If you get the structure right before you start, you will have less editing later. Allow time for revision and, if possible, ask someone else to read it before submission. When asked to make a presentation in support of a written report, assume that your audience has not read the report. However, your presentation must not consist of a repetition of the written version.

The art of listening

Communication depends on the receiver being able to interpret accurately what the sender of a message says. There are six things you can do to be an effective listener:

▶ **Stop talking**, especially that internal, mental silent chatter. Let the speaker finish. Hear them out. It is tempting in a familiar situation to complete the speaker's sentence for them and work out a reply. This assumes that you know what they are going to say, when you should instead be listening to what they are actually saying.

▶ **Put the speaker at ease** by showing that you are listening. The good listener does not look over someone's shoulder or write while the speaker is talking. If you must take notes, explain what you are doing. Take care, because we all rely on the other person's facial expression while we are speaking to them. The speaker will be put off if you look away or concentrate on your notes instead of nodding reassuringly.

▶ Remember that your **aim is to understand** what the speaker is saying, not to win an argument.

▶ Be aware of your **personal prejudices** and make a conscious effort to stop them influencing your judgement.

▶ Be alert to **what the speaker is not saying**, as well as what they are. Very often, what is missing is more important than what is there.

▶ **Ask questions**. This shows that you have been listening and encourages the speaker to develop the points you have raised. It is an active process, never more important than when you are meeting someone for the first time – when your objective should be to say as little and learn as much as possible in the shortest time.

7.10 Recap

Content agenda

The quality of information available to managers in dealing with the content agenda reflects communication processes. To develop objectives and planning to achieve them, managers need useful information about external events and internal resources. This comes from many sources and needs to be received and accurately decoded. It could include non-verbal signals and the grapevine as well as more formal information sources. In generating action and motivation, ideas about the clarity of encoding and choosing the right medium are relevant. The more carefully these are considered, the more likely it is that people will know what is expected of them. Being aware of the micro- and macro-barriers to communication can help management ensure that people know what is expected of them. The quality of communication as people make proposals, express opinions, clarify ideas and get things done will affect performance. Management needs to create formal and informal systems to support communication required in the situation – such as lateral communication in changing environments, effective vertical or centralised systems in a stable environment.

Process agenda

The process agenda is about how people influence the behaviour of others. Influence depends on understanding the needs and interests of those being influenced. This can only come from observing, listening and correctly interpreting what they say and do. Taking care to encode the meaning, choose the right medium and to seek feedback is likely to support attempts to influence others as the message is more likely to be accurately interpreted and acted upon by individuals and teams. Stakeholders can be kept well informed through effective communication or they can be ignored. They may also be threatened by information and may distort it. Team briefings can help to ensure that all understand the objectives of the organisation. Information can be shared to encourage joint problem-solving – or it can be suppressed and retained within a centralised communication system. Management styles that depend on input need to ensure that communication is not blocked.

Control agenda

Information can also be used and sometimes distorted to control people, support particular interests and maintain an existing balance of power. As part of the control agenda, managers monitor performance and communicate corrective action. Organisational learning depends on information

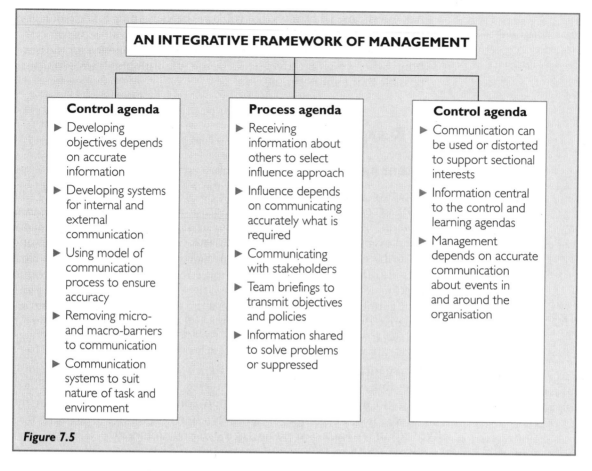

Figure 7.5

flowing around the enterprise: communcation barriers inhibit learning. Figure 7.5 summarises these points.

PART CASE QUESTIONS

▶ What are the main methods of communication in W.L. Gore and Associates and which methods does management encourage?

▶ Use the Lengel–Daft model to explain why communication practices differ between W.L. Gore and the 'command and control' system in the ambulance service.

▶ How could a groupware product such as that used at Price Waterhouse help W.L. Gore?

7.11 Review questions

1 Using examples of good and bad practice from your experience, explain why the quality of communication affects performance in organisations.
2 Use a communication episode you have experienced to illustrate each of the steps in Figure 7.1.
3 Which areas of the model caused most difficulty in that example of your experience, and what lessons can you take from that?

4 Take a message which you want to encode, and revise your approach in the light of the suggestions from Hellriegel and Slocum in the Noticeboard on page 227.

5 Give examples of non-verbal communication which (a) supported and (b) contradicted a verbal message.

6 What do you understand by the term 'media richness' and how does it affect the choice of communication method?

7 Compare the barriers to communication implied in the Dutch company in the Case Example on page 228 and in the ambulance service.

8 One of the barriers to communication stated is that information is a form of currency. Evaluate that view by reference to the ideas in Chapter 5.

9 How does feedback help or hinder communication?

10 How are the ideas in this chapter relevant to managing in an international context?

11 In view of the information in section 7.9, how would you improve your listening skills?

Further reading

To go deeper into some of the psychological aspects of communication, especially the non-verbal aspects, see Guirdham (1995). A classic (and short) work is Goffman's *Presentation of Self in Everyday Life* (1959).

In 1997, BT published an unusual short guide to communication called *Talkworks* which gives an excellent and well presented introduction with many practical tips.

A good source of examples of communication failure in organisations are the reports of public inquiries into accidents, business collapses or mistakes in healthcare and social service organisations. These often arise in part because separate agencies have not communicated as they should have.

How teams develop

CONTENTS

AIM

To outline theories of team development and to show how you can use these insights to increase your awareness of team processes.

OBJECTIVES

By the end of your work on this chapter you should be able to outline the concepts below in your own terms and:

1 List the functions that distinguish teams from other collections of people

2 Outline Homans's model of the interactions within a group and between the group and its environment

3 Give an example of the interaction between activities, interactions, sentiments and norms

4 Define formal and informal groups

5 Describe a theory of the stages of development through which groups pass, and evaluate a group by using this model

6 Summarise Schein's theory on how a group develops a distinct culture, and to test that approach against the experience of a group with which you are familiar

7 Distinguish between content, structure, culture and process in analysing a group, and illustrate how they affect each other

8 Accurately observe a group and compare patterns of communication and interaction within it

9 Explain Belbin's theory of team roles and use the model to distinguish different roles that people take in teams

10 Understand the implications of Belbin's approach for developing effective teamworking

11 Compare three alternative measures of group effectiveness

12 Outline the wider organisational factors which affect group performance

Consulting Engineers employed 600 people. The company consisted of five divisions based on broad professional disciplines, and each of these contained several groups of staff in separate subdisciplines. The information system used to control project costs had serious defects.

Management decided to install a new system to satisfy its needs for flexibility, detail and accessibility of information. The system would streamline administration and provide a more effective tool for managing the core consultancy activities. It would provide information on project costing and charging and would affect accounting, personnel and marketing departments.

Top management created a steering committee to co-ordinate the departments affected by the system. The committee had nine representatives from user groups and had powers to co-opt specialist expertise. The committee met regularly during the early stages of the project to prepare the specification and to choose a supplier. The committee would eventually transfer the running of the system to a system manager.

A manager from one of the technical departments chaired the committee, and he tended to dominate the group. He actively invited comment from other members, but in a way that some found intimidating. He did not always get a balanced and considered view from the committee.

The representative from the accounting function was young, unfamiliar with the kind of system planned, and was reluctant to voice his views. He limited his contribution to expressing satisfaction with progress, and gave assurances that his part of the project would be successful. Not surprisingly, other members lacked confidence in him. The system would integrate the accounting modules with other components so they had to be there from the beginning. Others depended on accounting which the team could not treat in isolation. It emerged during tests that the system designers had fundamentally misunderstood the internal procedures of the accounting function.

Members had different degrees of commitment to the project. The system manager supported the project and devoted all his time to it. The senior manager representing consultants and project leaders was less enthusiastic and often failed to do things to which he had agreed. There were other demands on his time and he gave low priority to this project, but another representative might not have carried the same seniority.

No one person had a clear overview of how the company's functions related to each other or how the internal functions of the information system related to each other. This made it difficult to establish a balance between the sometimes conflicting requirements of different functions. While the system did provide significant benefits once it was in operation, many users said the project was a lost opportunity to make more radical use of IT.

CASE QUESTIONS

▶ Have you, or someone you know, experienced a team like this? Why do you think it failed to deliver?

▶ What would you suggest that someone setting up a similar team should do to avoid these problems?

8.1 Introduction

This chapter introduces the following ideas:
- ▶ Group
- ▶ Team
- ▶ Formal and informal groups
- ▶ Content
- ▶ Structure
- ▶ Process
- ▶ Culture
- ▶ Activities
- ▶ Interactions
- ▶ Sentiments
- ▶ Norms
- ▶ Preferred team roles
- ▶ Team-based rewards
- ▶ Observation

Most work in organisations depends on people working together rather than as isolated individuals. A team or group is responsible for an area of work and deals with many practical issues itself rather than waiting for detailed instructions from a manager. Exceptional tasks to deal with complex problems facing organisations or communities usually require people with different perspectives and skills to work together on a solution.

Some teams work to very high standards and levels of achievement. They are conspicuously successful and achieve more than was expected. Others fail, wasting both time and opportunity. The team set up to design the new management information system in the Case Study is an example of a team that did not achieve a result. It never became a properly functioning team. The differences in performance – in meeting business goals or in satisfying members – reflect how the members managed the team. Putting people together as a group does not ensure either performance or satisfaction.

C A S E   Q U E S T I O N S   8 . 1

- ▶ What do you think went wrong in the team at Consulting Engineers? Why should a group of intelligent and well intentioned managers achieve so little when brought together to work in a team?

- ▶ Have you had similar or contrasting experiences? Can you think of a team that worked particularly well? And one that did not?

- ▶ Reflecting on all these examples, what is your theory about the factors that help a team to succeed or fail? Keep your notes ready, as you will be able to compare your conclusions with some other research on team development and performance later in the chapter.

The diversity of backgrounds that makes a team worthwhile also makes it harder for the team to work. Creating a team (or 'group', 'section', 'task-force' or 'working party') is only the start. Members then need to learn to work together collaboratively to reach a target. They need to integrate and focus effort rather than diffuse it. That is hard enough for any group of people, but they will also bring into the team differences of power, status, role and gender. Increasingly, team members come from different nations and cultures, with different ways of operating. The greater the diversity, the greater the challenge it will be to make the team work.

Studies of groups give some clues about building effective teams (Belbin, 1993; Hastings *et al.*, 1986; Hackman, 1990; Hayes, 1997). Belbin showed how, even in identical external circumstances, some teams perform effectively while others fail. He explained this by differences in how members choose to work. This chapter outlines the main concepts and methods which are available, dealing both with their academic sources and their practical implications

8.2 Defining groups and teams

A problem in studying groups and teams is that these labels are used in everyday speech to refer to a huge variety of social and organisational arrangements. To make their study manageable, researchers need to narrow the field and set some approximate boundaries. Some writers distinguish between groups and teams using the latter term for those which perform better than the former. Most use the words interchangeably, and this book does the same.

Nevertheless, groups and teams do need to be distinguished from other social arrangements. A group (or team) is not just any collection of people. A crowd in the street is not usually a group: they are there at the same time by chance, and will have little if any further contact. They are there for their own purposes, will accomplish them on their own, and will then go their separate ways. Are 150 students in a lecture theatre a team? What about the staff in a supermarket? In a takeaway restaurant? In the same section of a factory? They are not a crowd: they have some things in common, and may be referred to as a group by management. Compare them with five people designing some software for a bank, each of whom brings distinct professional skills to their collective discussions of the most suitable design, or with seven students who are working on a group project, or with six people in an electronics company who are solely responsible for packing products as they leave the assembly line and moving them into the freight containers. They handle the whole process, work largely on their initiative, and move easily between all the tasks, helping each other as needed.

---

n o t e b o o k   8.1

Note down a few words that express the differences between the examples given. Do some sound more like a group than others?

A group or team consists of two or more people with some shared purpose who assume different responsibilities, depend on each other, co-ordinate their activities, and see themselves as part of the unit.

One difference is in the extent to which they share a common purpose. Groups aim to produce some outcome to which all members have contributed, and for which they share some collective responsibility. A second difference is in the extent to which members share ideas and activities to get the job done. A group can add value to what any individual could do by exchanging ideas, information and effort. Thus there is a degree of continuing interdependence, which leads them to feel a sense of membership, and of being (temporarily) distinct from outsiders.

---

n o t e b o o k   8 . 2

Teams or not?

Consider a Davis Cup tennis or Ryder Cup golf 'team', in which most of the action takes place between individual participants from either side. No significant coordination occurs between the members during each of the matches. In what ways would such teams meet the definition above?

Can you think of other examples of people who work largely on their own but are commonly referred to as a team?

A team may not be physically obvious. People may work on their own but at the same time be part of a tight network. They may, for example, be part of a widely dispersed project team, who communicate intensively by electronic means and meet all the other criteria of a team. They may be working on their particular part of a production process. In order to do so effectively they take account of the needs of those in earlier or later stages, and try to work in with them. The definition says nothing about the physical location or closeness of members.

8.3   The basics of effective teamworking

The definition of a team that was given above can be used to establish some of the basic tools that team members need to develop.

Small number

Some teams are bigger but, in practice, collections of more than about twelve have great difficulty operating as a coherent team. It becomes harder for them to agree on a common purpose. The logistical problems of finding a place and time to work together become steadily greater as numbers increase. Hence most teams have between two and ten people – with between four and eight probably being the most common range. Larger groups, if formed, are more likely to divide themselves into subgroups.

Shared purpose

Teams are unlikely to work well towards achieving their common purpose unless members spend time and effort clarifying what that purpose is. They need to express it in clear and measurable performance goals. The two go together: balancing the broad, longer-term vision that sets the tone and aspiration levels with more immediately achievable goals. Clear purposes and goals help to focus the energy of the group on activities that support their achievement. They also help communication between members, since people can interpret and understand their contributions better if they share the same aims. Clear and measurable goals can themselves have a positive effect on the effort which team members make. This works even better if the team uses small wins to show progress.

Common approach

Teams need to decide how they will work together to accomplish their common purpose. This includes agreeing both the administrative and social aspects of working together. The former includes deciding who does which jobs, what skills members need to develop, and how the group should make and modify decisions. In other words, the team needs to agree the work required and how to integrate their skills and use them co-operatively to advance performance.

The common approach includes supporting and integrating new or reticent members into the team. It also includes practices of remembering and summarising group agreements and discussions. Working together on these tasks helps to promote the mutual trust and constructive conflict necessary to team success. Teams need to spend as much time on developing a common approach as they do on developing a shared purpose.

Complementary skills

Teams benefit from having three types of complementary skill available within their membership. First, there are *technical*, *functional* or *professional skills*, relevant to the subject of the group's work. A group implementing a networked computer system will require appropriate IT skills, while one developing a new strategy for a retailer will have strategic or business development skills. It is worth noting that Belbin's later research on teams included the role of specialist as an essential team role (see below).

Secondly, a team needs to have within it people with *problem-solving and decision-making skills*. These enable the team to approach a task systematically, using appropriate techniques of analysis. These include SWOT analysis, project management methods, cost/benefit analysis, diagramming techniques, and flowcharting. A single team will need only a few such techniques, but being able to use them helps speed the group's work.

Finally, a team needs people with adequate *interpersonal skills* to hold it together as a human institution. Members' attitudes and feelings towards each other and to the task change as work continues. The changing degree of commitment may generate irritation and conflict. To bring these feelings into the open or to smooth disagreements, and generally to be aware of developing relationships are essential skills within a group.

How important are these skills when selecting team members? The functional and technical skills need to be available, but team members can develop many of the others on the job as they identify a need. Working together towards a common purpose motivates learning within teams.

NOTICEBOARD Group problem-solving processes

Mike Robson (1993) offers more detail on the skills which group members need to develop as a common approach to getting things done. His model combines both analytical and creative methods, and team members often need both. The elements he suggests are:

▶ **Brainstorming**   A well known but often badly used technique to generate many ideas in a short time, and to ensure that everyone contributes.

▶ **Define the problem clearly**   People often pay too little attention to defining the real problem. Problem statements may be thinly disguised solutions; or may tackle the wrong issue because of the assumptions made. He recommends spending time to get at the root cause, by rigorously asking exactly what issue would be solved by dealing with the stated problem.

▶ **Multiple causes and solutions**   Analyse the problem by methods that help to identify a wide range of possible causes and solutions. Successful groups do not accept the obvious causes but think their way around the problem thoroughly. One technique here is to have six headings – people, environment, methods,

plant, equipment, materials – and assess how each of these (or other items) can be a possible cause of the difficulty.

▶ **Collect data**   Facts not opinion, and gather in a single document.

▶ **Interpret the data**   Use some organised tools for looking at the data and exploring what it means – Pareto charts, histograms. These allow data to be organised in descending order of priority, so indicating where to concentrate effort.

▶ **Find or generate possible solutions**   Use a fishbone diagram to generate ideas via brainstorming or techniques like force field analysis.

▶ **Agree the best solutions**   Ensure, too, that the criteria for selection are specified.

▶ **Cost/benefit analysis**   To establish what costs will be incurred, and what benefits obtained.

▶ **Implement solutions**   Often the most difficult part of the whole exercise.

▶ **Monitor and evaluate**   To check on progress and to learn lessons for the future.

Source: Robson (1993)

n o t e b o o k   8.3

Does your experience of teams support or contradict Robson's propositions? Which, if any, of the practices did the teams use? Did that help them to be effective? Did not using them explain their failure? Which two of these practices would have been most useful to the team in the Case Study?

If you work in teams on your course, you could try out some of these and other ideas in this chapter in order to see how helpful, or otherwise, they are.

Mutual accountability

The final point is that a team cannot work as one until its members willingly hold themselves to be collectively and mutually accountable for the results of the work. People joining a team or group are wisely cautious at first, since they do not know enough about the others to make a sensible judgement about their energy, reliability, commitment and so on. As people do real work together towards a common objective, commitment and trust usually follow.

8.4 What are the elements in a group?

George Homans's model

To understand the sources of group performance, it is necessary to have some tools with which to analyse their inner structure. One of the first writers to begin providing those tools was the sociologist George Homans (1950). He pointed out that, while groups performed much industrial work, there had been little study of their inner workings. He was a member of Elton Mayo's department at Harvard Business School and so was familiar with the Hawthorne studies. Drawing on this study and four other groups, he presented a general theory of the way groups develop.

Throughout his book *The Human Group* he stressed the complexity of the process, which arose from the constant interaction between each of the elements. This endless interweaving of the elements making up the group, and the interaction between them and the outside world, made the group an inherently fluid institution. He quoted with approval Mary Parker Follett's observation that 'the unity of the situation IS the interaction of the parts, not the result of the interaction'. A group is not the final static product of interacting events – it is itself made up of that interaction.

He proposed that we should analyse a group, like any social system, with four elements:

▶ **Activities**   The physical or mental tasks which people undertake, for example preparing a report, assembling a component, presenting a performance, completing a project.
▶ **Interactions**   When people communicate with each other in some way. What group members do or say to each other, who they talk to and how frequently, and whether discussions are relatively formal or spontaneous.
▶ **Sentiments**   Include the day-to-day feelings of irritation or enthusiasm and deeper ones such as trust and closeness, or the opposite. The feelings, emotions and attitudes that members have towards each other.
▶ **Norms**   The informal rules that group members share and enforce, specifying how members should behave. These set standards for how members behave in particular circumstance, and the enforcement mechanisms that ensure acceptance of those standards.

Any group exists in an environment, and for the group to survive it must meet to some degree the expectations of this environment. He identified three external elements that influence the demands on the group:

▶ **Physical**   Geography, terrain, climate, location.
▶ **Technological**   Knowledge, equipment, machinery.
▶ **Cultural**   Values, goals, customs.

These external forces (and including economic or financial conditions, union agreements, past practice and so on) shape what others require the group to do in terms of specific activities, interactions, sentiments and norms. He called this the 'external system' of the group, since it reflects external influences. It corresponds to what others have called the formal system of the organisation.

Management will specify and define activities (including targets) and interactions (the pattern of communications and reporting links) for a range of departments and other groups. So they are part of the visible, written structure of the organisation, specifying what groups in the business should do to achieve certain goals.

Activities are the physical or mental tasks that people undertake. Interactions are the communications that people have with each other in any way. Sentiments are the feelings, emotions and attitudes that people have towards each other. Norms are the informal rules that express beliefs about how people should behave.

A formal group is one that management has deliberately created to perform specific tasks to help meet organisational goals.

At the same time, the personal characteristics of the individuals occupying particular roles influence what happens. The required and personal systems interact. People develop new norms of behaviour and new sentiments towards each other as they take part in the required activities and interactions. They also develop new activities and patterns of interaction, which, like the norms and sentiments, are not required by the rules. These emergent activities or interactions may support or disrupt the required task system. They may also contribute to the satisfaction of individual needs. Homans termed this new pattern of emerging behaviour the 'internal system' of the group – corresponding to what others have called the informal system.

Informal groups are those which develop as the day-to-day activities bring people into contact with each other – and who then discover common interests or concerns. These may be unrelated to work – people find they share a common sporting or social interest with others in the organisation, and form a set of relationships with them through arranging outings or competitions. Informal groups form directly during work when people in different formal groups start exchanging information and ideas. Staff using a software package may begin to pass around problems or tips. Staff in separate departments dealing with a customer may start passing information to each other to avoid misunderstandings even though this is not part of the specified job. Informal groups may also develop in opposition to manage-

An informal group is one that emerges when people come together and interact regularly.

NOTICEBOARD Informal networks: the company behind the chart

According to Krackhardt and Hanson (1993):

If the formal organization is the skeleton of the company, the informal is the central nervous system. This drives the collective thought processes, actions and reactions of the business units. Designed to facilitate standard modes of production, management create the formal organization to handle easily anticipated problems. When unexpected problems arise, the informal organization becomes active. Its complex web of social ties form every time colleagues communicate and solidifies over time into surprisingly stable networks. Highly adaptive, informal networks move diagonally and elliptically, skipping entire functions to get work done.

Using network analysis management can translate a myriad of relationship ties into maps that show how the informal organization gets work done. Managers can produce a good overall picture by diagramming three types of relationship network:

▶ The advice network shows the prominent players in an organization on whom others depend to solve problems and provide technical information.
▶ The trust network tells which employees share delicate political information and back one another in a crisis.
▶ The communication network reveals the employees who talk about work-related matters on a regular basis. (pp.104–5)

The authors argue that these informal networks can either foster or disrupt communication processes. They recommend that managers try to understand them in order to make use of their strengths, or even adjust aspects of the formal organisation to complement the informal. Researchers gather data by questionnaires that ask employees to record who they communicate with, about what, and how often. Software packages can process the data to provide diagrams of the structure and membership of the different networks.

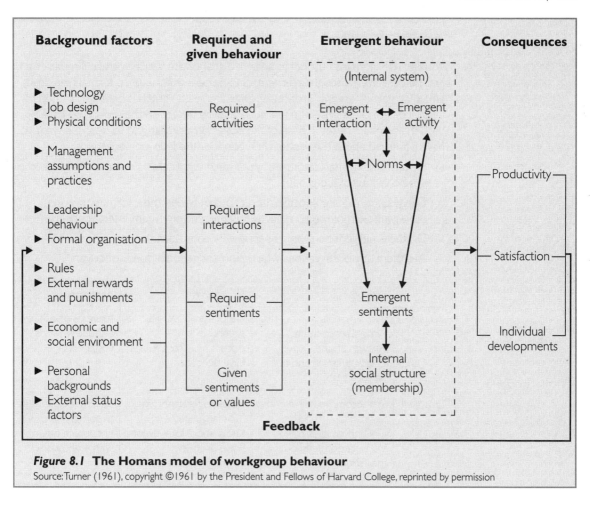

Figure 8.1 The Homans model of workgroup behaviour
Source: Turner (1961), copyright ©1961 by the President and Fellows of Harvard College, reprinted by permission

ment – as when people believe they are being unfairly treated, and come together from across groups to express a common dissatisfaction with a management policy.

These required and emergent behaviours have effects on productivity, satisfaction, or personal growth of the group members. These in turn feed into the background environmental factors, which in turn affect later behaviour, as the external and internal systems are constantly interacting and interdependent. Changes in the environment produce changes in both the formal and the informal systems; and the activities and interactions in the internal system lead to changes in the group's environment. Figure 8.1 summarises these factors.

CASE QUESTIONS 8.2

▶ What were the required activities and interactions in the Consulting Engineers case?

▶ What were the emergent activities?

▶ List these in the format of Figure 8.1 to help you become familiar with the model.

n o t e b o o k   8.4

You can use Homans's model to analyse a group with which you are familiar. The grid below summarises the elements that he believed made up formal (required) and informal (emergent) groups. As an example, the grid has been completed for a hotel reception team. As an individual activity, reflect on the group you have chosen and make notes in each of the boxes on a similar grid to describe what you have observed about the group. Then consider the following questions:

▶ How have external factors – physical, technological and cultural – influenced the behaviour of the group?

▶ Can you identify any specific interactions between the information in the boxes, for example required activities affecting emergent interactions?

▶ Do the emergent behaviours support or contradict the required ones?

▶ Are there any observations which Homans's model does not cover?

	Activities	*Interactions*	*Sentiments*
Required	Work in shifts Accept reservations Answer phone Check guests in and out Balance cash	Report problems to supervisor Accept mail from guests Give directions	Maintain a positive attitude towards customers
Emergent	Sell accommodation Sell restaurant and function facilities Work late to send out mail-shot	Speak to foreigners in their language Know about local events Solve problems Form subgroups	Keen to help others to solve problems Encourage others with enthusiasm

8.5   Stages of group development

Putting people into a group does not mean they perform well immediately, as teams need to go through stages of growth. Some never perform well. Tuckman and Jensen (1977) developed a theory that groups can potentially pass through five fairly clearly defined stages of growth and development. Figure 8.2 shows these.

Teams need to have the chance to grow up and to develop trust amongst the members. As the work makes progress, people will learn about each other, and how they can work well together. The closer they get, the easier that forming trust usually becomes.

Forming

Forming is the stage at which members choose, or are told, to join a team. Managers may select them for their functional and technical expertise or for some other skill. They come together and begin to find out who the other members are, exchanging fairly superficial information about themselves, and beginning to offer ideas about what the group should do. People are trying to make an impression on the group and to establish their identity with the other members.

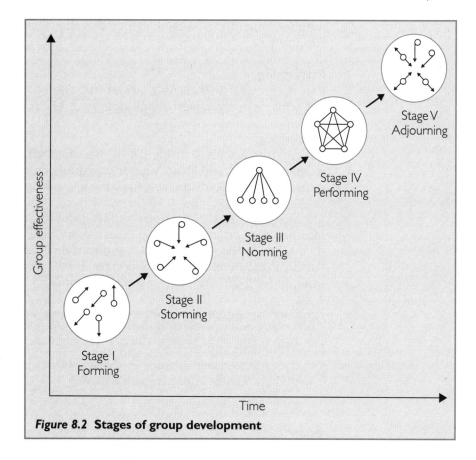

Figure 8.2 Stages of group development

Storming

Conflicts may occur at the storming stage, so that it can be an uncomfortable time for the group. As the group gets down to the actual work, members begin to express differences of interest that they withheld or did not recognise at the forming stage. People realise that others want different things from the group, or have other priorities and, perhaps, hidden agendas. Different personalities emerge, with contrasting attitudes towards the group and how it should work. Some may experience conflicts between the time they are spending with the group and other calls on their time. As they work, differences in the values and norms which people have brought to the team become clear. Some groups never satisfactorily get past this stage. They may accommodate or repress differences, or they may openly and vigorously debate them. Eventual performance depends on someone being able to do or say something that leads on to the next stage.

Norming

Here the members are beginning to accommodate differences constructively and to establish adequate ways of working together. They develop a set of shared norms – expected modes of behaviour – about how they should interact with each other, how they should approach the task, how they should deal with differences. People create or accept roles so that responsibilities are clear. The leader may set those roles formally or members may accept them implicitly during early meetings. Members may establish a common language to guide the group and allow members to work together effectively.

Performing

Here the group is working well, gets on with the job to the required standard and achieves its objectives. Not all groups get this far.

Adjourning

The group completes its task and disbands. Members may reflect on how the group performed, and identify lessons for future tasks. Some groups disband because they are clearly not able to do the job, and agree to stop meeting.

The model reminds us that open conflict is not the only signal of problems. Members may believe the group is performing well – but may be deluding themselves. If the group does not confront disagreements it will probably remain at the forming or storming stage. It will probably do no significant work, and will fall behind more successful teams.

C A S E   Q U E S T I O N S   8.3

▶ Which stage of group development did the system development team reach?

▶ If you had been a member of the team, what would you have tried to say or do to help it move to a more productive stage?

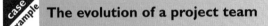

The evolution of a project team

A local authority created a project team to select and implement a computer-based housing management system. The chief executive appointed the assistant head of the information technology (IT) department as project leader, who then asked some members of the housing department to join the team. The director of the housing department allocated some project duties to his staff without reference to the project leader. The housing department believed the IT department was invading its territory. Both incidents caused relationship problems until managers clarified roles and expectations. To help gain the group's commitment, the project leader explained the plan to the team. They discussed and agreed it in principle.

The group members pointed out that they could not work on the project as well as on their normal duties. They believed that working in their normal open-plan offices alongside other housing staff would distract them. The chief executive agreed to a limited amount of time off for the project, and allocated a separate room for those working on it. One member still refused to commit to timescales. The other members told him forcefully that they were equally busy but able to comply, implying his behaviour was affecting team performance. This was enough to persuade him to participate more fully. There was another early conflict when members of two functional groups put forward opposing system requirements and were reluctant to specify in writing what their joint requirements would be. The team, with the encouragement of the project leader, established some guidelines on the working practices they would use.

Members contacted suppliers and other sites that had installed similar systems, to gather information about potential systems. The project leader noted that team members enjoyed these visits, and she used them as a motivator to encourage the completion of more boring but essential tasks like systems documentation. Performance improved as the project continued. Each member had prepared a checklist for meetings with suppliers and users. As they learned how each other worked, this process improved, with each evaluation increasing their effectiveness as a team. They completed document preparation, evaluation and recommendation on time and to the level of performance required. The group adjourned once they had implemented the project.

---

n o t e b o o k   8.5

Make a note of examples of Tuckman and Jensen's behaviour categories and the actions that helped the group in the Case Example move to the next stage of development.

8.6   Factors affecting group performance

As groups develop through the five stages, some features become more regular. These can be observed and distinguish one group from another. If you know what these are, and what to look for, you can see more clearly how a group is working and what is affecting performance. Four features are described – content, structure, culture and process.

Content

Content refers to the task of the group or the substantive deliverable work it must achieve, such as to design a product, agree a new organisation structure or set up a new process. In the Consulting Engineers case study, the content of the group's work was the design of the management information system, and all the technical and organisational issues associated with that.

> Content is the specific substantive task that the group is undertaking.

When a group is sharing ideas about some aspect of the job, they are said to be dealing with content issues. These are often to do with immediate, tangible questions, such as where to place the machinery, what software package to use, who will be responsible for checking quality. The group needs to have members who are able to deal with these aspects skilfully – but this is not usually sufficient. Observation of groups at work shows they also face issues of structure, culture and process.

Structure

Group structure refers to regularities in the group's organisation, including how it divides and co-ordinates the task. Management will usually establish some aspects of structure when it creates the group. Other aspects emerge as the group works together. For example, management designates one member of the group to be the formal leader. It then realises that one member has particular expertise in one aspect of the work, so she becomes the informal leader when the group discusses that topic. Structure does not only relate to the leadership of the group, but also includes questions about what other roles to create, who are the members, how often it meets, and to whom it reports.

Structure is the regularity in the way the group is organised, such as the roles that are specified.

Culture

Culture is the pattern of basic assumptions developed by a group as the correct way to perceive, think and feel in doing a task.

Edgar Schein (1985) believed that teams that work together develop a distinctive culture, which he defined as the

> pattern of basic assumptions ... developed by [a group] that has worked well enough to be considered ... as the correct way to perceive, think and feel in relation to ... problems. (p.9)

Culture develops as group members share enough experiences to form a view of what works and what does not. This view then shapes how members expect each other to behave. Culture is more intangible than structure, but the common assumptions and beliefs can exert a profound influence on how the group performs.

Process

Process refers to the way the group goes about the task it is doing: if content refers to *what* the group does, process refers to *how* it does it. It is similar to

---

NOTICEBOARD Edgar Schein on the cultures of groups

The main beliefs that Schein identified were those concerned with:

▶ **Mission and strategy** Beliefs about the overall mission and its reason for being.
▶ **Goals** What the operational goals should be so as to meet the broader mission.
▶ **Means** How the group is to meet its goals.
▶ **Criteria for measuring results** Consensus on how performance is to be measured.
▶ **Remedial strategies** The prevailing assumption about how to put things right – kept quiet, constructively discussed or fought out in public.

Schein also suggested aspects of culture which distinguish how a group works:

▶ **Common language and conceptual categories** A mutually understood terminology.

▶ **Group boundaries** Who is in, and who is beyond the margin.
▶ **Power and status** How these are allocated within the group – by success or rank?
▶ **Relationships** Norms about how authority and peer relationships should be managed.
▶ **Rewards and punishments** What rewards are used and the signals they give.

Schein believed that these cultural assumptions act as a filter for coping with information and provide members with a common set of guidelines which they use to work out how to make a contribution. The more clearly members work through these issues to develop a common understanding the better the group will perform.

Source: Schein (1985)

Process is the way the members interact with each other in performing the substantive task, such as how they make decisions.

the prescribed and emergent patterns of interaction described by Homans. A group's process can be analysed on the balance of contributions to the discussion and whether members listen or constantly interrupt. Do members speak in a competitive, aggressive way or is the style one of mutual co-operation? Process covers both the verbal and non-verbal behaviour of members, how they solve problems and how they reach decisions. The extent to which the members pay attention to process as well as to task issues is itself an aspect of process and is examined fully in the following sections.

In the Case Study, the fact that some members have stopped attending suggests that some process issues need urgent attention. It can also be seen that many make no contribution at the meetings, and that the chairman makes no attempt to bring them into the discussion.

Figure 8.3 summarises how the four elements of groups affect each other.

Schein's model is a way of describing groups as they form and develop. It is also clear from everyday observation that some groups work and others do not. What affects their performance? There is plenty of anecdotal evidence about this, and your experience in groups will probably have suggested some of the reasons for success and failure. You can compare that with more formal research into groups, of which an example is given here. Guzzo and Shea (1992) reviewed a long history of research on groups and concluded that most researchers analysed them as open systems. That is, they examined the relationships between their inputs, processes and outputs. These are illustrated as:

▶ **Inputs**   Knowledge skills and abilities of group members, composition of the team, and aspects of the context of the team, such as the reward system.

▶ **Processes**   Interactions among group members, information exchange, participation in decision-making, and social support within the group.

▶ **Outputs**   Products of the group's work, its well-being and survival, and the satisfaction of the members.

In this tradition, West and Anderson (1996) conducted a long-term study of twenty-seven senior management teams within the UK National Health Service. Their aim was to establish empirically the relative importance of input factors (such as the characteristics of team members) and group processes (such as participation) on output (in this case, innovation). Interview and questionnaire data about the innovations introduced by the teams

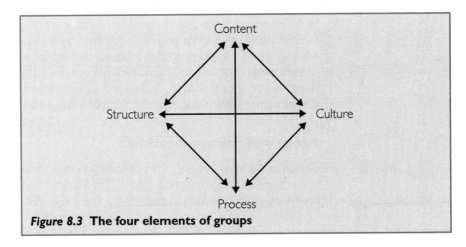

Figure 8.3 The four elements of groups

were gathered over a period of six months. People familiar with the sector assessed these innovations.

The data gathered in the questionnaires covered numerous aspects of team composition and structure. These included how long the team had existed, the number of members, and the hospital budget. The study also tried to identify the processes that the teams used. These included measures of:

▶ understanding of and commitment to team objectives,
▶ team participation,
▶ commitment to excellence within the team,
▶ behaviours that supported innovation,
▶ data from tape recordings of team meetings and documents.

Statistical analysis showed that group size, tenure and organisational resources had no effect on overall levels of innovation. Group process factors had much more significant effects. In particular, the set of practices (time, co-operation, verbal support and resources that team members gave to implement new ideas and proposals) emerged as the main indicator of innovation. The researchers point out that this should not be surprising. The ratio specifically includes measures of 'the extent to which support for innovation is perceived to be enacted as well as verbally expressed' (West and Anderson, 1996, p.690). Participation predicted the number of innovations introduced (the more participation, the more innovation).

8.7 Communication within groups – patterns and content

Observing groups

Observing is the activity of concentrating on how a team works rather than taking part in the activity itself.

A key step in understanding a group is to identify the communication processes. This provides information about communication events (who speaks to whom), and allows the observer to draw some inferences about the structure of the group. It shows if the group has a centralised communication structure or a decentralised one. People can develop their ability to observe groups by concentrating on this aspect rather than on the content of the immediate task. They work slightly apart from the team for a short time and keep a careful record of what members say or do. They also note how other members react and how that affects the performance of the team.

With practice, and in the reality of the workplace, skilled members of a team are able to observe what is happening at the same time as they work on the task itself. They can do this more easily and powerfully if they focus their observations on certain behaviour categories. These will vary with the purpose of the observation. A commonly used example is given here to help identify the patterns and content of communication.

Pattern of communication

Group members depend on information and ideas from others to help them perform the group task. Shaw (1978) identified five distinct patterns of communication, shown in Figure 8.4.

In the chain pattern, each person only passes information to the next member, while in the circle or star patterns information flows much more

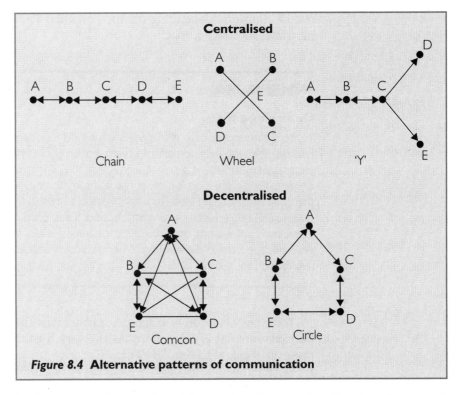

Figure 8.4 Alternative patterns of communication

freely amongst the members. The previous chapter described how Baron and Greenberg showed that different patterns of communication seem better suited to certain types of task: centralised networks seem to work best if the tasks are simple and routine; decentralised patterns are more effective in complex and uncertain tasks. It appears that allowing information and ideas to flow freely around the group produces better results in that kind of task.

Content of group communication

Observing the pattern of contributions gives some insight into the processes of a group, but it is only a start. The next step is to explore what kind of contribution people are making, and whether it helps the group to manage the task. To study and learn how people behave in groups, we need a precise and reliable way to describe events. There are many such models and you

Table 8.1 Content of group communication

Category	Explanation
Proposing	Behaviour which puts forward a new suggestion, idea or course of action
Supporting	Behaviour which declares agreement or support for an individual or an idea
Building	Behaviour which develops or extends an idea or suggestion from someone else
Disagreeing	Behaviour which states a criticism of another person's statement
Giving information	Behaviour which gives or clarifies facts, ideas or opinions
Seeking information	Behaviour which asks for facts, ideas or opinions from others

can develop one depending on the particular focus of interest. Table 8.1 illustrates such an approach.

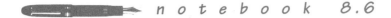

n o t e b o o k   8 . 6

Observing a team

Try to create an opportunity to use the method for observing how a team works. For example, you may be part of a team working on a project (connected with your studies or in some other capacity). Ask the other members if you can observe their discussion for about half an hour. During that time take no part in the discussion. Instead listen to what members say, and decide which of the categories best describes each contribution. If you produce a small chart with the members' names along one side and the categories along the other, you will gradually see a pattern emerging. When you have finished, offer to share the results with the team.

There are many other diagnostic instruments that can help observers to understand what is happening. At the very least, members can reflect on these questions at the end of a task:

▶ What did people do or say which helped or hindered the group's performance?
▶ What went well during that task that we should try to repeat?
▶ What did not go well, which we could improve?

8.8 Roles within a group

A key element in understanding group structures and processes is the roles which people play. One of the purposes of bringing people together in teams is to make use of particular types of talent and a variety of skills and interests. So the contributions people make vary, and when those contributions are of a particular kind, the individual is usually taking on a distinct role within the group. These people make different contributions to the task or content of the group by using their skills to deal with process issues beyond their functional expertise.

Meredith Belbin conducted a series of studies in which colleagues systematically observed several hundred small groups while they performed a task. From these observations he concluded that each person working in a group tends to behave in a way that corresponds closely to one of nine distinct roles that the study identified. The balance of these roles in a group affects how well or badly the group performs.

The research originally arose from the practice at the Henley School of Management of basing much of their training on work done by managers in teams. Groups of up to ten managers would work on a series of exercises or business simulations as part of the training events. The organisers had long observed that some teams achieved better financial results than others, irrespective of the abilities of the individual members as measured by standard personality and mental tests. The reasons for this were unclear and the subject of much debate. Why did some teams of individually able people perform less well than teams that appeared to contain less able people?

Belbin therefore undertook a study in which carefully briefed observers, drawn from the course members, used a standard procedure to record the types of contribution which members made. Team members voluntarily took the psychometric tests, and the researchers recorded quantifiable results of the team performance in the exercises. They tested and refined the conclusions in other settings (which included individual companies and a similar training establishment) as results from the exercises accumulated.

Some clues as to the eventual results occurred when the researchers formed teams of members with well above average mental abilities, and compared their performance with the other teams. The 'intelligent' teams usually performed less well than the others. Of twenty-five such teams observed, only three were winners, and the most common position was sixth in a league of eight teams. On average they performed worse than the other teams, often finishing last. The explanation seemed to lie in the way such teams behaved in carrying out the task, as noted by the information recorded by the observers. Typically, the team members spent much time in debate, arguing for their point of view to the exclusion of other opinions. Members in these teams of highly intelligent people were typically good at spotting flaws in other members' arguments. They then became so engrossed in these arguments that they neglected other jobs that they needed to do. Their failure usually led to heated recrimination. The important lesson from this was that the kinds of behaviour which people display during a task affect the performance of the group.

The researchers continued to construct teams of people with particular personality characteristics, and observed their performance in competition with others. This process enabled them to identify a variety of different types of behaviour which people displayed in teams – their preferred team roles. Some were creative, full of ideas and suggestions. Some were much more concerned with detail, ensuring that the team had dealt with all aspects of the situation and that quality was right. Others spent most of their time keeping the group together, encouraging withdrawn members to take part, smoothing conflicts. The first book published from the research in 1981 identified eight team roles. The research continued, and Belbin published a further book bringing the results up to date in 1993. The book renamed some of the earlier roles and added a ninth (the specialist). Table 8.2 lists the nine roles used in the 1993 report.

Preferred team roles are the types of behaviour that people display relatively frequently when they are part of a team.

Belbin and his colleagues observed that the composition of teams was crucial to their success. The types of behaviour which people display are infinite, but the range of behaviours that contribute to team performance is finite. Belbin grouped these performance-enhancing behaviours into clusters, which he then referred to by the term 'role'. Winning teams, those that came out most prominently at the top of the results, had a balance of roles that was different from the less successful ones.

Belbin outlined in the 1981 book how members with the different preferred team roles would make their mark on the team. Companies with a high proportion of (using the 1993 terminology) *implementers* did best in the competitive exercises. Such people worked for the company rather than their self-interest, and operated in a practical and realistic way. They then identified the contribution which two sets of paired roles made to teams.

Table 8.2 **Belbin's team roles**

Type	Typical features
Implementer	Disciplined, reliable, conservative and efficient. Turns ideas into practical actions
Co-ordinator	Mature, confident, a good chairperson. Clarifies goals, promotes decision-making, delegates well
Shaper	Challenging, dynamic, thrives on pressure. Has the drive and courage to overcome obstacles, likes to win
Plant	Creative, imaginative, unorthodox – the ideas person who solves difficult problems
Resource investigator	Extrovert, enthusiastic, communicative – explores opportunities, develops contacts, a natural networker
Monitor/evaluator	Sober, strategic and discerning. Sees all options, judges accurately – the inspector
Teamworker	Co-operative, mild, perceptive and diplomatic. Listens, builds, averts friction, calms things – sensitive to people and situations
Completer	Painstaking, conscientious, anxious. Searches out errors and omissions. Delivers on time
Specialist	Single-minded, self-starting, dedicated. Provides scarce knowledge and skill

Source: based on Belbin (1981, 1993)

The *shaper* usually provided leadership – challenging, goading the group into action. Sometimes the *co-ordinator* did this, pulling the group together, and helping it to unify in pursuit of common objectives. In addition, groups needed ideas, which were most likely to come from a *plant* quietly devising a solution, or the *resource investigator* who would go out looking for ideas and inspiration elsewhere.

---

n o t e b o o k   8 . 7

Which of the descriptions in Table 8.2 most closely matches your own preferred role when working within a team? Can you identify any of the other roles being taken by other members of teams you work in regularly? What happens if some of the roles are missing?

You might expect that a team with these five roles (implementer, co-ordinator, shaper, plant and resource investigator) in reasonable balance would be enough for success. Not so, claimed Belbin, as some roles would still be missing. The ideas produced could well be more than the team could handle. So the role of monitor/evaluator to take all aspects of the situation into account would be valuable. The teamworkers would also be valuable then as, with their strong sensitivity to people, they would be able to hold together a diverse group of people. Then the completer, to make sure that the group finishes what it starts, meets obligations and deals with details. Finally, in the 1993 book Belbin added the role of the specialist, bringing particular technical or professional expertise to the team, especially relevant in project work.

Belbin concluded that a team with good examples of all eight roles would be adequate for any task, though teams do not necessarily need all eight. The important point is that the composition of the team should reflect the task in hand:

> The useful people to have in a team are those who possess strengths or characteristics that serve a need without duplicating those that are already there. Teams are a question of balance; what is needed is not well-balanced individuals but individuals who balance well with one another. In that way human frailties can be underpinned and strengths used to full advantage. (Belbin, 1981, p.77)

Particularly successful teams were those that had:
▶ a capable chairman,
▶ a strong plant – a creative and clever source of ideas,
▶ at least one other clever person to act as a stimulus to the plant,
▶ a monitor/evaluator – someone to find flaws in proposals before it was too late.

Ineffective teams usually had a severe imbalance in the preferred roles of members, such as:
▶ a chairman with two dominant shapers – since the chairman will almost certainly not be allowed to take that role,
▶ two resource investigators and two plants – since no one listens or turns ideas into action,
▶ a completer with monitor/evaluators and implementers – probably slow to progress, and stuck in detail.

Belbin developed an instrument that enables anyone to identify their primary and secondary preferred team roles. Management trainers use the model widely to enable members to evaluate their own preferred roles. They also consider how the balance of roles within their teams at work has affected performance. The model helps people to reflect on and understand their roles. Some managers use it when filling vacancies. For example, a personnel director recently joining a company might notice that management often started initiatives and programmes but usually left them unfinished when it switched its attention to something else. The personnel director could resolve that in recruiting new staff she would look particularly for those who seemed most likely to bring the characteristics of the completer/finisher into the organisation.

However, there is little evidence that companies deliberately use the model when forming teams from existing staff. Managers typically form teams on criteria of technical expertise, departmental representation, or who is available. How the team processes will work is a secondary consideration. A team where members are capable and committed to the mission will ignore individual status or ego issues. People will be able and willing to cover roles if one seems to be lacking.

Belbin's recommendation for individual managers is that they should seek to develop their skills in at least one role other than their preferred one. They can then try to fill serious gaps in a team of which they are a member. However, whether widely used or not, there are some clear hints that a manager responsible for a team may find the work goes better if he or she puts effort into securing the most suitable mix of members.

The final model of team roles to be introduced is that which makes a distinction between task and maintenance roles. If the pattern of contributions in a

---

NOTICEBOARD Charles Handy on teams

Charles Handy has written extensively about teams. He argues that teams need a captain, someone who is able to gain the respect and support of all the members. He or she needs to ensure that the team is clear about its goals and committed to them. He or she also needs to ensure that the team members build up a sense of trust with each other, and that they maintain their enthusiasm through difficulties and disappointments. Not everyone has these skills, and if the nominated leader of the team does not have them, the team will suffer unless another member is able and willing to help.

Someone else needs to be able to look after the administrative work of the team. In the enthusiasm of the task it is easy to forget that records need to be kept and documents filed where someone can find them. A team needs to manage its communications with other teams. The teams will waste time if someone is not dealing with these aspects. It can also disrupt good relations if the team forgets to invite people to relevant meetings, or if it ignores their questions or suggestions.

While the captain will be keeping the whole thing working together, getting a good result depends on having at least one person in the team who is the driver or pusher. A team in difficulties may engage in lengthy and unfocused discussion. Members may become absorbed in some interesting aspect of the topic and ignore more mundane matters that need attention. Someone needs to act as the driver, constantly challenging it to keep going. Drivers encourage members to raise their sights, press for targets and deadlines, and try to move from debate to action.

Finally, the team will fail unless it has at least one member able to come up with a flow of ideas and proposals about the job in hand. Some will be impracticable, and in a team made up of experts from different backgrounds, there will often seem to be too many ideas rather than too few. It is critical that the people with the brightest ideas join the team and are encouraged to bring out their ideas. Otherwise the team will opt for the safe or conventional solution.

Source: Handy (1993)

---

team is observed, it may be seen that some people focus on task issues, getting the job done, hitting targets, while others put most of their energies into keeping the peace and ensuring the group stays together. The activities that characterise the two roles can be summarised as follows:

Emphasis on task	*Emphasis on maintenance*
Initiator	Encourager
Information-seeker	Compromiser
Diagnoser	Peacekeeper
Opinion-seeker	Clarifier
Evaluator	Summariser
Decision-manager	Standard-setter

Teams need people in both roles, and skilful managers try to ensure groups perform both.

8.9 Group structure and external design factors

The discussion so far has looked at research into how the internal processes of groups affect their performance. Other complementary perspectives focus on the influence of group structure and certain external aspects of a group. A study by Hackman gives some valuable pointers to these issues, based on an intensive study of twenty-seven groups (Hackman, 1990).

The study emphasised again the problem of identifying single factors affecting performance. The systems idea of equifinality states that a complex system can follow many routes to the same outcome – all of which may be equally satisfactory. Homans proposed that groups are continually renewing themselves through internal interactions and through their interactions with their environment. It therefore becomes impossible to specify with any certainty the effects of a single change in group structure or practice on effectiveness. The factors are many and tangled. A factor that seems influential in one group may not apply elsewhere: 'each factor loses its potency when examined in isolation from other conditions also in place for the groups under study' (p.8). The 'other conditions' may include external factors affecting performance, which have nothing to do with the way the group itself operates.

Hackman therefore took a different approach. He did not attempt to predict the effects of the complex internal processes of groups, including their unique behavioural styles and performance strategies. Instead he chose to focus on identifying the structural and external conditions that support performance. He claimed the research identified those aspects of group structure, and the organisational conditions surrounding the group, which encouraged (or discouraged) the group itself to develop appropriate effort, skills and strategies. The important aspects of *group structure* in promoting competent work were:

▶ **Task**   Is it clear, consistent with the wider purpose of the organisation, and will it meet the motivational needs of members as suggested by the Job Characteristics Model (see Chapter 6)? For example, how much responsibility and autonomy does a team have in deciding how to go about the task? How much feedback does it get? Wickens (1995), argues that, 'A team begins with individuals whose contributions are recognised and valued, and who are motivated to work together to achieve clear, understood and stretching goals for which they are accountable'.

▶ **Composition**   Is the group of the right size for the task and do members have the right skills? Are they too similar in outlook, or so diverse that they are unlikely to agree a solution? Is there an acceptable balance between part-time and full-time members?

▶ **Norms**   Do the members bring into the group norms about acceptable behaviour that will contribute to the task? Are they willing to work as a team towards a jointly acceptable solution, or are they merely defending a sectional interest? Do the norms include a willingness to reflect on group performance and develop improved strategies?

Influential aspects of the *organisational context* in supporting effectiveness were:

'Team-based rewards are payments or non-financial incentives provided to members of a formally established team and linked to the performance of the group.' (IPD, 1996)

▶ **Reward system**   Does this recognise group performance and provide incentives to members to work as a team, or is the emphasis on rewarding individual performance? As teamwork becomes more significant, can management redesign the reward system to support this by some form of team-based reward? The argument is that individual pay discourages teamwork and encourages managers to focus on the individuals in a team. The emphasis should be on whether rewards relate to what the team is achieving, and whether they support team performance. A survey by the UK Institute of Personnel Development identified many examples of such schemes in operation (IPD, 1996).

Where teams are responsible for a complete task with a high degree of autonomy, do they need a leader. If so, what should those leaders do? Research suggests that teams, even semi-autonomous ones, still benefit from some form of leadership.

Manz and Sims (1987) studied a plant made up of self-managing teams. Each team had between eight and twelve members with an elected team leader, who for most of the time did the same work as team members. In addition there were a small number of team co-ordinators, each responsible for the performance of several teams. The research focused particularly on the role and effectiveness of the co-ordinators (the 'external leaders') using questionnaires and observational

methods. The conclusion was that their role was distinct from that of the conventional supervisor and, in particular, they encouraged the teams to set their own targets, deal with disciplinary matters within the team and to develop their internal problem-solving skills. The overall pattern was to encourage members to do things themselves rather than expect the co-ordinator to do it for them, and to foster independence rather than dependence. The effective co-ordinators spent relatively large amounts of time encouraging self-reinforcement, self-observation and evaluation, and rehearsal.

Source: Manz and Sims (1987)

Some were confident that team pay had encouraged closer teamworking and co-operative behaviour. Others were sceptical, citing examples where team pay had reduced the motivation of high performers.

▶ **Educational system** Is assistance available to help members develop the skills they need?

▶ **Information system** Does this provide the information the group needs to do the work, or does it cut across the issues being dealt with by the group, leaving them without adequate data?

▶ **Coaching and consultation** Coaching and consultation should be available to provide support and guidance to the team in dealing with problems.

The Noticeboard describes research in this area by Manz and Sims, and Table 8.3 summarises the model.

Table 8.3 **Hackman's model of external leadership**

Criteria of effectiveness	Group structure	Organisational context
Effort	Motivational structure of group task	Remedying co-ordination problems and building group commitment, e.g. rewards
Knowledge and skill	Group composition	Available education and training, including coaching and guidance
Performance strategies	Norms that regulate behaviour and foster review and learning	Information system to support task and provide feedback on progress

Source: based on Hackman (1990, p.13)

▶ Use Hackmanís model to suggest some specific actions which management could have taken to improve the performance of the team.

▶ Are there any features of the situation for which the model may not account?

8.10 Improving your skill in meetings

Few meetings involve excitement and drama. Most are mundane affairs that keep the everyday business of the organisation going. People make progress reports to colleagues, settle disputes that arose last month or announce what they hope to do next month. Nevertheless, they are still places where people make things happen. Successful operators treat regular meetings as invaluable sources of information and opportunities to rehearse their skills in handling meetings.

To make things happen you have to be able to control a meeting effectively. That is, you need to ensure that it is conducted along the lines that suit your purpose without participants feeling they are being manipulated. Here are a couple of observations that may help you achieve this:

▶ People are easier to persuade when they are feeling good about being in a meeting.

▶ Ask members at the beginning if there are items they would like you to add to the agenda.

Meetings are more likely to succeed if:

▶ they are scheduled well in advance,

▶ have an agenda,

▶ have a starting and finishing time,

▶ follow prearranged time limits on each item.

The quality of regular meetings improves if someone assesses regularly the:

▶ clarity of objectives,

▶ performance and progress made,

▶ teamwork,

NOTICEBOARD Teams in world-class companies

Research by Arthur Andersen and Cardiff Business School (1995) provides more evidence on the structural aspects of teams. A study of world-class manufacturing companies concluded that those with lean manufacture had created much more active structures for shopfloor problem-solving and improvement than others. Such companies made extensive use of teams that were working towards the continuous improvement of their methods and processes. Companies that persevered with problem-solving teams always found that this enhanced the quality of the solution and the commitment to implementing it.

The most significant point was the role played by the leaders of the production teams. The empowered team leader played a pivotal role in achieving results and being a living embodiment of the organisation's corporate culture. Team leaders had real power and decision-making autonomy. The authors of the study concluded that this was a more significant influence on performance than the detailed internal processes of the team.

- level of participation,
- ways of improving output.

Meetings go wrong when:

- participants stop listening to each other,
- people are allowed to repeat themselves,
- people raise irrelevant issues, or backtrack,
- timings are allowed to drift,
- decisions lack clarity and are not recorded.

Another tool you can use is to consider how well a team is performing in terms of the following characteristics:

- **Performing appropriate leadership roles**   The leader discusses issues, gets facts and opinions before decisions are made, encourages initiative.
- **Having the right members**   The team members possess a mix of skills and abilities suited to produce high levels of performance.
- **Winning the commitment of members**   Members have a strong sense of belonging to the team and identify with its goals.
- **Building a climate of trust and openness**   A healthy level of trust and openness exists among team members. When interpersonal problems arise, they are dealt with candidly and honestly before they are allowed to disrupt the positive climate.
- **Clarifying the mission**   The organisation understands and respects contributions made by the team and would experience a substantial loss if the team did not exist. The mission of the team is known to members and non-members alike. The objectives of the team are integrated into the objectives of the entire organisation.
- **Using meetings to build teamwork**   The time spent at meetings is used effectively in resolving conflicts, solving problems and building commitment. The decisions reached and plans made are followed up and acted upon by members. Meetings are run using a methodical approach understood and supported by team members.
- **Developing relationships**   Team members have developed effective ways of working together and know how to use one another as resources. Members know how their roles relate to the roles and responsibilities of other team members. As the team develops, interpersonal relations among members are improved and strengthened.
- **Cultivating job satisfaction**   Members experience a great deal of satisfaction and pride in being part of the team and do not choose to belong to another team. Being a member of the team means receiving psychological (intrinsic) and financial (extrinsic) rewards. Team morale is high and stays that way even when problems arise.
- **Improving the quality of feedback**   The team views mistakes as learning experiences. Team performance is reviewed in a constructive and objective manner. Members give and receive feedback and suggest how to improve team performance. Reviews of team performance do not jeopardise working relationships.
- **Training and developing the team**   Team members have many opportunities for growth and enlargement of their skills and abilities within and beyond their area of speciality. Members initiate self-development programs to benefit team performance. The team is trained in techniques such as problem solving and decision making.

8.11 Recap

Content agenda

Groups are not just collections of individuals but are created to achieve some goals. Their performance depends on managing themselves so that they develop common agreement to such goals. If the members of a group or team develop and maintain a commitment to a shared culture their cohesion will be even greater. The objectives of a group may or may not be consistent with those of other groups in the organisation. Management attempts to align group objectives with organisational objectives but success cannot be taken for granted. External influences also shape the organisation and performance of the group, such as the role of the external leader and through the forces identified by Homans. Groups also benefit if they develop a commonly understood structure and way of organising how they operate,

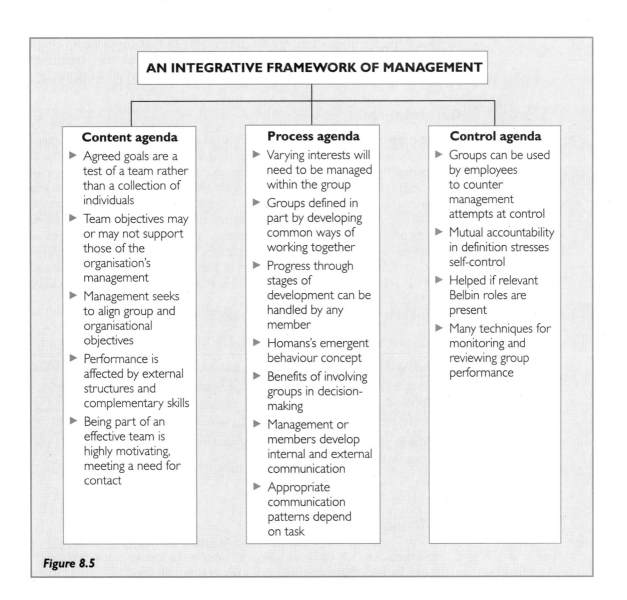

AN INTEGRATIVE FRAMEWORK OF MANAGEMENT

Content agenda
- ► Agreed goals are a test of a team rather than a collection of individuals
- ► Team objectives may or may not support those of the organisation's management
- ► Management seeks to align group and organisational objectives
- ► Performance is affected by external structures and complementary skills
- ► Being part of an effective team is highly motivating, meeting a need for contact

Process agenda
- ► Varying interests will need to be managed within the group
- ► Groups defined in part by developing common ways of working together
- ► Progress through stages of development can be handled by any member
- ► Homans's emergent behaviour concept
- ► Benefits of involving groups in decision-making
- ► Management or members develop internal and external communication
- ► Appropriate communication patterns depend on task

Control agenda
- ► Groups can be used by employees to counter management attempts at control
- ► Mutual accountability in definition stresses self-control
- ► Helped if relevant Belbin roles are present
- ► Many techniques for monitoring and reviewing group performance

Figure 8.5

and norms for the way that members behave towards each other. Belbin's role models highlight the benefits of complementary skills. The ability of effective groups to generate action from members is well established. Being mutually accountable for results also generates motivation.

Process agenda

A group will often include stakeholders with different interests in the task, and these differences have to be managed as part of the group's process. Groups are defined in terms of developing a common approach and way of working together to achieve their task. They typically progress through stages, and effective groups are those that manage to progress beyond the storming stage. If members have fundamental differences about the group, they express them at what is then the storming stage. The issues can be reconciled during the norming stage. The management activities to move a group forward can be taken by any member – they do not have to depend on a formally appointed leader. Research demonstrates the benefits to management and the members of involving groups fully in making decisions about work arrangements and similar matters. Management or the team itself establishes the formal communication processes and others arise informally.

Control agenda

Groups have often been used by employees as a way to balance management control, by establishing and enforcing output standards independently of management expectations. The mutual accountability in the definition of groups emphasises how effective groups are able to exercise self-control over their work. This can be strengthened if the Belbin roles related to control (such as monitor/evaluator) are well represented in the group. Many other methods of monitoring group performance are available, ranging from *ad hoc* process observation techniques and behaviour category analysis to formally validated instruments. Choice of methods depends on the purpose of the observation. Self-managing teams typically take corrective action, rather than it being externally imposed.

These points are summarised in Figure 8.5.

PART CASE QUESTIONS

▶ What are the required activities, interactions and norms likely to be within W.L. Gore and Associates?

▶ How do they compare with those at Consulting Engineers?

▶ What external factors support (or perhaps hinder) the working of project groups at W.L. Gore?

8.12 Review questions

1 For a team of which you have been a member, what lessons or insights about its development have you been able to draw from this chapter?

2   Why is a group of passengers on an airliner not usually considered to be a team? What change in circumstances would make it possible for them to become one?

3   Compare the bases of effective teamwork outlined earlier with your experience of being part of a team.

4   Compare the four elements in a team identified by Homans? What did he mean by emerging forms of these elements? Give some real examples of your own.

5   Teams go through how many stages of development? Compare, in terms of what happened at each stage and what was done to move to the next stage, two teams that have tried to develop.

6   List the main categories of behaviour that can be identified in observing a group?

7   Compare the meaning of the terms 'task' and 'maintenance roles'?

8   Evaluate Belbin's model of team roles? Which three or four roles are of most importance in an effective team? What is your own preferred role?

9   Give examples of the external factors which affect group performance? Compare the model with your experience as a group member.

Further reading

Nicky Hayes (1997) provides a lively and well referenced account of many of the issues covered here, as does Mike Robson's earlier book on more specific problem-solving methods in groups (Robson, 1993). Belbin (1993) gives a readable account of the experiments that led him to develop the roles described earlier. For a fuller discussion of some of the theoretical aspects of teams and their development, see Buchanan and Huczynski (1997).

Managing through teams and groups

AIM

To illustrate how teams are being more widely used as the basic building block of organisations, and to provide a way of evaluating this practice.

OBJECTIVES

By the end of your work on this chapter you should be able to outline the concepts below in your own terms and:

1 Give examples of the different types of group, and the unique difficulties that each is likely to face

2 Describe the balance between individual and co-operative work, and give examples of organisations moving towards self-managing teams

3 Summarise the business and motivational explanations for the greater use of teams

4 Summarise Mary Parker Follett's views on the significance of groups to the individual and to society

5 Summarise why Likert believed that management should use the principle of supportive relationships in building a team-based organisation

6 Compare some stated advantages and disadvantages of groups with your own experiences of teamwork or with published evidence

7 Describe the meaning of 'groupthink', and give some examples of its symptoms

8 Use a theory for checking whether a team is always appropriate

9 Describe the spread of distant and global teamworking

Opel Eisenach GmbH – creating a high-productivity workplace

In 1990, the German car company Opel began to redevelop its Eisenach plant. The plant would make three popular models, and the target was an annual output of 150,000 cars by 1994.

Opel Eisenach started as a unique experiment. It would provide full job control within a team structure and use skill-based pay to reward quality and encourage flexibility. Opel's objectives included aggressive use of lean production methods and labour relations patterns based on flexible teams and continuous improvement. At the heart of the system was an attempt to offset high German labour costs by achieving very high productivity. It would do this by focusing on people and teams. The plant moved away from traditional mass production techniques and put the people – their commitment and personal initiative – into the forefront of the new production system. One premise was that working in small teams would foster people's involvement and personal contributions. Another, that working on a larger sequence of the production line would give people greater satisfaction. So operators have full responsibility over an area of work including quality control, equipment maintenance and ordering supplies.

Within the new work environment, Opel relied on front-line people to decide details of the manufacturing process, based on their experience. Management's role changed to one of coach and adviser, assisting in moments of difficulty. From the outset, Opel gave staff the opportunity to examine all work procedures and restructure the workflow to make it more efficient. Listening to people's ideas and suggestions brought vast increases in productivity.

Opel Eisenach operates with about 200 production teams, each with six to eight members. Each team covers a particular sequence of the production line, called a 'cell', and owns full responsibility for the work within the cell. Because flexibility is an important objective, the company trained team members to handle each workstation within the cell. Acquiring new skills and becoming more flexible is important for people's performance evaluation.

Once a team achieves a desired level of flexibility, the team may send one of its members to another unit – a temporary exchange that expands flexibility across the team structure. The flexibility and the interchanges between teams also help everyone to understand the entire production system.

The teams are responsible for quality control and faultless workmanship. Practically all cars on the assembly line are based on customer orders so they come in a variety of models, colours and options. The team has to make sure that they assemble each car using the right parts. In 1995, the plant produced 160,000 cars and was rated as the most efficient in Europe, with production of 59.3 cars a worker each year.

Source: based on Haasen (1996)

CASE QUESTIONS

▶ How does this compare with your image of what work in a car plant is like?

▶ How is teamwork helping performance?

▶ What wider changes in the management of the plant are likely to be the result of this teamwork?

9.1 Introduction

This chapter introduces the following ideas:

▶ Group
▶ System of supportive relationships
▶ Groupthink
▶ Concertive control
▶ Working groups
▶ Pseudo-teams
▶ Potential teams
▶ Real teams
▶ High-performance teams
▶ Distant teams

The chapter examines teams as an aspect of organisational design. Management can divide the work so that people have little contact with others, or they can arrange it as a co-operative activity in which several people contribute their ideas and skill to a collectively delivered end-result. Why do they choose one way rather than the other? What degree of co-operation is there, and what influences that? Is teamwork always more effective than individual work?

---

n o t e b o o k   9.1

Learning as individual and team activities

Reflect on the work you do as a student. List some of the study or learning tasks that you do on your own. Now list some which you do as a group.

Why did the course team decide on that division between individual and group work? Who decided it? What factors influenced the decision? What assumptions did the team make?

Is the present balance between individual and group work the right one for. managing your learning? If not, how would you want to change it?'

Neither individual nor group work is the right approach for all situations. In order for either approach to be effective, other parts of the system must support them, or at least not undermine them. The issues must be dealt with as the use of teamworking becomes more widespread.

9.2 Types of group

A group or team consists of two or more people with some shared purpose who assume different responsibilities, depend on each other, co-ordinate their activities, and see themselves as part of the unit.

Once you begin to look at teams in organisations you find many types, with different purposes and different relationships between the members and the team. Consequently, different management issues arise. Hackman (1990) distinguished seven types of team. Table 9.1 summarises the risks and opportunities associated with each.

We can also distinguish amongst teams by the relationship which the members have to each other and to the team. Four varieties are worth considering as these also raise distinctive team management issues.

Table 9.1 **Hackman's classification of team types and their associated risks and opportunities**

Type	Risks	Opportunities
Top management teams – to set organisational directions	Underbounded; absence of organisational context	Self-designing; influence over key organisational conditions
Taskforces – for a single unique project	Team and work both new	Clear purpose and deadline
Professional support groups – providing expert assistance	Dependency on others for work	Using and honing professional expertise
Performing groups – playing to audiences	Skimpy organisational supports	Play that is fuelled by competition and/or audiences
Human service teams – taking care of people	Emotional drain; struggle for control	Inherent significance of helping people
Customer service teams – selling products and services	Loss of involvement with parent organisation	Bridging between parent organisation and customers
Production teams – turning out the product	Retreat into technology; insulation from end users	Continuity of work; able to hone team design and product

Source: Hackman (1990)

C A S E   Q U E S T I O N S   9. 1

▶ What kinds of team do those described in the Opel Eisenach case represent in Hackman's typology?

▶ What other kinds of team from the list would you expect the company to have created?

Permanent or temporary teams

Permanent teams give some continuing shape to the structure of an organisation even though individual members come and go. The Opel Eisenach teams are an example of this. Other teams provide regular professional support (such as a legal group) or deliver customer services like health care or concerts. Others are top teams responsible for the overall direction and strategy of the business.

Temporary teams are those created to deal with a one-off project or problem and are often what Hackman refers to as taskforces. They disband when the task is complete. Such teams face particular problems which Boddy and Buchanan (1992) identified as:

▶ A **temporary assignment**, so they are likely to have one eye on the next job as well as on the current work.

▶ **Varied technical skills**: those less familiar with the technical aspects, perhaps because they come from a user-department, will usually be reluctant to air their questions in the public forum.

▶ **Other jobs to do**, because in most cases they will only be part-time members of the project team.

▶ **Political** and possibly **personal agendas**, being there as representatives of a department or function rather than as individuals.

NOTICEBOARD **Topics for temporary teams**

Ashridge Teamwork Services, a British consultancy firm with wide experience of developing teams, identified these examples of the tasks for which management used temporary teams:

▶ **Strategy development and implementation** With growing business complexity, it becomes difficult for a single top team to cope with all aspects of strategy and its implementation. Many try to involve more people in the process by creating cross-departmental teams, with varied expertise and perspectives.

▶ **Restructuring** Major organisational changes, especially in times of wider uncertainties, usually have many hidden dimensions, and so are unlikely to succeed if driven from a single perspective. Management therefore creates teams to design solutions to a new business opportunity or a change in market. This is often a prelude to working in the new structure and ensuring that it works.

▶ **New products and systems** When organisations innovate by developing new products, systems or technologies, they usually do so by creating temporary teams or task-groups, with people from different jobs working together on the innovation or problem.

Source: Hastings et al. (1986)

Diversity of membership

Diversity of membership refers to the range of different people who join the team. This varies from teams in a single department to those from across the globe. Effective performance often requires people from different professions or functions to work closely together in order to deliver a service. Closely allied to this are innovations like quality circles, where a manager's remit spans more than one department. As business becomes more international, teams made up of people from different nationalities and cultures become more common. The diversity of membership – which is their main benefit – brings with it additional issues of team management.

---

n o t e b o o k   9 . 2

Cultures and teams

Geert Hofstede reported how students from Germany, France and Britain analysed a case concerning conflict between sales and production departments. The majority of French students recommended referring the problem to the next level in the hierarchy. The majority of British students recommended training programmes so that the two departments would be better at dealing with interpersonal communications. The majority of German students recommended estabishing a clearer written policy.

This is an example of now well-documented differences in the way people from different cultures work. What would the implications be of those students (or other people from their nations) working in a team?

Similar differences can occur when people from different professions have to work together. Have you any experience of working in a team (where an identifiable output was required) with people from different national or professional cultures? What lessons can you draw from the experience?

Face-to-face or sequential

We usually assume that teams operate in the same place or at least have regular *face-to-face* discussion. There are also teams that meet our definition – except that the members have to work in a particular *sequence*, rather than simultaneously. The printer cannot start work until the journalist has finished; distribution cannot start until the printing is complete. How good or timely the finished product is depends on how well those at each stage do their work. A management issue in this situation is whether those in the separate parts see themselves as a team or as isolated operators.

Formal teams and informal networks

Management often creates teams to do a specified task. In addition, managers have long been aware that informal teams develop as people work together across the lines created by formal structures. Krackhardt and Hanson's (1993) research has confirmed many earlier studies showing how informal relationships build up amongst members of the organisation. These relationships form as a result of regular contact amongst staff as they work towards a common objective. They too would come close to our definition – even if the members rarely meet as a complete team. Krackhardt and Hanson's analysis indicated three overlapping types of network:

▶ The **advice network** shows the prominent players in an organisation on whom others depend to solve problems and provide technical information.

▶ The **trust network** tells which employees share delicate political information and back one another in crisis.

▶ The **communication network** reveals the employees who talk about work-related matters on a regular basis.

Krackhardt and Hanson's work implies that not all teamwork goes on in regularly established arrangements. Understanding teams depends on understanding these informal and invisible teams as well.

9.3 The spread of teamwork

The team is no longer mainly a temporary affair to cope with a short-term issue: it is becoming the basic organisational unit for delivering products and services – as the Opel case illustrates.

As was described in Chapter 6, management often introduces self-managing teams to gain commitment from employees and enhance productivity. Instead of being told individually by a supervisor what to do, workers in self-managing teams (typically with between five and fifteen members) are expected to use their initiative. They must gather and interpret information, act on it and take collective responsibility for their actions. Senior management provides overall guidelines on what they expect, but beyond that, teams may have considerable freedom in how they operate, including the selection of new members. They may direct their work and co-ordinate with other areas of the company. They are usually responsible for completing a well-defined function, whether in production or service. Members are

NOTICEBOARD **A historical perspective on teams**

Early forms of economic organisation – tribes of nomadic hunter-gatherers – appear from archaeological evidence to have worked as teams. Many pre-industrial forms of activity depended on people working co-operatively together. For example, the pre-industrial textile industry in Britain, before the invention of steam-powered machinery, operated a system of outworking in which entrepreneurs subcontracted work to family units. Entrepreneurs delivered raw materials to outworkers' homes where the family processed the material. The merchant collected the finished products and paid for the work.

The factory system sometimes resulted in established group and craft loyalties being fragmented. As manufacturers recruited skilled artisans to their workshops, many believed that in order to control work processes and costs they needed to replace craft autonomy by managerial control. They reduced their dependence on craft skills by dividing the task and requiring workers to perform repeatedly one small and carefully prescribed part. Workers had little need to interact with others, and their pay often depended on their output. The emphasis was clearly on allocating work and responsibility to the individual,

preventing or actively discouraging teamwork and co-operation amongst workers.

Management's search for control did not always lead this way. In coalmining the basic unit of organisation at the coal face remained the small group – a hewer, his mate and a boy. The hewer made an individual contract with the colliery management and then worked the face with his team – sometimes in close co-operation with two or three other such groups. This 'had the advantage of placing all the responsibility on the shoulders of a single, small, face-to-face group that experiences the entire cycle of operation within its membership' (Trist and Bamforth, 1951, p.6). The large, nineteenth century railway engineering workshops often used a similar system of subcontracting, in which the companies allocated work not to their employees but to independent subcontractors who did the work on the employer's premises alongside other staff employed directly by the railway company. In one workshop, management tried to diminish craft identity by 'establishing manufacturing processes obliging men of different trades to work together' (Drummond, 1989, p.17) – an early example of the cross-functional team?

cross-trained to do a wide range of tasks, and have the authority to make decisions essential to complete the work.

C A S E   Q U E S T I O N S   9.2

▶ Make a list of the tasks that management at Opel expects its work-teams to perform besides the traditional operating ones.

Rosabeth Moss Kanter observed in her study of unusually innovative and entrepreneurial organisations that it was common to give assignments with the most critical change implications to teams rather than to individuals. She found that teams of managers from different functional units were especially effective. Long-established businesses were also turning to teams. She quotes the experience of a retail company whose top executives attributed their recently improved performance to a new management style involving teamwork. The mechanism was a series of overlapping groups – some permanent, some temporary – dealing with strategic and operating problems.

These not only dealt with the problems, but 'laid the foundation for a more informed, versatile and integrated management' (Kanter, 1983, p.167).

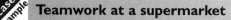

A team hospitality programme

Whitbread Inns operates a chain of pubs where half the staff work part-time and many more are seasonal. Coupled with high turnover, the company had found improving customer service to be a major challenge. The board decided to try a new approach by integrating existing work on raising standards, team-briefings and training. Whereas previous work had focused on individuals, the emphasis now was to be on team-building. With support from training staff, teams of employees from all levels of the company worked to define standards of good practice. These varied for the different types of pub in the company. The manager and a member of staff from each pub received training in group-training skills. They then trained their staff on the requirements of the new standards, using a common, structured format to ensure consistency.

Individual and team incentives support the training. Staff who pass multiple-choice tests on the standards receive additional pay, and pubs where 80 per cent of staff achieve a certain level on this test are eligible for a Team Hospitality Award. To attain this the pub also has to meet standards covering service delivery, effectiveness of team meetings and customer satisfaction (the last being assessed by 'mystery drinkers or diners'). Staff choose whether to celebrate their achievement of the award with a party or to receive vouchers that they can exchange for goods from a catalogue.

The company regards the combination of individual reward and team recognition as highly effective. When the company launched the scheme early in 1995 it identified a number of control houses that matched those in the pilot scheme. These were assessed on the same measures as the pilot houses, though they did not benefit from the training events. Sales rose in both groups, but were significantly higher in the pilot pubs, as were the customer satisfaction scores. Staff turnover had also decreased in the pilot houses.

Source: based on Arkin (1996, pp.36–7)

Teamwork at a supermarket

As part of a major effort to change the culture in the Asda supermarket group, management has moved strongly towards a team structure. Each in-store bakery or fish department is a team effort, with a profit and loss account. Instead of an old-style weekly managers' meeting, there are now twice-daily 'huddles'. Managers and their working teams in the stores meet to plan the next set of actions. As one said: 'In this business you've got to move quickly to invent the next thing: the team-based approach is one way of speeding things up.'

Source: *Management Today*, December 1995, p.54

There are many examples of both successful and unsuccessful teams (see, for example, Sandberg, 1995; Reich, 1987; MacKinlay and Starkey, 1993; Wickens, 1995; Sengenberger, 1992). Some are given below, but inevitably these are distant summaries of what happened. You will learn more if you can compare some of these accounts with evidence you have collected yourself about how organisations use teams. Notebook 9.3 outlines how you could do this – perhaps as a team activity.

 n o t e b o o k   9.3

Gather some original information on how at least two organisations have used teams to get work done, or where an organisation has abandoned teamwork. Use the questions below as a starting point for your enquiry. The data you collect may be useful in one of your tutorials, as well as adding to your knowledge of teams.

What is the main task of the organisation or department?

How are the staff in the area grouped into teams?

Use the definition (page 282) to describe the team – how many people are in the team, what is their shared purpose, how do they share and co-ordinate responsibilities, do they see themselves as part of the group?

What type of team is it (using the ideas in section 9.2 as a guide)?

What do management and team members see as the advantages and disadvantages of teamworking in this situation?

Have there been any recent changes in the organisation of the teams, such as members taking on new tasks? If so, why?

Teams are also controversial – they can threaten established interests and customs, and potential members may have anxieties about working in this new way. Hence management seeking to increase its use of teams may face challenges from those with different priorities. Here are two Case Examples where management attempts to introduce teamworking ran into difficulty.

case example The Volvo plant at Uddevalla

The Swedish vehicle-maker Volvo has created many innovative production methods while continuing to use very traditional assembly lines in some plants. In 1985, management decided to build a new plant at Uddevalla to manufacture part of its range of saloon cars for which demand was growing. Unemployment was low in Sweden and it had been hard to recruit labour to work on traditional assembly lines. The planning team (which included union leaders) initially proposed an assembly line method with workers each doing ten jobs in a flow-line. Each job would take about two-minutes to complete. Management rejected this fairly quickly and reviewed several other options before choosing one. The plant opened in 1989 with a radical team-based production system.

The production area consisted of two workshops, in each of which there were eight product areas, with a group of between seven and ten workers in each. Members worked in pairs to build the entire car on a fixed platform, taking about two hours to complete the task. All members were able to build, and in addition some of the team were able to do complementary tasks such as personnel work (e.g. arranging recruitment or time off), quality, maintenance and training. The team also elected one of its members to be team leader. These additional jobs earned extra pay and rotated around the group members who had the necessary skill – but all members spent most of the day building cars.

A shop manager was in charge of the eight groups in that workshop. The factory manager was at the next level above. So the hierarchy was relatively flat and the workgroups made many decisions. Productivity and quality were claimed to be as high and possibly better than at other Volvo plants. The plant attracted worldwide interest, and some hailed it as the direction which modern manufacturing should take.

That was not how it ended. Volvo closed the Uddevalla plant in 1993 and another innovative plant at Kalmar in 1994. There are many possible reasons for this decision. The company claimed the car business now had too much capacity and that they could meet demand more cheaply at its larger and more conventional plants. Others believe that the decision represented the latest stage in a long-running battle of ideas between traditionalists and modernisers within the company – and this time the traditionalists won.

Source: Sandberg (1995)

 A community mental health team

The management of a unit in the UK National Health Service decided to reduce radically the number of hospital places available. It would also increase the resources available for community care. As part of the change, a resource centre was established in one area containing multidisciplinary teams, each with about thirty staff. These teams would provide a round-the-clock service for the severely mentally ill in the community. The service was to be patient-centred and would use a team approach with a flattened hierarchy and greater mutual accountability. A nurse became general manager. There were many team-building and similar activities.

Problems soon arose, and clear signals were given that many staff could not cope with the extra responsibility and shared decision-making of empowerment. The job is difficult and sometimes dangerous, and one in which people's lives are at stake. Management changed the system to give a stronger role definition to each member of staff and a clearer structure of authority and management. It also recognised that while teamworking may be an ideal to aim for, it has limitations. It needs to be supported by effective inter-team functioning and by broader management structures.

In summary, the Volvo and NHS experiences show that creating teams as part of the structure is not an easy option. Some people resent the shift in power that it implies and others find the extra responsibility hard to take.

In the light of the data you collected in Notebook 9.3 and these other Case Examples (including the W.L. Gore and Opel Eisenach cases), what three or four issues about the management of teams seem to you to be the most significant? You can use these as a focus for your study of the rest of this chapter.

9.4 Advantages of groups

There are both business and motivational reasons for the more widespread use of teams by management.

Business reasons

These follow from the great complexity and change facing organisations, which imply big changes in the way that individuals across an organisation may need to work. Size itself brings complexity, with different plants or national interests involved in shaping a policy. As scientific or technical knowledge grows, it becomes more fragmented between different professional groups, hence solving many technical, production, social, health and other types of problem is likely to involve several disciplines. Even if staff remain within their separate hierarchical structures, management will often create multidisciplinary teams to work together in delivering a service or on resolving some common problem. Teams can bring complementary skills beyond those which any of the individual members could bring.

> **Most big ideas come from teams …**
> ❛ Rarely do even Big Ideas emerge any longer from the solitary labors of genius. Modern science and technology is too complicated for one brain. It requires groups of astronomers, physicists and computer programmers to discover new dimensions of the universe: teams of microbiologists, oncologists and chemists to unravel the mysteries of cancer. With ever more frequency, Nobel prizes are awarded to collections of people. Scientific papers are authored by small platoons of researchers. ❜

In the area of health care, there is a long tradition that professional groups work independently and autonomously – and 'each has its own view of the patient, and its own view of the solution. Each profession has been given its own spectacles through which to view the world' (Soothill *et al.*, 1995, p.6). Yet there is growing interest in developing collaborative and teamworking practices between the various professions involved in delivering some aspect of patient care. One reason has undoubtedly been the unnecessary suffering caused by different groups failing to pass on information. Others have been the need to improve the general quality of care provided and the need to make better use of the available resources. Many believe that these can best be achieved by the different groups working more as teams than as independent professionals. There may also be an unstated desire in some quarters to undermine established and expensive demarcation lines, such as when closer teamworking between doctors and nurses enables the latter to take on some of the duties previously done by the former.

Teams are also used when organisations need to make large improvements in performance quickly, or to enhance permanently their flexibility and responsiveness. They seem especially attractive where an organisation faces great uncertainty. Top management cannot have all the knowledge and information that is needed to specify in advance how an issue should be managed. Creating a group allows it to benefit from the insights and enthusiasm of people across the organisation – who are more likely to produce a solution than managers or professional staff working on their own. Creating a team with appropriate authority gets talent working on organisational problems much more quickly than hierarchical structures could. So teams are often seen by management as a way of using the talent and resources within the company more effectively than through more prescriptive, individual-centred styles.

Another less public reason encouraging teamworking is the belief that it is a way of cutting costs. Skills may be more interchangeable within a team than if staff are located in separate departments, so fewer may be needed. If teamworking is used to encourage operators to take on more decision-making responsibility, management can reduce the number of supervisory or support staff. It may also be seen as a way of undermining professional autonomy. Hence, while sold on the basis of customer service or business improvement, teams may be implemented for other reasons – making some suspicious of teamworking.

CASE QUESTIONS 9.3

▶ What were the business reasons which led Opel to introduce teams so extensively in its new plant?

▶ What were the motivational reasons?

▶ What evidence is there in the account that Opel's assumptions were correct?

▶ Using your library or Internet resources, try to find out recent information about the Opel plant to see if the experiment is still working. If it is not, try to find out what has changed.

Motivational reasons

This explanation for the popularity of teamworking is based on the belief that people will be more committed to their work if they are part of a team. This was the focus of the Hawthorne studies described in Chapter 2, which led to the conclusion that the operation of the workgroup itself was a far more important influence on performance than physical conditions. Further, as was shown in Chapter 6, people have social instincts which they seek to satisfy by being acknowledged and accepted by other people. This can be done on a person-to-person basis (mutual acknowledgement or courteous small-talk on the train), but most people also put some effort into being a member of several relatively permanent and durable arrangements in which people co-operate with each other. These give people the opportunity to express and receive ideas and to reshape their views by interacting with others. Acceptance by a group met an important human need which had been overlooked by scientific management, and implied that management should take account of this need in arranging work.

Mary Parker Follett and Chester Barnard developed these ideas on the social nature of people and on the benefits of co-operative action. They saw the group as an intermediate institution between the solitary individual and the abstract society, and argued that it was through the institution of the group that co-operative action was organised. Writing in 1926, Follett argued that:

> Early psychology was based on the study of the individual; early sociolgy was based on the study of society. But there is no such thing as the 'individual', there is no such thing as 'society'; there is only the group and the group-unit – the social individual. Social psychology must begin with an intensive study of the group, of the selective processes which go on within it, the differentiated reactions, the likenesses and the unlikenesses, and the spiritual energy which unites them ... Modern business ... needs above all men who can unite, not merely men who can unite without friction but who can turn their union to account. The successful businessman of today is the man of trained co-operative intelligence. (Mary Parker Follett, quoted in Graham, 1995, p.230)

The potential of groups as a basis for organising work was explored most fully by Rensis Likert. He had noted that the Hawthorne study showed that groups could either support or counter management interests, by enhancing or restricting output. He offered management a way out of this dilemma, by focusing on the way that groups could be managed.

Likert observed that while effective managers used many of the traditional tools of scientific management, they did so in a way that did not emphasise compliance by using hierarchical and economic pressures. Instead they encouraged participation by group members in all aspects of the job and work, including setting goals and budgets, controlling costs and organising work. Above all, effective managers were those who developed their subordinates into a working team with high group loyalty. Effective managers used participation and other kinds of group-leadership practice.

NOTICEBOARD **Mary Parker Follett and Japanese management**

According to Tokihiko Enomoto, Professor of Business Administration at Tokai University, Japan:

Follett's work has become part of our teaching on management, and is well-known to quite a number of ... managers in our government institutions and business organisations. Much of what Follett says about individuals and groups reflects to a substantial extent our Japanese view of the place of individuals in groups, and by extension their place in society ... She sees individuals not as independent selves going their separate ways, but as interdependent, interactive and interconnecting members of the groups to which they belong. This is something close to the Japanese ethos. We can fully agree with Follett when she writes that 'the vital relation of the individual to the world is through his groups.

Source: quoted in Graham, 1995, pp.242–3

These ensured that team members had relatively high levels of skill in personal interaction and the functioning of groups. These skills also permitted effective participation in decisions on common problems.

Why were these groups effective? Likert suggested the explanation lay in what he called the *principle of supportive relationships*. He agreed with Abraham Maslow that people value receiving a positive response from others who matter to them, as this helps to build and maintain their self-esteem. The interactions and relationships which people experience within an organisation can build and maintain their sense of worth and importance, making up what Likert called a system of supportive relationships.

A system of supportive relationships refers to the interactions and experiences that build a person's sense of personal worth.

CASE QUESTIONS 9.4

▶ What are the benefits which W.L. Gore gains from its team-based organisation?

▶ What, if any, differences are there between Gore's approach and that used by Opel?

▶ What lessons about the benefits can you draw from the two examples?

Since most people spend much of their time with their workgroup, these groups provided the route to the supportive relationships that people value. Likert found that effective organisations had developed what he called a highly effective social system for interaction and mutual influence. This consisted of a tightly knit system of interlocking groups with a high degree of group loyalty amongst the members. Their managements had made deliberate attempts to build such groups and to link them by people who had overlapping membership of more than one group. He therefore advocated that management should ensure that 'each person was a member of one or more effectively functioning workgroups that have a high degree of group loyalty, effective skills of interaction and high performance goals'.

These ideas continue to influence views of teams. Katzenbach and Smith (1993) observed that people who as members of a team surmount problems together build trust and confidence in each other. They benefit from the buzz of being in a team, and of 'being part of something bigger than myself'. They also predict that changing behaviour is easier if people are in a team, with support and encouragement available, than if a person is isolated and feels more need to defend a position.

n o t e b o o k   9.5

Do you agree that teams are less threatened by change than are individuals? Can you think of examples from your study which would support or contradict that conclusion?

Interaction of business and motivational reasons

Having set out the two sets of reasons separately, it is clear that they reinforce each other. Many managements, especially in sectors facing severe competition, see teamwork as a way of reaching a new synthesis between high efficiency and high-quality jobs (Wickens, 1995). Teams can *provide a structure* within which individuals can contribute both to their own and to organisational goals. They provide a forum in which issues or problems can be raised and dealt with – rather than being left unattended.

While an individual may find a solution on his or her own, no one can be familiar with all sides of an issue, so bringing in more people *increases the perspectives* available. Ideas can be tried on other members and encouraged or discarded in the light of their reactions and other sources of knowledge.

Good teams are *collections of differences*. There is little point in having a team made up of people who all approach a job in the same way. A team usually benefits not only from getting people with different knowledge and technical skills to work together, but even more so from those with radically different perspectives. They can challenge the accepted wisdom and propose completely new ways of working on the problem.

Teams in advertising

An advertising agency which prides itself on its team approach claims that it works hard at getting account managers (who deal with the business aspects of each contract or client) to work well with the creative people (who create and design campaigns for the client) and the media department (who assess the most effective media to use for an advertising campaign, and who are therefore very quantitative and analytical in their work). A creative designer commented, 'even the media department are creative in their own way; they're different – but still creative'.

Teams can encourage *acceptance and understanding* of the problem and the solution proposed. If those closely affected by a decision have been able to express their views then they are more likely to accept the result than if it had been imposed. They will know more of the constraints and limitations, and probably be more committed to implementing the result. Taking part in a group effort usually builds a sense of ownership in overcoming difficulties and achieving a result.

Teams can *promote learning*. As people work together to solve problems, they not only deal with the present task but also reflect on what they can learn from the experience, and perhaps see how they could do the job differently next time. While learning established facts and theories can be done effectively by a person working alone, most management learning is not of that sort. It is unstructured and unpredictable, and more to do with the art of asking the right questions of a situation, and coping with the ambiguity of management problems. People often use tacit knowledge to reach solutions; working in a team is more likely to lead to those assumptions being challenged and tested against reality, rather than continuing to be applied in an established way. Thus learning new ways of dealing with open problems is most likely to take place in groups. It happens as people work together on a common problem, able to challenge and support each other in the search for a solution. In the course of doing that, they may learn something of value to future tasks. (For a discussion of the idea of 'action learning', which is centred on using groups to learn together, see Weinstein, 1995.) To sum up, Katzenbach and Smith enthuse that:

> When teams work, they represent the best proven way to convert embryonic visions and values into consistent action patterns because they rely on people working together. They are also the most practical way to develop a shared sense of direction among people throughout an organisation. Teams can make hierarchy responsive without weakening it, energize processes across organizationl boundaries, and bring multiple capabilities to bear on difficult issues ... most models of the 'organization of the future' are premised on teams surpassing individuals as the primary performance unit of the company. (1993a, p.19)

9.5 Disadvantages of groups

For all of the undoubted benefits which a team can bring, it can also be a source of danger and threat to the individual and the organisation. These dangers can be overcome by good management of the group – but that depends on being alert to the possible threats.

Take on their own purpose

Sometimes referred to as goal displacement, groups sometimes take on a life of their own and become too independent of the organisation which created them. The positive side of groups created to perform a particular task is that they generate enthusiasm and commitment. The potential danger is that they then become harder to control, and may divert the project so that it meets goals of more value to the project team than to the management that created it. As experts in the particular issue, the team members can exert great influence over management by controlling or filtering the flow of information to the organisation as whole, so that the team's goals become increasingly hard to challenge. Its work becomes relatively isolated from other parts of the organisation, with the danger that its agenda becomes out of line with the issues facing the organisation.

Time

Gaining the benefits of a wider range of knowledge and perspectives depends on discussion – which inevitably takes longer than if an individual alone made the decision. If the discussion is well handled, the time spent will be seen as acceptable. If it is poorly managed, the potential benefits of a wide range of inputs will not be seen, but the time spent on fruitless discussion will be. In fast-moving situations, the time may simply not be affordable. Time spent in discussion may also be used to encourage participation and acceptance, but again this only works if it is done properly. If discussion is allowed to stray over unrelated issues, or to go over matters that have already been decided, time is lost. This can also be an opportunity for members opposed to the project to prolong group discussion and the search for agreement as a blocking tactic.

Domination by an individual

Some teams allow themselves to be dominated by one member. This may be the formal leader of the group in a hierarchical organisation, where people are not used to challenging those in a position of authority, or it can be a technical expert who is allowed to take over the group because others are afraid to show their lack of knowledge or to ask for explanations. In either case, the group will not draw on the experience available and will probably be a dissatisfying and unproductive experience. It may produce a worse result, and be more costly, than if the issue had been decided by a single manager.

Conformity and groupthink

'[Groupthink is] a mode of thinking that people engage in when they are deeply involved in a cohesive in-group, when the members' striving for unanimity overrides their motivation to realistically appraise alternative courses of action.'
(Janis, 1977)

Teams can become too cosy. The close-knit ideal can be taken too far and a team can become complacent and inward-looking, with people unwilling to challenge the prevailing direction of the group. People come to value their inclusion in the group so highly that they are reluctant to voice criticism in case this is seen as disloyalty, leading to isolation. This means that counter-propositions or inconvenient evidence is ignored or played down – perhaps leading the group to the wrong conclusion.

An influential analysis of how such *groupthink* occurs was put forward by the social psychologist Irving Janis. His research began by studying some major and highly publicised failures of desision-making, looking for some common theme which might explain why apparently able and intelligent people were able to make such bad decisions – such as President Kennedy's decision to have American forces invade Cuba in 1961. One common thread he observed was the inability of the groups involved to consider a range of alternatives rationally, or to see the likely consequences of the choice they made. Members were also keen to be seen as team players, and not to say things which might end their membership of the group. Janis termed this phenomenon 'groupthink', and defined it as follows:

> [Groupthink is] a mode of thinking that people engage in when they are deeply involved in a cohesive in-group, when the members' striving for unanimity overrides their motivation to realistically appraise alternative courses of action. (Janis, 1977)

He went on to identify the main symptoms of groupthink as a warning to those involved in team-decisions. These are summarised in the Noticeboard together with his suggestions for avoiding each one.

Control by self-managing teams can be oppressive

Much of the argument in favour of teams is based on the idea that organisations and their members will benefit if more of the control of operations is conducted not by remote management but by forms of self-governing teams. This represents a shift from control by management to control by the workers themselves, who collaborate to develop their own means of control. This is seen as consistent with values of responsible workers welcoming greater autonomy in how tasks will be done. The expectation is that they discuss among themselves how the work is to be done, how interactions are

NOTICEBOARD Irving Janis on the symptoms and prevention of groupthink

Janis (1977) identified eight symptoms which give early warning of groupthink developing – and the more of them that are present, the more likely it is that the disease will strike.

Symptoms

▶ **Illusion of invulnerability**   The belief that any decision they make will be successful.

▶ **The illusion of inherent morality** Justifying a decision by reference to some higher value.

▶ **Rationalisation**   Playing down the negative consequences or risks of a decision.

▶ **Stereotyping out-groups**   Characterising opponents or doubters in unfavourable terms, making it easier to dismiss even valid criticism from that source.

▶ **Self-censorship**   Suppressing legitimate doubts in the interest of group loyalty.

▶ **Direct pressure**   Strong expressions from other members (or the leader) that dissent to their favoured approach will be unwelcome.

▶ **Mindguards**   Keeping uncomfortable facts or opinions out of the discussion.

▶ **Illusion of unanimity**   Playing down any remaining doubts or questions, even if they become stronger or more persistent.

Preventive measures

▶ **Open climate**   The leader should encourage free discussion and divergent opinions.

▶ **Avoid the isolation of the group**   Bring in independent-minded outsiders.

▶ **Assign the role of critic to members** With the responsibility to challenge untested assumptions if they are made.

▶ **Avoid being too directive**   The formal leader moves out of the role for the discussion if they feel their views are carrying too much weight, and are not being challenged enough.

Source: based on Janis (1977; 1982)

---

to be conducted, how team members will behave towards each other, how difficulties will be handled, and so on.

A detailed study of an organisation which introduced such teams indicates that members of self-managing teams can experience control just as tightly as if they were subject to the traditional, management-determined rules (Barker, 1993). The self-managing teams worked hard to create shared values and ways of working, which all accepted. This gradually evolved into a set of relatively formal rules, with the additional force that, as they had been created by the members themselves, they were backed up by peer pressure. Anyone breaching the rules was subject to much more intense pressure than would normally be experienced if he or she broke a management-created rule:

> Concertive, value-based rules increased the overall force of control in the system, making it more powerful than bureaucratic control had been. Unlike the bureaucratic hierarchy, authority and the possibility of appeal first and finally resided in the peer pressure of teams ... concertive control is much more subtle than a supervisor telling a group of workers what to do. In a concertive system, the workers create a value-based system of control ... and willingly submit to their own control system [which] winds tighter and tighter about them as the power of their value consensus compels their wilful obedience. (Barker, 1993, pp.434–5)

Concertive control occurs when team members create a system of values and norms which members submit to.

Altering the power balance

Creating teams or groups is not a politically neutral act. Opting for teams has political implications. To the extent that groups are created and expected to act with more autonomy or discretion than the individual members previously had, there is likely to be some sense of loss by other players. Creating a self-managing team with greater autonomy may remove some power, influence and status from supervisors or middle managers. Removing some management levels alters the career prospects of those who expected to move up the hierarchy. It may be seen as an attempt to merge skills and to undermine professional autonomy, or as an attempt to cut costs. It may also be seen as a way of undermining traditional trade union interests in representing and reaching collective agreements on behalf of their members. Trade unions have traditionally sought to limit management power by ensuring that detailed working arrangements can only be changed by negotiation with union representatives. If teamworking leaves such issues to the discretion of workers themselves, trade union representatives will be bypassed.

case example: Teamworking sparks conflict at Royal Mail

Although the following dispute was eventually resolved in a way satisfactory to both parties, it is a good example of the political aspects which teamwork raises in some situations.

The management at Royal Mail planned to introduce a range of new management practices including teamworking, continuous improvement and the abolition of job demarcations. In return it offered increased pay, shorter working hours and greater job security. 'We are hoping to provide individuals with the opportunity for their own development so they can do tasks outside the job in hand,' a management spokesman said. 'It is designed to make the jobs people do more varied and interesting and end rigid definitions.'

The executive of the Union of Communication Workers initially rejected the deal, saying that no deal involving teamworking would be acceptable. A union spokesman said: 'There is deep suspicion within the activists of the union that one of the principal motivations for teamworking is to lessen the influence of the union.' Teamworking was seen by a majority of the executive as an attempt to undermine shopfloor organisation and remove many long-established agreements. In addition, some union members would become team leaders, which the executive saw as being divisive.

Source: based on *People Management*, 4 April 1996, p.8

We can see, then, that teams have costs. They have a cost in the sense of the training and other costs necessary to develop the skills unique to working in this way. There are also costs of the kind just outlined that may arise even in teams that on some criteria may be working well. Management, therefore, needs to exercise a deliberate choice in how far to go in introducing teamworking.

9.6 Choosing whether to invest in teams

Management evidently has choices over whether to introduce teams as the basic unit for organising work. These choices becomes clearer if we distinguish between different levels of group or team performance. In some situations a relatively low level of interaction amongst staff may be adequate, so it may be wasteful and dissatisfying to spend effort on team-building activities. In other situations these are essential.

A useful model for considering this was developed by Katzenbach and Smith (1993b). They illustrate differences in team performance by locating them on what they call the team performance curve. Figure 9.1 shows this.

Working groups rely on the sum of individual efforts for their performance. Members interact mainly to share information and best practices. They make decisions that help members of the group to perform well within their own area of responsibility. Beyond that there is no pressure to create a common purpose or tight performance goals, so there is no need for members to work closely together or to feel jointly accountable for results.

A working group is a collection of individuals who work mainly on their own but interact socially and share information and best practices.
A pseudo-team is a collection of individuals who could perform more effectively but have shown no interest in developing the necessary skills and methods.

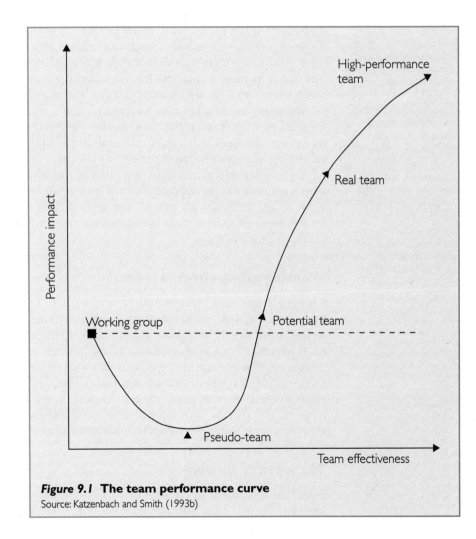

Figure 9.1 The team performance curve
Source: Katzenbach and Smith (1993b)

Pseudo-teams are teams where there could be significant benefits from group development but the members have done nothing to achieve them. They express no interest in setting common purposes or specific goals, even though they or their management may call themselves a team. They may even contribute less than working groups, as the time they spend in team meetings detracts from individual performance without delivering any added value or joint work products. The whole is less than the sum of the parts, and the members will probably regard the experience as unsatisfactory. Such groups have chosen to call themselves teams, and in doing so need to commit to the risk of conflict, to developing joint work products and to an agreed method of working. Otherwise they will remain a pseudo-team.

C A S E   Q U E S T I O N S   9.5

▶ Review the Consulting Engineers Case Study at the start of Chapter 8. What category of team does it most closely correspond to?

Potential teams are those for which there is a significant performance need, and that are genuinely attempting to improve performance. For example, they may require more clarity about purpose or about performance goals; or the goals may be clear, but a common method of working is not. Trying to be a fully functional team inevitably means that members will confront difficulties in these areas, which some teams overcome, while others do not. The latter revert to being pseudo-teams or working groups.

Real teams are small groups with complementary skills who have become committed to common purposes, goals and working methods. They have learnt how to meet both organisational and members' needs; they may be exceeding what management expected of them.

High-performance teams were described by Katzenbach and Smith as those which meet all the requirements of real teams, but in addition show commitment to the personal growth of members. They perform well beyond the expectations of others and, though rare, they provide a model to which other teams may aspire.

> A potential team is a collection of individuals who could perform more effectively and are putting effort into developing the necessary skills and methods.
> A real team is a collection of individuals with complementary skills who have become committed to common purposes, goals and working methods.
> A high-performance team is a team which meets all the requirements of a real team, but in addition shows commitment to the personal growth of members and performs beyond expectations.

Working groups or real teams?

Katzenbach and Smith raise the question of whether teams as they have defined them are always necessary for effective performance. Many tasks are such that an individual may be as capable of carrying them through. An example is where a task requires the application of a particular expertise to a narrowly defined technical issue with no wider implications. For such purposes an effective working group can meet the performance required. There is no need to invest the extra effort needed for team performance. In other cases the task requires people to work together to create joint work products in addition to individual contributions. Then the risk and cost of creating a team will be worthwhile.

The work to be done

Teams are expensive to create and develop properly, so whether the task is one that needs a team should be carefully considered. Critchley and Casey,

NOTICEBOARD **Assessing team effectiveness**

How can a group's performance be assessed? If a task is a relatively well defined, tactical or operational one, direct measures of output, quality and cost can be used. However, many organisational tasks have no correct answer, so Hackman (1990) argues that people should not measure effectiveness on a single dimension. He suggests a 'three-dimensional conception of group effectiveness':

▶ **Productive output** The degree to which the product, service or decision of a group meets the standards (however measured) expected by those who receive or use them. In other words, self-ratings by the group are not sufficient – the group should also take account of what clients think of their performance.

▶ **Group capability** The extent to which the group has developed collective skills of working together as a group, capable of further improving its performance on future tasks. Or has the experience been so bad that the group would be incapable of working together again?

▶ **Individual growth** The extent to which the experience of working with the group contributed to the personal growth and satisfaction of individual members. Did it provide new opportunities to satisfy valued needs, or was it a source of frustration and demotivation?

two British consultants specialising in developing teams at senior level raised the same dilemma. Reviewing the many teams with which they had worked, they concluded that teams were not always necessary, and may have represented an expensive solution to simple problems. The necessity of creating a team depended on the nature of the task being undertaken:

▶ **Simple puzzles of a technical nature** These could be done quite effectively by members working independently of each other, on the basis of their technical expertise; they need only a reasonable degree of polite social skills.

▶ **Familiar tasks with moderate degrees of uncertainty** Some sharing of information and ideas is required, but main requirement is reasonable co-operation between the people concerned using skills of negotiation and co-ordination.

▶ **Tasks with a high degree of uncertainty and relatively unknown problems affecting all concerned** High levels of information-sharing and of good interpersonal skills required to cope with the 'shared uncertainty', implying a high level of team skills.

John Adair (1986) has suggested that a team is only needed when the task requires the complementary efforts of other people. If this is not the case, then the work will best be done by well organised individuals.

n o t e b o o k   9 . 6

Reflect on a team that you have been part of. Where, on the scale between working group and high-performance team, would you place it?

Was a working group appropriate for the task? In other words, would any more intense type of team activity have been counterproductive? Could one person have done the job better?

Do your conclusions support the views of Critchley and Casey and of Adair, or not?

9.7 Teamwork at a distance – the spread of global teams

A development of teamworking, which is becoming increasingly common, is the geographically dispersed team. Most studies of teams have been based on those which were physically close and able to engage in face-to-face discussions. Project teams are often drawn from widely separate parts of the company, or from separate organisations, but typically they have done significant parts of their work in face-to-face meetings.

Teams nowadays are becoming more geographically spread. Companies operate internationally, dealing with markets and competitors across many national boundaries, time zones and cultures. Whether they work independently or through joint ventures, working transnationally can be severely impeded by a traditional hierarchical structure. The tension is that managers at the centre seek to maintain overall control, while managers in operating units around the globe, and their equally dispersed customers and suppliers, seek to respond rapidly to changing situations. Whyte and Poynter (1990) argue that the variety and complexity of the decisions required in the multinational firm cannot be supported by a predominantly vertical information flow. A different organisational approach is required which encourages managers to deal with issues at their level by building contacts with managers in other units directly involved in or affected by the issue. They will typically have specific projects to deliver against tight deadlines, but are unable to meet face-to-face because of cost and time constraints. Meeting deadlines can be supported by a system of 'lateral decision-making processes, horizontal networks and a common set of shared premises on which decisions were based' (p.98). Such lateral decision-making processes bring together in a collaborative effort the people most affected by the outcome, creating a flexible and overlapping set of teams.

Distant teams are those that meet the definition of teams but work with little, if any, face-to-face interaction because members are widely spread geographically.

Members of these widespread teams may be drawn from the same company, such as when members of several parts of the company work together to develop a new product or operating procedure. They may also be from different companies: closer collaboration between customers and suppliers, often over much greater distances than before, usually requires the creation of joint teams with representatives from both companies to deal quickly and continuously with technical, scheduling or commercial matters. Alliances between companies developing a new product – such as the European Airbus – inevitably requires teams made up of representatives from several companies and countries.

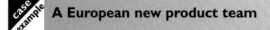

case example   **A European new product team**

Senior management in a semiconductor business decided to enter a new market, and created a new division of the company to handle this. Part of the project was to be handled by the company's European manufacturing plant and a development team was created there to develop expertise in the new tools. The team would also support the European design network which would promote the product to potential customers.

    The local manager arranged for four of his managers to participate in the project. He was excited about the possibility of getting his team

involved in this state-of-the-art design development, as it would make the European group stronger, enhance its skills and result in even more challenging work in future.

Traditionally, members of such teams would have travelled to meetings, with interaction between those infrequent encounters being conducted by telephone or letter. Not any longer. Developments in information technology are making it easier (though not necessarily *easy*) for members of a project or task team to work together with little face-to-face interaction. Voice and video-conferencing, e-mail and other forms of groupware make it feasible to exchange information during the course of an activity without the time and cost involved in travelling to meetings. Desk-top video systems will increase the practice.

As with all teams, though, merely creating them does not ensure that they work effectively. Globally dispersed teams face particular problems of differences in culture, working times and the balance of different local interests. They also lack the informal interaction which is so much a part of meeting and building an effective team. Given a high degree of individual diversity in a team, what does that imply for their management?

Some insight into the practical issues which arise was given by a report of an experiment in which a 'globally distributed team' (GDT) was created. The team consisted of MBA students at three business schools – in Spain, the UK and the United States. Their task was to create a global marketing plan for an international company. The major innovation in teamworking was to conduct their meetings using a video-conferencing facility. Some of the lessons learned are presented here:

Process issues need more attention when cultures 'meet' electronically
❛ A simple thing, such as the length of a lunchbreak, is easily resolved when all are meeting face-to-face. When working in a GDT to tight deadlines, Americans may not be aware that the Spanish team signing-off for lunch is unlikely to be back for a few hours, though it will then be happy to work long after the UK team has reached its traditional end of day. ❜

Poor technical support
❛ Many telecommunication companies offer video-conferencing services [but] ... we found that a number of these were unable to deliver to an acceptable level. Unquestionably the most frustrating aspect is that the technology is not within the control of the GDT members themselves. We found ourselves waiting for hours while technicians were trying to connect all three teams for a live discussion. ❜

Interruptions
❛ Most multi-point systems are voice-activated, in which the camera focuses on the person speaking the loudest. Time and focus are easily lost if more than one person attempts to speak. ❜

Lack of data transfer
❛ While data are easily handled in traditional teams, the same is not true of GDTs. It is difficult to create real-time knowledge in GDTs because the technology does not yet easily allow the transfer of information. ❜

Leadership

❛ The leadership role within the team is constantly changing. It moves easily from one member to another (and hence from one geographical site to another). If not properly managed this can lead to a waste of time and power-posturing. ❜

Role of culture

❛ We found that teams operate within their own culture (national and organisational). The transient nature of GDTs and the short duration of projects mean it is not feasible to build a team culture. ❜

(Based on Miller et al., 1996)

9.8 Recap

Content agenda

As management faces new expectations about cost and quality, many see teams as a way of using the talents and experience of the organisation more fully, to meet these tougher objectives. The organising tasks that were traditionally performed by specialist groups of managers can be done by teams themselves. Many see organisations structured around teams as the way to improve both performance and the quality of working life. Teams also meet important motivational needs – for social contact and to be part of a collective achievement. Teams are often becoming the basic vehicle through which management is performed. In that sense they reintegrate some management functions with direct work. They then make the task of generating action and motivation less problematic. Powerful teams can also pursue their own objectives at the expense of those of management or other stakeholders. Decisions on whether to invest in teams rather than working groups depend on wider strategy.

Process agenda

Teams are a way of making sure that relevant stakeholders are visible and represented in management processes. Selecting membership, and indeed whether a team or a working group (Katzenbach and Smith) should do the work, is a potentially far-reaching management decision. Teams can develop lives of their own and set their own agendas. Decisions about the external and internal team processes (see Chapter 8) are also problematic. The structural links between the team and the rest of the organisation will affect communication between teams. Particular aspects of the team concept, such as team-briefings, are used by management to try to ensure that a management message is passed rapidly thoughout the organisation.

Control agenda

Creating teams, and reallocating functions to them, often threatens other stakeholders who may fear their power sources (personal or organisational resources and knowledge) will be eroded. Indeed, teams may be proposed in order to enhance the power of some players relative to that of others. The latter may be able to resist this, irrespective of the working benefits expected.

AN INTEGRATIVE FRAMEWORK OF MANAGEMENT

Content agenda

▶ Teams are seen as a way of raising performance and quality of working life

▶ Specialist management tasks can be reintegrated into the work of teams

▶ Teams are becoming the basic unit of work in many organisations

▶ Teams are not always supported by human resources policies

▶ Teams are costly and not always worthwhile – so decision to create is significant

▶ Teams may pursue own objectives and agendas

▶ Teams meet basic motivation needs of many people for contact and shared achievement

Process agenda

▶ Teams are a way of making stakeholder interests visible

▶ Who to involve in decisions on internal and external team structures?

▶ Structural links affect communications between teams

▶ Team-briefings are a means of organisational communication

Control agenda

▶ Power distribution may be threatened by creating teams

▶ Teamwork may be a deliberate/covert attempt to gain power and reduce that of others

▶ Concertive control by members may be more oppressive than management control

▶ Groupthink can prevent effective monitoring and corrective action

▶ Self-monitoring of performance becoming widespread (technology helps)

▶ Teams are a powerful vehicle for mutual learning

Figure 9.2

Team-briefings may also be used to exercise power within the organisation, making it harder for alternative messages to be transmitted.

Many self-managing teams take on responsibility for monitoring performance. In this respect there is some evidence that they can be more oppressive than management would be to team members who are seen as underperforming. The bases and methods of measurement may be jointly agreed between the team members and management. Groupthink may lead members of a team which is too cohesive to ignore or fail to recognise the need for corrective action. Teams can powerfully support organisational learning by passing ideas across functional boundaries.

These points are summarised in Figure 9.2.

PART CASE QUESTIONS

- ▶ What kinds of team do those described in W.L. Gore represent in Hackman's typology?
- ▶ How do they compare with those at Opel Eisenach? What are the similarities and differences in the two examples?
- ▶ What are the benefits that W.L. Gore and Opel obtain from their team-based organisation?

9.9   Review questions

1   Several types of team are listed at the start of the chapter. Take two or three of these and try to find out more about them from someone who has worked in that type of team. Were the risks and opportunities similar to those suggested in Table 9.1?

2   Historically, what factors shaped the balance between individual work and group-work? Compare these with factors that affect that balance today.

3   Why has the balance shifted recently in favour of teamwork? What are the main business and motivational reasons?

4   Compare your own experience of teams with some published examples. What additional lessons can you learn from your examples beyond those in the published stories?

5   Evaluate the argument that teamwork sometimes causes stress to members in the light of teams you have observed or read about.

6   What are the disadvantages of teams?

7   Try to identify two examples of the symptoms of groupthink in a meeting which you attend.

8   Katzenbach and Smith distinguish between working goups and real teams. Compare their argument, that real teams are often not necessary, with that of Critchley and Casey.

9   W.L. Gore and Associates is beginning to form more distant teams. Compare management issues raised by this form of team with those arising when teams are in the same place.

Further reading

Hackman (1990) and Katzenbach and Smith (1993a) contain many good examples of the use of teamwork in modern organisations. Sandberg (1995) offers a very wide range of perspectives on the Volvo story. You could add to these by looking for more recent examples in the *Financial Times*, *Management Today* or *People Management*.

W Website addresses

Asda   http://www.asda.co.uk
To provide the wider context for one of the examples of teamwork quoted in the text, you could visit the Asda Website. This contains five-year performance information and other material about the company.

part three

Planning the business

3

Introduction

This part examines some of the issues involved in setting out the overall direction of an activity and planning how to implement it. As before, the essential tasks to be done apply to most human activities. Whatever they are, they will usually work better if some thought is given at the outset as to what the objectives are, what are the alternative ways of achieving them, which to choose, and how to implement the decisions made. All of this takes place within an environment, a particular context.

A key management responsibility (whether conducted by all involved or by a specialist occupational group) is to be familiar with that environment. The environment need not be accepted passively, as it can be influenced – by lobbying key players, by reaching agreement with competitors and so on. Nevertheless, since the organisation draws its resources from the external world, it needs to deliver goods or services well enough to persuade decision-makers in that environment to continue their support. This is most obvious in commercial organisations. It is equally relevant in the public service: if a department set up to deliver care is managed badly, it will not deliver. Taxpayers or clients will bring pressure on their elected representatives to improve performance, and they in turn are likely to demand improved performance

from management and staff. All those involved with the organisation have some expectations of it. How satisfied they are will affect whether or not they are willing to continue their support. If they do not, the enterprise will fail.

Sensing what the players in the environment want, and developing a strategy to meet those requirements are prominent tasks. Issues of strategy development and understanding the external environment are dealt with in Chapters 10 and 11. That leads to an aspect of management which is in essence outward-looking, that of marketing, dealt with in Chapter 12. Organisations can no longer act as if their shareholders were the only legitimate interests. Pressure from interest groups and many consumers has encouraged some companies to take a positive approach to issues of corporate social responsibility and ethical behaviour. There are conflicting interests here and difficult dilemmas: Chapter 13 presents some concepts and tools which help to consider these issues in a coherent and well informed way.

The case is the story of Glenlight Shipping, owned by Clyde Shipping Company, a subsidiary of Cathay Pacific. This is an international trading business based in Hong Kong. Glenlight illustrates the dilemmas that management faces in dealing with not only a changing market but also a changing government policy on public expenditure and environmental issues.

Glenlight Shipping Limited

Background

The geography of the western seaboard of Scotland graphically illustrates the obvious problems in servicing the communities' transport needs. There are over thirty islands, ranging from Arran in the south, to Lewis in the north whose sizes vary from small, e.g. Eigg, to the largest, Skye and whose populations vary broadly in line with the islands' dimensions. Communities require basic materials to survive in addition to the obvious necessities such as food and medical services.

For the past 150 years, the areas of the Western Highland and Islands have been serviced by small cargo vessels, nicknamed Puffers, which literally puffed their way through to these far flung settlements. The 'puff' came from the black smoke emitted from the funnel and it was the signal to the community that the ship was on its way with a cargo of coal or building blocks or another essential material required by the villagers. These ships had flat bottoms so that they could sit on the beach to discharge their cargo onto wagons or vehicles for onward delivery. Thus puffers had become part of the fabric of Highland society and played an essential role in sustaining the remaining population as young people left these remote communities to settle further afield.

Glenlight Shipping

Glenlight Shipping Limited (the last of the puffer companies) was formed in 1968 out of economic necessity by the merger of two family-owned fleets of puffers. Glenlight's shareholding was split 50/50 between the two owner-families and the ships of both fleets were hired to Glenlight at a rate which included a return on capital to the families. The management was merged and worked well: indeed, Glenlight operated better in the operations room than in the boardroom. The vital supplies of coal, stone, building materials and road salt to the communities on Islay, Skye, Mull, Tiree, Benbecula and Harris comprised the Northerly route (emanating from ports close to Central Scotland or Northern Ireland), and Southerly return cargoes consisted of seaweed and whisky. A round trip of the puffer was the owners' profit – a single leg voyage meant break-even at best.

In the late 1960s, the introduction of roll-on roll-off ferries took away one of those Southerly legs, namely whisky, and the 1970s saw the development of the national ferry company, Caledonian MacBrayne, which then removed the seaweed cargoes. By the late 1970s, apart from some profitable years serving the oil platforms at Ardyne and Loch Kishorn, Glenlight struggled to make ends meet.

Since 1968, Glenlight had had a contract with the American Navy who were at that time based in a deep water loch in the west of Scotland, servicing nuclear submarines that were used to patrol NATO waters. The contract required Glenlight to have on hire at least one ship available to the US Navy 24 hours a day, 365 days a year and to have at least four other ships available for a minimum period of five days per month every month of the year. On average, during the period 1981 to 1986, the US Navy represented about 40 per cent of Glenlight's turnover and was the largest single profit centre. Glenlight had a third market segment – traditional shipping business – the sorts of cargo carried by many shipping companies to ports around the UK. This segment too was profitable.

In 1976 Glenlight became a wholly-owned subsidiary (having been 50 per cent owned in 1968) of a Scottish based mini-conglomerate whose wider interests included harbour towage, leisure marine, quarrying and property. The core competence of the group was widely regarded as tug-owner having established joint venture arrangements with other organisations which resulted in significant contracts. These included one with BP for towage services at Sullom Voe in Shetland and the Hound Point oil terminal in the Firth of Forth. Towage was the 'cash cow' of the group.

This mini-conglomerate had been established in 1815 and was controlled by the descendants of the two original families who had then grown and diversified the group over the years. The family dominated the main board of directors and the culture of the group was one of autonomy to each of the subsidiary chief executives who then reported to their own respective boards containing main board representatives. The main board representatives then reported the activities of that subsidiary to the parent board, with meetings, on average, five times per year. The organisational structure was hierarchical, with service contracts and a share option scheme for senior employees. Long service within the group was the norm.

Table 1 shows the parent group's performance record during 1981 to 1986. In 1987 the group appointed its first non-family CEO; the new CEO having been an executive director since 1975.

Table 1 Summary of group results 1981–86 (£000)

	Turnover	Profit before tax
1986	37,415	1,524
1985	29,032	1,063
1984	27,120	1,424
1983	24,585	1,757
1982	21,602	1,546
1981	14,373	1,232

Glenlight's years of plenty 1981–86

In 1979, efforts were made to have the then Conservative government recognise the lifeline services of Glenlight to the Highland communities and, after some delays, in January 1981 a bill in Glenlight's name was passed through Parliament giving the Scottish Office the power to assist Glenlight financially. This power had three strands:

▶ To assist the company annually with losses in maintaining the lifeline services to the Highland and Islands area (deficit grant).
▶ To give a percentage of the rates that Glenlight charged for its services back to the customer, as a discount, in an

attempt to stimulate demand for the services and control the high cost of living in the area (Tariff Reduction Scheme, TRS).
▶ To receive from Glenlight submissions for capital funding on replacement vessels in order that the service could be maintained without fear of the ships becoming elderly and uneconomical and as a consequence adding to the deficit grant.

Glenlight hit record profits in 1986, but the impending reduction in subsidy levels through government spending cuts and the end of the Cold War bringing pressure on the US naval spending threatened the future. Other problems included Glenlight's ageing fleet of ships and competition from roll-on roll-off ferries. Finally the government had decided to modernise Caledonian MacBrayne's fleet in the light of the *Herald of Free Enterprise* disaster, which left Glenlight in an uncomfortable and exposed situation.

1987–91 Timber boom

One part of Glenlight's market that appeared to be growing was timber. In the late 1940s, land was cheap in Scotland, particularly in the west and the north. Consequently, the newly formed Forestry Commission planted trees in areas such as Islay, Skye and Mull as well as along the western fringes of the Scottish mainland. With growing times around 35–40 years, the late 1980s through to the middle 1990s were expected to see the full-scale production of significant volumes of timber for the home market. The western location was ideal for growing, thanks to the damp climate, but less than perfect for transportation by road as the main systems from the west were predominantly single track or A-class at best. Some of the largest users of timber were also located on the western seaboard, in total accounting for more than one million tonnes of timber per annum – all of which had to be transported into the appropriate mill.

TRS was a subsidy to the customer and an inducement to use Glenlight's service, but it was also restricted to commodities considered by Scottish Office officials to be essential (such as coal, etc.). Glenlight initially persuaded the Scottish Office that timber was such a commodity and thereby applicable to TRS, but perhaps more importantly, the flow of timber cargoes would be 95 per cent southbound thereby returning the company to the round trip of coal north and timber south, improving the economics of the company significantly.

Government policy on shipping subsidies, 1987–91

As Glenlight's then chairman and group CEO wrote later:

> The fact that Glenlight had an undertaking with the Scottish Office was not popular with other shippers who were engaged in the west coast trade to a greater or lesser extent. In 1982, other companies had received undertakings from the SDD [Scottish Development Department of the Scottish Office] to allow them to apply TRS to their cargoes in the area covered by the Highlands and Islands Development Board (HIDB). However, none of them were given the right to receive either deficit grants or assistance with capital investment. This rankled in some quarters. It was not any part of Glenlight's stand that others should not have equal rights with it and said so on many occasions. Sadly, and negatively, some shippers concentrated on attacking Glenlight's 'unfair advantage' rather than seeking parity. (Such a debate would have made the government face the question of what the policy on bulk shipments to the area was to be.) This did no one any good and certainly worked to the disadvantage of the trade to the Highlands and Islands. SDD announced that deficit support was to cease on March 31, 1987, i.e. within three months of the end of Glenlight's financial year ... The problem was that Glenlight was spending half its operating time and earning half its income from the HIDB area. Under the SDD's injunction, half of its management resources and employed capital would

become unproductive and drag down the rest of the company.

A government consultative document on the operation of the TRS system was issued for public debate and comment with the intention that a revised system should be introduced for April 1988 ... The April 1988 deadline was not met but the deficit payment stopped on time. The life of the 'old' TRS system was extended until October ... The intended system was much more complex than the original and looked to be complicated to administer for both user and the SDD. For the first time differential rates were to be applied for northbound and southbound cargoes and between the mainland and the islands together with a range of commodity rates. The rate for cargoes carried to the Islands was increased [from 30 per cent] to 40 per cent but all 'imports' to the mainland of the HIDB jurisdiction were to be disqualified completely. (A 40 per cent discount was to be available on the freight for goods delivered to Kyleakin on Skye but not to Kyle of Lochalsh on the mainland half a mile across the strait.) Some commodities, like timber, were restricted to a tonnage limit for the availability of TRS, but most importantly from Glenlight's point of view, *all* cargoes intended for local authorities were to be excluded from the scheme. Given that the company had contracts to take up to 30,000 tonnes of road salt each year from Northern Ireland to all the local authorities in the Highlands and Islands, this was a disastrous decision. A recalculation of the 1987 cargoes showed that if the new system had been in force that year Glenlight's customers would have lost £180,000 of discounts.

Cynics saw in this the fine hand of the Treasury trying to make savings on transport to the Highlands. The even more cynical saw the disqualification of discounts to the local authorities, in the run up to the introduction of the Community Charge, popularly known as the Poll Tax, as a way of exposing these bodies to the true costs of providing their services ... Glenlight was concerned that a major customer, faced with a large increase in the freight cost of its salt, would use another transport mode. What is more, the viability of the pricing structure of the southbound timber cargoes depended on the ships being in the north, with salt for example.

A fierce debate between Glenlight and the Scottish Office raged over the period 1987–94, typified by a letter to the minister responsible, at the end of 1988:

> In 1987 Glenlight transported over 77,000 tonnes of commodities to and from forty-six Highland and Island ports. Of this total, roughly 65 per cent was northbound. Virtually all of the southbound cargoes were logs carried on the return legs of the northbound loads, almost half of which were road salt for local authorities. We hope that it will now become clear why in previous correspondence to you we have talked of the revision of the TRS system increasing our loss in the HIDB area by over £200,000 per annum ... There is nothing in this sorry story that will encourage the future investment of private capital in transport services to the HIDB area ... We urge you to reconsider the recent decisions on the restructuring of the TRS system.

A minor compromise was reached when TRS was allowed in certain conditions on mainland shipments and a reduced rate of TRS at 20 per cent was allowed on salt shipments, but only for a six month period. It would then reduce to 10 per cent for one year, then zero. Deficit funding was never restored.

Glenlight's fleet 1987–91

On 1 January 1987 Glenlight had eight vessels, three of which were considered small by coastal standards and were being kept because of the US Navy contract. The bulk of its trade was carried out by four sister ships, built in 1969/70, and its largest vessel, built in 1976. These five coasters had a carrying capacity of 2,500 tonnes; three were fitted with made-to-measure timber cranes that sat on a travelling gantry whilst the other two had ordinary marine cranes. The coasters and their expensive cargo-handling equipment had been purchased during Glenlight's good times, but by 1987 they were getting relatively old, with the exception of the largest vessel which had been refurbished during 1986. The prospect of replacing these assets with larger and more modern vessels that were less expensive to operate was remote.

In 1989, one of the four sister ships sank in the Irish Sea. No lives were lost, and another coaster was purchased, with the insurance proceeds. The new vessel was larger than the one lost and fitted with a made-to-measure timber crane. This purchase, along with disposals of older vessels meant that by the end of 1990 Glenlight had three coasters, each with timber cranes and a carrying capacity of 1,700 tonnes.

Strategic development 1992–94

Glenlight had by now been beaten down through the government doctrine of public sector spending cuts, the US Navy contract was gone completely, fleet size reductions and employee redundancies. The question was asked, where do we go from here?

> The tonnage [of timber] being moved from west coast forests had reached an annual rate of 35,000 and projections were that this was to increase to 100,000 by 1995 and eventually to 300,000 by the end of the century if, as was expected, papermaking capacity in Scotland was doubled. In considering how to cope with such an increase Glenlight very quickly came to the conclusion that its conventional Highland shipping technique was not the answer.
>
> The area had no suitable port, and up to ten possible loading sites adjacent to mature forests had been identified. Parcels were likely to be in the range of 400–600 tonnes and, for various technical reasons and time constraints, it was

essential to load the timber as close to the forest as possible. Usually timber was felled, loaded to trucks, unloaded to a pier and when enough had been stored to justify a full hold, a ship was put alongside to load herself from the jetty and sail. The process was slow, involved double-handling and was restricted to places becoming ever more rare in the west Highlands – where there was adequate quay space ... The proposed solution was a tug and barge system. The barge would be beached on the forest's shores – a technique which was second nature to a puffer company – and loaded directly by road vehicle without double-handling. The tug would be supplied by Glenlight's sister company ... So puffer know-how would be married to equally venerable towage skills to solve the problem.

The concept envisaged one tug servicing three barges, on the basis of having one loading, one on passage and one discharging, thereby economically providing one motive unit for three cargo-carrying units totalling 1,800 tonnes ... It was not envisaged that the barge system would entirely replace the traditional ship. The two systems would complement each other and share the increasing load as the tonnages increased and the barging went through its proving trials.

The first barge was ordered in 1991 and delivered in January 1992. The SDD had reintroduced TRS for timber on the news of this environmentally friendly way of transporting a low value, bulky material, given that one barge-load of timber from Kintyre would save approximately 7,000

timber lorry miles on the road. A second barge was introduced in August 1993.

Glenlight's sister company operated fleet of tugs in conjunction with another (non-group-company) fleet, through a conference arrangement whereby both companies supplied a stated number of tugs to satisfy the demand of the market and remove competition. The business was profitable even though the tugs were only used 40 per cent of the time. Looking at it another way, 60 per cent of the time they sat doing nothing. The cost structure of the business was 90 per cent fixed cost and 10 per cent variable cost, therefore if the under-utilised tugs could be used during the 60 per cent idle time for an income that was greater than the variable 10 per cent cost, then the concept of marginal costing would bring profits to the group, given that Glenlight's costs of running the barge were also covered.

In 1992, the group appointed a 30 year old non-executive 'family' board member.

Government policy on shipping subsidies 1992–94

Glenlight required a third barge and some stabilisation in the TRS scheme in order to fully demonstrate the longer-term viability of the barging concept and the deep-seated belief within its management that, with a rising demand for timber, the barging and shipping system should be subsidy-free by the year 2000. Another government TRS review was carried out in 1993, this time conducted by outside consultants, but it had a sting in its tail – the review had to include the state ferry company. This brought a public outcry that the Scottish Office was seeking to privatise

Table 2 Source of operating profit 1987–93 (%)

	1993	1992	1991	1990	1989	1988	1987
Towage	58	59	54	47	46	57	39
Coastal shipping	(34)	(7)	(7)	(10)	(5)	(9)	(5)
Quarrying	35	22	31	31	27	29	31
Leisure	29	18	16	21	22	26	18
Property	12	8	6	4	3	2	0
Businesses sold	0	0	0	7	7	(5)	17
	100	100	100	100	100	100	100

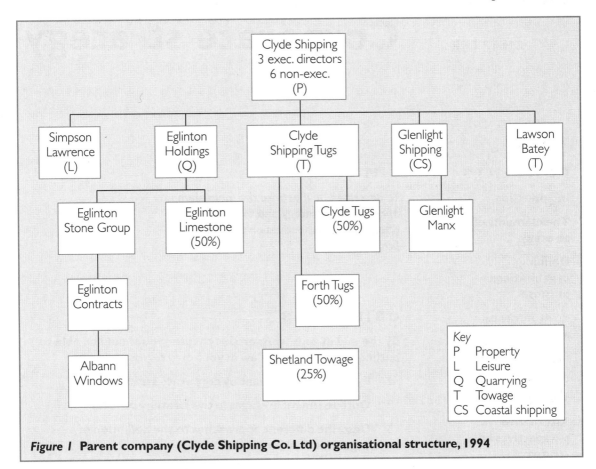

Figure 1 **Parent company (Clyde Shipping Co. Ltd) organisational structure, 1994**

the ferry company to cut government subsidies and services to the Islands. Glenlight reacted by mobilising its own campaign which culminated in a BBC documentary broadcast in November 1993 on the company and explained its worries for the future.

Table 2 shows Glenlight's parent group's profit sources during the period 1987–93.

In July 1994 at the group's AGM, the chairman announced to the shareholders that, with immediate effect, a strategic review of the group would take place. This review would be completed by July 1995 in time for the next AGM. In December 1994 the 'new' non-executive director (who was given the task of the strategic review) was appointed CEO of the group following the resignation of the previous incumbent. The parent company's organisational chart at 1994 is shown in Figure 1.

PART CASE QUESTIONS

▶ What new aspects of management do you think this case has introduced?

▶ What appears to be the main preoccupation of senior management during the years described?

▶ How have wider changes in government policy affected the company?

10

Corporate strategy

AIM

To describe and illustrate the main elements of corporate strategy and to introduce alternative perspectives on the strategy process.

OBJECTIVES

By the end of your work on this chapter you should be able to outline the concepts below in your own terms and:

1 Explain what is meant by corporate strategy

2 Outline the main stages in the strategy process

3 Describe different approaches to the definition of organisational purpose

4 Outline the purpose of environmental analysis

5 Explain what is meant by competitive advantage and how its meaning might differ in the public and private sectors

6 Explain Porter's concept of 'generic strategies'

7 Demonstrate how the product/market matrix can be used to identify alternative strategic directions

8 Assess the alternative means by which new directions can be pursued

9 Draw a distinction between strategic planning and strategic management

10 Summarise Mintzberg's critique of strategic planning

11 Contrast the planning view with the learning and political perspectives on strategy

Scottish Homes
The national housing agency in Scotland

Scottish Homes is a quango (quasi-autonomous non-governmental organisation) which was set up in 1989 to assist in meeting central government housing policy objectives. Like most public sector organisations, strategic planning now plays an important part in running the organisation. The Secretary of State for Scotland requires the agency to produce an annual strategic plan that sets out the agency's purpose, strategic objectives and strategies. The strategic plan forms the basis for agreeing with government – in this case the Scottish Office – the activities that the agency will undertake. It must also produce a strategic investment plan that indicates the level of public resources it will need to enable it to meet its objectives.

Scottish Homes is primarily an enabling agency. Its principal activity is to allocate government funds to external housing providers – mainly non-profit housing associations, but also private developers – for the provision or renovation of rented and owner-occupied housing. In order to receive funding, housing projects must meet a number of criteria: first, projects must meet housing needs as identified by Scottish Homes and reflected in its Strategic and Regional Plans and objectives; secondly, providers must be able to demonstrate value for money in the use of public funds.

In order to guide the allocation of its investment programme funds throughout Scotland, Scottish Homes developed a highly structured corporate planning framework. The planning process, which is carried out annually, leads to the production of a range of plans and other related documents:

▶ A *national database* and *context statement* are derived from an environmental analysis – principally of external factors – and are used to inform the agency's objectives.

▶ A *strategic plan* contains explicit statements of the agency's overall aim and supporting strategic objectives (see below).

▶ *Regional plans* translate national objectives into more detailed strategies at a local scale.

▶ *Strategic option analysis* signifies the assessment and comparison of alternative investment opportunities.

▶ *Strategic agreements*, reached between Scottish Homes's Regional Offices and relevant local authorities, set out shared priorities for investment.

▶ *Statements of activities*, produced at local level, describe the actions which will be taken in pursuit of strategic objectives.

▶ *Impact assessment* takes a number of forms. A research programme includes evaluation studies to assess whether particular housing initiatives or projects have met their objectives. Performance in meeting investment and output targets is also monitored annually.

Source: Scottish Homes Planning Framework

CASE QUESTIONS

▶ How would you describe Scottish Homes's approach to strategic planning?

▶ What degree of freedom is Scottish Homes likely to have in determining its own strategy?

▶ What do you think are the major external influences on Scottish Homes's strategy?

10.1 Introduction

This chapter introduces the following ideas:
- Strategy
- Corporate strategy
- Operational strategy
- Competitive advantage
- Competitive or business strategy
- Value for money
- Institutional advantage
- Generic strategies: cost, differentiation and focus
- Strategic planning
- Strategic management
- Logical incrementalism
- Emergent strategy

What is strategy?

Strategy is concerned with deciding what business an organisation should be in, where it wants to be, and how it is going to get there.

Smith (1994) describes the literature on strategy as 'a terminological mine-field'. Terms such as *strategic planning*, *corporate planning*, *corporate strategy*, *strategic management*, *business strategy* and *business planning* are widely, and often interchangeably, used. Although some writers make great play of the distinctions between these terms (some of them are defined in this chapter), each deals with the same general idea. Harrison *et al*. (1995) explain that 'strategy is about clarifying your mission, setting clear long-term objectives and formulating a comprehensive and integrated set of steps to achieve it'.

Why should organisations wish to plan in this way? Smith (1994) argues that there are four main reasons:
- **To give clarity of purpose**   If an organisation is to maximise its chances of success, it needs a well understood sense of direction, supported by clear objectives and priorities.
- **To create unity of purpose**   Any organisation will wish to ensure that all of its divisions or departments are moving in the same direction and towards achieving the same set of goals. A clearly articulated strategy conveying a sense of common values helps to facilitate a united or corporate approach (hence the use of the term *corporate* strategy). A strategy is, however, not enough on its own. Good communication and commitment throughout the organisation are also necessary if plans are to have any chance of being implemented successfully.
- **To facilitate the achievement of purpose**   Even the most well conceived and widely communicated strategy can fail if people do not consider it is feasible. Management needs to assess whether it has the financial, staffing and other resources necessary to put into action.
- **To provide a framework for day-to-day decisions**   although focused on the long-term direction of the business, strategy must also address the short term. Grand ideas or master plans serve no purpose unless they can provide a clear guide to action and a basis for monitoring progress.

So if strategy provides a context for day-to-day decisions, what are 'strategic' decisions? Strategy is concerned with 'the *direction* and *scope* of an organisation over the long term' (Johnson and Scholes, 1997) and raises the following types of question. Should the organisation concentrate on one activity, or undertake several? Should it operate in one or several markets, as in the case of multinational conglomerates? What should the boundaries of the organisation be? For example, should a company make or buy the components required to assemble the product? Should it employ the staff to carry out certain functions or should it contract with another organisation for this purpose? These types of decisions are strategic: they concern the future, have long-term effects, often involve major resource commitments, and usually bring in their wake a need for a series of operational decisions throughout the organisation. Strategic decisions are 'likely to be complex in nature ... to involve a high degree of uncertainty, ... to demand an integrated approach to managing the organisation [and] may also involve major change in organisations' (Johnson and Scholes, 1997).

In contrast, day-to-day or 'operational' decisions are more action-centred, often more routine in nature and usually affect only part of an organisation. Operational decisions are important but take place within the context of an overall strategy.

These definitions illustrate that objectives and strategies exist at different levels within an organisation. Sometimes the distinction between the different levels can be confusing.

> Corporate strategy 'is concerned with the firm's choice of business, markets and activities' (Kay, 1996), and thus it defines the overall scope and direction of the business.

> Operational strategies are those deployed by the different functions of the organisation, such as manufacturing, marketing, finance and human resource management, and which contribute to the achievement of corporate strategy.

Scottish Homes – the case continues
Central and local planning

Four central divisions – Strategy and Performance, Finance and Regulation, Organisational Development, and Communications – each produce business plans which tie into an annual corporate plan. These plans indicate the ways in which central activities support the implementation of Scottish Homes's objectives. Corporate planning is co-ordinated by a central team but responsibility for the production of regional plans is devolved to local teams.

Regional plans (there are five regional divisions) translate national objectives into more detailed strategies at a local scale. Important inputs to these plans are:

▶ **Local housing system analysis   Aims to identify trends in the external environment (for example, changes in population, households, employment levels and housing stock quality) and to establish the main types of housing need in different areas within the region.**

▶ **Partners' plans   These include the plans prepared by local authorities (both housing and structure plans), housing association plans (which include bids for a share of the agency's resources), community care plans, and the plans of local enterprise companies (which have responsibilities for employment and economic development).**

The annual planning process for the investment of public funds in housing involves many organisations. A number of questions arise:

▶ **Whose objectives are being met? Local authorities, housing associations and others have their own objectives that may not always coincide with those of Scottish Homes, but its control over a substantial pot of public money puts the agency in a powerful position.**

▶ **How does Scottish Homes decide which areas and which organisations will receive a share of its funds?** There are always more potential projects than money available to fund them, so that tensions can arise if it is perceived that some locations are favoured over others.

▶ **How can separate organisations plan and work together?** Current government policy favours a partnership approach to the regeneration of run-down areas. This involves not just housing providers but also other organisations concerned with raising employment and education opportunities, and with improving health and social care.

The best way to think about these different levels is in terms of a hierarchy. The top level represents the organisation as a whole, below which are different divisions, business units or departments. There will be different sets of objectives and strategies at each level. These are likely to become more specific in their terms as they move down the organisation (a process sometimes referred to as 'cascading'). They should be consistent with those set for the organisation as a whole.

Confusion sometimes arises over the use of the word 'strategy' itself. Organisations use the term in different ways and sometimes interchangeably with other terms such as 'aims' and 'objectives'. It is important not to become obsessed about precise definitions, but one distinction can be made that is sometimes helpful: that between *what* an organisation aims to achieve (its objectives or *ends*), and *how* the organisation intends to achieve these objectives (the *means* by which it will achieve the objectives). Marks & Spencer, for example, declares that 'our strategy is to accelerate expansion overseas'; this sets out *what* the company seeks to achieve. British Airways says that its strategy is 'to expand our core business globally by creating marketing alliances or by investing in other airlines'. This statement tells us both *what* it seeks to achieve and *how*.

Competitive advantage

'Competitive advantage arises from discovering and implementing ways of competing that are unique and distinctive from those of rivals, and that can be sustained over time.' (Porter, 1994)

Strategy, then, is concerned with defining and achieving organisational purpose. Organisations do not operate in a vacuum but, for the most part, in a competitive marketplace. Thus managements want their organisations to perform well not just in their own terms but against their competitors. This raises a concept of central importance in discussion of strategy, that of *competitive advantage*. Introduced by Porter (1980b, 1985), the approach attempts to identify the factors that give an organisation an edge over its competitors. Usually this means that organisations will seek to produce goods or services that are differentiated from those of their competitors. The difference may be in the price charged or in other factors such as unique product features.

Competitive or business strategy 'is concerned with the firm's position relative to its competitors in the markets which it has chosen.' (Kay, 1996)

Strategy defined in this competitive sense and which seeks to identify and sustain sources of competitive advantage is often called *competitive strategy* or *business strategy*. Because of the importance of competitive advantage in the development of strategy, this chapter and the next examine the different bases of competitive advantage and the ways in which organisations might identify the advantages they hold.

The position of not-for-profit organisations needs also to be considered. Goold (1997) argues that competitive advantage assumes firstly the existence of competitors and secondly that organisations and their competitors share a common goal of maximising profitability. Neither of these assumptions, he argues, is valid for not-for-profit organisations. On the face of it, this seems a plausible argument since, for organisations such as the Benefits Agency or local councils, it is difficult to identify who the competitors are. Yet while public and voluntary organisations may not compete for customers they are increasingly competing for resources. In the UK, for example, there has been a rapid growth in competitive projects, such as the challenge funding initiatives, which invite local authorities and other public service organisations to compete for limited public resources. This contrasts with the traditional method that is to allocate resources in line with the identified need of different geographical areas.

Where public service organisations compete for resources a central concept is *value for money*. To win resources, organisations have to demonstrate – to government or whomever else is controlling funding – their ability to perform their tasks efficiently and effectively. In such cases, where organisations are dependent on external bodies for funding support, strategy may be driven more by powerful external interests than by the organisations themselves. This issue is considered in section 10.7.

Consider also the position of charities. It is clear that they do compete with each other for the public's donations, *and* for customers through shop and mail-order networks. Porter (1990) has also written about competition between nations. Nation-states and, within them, individual cities compete with each other. The prizes include inward investment by multinational companies; the right to host events such as the Olympic Games; or to hold titles such as 'European City of Culture'. Such events can bring major employment and income benefits.

The idea of competitive advantage, then, *is* relevant to the not-for-profit sector. Goold prefers the term 'institutional advantage' which 'is held when a not-for-profit body performs its tasks more effectively than other comparable organizations'. The important point to recognise is that the nature of competition differs between the public and private sectors. In aiming to improve value for money, not-for-profit organisations are seeking institutional advantage by gaining a greater share of available funds. In this sense, value for money is analogous to the idea of competitive advantage. This theme is returned to later.

A service that represents value for money is one that is provided economically, efficiently and effectively.

'Institutional advantage is when a not-for-profit body performs its tasks more effectively than other comparable organizations.'
(Goold, 1997)

Nature of the strategy process

There are a number of views on the nature of the strategy process (see, for example, Johnson and Scholes, 1997) each of which lies somewhere on a continuum. At one end of the continuum are views that are *prescriptive* in that they seek to explain how management *should* make strategy. Towards the other end are the more *descriptive* views that attempt to describe how management *does* make strategy in practice.

The traditional, 'planning view' of strategy is prescriptive and stems from the rational planning process articulated many years ago by writers such as Herbert Simon (1947). Simon's interest was in how people in organisations take decisions. In contrast to the concern of earlier classical theory, he emphasised the importance of *process* rather than organisational structure in effective decision-taking. Simon's view was that the complexity of strategic decisions required an explicit and formalised approach to guide management through the process. His ideas were influential in the emergence in the 1960s and 1970s of a wide literature on the subject of corporate strategy, most notably the work of Ansoff (1965). At this time, strategy was seen as a highly systematised process, following a prescribed sequence of steps and making extensive use of analytical tools and techniques. This was the 'one best way' to develop strategy which, if followed, was believed almost to guarantee corporate success. Although writers criticise the rigidity of these early approaches, contemporary texts still portray strategy in the same broad steps. However, these models of the strategy process are no longer intended to be prescriptive but to provide a framework for analysing real processes. The framework is outlined in the next section.

10.2 The elements of strategy

Figure 10.1 identifies seven stages in the strategy process. Each stage links to one of a series of basic questions that form the essence of strategic decision-taking. The process begins with an articulation of the organisation's purpose; management often expresses this as a mission or aim. The next stage is to analyse the business environment, which encompasses a range of internal and external factors. Environmental analysis enables management to develop its broad aim into more detailed objectives. These specify more clearly what they wish the organisation to achieve.

> **Strategy at ENI, an Italian natural gas and chemicals group**
> ❛ **Group strategy is to concentrate on activities in which it deploys, or has the prospect of deploying, world class skills. The aim is to secure positions among the international market leaders in terms of business performance, technology, productivity and cost structure.** ❜
> (ENI Annual Report 1994)

Once there are some clear objectives, the next stage is to formulate strategies that specify how the organisation will achieve the objectives. Since it might be necessary to make a choice between different strategies, the process includes an 'options analysis' stage. Once selected, management puts the chosen strategies into action (the implementation stage). Finally, to ensure that the organisation remains on track, management needs to put mechanisms in place to monitor and control performance and progress.

Figure 10.1 also shows the seven stages as just two broad phases: strategy formulation and strategy implementation. The relationship between these two phases is important and is discussed later.

C A S E   Q U E S T I O N S   10.1

▶ Scottish Homes's Corporate Planning Framework is an example of a strategic planning system. How does the framework compare with the model in Figure 10.1?

▶ Which of the different stages in the strategy process can you identify?

▶ Can you also identify a 'family' of plans and the relationship between them?

Stage of strategy process	Questions	Description
STRATEGY FORMULATION		
Mission statement **Statement of aim(s)** **Statement of values**	What is our purpose? What kind of organisation do we want to be?	A clarification of the purpose of the business, often resulting in a statement of mission or aims. Some organisations also determine the values to which they wish to subscribe
Environmental analysis	Where are we now?	Environmental analysis involves the gathering and analysis of 'intelligence' on the business environment. This encompasses the external environment, the internal environment (staffing, resources, performance relative to competitors), and stakeholder expectations
Objectives	Where do we want to be?	Objectives provide a more detailed articulation of aims; sometimes objectives are expressed in quantitative form, setting a target for the organisation to achieve
Strategic choice **(a) Strategies**	How are we going to get there?	Strategies describe how the objectives are to be achieved
(b) Options analysis	Are there alternative routes?	Alternative strategic options may be identified; options require to be screened and appraised in order that the best can be selected
STRATEGY IMPLEMENTATION		
Actions	How do we turn plans into reality?	A specification of the operational activities and tasks required to enable strategies to be implemented
Monitoring and control	How will we know if we are getting there?	Monitoring performance and progress in meeting objectives, taking corrective action as necessary and reviewing strategy

Figure 10.1 Stages in the strategy process
Source: adapted from Catterick (1995, p.14) and Johnson and Scholes (1997, p. 13)

The conclusion of each stage in the process may be marked (but need not be) by the production of a physical document. Many organisations produce separate mission statements and statements of aims, objectives and strategies. Sometimes a single document, the strategic plan, will contain all of these. Following the principle of a hierarchy of objectives and strategies for different parts of the organisation, there may be a consistent set or 'family' of plans.

Strategy models portray an over-simplified caricature which does not convey the complexity of strategy making in practice. Yet there are many examples of similar frameworks in the real world. Many public and voluntary organisations have started to use strategic planning systems as their managements have adapted to the demands of a more business-oriented culture. This has resulted from various government policy changes designed to increase the efficiency and effectiveness of public service provision.

A glance through the annual report of any large public limited company will also reveal a widespread use of the language of strategy, as the Case Example demonstrates.

Strategy at Marks & Spencer

Marks & Spencer has four core businesses: clothing, footwear and gifts; home furnishings; food; and financial services. The company also has a strong sense of social responsibility, placing particular emphasis on caring for the environment and contributing to the development of local communities. The following statements illustrate the way in which the company expresses *what* it aims to achieve, *how* it intends to achieve these objectives and the *values* to which it subscribes. There are also examples of *actions* consistent with the company's stated intentions. Some of the objectives, strategies and actions relate to the whole business and others to specific business sectors and markets. In moving from the general to the specific, a 'hierarchy' of objectives and strategies begins to develop.

Aim

　　Marks & Spencer aims to become the world's leading volume retailer with a global brand and global recognition.

Values

　　Customer service is the priority for the 21st century.

　　Quality is the key, in clothing, homeware and food.

　　We believe that business must accept *social responsibility*.

Goals (objectives)

　　Our goal is to continue growing the business.

　　The goal is to produce quality foods by methods that do not disrupt the balance of nature.

Strategies

　　Our strategy is to accelerate expansion overseas while continuing to exploit the many opportunities for growth here in the UK.

　　We will provide new and upgraded stores in many UK towns and cities, offering our customers excellent shopping facilities in attractive and secure surroundings.

　　Investment will continue – in people, training, technology and the logistical infrastructure that supports our business, so that the quality of the shopping experience matches the quality of the products on which our reputation is based.

Actions

　　during the year [1997] the Group opened a record 250,000 square feet of new selling space outside the UK ...

We have recruited 4,000 additional people in UK stores to enhance customer service ...
Spending on community involvement ... was nearly £10 million.

Source: Marks & Spencer plc Annual Report and Financial Statements 1997

10.3 Defining organisational purpose

The initial stage in strategy development tries to identify organisational purpose or choice of business. Smith (1994) considers that this is likely to be a more prominent component of the strategy process for public sector organisations. Private companies generally have freedom to choose which business they want to be in within the bounds of legality. Public service organisations such as local authorities and executive agencies must perform specific functions. Legislation, statutory instrument and other forms of regulation stipulate the main duties. These also set out other discretionary powers and activities making it clear what the organisation can and cannot do.

Missions, visions, aims and objectives

An expression of an organisation's overall purpose may take a variety of forms:
► mission statement
► vision statement
► short statement setting out a single overall aim
► a set of strategic objectives

The first three of these normally express organisational purpose in very general terms. Management must then develop them into more specific objectives. Vision statements tend to set out the desired end-states. They describe what the management of the organisation would like the future to be like. The following are some examples of the way in which organisations express their underlying purpose:

Barclays plc
❛ Barclays' objective is to be one of the best financial services groups in the eyes of customers, staff and shareholders. ❜

Royal Dutch/Shell Group
❛ The objectives of Shell companies are to engage efficiently, responsibly and profitably in the oil, gas, chemicals and other selected businesses and to participate in the search for and development of other sources of energy. Shell companies seek a high standard of performance and aim to maintain a long-term position in their respective competitive environments. ❜

Higher Education Funding Council
❛ The HEFC's mission is to promote high quality, cost effective, teaching and research within a financially healthy higher education sector, having regard to national needs. ❜

Volvo Car Group
❛ Volvo Car should be among the world's leading specialist car manufacturers, with safety, concern for the environment and quality constituting the base for the development of new products and services. ❜

Scottish Homes – the case continues
Aims and objectives

Our aim
We aim to make sure the quality of housing and variety of housing options available in Scotland are substantially improved.

Our objectives
Our objectives are designed to support the achievement of this aim. We will promote housing choice by:
- *promoting home ownership*
- *promoting the development of a more diverse rented sector*

We will respond to people's housing needs by:
- *assisting those with particular housing needs*
- *making an effective contribution to the reduction of homelessness*

We will create sustainable and balanced communities by:
- *contributing to improved quality in housing and its management*
- *making an effective contribution to community regeneration strategies*

Targets
Each of the agency's objectives is developed to include specific targets for achievement. For example, in 'contributing to improved housing quality', the target for 1995/96 was to effect the improvement, repair or replacement of 1,200 substandard houses.

Monitoring progress
The agency's annual reviews report progress in meeting annual targets set by the Secretary of State for Scotland. Financial year 1996/97 was heralded as 'a year of achievement': it funded 7,015 new or improved homes against a target of 6,250; it contributed to providing 5,009 homes (target 4,725) for low cost home ownership (almost 2,000 of these were existing houses bought by tenants under the Right-to-Buy or other discount schemes); it contributed to meeting the particular housing needs of elderly and disabled people by funding the creation of 1,210 new homes (target 1,200); 2,656 homeless people were housed (target 2,600); and its investment programme levered in £191.3 million of private finance against a £160 million target.

Sources: Scottish Homes Strategic Plan 1995–1998, and Annual Review 1996/97

CASE QUESTIONS 10.2

Consider the statement of Scottish Homes's aims and objectives.

- Do you consider it to be a clear statement of its organisational purpose?
- Do you consider it to be a clear statement of its overall aims or objectives? What, if any, ambiguities does it contain?
- Would you say that its performance targets emphasise quantity or quality? Can you think of alternative targets that could be set?

Organisational values

Statements of purpose often express an organisation's values. Amongst the purposes of planning is a desire to create clarity and unity of purpose within an organisation. One means of trying to achieve this is to identify a set of values to which people involved with the organisation can subscribe, and which define what the organisation wants to represent. Values often relate to promoting success in business but many also seek to convey the organisation's image and its reputation as an employer. Public service organisations often stress values relating to fairness, equality and community involvement.

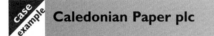 **Caledonian Paper plc**

Caledonian Paper plc is part of the UPM–Kymmene Group of Finland. Part of the Caledonian strategy is what it describes as 'Our values'. The value statements aim to inform any interested party of what type of organisation Caledonian is and what to expect from the company, whether as employee, customer or supplier.

> **'Excellence through innovation**
> **Care and respect for customers and individuals**
> **Honour commitments**
> **Recognise success**
> **Acting always in Caledonian's best interests**
> **Commitment through involvement**
> **Achievement through teamwork**
> **Best practice is our aim'**

Stakeholder expectations

Statements of organisational purpose and values will reflect the expectations of stakeholders, both inside and outside the organisation. As discussed in further detail in Chapter 11, the degree to which individuals, groups or society at large can actually influence what organisations do will depend on their relative power. The reaction of Shell to pressure from environmental groups is an example of the power that stakeholders can exert. The pressure groups' actions forced Shell to acknowledge that 'externally the Group was challenged over the proposed deep-water disposal of Brent Spar as well as environmental and human rights concerns elsewhere ... [and] we learned that we need to have greater external focus if we are to create a better acceptance of the Group's business among varied audiences' (Shell Annual Report, 1995).

The core beliefs and assumptions held within an organisation are equally if not more important. The ability of groups or individuals either to promote or to prevent change in organisations should never be underestimated. As discussed later in the chapter, cultural and political tensions exist in all organisations, exerting influence at all stages in the strategy process.

Goals at Hoechst, a German chemicals company
❝ Our common goal is a long-term sustainable increase in the value of the Hoechst Group which will benefit our shareholders and stakeholders alike. We are focusing on profitable core activities and aim to be one of the global leaders in this business. ❞
(Hoechst Annual Report 1996)

n o t e b o o k   1 0 . 1

Examine the annual report of an organisation with which you are familiar. Can you identify the range of stakeholders whose interests are mentioned? Do you sense that the organisation's aims and values rank the interests of certain stakeholders above others?

Wish-driven strategy

Although many organisations have mission statements, some writers question their value. Kay (1996) asserts that visions or missions are indicative of a 'wish-driven strategy' which fails to recognise the limits to what might be possible given finite organisational resources. He cites the case of Groupe Bull, a French computer company (see below).

Groupe Bull

'European politicians and businessmen have long dreamt of creating a European IBM. The British government promoted ICL, the Germans Nixdorf and Siemens, the Italians supported Olivetti. These companies have succeeded only in subsectors of the computer market. The European government most determined to resist IBM's hegemony across the full range of computers has been the French, and the European company most determined to resist it has been Groupe Bull.'

For many years, backed by the French government, Groupe Bull sought to challenge the supremacy of IBM, particularly in the large US market. Bull enjoyed success, and gained a worldwide name in the 1960s with its Gamma Sixty range of computers. Its later Ninety range, however, did not live up to expectations. 'The company recognised that it lacked the technical capacity to challenge IBM alone and that the USA would be by far the largest geographic market for computers.' To penetrate the North American market, Bull entered into partnerships with two US companies, first General Electric and then Honeywell. 'General Electric came to an early conclusion that the computer market was IBM's, and quit it completely ... [and] eventually Honeywell too gave up the chase' – and was bought out by its partner Bull.

In 1989, Bull's new chief executive 'reasserted the company's primary objective. This was "to become the major European supplier of global information systems" – the emphasis had shifted slightly from a French to a European base, but the central message remained the same. But by now even IBM was faltering. IBM's distinctive capabilities remained strong, but markets had changed. A computer had become a commodity, not a mystery, and there could be one on every manager's desk. In 1990, Bull posted large losses, and 1991 was a worse year still. Early in 1992 Bull announced an alliance with IBM, and [the chief executive] left the company soon after.'

Kay's analysis is that for thirty years Groupe Bull was 'driven not by an assessment of what it was but by a vision of what it would like to be.

Throughout, it lacked the distinctive capabilities that would enable it to realise that vision. Bull – and the other attempts at European clones of IBM – epitomises wish-driven strategy, based on aspiration, not capability.'

Source: extracts from Kay (1996, pp.41–3)

Referring to the experience of local government in Britain, Leach (1996) notes that mission statements and strategic visions 'are beginning to approach the status of an orthodoxy'. He points to Newman and Clarke's assertion that 'no self-respecting chief executive would be lacking in a strategy, vision, or mission statement'. Leach found that, in some authorities, mission statements appear to have made a real impact in clarifying organisational values and culture. However, many remain sceptical and argue that mission statements amount to no more than symbolic public relations documents that have little or no effect as a management tool. The danger is not just that missions are unrealistic and fail to recognise an organisation's capabilities, but also that management fails to communicate the vision or mission and to translate it into day-to-day action for the organisation. Mission statements and objectives for business must be accurate, achievable, and should serve to motivate whilst providing direction to all employees.

The Case Example describes how the City of Glasgow Council has begun the translation process by developing its vision statement into more specific objectives and strategies. It then needs to develop the council-wide objectives and strategies in the context of the individual council departments that will contribute towards making the vision a reality.

Glasgow City Council's vision, objectives and strategies

case example

The Council wants Glasgow to flourish as a multicultural international city where people choose to live, learn, work and play. It wants employment opportunities, social justice and a good quality of life for all Glaswegians. Seven key objectives ... have been adopted to make this happen.

1 **To achieve high quality services.**
2 **To improve the quality of city life for all Glaswegians.**
3 **To regenerate Glasgow's economy, increasing job opportunities and improving access to education and training.**
4 **To tackle deprivation and disadvantage in Glasgow.**
5 **To improve Glasgow's environment and make it a safe and healthy place.**
6 **To fight discrimination and encourage a vibrant, multicultural Glasgow.**
7 **To be open and responsive by involving local people.**

Alongside each strategic objective the Council lists a series of strategies that it intends to follow. In relation to the last objective, for example, it is stated that

'the Council will:

▶ **pursue meaningful community involvement and consultation on local policy issues,**

> ▶ **engage with service users in the design, review and management of service provision,**
> ▶ **develop appropriate support for the voluntary sector and consult on a strategy and code of guidance,**
> ▶ **maintain dialogue with special interest groups and sections of the community such as the elderly, young people, ethnic and other organisations,**
> ▶ **consult widely on decentralisation and implement a scheme, and**
> ▶ **develop its links with Community Councils, Tenants Associations and other community groups.'**

Source: Glasgow City Council *Key Objectives 1996 to 1999* (1996)

notebook 10.2

Find out if your local authority has a vision or mission statement. Do more detailed statements of objectives and strategies support these visions?

Once management has defined the broad organisational purpose, it must translate this into specific objectives that explain in precise terms what the organisation wishes to achieve. This involves 'cascading' the corporate-level objectives down to the levels of business units or departments and, often, to individuals. Such objectives often include targets – relating for example to sales or turnover – which quantify what the organisation seeks to achieve over a certain time. Before management can establish these detailed objectives, however, it needs to undertake the next stage in the strategy process – environmental analysis. Organisations operate within the context of a business environment that creates both opportunities and constraints. Management must take these into account in formulating objectives and strategies. Knowledge of the business environment will underpin the specification of 'core', corporate-level objectives that flow from the broad statement of organisational purpose. It will also help to identify 'change' objectives that reflect what management wants to do differently or better.

10.4 Environmental analysis

Against the backdrop of agreed organisational purpose, environmental analysis is 'concerned with understanding the strategic position of the organisation'. It aims 'to form a view of the key influences on the present and future well-being of the organisation and therefore on the choice of strategy' (Johnson and Scholes, 1993).

Kay (1996) defines a firm's strategy as 'the match between its internal capabilities and its external relationships. It describes how it responds to its suppliers, its customers, its competitors, and the social and economic environment within which it operates.' This definition points to the three main elements that environmental analysis addresses:

▶ The ways in which socioeconomic forces in the wider external environment both create opportunities and impose constraints on organisations.

- ▶ The influence of important stakeholders (particularly customers and suppliers) and competitors on organisational strategy.
- ▶ The strengths and weaknesses of the organisation's own internal resources and capabilities in relation to its competitive environment.

Since these factors form the basis for Chapter 11 they are only summarised here.

The wider external environment

Strategy aims to map the organisation's future, so it is vital to understand the external forces that might work in favour of or against the organisation. Most of these influences are beyond the organisation's control but will nevertheless affect organisational performance and play an important part in determining the type of strategy it should pursue. For example, changes in factors such as demography, consumer tastes and personal tax rates are likely to affect demand for the goods or services which the organisation provides. Supply-side factors such as advances in technology could lower production costs and enhance competitiveness.

CASE QUESTIONS 10.3

- ▶ Give some examples of external factors which you believe would be relevant to Scottish Homes in developing its strategy.

Stakeholders and the competitive environment

The competitive environment is a subset of the external environment. It comprises the organisation's external stakeholders and its competitors or rivals. External stakeholders such as suppliers and buyers may be in a position to influence or be influenced by the organisation. They can influence the supply or purchase of materials, goods or services. Large retail stores often dominate their small suppliers. Management needs to consider the impact of these relationships on their future strategy. Just as important are the actions of competitors. Managers and staff need to develop a good understanding of the way their industry operates and of the strategies and tactics of their competitors.

In the sphere of public services, external stakeholders often play a major role in strategy development. As noted in section 10.3, strategies followed by local government and public agencies are often dictated by legislation and by general government policy objectives. The privatisation of many former public corporations, such as the public utilities, is a further example of the way in which strategy can be imposed on organisations rather than developed by choice.

Internal resources and capabilities

A third set of influences, which Kay refers to as internal capabilities, are those within an organisation's internal environment, and they relate to its physical, financial, human and other resources. Organisations need to address the quantity, quality and organisation of their resource base. This includes the structure of the organisation and form of its business processes. These will affect efficiency and performance. In assessing capabilities, management needs to understand both the strengths and weaknesses of its business processes, particularly in comparison with their competitors. The *resource-based theory of strategy* (also discussed in Chapter 11) emphasises the importance of internal resources as sources of competitive advantage.

The aim of environmental analysis is, as Kay suggests, to identify the degree of match (or mismatch) between the organisation's capabilities and the demands imposed by the competitive and wider external environments. If management can develop its understanding of what is necessary to be successful in its chosen markets, it will be in a better position to meet the challenge. Several of the techniques developed to help organisations with the complex analytical task are discussed in the next chapter.

10.5 Strategic choice

Johnson and Scholes (1997) note that 'strategic analysis provides a basis for strategic choice [and that] in many ways strategic choice is the core of corporate strategy. It is concerned with decisions about an organisation's future and the way in which it needs to respond to the many pressures and influences identified in strategic analysis. In turn, the consideration of future strategies must be mindful of the realities of strategy implementation, which can be a significant constraint on strategic choice.'

Choices exist at two main levels within an organisation. First, there are choices about which objectives to pursue, i.e. answering the basic question what business are we or should we be in? Should the organisation, for example, provide a wider range of goods or services or concentrate on a narrower range? These first-order choices, concerned primarily with the organisation's scope, will be reflected in its statements of organisational purpose. Decisions on organisational scope, in turn, define organisational boundaries and shape decisions on organisational structure and ownership. These are typically corporate-level choices. Secondly, there are choices between different strategies or means to achieve organisational objectives. Alternative strategies are likely to require detailed analysis and appraisal before a choice can be made. The final selection should reflect whatever the organisation believes is necessary to create and sustain competitive advantage in its chosen markets. The fact that an organisation may operate in more than one market implies that the process of identifying and evaluating strategic options is likely to be conducted at the level of individual business units or departments.

Identifying strategic options

In considering possible strategies to achieve its objectives, management faces a further three choices:

▶ On what basis do they wish to compete with or differentiate themselves from their competitors? This is sometimes referred to as deciding a *positioning* or *generic* strategy.

▶ Should they develop new products or services, new markets or a combination of the two, and should they drop certain activities? This concerns choosing a *strategic direction*.

▶ Having made the first two sets of decisions, how should they develop the new services, products and/or markets? This concerns choosing the *means* of developing strategy.

The choices available can be categorised as shown in Figure 10.2.

Generic strategies

Porter (1980b, 1985) identified two basic types of competitive advantage that a firm can possess: low cost or differentiation. From this he developed the idea that there are three generic strategies or means by which companies could position themselves to develop and maintain competitive advantage. The first, *cost leadership*, is a strategy whereby a firm aims to produce its product or service at a lower cost than its competitors can. This could mean developing a large market share to bring economies of scale in production costs, so that cost leadership does not necessarily mean low price. As Johnson and Scholes (1993) point out, a low cost base will not in itself bring competitive advantage. What matters is the value perceived by the customers or users of the product or service.

The second generic strategy is *differentiation*, whereby a company aims to offer a product or service that is distinctive – and valued as such by customers – from those of its competitors. Porter argued that differentiation is 'something unique beyond simply offering a low price' that allows firms to command a premium price or to retain buyer loyalty during cyclical or seasonal downturns in the market. Firms that develop a reputation for reliability, for example, may be able to enhance their market share or to achieve higher margins by charging slightly higher prices which consumers are willing to pay. We also noted earlier that cities compete with each other in various ways. They do so on the basis of factors such as a skilled workforce, building land, transport quality, recreational facilities or hotel accommodation. These may be more important to inward investors or event

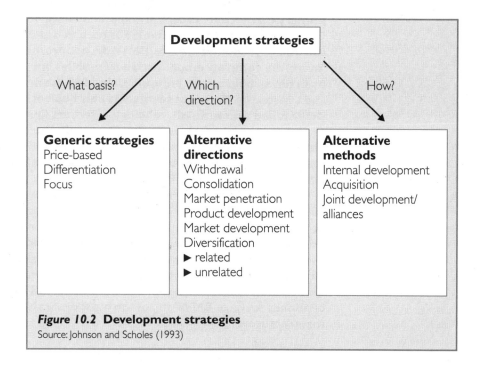

Figure 10.2 **Development strategies**
Source: Johnson and Scholes (1993)

organisers (and, indeed, to potential residents) than cost factors such as the cost of living in particular areas.

The third, *focus*, strategy occurs when management applies either cost leadership or differentiation to a narrow market segment (see Chapter 12) rather than to a whole market. Porter refers to two variants, cost focus and differentiation focus. Since this is really a hybrid strategy it is simpler to think of the distinction between cost and differentiation.

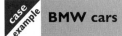

BMW cars

BMW cars are not the most powerful, or the most reliable, or the most luxurious on the market, although they score well against all these criteria. No one has ever suggested that they are cheap, even for the high level of specification that most models offer. Although BMW rightly emphasises the quality and advanced nature of its technology, its products are not exceptionally innovative. The design of the company's cars is conventional and the styling of its models is decidedly traditional.

The achievements of BMW are built on two closely associated factors. The company achieves a higher quality of engineering than is usual in production cars. While robots or workers from low-wage economies do most car assembly work, BMW maintains a skilled German labour force. The company benefits, as many German firms do, from an educational system that gives basic technical skills to an unusually high proportion of the population. Its reputation has followed from these substantial achievements. In this, BMW is representative of much of German manufacturing industry.

Yet BMW's success was neither easy nor certain. In 1945 the company was Germany's leading manufacturer of aero-engines. Its primary market and its capital equipment were both in ruins ... While German recovery through the 1950s occurred at a pace that attracted the title of economic miracle, BMW did not prosper. Uncertain of its future, the company emphasised automobiles but its products ranged from tiny bubble cars to limousines. In 1959 the firm faced bankruptcy and a rescue by Mercedes seemed its only hope of survival. Instead, BMW found a powerful shareholder – Herbert Quandt – who perceived the company's inherent strengths. The turning point came when the firm identified a market that most effectively exploited its capabilities – the market for high-performance saloon cars, which has since become almost synonymous with BMW.

The BMW 1500, launched in 1961, established a reputation for engineering quality in the BMW automobile brand. The brand in turn acquired a distinctive identity as a symbol for young, affluent European professionals. That combination – a system of production which gives the company a particular advantage in its chosen market segment, a worldwide reputation for product quality, and a brand which immediately identifies the aims and aspirations of its customers – continues to make BMW one of the most profitable automobile manufacturers in the world.

Source: Kay (1996, pp. 37–8)

What sort of strategy is BMW following?

Porter (1985) argued that a firm had to choose between the two basic strategies of cost leadership and differentiation (permitting higher prices to be charged) but this point has been widely disputed. Many believe that companies follow both strategies simultaneously. For example, by controlling costs better than competitors, companies can reinvest the savings in unique features that will differentiate their products or services. Porter (1994) has since offered some clarification: 'Every strategy must consider both relative cost and relative differentiation ... a company cannot completely ignore quality and differentiation in the pursuit of cost advantage, and vice versa ... Progress can be made against both types of advantage simultaneously.' However, he notes that there are trade-offs between the two and that companies should 'maintain a clear commitment to superiority in one of them.' The scope for degrees of trade-off gives rise to a range of possible strategy choices. Johnson and Scholes (1997, pp.250–64) illustrate eight possibilities, each attaching a different degree of importance to price and added value or differentiation, the two key dimensions of consumer value.

Choice of the bases for competitive advantage is complex and requires from environmental analysis a clear understanding of who the competitors are (that is, of the relevant markets or market segments) and of consumer demands, needs and values. Ultimately, user value will determine the organisation's ability to sustain competitive advantage. In the public and not-for-profit sectors, however, the idea of user value is more complicated. Often it is not the ultimate service users but government agencies or departments who pay for the goods or services. This means that public and non-profit strategies may pay as much attention to the interests of their sponsors as to those of their end users. A common problem is that the main interest of government or its agents is in the concept of value for money. This tends to emphasise cost efficiency over product or service effectiveness.

Kay (1996) makes the further point that competitive advantage derives not just from the capabilities of firms themselves but from the structure of the industry. He observes that 'there can be no greater competitive advantage than the absence of competitors'. In a very competitive market, even where firms have obvious competitive advantage this may not yield substantial profit. Yet mediocre service can bring large profits where competition is weak or absent – as in many of Europe's remaining monopolistic public utilities. Competition provides the incentive to control costs or to provide a better service to gain custom. For example, in the run up to deregulation of the market for domestic gas supply in Britain, British Gas (the incumbent monopoly) is being forced to review its strategy. Other companies are now competing for business largely by offering lower prices.

Strategic directions

The second set of choices facing organisations concern the direction of strategy development. Options can be set out in a product/market matrix as

	Existing products/services	New products/services
Existing markets	Consolidation Market penetration Withdrawal	Product/service development
New markets	Market development	Diversification: ▶ horizontal ▶ vertical ▶ unrelated

Figure 10.3 Strategic directions – the product/market matrix
Source: adapted from Johnson and Scholes (1993)

shown in Figure 10.3. This type of matrix, originally developed by Ansoff (1965), tends to assume the existence of growth opportunities, which may not always be the case. For many public service organisations dependent on limited public resources, growth may not be an option. Instead, decisions may be about altering the service mix to use existing resources more efficiently and effectively.

Existing markets, same product/service

Organisations may choose to focus on their current product/service and markets. Choice will depend among other things on whether the market is growing, in decline or has reached maturity.

▶ **Consolidation**   In a growing market, consolidation would aim to increase business in order to retain market share, whereas in mature markets firms might focus on improving cost efficiency and customer service. In declining markets, management might take the opportunity to acquire companies, withdraw from the market or to streamline operations. For public services faced with resource shortage, introducing charges may be an appropriate strategy to cope with growing demand for a service.

▶ **Market penetration**   As a strategy, market penetration is designed to increase market share, which may be easier in a growing than a mature market. Strategies may involve reducing price, increasing advertising expenditure, or improving productivity or distribution channels.

▶ **Withdrawal**   Complete or partial withdrawal from a market is a legitimate strategic option in certain circumstances. The demerger of the Hanson Group is an example of a withdrawal strategy (see Case Example). In the public sector the strategy is illustrated by the withdrawal by Health Boards of accident and emergency services from some hospitals in order to use resources better.

case example The demerger of Hanson plc

In 1996, industrial conglomerate Hanson plc decided to demerge its energy, chemical and tobacco divisions to concentrate on a core building materials and equipment business. The company had grown over more

than thirty years to become one of the UK's top ten companies. But by the early 1990s, poor cash flow and a heavy debt burden from recent acquisitions resulted in declining profitability. The size of the company and the nature of its businesses were such that its acquisition-driven strategy, the foundation of its success, was no longer a winning formula. Hanson decided to withdraw from three markets in the belief that separation of the businesses would allow the 'greater management focus' necessary to improve operations, profitability and long-term prospects.

Existing market, new product

A strategy of product (or service) development allows a company to retain the relative security of its present markets while altering products or developing new ones. The recent shift by several retail supermarkets into banking or other types of financial service is an example of product development. Similarly, several of the privatised utility companies in the UK are seeking to become multi-utility companies, using the strength of their existing customer base to develop new product lines. Johnson and Scholes (1997) note that new product development can be expensive and risky and may also require the development of new organisational skills.

New market, present product/service

In the case of market development, the company is seeking new markets for existing products or services. This could mean 'new demographic markets – new groups of customers, by age, socioeconomic grouping, education, lifestyle, interests, etc.' It could also mean 'new purchasing markets. For example, the retail fashion group Next introduced the Next directory in order to extend its customer base and to reach customers who prefer to buy clothes and accessories from catalogues' (Harrison *et al.* 1995). Business can also extend geographically. Marks and Spencer, for example, in pursuit of its aim to become the leading volume retailer in the world is currently expanding its operations in several countries.

Diversification

Diversification takes three basic forms:

▶ **Vertical integration**   Moving either backwards or forwards into activities related to the organisation's products and services. A manufacturer might decide to make its own components rather than buy them from elsewhere. Equally, it could develop forward, for instance, into distribution, repairs or servicing activities.

▶ **Horizontal integration**   Developing competing or complementary activities, such as the move made by many mortgage lenders into the insurance business. With both vertical and horizontal integration, there is some link between existing and new activities. This is sometimes called related diversification. Advantages include the ability to exercise greater control over the quality of inputs or servicing or simply an opportunity to expand the business by making use of existing skills in related businesses.

▶ **Unrelated diversification**   Developing into new products or markets outside the present industry. A strategy illustrated by the operations of conglomerate companies. Amongst other reasons, unrelated diversification may be undertaken as a means of spreading risk or to achieve further growth where existing markets have reached saturation.

Alternative means of developing strategy

The chapter so far has considered the basis on which organisations might opt to create competitive advantage as well as the different directions (new product/market mixes) in which to go. A final set of decisions concerns the means by which organisations pursue the chosen strategies.

Internal development

Many organisations favour this method as they believe that all aspects of the development of new products or services are totally within their control and under the influence of their management and production expertise. This is particularly true where the product is highly technical in the design and manufacturing processes. Internal development used often to be favoured by public service organisations. For instance, many local authorities in the UK created their own in-house direct service organisations (DSOs) to under-take activities such as repair and maintenance of council buildings. In today's 'contract culture', DSOs are usually required to compete with outside contractors. Similarly, many parts of local government and the civil service – for example, legal services and Her Majesty's Stationery Office – have been privatised. The present climate for public services is not conducive to internal development. It is much more likely that attempts to meet new or growing demands will involve some form of joint venture or alliance (see below).

Acquisition (and merger)

A key reason for acquisition is that it allows rapid entry into new product/market areas. It may also be an appropriate strategy to take advantage of new market opportunities where the acquiring company lacks the necessary in-house skills and resources. Financial motives are often strong, particularly where there are opportunities to increase cost efficiency. The ability to tap into new markets and save costs (mainly by closing branches) encouraged many banks and building societies in Britain to merge. A different example is the case of not-for-profit housing associations and trusts. Organisations seeking growth normally depend on government grants to subsidise the production cost of new rented homes. In recent years, cuts in the govern-ment budget for grant-aiding new housing has hampered this method of growth. An alternative opportunity emerged when local authorities decided to sell properties to non-public-sector landlords. The prospect of taking over former council property offers housing associations a fast track to growth and the potential to generate cost efficiencies.

Joint developments and alliances

Faced with either internal resource problems or unacceptable levels of risk in complex environments, organisations may turn to partners to co-operate in developing products or services. Arrangements can vary from highly formal contractual relationships to looser forms of co-operation based on the less tangible bonds of mutual advantage and trust. Examples of joint develop-ments or joint ventures are common in large construction or civil engin-eering projects. Other forms of joint development include franchising, licensing (for example, building under licence) and subcontracting. Franchising is a common form of development in many retailing activities (see the cases on The Body Shop and Benetton).

Strategic alliances or partnerships have also become commonplace in the provision of public services, as the role of the state as direct provider of services has contracted. Instead there has been a growing use of contracts and partnerships between public sector bodies and various private or voluntary organisations. The public bodies act as enablers or commissioners rather than as direct providers. The Case Example illustrates this.

City Challenge: the North Kensington Partnership

The City Challenge programme was introduced by the UK government to deal with the problems experienced in many run-down areas of cities – high unemployment, poverty, poor health, crime and a general sense of low morale. The government recognised that a multi-agency approach would be required if the areas were to be renewed, not just because many of the problems are inter-related, for instance poverty, often caused by joblessness, contributes to poor health, but also because no single organisation has the power or resources to tackle these problems alone.

In common with other organisations, the Partnership has a vision for the area. It is 'To link the North Kensington City Challenge Area with the rest of the Royal Borough and to create there a self-confident community at one with itself, well housed and with a vibrant legitimate local economy, based in a safe, welcoming and attractive environment.'

In North Kensington, as in all other areas which won City Challenge status, the approach has been to set up a partnership board. Its function is to set strategic objectives (designed to achieve the vision) and to oversee and monitor the implementation of strategy. In North Kensington's case the decision was to set up a company limited by guarantee, the North Kensington City Challenge Company Limited. The company's board structure (Figure 10.4) illustrates the partnership approach by the wide range of statutory, voluntary and private organisations that are represented.

CASE QUESTIONS 10.4

▶ Can you identify the ways in which the Scottish Homes Planning Framework demonstrates a partnership approach to its activities?

▶ Who are the major external stakeholders?

Screening and appraising options

As it develops a strategy, management is likely to identify or generate alternative options. Since most options will be mutually exclusive, management must evaluate suitability, feasibility and acceptability. Many tools and techniques are available to assist these decisions (see Johnson and Scholes, 1997; Hogwood and Gunn, 1984). Some, including ranking, decision trees and scenarios, assist the initial screening process. This narrows down the number of options to a more manageable list that a strategy team can appraise in

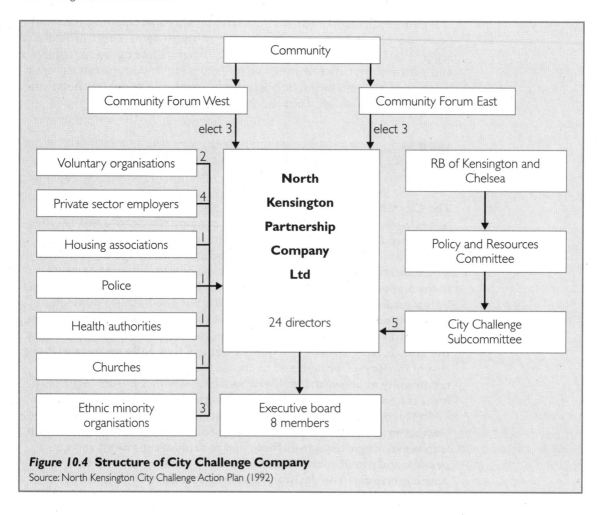

Figure 10.4 Structure of City Challenge Company
Source: North Kensington City Challenge Action Plan (1992)

more detail. Others, such as profitability and cost/benefit analysis, assess the feasibility of options as well as their acceptability in terms of likely risks and rates of return. Another task is to assess the acceptability of options to stakeholders. Such processes, with their scientific connotations, are associated with the prescriptive schools of strategy.

10.6 Strategy implementation

There is a close relationship between formulating and implementing strategy. Clearly, the implementation phase is concerned with translating strategy into action. However, as Johnson and Scholes (1997, p.363) note, 'strategic change does not take place simply because it is considered to be desirable; it takes place if it can be made to work and put into effect by members of the organisation'. It is wrong to assume that, once plans are formulated, they will be implemented. Sometimes there is an 'implementation deficit', which means that either strategies have not been implemented at all or they have been only partially successful. The reasons for this are numerous but include external constraints, inadequate time or resources, an inappropriate combination of resources, poor communication or resistance on the part of those expected to implement strategy (Hogwood and Gunn, 1984). Managing implementation is complex (see Chapter 17). Johnson and Scholes (1997) consider that there are three main tasks:

- ▶ **Planning and allocating resources**   Here decisions include the required resource mix (physical, financial, human, etc.) and how these should be allocated amongst different divisions or departments and how new production facilities are to be financed.
- ▶ **Organisation structure and design**   Strategic change also requires consideration of appropriate organisational structure and design. This includes deciding on the responsibilities of different departments, operational and control systems, and staff training and development needs.
- ▶ **Managing strategic change**   This is also concerned with a range of behavioural and cultural issues, such as overcoming resistance to change. In the words of Machiavelli, 'there is nothing more difficult to take in hand, more perilous to conduct, or more uncertain of success than to take a lead in the introduction of a new order of things, because innovation has for enemies all those who have done well under the old conditions and lukewarm defenders in those who may do well under the new' (quoted in Ansoff, 1987).

From strategic planning to strategic management

Strategic planning is the process of formulating objectives and strategies. Strategic management is an organisation-wide task involving both the development and implementation of strategy. It demands the ability to steer the organisation as a whole through strategic change under conditions of complexity and uncertainty.

It is at this point that the distinction between strategic planning and strategic management starts to become apparent. While the former is the process of formulating objectives, priorities and strategies, the latter includes developing strategy and managing its implementation. 'Strategic management is characterised by its complexity … arising out of ambiguous and non-routine situations with organisation-wide rather than operational specific implications' (Johnson and Scholes, 1997).

Alternative perspectives on strategy often centre on what some writers refer to as the 'formulation/implementation dichotomy' which is discussed more fully in the next section.

Monitoring progress

The final stage in the strategy process, as depicted in Figure 10.1, is to monitor the implementation of strategy. This requires creating information systems which allow management to monitor progress. Organisations will normally assess achievements in terms of their own objectives and targets, for example by monitoring turnover, operating costs and other financial information against budget. They will also wish to compare their performance with their competitors. Managers may judge performance in both quantitative and qualitative terms, perhaps by using customer satisfaction ratings. Chapter 11 discusses the assessment of organisational performance and competitive position in more detail. A point to note, however, is that although this is the last stage in the strategy model, it is not the end of the strategy process. As emphasised in the final section, strategy is a continuous process as organisations adapt and adjust to the changes in their business environment. Monitoring and review is just one element in that process, providing new information that loops back to the reformulation of strategy.

10.7 Alternative perspectives on strategy

The elemental approach to strategy discussed in this chapter is closely associated with the planning view of strategy. Implicit in this latter view are assumptions that human beings always behave rationally and that events, facts and the world in general can be viewed and interpreted in purely objective terms. Points made earlier in this chapter and in Chapter 4 have already indicated that pure rationality and objectivity rarely pertain in the real world. Two alternative perspectives – the learning and the political – highlight the weaknesses of the traditional planning view and illustrate further the difficulty in separating formulation and implementation.

Learning view

The message of the learning view is that strategy is an *emergent* or adaptive process. The idea can be illustrated by summarising Mintzberg's (1994a,b) critique of the formalised approach to strategy. In his opinion, strategic planning – which he refers to as the planning school – suffers from what he terms three 'fundamental fallacies':

▶ **The fallacy of predetermination** This criticism is founded on the planning school's assumptions on predetermination: 'the prediction of the environment through forecasting … the unfolding of the strategy formation process on schedule … and the imposition of the resulting strategies on an acquiescent environment, again on schedule' (1994a, p.228). Mintzberg contrasts the planning school's desire for predictability with the acknowledged inaccuracy of long-range forecasting, in particular the inability to forecast 'discontinuities' (which, by definition, could not be forecast by extrapolation) 'such as technological innovations, prices increases, shifts in consumer attitudes, government legislation' (p.231). He further contrasts the stability assumed by planners, who are said to expect 'the world … to hold still while the planning process proceeds' (1994b, p.16) with the dynamic nature of the internal and external environments which ensure that, in reality, plans rarely unfold as intended.

▶ **The fallacy of detachment** Mintzberg argues against the central thrust of strategic planning which is (as noted earlier) to separate formulation from implementation, to employ centralised teams of strategic 'thinkers' isolated from operational activities. As he puts it: 'The ultimate prescription is that organisations should complete their thinking before they begin to act [whereas] effective strategists are not people who abstract themselves from the daily detail but quite the opposite: they immerse themselves in it while being able to abstract the strategic messages from it'. Effective strategy-making requires that implementation informs formulation.

▶ **The fallacy of formalisation** A third error in the planning view is the analytical, scientific approach to strategy, with its prescribed series of steps or boxes, and array of checklists. Strategy, according to Mintzberg, requires insight, creativity and synthesis, all the things that formalisation discourages: 'intuition and innovation cannot be formalised or institutionalised … strategy-making, like creativity, needs to function beyond boxes'. He also contends that structured planning tends to inhibit innovation by introducing 'a bias in favour of incremental change, of generic strategies, and of goals that can be quantified … thus, the popularity of strategic planning may have favoured so-called cost leadership strategies over ones of product leadership, simply because innovative design or high quality are more difficult to measure and formalise than straight cost-cutting' (1994b).

Mintzberg's criticisms are deliberately pointed in order to emphasise his argument that, in contrast to the structured analytical approach advocated by Ansoff and others, there is no one best way to develop strategy. He regards strategic planning as 'strategic programming', a system developed during a period of stability (in contrast to the rapidly changing environment of the 1980s and 1990s) and designed primarily for what he calls 'the machine organisation' – the classic formalised, specialised and centralised bureaucracy typically found in manufacturing industry. This style of planning, he argues, may be appropriate for certain types of organisation but not for others. Thus, what is required is a flexible approach to strategy.

Other writers share similar views. Hogwood and Gunn (1984) cite Etzioni's case for a contingent approach to strategy which distinguishes fundamental decisions which 'lend themselves to a much more planned or analytical approach' from incremental decisions, and conclude that 'there is no one best way of decision-taking just as there is no universal prescription for "good organization"'. In a similar vein, Kay (1996) notes that there are 'no recipes and generic strategies for corporate success … there cannot be, because if there were, their general adoption would eliminate any competitive advantage … the foundations of corporate success are unique to each successful company.'

The success of Honda in the US motorcycle market has become a classic case in corporate strategy. Kay (1996) notes that there are two perspectives on the company's achievement. The first, an assessment by the Boston Consulting Group, was that the success was simply another example of Japanese penetration of western markets. Richard Pascale's account (see the Case Example) was very different.

The Honda Motor Company

Richard T. Pascale of Stanford University (1984) has described the entry of Honda into the US motorcycle market. When Honda executives arrived in Los Angeles from Japan in 1959 to establish an American subsidiary, their intended strategy was to focus on selling 250cc and 350cc machines rather than the 50cc Honda Cubs which were a big hit in Japan. Their instinct told them that the Honda 50s were not suitable for the US market, where everything was bigger and more luxurious.

However, sales of the 250cc and 350cc bikes were sluggish and the bikes themselves were plagued by mechanical failure. It looked as though Honda's strategy was going to fail. At the same time, the Japanese executives were using the Honda 50s to run errands around Los Angeles, attracting a lot of attention. One day they got a call from a Sears Roebuck buyer who wanted to sell them to a broad market of Americans who were not necessarily already motorcycle enthusiasts. The Honda executives hesitated over selling the 50cc bikes, for fear of alienating serious bikers, who might then associate Honda with 'wimp' machines. In

the end they were pushed into doing so by the failure of the 250cc and 350cc machines. The rest is history. Honda had stumbled on a previously untouched market segment that was to prove huge. It had also found a previously untried channel of distribution: general retailers rather than speciality motorbike stores. By 1964, nearly one in two motorcycles sold in the USA was a Honda.

Source: Quinn (1980), adapted by Harrison et al. (1995)

Kay's (1996) perspective is that 'we shall never know the extent to which Honda's success was truly the result of chance or rational calculation [but] like all successful strategies, it was based on a mixture of calculation and opportunism, of vision and experiment.' The important point is that strategists and managers should not expect rigid adherence to 'the plan', but should anticipate that some departure from it is inevitable, owing to unanticipated events and the emergence of new opportunities.

To underline this point, Mintzberg makes a distinction between intended and emergent strategies (see Figure 10.5). He acknowledges the validity of strategy as a plan, setting out intended courses of action, and recognises that some deliberate intentions may in fact be realised. But he challenges managers to review just how closely their realised strategies mirror their original intentions. As well as the realisation of deliberate strategies, it is also likely that some plans failed to be implemented at all (unrealised strategies) and that others which he describes as 'emergent strategies' were not expressly intended but resulted from 'actions taken one by one, which converged in time in some sort of consistency or pattern'. A flexible approach to strategy is one which recognises that 'the real word inevitably involves some thinking ahead of time as well as some adaptation en route'. The essence of the learning view is this process of adaptation, the ability to react to unexpected events, to exploit or experiment with new ideas 'on the ground'. Mintzberg gives the example of a salesperson coming up with the idea of selling an existing product to some new customers. Soon all the other salespeople begin to do the same, and 'one day, months later, management discovers that the company has entered a new market.' This was not planned but learned, in a collective process. People learn in the process of implementation.

Political view

The view of strategy as an emergent process has much in common with political perspectives on strategy. While the former tends to be based on the logic that 'prior thought can never specify all subsequent action' (Majone and Wildavsky in Mintzberg, 1994a, p.289), the political view adds the further dimensions of power, conflict and ambiguity.

Drawing on his experiences in the public policy sphere, Charles Lindblom (1959) was an early proponent of the political view. Lindblom's thesis was that the rational approach described by Simon (1947) was unrealistic. He argued that limits on the intellectual capacity of humans, sources of information and resources were such that comprehensive rational planning, involving extensive analysis and detailed evaluation of alternative strategies, was impossible. Simon (1957) also recognised these limitations, putting forward the concept of 'bounded rationality'. The idea here is that policy-

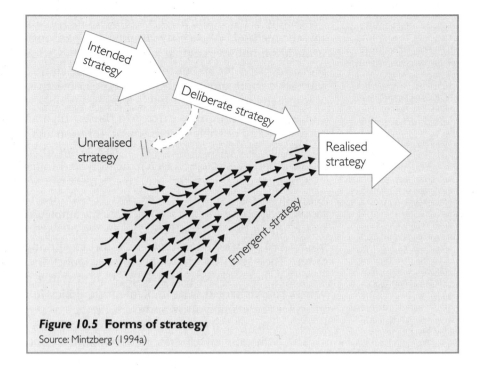

Figure 10.5 Forms of strategy
Source: Mintzberg (1994a)

makers seek to be rational but are constrained into 'satisficing' behaviour – performance which is considered acceptable rather than exceptional – because of psychological, organisational and cost limitations. However, Lindblom's arguments go beyond identifying the limits of true rationality (Hogwood and Gunn, 1984). He draws attention to the ways in which value judgements pervade and influence the planning process and points to the sectionalism or conflicting interests among stakeholders (noted in Chapter 4), so characteristic of public policy, which frustrate attempts to reach agreement on objectives or on particular strategies to be pursued. He argued that the identification of values or objectives (ends) prior to the analysis of alternative strategies (means) to achieve them was an artificial construct because all strategies encompass implicit value judgements.

For example, most people would agree that the elimination of poverty is a valid objective for society to pursue, but there might be considerable difficulty in agreeing *how* the problem should be tackled. Some politicians or other policy-makers might favour an increase in income-related benefits, but others might see this solution as encouraging the poor to continue living at state expense. They might instead prefer to support initiatives aimed at getting the poor off benefits and back into work. Value judgements (assumptions about the poor) are embedded in each potential strategy. The complexity of many social problems is such that identifying cause and effect and thus appropriate policy solutions (strategies) is difficult. But there remain fundamental differences in values between individuals and groups in society, and the relative power of these groups will ultimately determine which strategies and options are favoured.

On the basis of these observations, Lindblom concluded that policy- or strategy-making was not a scientific, comprehensive or rational process, but an iterative, incremental process, characterised by restricted analysis and bargaining between the players or stakeholders involved. Lindblom labelled this the method of 'successive limited comparisons' whereby 'new' strategy is made simply by marginal adjustments to existing strategy. 'Policy is not made once and for all but made and remade endlessly through a process of successive approximation to some desired objective.' Strategic choice is not a comprehensive and objective process but takes the form of a limited comparison of options, restricted to those which are considered politically acceptable and possible to implement. Johnson and Scholes (1997) consider Lindblom's account to be close to the *logical incrementalism* described by Quinn whereby 'strategy is seen to be worked through in action.'

Conflicting values often lead to intentions or actions being couched in vague or ambiguous terms. Baier *et al.* (1994) note that a 'common method for securing policy support is to increase the ambiguity of a proposed policy ... it is commonplace that difficult issues are often "settled" by leaving them unresolved or specifying them in a form requiring subsequent interpretation.' They add that 'the ambiguity of a policy increases the chance of its adoption, but at the cost of creating administrative complications.' In other words, those charged with implementing policy find themselves having to interpret these ambiguities and clarify policy as implementation proceeds, so that strategy is, in effect, made by the people who implement it.

The political view of strategy development is of particular relevance to public sector organisations as well as to other non-profit and private organisations dependent on government support for their activities. Such organisations, which Johnson and Scholes (1997, p.64) describe as 'externally dependent', find that their strategy is often imposed on them from outside and their freedom of choice is restricted. Strategy is not only characterised by political bargaining but also constrained by the demands of the more powerful players. In other words, the ability to bargain successfully is dependent on the relative power of the organisations involved.

---

n o t e b o o k   10.4

Refer back to the examples of missions, aims, objectives and strategies in earlier parts of the chapter. Do you consider any of these stated intentions or planned actions to be unclear or vague? If so, consider why they might have been expressed in this way.

C A S E   Q U E S T I O N S   10.5

- ► To what extent do you consider it likely that the objectives and strategy of Scottish Homes are dictated by players outside the organisation?
- ► Consider also the impact of external constraints on the strategy of housing associations that depend on Scottish Homes for funding support.

While the learning view has its origins in the experiences of profit-making companies, and the political view its roots in public policy and the public sector, the views are closely related. Both believe in adaptive strategy, in the impossibility of predicting the future, and in the ability of implementors to use their discretion to interpret and adjust strategy in the course of implementation. Both oppose the rigid planning view of strategy, but ultimately accept that a structured approach to strategy has its place. 'Too much planning may lead us to chaos, but so too would too little, more directly' (Mintzberg, 1994a). This view is reflected in several recent contributions (e.g. Taylor, 1997) to the literature on strategy which have mused upon the rise and fall, or death and reincarnation of 1960s style 'strategic planning'. Just as organisations adapt to the changing environment, so too do approaches to strategy. Moncrieff and Smallwood (1996) note that different planning styles emerge in response to different economic and social conditions. The planning style of the 1960s seemed to suit the relative stability which characterised the period. The highly competitive, increasingly global and fast-moving markets which characterise the late 1990s may be better matched by a learning, adaptive or even 'real time strategy' (Taylor, 1997). As a final observation, it should be noted that the different styles are not mutually exclusive: today's organisations develop strategy through a mix of these processes.

10.8 Recap

Content agenda

Management needs to make plans for its organisation's future direction to help the enterprise to survive. A strategy, sometimes expressed in a formal strategic plan, sets an overall direction. Drawing on information about the external environment and internal capabilities helps to shape the long-term direction and scope of the organisation. This provides a basis for consistent action throughout the organisation and a framework within which operational decisions can be made. Management chooses whether to follow low cost or differentiation strategies or one that delivers both. It also guides the overall strategic direction to follow in terms of the balance to strike between existing or new markets and products.

Developing a strategy also involves planning how the organisation is to achieve the objectives set. Management needs to set out how internal resources and capabilities will be deployed or changed so that they support the strategy. It also needs to decide whether other organisations are to be part of the plan – such as through mergers or joint ventures of some form. One of the benefits of a clear, if flexible, strategic plan is that it helps management to generate commitment and effort towards achieving the goals set out in it.

Process agenda

The strategy developed usually reflects the interests of powerful individuals or groups. Strategy-making is not an objectively rational activity. Strategy models depicting the key stages in the process should not be regarded as prescriptive but as frameworks which serve both as a guide to managers and as an analytical tool. Strategy rarely unfolds as intended. Rather, it is an emergent process, which must be capable of adapting in complex, changing and ambiguous situations. As well as the traditional approaches to strategic planning, learning and political models are offered as more accurate ways to represent the process.

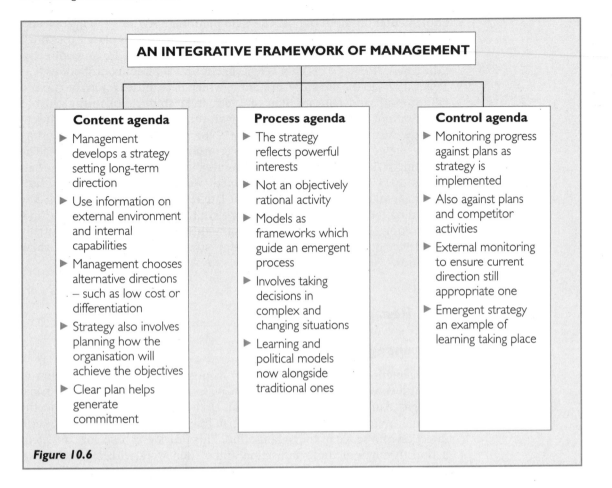

AN INTEGRATIVE FRAMEWORK OF MANAGEMENT

Content agenda
- ▶ Management develops a strategy setting long-term direction
- ▶ Use information on external environment and internal capabilities
- ▶ Management chooses alternative directions – such as low cost or differentiation
- ▶ Strategy also involves planning how the organisation will achieve the objectives
- ▶ Clear plan helps generate commitment

Process agenda
- ▶ The strategy reflects powerful interests
- ▶ Not an objectively rational activity
- ▶ Models as frameworks which guide an emergent process
- ▶ Involves taking decisions in complex and changing situations
- ▶ Learning and political models now alongside traditional ones

Control agenda
- ▶ Monitoring progress against plans as strategy is implemented
- ▶ Also against plans and competitor activities
- ▶ External monitoring to ensure current direction still appropriate one
- ▶ Emergent strategy an example of learning taking place

Figure 10.6

Control agenda

Strategy does not end when plans have been drawn up. Progress needs to be constantly monitored as the plans are implemented. Activities and achievements need to be checked against plans and against competitors' activities. Managers also need to exercise control in the sense of monitoring the plans against market and other developments to ensure that the direction chosen is still appropriate. Figure 10.6 summarises these points.

P A R T   C A S E   Q U E S T I O N S

- ▶ What environmental influences have particularly affected Glenlight Shipping?
- ▶ Which of these are similar to, and which different from those facing Scottish Homes?
- ▶ Which generic strategy would it be most appropriate for Glenlight to have followed at different periods in its history?
- ▶ How does Glenlight Shipping's strategy process compare with that of Scottish Homes? On balance, does the Glenlight story support the planned or the emergent view of strategy?
- ▶ In what ways was the strategy of Glenlight Shipping shaped by outside forces?

10.9 Review questions

1   What are four benefits that an organisation can gain from having a strategy?
2   Distinguish between a corporate and an operating strategy.
3   In what ways, if any, does the concept of competitive advantage apply to not-for-profit organisations?
4   Describe the main stages of the strategy process in your own terms.
5   Discuss with a manager from an organisation how his or her organisation developed its present strategy. Compare this practice with that set out in the model. What conclusions do you draw from that comparison?
6   Compare the strategies of Marks & Spencer and The Body Shop, and list any similarities and differences.
7   What are the main steps to take in analysing the organisation's environment? Why is it necessary to do this?
8   The chapter described three generic strategies that organisations can follow. Give examples of three companies each following one of these strategies.
9   Give examples of company strategies corresponding to each box in Ansoff's product/market matrix.
10 Compare the main ideas of the learning and political approaches to strategy with traditional models.

Further reading

There is a vast array of textbooks and papers on the subject of corporate strategy making it difficult to select just a small number. However, with a European audience in mind, Johnson and Scholes (1997) is indispensable. Kay (1993, 1996) presents interesting and readable accounts of competitive strategy written from an economic perspective, illustrated by a wide range of European and other international case examples. Porter's original work on competitive strategy and competitive advantage (1980a,b, 1985) is detailed but often summarised in other texts. Mintzberg's account of the rise and fall of strategic planning is summarised in Mintzberg (1994b,c). In the same issue of *Long Range Planning* a short piece by Ansoff (1994) debates, with Mintzberg, the different approaches to strategy. Texts dealing specifically with the public and non-profit sectors include Bryson (1995) and Smith (1994). Caulfield and Schultz (1989) cast a practical perspective on strategic planning in British local government.

W Website addresses

Scottish Homes   http://www.scot-homes.gov.uk

CHAPTER 11

Analysing the business environment

CONTENTS

AIM

To identify major external and internal influences on organisations, and to examine approaches and techniques which organisations can use to analyse patterns and change in their business environment.

OBJECTIVES

By the end of your work on this chapter you should be able to outline the concepts below in your own terms and:

1 Give examples of the ways in which stakeholders might seek to influence strategy and demonstrate why an understanding of stakeholder power is important in determining their ability to do so

2 Identify the broad sets of forces exerting influence on organisations

3 Conduct a **PEST** analysis for an organisation with which you are familiar

4 Explain the usefulness of Porter's five-forces model in analysing the competitive environment

5 Outline the nature and benefits of value chain analysis

6 Describe the purpose of portfolio models such as the Boston matrix

7 Discuss the ways in which organisations can assess their internal performance and competitive position

8 Explain the purpose of **SWOT** analysis

9 Assess the contribution of internal resources or capabilities to successful strategy

Virgin is known all over Europe and is seen by the public as fun, daring and successful. The first record shop was opened in 1971 and the record label launched in 1973. Virgin Atlantic Airways began operating in 1984, quickly followed by Virgin Holidays. In 1995 the company entered a joint venture offering financial services. By 1997 it was an established global corporation with airline, retailing and travel operations worldwide.

The original record business was launched shortly after the UK government had abolished retail price maintenance, a practice which had limited competition and kept prices high. Branson saw the opportunity and began a mail order business offering popular records at prices about 15 per cent below those charged by shops.

The business prospered until a postal strike occurred. Branson's response was to open a retail outlet. This was an immediate success and was the start of Virgin Retail. In 1973, Virgin released the hugely successful album *Tubular Bells*. The ensuing inflow of funds enabled the record business to expand under Branson's colleague Simon Draper. It led to ventures in recording studios, book publishing and cinemas. By the late 1980s, the high annual growth that the record industry had experienced was coming to an end. This affected Virgin which was still a relatively small player.

In the early 1980s, Branson was approached by Randolph Fields who was seeking additional finance for a cut-price airline he had founded. The airline business then was tightly regulated, with routes, landing rights, prices and service levels established and maintained by intergovernmental arrangements. Decisions on these and other regulations were mainly used to protect inefficient, often state-owned, national 'flag carriers'. This had kept most air fares high. After three months of intense activity Branson and Fields had gained permission to fly, arranged to lease an aircraft and built up a staff. The first flight was in June 1984. To grow, he needed more landing rights, and would need to persuade government ministers to get them (at both ends of each route). Those ministers would also be being lobbied by the established airlines, who could also try to pursuade them not to approve the low fares which Branson was proposing. Alternatively, they could undercut his fares and subsidise the losses from profits on other routes.

By the early 1990s the airline had become the focus of Branson's interests (Virgin Music had been sold in 1992) and was becoming a serious threat to the established airlines, shown by the acrimonious relationship with British Airways. Branson had been helped by the UK government's commitment since 1979 to freer competition, which allowed him to secure more landing rights, despite opposition.

CASE QUESTIONS

▶ **Note down examples of the relationship between Virgin and the business environment.**

▶ **Would you describe its strategy as planned or emergent?**

▶ **What is the relationship between Branson's many publicity activities and the business?**

11.1 Introduction

This chapter introduces the following ideas:
- ▶ Stakeholder power
- ▶ PEST analysis
- ▶ Macroenvironment
- ▶ Forecasting
- ▶ Scenarios
- ▶ Critical success factors
- ▶ Organisational capability
- ▶ Organisational competences
- ▶ Resource base
- ▶ Value chain analysis
- ▶ Growth/share matrix
- ▶ Benchmarking

In Chapter 10 it was noted that strategy can be defined as the match between an organisation's internal capabilities and its external relationships. Johnson and Scholes (1997) explain this further: strategy 'achieves *advantage* for the organisation through its configurations of *resources* within a changing *environment*, to meet the needs of *markets* and to fulfil *stakeholder* expectations.' These definitions recognise that organisations do not operate in a vacuum but are part of an open system in which they are in constant interaction with other organisations – including their customers, suppliers, financiers and competitors – and exposed to continual change and uncertainty in the wider legal, regulatory, technological and other environments.

Much of management theory is concerned with the way in which organisations cope with change in the business environment and, in particular, with the way in which strategies and structures are adjusted in response to environmental changes. Developing an understanding of the business environment is a critical early stage in the strategy process, which was referred to in Chapter 10 as 'environmental analysis'. The analysis stage can itself be broken down into three main elements which form the subject matter for this chapter. Management has to decide how each of the following affects the strategies which are pursued:
- ▶ what stakeholders expect of the organisation,
- ▶ the forces at work outside the organisation,
- ▶ the organisation's internal resources or capabilities.

The chapter examines the nature of these forces and their relevance to strategy development. In each case, approaches and techniques are outlined which can be used to facilitate analysis.

11.2 Stakeholder analysis

All organisations have a wide range of stakeholders, both internal and external, and the interests of these different stakeholders will often conflict. This is because, as groups or as individuals, stakeholders are themselves subject to a wide range of influences which will condition or shape their views and what they expect of organisations. These influences include the culture and values of society as a whole (which often vary between different countries) and of particular political, social or other groups in society. Organisations themselves can develop internal cultures (see Chapter 14 or Handy, 1993) which affect the way in which the board and staff perceive the organisation and what it is, or should be, doing. Johnson and Scholes refer to a 'cultural web' of an organisation – a complex product of the values, beliefs and assumptions held within an organisation, its internal structure, its power relationships and its ways of doing things. The web develops over time into a dominant culture which is a powerful force in shaping organisational strategy.

External stakeholders too – including suppliers, financiers, central and local government, shareholders and customers – have expectations of organisations and will seek to influence strategy in various ways. They may be able to influence staff or board members directly through personal contact, or they may seek to exert influence indirectly, for instance by the use of the press and other media to raise issues of concern. A means increasingly adopted by organised groups of shareholders is to attend company annual general meetings with the intention of influencing the outcomes of decisions. Figure 11.1 indicates the different expectations that stakeholders may have.

Stakeholder power

Any analysis of the business environment must include not only the identification of stakeholders and their expectations, but also an assessment of the strategic importance of these expectations One approach to this task is to undertake *stakeholder mapping*. According to Johnson and Scholes, this aims to assess:

▶ the likelihood of each stakeholder group seeking to impress its expectations on the organisation,

---

Shareholders
▶ Growth in dividend payments
▶ Growth in share price
▶ Consistent dividend payments
▶ Growth in net asset value

Customers
▶ Price always competitive
▶ Emphasis on product/service quality
▶ Return and replacement policies
▶ Warranty/guarantee provisions
▶ Product reliability

Suppliers
▶ Timely payment of debt by company
▶ Adequate liquidity
▶ Integrity and public standing of directors
▶ Negotiating ability of the purchasing manager

Employees
▶ Good compensation and benefits
▶ Job security
▶ Sense of meaning or purpose in the job
▶ Opportunities for personal development
▶ Amount of interesting work

Government
▶ Efficient user of energy and natural resources
▶ Adhering to the country's laws
▶ Paying taxes
▶ Provision of employment
▶ Value for money in the use of public funds

Lenders
▶ Liquidity of the company
▶ Character and standing of company management
▶ Quality of assets available for security
▶ Potential to repay interest and capital on due date

Figure 11.1 **Examples of possible stakeholder expectations**

▶ whether each group has the capability or means to do so,
▶ the likely effect of these expectations on future strategies.

Stakeholder mapping is, in essence, concerned with the relative power of each stakeholder group which, ultimately, will determine its ability to influence organisational strategy. As described in Chapter 5, there are several sources of power within and outside organisations. Some examples of the way in which power can be used by external stakeholders are given below:

▶ **Formal power**   May be exercised by stakeholders who are members of influential outside bodies or committees such as those concerned with legislative or regulatory matters.

▶ **Resource power**   Many small companies are dependent on large manufacturers, such as those in the car and electronics industries. These large buyers often dictate product quality and prices. Some suppliers may exercise control over strategic assets: an example is the collective power of oil-producing countries to control world oil prices. Resource dependence is also a key feature of public services: those who control the purse strings (usually government or its agents) are in a strong position to shape the objectives and strategies of organisations dependent on them for funding.

▶ **Expert power**   Superior knowledge of customers held, for example, by distribution companies may enable them to dictate terms (say on design, quality or price) to manufacturers.

Much of the literature on strategy conveys the impression that organisations should aim to balance the interests of stakeholders, but opinion on what this means is divided. Campbell (1997) argues that the achievement of purpose and, ultimately, survival, requires companies to win 'the loyalty of all the "active" stakeholders – shareholders, customers, employees and suppliers' because companies compete in each of the relevant markets, for capital, labour and goods.

Argenti (1997), on the other hand, seems to equate 'balance' with 'equality' arguing that 'some stakeholders are vastly more equal than others'. He considers, for example, that a retailer contemplating longer opening hours will '*not* attempt to balance the convenience of his employees with that of his customers', but will instead 'ask himself what effect each decision might have on his profits. That is how all legitimate decisions are made in companies – they are, by definition, profit-making organisations.' Since profit is the objective criterion by which 'the capitalist company' will act, shareholders are, in Argenti's view, the stakeholders whose interests should come first. While he recognises that performance would suffer were companies to fail to engage everyone affected by their operations, he maintains that 'an organisation designed to serve more than one set of people will fail to satisfy any'. This observation is just as applicable in the public service sphere as to profit-making concerns.

Both Campbell and Argenti make valid points. Perhaps the overall message to be abstracted from such debates is that embracing stakeholder expectations *is* important to the long-run success of organisations, but that the degree of priority accorded to each is likely to be unequal and to change over time, as the business environment evolves and changes. A further point to recognise is that the exercise of power between organisations and their stakeholders is a two-way process. Just as external stakeholders seek to influence the people inside the organisation, the organisation can itself take steps to change the perceptions and expectations of its external stakeholders. Furthermore, in some organisations a joint approach to strategy development, involving major external players, is actively encouraged. The growth in various forms of strategic alliances and partnerships (as discussed in Chapter 10) demonstrates this type of collaboration between stakeholders.

11.3 Analysing the external environment

In addition to external stakeholders, there are many other forces at work outside the organisation. Not only are these numerous but they also interact with each other, producing complex cause-and-effect relationships. Thus, it is often difficult to gauge precisely how these forces have affected the organisation and its markets in the past, and virtually impossible to know how they will continue to do so in future. Strategists charged with analysing the external environment are therefore confronted with the twin problems of complexity and uncertainty. Nevertheless, efforts must be made to develop an understanding of the external environment, in order that strategy can be adjusted to reflect changes and developments in the outside world.

The task involves the collection, analysis and interpretation of information from a wide range of sources, which will include published statistics and various forms of externally or internally commissioned surveys or market research studies. It is useful to think of this information at two levels. First there is information pertaining to the 'macroenvironment', that is, wider environmental factors over which the organisation may have little or no control but which can nevertheless exert major influence on the organisation's activities. Secondly, there is a vast array of information relating to the organisation's microenvironment, that is the immediate operating environment involving its own customers, suppliers and competitors. Organisations are more likely to be able to exert some control over the factors operating at this level.

At both levels the aim is to use the information to answer the following questions:

▶ How is the external environment changing?
▶ What impact will these changes have on the organisation, its customers and markets?
▶ How should strategy be adjusted to take account of the opportunities and threats posed by the changing environment?

PEST analysis

A common approach to trying to make sense of what is happening in the macroenvironment is to undertake a PEST (political/legal, economic, sociocultural and technological) analysis. As a first step, the technique aims to identify the main external sources of influence on organisations. Some examples are shown in Figure 11.2.

The macroenvironmental factors listed in Figure 11.2 will influence the strategy of the business in a variety of ways and have a changing effect over time in relation to the size, shape and growth stage of the organisation. The cause and effect of these changes should be considered in relation to their impact on competitive positioning. The aim of PEST analysis is not just to produce a list of environmental influences although, as a checklist, it does

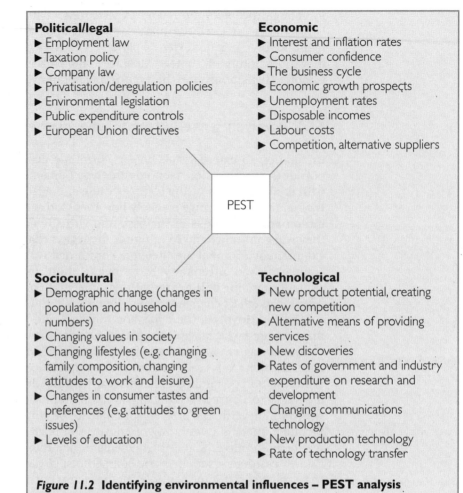

Political/legal
► Employment law
► Taxation policy
► Company law
► Privatisation/deregulation policies
► Environmental legislation
► Public expenditure controls
► European Union directives

Economic
► Interest and inflation rates
► Consumer confidence
► The business cycle
► Economic growth prospects
► Unemployment rates
► Disposable incomes
► Labour costs
► Competition, alternative suppliers

PEST

Sociocultural
► Demographic change (changes in population and household numbers)
► Changing values in society
► Changing lifestyles (e.g. changing family composition, changing attitudes to work and leisure)
► Changes in consumer tastes and preferences (e.g. attitudes to green issues)
► Levels of education

Technological
► New product potential, creating new competition
► Alternative means of providing services
► New discoveries
► Rates of government and industry expenditure on research and development
► Changing communications technology
► New production technology
► Rate of technology transfer

Figure 11.2 **Identifying environmental influences – PEST analysis**
Source: adapted from Johnson and Scholes (1997, p.96) and Smith (1994, p.54)

help to ensure that important factors are not overlooked. Management also uses the framework to:

► identify changes or trends in environmental factors,
► focus on those forces and trends which seem to be the most relevant and critical to the organisation's business,
► think through the implications of these changes for the future direction and strategies of the organisation.

The use of PEST analysis should heighten the awareness of the environmental influences on strategy. It should underline the dynamic nature of the business environment and demonstrate the need for strategy to be revisited and not set in tablets of stone for all time. Returning to the earlier discussion of stakeholders, it is worth noting that a PEST analysis should also serve to highlight that changes in the external environment will affect and alter the pattern of stakeholder power and influence over time.

This approach to understanding the environment is just as relevant to public and voluntary sector organisations as it is to profit-making companies, although in some respects there may be a difference of emphasis. The central focus of companies is on profitability, and so forces which impact upon the bottom line will be of importance. Public service organisations tend to be in business to meet needs or to solve problems which are not catered for by market systems (although these organisations are increasingly subject to a range of market forces). For them, PEST analysis serves to identify the problems which society may wish to solve and the ways in which such problems or needs are changing. Strategists must then consider the strategic implications of such change. An obvious example is the changing age structure of the population, with growing numbers of elderly people which will impact upon several services such as care in the community, the welfare benefits system and hospitals. As noted in Chapter 10, public sector organisations are often unable to expand their operations where new problems or needs are identified, but instead can use the results of analysis to better target scarce public resources and/or to influence the views and actions of powerful stakeholders.

C A S E   Q U E S T I O N S   11.1

▶ Gather some information from current newspapers about the airline industry in general. What are the main factors (be specific) that are affecting the airline industry as a whole?

▶ Also collect information on Virgin Atlantic and the part of the market in which it is operating. What are the specific PEST factors that management needs to be taking into account?

Forecasting and scenarios

It was implied above that it is not sufficient to consider environmental forces only in a static sense. Forces must be subject to trend analysis as a means of identifying rates of change which might help in predicting their future course. But it must be recognised that past trends cannot be assumed to continue and that analysis must extend to some consideration of the future. The planning model of strategy (discussed in Chapter 10) places considerable emphasis on forecasting with the use of techniques such as time-series analysis and econometric modelling to predict the future. However, many so-called forecasts are in fact extrapolations of past trends so that provisos are required. For example, a government department with responsibility for demographic forecasting attaches the following proviso to its published household projections:

> The projections are based on trends in household formation and population change observed in past years and if these trends have not continued then the number of households in future years may differ from that shown by the projections. *The projections should not, therefore, be treated as forecasts but as an indication of what might happen if past trends continue.*

Another popular approach is to build up a number of possible *scenarios* of what the future may look like. Johnson and Scholes (1997, p.103) note that:

> scenario-building is not just based on a hunch, but tries to build plausible views of different possible futures for the organisation based on groupings of key environmental influences and drivers of change which

have been identified. The result is a limited number of logically consistent, but different scenarios which can be considered alongside each other.

Scenarios will typically be developed for best case, worst case and some level of intermediate outcomes. These would be discussed and debated within the organisation with a view to reaching a consensus on which is most likely. No one can predict the future, and the main benefits of scenario-building are that it discourages reliance on what is sometimes referred to as 'single-point forecasting', that is a single view of the future, and raises awareness within organisations of the need for adaptive strategy in a constantly changing environment.

The competitive environment

Developing an understanding of broad macro-level socioeconomic and political factors which shape the organisation's operating environment is a first step in environmental analysis. Of more specific concern are those factors which shape the immediate competitive environment and affect the organisation's ability to compete effectively in its chosen markets. Analysis of the forces at work in this competitive environment – the microenvironment – underpins the development of an organisation's competitive strategy.

The ultimate aim of competitive strategy is to increase profitability (or in the case of non-profit organisations, to improve 'value-for-money'). According to Porter (1985) profitability depends on two key variables:

▶ the structure of the industry in which the organisation operates,
▶ the organisation's own position, or relative performance, within that industry.

Analysis of these variables will help a firm to identify areas where it enjoys, or where there is scope to create, competitive advantage (discussed in Chapter 10) relative to its competitors. Porter himself developed a series of tools designed to assist in the analysis of the competitive environment: the first of these, the five-forces model, provides a useful framework for the analysis of industry structure (Figure 11.3).

The five forces are:

▶ **Entry barriers** These reduce the threat of new organisations entering a market. Barriers include high entry costs (where significant capital investment is required, typically in plant and machinery), difficulties of access to distribution channels, a strong experience curve effect (see section 11.4), legislation or other government action, such as selective subsidies, which benefit the organisation relative to its competitors (examples include the monopoly situation formerly enjoyed by the public utilities, and subsidies – no longer permitted within EU law – given to prop up industries such as steel), and strong product or service differentiation.
▶ **Bargaining power of buyers** This is low when there are relatively few buyers in the market and few alternative sources of supply, where the organisation's input to the buyer's final product is a small percentage of the buyer's total cost, and where there is no threat of backward integration by the buyer if they cannot obtain satisfactory prices or suppliers.
▶ **Bargaining power of suppliers** This is usually low when there is a fragmented source of supply, where the costs of switching from one

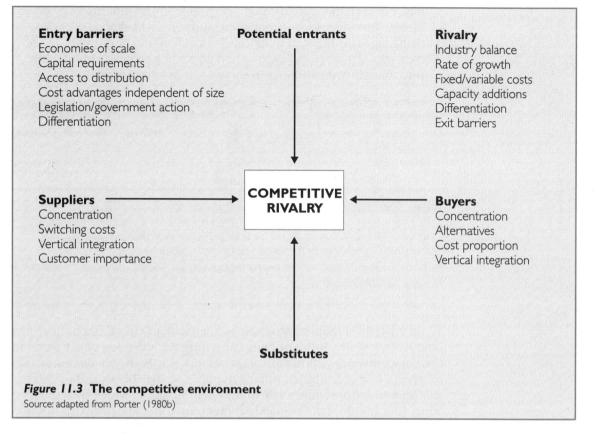

Figure 11.3 **The competitive environment**
Source: adapted from Porter (1980b)

supplier to another are low, where there is little possibility of the supplier integrating forward if it does not obtain the prices it seeks, and if the organisation is an important customer to the supplier, so that the supplier is likely to regard the long-term future of the customer as of particular importance.

▶ **Threat of substitute products or services** This can undermine industry attractiveness, particularly by placing constraints on key variables such as price. Substitutes may take the form of direct imitations of a company's products or services. This may be fought off by differentiation (a strong brand name, for example) or a low-cost profile. Technological change, on the other hand, means that alternative products or services, are continually being developed – as seen, for instance in the telecommunications industry – bringing the risk of product/service obsolescence and underlining the need for external analysis to pay particular attention to technological factors. There is also the possibility that the organisation's own products/services could find new markets as substitutes for those of other organisations.

▶ **Degree of rivalry between existing firms in the market** This is also of importance in developing strategy. Not only will a competitive market be one in which the threats of new entrants and of substitution are high and supplier and buyer power strong, but it will also reflect other factors. Strong rivalry is likely to exist where no one competing company is dominant, where the market is growing slowly (and there is therefore a scramble to increase market share), where there are high fixed costs or high exit costs (both often found in capital-intensive industries), or where there is little scope for differentiation (and hence a likelihood of customers switching easily between suppliers). Porter identifies the degree of competitive rivalry as a key force in determining company profitability, since intense competition is likely to result in lower margins.

C A S E   Q U E S T I O N S   1 1 . 2

▶ Conduct a five-forces analysis for Virgin Atlantic in 1998 or for Glenlight Shipping in its 1992 position.

---

n o t e b o o k   1 1 . 1

Conduct a five-forces analysis for an organisation with which you are familiar. Discuss with a manager of the organisation how useful he or she finds the technique. Does it capture the main competitive variables in his or her industry? Are any variables missing?

An analysis of industry structure is, therefore, of crucial importance in a number of respects. By identifying the nature and direction of key forces in the competitive environment, organisations will be better placed to take advantage of opportunities, to take steps to counter threats and to develop strategies which are appropriate to the environment in which they are operating. For instance, can the organisation do anything to improve its position by building barriers to entry or increasing its power over suppliers or buyers? Industry analysis will also enable judgements to be made about the intrinsic profitability of different industries, considered by Porter to be a key determinant of company profitability. Analysis will therefore influence strategic choice, including the possibilities of withdrawal from some markets or development of new markets.

A combination of PEST and five-forces analysis should ensure that all major influences in the external environment are recognised and their impact on strategy considered. It should also draw attention to the fact that an adjustment to the organisation's own strategy will impact on the industry itself and perhaps also on the wider environment. For example, the decision in 1992 by British Steel to close its Ravenscraig plant in Scotland was part of the organisation's strategy to improve profitability. But the decision also impacted on the industry, which had to adjust to the loss of a major production unit, and on the local Lanarkshire economy, which had to cope with the spillover effects of unemployment and reduced household incomes.

Analysis of the competitive environment is, as noted above, the first step towards developing competitive strategy. Before taking any decisions, organisations must also review their own competitive position relative to others within the industry. This is discussed in section 11.4.

Analysis of consumer needs and demands

Porter's framework identifies buyers as a key force in the competitive environment, placing particular emphasis on the ways in which they can exercise power over organisations. However, given the centrality of buyers or customers to the very existence of organisations, it is important to recognise the role of external analysis in identifying consumer needs and demands. Organisations need to understand what factors shape overall demand for their products or services as well as how individual consumers value their products or services. Since demand is a function of several factors, this means that organisations have to consider, amongst other things, demographic trends, changes in incomes, tastes and preferences and the role of prices (of both their own and substitute goods and services) in determining appropriate future strategy.

Many of these factors will have been identified in the course of the PEST analysis, but a much more detailed analysis is also necessary. Potential sources of information include surveys or market research – which might examine individual shopping patterns, attitudes towards particular firms or brand names, or satisfaction with existing products or services – and the use of focus groups, which might be used to test consumer reaction to new products. In addition, there are several valuable sources of information held internally, including rates of customer enquiries and sales, which can be used to determine changing patterns of demand.

In business management terms, these tasks are usually regarded as part of the marketing function and so are discussed in detail in Chapter 12.

11.4 Internal analysis

The third key dimension of the business environment is the organisation's internal environment. Internal analysis aims to answer questions such as:

▶ Is the organisation producing the right products or services?
▶ Is it producing them as efficiently and effectively as possible?
▶ Upon what critical success factors does the achievement of objectives depend, and does the organisation have the ability to match them?
▶ Which features of the organisation will help or hinder in the pursuit of its overall objectives and strategy?
▶ What could the organisation do better?

'Critical success factors are those aspects of strategy in which an organisation must excel to outperform competition.' (Johnson and Scholes, 1997)

Resources and capabilities

These questions are concerned with the organisation's capabilities and competences which it must seek to understand before it can pursue any form of strategy or undertake any strategic change. Johnson and Scholes (1997, p.137) argue that strategic capability stems from three main factors:

▶ the resources available to the organisation,
▶ the competence with which it pursues its activities,
▶ the balance of resources, activities and business units in the organisation.

Assessment of capability must, therefore, have regard to the overall balance of resources and mix of activities in the organisation as a whole, as well as to the quantity or quality of the different resource inputs (e.g. buildings, machines, people). Above all, however, capability is determined by the way in which the *separate activities* involved in designing, producing, marketing, delivering and supporting the organisation's products or services are performed and by the *linkages* between them. This can be related to Hamel and Prahalad's

Organisational capability is a function of the organisation's resources and competences.

Organisational competences arise from the way in which knowledge, skills and/or technologies are combined in performing business activities.

definition of a competence as a 'bundle of skills and technologies' which stresses the integration of those skills and processes. Thus a competence is unlikely to be held in its entirety by one individual or even a small team.

In order to develop an understanding of its capabilities, an organisation needs to:

▶ assess its resource base,

▶ examine the way in which resources are used and linked together in the different activities which create each product or service,

▶ assess whether its range of products or services is appropriately balanced.

A means must then be found of putting these capabilities in context. As Johnson and Scholes point out, it is not easy to assess organisational capability in absolute terms, so that assessment is more meaningful if gauged in relative terms against the performance of competitors. Indeed, if we bear in mind the central importance of competitive advantage (Chapter 10), then some form of comparative analysis is essential. Hamel and Prahalad (1994) note that although organisations may have many competences, management needs to focus on those which are critical to long-term success. These are the factors which distinguish the organisation from its competitors or, in the context of many public services, those factors which are key determinants of value for money. Such distinguishing factors which create competitive advantage are often referred to as *distinctive capabilities* or *core competences*.

Internal analysis is thus concerned to identify the organisation's distinctive capabilities (and, by implication, activities which are not distinctive and might be done better). With an eye to identifying sources of competitive advantage, the focus throughout the analysis is firmly on performance relative to competitors. A variety of tools and techniques have been developed to enable strategists to assess organisational capability. Some of the most widely used are discussed below (but for a more comprehensive account, see Johnson and Scholes, 1997).

Assessing the resource base

Johnson and Scholes (1997) suggest that a first step in understanding capability is to conduct a resource audit, covering the organisation's physical, human, financial and other resources. This should include resources which are not 'owned' by the organisation, but to which it has access. The audit would address the following types of questions:

▶ Are production facilities up-to-date?

▶ Are they suitably located?

▶ Is the staff mix right?

▶ Are staff appropriately qualified and skilled?

▶ Does the organisation have an appropriate financial structure (debt/equity mix)?

▶ Are financial control systems (such as credit and debt control) effective?

▶ Does the organisation have important intangible resources (such as goodwill)?

▶ Are there important resources outside the organisation (such as good relationships with key customers or suppliers)?

Analysis must then proceed to develop a deeper understanding of the way in which these resources are deployed in the various activities of the organisation. A widely adopted method is value chain analysis.

Value chain analysis

The concept of the value chain, introduced by Porter (1985), is derived from an established accounting practice of calculating the value added to a product by individual stages in a manufacturing processes. Porter applied this idea to the activities of an organisation as a whole, arguing that it is necessary to examine activities separately in order to identify sources of competitive advantage.

As shown in Figure 11.4, activities are divided into two categories. Primary activities relate directly to production or service delivery, and include what Porter terms 'inbound logistics' (activities such as materials handling, warehousing and inventory control), 'operations' (activities which create the product, such as machining and packaging), 'outbound logistics' (such as storing finished products, order processing and distribution), 'marketing and sales' (the activities which create consumer awareness of the product) and, finally, 'service' (including activities such as installation, training support, and repairs service). Support activities include human resource management (involving recruitment, training and development, etc.) and 'firm infrastructure' (including organisational structure, strategic planning, and financial and quality control systems).

Johnson and Scholes observe that few organisations undertake all activities from product or service inception through to distribution to the consumer themselves, but that the value chain exercise must incorporate the whole process, that is the entire *value system*. This means, for instance, that even if an organisation does not produce its own raw materials, it must nevertheless seek to identify the role and impact of its supply sources on the final product. Even if it is not responsible for after-sales service, it must consider how the performance of those who deliver the service contributes to overall product/service quality.

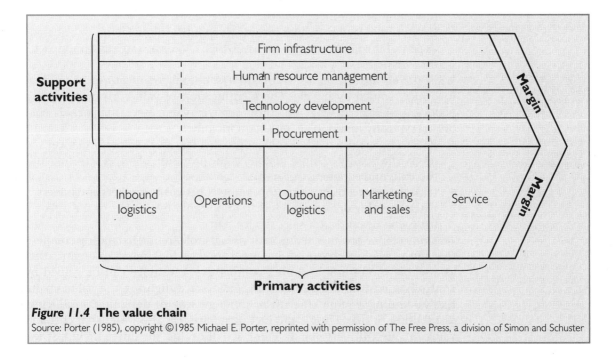

***Figure 11.4* The value chain**

Source: Porter (1985), copyright ©1985 Michael E. Porter, reprinted with permission of The Free Press, a division of Simon and Schuster

The usefulness of value chain analysis is that it recognises that individual activities in the overall production process play a part in determining the cost, quality, image and so on of the end-product or service, that is 'each ... can contribute to a firm's relative cost position and create a basis for differentiation' (Porter, 1985). These are the two main sources of competitive advantage identified by Porter (and discussed in Chapter 10). Analysing the separate activities in the value chain helps organisations to identify what underpins competitive advantage by addressing the following issues:

▶ Which activities are the most critical in reducing cost or adding value? For example, if quality is a key user value, as in the case of Marks and Spencer, then ensuring the quality of supplies is a critical success factor.

▶ What are the key cost or value drivers in the value chain?

▶ What are the most important linkages in the value chain, which either reduce cost or enhance value, and which discourage imitation, and how do these linkages relate to the cost and value drivers?

Porter identified several key factors which 'drive' cost efficiency and value. Amongst the most important cost drivers are:

▶ Economy of scale (also associated with the experience curve – see 'Portfolio models' below).

▶ The pattern of capacity utilisation (including the efficiency of production processes and labour productivity).

▶ Linkages between activities (for example, arrangements governing the frequency and timing of deliveries affect storage costs).

▶ Interrelationships (for example, joint purchasing by different business units to achieve lower input costs).

▶ Geographical location (for example, location can affect an organisation's labour and other input costs; proximity to suppliers may also be an important inbound logistical cost).

▶ Policy choices (such as the choices on the mix and variety of products offered, the number of suppliers used, wages costs, skill requirements and other human resource policies).

▶ Institutional factors (which include the political/legal factors considered as part of the PEST analysis, each of which can have a significant impact on costs).

Value drivers are analogous to cost drivers, but relate to features, other than low price, valued by buyers. The identification of value drivers requires a good knowledge of what determines buyer value (see Chapter 12), but drivers typically found to be important include:

▶ Policy choices (on matters such as product features and performance levels, the quality of input materials, the provision of buyer services, and the skills and experience of staff).

▶ Linkages between activities (for example, between suppliers and buyers where meeting delivery times is an important buyer value, or the links between sales and after-sales service staff).

The importance of value chain analysis is its role in understanding competitive advantage, which cannot be understood by looking at an organisation as a whole. According to Porter, competitive advantage can be gained by controlling cost or value drivers and/or by reconfiguring the value chain, that is, finding a more efficient or different way of designing, producing, distributing or marketing a product or service. He also notes that cost and value drivers will vary for different activities and for different industries,

'The value chain divides a firm into the discrete activities it performs in designing, producing, marketing and distributing its product. It is the basic tool for diagnosing competitive advantage and finding ways to enhance it.' (Porter, 1985)

and, given the dynamic nature of the environment, that they will also change over time. The fluidity of the external environment means that organisations must also address the question of 'sustainability', by finding ways of ensuring that their competitive advantages are 'difficult for competitors to replicate or imitate' (Porter, 1985, p.97).

Although his original work stressed the scope for reconfiguring the value chain, Porter has since expressed concern that too often this has been interpreted as improving operational efficiency. But operational improvement, he says, 'is doing the same thing better' whereas strategy involves choosing, and 'choice arises from doing things differently from the rival ... strategy is about trade-offs, where you decide to do this and not that ... strategy is the deliberate choice not to respond to some customers, or choosing which customer needs you are going to respond to' (*Financial Times*, 19 June 1997). Tools designed to improve operational effectiveness 'are complementary to competitive strategy because they can help organisations implement better whatever strategy they have chosen', but they should not 'get mistaken for strategy' (Porter, 1994).

This view is shared by Hamel and Pralahad (1994). They argue that, in the quest for competitiveness, much management effort in the 1980s and 1990s has been devoted to restructuring (especially 'downsizing') and re-engineering of business processes but that these processes are focused on preserving the past rather than creating the future. 'It is entirely possible for a company to downsize and re-engineer without ever confronting the need to regenerate its core strategy, without ever being forced to rethink the boundaries of its industry, without ever having to imagine what customers might want in ten years' time, and without ever having to fundamentally redefine its "served market"'. Strategy is about creating a foundation for future success, so that

> it is not enough for a company to get smaller and better and faster, as important as these tasks may be; a company must also be capable of fundamentally reconceiving itself, of regenerating its core strategies, and of reinventing its industry. In short, a company must also be capable of getting different.

Portfolio models

Analysis of organisational capability, as noted above, also involves an assessment of the organisation's product or service mix. Johnson and Scholes (1993, p.118) note that 'very often an organisation's strategic capability is impaired, not because of problems with individual activities or resources but because the balance of these resources is inappropriate. For example, there may be too many new products, resulting in cash flow problems.' A number of models aim to assess the balance of an organisation's product/service portfolio. Separate consideration should be given to each of the markets or market segments in which an organisation operates.

A useful model, developed by the Boston Consulting Group (BCG), is the growth/share matrix (sometimes referred to as the Boston matrix) which examines the market share of individual products or services in relation to the growth rate in their particular markets (Figure 11.5). Harrison *et al.* (1995) note that 'the underlying assumptions [of the matrix] equate high market share with higher profitability/competitive advantage and prescribe that growing markets

	Competitive position (market share)	
	High	Low
High	**Stars** (develop)	**Question marks** (investigate)
Low	**Cash cows** (milk)	**Dogs** (divest)

(Market growth on vertical axis)

Business type	Profitability	Growth opportunities	Typical net cash flow
Star	High	Yes	Balanced to negative
Cash cow	High	Limited	Positive
Dog	Low	Limited	Balanced to negative
Question mark	Low	Yes	Very negative

Figure 11.5 **The Boston portfolio matrix**

are more commercially attractive than static or declining markets. Strategists use the BCG matrix to help position the products/services of companies'.

The model's assumptions are underpinned by the concept of the *experience curve*, which holds that companies already in a particular market for a significant period of time have learned from their experience how to produce and deliver their product or service more efficiently and effectively. They are likely to have built a strong market share, and on the basis of both the associated economies of scale and their 'experience', to have achieved relatively low unit costs. Thus the matrix tends to associate a high market share with an ability to generate large, positive cash flows.

The matrix descriptors are explained as follows:

▶ **Cash cows**   Have high market share in a mature market; probably 'stars' of the past now in maturity, they occupy a leading position, with little need for investment in production capacity or marketing. They are likely to be cash generators which can be 'milked', contributing to the development of future stars.

▶ **Stars**   Have a high market share within a growing market but expenditure may be high so that the product or service both generates and uses cash. They are likely to be the cash cows of the future.

▶ **Question marks**   Also found in growing markets, but have a low market share. They are typically products or services that are at an early stage in life requiring substantial amounts of cash to be spent in an effort to increase market share; however, the payback from high spending is uncertain.

▶ **Dogs**   Experience low market share in low-growth markets, and are likely to be draining the organisation of cash and using a disproportionate amount of management time.

A portfolio of products and/or services which is balanced in terms of this matrix is crucial to the survival of the business because investment for growth must be, in part, internally generated – the role of the cash cow – while the star and perhaps the question mark are essential to future success. Although the dog, as a drain on resources, is often regarded as a candidate for speedy elimination, Johnson and Scholes (1997) caution against immediate action without further consideration, such as whether a product is a necessary element in a complete product range, or whether dropping a service will be politically acceptable. In other words, there might be good reason to retain a loss-making product or service.

Although portfolio models such as the Boston matrix were designed for use by profit-making companies, Smith (1994) notes that they may also be of use to public sector organisations, particularly where these are subject to some degree of competition. He suggests that where profitability and thus the generation of cash surpluses is not applicable, a growth/turnover matrix may be more useful, especially if full privatisation is a future possibility. If analysis reveals the majority of the turnover is in low-growth products/ services, the implications for the success of privatisation would need to be considered.

The concept of a portfolio matrix can also be tailored to the circumstances of other public service organisations which have no direct profit motive. The example shown in Figure 11.6 was developed by Montanari and Bracker (1986). Here, the growth/share dimensions are replaced by those of political support (which brings funding support) and ability to serve effectively.

The idea is that a service with high priority among the public and other stakeholders (especially those who control resource allocation) is likely to be well funded and this, in turn, will enable those responsible to provide an effective service. This is a 'public sector star'. A current example could be the provision of closed circuit television systems in many shopping centres: the level of concern over crime in these areas has mobilised funding support for what are proving to be effective surveillance systems. In contrast, a low priority, thus inadequately funded, service will impede staff's ability to do a good job (a 'back drawer issue'), further decreasing the likelihood of support. A service unit or department with too many back drawer issues will be vulnerable to funding reductions.

A 'political hot box' is a service in high demand but too new or inadequately resourced to be provided effectively. An example might be the Care in the Community programme in Britain: where, in the face of public concern, housing, health and social care services appear both under-resourced and inadequately co-ordinated to cope with the demands arising from a growing elderly population and from the closure of long-stay hospitals.

In terms of a 'master strategy', a service unit or department would wish to ensure that its portfolio contained at least some star services. Not only are these well funded, but the demonstration of value for money enhances the service unit's reputation and the likelihood of further political and funding support for further service development. Star services, according to Montanari

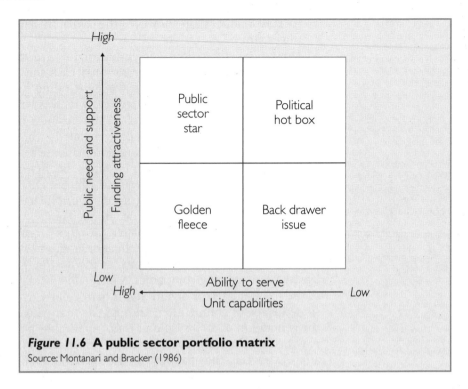

Figure 11.6 A public sector portfolio matrix
Source: Montanari and Bracker (1986)

and Bracker, provide resource flexibility which 'can be used to build the capabilities for a "hot" new service' or to 'increase public awareness of a back drawer service'.

The 'golden fleece' service is one which is well resourced but no longer meeting a key public need. It is likely to be viewed as an excess capability, overstaffed and a drain on resources. Unless support can be revitalised it is likely to suffer budget cuts.

The portfolio approach can help service units to direct their effort in building, maintaining or rebuilding support for specific public services. It also serves to illustrate the types of instances in which organisations might seek to shape the perceptions of their stakeholders to their own advantage.

n o t e b o o k   11.2

Find out about the services provided by one of the departments in your own local authority. Try to categorise its service portfolio according to Montanari and Bracker's model, and consider what implications the service mix might have for the future of the department.

Analysing organisational performance

A key stage in the overall strategy process (depicted in Figure 10.1) is to assess whether strategies designed to meet particular objectives are proving effective or whether some sort of corrective action needs to be taken. This chapter has stressed the need for organisations to assess their capability within the context of the industry in which they operate. The purpose of performance assessment is therefore twofold: first it is concerned to establish whether an organisation is meeting expectations defined in terms of its own objectives and strategies; secondly, the aim is to establish how these performance levels compare with others within the industry and perhaps also beyond. Competitive advantage can be defined only in these relative terms.

A term which has come into fashionable use in the 1990s to describe performance assessment is *benchmarking*. Bendell *et al.* (1993) note that the term 'clearly means different things to different people'. Often it is interpreted to mean only measures of output performance which can be defined in 'hard', quantitative terms. Such measures include comparisons of financial performance, key financial ratios and other measures of output such as market share, production throughput and number of sales calls or repairs undertaken in a given period. However, there are also more qualitative or 'soft' dimensions of performance. These are the less tangible features of performance which result in quality or satisfaction, such as attitudes towards customers, and are particularly important in service organisations. Assessment of these features is more difficult and it can often be done only by direct observation or by undertaking a survey of users. Benchmarking, according to Bendell *et al.* should include hard and soft measures of performance, and its emphasis should be on continuous quality improvement not just in terms of output performance but also in relation to internal processes. 'Perhaps most fundamental of all, benchmarking should be a team-based activity, integrated with other quality improvement activities within the organisation and closely connected to the planning activities going on at the top' (p.12).

Intra-organisational performance or internal benchmarking

Most organisations will undertake some form of internal monitoring of their own performance in order to identify significant variations in key business areas over time. This may mean looking at the performance of the organisation as a whole, or comparing the performance of different individuals, teams or business units with each other. In the corporate sector, the traditional focus is on financial performance involving the comparison of key financial ratios. A glance through company annual reports gives a clear illustration of some of the indicators used. For example, the Great Universal Stores plc records the following 'financial highlights of 1997':

Indicator	1997	1996
Turnover	£2,855m	£2,758m
Profit before tax	£570.6m	£581.1m
Profit after tax	£378.5m	£386.3m
Earnings per share	37.6p	38.4p
Annual dividend per share	18.0p	16.5p

Although these tend to be the 'headline' profit and loss indicators which are of particular interest to shareholders and to industry analysts, annual reports usually contain many other measures of performance. Marks and Spencer, for example, also reports on its performance in respect of its commitment to social responsibility:

Marks & Spencer and social responsibility

The community

Each year, Marks & Spencer receives thousands of appeals for assistance. During 1996/97, the Company donated £9.8m in cash, kind and staff secondments.

The following are examples of the contributions made:

In total, Marks & Spencer made donations to over 1,200 organisations during the year, supporting initiatives in health and care, community development and environment, the arts and heritage.

We currently have 35 staff on full-time secondments, ranging from city centre managers to those working with community groups and government departments. Secondment represents a total cost to the business of £2.6m.

Over 200 staff are participating in 100-hour community assignments as part of their training and development.

The environment
The company believes that caring for the environment makes sound business sense. Its report draws attention to performance in this area:

Our stores incorporate energy conservation features and we invested more than £1m during 1996/97 in new lighting and refrigeration developments. The cost of this technology will be recovered over three years by saving some six million units of electricity and 4,200 tonnes of carbon dioxide pollution.

90% of all transit packaging is reused or recycled (99% by 1998).

1,800 tonnes of plastic was saved by recycling hangers.

8,000 trees have been saved over the last two years by collecting 40 tonnes of paper a month from our Head Office and Marks & Spencer Financial Services headquarters for recycling and waste management.

Source: Marks & Spencer Annual Report and Financial Statements 1997

Performance monitoring is a continual process. Shareholders, analysts, management and others with an interest in the organisation's business will wish to compare performance results over time in order to reveal trends in business performance. It is only by tracking trends that a view can be taken on whether performance is in line with expectations or whether there is a need for corrective action to be taken. Management's interest in performance will be far more extensive than that found in published reports, which tend to relate to overall organisational performance. In line with the concept of the value chain, managers will be concerned to assess the performance not only of individual business units but also of the individual activities involved. Part of this process will involve regular analysis (quarterly, half yearly and annual) of outturn performance against targets, e.g.

financial performance against budget, sales and production achievements against target.

Stemming from central government's desire to increase competition and/ or value for money in the provision of public services, performance assessment is also a common feature of public sector management in the 1990s. The nature of public services is such that financial performance may not be regarded as critical, at least by some stakeholders. As illustrated in Chapter 4, the problem for public sector managers is in managing the conflict which arises between measures of economy and efficiency – which do stress financial performance – and measures of effectiveness, which are concerned with the quality and fairness of service outcomes. This is a reflection of the differing values held among the multiple-constituency of stakeholders. Stewart and Walsh (1994) encourage public service organisations to view the conflict as desirable rather than confusing, as the different measures each have a valid role in assessing organisational performance. (For a further discussion of the difficulties in public sector performance measurement, see, for example, Flynn, 1997.)

A further form of performance assessment – the evaluation study – is common in the public sector. With the degree of emphasis placed on obtaining value for money from the investment of public resources, it is common for government departments or agencies to commission specific studies to examine whether this has been achieved. Studies typically seek to establish whether particular spending programmes or initiatives have been implemented economically and efficiently and also whether they have been effective in meeting the programme's objectives. Given the conflicting perspectives on these measures, evaluation studies in the public service sphere are often complex (for a detailed discussion of the difficulties faced, see Hogwood and Gunn, 1984).

Inter-organisational performance or external benchmarking

It is just a short step from an analysis of internal performance trends to a comparison with other organisations, although as Smith (1994) points out, organisations first need to decide:

▶ what activities or other dimensions of the organisation should be compared with others,

▶ who the other organisations should be,

▶ how information on other organisations can be obtained.

In an ideal world without constraint on time or other resources, organisations might elect to investigate their competitors in some depth. Johnson and Scholes (1997) note, for instance, that a knowledge of competitors' objectives and strategies and the assumptions underpinning these is required, as well as some insight into their resource strengths (following the line of value chain analysis). In reality it can be time consuming and sometimes difficult to get hold of this type of information, although published documents such as annual reports and strategic plans would contain much of the information in summary form.

As alluded to above, there are many other sources of published information on organisational performance. In the private sector, companies such as Dun and Bradstreet specialise in the provision of statistical information on industry and company performance which can be accessed (usually at a cost) by others wishing to analyse their business environment. In relation to many public services, there are also regular publications – often referred to as league tables – which chart specified indicators of performance in key service areas. The Case Example shows the type of information used to assess and compare local authority performance.

CASE QUESTIONS 11.3

▶ What factors would you suggest Virgin Atlantic should include in a benchmarking exercise?

▶ What other businesses would it need to work with to benchmark its performance?

Strategy texts normally advise that analysis target organisations following similar strategies or competing on similar bases. Sometimes, though, there is a difficulty in identifying such organisations, and this is one reason why league tables in the public service sphere often generate heated debate. One question asked is whether it is fair to compare the performance of authorities working in areas of high socioeconomic deprivation with that of counterparts operating in more affluent areas because the environmental context in which the authorities operate is a major influence on performance. Since public resources are increasingly distributed on the basis of performance (rather than need), it is easy to understand concerns about comparing organisations in this way. Although such problems are recognised by regulatory bodies, the widespread adoption of this type of benchmarking in public services is nevertheless seen as a spur to efficiency in the absence of market forces.

Performance of London borough councils in selected service areas

Borough Council	Education		Housing		Recycling	Taxation and expenditure	
	3–4 year olds with a school place (%)	Expenditure per primary school pupil (£)	Average time taken to re-let dwellings (weeks)	Housing benefit claims processed in 14 days (%)	Household waste recycled (%)	Cost of council tax collection (£/dwelling)	Total expenditure by authority (£/head of popn)
Inner							
Camden	52	2,214	10.0	95	8.8	23	1,088
Ken. & Chelsea	40	2,569	6.0	98	5.2	32	932
Tower Hamlets	85	2,466	13.8	75	1.8	63	1,413
Westminster	42	2,298	6.3	76	6.8	25	1,090
Outer							
Brent	85	1,484	12.2	98	2.0	40	1,049
Ealing	68	1,850	8.6	82	6.2	27	886
Richmond-upon-Thames	47	1,763	8.4	43	13.9	18	576

Source: *Public Finance Supplement,* 31 March 1995

Notwithstanding possible comparability problems – which exist in both the private and public sectors – most organisations will wish to assess their own performance relative to industry norms. They may do this with reference to industry averages or to the performance of the best-performing organisations. In some circumstances, there may be merit in drawing comparisons with organisations in quite different businesses. Johnson and Scholes note that a danger in relying solely on industry-norm analysis is that 'the whole industry may be performing badly and losing out competitively to other industries that can satisfy customers' needs in different ways, or to different countries' (1997, p.165). Obviously the scope for cross-industry comparison will be more limited but could relate, for example, to employee costs or to research and development expenditure.

The many exercises in the market testing and compulsory competitive tendering of public services are based on the idea of cross-industry comparison. In these cases, at least part of the objective has been to assess whether in-house provision of services – ranging from direct services such as cleansing and building repair and maintenance to support services such as personnel, training and development, and legal services – provide the taxpayer with value for money.

11.5 Matching the internal organisation to external demands

Having undertaken an analysis of environmental influences, including the nature of the competitive environment, and of internal resources and capabilities, some means has to be found of bringing the results together and drawing out the strategic messages. This is often described as a process in which the key issues are identified, or one in which the 'fit' between the organisation's internal capabilities and its external environment is assessed. A technique often used to assist managers in this process is SWOT analysis.

SWOT analysis

SWOT stands for strengths, weaknesses, opportunities and threats, and is perhaps the most familiar of all performance assessment techniques. Strengths and weaknesses are usually pinpointed in the course of internal analysis so that the results of the value chain and portfolio analyses would be pertinent. Opportunities and threats relate to trends and likely developments in the external environment and would be identified in the PEST and five-forces exercises. Thus, a strength might be a highly skilled workforce and a weakness out-of-date plant and machinery; while a new product line might constitute an opportunity, but competition from cheaper imports could pose a threat. Johnson and Scholes see the role of SWOT being 'to identify the extent to which the current strategy of an organisation and its more specific strengths and weaknesses are relevant to, and capable of dealing with, the changes taking place in the business environment' (1997, pp.174–5).

The SWOT approach is enhanced when all factors are considered in the context of the competitive environment, so that the judgements reached reflect the organisation's assessment of its performance relative to that of its competitors. Thus the exercise will be concerned to relate what the organisation had identified as its competences to critical success factors, to the changes taking place in the external environment and to the performance of its competitors. Particular consideration would be given to the identification of those strengths which appear to give the company an edge over its competitors and are likely to constitute its core competences or distinctive capabilities. Management will be concerned to consider whether these distinctive capabilities are sustainable in the long term or whether there are factors identified by the external analysis which suggest the erosion of advantage – can they be enhanced or protected from imitation (e.g. patenting of innovation) or is erosion inevitable and a new strategy required? Similarly, SWOT can be used to identify areas of particular weakness which are to be avoided, or which can be improved

The Case Example illustrates how a company reacted to external changes in their market, in their customers' requirements and in technology. It changed its structure to support a change in strategy from operating as a multinational to that of a global player.

 Philips, a Dutch electronics giant

Philips is one of the world's largest companies. In 1990 it had business interests in some sixty countries and included every major land mass of the world. Historically, Philips's organisational structure was different from that of many international companies. It was markedly less integrated in logistics and manufacturing and maintained a high diversity of products and services. It encouraged a strong national independence in its companies. The existing structure had evolved over many years and supported federalism. In many countries, resources were duplicated, operational decisions were restricted by national boundaries and new technologies, often well researched, were underutilised for corporate growth and prosperity. The style of the organisation increasingly hindered the company's development to become an efficient trading company.

Between 1986 and 1990, Philips experienced a change in net sales pattern with the concentration of activities in core business. This coincided with a programme of divestment for non-core activities and a series of acquisitions of businesses that strengthened its core concentration and offered the greatest potential for growth. These disposals and acquisitions were part of a programme to produce a product range in accordance with the new strategy centred around four major areas:
- ▶ Lighting, a separate business and technology
- ▶ Components, fundamental to all other activities
- ▶ Consumer electronics, the major activity
- ▶ Information technology and communications

The Philips president is quoted as saying, 'we must develop a better equilibrium of our portfolios'. This change in strategy was to develop Philips as a global competitor and move it away from its multinational style of operation. Changes in the global environment, such as falling market prices, revealed the need for a new strategy, but above all, the need to avoid duplication of costly production and support. A new organisation was required to bring together under one management the

information and decision-making functions required to optimise development and production across a worldwide stage.

This was effected in 1987 and Philips's move to a more classical structure with a strengthening of central authority. A group management council was created which was to set the general policy of the company and monitor the competitive strategy, with the product divisions directly responsible for worldwide activity and profit. The new operational structure evolved over a number of years and has fewer managers and fewer staff.

The total effect of the restructuring was a reduction in the number of staff needed now and in the future, leading to lower expense and a more efficient operation. The company was now much leaner and the new organisational structures were strengthened to concentrate on the core competences. For each competence, every issue, from whichever function, can now be brought to the same discussion table.

Resource-based theory of strategy

Some writers contend that too much emphasis has been placed on the impact of external environmental factors in influencing strategy, arguing that strategies based on an organisation's internal resources or capabilities form a stronger foundation for future success. Kay (1996) outlines the main elements of the resource-based theory as follows:

▶ Firms are in essence collections of capabilities.
▶ The effectiveness of a firm depends on the match between these capabilities and the market it serves.
▶ The growth, and appropriate boundaries, of a firm are limited by its capabilities.
▶ Some of these capabilities can be purchased or created and are available to all firms.
▶ Others are irreproducible, or reproducible only with substantial difficulty, by other firms, and it is on these that competitive advantage depends.
▶ Such capabilities are generally irreproducible because they are a product of the history of the firm or by virtue of uncertainty (even within the firm itself) about their nature.

From his studies of successful companies, Kay has identified only three largely irreproducible, and thus distinctive, capabilities: innovation, reputation and 'architecture', which he describes as 'the system of relationships within the firm or between the firm and its suppliers and customers, or both'. All are products of organisational resources. Through the use of examples, Kay demonstrates how the success of many well known firms is based on one or more of such distinctive capabilities.

 Competitive advantage: the importance of 'architecture'

Observers of the rise of Toyota from second-line manufacturer of sewing machines to dominance of the world automobile industry in a period of forty years have emphasized the role Toyota's keiretsu – the

integrated but nevertheless independent group of suppliers which underpins Toyota's exceptional reputation for reliability – their pioneering of just-in-time inventory management, and their shortening of the traditional model cycle ... The keiretsu involves a complex structure of implicit contracts – long-lasting understandings whose context is not, and cannot be, written down. The nature of these relationships enables Toyota to be confident in the quality of its suppliers' parts, unconcerned about its potential vulnerability to component shortages, and ready to share proprietary knowledge in order to accelerate design and retooling ... Despite the internationalization of markets ... there are still things that are done best by people who find themselves frequently in the same room. The most important of these are the transfer of skills and knowledge and the development of trust between individuals. It is on success in creating networks which facilitate these exchanges that many competitive advantages in today's world depend.

Source: Kay (1996, p.74)

Clearly, internal capabilities can create powerful competitive advantages, but Porter (1994) argues that the resource-based view of the firm and other recent theories based on competences and capabilities have merely shifted the focus from the external to the internal environment, and he remains convinced that industry structure and the competitive environment are important influences on strategy.

Any company can identify some positive qualities and skills – but the real question is how these qualities result in competitve advantage. Industry structure and competitive position define the value of competencies, capabilities and resources [so that] ... identifying [them] in the abstract, decoupled from particular markets, is meaningless.

There can be little doubt that the context provided by the external environment in which organisations operate is important. As a supporter of the resource-based view, Kay is also clear on this when he refers to the match between capabilities and markets. But by turning the focus towards internal resources, there can also be little doubt that the resource-based theory of strategy has added new perspectives to the study of what gives organisations competitive advantage.

11.6 Recap

Content agenda

A major responsibility of management in public and private organisations is to assess how developments in the macroenvironment and in the more immediate competitive environment will influence strategy and competitive positioning. While, in the private sector, strategy is directed towards an acceptable level of profit, in the public sector the focus is on more ambiguous targets related to value for money. In either case, environmental analysis becomes ever more important as the volatility and uncertainty of external conditions increase. Several techniques such as the PEST model and various forecasting and scenario planning approaches, can be used to

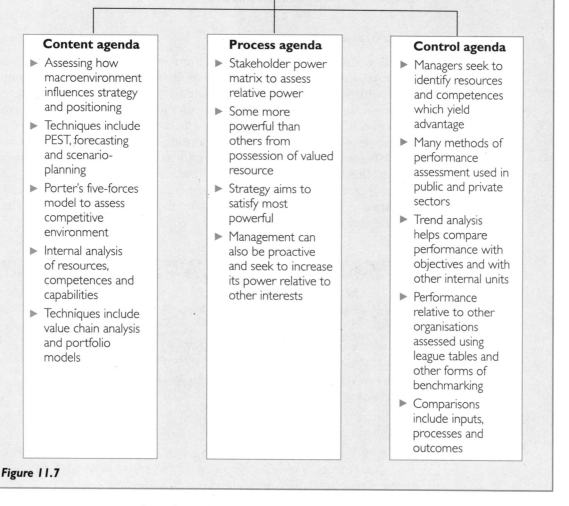

AN INTEGRATIVE FRAMEWORK OF MANAGEMENT

Content agenda	Process agenda	Control agenda
▶ Assessing how macroenvironment influences strategy and positioning	▶ Stakeholder power matrix to assess relative power	▶ Managers seek to identify resources and competences which yield advantage
▶ Techniques include PEST, forecasting and scenario-planning	▶ Some more powerful than others from possession of valued resource	▶ Many methods of performance assessment used in public and private sectors
▶ Porter's five-forces model to assess competitive environment	▶ Strategy aims to satisfy most powerful	▶ Trend analysis helps compare performance with objectives and with other internal units
▶ Internal analysis of resources, competences and capabilities	▶ Management can also be proactive and seek to increase its power relative to other interests	▶ Performance relative to other organisations assessed using league tables and other forms of benchmarking
▶ Techniques include value chain analysis and portfolio models		▶ Comparisons include inputs, processes and outcomes

Figure 11.7

analyse these trends. Porter's five-forces model is also helpful as a way of assessing the competitive environment and identifying sources of competitive advantage.

Managers can focus their analysis of the internal environment on their resources and competences/capabilities. These can include not only human factors but also technologial or structural resources that can be used to support strategic objectives. Value chain analysis can be used to identify resource usage and competences in separate and linked activities, while portfolio models help assess balance in the range of products/services offered. All may be significant sources of competitive advantage or weakness.

Process agenda

Management can assess the relative power of internal and external stakeholders using the stakeholder power matrix, which acknowledges that some stakeholders have more power because of their easier access to some valued resource. Strategy will probably aim to satisfy the powerful rather than the weak stakeholders. Management is not passive in relation to external sources of influence. It can try to influence both the power and the behaviours of some external stakeholders if it so chooses.

Control agenda

As well as scanning the external environment for opportunities to build advantage, managers seek to identify those internal resources and competences which yield advantage. These must be assessed in relative terms. Numerous methods of performance measurement and assessment are available to both public and private sector managers. Internal trend analysis helps to see whether their area of responsibility is meeting its objectives or how it stands in comparison with other units. To measure their performance against other organisations, managers can access published statistical data and/or league tables or undertake benchmarking to gather comparable performance data on a range of inputs, processes and outcomes. These points are summarised in Figure 11.7.

PART CASE QUESTIONS

▶ Make a list of stakeholders for Glenlight Shipping Limited. Assess their sources of power, and rank them according to the likely degree of influence which they hold.

▶ Construct PEST analyses for Glenlight Shipping for 1981 and 1994. Compare them to identify significant similarities between the two periods.

▶ Compare your PEST analyses of Glenlight with the one you made for Virgin Atlantic (Case Question 11.1).

▶ Construct a portfolio matrix of the Clyde Shipping Group, highlighting the areas where you would need more information.

▶ Construct a SWOT analysis for Glenlight Shipping Ltd in 1992. Taking account of factors in the competitive and wider external environment, identify Glenlight's core competences and other sources of competitive advantage.

▶ Obtain a copy of The Body Shop's annual report. Make a list of the performance achievements which are highlighted in the report. Can you make a distinction between hard and soft measures of success? Which of the Body Shop's stakeholders do you think the performance information is targeting?

11.7 Review questions

1 Illustrate the stakeholder idea with an example of your own, focusing on what affects the relative power of the stakeholders to influence an organisation's policy.
2 Evaluate Argenti's comment on stakeholder power in view of your answer to question 1.
3 How should managers decide which of the many factors easily identified in a PEST analysis they should attend to? If they have to be selective, what is the value of the PEST method?

4 Identify the relative influence of Porter's five forces on an organisation of your choice and compare your results with a colleague's. What can you learn from that comparison?
5 What are the main elements in an organisation's resource base?
6 Can you describe clearly each of the stages in value chain analysis and illustrate them with an example? Why is the model useful to management?
7 Explain the meaning of the Boston portfolio matrix and decide into which categories you would put the various businesses mentioned in the Glenlight Shipping and Virgin Atlantic cases.
8 Why do firms conduct benchmarking exercises? What difficulties can arise in external benchmarking?
9 Compare the ideas of the resource-based approach to strategy with the perspectives which emphasise external factors. Evaluate the strengths and weaknesses of each approach.

Further reading

Detailed coverage of the material in this chapter can be found in Part II of Johnson and Scholes (1997). Porter (1985) explains the concept of the value chain in detail and also summarises his earlier work (1980) on the analysis of the competitive environment. Kay (1993, 1996) analyses many aspects of strategic capability and uses well chosen case examples to illustrate the ways in which corporate success is underpinned by distinctive capabilities. Hamal and Prahalad (1994) also discuss in detail the importance of internal resources and competences in building strategic capability. A comprehensive account of benchmarking is given by Bendell *et al.* (1993), while the particular difficulties of performance assessment in the public sector are discussed in Flynn (1997) and Stewart and Walsh (1994).

Managing marketing

CONTENTS

AIM

To discuss marketing as both an organisational philosophy and a functional area within the organisation.

OBJECTIVES

By the end of your work on this chapter you should be able to outline the concepts below in your own terms and:

1 Detail the ways in which a marketing philosophy differs from alternative organisational philosophies

2 Explain, with the use of illustrative examples, the benefits which can accrue to organisations of all types and sizes when they embrace the marketing philosophy

3 Debate whether marketing is an activity which contributes to consumer choice or an exercise in consumer manipulation which encourages materialism and contributes towards social decay

4 Outline the roles and responsibilities of the effective marketing manager and the effective management of the marketing function

5 Explain why marketing can be described as an information-intensive activity

6 Describe component parts of the marketing environment and suggest ways in which each part can impact upon an organisation's marketing activities

7 Outline the process of segmenting markets to identify opportunities and select target markets which offer the greatest potential for achieving organisational goals

8 Describe component parts of the marketing mix and explain the role of the marketing mix in positioning products in the marketplace

Nescafé Italy

The marketing manager for Nescafé Italy was considering the marketing strategies he could use to improve the performance of the brand. It had been sold in Italy for about thirty years but had not established a significant or profitable share of the coffee market. Leaving the market was one option to be considered.

Nestlé SA is based in Switzerland and operates around the world. It has a decentralised organisation structure which allows the operating companies considerable freedom in establishing policies which suit local conditions. At the time of the case there were some two hundred separate companies within the Nestlé group. Nestlé Italy is run from Milan and operates in ten different industries with more than eighty products. One of these is instant coffee, where the company has an 80 per cent share of the Italian market. This represented 1.5 per cent of Nestlé Italy's total revenue.

Coffee companies sell coffee to four groups of customers: families, coffee houses, hotels and restaurants. In the 'family' segment competition is fierce among the major companies. Their strategies focus on:

▶ intensive advertising to enhance the brand image,
▶ growing use of modern distribution channels such as supermarkets,
▶ strong promotion at points of sale,
▶ segmentation of the market by quality, price and form of use.

The companies compete in various ways. They can choose whether to offer coffee as whole beans, ground or instant. It can be packaged and presented to the consumer in bags, tins or jars, all in various sizes. The image of a brand is important, especially in supermarket sales. An image that is strong in the CHR (coffee houses, hotels and restaurants) segment will help sales in the family segment. Price is an important competitive weapon in some segments of the market – but in the CHR segment service and reliable delivery are more important. Advertising is heavy, especially by the larger companies who can afford to spend more, as the cost represents a smaller share of total sales.

The Italian market has a distinctive coffee culture, with the type of coffee used and the degree of roasting different from other European countries. When Nescafé launched its instant brand, the company hoped the brand would be identified with the qualities of 'real' coffee. Marketing was aimed at overcoming the suspicion towards a coffee that was simultaneously 'good, convenient and easy to use'.

Market research for the Italian company showed that 80 per cent of Nescafé sales were to people over 55, who only consumed one cup a day. Younger families saw it as an emergency provision (such as when on holiday), rather than as their main source of coffee.

Source: adapted from Constabile *et al.* (1994)

CASE QUESTIONS

▶ What obstacles is the marketing manager likely to experience in building the brand?

▶ What alternative customer groups could he aim for?

▶ How would his choice of target affect the way he persuades them to buy the product?

12.1 Introduction

This chapter introduces the following ideas:
▶ Organisational philosophy
▶ Marketing philosophy
▶ Consumers
▶ Consumer-centred organisation
▶ Transactional marketing
▶ Relationship marketing
▶ Marketing environment
▶ Marketing information system
▶ Market segmentation
▶ Target market
▶ Product
▶ Product position
▶ Marketing mix

---

n o t e b o o k   12.1

What is marketing?

Before you start reading this chapter, write a few sentences or notes on what you think marketing is. You might find it helpful to think of some recent purchases you have made and consider the different ways in which you came across marketing before, during or after your purchase. Keep your definition of marketing safe as you will use it again at the end of this chapter.

If you ask the chief executive of any successful organisation why it has been a success, he or she will often stress the role that marketing has played. While, in 1982, Peters and Waterman noted that excellent firms shared a commitment to marketing, ten years later it was established that very few of these companies were still successful. Cannon (1996) argues that this high-lights the importance of a *continued* commitment to marketing. Taking this argument further, Doyle (1994) argues that if organisations are to achieve success in the long run they need to change how they measure success. He believes it is essential that companies replace the financial measures on which they commonly judge success with measures of their commitment to the consumer. Consumers are the source of an organisation's profit, growth and shareholder value.

This chapter looks at marketing firstly as an organisational philosophy and then as a functional area that requires to be effectively managed. It argues that if organisations are to achieve success in the long term it is not enough to create a dedicated marketing function. Organisations also need to instil throughout the whole organisation a marketing philosophy. Having examined the benefits that adopting a marketing philosophy can bring to organisations of all types and sizes, the chapter discusses marketing as a functional area within the organisation. It pays particular attention to the roles and responsibilities involved in managing marketing.

12.2 What is marketing?

When speaking about marketing people commonly discuss such issues as: the latest Benetton advert, Richard Branson's attempt to fly round the world in a Virgin hot air balloon, the controversy implied by cigarette companies' sponsoring of sports events and the tactics used by politicians to attract the support of voters. These examples illustrate the various ways in which marketing is used by organisations to attract and retain consumers. The study of marketing and the role it plays within the organisation reveals that marketing involves much more than the use of innovative promotional techniques, creative company logos and product brand names.

Marketing is defined in different ways. The UK Chartered Institute of Marketing and the American Marketing Association both stress that marketing is a management process:

> Marketing is the management process which identifies, anticipates and supplies consumer requirements efficiently and effectively. (Chartered Institute of Marketing)

> Marketing is the process of planning and executing the conception, pricing, promotion, and distribution of ideas, goods, and services to create exchanges that satisfy individual and organisational goals. (American Marketing Association)

Gurus such as Peter Drucker and Philip Kotler go much further. Drucker (1973) argues that:

> Marketing is so basic that it cannot be considered a separate function ... It is the view of the business seen from the point of view of its final result, that is, from the consumer's point of view.

While Kotler (1997, p.19) sees marketing as:

> the key to achieving organisational goals.

Marketing can be regarded as a *functional area* within the organisation and as a *philosophy* adopted by the whole organisation.

Marketing as an organisational philosophy

In organising their activities and planning their structure, many organisations are guided by an overriding philosophy. This is the set of principles, values and beliefs which guide the organisation's approach to business. In the search for competitive advantage many organisations are not only investing in marketing as a functional department. They are adopting a marketing philosophy. Organisations which adopt a marketing philosophy concentrate their activities on the marketplace and the consumer. They are 'consumer centred' or 'consumer driven' (Kotler *et al.*, 1996).

Organisational philosophy is a set of principles, values and beliefs which guide the approach which organisations adopt towards their activities.

Marketing philosophy is an organisational philosophy which believes that organisational success is most effectively achieved by the organisation's satisfaction of consumer demands.

Universities becoming consumer centred

There is growing competition among universities to fill their places. Many universities have replaced their traditional product-led approach to education with a consumer approach. Their move towards the

marketing philosophy can be identified in a variety of ways. In developing courses, universities gather data from employers and past and potential students. In promoting their courses many universities supplement open days and the UCCA handbook with radio, television and billboard advertisements. In identifying what employers look for in graduates and in using such marketing tools as advertising, many universities have successfully responded to increased competition.

Companies such as Dorothy Perkins have repositioned themselves as a successful fashion retailer by making marketing a central organisational activity. They respond to the changing needs, wants and demands of consumers. Charities such as the Worldwide Fund for Nature have attracted wide support for their cause. Ferry operators such as P&O have defended their position against competition from the Channel Tunnel. By adopting a marketing philosophy they have experienced success in *continually* achieving their organisational goals.

Identifying a marketing-oriented organisation is not easy. An organisation's involvement in public relations or advertising does not necessarily mean it has adopted a marketing orientation and is consumer-centred. While an organisation might use marketing tools such as public relations and advertising, it might be doing so superficially. Table 12.1 summarises the organisational philosophies identified in the marketing literature (Dibb *et al.*, 1997; Lancaster and Messingham, 1993).

Those who support a marketing philosophy believe that organisational success depends on a continual focus on the consumer. By identifying and

Consumers are individuals, households, organisations, institutions, resellers and governments which purchase the products offered by other organisations.

A consumer-centred organisation is focused upon and structured around the identification and satisfaction of the demands of its consumers.

Table 12.1 Alternative organisational philosophies

Organisational philosophy	Focus	Benefit	Disadvantage
Product	Product features	High-quality products	Research has not identified demand for the product and it may not sell
Production	Production efficiency	Low costs	Price and level of production are determined by costs, not consumer demands. Amount produced might exceed or not be enough to satisfy consumer demands
Sales	Turnover and shifting product	Sales targets met; good for cash flow in the short term	Hard-pressure sales techniques might achieve current sales targets but lose future ones due to dissatisfaction with the product
Marketing	Continually on consumers and consumer demands	Product offering determined by consumer demands; organisational goals achieved	Initial investment in becoming consumer-centred

understanding consumer demands, organisations with a marketing philosophy anticipate changes in consumer tastes. Then they respond to them quickly. They do not develop and offer products that they assume or expect consumers will buy. Instead they use information about consumer demands to develop and offer products which satisfy their demands. The food industry provides many examples of the benefits of a marketing philosophy. The German Müller became aware that more consumers seek a healthy diet, so the company extended its range of desserts to include low-fat, low-calorie yoghurts. Similarly, McVities introduced a low-fat range of biscuits.

The following comparisons illustrate the advantages that a marketing philosophy has over alternative approaches to guiding the activities of an organisation.

Marketing philosophy and product philosophy compared

Organisations operating under a product orientation focus their activities on the technological strengths and expertise of the organisation. They stress the products and product features which these strengths allow them to make. They pay less attention to the demands of the market and can often find themselves in a position similar to that of the De Lorean car.

De Lorean
❨ **This stainless steel car was built in Northern Ireland with UK grant money and Lotus expertise. It was targeted for the American market. It received much free publicity from its appearance in the film *Back to the Future*. When the manufacturers introduced the car to the market they found that there was no demand. Nobody wanted to buy the car. ❩**

(*Car Magazine*, supplement, April 1997)

Baker (1991) argues that by adopting a marketing philosophy 'which puts the consumer at the beginning rather than the end of the production–consumption cycle', organisations discover what consumers want. They can then decide how to best use the strengths of the organisation to meet these demands. They then *return* to the marketplace with a product for which a demand exists.

While a product philosophy is focused on products for which there may or may not be demand, a marketing philosophy is focused on identifiying consumer demands for particular products.

Marketing philosophy and production philosophy compared

An organisation operating under the production philosophy uses production efficiency and cost of materials to determine the quantity and price of goods to be produced. An organisation operating under the marketing philosophy uses information from the market about demand and the price that consumers are prepared to pay. They use that to determine how much to produce and what the costs must be to offer a price that consumers will accept.

While the production philosophy focuses on efficiency and costs, the marketing concept focuses on effectiveness and the price at which consumers demand particular products.

Marketing philosophy and sales philosophy compared

An organisation operating under the sales philosophy aims to shift as much of a product as it can as quickly as possible. One operating under the marketing philosophy focuses on selling products that will satisfy consumer demands. Levitt (1960) provides a clear understanding of the differences between selling and marketing philosophies:

> Selling focuses on the needs of the seller; marketing on the needs of the buyer. Selling is a preoccupation with the seller's need to convert his product into cash; marketing with the idea of satisfying the needs of the consumer by means of the product and the whole cluster of things associated with creating, delivering and finally consuming it.

The holiday timeshare industry has been widely criticised for its selling techniques. Industries which have traditionally been regarded as adopting a sales philosophy (such as insurance and car retailing) have begun to adopt a marketing philosophy. They hope this will achieve lasting rather than short-term success. While the sales philosophy focuses on shifting products, the marketing philosophy focuses on satisfying consumers and building long-term, mutually satisfying relationships with consumers.

---

n o t e b o o k   1 2 . 2

Benefits of the marketing philosophy

The marketing philosophy suggests that organisational success is best achieved by focusing on the consumer. Identify each of the following organisations' consumers and suggest the benefits that a focus on their consumers will bring to each organisation: Sony, The Body Shop, Save the Children Fund, Lufthansa Airlines, and your university or college.

12.3 Benefits of a marketing philosophy

As an organisational philosophy, marketing asserts that the most effective way of achieving organisational objectives is through consumer satisfaction. It is a philosophy that uses the demands of consumers to determine products, levels of production, prices charged and sales techniques used. This means that organisations selecting marketing over alternative philosophies still assess product features, efficient levels of production and sales targets – but they do not make decisions about these matters the focus of organisational activities. Consumer demands determine product development, levels of production and sales targets. Meeting these demands brings consumer satisfaction and organisational success.

The adoption of a marketing philosophy ensures that the whole organisation commits to achieving organisational goals by *continually* satisfying consumer demands. Aware of this objective and of their contribution towards it, different areas within the organisation are able to co-operate and co-ordinate their activities. Organisations like Safeway, Microsoft and P&O Ferries, which appreciate that consumer demands are continually changing, anticipate these changes and are more open and flexible in their approach to developing new products.

Apple MacIntosh

Apple MacIntosh was at the forefront of innovation in the computer software industry. Given that and the quality of Apple MacIntosh's products, it came as a surprise to many that its competitor, Microsoft, went on to dominate the software market. Why did Microsoft achieve such domination? Unlike Apple MacIntosh it adopted a marketing orientation that paid attention to both consumers and product innovation. As a consequence, by combining product innovation with effective marketing, Microsoft was able to take the lead in the global computer software market.

By identifying and monitoring consumer demands, marketing-oriented organisations are able to respond to these demands and ensure that the products they offer satisfy consumer demands. Above all else, the adoption of the marketing orientation offers stability in the marketplace (Figure 12.1).

Authors such as Cravens (1991) stress the pace and magnitude of changes in consumer demands. This is such that, for organisations to remain competitive they must monitor these changing demands and respond by producing goods that satisfy them. Doyle (1994) agrees that as 'consumers can choose from whom they buy, and unless the firm satisfies them at least as well as competitors, sales and profits will quickly erode'. Indeed, he goes further, distinguishing between *transactions* and *relationships*. He argues that in order

Transactional marketing is an approach which focuses upon one-off exchanges with consumers. Relationship marketing is an approach which focuses on developing a series of transactions with consumers.

Figure 12.1 **Benefits of marketing as an organisational philosophy**

to ensure a stable position in the marketplace many organisations have replaced their focus on transactions with one that seeks to develop mutually satisfying, long-term relationships with their consumers. Doyle argues that a focus on one-off transactions encourages organisations to concentrate on the short-term maximisation of profit. They then pay less attention to their long-term position in the marketplace. Organisations that move towards a relational focus have a better understanding of consumer needs. They concentrate on developing a 'long-term, continuous series of transactions' that helps them maintain stability in the market and achieve their objectives in the long term.

It is through the continual satisfaction of consumer demands that marketing-oriented organisations are able to continually satisfy organisational goals. Many marketing-oriented organisations are replacing a focus on transactions with a focus on long-term relationships with their consumers.

case example: Supermarkets seek to develop relationships with their customers

The idea of building relationships with consumers has historically been most evident in industrial markets in which organisations sell to other businesses and government. The supermarket industry provides an excellent recent example of organisations seeking to develop relationships with individual consumers.

Loyalty cards aim to encourage the customer to buy from the same store by awarding points for every pound spent there. The cards also offer supermarkets a powerful tool with which to develop relationships with individual consumers. Passing a card through the electronic point-of-sale (EPOS) terminal at the checkout provides the companies with valuable information about the customer's shopping habits. It will show how often the person visits the shop, how much he or she spends and on what. The stores can then design messages and sales promotions to satisfy the shopping patterns and demands of individual consumers. So loyalty cards are used by retailers in many countries to build relationships with customers in two ways: they reward them for their repeat business and provide the stores with information to satisfy their precise demands more effectively.

While loyalty cards are widely used, can their value be overstated? For example, they can only supply data on goods that are offered by the store. They do not tell the store if the customer wanted a particular product which was not stocked or if any of the goods bought were second-choice alternatives. Either of these would imply that too much reliance on loyalty card data will lead to stores dictating what the consumer can buy, limiting the choice to the most frequently bought lines. These are not necessarily what they or other consumers actually wanted.

12.4 What types of organisation can use marketing?

The benefits offered by the marketing philosophy apply to all types of organisations. Irrespective of size, ownership, consumer or industrial focus the concepts equally apply. Those managing not-for-profit organisations, charities, churches and sports teams can all benefit from the marketing philosophy.

The marketing philosophy was traditionally adopted by organisations seeking to satisfy the demands of individual consumers. More recently it has been adopted by organisations seeking to satisfy the demands of other business organisations to whom they sell. For example, IBM and Compaq adopt a marketing philosophy for the purposes of satisfying the needs of both their individual and organisational consumers, which include hospitals, universities, banks, among many others.

Marketing health care

❝ The present day marketing concept views marketing as a social process ... [to identify] consumer needs and satisfy them through integrated marketing activities ... Marketing thinking will lead to a better understanding of the needs of different client segments; to a more careful shaping and launching of new services; to a pruning of weak services; to more flexible pricing approaches; and to higher levels of patient satisfaction.

Some health care organizations are now beginning to apply marketing to a broader set of problems by trying to answer critical questions such as:

Where should the hospital locate a clinic or an ambulatory care unit?
How can the hospital estimate whether a new service will draw enough patients?
What should the hospital do with a maternity wing that is only 20% occupied?
How can the hospital attract more consumers to preventive care services such as annual medical check-ups and cancer-screening programmes?

The acid test for the implementation of a marketing orientation in the health care sector is based on the existence of an orderly, systematic and complete strategic marketing plan. ❞

(Moutinho, 1995)

case example Saint Honoré Hospital, Brussels

Saint Honoré Hospital is situated in a suburban area of Brussels. The administrator has for some time felt that he needs to pay closer attention to the marketing aspects of the operation. He feels this will ensure the successful use of facilities and will help the future development of the hospital. As a first step towards developing a comprehensive marketing strategy he arranged for some market research to be done. One of the questions he was particularly interested in was the factors which patients and doctors used in deciding which hospital to go to.

Amongst the data which the research produced was the following table:

Consumers' choice criteria in selecting a hospital.

Aspect of the hospital	Very important (%)
Good doctors	**95.7**
Good nursing care	**88.2**
Good emergency room	**86.5**
Latest medical equipment	**81.3**

Keep patients informed about their care	71.4
Good reputation	68.7
Prices of services	59.1
Overall hospital management	56.3

---

n o t e b o o k   12.3

How might the information affect the decisions taken by the management of Saint Honoré Hospital? What other information would they be wise to take into account alongside this on the views of patients?

Can you identify another social care organisation that could use market research to assist it?

The marketing philosophy has also been more recently adopted by organisations with social or charitable aims. These include raising awareness of the dangers of smoking, increasing charitable donations and promoting the benefits of an active lifestyle (for example, see Lovelock, 1991; Carson *et al.*, 1995; Meidan *et al.*, 1997; Kotler and Levy, 1969). Not-for-profit organisations focus on understanding the opinions, perceptions and attitudes of those individuals whose opinions and attitudes they want to change or whose support they seek.

Using the marketing philosophy to raise awareness of domestic violence

The hard-hitting Zero Tolerance Campaign adopted the marketing philosophy to increase public awareness of the scale and extent of domestic violence in the UK. The campaigners recognised that to achieve their objective they needed to understand public perceptions on the topic. Their research showed that the public believed domestic violence was much less widespread than it was. Knowing this, they were able to identify different target audiences within society. They then developed a series of messages which aimed to change these perceptions and increase awareness of the widespread problem of domestic violence.

The Case Example shows that the fundamental marketing philosophy – of understanding consumers before trying to sell a product or message – applies just as much in social as commercial areas.

---

n o t e b o o k   12.4

Identifying consumers

For each of the following organisations, identify whether they market their products towards individual or organisational consumers or both: Quantas, Avis, Hanson, Nestlé.

12.5 Implementing a marketing philosophy

Michaels (1982) warns that: 'No one person, system, or technique will make a company marketing orientated' and stresses that a marketing orientation cannot be achieved overnight. Advising on the implementation of a marketing philosophy, Michaels emphasises the following requirements:

▶ **Investment by top management**   Before marketing can be instilled throughout the whole organisation, senior managers must commit themselves to the marketing philosophy. Without their support other managers will not implement the necessary changes.

▶ **Injection of outside talent**   Michaels notes that, in his experience, managements implementing a marketing philosophy successfully have brought in new personnel. These have helped to educate other staff about the possible benefits of the new philosophy.

▶ **A clear sense of direction**   As with any change, it is essential that management take a planned approach to its implementation. It must set objectives and timescales to guide the introduction.

Kotler (1997) also stresses the importance of restructuring the organisation to focus on the consumer. Managers need to educate themselves and their staff about the idea and how it may support long-lasting success in the marketplace. This applies to all levels and functions who must share a common commitment if they are to work together in the interests of the consumers. Without the support of top management, the focus on consumer satisfaction advocated by the marketing philosophy will not become the guiding philosophy for organisational decisions.

The structure of the organisation may have to change to allow all departments to become focused on and work together for the achievement of

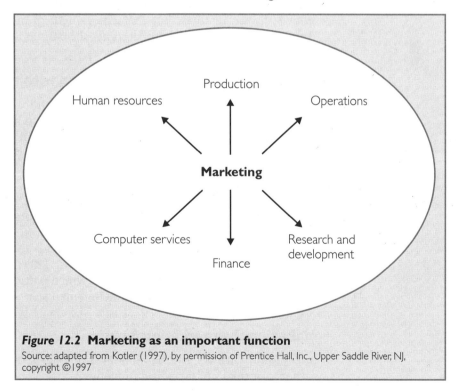

***Figure 12.2* Marketing as an important function**

Source: adapted from Kotler (1997), by permission of Prentice Hall, Inc., Upper Saddle River, NJ, copyright ©1997

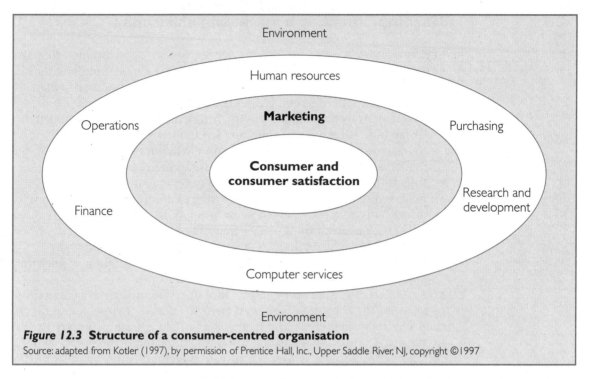

Figure 12.3 **Structure of a consumer-centred organisation**

Source: adapted from Kotler (1997), by permission of Prentice Hall, Inc., Upper Saddle River, NJ, copyright ©1997

consumer satisfaction. Compare Figures 12.2 and 12.3. Figure 12.2 shows marketing as an important function within the organisation and Figure 12.3 is the structure required if an organisation is to become consumer-centred. Such restructuring includes putting in place systems and procedures to collect, analyse and distribute data about the changing demands of consumers. It also requires that the achievement of organisational objectives through consumer satisfaction becomes the basis of decisions.

12.6 Marketing as a functional area within the organisation

The effective implementation of a marketing philosophy requires that as a functional area within the organisation marketing has the central position displayed in Figure 12.3. The continual satisfaction of changing consumer demands relies upon information about consumer demands passing to the whole organisation. It is for this reason that marketing professionals claim that marketing requires to have a central position.

Within marketing-oriented organisations, the marketing department links the consumer and the enterprise. It monitors changes in consumer demands and alerts other areas of the organisation to things that may require a response. Marketing studies the market and decides which consumer demands the organisation can satisfy most effectively. Decisions about which consumer demands to satisfy and which particular marketing tools to use are the responsibility of the marketing manager.

Managing the marketing function

In common with other functional area managers, the marketing manager gathers information, takes and implements decisions, monitors results and

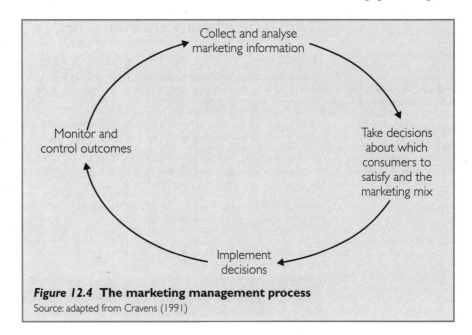

Figure 12.4 The marketing management process
Source: adapted from Cravens (1991)

takes corrective action. The focus in marketing is on the marketplace. It is on deciding which consumer demands the organisation can satisfy, selecting the right mix of marketing tools and monitoring their effectiveness. Figure 12.4 outlines the processes involved in marketing management.

CASE QUESTIONS 12.1

▶ What customer demands was Nescafé satisfying in Italy at the time of the case study?

▶ What other demands could the instant coffee brand try to meet?

▶ What marketing tools are mentioned in the case?

The figure shows that the marketing function is responsible for:
▶ identifying those consumers whose demands the organisation can satisfy most effectively;
▶ selecting the marketing mix which will satisfy consumer demands and succeed in achieving organisational objectives.

In order to take these decisions, information about consumer demands, competitor strategies and changes in the environment which are likely to impact upon consumer tastes and demands is required. It is marketing's responsibility to provide this type of information on a regular basis which makes it an *information intensive activity*. Information collected about the marketing environment is used to assist the marketing manager in taking decisions. These could concern the products that will satisfy consumer demands and the distribution outlets which consumers prefer to use. Other functional areas will also use the information. Manufacturing may use it to determine levels of production, or finance to estimate the capital required to finance raw materials if the data indicate a big increase in demand. The information usually relates to changes in the organisation's marketing environment and its several components.

12.7 The marketing environment

d

The marketing environment consists of all those forces which impact upon the marketing activities of an organisation. It includes both micro and macro components.

There has recently been a noticeable increase in the number of hair products and deodorants that no longer contain CFCs which damage the ozone layer, and the number of car manufacturers that install air bags and side-impact bars as standard equipment in new cars. Why have organisations such as Unilever and Nissan invested in new innovative packaging and additional product features? Why was The Body Shop so successful, and the idea of buying natural beauty products such a money-spinner?

The answer to the above questions and others like them lies with the number, range and extent of changes taking place in the marketing environment. Growing interest in healthy eating, concern over car safety, awareness of environmental degradation, together with legislation, have affected consumer demands. These have obliged organisations to respond by adapting their marketing strategies and tactics.

case example **Fast-food restaurants respond to the British beef crisis**

In response to the crisis that hit British beef, which peaked at the beginning of 1996, fast-food giants, McDonald's and Burger King responded in very different ways. McDonald's began to import beef from Holland and, in order to combat a drop in consumer demand for beefburgers, introduced a 'veggie' burger. Burger King, however, responded by slashing the price of its 'Whopper' burger and announcing to consumers its confidence in British beef. The fact that the two organisations altered their marketing mix (McDonald's by introducing a new burger and Burger King by reducing prices) illustrates that the marketing environment can affect marketing decisions.

Kotler and Armstrong (1997) define an organisation's marketing environment as:

> the actors and forces outside marketing that affect the marketing manager's ability to develop and maintain successful relationships with its target consumers.

The influence of the environment on an organisations' marketing effort can be both positive and negative. The marketing environment contains *opportunities* such as those presented to multimedia organisations by technological developments in the Internet. It also contains *threats* such as Ben & Jerry's entry into the British market to compete head-on with Haagen-Daz for the superior ice-cream market. Kotler and Armstrong suggest that the environment consists of micro and macro elements.

Microenvironment

This is the part of the environment close to the organisation. It contains those parts of the marketing environment with which the organisation interacts regularly and over which it can exercise some control. Some describe it as the operating or controllable environment. Figure 12.5 shows the components. The microenvironment is unique to individual organisations.

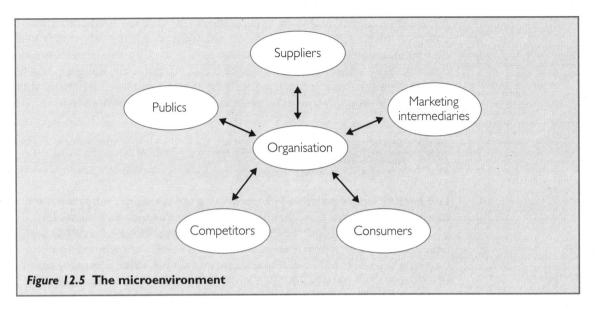

Figure 12.5 **The microenvironment**

While it may be similar to the microenvironment of a competitor, no two are the same. Some of the ways the microenvironment can affect marketing activities are described below.

Organisation

An organisation's marketing effort can be affected by the internal relationships and dynamics of the organisation. If the organisation has not fully embraced the marketing philosophy, the marketing manager may find it difficult to convince other functional areas of what they need to do differently to satisfy consumers. For example, when developing new products, teams from several departments work together. If staff from R&D do not use the information provided by marketing staff about consumer demands then they are less likely to develop something that people want to buy.

Suppliers

The suppliers of an organisation's raw materials and resources can exert bargaining power over the organisation, and vice versa. The bargaining power between organisations and their suppliers normally lies with the larger of the two. An organisation's bargaining power determines the extent to which it can demand, for example, specific delivery dates, advantageous payment terms and the quality of the goods and services supplied. The greater the bargaining power of suppliers, the more influence they can exert over the marketing activities of an organisation and vice versa.

Competitors

Competitors are all those organisations producing and offering similar products to the same consumers. Competitor strategies evidently affect the effectiveness of an organisation's marketing effort. When Clinique cosmetics offers a special bonus pack with two or more purchases from its range of cosmetics, competitors such as Lancôme and Clarins can expect this to have an impact upon their sales. Competitor strategies have serious implications for an organisation. When competition is based on price, the threat of a price war amongst competing organisations can damage both the organisations involved and the industry. An example of a price war which had detrimental effects for one organisation is provided by the UK newspaper industry. Following many months of competing in an industry where competition was based on price, the *Today* newspaper closed when, despite reductions in its price, consumers were not encouraged to switch to it.

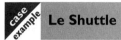

Le Shuttle

Le Shuttle began service in 1994, providing rail transport for private and commercial vehicles from Britain to mainland Europe, via France. It posed a serious competitive threat to ferry companies such as P&O and Stena Sealink which provided passenger and vehicle transportation between the ports of Dover/Folkestone and Calais. With a journey time of only one hour between British and French motorway links, Le Shuttle had a competitive advantage: it was the fastest means of transport for travellers wishing to take their car with them on their journey.

The British and French governments announced in 1986 that they would build the Channel Tunnel. Since then, ferry operators had been planning how best to use their marketing strategies and tactics to meet the new challenges that the tunnel would pose. Many of these efforts concentrated on shortening cross-channel ferry times. P&O used computer systems to reduce check-in-times to 20 minutes. It also used new ferries to reduce the time spent at sea to 75 minutes on the fastest journey. Despite these measures, Le Shuttle still had the time advantage.

Recognising that it was unable to match Le Shuttle's journey time, P&O changed its marketing strategy. It decided to invest in a strategy of diversification and reinvested its marketing efforts towards a particular type of customer – the traveller who viewed the channel crossing as a pleasure to be enjoyed rather than a chore to be endured. In order to attract this type of consumer, P&O improved the quality of its service by investing £650 million in new ships, training and refurbishment of its terminals. To make the ferry crossing more of a welcome break, it also improved its restaurants and duty-free shopping facilities. The same happened to cinemas and children's play areas. It also reduced the price of its fares from £126 in 1994 to £118 in 1997, in a bid to compete with the £160 cost of Le Shuttle.

Source: *Financial Times*, 11 January, 6 May and 19 November 1994; P&O Spring brochure 1997

Marketing intermediaries

These are the go-betweens who distribute goods and services for an organisation. They include wholesalers, retailers and agents such as insurance brokers. Distributors play a key role in ensuring that a product reaches the consumer in time, at the correct price and in good condition. Organisations that use wholesalers and retailers to distribute their products use a recommended retail price which ensures that wholesalers and retailers receive an adequate margin from their resale of a product. It also indicates to consumers what the manufacturers perceive the value of the product to be. A recent example that illustrates how determined some distributors are to maintain the recommended retail price is provided by the perfume industry. The perfume manufacturers believed that the low price at which their products could be bought did not fit with the expensive image they had tried to create. Consumers who were able to buy from cut-price outlets did so, but the perfume companies retaliated by trying to cut supplies to them.

n o t e b o o k   1 2 . 5

Would you prefer to have the choice of buying a product from whatever outlets choose to offer it, or to buy only from outlets set by the manufacturer?

How does the practice of the perfume houses fit with the earlier discussion about the benefits of marketing philosophy?

Consumers

Consumers' tastes change, and this has a powerful effect upon an organisation's marketing activities. It is essential that an organisation anticipates these changes and responds by altering products, prices, packaging or promotion.

Publics

Organisations are surrounded by a number of different publics – any group which has a specific interest in the organisation. They include the general public and also pressure groups. The anti-smoking lobby is an example of the latter which tries to influence the activities of tobacco companies. Companies may therefore have to respond to such pressure and perhaps make changes in the marketing mix that have not been demanded by the final consumer.

Macroenvironment

The macroenvironment is more remote from the activities of the organisation than the microenvironment. It contains those parts of the marketing environment to which the organisation is indirectly related and over which the organisation has no direct control and often, very little indirect control. The components of this environment can, however, exercise great indirect control over an organisation's marketing activities. For these reasons some writers refer to it as the *uncontrollable* environment. The main components of this wider environment are set out in Figure 12.6.

n o t e b o o k   1 2 . 6

Turn back to Figure 12.5 on page 393. Identify one specific example of a recent change in each of the components of the microenvironment which have implications for the marketing activities of an organisation with which you are familiar.

The macroenvironment of an organisation is very similar to that of its competitors. For most organisations, the macroenvironment is to a great

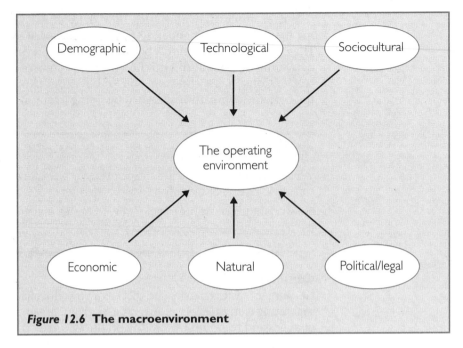

Figure 12.6 The macroenvironment

extent a given fact of their business. Examples of the way these external factors influence marketing management are listed below.

Demographic factors
These include a population's age structure, educational levels and size of family unit. For example, an increase in the number of women with children who are returning to employment has created opportunities for organisations offering personal services such as child care and home care.

Economic factors
These include interest rates, disposable income and saving patterns. For example growth in wealth has stimulated a growth in demand for home ownership throughout Europe. This in turn has created opportunities not only for builders but also for furnishing chains, do-it-yourself stores and garden centres.

Natural factors
The natural environment is one part of the macroenvironment that is nowadays much more prominent in organisations' marketing activities. Responding to concerns over the ozone layer, many organisations have altered the packaging of their products by removing any CFCs that they contain and ensuring that packaging materials are biodegradable. While some have changed the packaging others have created new products such as recycled paper and unleaded petrol to appeal to the green consumer.

Technological factors
From the checkout scanners seen at most stores to advertising on the Internet, managements have been using technology to support their marketing efforts. Other organisations have experienced the threats presented by technological advances. For example, those in the newspaper industry have had to respond to the ability of the Internet to bring up-to-date news to readers at their desks.

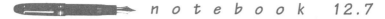

n o t e b o o k   12.7

Access the Internet for company information

To find out how each of the following organisations have responded to the opportunities that have been made available to them by the Internet, log onto the World Wide Web and locate their Web pages: Nike, Burger King, Greenpeace, McDonald's and Reebok.

Which pages did you think were best? The worst? Why did you reach that conclusion?

Political and legal factors

Organisations have always had to be aware of and adhere to legislation surrounding their particular industry. Regulations from the European Commission now often require products to meet higher health standards, have more accurate labelling and to contain more information on their contents. These affect how marketing managers are able to position and promote their products. The politics of the party in power can create opportunities for some organisations and pose threats to others. Many European governments are now privatising former state monopolies and allowing new entrants to compete with established players. Examples include the French government's plans to privatise France Telecom, Air France and Renault. Many people connected with those companies oppose the change.

The EC directive establishing the single European market in 1992 affected many companies. The Case Example illustrates the effect on Volvo Trucks.

Volvo Trucks Europe

In early May 1989, Ulf Selvin, vice-president of marketing, sales and service for Volvo Trucks Corporation, Europe Division (VTC Europe), was deep in thought. European Community directives aimed at creating a single internal EC market by the end of 1992 were reshaping the truck market in Europe. Truck buyers' sales support and service needs were changing and becoming more pan-European. Large European trucking companies had begun to demand that truck producers supply consistent sales and service across Europe. Fleet owners often attempted to negotiate Europe-wide prices and it was likely that, eventually, new trucks would be built to a common standard. Competition was growing fiercer and increasingly pan-European as well.

VTC Europe had historically operated as a multi-domestic marketer, with each national importer management team responsible for the marketing, sales and service of Volvo trucks within its country. Recently, however, programmes had been initiated at both headquarters and importer level that were aimed at moving VTC Europe towards pan-European marketing. As Mr Selvin reviewed the progress of these programmes he deliberated over whether or not VTC Europe should attempt to become a Euro-marketer and, if so, what the appropriate mix was among VTC Europe, regional and national marketing of Volvo trucks in Europe. If he and his management team decided to move VTC Europe from multi-domestic to pan-European marketing they would have to identify the critical steps ... to make such a transition successful (there were implications for VTC Europe's marketing strategy, marketing organisational structure, marketing information systems and human resource development policies).

Source: Lambin and Hiller (1994, p.105)

Sociocultural factors

Organisations such as Benetton that compete globally need to be aware of and sensitive to the belief systems of particular nationalities and cultures. It was these differing values that led consumers in several countries to be offended by a Benetton advert which contained the image of a newborn baby. An organisation's ability to identify and respond to the values and beliefs of its consumers is crucial in maintaining consumer satisfaction.

> **Cultural differences and the markets for coffee**
>
> ❝ A wide variety of blends, degrees of roasting, methods of preparing and habits of consuming coffee can be found in different countries. Each nation has adapted coffee to its culture and traditions, in particular to its traditional forms of nutrition and food consumption. Thus in certain countries coffee is consumed not only for its stimulating properties, but also as a thirst-quencher; in other parts of the world it is drunk with very little water, as if it were an 'elixir'.
>
> The highest per capita consumption occurs in northern Europe (ranging from 12 kg per head per year in Sweden and Norway to 6 kg in France and Switzerland). In Italy, where most people perceive themselves to be heavy consumers of coffee, the level of consumption is equal to that of Canada, about 4.3 kg. ❞
>
> (Constabile et al., 1994, p.69)

🖋 n o t e b o o k   12.8

Analysing the marketing environment

For each of the following organisations, outline those parts of their micro- and macroenvironments that have most impact upon their marketing activities and recommend ways in which they should respond to these environmental influences: IKEA, IBM, a university bookshop and Philips.

🖋 n o t e b o o k   12.9

Form a group of colleagues from different countries and record on a chart the different patterns of coffee consumption experienced.

What do such differences mean for the management of marketing in global or international consumer goods companies?

12.8 Managing marketing information

If organisations are to continually satisfy consumer demands and achieve organisational goals, the above examples illustrate that it is important that they are aware of what is happening in the marketing environment. To monitor and anticipate changes in the marketing environment, marketing-oriented organisations use systematic procedures for collecting and analysing information about that environment. This is often called the marketing information system.

Marketing information systems

To keep in touch, marketing managers need to have imaginative and up-to-date information. They need to have systematic processes to collect, analyse and distribute the information throughout the organisation. Cannon (1996) defines a marketing information system as:

> The organised arrangement of people, machines and procedures set up to ensure that all relevant and usable information required by marketing management reaches them at a time and in a form to help them with effective decision making.

Figure 12.7 details the typical component parts of such a system.

A marketing information system contains internal and external sources of data and mechanisms to analyse and interpret the data. Data should not

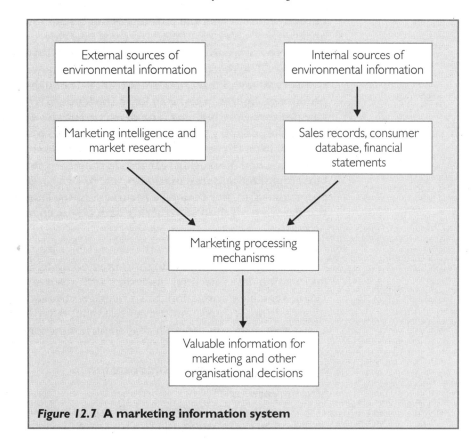

Figure 12.7 A marketing information system

be confused with information. Data are the facts and figures collected from the marketplace. In their raw form, data do not mean anything. For example, the data about consumer awareness of an organisation's leading product in February 1996 may discover that 59 per cent of the sample asked about the product were aware of it. The raw figure of 59 per cent does not mean anything. It does not reveal whether this is a positive or negative finding. For raw data to become meaningful they need to be analysed, interpreted and converted into information. When marketing staff set the February 1996 figure against that for February 1995, then 59 per cent may mean something. The marketing process mechanisms turn raw data into information.

Marketing information on VTC Europe

VTC Europe did not have a standardised method of forecasting sales across Europe. Each importer developed its annual sales forecast using its own forecasting technique. The importers' forecasts were sent to VTC Europe's marketing planning and logistics department, which used them as a starting point for making a total forecast. Forecasts were used to plan production and for long-term capacity planning. In 1987 and 1988, several importers under-estimated annual sales by as much as 25 per cent, leading VTC Europe to under-estimate its total sales substantially.

VTC Europe's market planning and logistics department conducted market research and market analysis. Market research included both Europe-wide surveys and individual country surveys. Much of it was qualitative research intended to reveal how Volvo was performing relative to competitors. Results were shared with importer marketing managers. The department regularly tracked new truck registration statistics to try to discern market trends. It bought competitive production figures in order to learn the kinds of truck which Volvo's competitors were building. The department also tracked Volvo's production, delivery precision, turnover rate and market share by country.

In addition to research conducted by headquarters, importers commissioned marketing research in their own countries as needed. Most importer-initiated market research was conducted on a project-by-project basis, rather than on a recurrent basis. There was no standardised method of gathering data across countries.

Source: Lambin and Hiller (1994)

The purpose of a marketing information system is to produce valuable information by collecting, analysing and interpreting raw data (Fletcher 1990). Valuable information assists managers by reducing the uncertainty in their decisions. Hence it must meet two main criteria: it must be available in a form that managers can understand and in time for them to act on it.

Sources of marketing information

Internal records

The first sources of data for a marketing information system are the internal records of an organisation. Data on the size and regularity of consumer orders and the cost of certain levels of production track the pattern of consumer purchases and help management decide how best to meet fluctuating demand. For a small organisation, internal records may be the source of marketing data that is relied upon most heavily.

Marketing intelligence

A common source of external marketing data is marketing intelligence, that is current data about the micro- and macroenvironments. Marketing intelligence tends to be secondary data which are collected from newspapers, trade associations and industry reports. It is in various degrees of formality. As a rule, the larger an organisation and the greater its resources, the more opportunity it has to employ staff dedicated to collecting marketing intelligence. In smaller organisations a great deal of intelligence can be collected without formal procedures. One way is to make all staff aware of the value of noting and reporting potentially relevant events in the market. They may spot new incentives which competitors are offering customers or distributors, or a new industrial customer opening nearby.

Market research

Another source of data is market research. When marketing managers want to understand a specific problem they use the more focused approach of market research. The processes involved in a market research project are outlined in Figure 12.8.

The first stage involves the client specifying the type of information that he or she wants to receive. If, for example, the marketing manager of a Nissan garage wanted to know how many people within a specific income bracket and living in the area had bought a new car last year he would use market research to find out.

The second stage is to develop hypotheses that can be tested by analysing the data collected. For example, if sales of a particular model of car have fallen over the past eighteen months, the manager might hypothesise that this fall was due to less sales promotion or higher insurance premiums. Once hypotheses have been developed, research staff can collect data to refute or confirm them.

The data may be quantitative or qualitative. Quantitative data, such as that collected by a postal, telephone or personal survey, are easy to analyse and can provide precise information on the issues. Qualitative data, such as those collected when a small number of actual and potential consumers are brought together to form a focus group, are more troublesome to analyse. Their advantage is that they can provide a greater level of detail and a better understanding of consumer motivations than quantitative approaches.

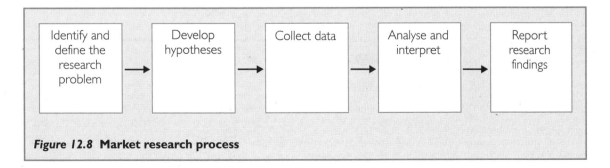

Figure 12.8 **Market research process**

Once collected, research staff use several techniques to analyse the data. Standard software packages process quantitative data to provide statistical tests of the hypotheses. Researchers use less formal methods to identify common themes and issues in qualitiative data. The final stage is to present the findings of the research to the decision-makers who requested the information. The points made earlier about form and timeliness apply here.

CASE QUESTIONS 12.2

▶ As part of the effort to build the Nescafé brand in Italy the marketing manager wants to gather some additional marketing information. What do you think are the most important areas to investigate? Use the model in Figure 12.8 to outline how you would conduct that market research project.

Marketing processing mechanism

This part of a marketing information system is most common in larger organisations that regularly collect large amounts of marketing data. Its role is to analyse data and to store and distribute marketing information throughout the organisation. Sophisticated packages may enable the marketing staff to simulate situations and plan marketing activities on different scenarios. Using the data collected, software packages can provide answers to various 'what if?' questions such as 'What will happen to car sales on model A if we increase the advertising budget for this model by 15 per cent over the next 6 months?' By running a number of different scenarios, the marketing manager can prepare the organisation for any number of possible situations.

Another role of the marketing processing mechanism is to provide an information retrieval service. Information produced by data analysis and interpretation is not only distributed throughout the organisation, but is also stored in the marketing information system for future access through the organisation's computer network.

12.9 Understanding the consumer – buyer behaviour

The marketing information system provides information on the marketing environment. The results of market research projects indicate solutions to precise marketing questions. Organisations with a marketing perspective also want to understand how customers decide to buy something.

---

n o t e b o o k   12.10

Why did you buy that?

Pick a product which you buy on a regular basis, for example, toothpaste, a soft drink or a chocolate bar. Think of the last time you bought that product and try to identify the factors which influenced your choice.

Research into buyer behaviour (Engel *et al.*, 1978; Howard and Sheth, 1969) has identified that consumers work through a series of decisions. Figure 12.9 presents a model of these decisions.

Awareness of unsatisfied need

Consumers become aware of a need that they want to satisfy in two ways. The first is self-discovery. When your stomach rumbles and your throat becomes dry these are physical signals that you are hungry and thirsty and need to satisfy these feelings by eating and drinking. Consumers can also become aware of a need that is currently unsatisfied as a result of receiving some marketing communication from an organisation. For example, until 3M made you aware of 'Post-It Pads', did you identify the need to have a small piece of paper on which you could write messages and stick to a surface?

Needs are categorised in different ways. There are physiological needs, such as the need for food and drink to satisfy hunger and thirst, and there are psychological needs such as the need to feel loved and wanted. Needs can also be described as sought and unsought. An example of a sought need is something that you actively want to buy, such as a holiday or a new bicycle. An unsought need is something that you may not want to satisfy but is something that you must, such as insurance for your car or a television licence.

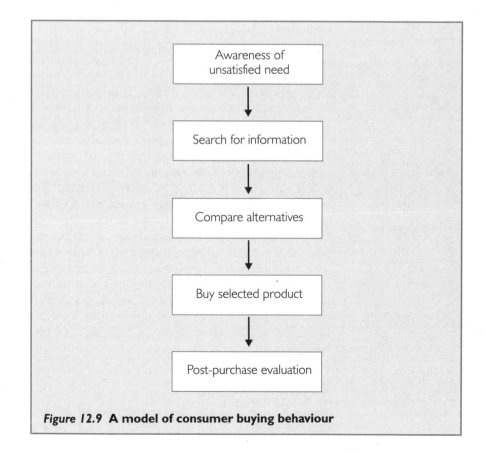

Figure 12.9 **A model of consumer buying behaviour**

Search for information

Having identified a need, consumers search for information that will help them decide which product to buy. Many sources provide this information. Their own experience is one powerful source. Family and friends' information on possible purchases is another. A third source of information is organisations themselves, through advertisements in all media including the Internet.

The source of the information provided at this stage in the buying process has great influence on the purchase decision. Passing on information about the poor service that a friend experienced at a restaurant will usually dissuade a potential customer from booking a table there.

---

n o t e b o o k   12.11

Buying an expensive product

Select from one of the following products: a car, a hi-fi, a computer or a pair of expensive running shoes. For your selected product, describe the type of information you would want before deciding which brand to buy, and why.

The amount of time spent on this stage of the consumer buying process depends on the type of product which consumers believe will satisfy their identified need. It also depends on how much experience they have of buying that product. Buying some products is more risky than buying others. The customers need more information to reduce the risk. The degree of risk depends on:

▸ how expensive it seems relative to other purchases – we need more information before we buy a CD player than before we buy a tin of soup,

▸ whether it is likely to affect their image – a purchase often affects our self-image and the image we wish to create for ourselves,

▸ how much they know about that type of product.

Depending on how often someone buys a product, their information search before a purchase is routine, limited or extensive. *Routine purchases* are those we make regularly – the daily requirements. This regularity provides the consumer with much experience so they need little or no information before making them. *Limited purchases* are made less frequently than routine purchases but are still bought regularly. Clothes, meals out, weekend breaks would be examples. Consumers have some experience on which to base their decision and need only this limited information in order to make a decision. *Extensive information searches* are required before infrequently purchased items such as a new house or car are decided upon. They want to be aware of the alternatives and to reduce the risk attached to such purchases.

Compare alternatives

Depending on whether a purchase involves a routine, limited or extensive search for information, the customer may not need to compare alternatives.

The more information a consumer has collected, the longer he or she will spend comparing different products against set criteria. For example, if a new television is to be purchased the main criteria may be brand name, Dolby sound, teletext and a reasonable price.

Buy selected product

Having compared all the alternatives and decided which product will most effectively satisfy their needs, the next stage is for consumers to make their selected purchase. Even at this stage of the buying process other factors may influence the purchasing decision. The product they intended to buy may not be in stock. A price cut on the product they had rated second or third might persuade them to buy it instead. The salesperson or point of sale promotional material may also influence decisions.

Post-purchase evaluation

Once a purchase is made, consumers enter the final stage of the buying process. This is when they compare how they expected to feel after they had made the purchase with how they actually feel. If the expectation equates with reality then the consumer is more likely to buy in the future. At this stage the communications with consumers can affect future decisions. The quality of after-sales service might convince the car-purchaser that she made the right decision – or not.

---

notebook 12.12

Marketing's impact on evaluating purchasing decisions

For each of the following products, what activities do you think an organisation should engage in to convince you that you made the correct choice?

▶ A can of Diet Coke

▶ A Compaq lap-top computer

▶ A bottle of Calvin Klein Eternity perfume or aftershave

▶ The course on which you have enrolled at university

Whilst the factors that consumers work through when deciding to buy or not are most obvious at the search and comparison stages of the model, they affect each of the decisions the consumer takes in the process. Figure 12.10 summarises these influences.

External influences

External influences, such as individuals' reference groups, culture, subculture, and the social class with which they identify can all influence the types of purchases that they make to satisfy their needs. A *reference group* contains other individuals with whom an individual identifies because of the opinions, social standards and beliefs that they hold. An individual's reference group can include family, friends and peers as well as individuals in social,

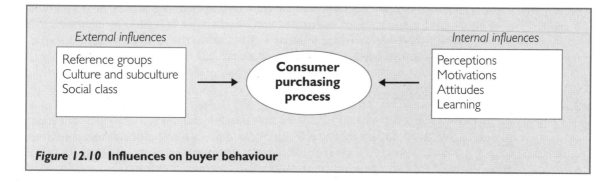

External influences

Reference groups
Culture and subculture
Social class

Consumer purchasing process

Internal influences

Perceptions
Motivations
Attitudes
Learning

Figure 12.10 **Influences on buyer behaviour**

professional and political groups of which they are a member. The individuals with whom we interact most frequently are a major source of information and advice, so the reference groups with which we identify can influence the purchases that we make. By being aware of the reference groups with which consumers identify, the marketing manager can influence and persuade consumers to buy particular products. For example, by sponsoring individual athletes, companies such as Nike use the influence that sporting personalities have over the buying decisions of other people: those who identify with the sponsored athlete will aspire to be like them by buying the products they endorse.

The *culture* and *subculture* to which an individual conforms influences the values they have and social norms to which they adhere. An individual's cultural identity can influence his or her buying decisions in very direct ways. For example, a Muslim will not buy pork as this product is prohibited by the Muslim religion. Subcultures exist within a larger culture and while more short-lived than national or religious cultures, they can influence the buying decisions of smaller numbers of individuals. Punk and Grunge provide good examples of the impact that subcultures can have on the purchasing decisions that individuals make about clothing and music.

The *social class* with which individuals identify themselves is another external influence on consumer buying behaviour. Individuals identify others' social class by such factors as income, educational background and where people live. People often decide to buy things that confirm and reaffirm to them the social class to which they believe they belong or to which they aspire.

Internal influences

Internal influences such as perception, motivations, attitudes and learning processes also affect purchase decisions. *Perception* is the way in which individuals collect and interpret information about the world around them and develop an understanding of reality. These perceptions are unique to them. Because perceptions influence whether people react positively or negatively to an advertisement, marketing managers try to understand how the groups they are hoping to influence perceive and interpret the world. Understanding the perceptions they have of particular images, words and colour, increases the chances of communicating the message successfully. As Chapter 7 shows, this only happens when the receiver – the consumer – receives a message with the same meaning as the sender – the marketing manager – intended.

Motivations are internal forces that encourage consumers to make certain purchasing decisions to satisfy a recognised need. In Chapter 6 we outlined the work of several scholars – Maslow, Alderfer and McClelland – to identify and group human needs. These theories of human needs can help explain why people buy a particular product or service. Marketing staff can use this insight to link their product to a human need. This will encourage people to buy it. Insurance companies eagerly remind consumers of the potential dangers to their home. This reminds people of their need for safety and at the same time offers them a way of satisfying that need by purchasing an insurance policy against fire or theft.

C A S E   Q U E S T I O N S   12.3

▶ Use this model of consumer buyer behaviour to identify the factors that the Case Study suggests have an influence on the purchase of Nescafé in Italy.

Attitudes are the opinions and points of view which individuals have of other people or institutions. Like perceptions, they develop from experiences and social interactions. They affect decisions to buy one product rather than another. The cosmetics industry realised that disapproval of the use of animals to test new cosmetics was growing, so many companies now try to influence purchases by ensuring, and claiming, that they do not test their products on animals.

How individuals *learn* about the environment around them also influences their purchasing decisions. Marketing staff need to understand these learning processes. Kolb suggests that individuals learn either through their

NOTICEBOARD   Needs, wants and demands

As an organisational philosophy, the marketing concept recommends that organisational goals are most effectively achieved by focusing on the consumer. This means that to satisfy the consumer it is necessary to identify the types of product for which there is *demand* and to understand the *needs* and *wants* which will be satisfied when a consumer buys a product. To understand why consumers are satisfied by some products and not by others, it is important to make the distinction amongst needs, wants and demands.

▶ **Needs**   These are the *core* feelings, both physical and psychological, which consumers 'need' to satisfy. For example, thirst is a physical need which needs to be satisfied.

▶ **Wants**   These are the preferences which individual consumers have about the ways in which they 'want' to satisfy the needs which they share in common with others. For

example, individual consumers will want to drink different liquids, according to their tastes, in order to satisfy their thirst which makes them need a drink.

▶ **Demands**   The amount of money which individual consumers have determines the types of drink which they are able to buy. For example, when an individual experiences the need to drink something, they may want to buy a Red Bull energy drink. The amount of money in their wallet may determine that the drink which they have the purchasing power to buy is an own-label soft drink.

In order to achieve consumer satisfaction, it is necessary for a marketing-oriented organisation to understand the needs, wants and demands of consumers. If they define too narrowly the demand which they are satisfying they may be unable to satisfy consumers.

direct experience of a situation or indirectly through other people's experiences (Kolb *et al.*, 1991). By understanding the ways in which consumers 'learn' about particular types of product, the marketing manager can influence their learning to encourage consumers to learn about particular products. Where consumers learn indirectly about products, the marketing manager has the potential to influence the purchases they make. A campaign may repeat an image of a product and each time remind consumers of the benefits attached to it. Another way in which marketing assists in consumer learning is by packaging products in distinctive and consistent designs and colours. Eventually the consumer learns to associate that design and colour with a particular product. Coke, for example, has taught consumers to associate the colours red and white with its particular brand of cola. Consumers all over the world associate the 'Swoosh' symbol with Nike.

12.10 Managing marketing – taking marketing decisions

The marketing manager now has information about the marketing environment, possible opportunities and threats, and the buying behaviour of consumers. The next stage is to decide which demands to satisfy and how to do it. The first decision is about market segmentation and targeting. The second is about choosing the correct mix of marketing tools to position products and make them attractive to consumers (Figure 12.11).

Segmenting markets

Organisations are increasingly using segmentation strategies to satisfy the different needs that exist within the marketplace. Airlines offer consumers the choice of flying first class, business class or economy class. Universities offer degrees by full-time, part-time and distance learning. Athletic shoe companies offer shoes specifically for running, aerobics, tennis and squash as well as 'cross' trainers for the needs of all these sports.

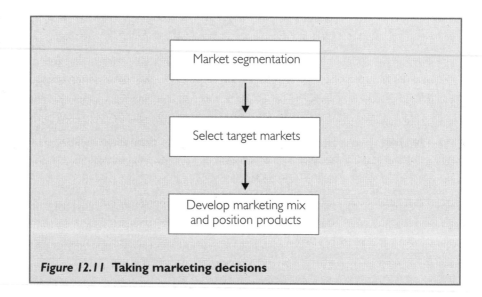

Figure 12.11 **Taking marketing decisions**

Market segmentation is the process of dividing markets comprising the heterogeneous needs of many consumers into smaller parts or segments comprising the homogeneous needs of smaller groups of consumers.

The logic behind segmentation strategies lies with the fact that consumers have different needs. The personal computer market consists of all the individuals who need a personal computer. Within that market people with similar needs can be grouped into distinct segments. Those who travel and need a lap-top form one distinct segment; those who want to use a personal computer to help their children learn, and so need one with CD-ROM facilities, form another. Segmenting the personal computer market (and any other market) relies on identifying the variables that distinguish consumers with similar needs:

▶ **Demography**   The easiest way to segment a consumer market is on the basis of demographic variables such as those discussed earlier (page 396). Magazine companies, for example, use gender and age variables to ensure that within their portfolio they have magazine titles which will suit the needs of females as well as males and those of different ages.

▶ **Geography**   This is common in organisations competing in a global market. By segmenting markets on the basis of country, organisations such as McDonald's have been able to 'think global but act local'. This means that while maintaining uniform global standards of service and hygiene, the company competes differently in each country by varying the product offered slightly to suit local tastes.

▶ **Socioeconomic**   Segmentation on the basis of socioeconomic variables – income, social class and lifestyle – is less straightforward as it is difficult to measure lifestyle and accurately pinpoint the social class with which consumers identify. Segmentation on the basis of lifestyle includes identifying groups of consumers who share similar values about the ways in which they wish to live their lives.

---

n o t e b o o k   1 2 . 1 3

Targeting market segments

For each of the following models of Nissan car, list the characteristics that would describe the individuals who would be likely to buy them: Micra, Almera and Primera.

What differences are there in the characteristics you have listed for each of these examples? Why do you think these differences exist?

When segmenting consumer markets, marketers commonly use a mixture of these variables to provide an accurate profile of distinct groups within a market. The magazine, *Marie-Claire*, for example, uses age, gender, education, lifestyle and social class to attract a readership of educated, independently minded women between the ages of 25 and 35, in income brackets ABC1.

---

n o t e b o o k   1 2 . 1 4

The benefits of segmentation

What market segments have the following organisations identified: EasyJet, Sky TV, The Disney Corporation, Mars, IKEA, P&O Ferries? What benefits do you think their segmentation strategies offer?

Uses and benefits of market segmentation

Many organisations now develop and offer products to meet the needs of particular segments within a market rather than trying to satisfy all requirements. Reasons include the diversity of needs and the pace of change in consumer markets mentioned earlier. In the past, consumers had less to spend and less access to information about the types of product they could buy. Demand was typically met by a few local suppliers offering a limited range to a small market. Rising wealth, developments in information and transportation technology, and the globalisation of much economic activity have brought great changes. Many consumers expect products to satisfy their specific needs. Market segmentation offers organisations a strategy for dividing markets composed of heterogeneous consumer needs into smaller groups of consumers sharing homogeneous needs. By segmenting markets, organisations can choose to satisfy the needs of several segments within the market rather than attempt to satisfy the needs of all consumers within the total market. By focusing on the needs of consumers within a segment, market segmentation offers the marketing activities of an organisation several advantages. They can collect more precise information on consumers selected from a market segment than from the total market. They can use this to design products that more effectively satisfy the needs of those within the segments they have identified.

Targeting selected market segments

Target market is the segment of the market selected by the organisation as the focus of its activities.

Having segmented a market using the variables described above, marketers have to decide which of those segments to target. Target markets are those segments of the market that an organisation selects as the focus for its activities. This decision guides subsequent decisions about products, communications and price. Target markets must meet three criteria: they must contain consumer demands that the resources of the organisation can effectively satisfy; they must be large enough and they must have the potential for future growth. Ultimately, segments selected as target markets are those which offer the greatest potential for achieving organisational goals.

C A S E   Q U E S T I O N S   12.4

▶ What market segments does the case identify within the overall Italian market for coffee?

▶ What are the target markets that Nescafé is considering?

▶ What might be the implications of different target markets for the marketing mix?

As market segments contain fewer actual and potential consumers than the total market, organisations can target more than one segment. This spreads the risk and achieves a greater share of the market than if they were to focus on one segment only.

Using the marketing mix to position products

The final decision facing marketing management is to select the mixture of price, product, promotion and place. This is known as the *marketing mix*. It positions products in the market in a way that makes them attractive to the target consumers. The position that a product has within a market reflects consumer opinions of that product and the comparisons that they make between that product and competing products. The aim is to position products *within the minds of consumers* as more attractive than competing products and better able to satisfy their demands than competing products. To position products effectively the marketing team develops a marketing mix. Kotler *et al.* (1996) define an organisation's marketing mix as 'a set of tools that work together to affect the marketplace'. Traditionally, the marketing mix consists of product, price, promotion and distribution decisions.

Marketing mix – product decisions

Product is a generic term used to identify both tangible goods and intangible services.

Decisions about which products to develop will establish the range of goods and services an organisation offers. Some are obviously physical products or intangible personal services. Most are a mixture of the two.

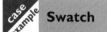

case example   Swatch

The story of the development and introduction of Swatch is a classic example of marketing techniques being used by a traditional industry to launch a new product. Faced with competition from low-cost producers, SMH, an old established Swiss watchmaker (brands included Longines and Omega) urgently needed a new product line. Its engineers successfully developed a radically new product which was much cheaper to make than traditional models. The company 'worked closely with advertising agencies in the United States on product positioning and advertising strategy. In addition to the name "Swatch", a snappy contraction of "Swiss" and "watch", this research generated the idea of downplaying the product's practical benefits and positioning it as a "fashion accessory that happens to tell the time". Swatch would be a second or third watch used to adapt to different situations without replacing the traditional "status symbol" watch.' By 1996 it had sold over 200 million units and was the most successful wristwatch of all time. Its parent company, SMH, is the largest and most dynamic watch company in the world.

Source: based on 'Swatch', Case No. 589-005-1, INSEAD-Cedep, Fontainebleau, and the Swatch Web page at http://www.swatch.com.

---

n o t e b o o k   12.15

Good or service?

Would you classify the following products as goods or services? A university degree, a new car, a compact disc, food bought from a fast-food outlet, a Channel ferry crossing.

The extent to which goods are tangible or intangible affects how marketing staff deal with them. Services present marketing with particular challenges because of their characteristics. These include perishability, intangibility, heterogeneity and inseparability.

Perishability refers to the fact that services cannot be held in stock for even the shortest amount of time. If a plane flies with some empty seats, these seats cannot be stored for another flight – empty seats are permanently lost sales.

The intangibility of services presents the marketing manager with the greatest challenge. Services cannot usually be viewed, touched, tried on or sampled before their purchase. The marketing manager has to devise some way for consumers to try out services before buying them. One way is to produce leaflets with attractive information on the benefits of the service. The financial services industry, for example, relies on the use of information packs to inform consumers of the features and benefits of such products as mortgages, insurance policies and bank accounts. Consumers also have little information on which to assess the product benefits relative to their demands. A common source of product information on services is that which reference groups provide. For example, in moving to a new town, the selection of a new doctor, dentist, hairdresser or sports club is commonly influenced by the information provided by reference groups. Aware of this, organisations like health clubs encourage existing members to invite friends and family to their fitness clubs for trial memberships.

The heterogeneity and inseparability of services relate to the fact that services are labour intensive. Many rely on the skills, competences and experiences of the people who provide these services, and this creates particular challenges for the marketing manager. In providing services, it is inevitable that service providers and buyers will meet, for some amount of time. When booking your car in for a service you discuss it with the staff in the garage. When having your hair cut or attending a doctor's appointment you have to be there with the person providing the service. Organisations operating through branch systems such as banks or fast-food restaurants have to overcome the hazards of inseparability and heterogeneity to ensure consistent delivery standards. Both service providers and consumers have personalities, opinions and values that make them unique. This can create differences in the levels of service and standards which consumers experience when buying services. Organisations like Pizza Hut and UCI Cinemas try to minimise differences by providing staff with company uniforms, decorating premises in a similar way and setting firm guidelines for the way staff deliver the service.

Consumer products (both goods and services) can by classified as convenience, shopping, speciality or unsought products. People buy *convenience* products regularly and easily and the products have low prices relative to other purchases. Examples include bread, milk and magazines. They are widely available and, if one brand is not available, consumers buy another. It is the 'brand switching' nature of the purchase of convenience products that presents the marketing manager with particular challenges. To raise consumer awareness and to convince them to buy a specific brand of, for example, toilet paper, organisations like Andrex invest in television advertising. To attract consumers towards their brand of diet cola, Pepsi unsuccessfully changed the packaging.

Products that are not as widely distributed as convenience products, which cost more and for which consumers will spend more time searching

Product position is the position in which consumers place a product relative to that of an alternative supplier.

are called *shopping* products. Products such as washing machines, televisions and cookers that people commonly buy when they move house are examples of shopping products. For most consumers, the brand name, product features, design and price of shopping products are important and they will spend time searching for the mix of these factors that best satisfies their demands. Advertising plays a part in convincing consumers to purchase, say, a brand of washing machine. A bigger factor is the level of service provided by salespeople, so companies invest heavily in training staff in techniques of personal selling.

Speciality products are bought infrequently, from fewer outlets and are more expensive than shopping products. In purchasing such speciality products as a diamond ring, a new house and a vintage car, consumers require a lot of product information. They will engage in extensive information searches before evaluating alternatives and deciding which to buy. Organisations selling speciality items with a brand name, such as Cartier or Rolex, try to protect the exclusivity associated with their products. The marketing manager will try to ensure that only recommended dealers distribute the product and that the image of the product is maintained and reinforced. They do this by focused advertising and distinctive packaging.

As was mentioned earlier, *unsought* products are those which consumers need to buy but do so without great enthusiasm. They include insurance or a product that is new to the market. It is necessary to make consumers aware of the existence of unsought products and to explain the ways in which consumers will benefit from making their purchase. Common tactics include the use of advertising and personal selling. These focus on explaining how the specific features of unsought products will benefit consumers by satisfying their demands.

The management of an organisation's product can involve decisions about individual product items, product lines and product mixes. A *product item* is an individual product that has different product features, packaging or image from any other product offered by an organisation. Nescafé Gold Blend is an example of a product item. A *product line* is a group of products that share similar characteristics. All the chocolate biscuits produced by McVitie's are grouped together under the same product line. An organisation's *product mix* consists of all the products offered by an organisation. Some university business schools include within their product mix undergraduate management degrees, MBAs, taught postgraduate courses and short courses for businesses. Nissan include within their product mix the product lines of Micras, Almeras and Primeras and within each of these product lines, the individual cars range from basic 'L' models to 'GLX' versions.

In managing the organisation's product mix, product lines and individual product items the marketing manager can use a concept called the *product lifecycle* (Figure 12.12). The central assumption upon which the product lifecycle rests is that all products have a limited life. Depending on the stage reached by a product in its lifecycle, a known set of competitive and consumer conditions exists which helps the marketing manager to specify the marketing activities required at that stage. Mapping the sales and profit generated, the product lifecycle suggests that products pass through the stages of introduction, growth, maturity and decline.

▶ **Introduction** This is the stage at which products enter the marketplace. Profits are negative because of the investment made in

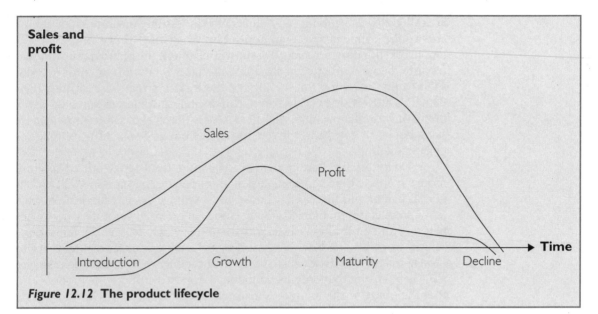

Sales and profit

Sales

Profit

Introduction · Growth · Maturity · Decline · **Time**

Figure 12.12 **The product lifecycle**

researching and developing the product. There are few consumers aware of and therefore interested in buying the product and few organisations involved in producing and distributing it. The aim of the marketing manager at this stage is to invest in marketing communication and make as many potential consumers as possible aware of the product's entry into the marketplace.

▶ **Growth** At this stage consumers have become aware of and started buying the product. It is during this stage that sales rise most quickly and profits peak. As people buy the product, more consumers become aware of it and the high profit levels attract new competitors into the industry. The aim of the marketing manager at this stage is to fight off existing competitors and new entrants. This can be done by encouraging consumer loyalty and distributing the product as widely as is demanded by consumers.

▶ **Maturity** With profits peaking during the growth stage, profit and sales start to plateau and then decline towards the end of this stage. By this stage in a product's lifecycle many consumers are aware of and have bought the product and there are many organisations competing for a decreasing amount of consumer demand for the product. The aim of the marketing manager is to fight competition by reducing the price of the product or differentiating it by, for example, altering its packaging and design. At this stage, product differentiation can successfully reposition products to an earlier stage in their lifecycle. It is also important that the marketing manager begins to consider ideas for replacement products and to select ideas for research and development.

▶ **Decline** By this stage in a product's life there is little consumer demand and all competing organisations are considering removing the product from the marketplace. In deciding when to remove products, the marketing manager must assess the extent to which residual consumer demand exists in order to determine whether to remove the product at once or to phase it out gradually. It is important that by this stage, the marketing manager has a new product ready to enter the marketplace and replace the product that is being removed.

An awareness of the stage at which a product is at in its lifecycle can assist the marketing manager in deciding upon the course of marketing action to take. For example, aware that a product is at the maturity stage, the marketing manager might decide to reposition the product by changing the packaging or image created by the branding of the product. Consider the recent repositioning of the UK high street clothing retailer Dorothy Perkins. The company achieved this by changing the shape and size of the letters used in the 'Dorothy Perkins' name and redesigning shop layouts. They also employed a well-known model to advertise newly designed clothing. Other examples of products which have been repositioned include Babycham as a young person's drink and Lucozade as a sports drink.

---

n o t e b o o k   12.16

Using the product lifecycle

State the stage that you believe each of the following products to be in and comment on how long, in years, you believe their lifecycle to be: a drawing pin, the Spice Girls, compact discs, umbrellas.

Notebook 12.16 addresses two of the major criticisms of the product lifecycle: that all products have a limited life and that all products follow each of the four stages of introduction, growth, maturity and decline. Clearly some products do not have a limited lifespan and other products can be repositioned to an earlier stage. Despite these criticisms, the product lifecycle offers the marketing manager a useful aid to many product decisions.

Marketing mix – price

> Marketing mix is the mix of decisions about product features, prices, communications and distribution of products used by the marketing manager to position products competitively within the minds of consumers.

Price is the value placed upon the goods, services and ideas that are exchanged between organisations and consumers. For most products, price is always measured with money, though consumers do not identify all the purchases they make as having a 'price'. The price, for example, of accessing BBC television programmes is the cost of a television licence, and the price of streetlighting and cleaning is the community charge which individual households are responsible for paying. A visit to the great public parks in Paris, Copenhagen and other European cities is free – but paid for by local taxpayers. In selecting the price of a product which will position it competitively within the minds of consumers, the marketing manager must be aware of the image which consumers have of the product. Consumers have price ranges which they expect to pay for certain types of product. In particular, for safety products, products for children, those associated with health or connected to their self-image, consumers have a minimum price they expect to pay. If the price is below this, consumers will not purchase the product because they perceive such products as being of inferior quality or lower value.

Marketing managers need to be aware of the psychological effects that different prices have on consumer perceptions. They must also ensure that the price charged covers the costs of producing, distributing and promoting products. It must not only provide the organisation with an acceptable profit but also offer an acceptable margin to distributors and retailers.

Marketing mix – promotion

Properly referred to as marketing communications, this part of the marketing mix involves deciding the type of information that will encourage consumers to buy a product. Decisions are also needed on how to present such information and where it should appear. Organisations can communicate with their target markets in many ways. Packaging can provide information, a company logo may transmit a particular message, and sponsoring a football team or a concert indicates an organisation's values and attitudes. The most common ways, however, of communicating with consumers for the purposes of encouraging them to buy products include advertising, sales promotion, personal selling and publicity.

Advertising is the form of communication commonly selected when an organisation wishes to transmit a message to a large audience. It is an impersonal form of communication as it does not involve direct communication between an organisation and a potential consumer. Advertising is effective in creating awareness of a good, service or idea but is less effective in persuading consumers to buy. For new products and products which have been repositioned, advertising is effective in making consumers aware of the product or changes. It requires the support of either sales promotion or personal selling to encourage consumers to buy. Advertisements can be placed on billboards, magazines, television and radio, and their public presentation makes them pervasive. If you follow the same route to work or university each day it is likely that over a period of weeks you will repeatedly see the same poster containing the same message. This means that the organisation has a number of occasions on which to attract your attention to their product and message. It is the pervasive and impersonal characteristics of advertising which makes it a cost-effective method of communicating with potential consumers in a mass market.

Organisations usually use *sales promotions* to encourage consumers who are considering a product to take the next step and buy it. The fast-food industry povides good examples of sales promotion. Both McDonald's and Burger King frequently offer special promotions to encourage consumers to buy their brand of fast-food. The unique characteristic of sales promotion is that it offers potential consumers an incentive to make a purchase within a certain time. By informing consumers that if they buy a product within a defined time, organisations are able to boost the sales of their product for that particular period. Companies also use promotions to encourage repeat buys, as in the cereal box containing a money-back coupon for the next box you buy. Sales promotion can also encourage consumers to try out new products which advertising has made them aware of but which they have not yet bought. When Müller introduce new flavours of yoghurt, for example, it entices consumers to try them by selling them at special introductory prices.

Marketing departments use *personal selling* when consumers require first-hand information and advice before making a purchase. It is particularly useful for infrequently purchased products (see above) such as hi-fi systems. Personal selling is a direct transfer of product and company information from the organisation or representatives of the organisation to potential consumers. It has the advantage of being able to respond to any questions which consumers might have and to explain complicated or technical product features. For many organisations, effective personal selling has provided them with the differentiation required for a competitive advantage. To be effective, however, personal selling requires that managers train salespeople properly, especially on specific product features. The cost and characteristics of personal selling make it useful for more expensive products and for products that are technically sophisticated or difficult to understand. In the sportswear industry, Nike has successfully differentiated itself by employing staff known as Ekins (Nike spelt backwards) to educate salespeople on the technical sophistication of its training shoes. This ensures that salespeople are able to provide a service valued by consumers, that of assisting them in buying the right sort of shoe for their purpose.

Publicity is effective in supporting a positive image of the organisation and its use is not particular to any specific stage in consumers' buying decisions. Publicity involves building good working relationships with the media and using them to promote a positive image of the organisation. The aim is to ensure that positive incidents in which the media might have an interest, such as launching a new product, are fully reported, and that negative ones do as little damage as possible.

Organisations often employ staff specifically to be in charge of publicity and responsible for maintaining relationships with the media. They often take part in particular events to encourage media interest, such as charity events sponsored by the organisation. The importance to the organisation of maintaining a positive corporate image with its various publics must not be underestimated.

Marketing mix – place

Place refers to decisions about the ways in which products can be most effectively distributed to the final consumer. Decisions about marketing channels concentrate on whether the distribution of products should be owned and organised by the organisation producing products or whether products should be distributed by external parties. These decisions are determined by the products involved and the costs of distribution. If the quality of a product is vital to its positioning in the marketplace and it is important that the organisation maintains some control over the distribution of its products, organisations may decide to manage the distribution of their products in-house. Paul Mitchell hair products, for example, maintains the quality image which consumers attach to the Paul Mitchell name by detailing on the product packaging that the authenticity of the product cannot be guaranteed unless it is purchased from an outlet approved by Paul Mitchell. Clearly, the distribution of a product must be consistent with the image which consumers have of the product and the position which consumers regard it as holding in the marketplace, relative to competing products.

A second consideration is the cost of using distributors. Having identified the price at which consumers demand to buy particular products, the costs involved in distributing products in-house relative to externally must be considered. For organisations producing consumer products it is more common for goods to be distributed through retailers. For example, manufacturers such as Heinz use the food retailers to distribute their products to final consumers rather than the more expensive option of having their own shops.

In describing the component parts of the marketing mix, the interrelated nature of decisions about product, price, promotion and place has been mentioned. In developing a mix that will place products competitively within the minds of consumers, the marketing manager must be aware that changes in one area will create changes in other areas. For example, if the price of a product is reduced, consumer perceptions of the product might change. Creating an effective marketing mix with which to position products relies upon integration and co-ordination of each tool used to position products. For example, in positioning their products as value-for-money, organisations such as EasyJet and Aldi (a German retailer) ensure that each part of the marketing mix supports and reinforces this image. This means that products must not be highly differentiated, prices should be low, promotion should stress the low price and value for money. The stores in which products are distributed should be simple in design. This avoids sending a message that the costs of creating a smart place in which to buy products will be reflected in the prices.

12.11 Criticisms of marketing

Managements that adopt a marketing philosophy can clearly bring significant benefits to the organisation. Others take a more critical view. They argue that it manipulates consumer choices and encourages materialism and over-consumption. In 1996, several drinks companies introduced products that were known as Alcopops. These were fruit-flavoured carbonated drinks which taste like soft drinks but contain alcohol equivalent to a 330 ml bottle of beer. This sparked a lively debate over marketing's role in society. The manufacturers argued that they were responding to the tastes of adults who enjoy alcohol but prefer the flavour of soft rather than alcoholic drinks. Rather than encouraging youths and children to buy these drinks, they had widened the choice of alcoholic drinks available to those over the legal age. The charity Alcohol Concern argued that the fruity flavour of such drinks and the bright colours used in their packaging serve to manipulate the under-age drinker into making unwanted or possibly harmful purchases.

The debate on marketing's role within society will run. Those concerned with environmental and public health issues will criticise organisations that they perceive to be damaging the environment or knowingly causing harm to people's health. Important, however, to this discussion is the consideration of whether organisations embracing the marketing philosophy are criticised on the grounds of their morality or on the ethics of their approach to business. While the morality of an organisation in terms of its values, attitudes and belief systems can be difficult to define and therefore criticise or otherwise, the degree to which an organisation is ethical in its approach to the marketplace is more readily measured. The adoption of a marketing philosophy, it can be argued, is not an issue of morality and, as long as it is used for its intended purposes of informing consumers and widening their choice, should not be regarded as an ethical consideration either. The adoption of a marketing philosophy does not advocate that consumers should be 'tricked' into making purchases. Where, for example, incidences of product misinformation occur and it is clear that an organisation has engaged in unethical practices, the marketing philosophy would advocate that a focus on consumer satisfaction has not been adhered to. Consequently, marketing thinkers would argue that such an organisation had failed to conduct its activities under the guidance of a marketing philosophy. Nevertheless, it is a fact that some people use marketing concepts to sell pornography, traffick drugs and invade privacy.

---

n o t e b o o k   12.17

Having completed this chapter, how would you define marketing? Compare this definition with the one that you were asked to make in Notebook 12.1 and comment on any changes.

12.12 Recap

Content agenda

Marketing represents an attempt by management to recognise explicitly the needs and interests of customers. It does so in the belief that meeting these needs is likely to add more value to the organisation's activities than ignoring them. It places particular emphasis on keeping in touch with external (micro and macro) developments that affect customers' needs and the organisation's objectives. Adopting a marketing philosophy wholeheartedly implies making the customer the centre of attention and is distinct from product, production and sales philosophies. It becomes a guiding philosophy for the whole organisation, with all committed to meeting customer demands and thus meeting organisational objectives. Implementing the approach involves increasingly precise target of defined segments of the whole market. It also implies restructuring to ensure that the whole organisation focuses on the customer and planning organisation-wide information systems to deal with marketing data.

Understanding buyer behaviour draws on motivational theories described in Chapter 6. Management uses this knowledge to design products that aim to satisfy one or more human needs. This is believed to help generate consumer commitment to buy a product.

Process agenda

The primacy of marketing advocated by its professionals needs to be seen in the light of the needs of other professional groups. Their relative status and position may be threatened by the primacy of the marketing group in organisations embracing the marketing emphasis: other departments are expected to suppport and be committed to the central position of marketing. It is also argued that marketing needs to be involved in major business decisions to ensure that management hears a consumer perspective. This implies creating mechanisms for involving the relevant players in decisions.

A major element in marketing is the management of communications. They need to ensure that information about external developments and customer needs is gathered, processed and transferred around the organisation. They also require various external means of communication to inform consumers about the product and to influence them to buy it.

Control agenda

Critical perspectives see marketing as an attempt to exert control over consumers. Management's aims are seen as suspect rather than benign, and as an attempt to manipulate the public in the interest of big business. Major marketing roles are those of testing the effects of decisions on the product mix and of gathering information to monitor consumer perceptions of the product prior to making changes.

The integrative framework is set out in Figure 12.13.

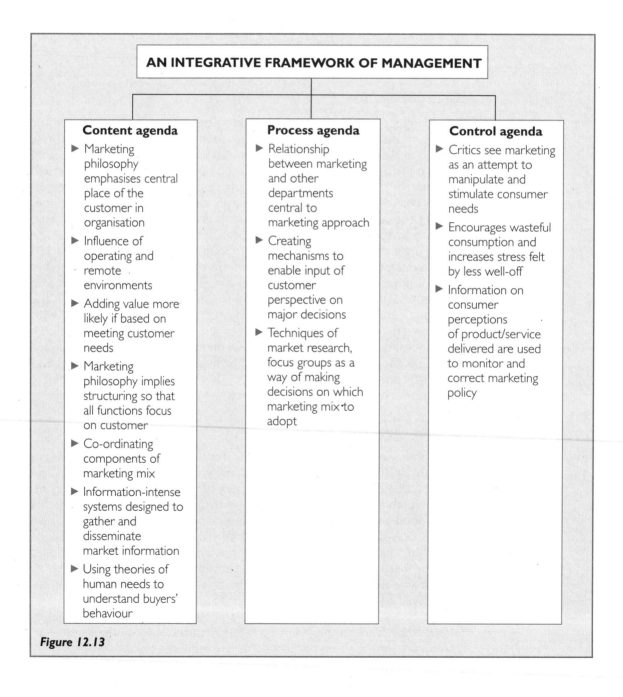

AN INTEGRATIVE FRAMEWORK OF MANAGEMENT

Content agenda
- ▶ Marketing philosophy emphasises central place of the customer in organisation
- ▶ Influence of operating and remote environments
- ▶ Adding value more likely if based on meeting customer needs
- ▶ Marketing philosophy implies structuring so that all functions focus on customer
- ▶ Co-ordinating components of marketing mix
- ▶ Information-intense systems designed to gather and disseminate market information
- ▶ Using theories of human needs to understand buyers' behaviour

Process agenda
- ▶ Relationship between marketing and other departments central to marketing approach
- ▶ Creating mechanisms to enable input of customer perspective on major decisions
- ▶ Techniques of market research, focus groups as a way of making decisions on which marketing mix to adopt

Control agenda
- ▶ Critics see marketing as an attempt to manipulate and stimulate consumer needs
- ▶ Encourages wasteful consumption and increases stress felt by less well-off
- ▶ Information on consumer perceptions of product/service delivered are used to monitor and correct marketing policy

Figure 12.13

▶ Was marketing important to Glenlight Shipping in its early days? To what extent had Glenlight implemented a marketing philosophy by 1994?

▶ How did the company market its new ideas?

▶ How did Glenlight alter its marketing strategies to the changing environment at successive stages of its history?

12.13 Review questions

1 What advantages does the marketing philosophy have over each of the following organisational philosophies: production, product and sales?
2 Outline the benefits which the marketing philosophy can offer each of the following organisations: a university, a charity and a high street retailer.
3 What are the key responsibilities of the marketing manager?
4 In what way is an organisation's microenvironment different from its macroenvironment? Comment on those areas of the following organisations' marketing environment which have the greatest impact upon their marketing activities: Yellow Pages, your local library, Golden Tulip Hotels and *The European* newspaper.
5 Outline various sources of marketing information and compare and contrast alternative ways of collecting and analysing information about an organisation's market environment.
6 Describe the process of buying decisions involved and identify the factors which might influence the purchase made of: a new car, a soft drink, a present for a friend's 30th birthday, a new outfit for work.
7 What are the advantages of market segmentation and what are the variables upon which consumer markets are commonly segmented?
8 How are target markets identified and what is meant by product positioning?
9 What position does each of the following have in the marketplace and what mix of marketing tools has each used to achieve this position? Carrefour, Tango soft drinks, Irn-Bru, Save the Children Fund, Surf washing powder.

Further reading

Dibb *et al.* (1997) and Kotler (1997) provide detailed introductions to marketing; they are widely used on introductory courses. Lovelock (1991) is recommended to students wishing to read more about services marketing. Finally, Baker (1991) contains an excellent selection of classic marketing articles.

W Website addresses

Benetton   http://www.benetton.com
This informative site shows in particular the importance of marketing and knowledge of consumers to Benetton's wider strategy.

Nestlé   http://www.nestle.com
The Nestlé Case Study can be put in the context of the company's wider operations by visiting its site, which profiles 'The World Food Company'.

Corporate social responsibility

AIM

To introduce the ethical, environmental and social responsibility dilemmas which management faces, and some concepts that help to clarify them.

OBJECTIVES

By the end of your work on this chapter you should be able to outline the concepts below in your own terms and:

1 Explain what is meant by the terms 'business ethics', 'enlightened self-interest' and 'corporate social responsibility'

2 Identify some of the major ethical issues within business practice

3 Give alternative views on the role of business within society

4 Outline the difficulties of making ethical business decisions

5 Explain the influence of consumers on corporate responsibility

6 Illustrate the potential competitive advantage which management can gain from socially responsible corporate practice

7 Outline the social and economic trade-offs inherent within corporate decision-making and business practice

8 Outline the complexities of being a socially responsible business

The Ford Pinto story

In the late 1960s, the American automobile industry's home market was under threat from overseas competitors. Lee Iacocca, then president of Ford, was determined to face the competition head on, by having a new car, the Ford Pinto, on the market by the 1971 model year. This meant reducing the standard 'concept to production' time of a year and a half, and making changes on the production line rather than the drawingboard

In testing its new design, Ford used current and proposed legislation. Crash tests indicated that the petrol tank tended to rupture when it was struck from behind at 20 mph, posing a significant risk to those inside. This contravened proposed national legislation that required that cars be able to withstand an impact at 30 mph without fuel loss. No one informed Iacocca of these findings, for fear of being fired. He was fond of saying 'safety doesn't sell'.

Management had to decide between production deadlines to meet competitive requirements, and passenger safety. The engineers costed the design improvements at $11 per car, and turned to cost/benefit analysis to help quantify the dilemma. Using government figures which estimated the loss to society for every traffic accident at $200,000, Ford's calculations were:

Benefits of altering design
Savings: 180 deaths; 180 serious injuries; 2,100 vehicles
Unit cost: $200,000 per death, $67,000 per serious injury; $700 per vehicle
Total benefit $49.5 million

Costs of altering the design
Sales: 11 million cars; 1.5 million light trucks
Unit cost: $11 per car; $11 per truck
Total cost: $137.5 million

From this calculation, Ford determined that the costs of altering the design outweighed the benefits, so they would produce the Pinto in its original form. They reasoned that the current design met all the applicable federal regulatory safety standards. While it did not meet proposed future legislation, it was as safe as current competing models.

Ford therefore launched the Pinto in 1971. Observers estimate that between 1971 and 1978 between 1,700 and 2,500 people died in fires involving Pintos. In 1977 the proposed fuel-tank legislation was adopted. Ford recalled all 1971–76 Pintos to modify their fuel tanks. Civil action was brought against Ford and resulted in a pay-out of $250 million in damage awards. Many courts concluded that the Pinto's design was legally defective. However, when charged with criminal homicide, Ford were found not guilty in 1980.

Sources: based on Shaw (1991) and Birsh and Fielder (1994)

CASE QUESTIONS

▶ As a marketing or production manager at Ford at the time, what dilemmas would you face?

▶ How would you express these dilemmas within the company?

13.1 Introduction

This chapter introduces the following ideas:

▶ Philanthropy
▶ Enlightened self-interest
▶ Ethical investors
▶ Social contract
▶ Deontology
▶ Utilitarianism
▶ Egoism
▶ Applied ethics
▶ Ethical relativism
▶ Corporate social responsibility
▶ Ethical consumers
▶ Ethical audits

Most of us only become conscious of business ethics when there is a problem. Events such as the collapse of the Maxwell Group, Bank of Credit and Commerce International and of Barings invoke consumer distrust of corporate bodies. The ensuing media debate invariably raises public awareness and displeasure, and ends in calls for legislation or court action. The stories of Persil Power, when clothes were said to have been slightly damaged when washed (German, 1995) and the British Airways 'dirty tricks' campaign against Virgin Atlantic, when BA used unusual tactics against a competitor (Glaister, 1991) make good reading: they also raise public questions about the ethics of such companies, and their sense of corporate social responsibility.

While such situations seem clear-cut, many issues in the corporate response to social and ethical problems are much more ambiguous and complex. The chapter uses current concerns and debates in business ethics to illustrate these complexities and trade-offs in corporate decision-making and responsibility. It exposes corporate action to critical review and highlights evidence about the costs of irresponsible actions. In using well known examples, it emphasises the issues that affect business at all levels, from human resource issues to environmental degradation.

CASE QUESTIONS 13.1

▶ Did Ford act unethically at that time? Should the law be the only influence on a corporation's actions? What responsibilities do you think a major company has?

▶ Ford used cost/benefit analysis to decide what to do – could this have been improved? Was it a useful decision tool in this case?

▶ Imagine you were Ford's management at this time. What would you have done, and why? List the social costs and benefits to the company and society of the alternatives to help you determine your answer.

▶ Imagine you worked for Ford as an engineer and were aware of this potential design fault. What would you do? What, if any, are your responsibilities to the customer and/or your employer?

These issues are integral aspects of management. The aim is to encourage informed consideration of the way management conducts business and the impact that business practice has upon society. While the issues are inescapable, there are no easy solutions, nor does the chapter prescribe any ideal management actions. The aim is to outline some concepts and tools for informed, critical thinking.

The possibly under-used influence of consumers upon corporate decisions is also demonstrated. Some companies have acknowledged this and have approached business in a responsible and ethical way – this may have helped them gain some competitive advantage.

13.2 The history of responsible business practice

❝ Ethics, in the broadest sense of the word, is rising to the top of the corporate agenda. ❞
(*Marketing Business*, July/August 1996)

While current newspaper headlines imply that business ethics has only just become an important issue, the Pinto case shows it has been around for years. Indeed there is a long tradition of ethical behaviour in business. From the very start of the Industrial Revolution some entrepreneurs acted philanthropically:

1803–1876	Titus Salt	Textiles	Employee welfare; Saltaire Village
1830–1898	Jeremiah Coleman	Mustard	Charities; Salvation Army; YMCA
1839–1922	George Cadbury	Chocolate	Employee welfare; Bournville Village
1836–1925	Joseph Rowntree	Chocolate	Employee welfare; New Earswick Village
1851–1925	William Lever	Soap	Employee welfare; Port Sunlight Village

Their approach to business recognised the social impact of industry and its potential to improve social conditions. By fostering an ethos of care, these industrialists developed the traditional notion of individual charity and redefined the responsibilities of business. They offered a different business model and showed society what was possible. The early philanthropists helped define enlightened self-interest as a viable approach to business. They were committed Quakers who believed it was morally unacceptable to exploit their workers to make money. They were also owner-managers and so free to give their own money to charitable aims if they desired. Managers of today's public companies are responsible to the shareholders and the communities in which they exist.

As business grew during the Industrial Revolution the original owner-managers required additional capital to finance the expansion. The method chosen in most western economies was to issue shares in the business to wealthy individuals. If growth continued, the number of separate shareholders grew and were often not individuals but financial institutions such as insurance companies and pension funds. This diverse group of shareholders rarely took an active part in managing the business – they appointed managers to do the work on their behalf. This led to a significant change in the nature of those companies. Management increasingly became separated from ownership. If owner-managers chose to be philanthropic, they could manage accordingly – they combined the two roles.

Separation of the roles reduced this possibility. The ownership role was spread among many individual or institutional shareholders. They were unlikely to have had a coherent view of philanthropy. Moreover, the institutional holders have responsibilities to their policyholders or pensioners. Their interests may be damaged by overgenerous donations to another group of people. So the responsibility for the philanthropy or otherwise of the modern company is more diverse and policy harder to set. The charitable ideals of the early philanthropists are rarely put into practice by modern corporations.

Another obstacle is that the problems identified within this area of applied ethics are complex, variable and constantly evolving. It is usually impossible to determine the definitively correct response to ethical issues in the workplace. Hence it is often easier to ignore the problem by invoking the economic imperative rather than struggle to apply ethical theories to business decisions.

The economic imperative argues that in business financial priorities rank far above social or environmental ones. It leads to the view that overt and significant philanthropy ought to be a responsibility of charity rather than of business. Those of this view maintain that the 'business of business is business'. Many managers and directors affirm that their primary duty is to maximise shareholder wealth.

Others believe that this does not inevitably preclude a strategy of enlightened self-interest. They do not accept that acting responsibly damages business interests. However, they do accept that returns will be in the long run rather than the short. These benefits could include increased employee motivation, customer loyalty, verbal recommendations, repeat purchases, improved public and/or media relations, and increased customer awareness of the product or company. All of these can support the long-term success of a business. They may increase productivity through more committed staff, reduce the expense of hiring new employees and increase sales in the long term by having loyal customers. They can save advertising costs if they receive good coverage from sponsoring sports or charities.

Some examples of prominent companies that have developed a clear policy of ethical behaviour are:

▶ Ford now has an environmental manufacturing policy.
▶ Tengelmann, one of the largest department store chains in Germany, is committed to offering products that are environmentally harmless and contain recycled materials as far as practicable.
▶ B&Q, a leading UK retailer chain, actively employs people who are otherwise often discriminated against because of their age. It also avoids stocking products whose production is environmentally damaging (such as peat).
▶ Ben and Jerry's Home-made Ice Cream Company and British Telecom produce audited social statements.
▶ Ciba-Geigy, a Swiss-based chemicals company, sets environmental protection as an equal goal along with product innovation and profitability.
▶ BP has a formal policy on business conduct with a code of practice.

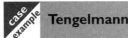

Tengelmann

Tengelmann, a German retailer with over five thousand branches around the world, combines profitability and ecological aspects in its approach to business. Environmental protection takes a high priority in management decisions. Many measures have been introduced by the company, often well ahead of their time, including:

- ▶ **converting to lead-free petrol,**
- ▶ **returnable bottles,**
- ▶ **phosphate-free washing powders,**
- ▶ **refusing to sell Icelandic fish, as a contribution to saving whales (which at that time were being destroyed by Icelandic fishing businesses),**
- ▶ **not stocking batteries containing mercury.**

Source: Hopfenbeck (1993)

---

n o t e b o o k   13.1

Collect at least two new examples of organisations that seem to be taking the matter seriously by introducing explicit policies on environmental, social or ethical matters. What aspects of the company's operations does the policy cover? How did management develop the policy (for example, which people or groups took part in forming the policy)? How does management ensure that people follow the policy and that it has the expected effects?

The ethical dimension can be reflected in all areas of business. It can guide decisions on hiring staff, design criteria, manufacturing policy, sourcing raw materials, marketing and sponsorship.

13.3 The role of business in society.

There are two major schools of thought on the role of business in society. One follows Milton Friedman, an American economist who believes that the role of business is to create wealth by providing goods, services and employment. The other is based on the idea of corporate social responsibility, where the emphasis is on public good rather than private gain.

The Friedmanite position

Milton Friedman disagreed with the corporate social responsibility approach to business, calling it a fundamentally subversive doctrine:

> There is only one social responsibility of business – to use its resources and engage in activities designed to increase profits so long as it stays within the rules of the game, and engages in open and free competition without deception or fraud. (Friedman, 1970)

As an economist, Friedman believed that operating business 'without deception or fraud' provided sufficient social benefit through the creation of wealth or employment. For a business to give money away to charitable purposes was equivalent to self-imposed taxation. He argued that those who had been put in charge of a business (the managers/board of directors) had no right to give away the owners' (the shareholders) money. They were employed to generate wealth for shareholders, not to give it away.

This stance sees the role of business in society as being solely concerned with operating in a competitive market economy. For an individual business to undertake any additional roles is to operate beyond the remit of business.

CASE QUESTIONS 13.2

▶ In view of Ford's actions during the 1970s, was Milton Friedman correct to suggest that 'the business of business is business'?

---

notebook 13.2

Ethical investors

Ethical investors do not invest in business activities that they consider unethical. They avoid investing in businesses with unethical characteristics, such as those in countries with oppressive regimes or which produce nuclear power, tobacco, alcohol, armaments or pharmaceuticals. Conversely, they actively seek out companies which have a positive record on issues such as animal testing, the environment, trade relations, working conditions and community or social involvement. Some unit trusts offer the opportunity to invest in ethical businesses: they have been very popular, earning good returns.

Can this growth in ethical investment be explained in the light of Friedman's assertions?

Others disagree with Friedman's argument that management should focus solely on profit considerations. They take the position that business does not have an unquestioned right to operate in society and to do as it wishes. In systems terms, they see business as one of many subsystems in the wider social system. Just as society depends on business organisations for goods and services, so business depends on society. It cannot operate without inputs from that society in the form of employees, capital, physical resources. It also depends on some explicit or implicit legal right to operate and a framework of institutions which allow it to do so – courts, banking systems, educational systems and so on. To be accepted as part of that society, business needs to respond to society's demands and expectations, which will not be confined to generating wealth. The link between business and society is more complex than Friedman suggests.

The corporate social responsibility approach

The social contract consists of the mutual obligations that society and business recognise they have to each other.

The corporate social responsibility perspective reflects this interdependency: society and business depend on each other and have mutual obligations.

The complexity is that the relationship is not static and there are many competing interests. However, corporate power has grown to the extent that citizens (and even individual shareholders) often appear to have little power to influence corporate decisions. The expansion of many nineteenth-century companies listed earlier has meant that their original ethical driver, responsibility to one community, has been diluted by the drive to meet the values of their shareholders.

Thus the social environment changes over time. As corporations change, so do society's expectations of them. The Pinto case indicated that producers were not overly interested in safety in the late 1960s. Equally, it would be fair to say that most motorists of the same era were just as oblivious to the protection of their own lives. Today many make a virtue of it by advertising safety features such as anti-lock brakes or airbags as their selling points. More broadly, legislation can be used to protect consumers. Society has become more sophisticated and demanding. For example, the public demand for recycled or more environmentally friendly goods has prompted changes in corporate behaviour, and in the composition of organisations' product portfolios. Recognition of the appalling working conditions for many of those who produce the raw materials for western goods has developed the notion of 'fair trade' and resulted in a range of corporate responses, such as:

▶ Typhoo tea changing its practices and being awarded the 'fair trade' mark.
▶ Café Direct successfully competing head-on with the coffee giants.
▶ Smaller brands such as Green and Black being able to enter the chocolate market.

The Noticeboard contains some evidence about consumer opinions.

CASE QUESTIONS 13.3

▶ Did Ford make the right decision *for that time?*
▶ Would it be the right decision *now?*

If you have given different answers, why is that?

Consumer and public expectations change. It appears that more European consumers expect ethical commitment or social responsibility to be demonstrated by large corporations. Management may damage rather than promote shareholder interests by ignoring its wider responsibilities to society. This raises numerous practical dilemmas about business ethics.

NOTICEBOARD Consumers, environment and ethics

▶ 60 per cent of consumers consider environmental issues in their shopping.
▶ 40 per cent of those believe themselves to be 'dark green' (very committed to environmental issues).
▶ The percentage prepared to pay more for eco-products increased from 53 per cent to 60 per cent during 1990–95.

▶ Environmental concern is now found across all socioeconomic groups.

Mintel predicts that it will be the demand for 'ethical goods' that shows the next significant growth.

Source: Mintel (1995)

13.4 What is business ethics?

Before looking at some tools for exploring the ethical dilemmas facing management, use Notebook 13.3 to locate your own ethical positions.

---

notebook 13.3

What are your ethics?

▶ You are walking down the street. There is no one nearby and you see: (a) a 50 pence piece, (b) a £5 note, (c) a £50 note, (d) a £100 note, (e) £1,000. Do you keep it? Yes or no?

▶ The money you find was actually in a wallet with the owner's name and address in it. Does this make a difference?

▶ That name indicates to you that it belongs to: (a) a wealthy person, (b) a pensioner of modest means, (c) a single parent. Does this make a difference?

▶ Suppose there were some people nearby. Does this make a difference?

Explore your reasons for each of your decisions.

Peter Drucker (1981) posed the question: What precisely is business ethics, and what could, or should it be? The challenge is not as strange as it may at first seem. There are two alternative positions, on whether business ethics refers to:

▶ applying ethical theory to business, or
▶ creating a separate set of rules about ethical behaviour in business that are distinct from those of society.

Some authors argue that business has its own ethics, describing it as 'the game of business' (Carr, 1968). Carr then suggests that like any game, business has its own rules. Using the analogy of the game of poker (where bluffing is a central part of the game itself), Carr suggests that 'no one should think any the worse of the game of business because its standards of right and wrong differ from the prevailing tradition of morality in our society' (p.139). He believes that all the bluffing and hyperbole which surround business dealings are central to its operation and that all parties expect it:

> Violations of ethical ideals of society are common in business, but they are not necessarily violations of business principles. (Carr, 1968, p.147)

CASE QUESTIONS 13.4

▶ Do you agree with Carr's comments?
▶ Does this help you take a different view towards Ford's action in the 1970s?
▶ Is the following quote from Nash (1990) the logical conclusion to Carr's view?

'Suppose you are a business (wo)man. Now suppose you are of ruthless and greedy character ... But I repeat myself.'

Conversely, others (see, for example, Drucker, 1981; Frederick *et al.*, 1992) believe that management should not make up their own definitions of what is right and wrong. They believe that, as part of society, managers are subject to the rules of that society and should run their organisations accordingly. This implies that business ethics 'requires that the organisation or individual behave in accordance with the carefully thought-out rules of moral philosophy' (Robin and Reidenbach, 1987, p.45). What are these rules?

There are four main schools of thought in moral philosophy, offering different approaches to solving ethical dilemmas. They can be summarised as follows (Honerich, 1995):

▶ **Deontology**   This is the 'ethics of principle', equating any decision with a moral law. This in effect means that any act is right if it is consistent with an accepted moral principle or law. Societies have developed certain rules which members generally accept (e.g. that people do not deliberately kill each other) which apply to many situations, including organisational ones, and are still valid (Honerich, 1995, pp.887–8).

▶ **Utilitarianism**   This follows the logic of the 'ethics of consequence'. It looks at the majority utility (or benefit) of any decision or action and deems it right if it has positive consequences for the majority, or the 'greater good'. In examining the probable results or outcome of a decision, utilitarianism suggests that what is good for most people, is right (Honerich, 1995, pp.890–2).

▶ **Teleology**   This is the 'ethics of purpose'. It considers the outcome that is achieved by an action (within the laws of the land as the lowest common denominator acceptable to ethical principles) and assesses it to determine whether it accomplishes the original goal. This uses the agent's vision as the criterion to judge the action. When applied, this would then suggest that if a reasonable act ensured the continuation of the corporation, then it was right.

▶ **Egoism**   This is the 'ethics of self interest', claiming that personal or corporate benefit is the only rational criterion for judging economic actions. The argument (first developed in the teachings of Adam Smith, 1776) is that if people follow this principle it will, perhaps paradoxically, result in the general good. The assumption is that people will only be able to maximise their personal self-interest if they do things which others value and are willing to pay for.

Deontology is the application of established general rules or moral laws to a decision.

Utilitarianism is the practice of evaluating a decision against the criterion of its consequences for the majority of people.

Teleology is the practice of evaluating a decision against the criterion of whether the outcome achieves the original goal.

Egoism is the practice of evaluating a decision against the criterion of whether it serves a person's self-interest.

n o t e b o o k   13.4

Think about times when you have justified a decision you have made on the grounds that it was: (a) for the good of the group/family/friends, (b) the right thing to do, (c) the best option for yourself, (d) the best way to get the job done. Which of the ethical philosophies outlined above matches each reason?

These tools from moral philosophy can be used to show how they can give us a more informed and analytical insight into management dilemmas. The problem with attempting this form of analysis is that you may be left with more questions than answers. The following list identifies some of the major questions that might arise with each philosophy:

Applied ethics is the application of moral philosophy to actual problems, including those in management.

▶ **Deontology**   In order to determine this, it is necessary to determine a generally accepted principle or code which can be applied to the situation. What might this be? Who should be declared the main corporate concern – workers, customers, shareholders – so that the principle can be applied?

▶ **Utilitarianism** If utilitarianism operates for the greater good, who is to define what that good is? Over what period of time? Does the benefit for the majority change if the time period is changed?

▶ **Teleology** If this suggests that the means justifies the end, who is to determine what the outcome will be, and whether that was justified?

▶ **Egoism** The question is whose self-interest is central to the debate? As management has become separated from ownership, will the interests of shareholders and management coincide or not?

What is the right course of action? Which approach provides you with the right answer? Management is likely to decide that the rationale of economic reasoning, while harsh, reduces the dilemma to a clearly understandable problem to which an apparently objective answer can be found. Other members of society may prefer a different logic which may be equally legitimate.

---

n o t e b o o k   13.5

Note down your initial reaction to the following question. Should a company close down an uneconomic plant in an area which depends heavily upon it for employment?

Now take each of the four ethical philosophies and note down the answer they imply, or the further information you would want to collect before recommending a decision. Which of these four philosophies seem to have shaped your initial reaction?

---

n o t e b o o k   13.6

The European motor industry

Consider the situation facing the European car manufacturers in early 1997. The industry has built too much capacity in Europe so that there was a gap of 7 million units between production capacity and forecast demand. Many manufacturers were considering the closure of one entire manufacturing plant.

Imagine you are the Chair of the Ford Motor Company. While Ford as a global company is profitable, Ford Europe is losing money. Your shareholders expect profits. You need to reduce costs across the group, and you are aware that this high level of overcapacity in Europe suggests closing a plant. You know that other car manufacturers are also considering this route.

There are 47 plants in Europe. What criteria should you use to select the one to close? Do you have enough information to make this decision? What other options are available? Do you ask for further information on the social impact that any closure might have? Might it be better to reduce the size of several plants rather than close one? Should you take social concerns into account in your decision?

Can you determine the solution provided by each of the ethical philosophies?

You could also do a similar analysis on other management dilemmas as they arise in your area. For example, the effects of out-of-town shopping centres on the quality of life in city centres is a topical issue that can be approached in a similar way to identify conflicting perspectives.

In this chapter, as in much of management, there are no right or wrong answers. What is important is that you appreciate this fact and that you are clear about the processes by which an answer is reached. By being able to use these philosophical tools you are better able to consider the implications of management decisions. Thinking about and debating these issues helps you to understand the complexities of business ethics and of major management decisions. Try reviewing public decisions against these theories to see which are being implicitly used. Notebook 13.7 introduces yet another level of complexity and highlights further the difficulties of applying moral philosophy to business problems.

---

n o t e b o o k   1 3 . 7

The world motor industry

What if the problem is not that of reducing capacity but of relocating it? Demand in the developing world is potentially immense, especially for more basic models. So the major companies are tempted to reallocate capacity to these areas. Should a plant be relocated from an economically dependent and deprived European region, to a country in South East Asia whose government is offering favourable incentives? The plant itself is currently not losing money but in the long term the financial returns will be higher in Indonesia or China. It could operate with a cheaper workforce, less demanding health and safety regulations, weak trade unions and few environmental conditions. It would also be contributing to the economic development and modernisation of the area.

Having considered some ethical philosophies and not found any easy answers, some argue that business ethics has simply not come to terms with the world of business practice. They criticise it for being too general, too theoretical and too impractical for a manager to apply (Stark, 1993), especially when compared with the economic clarity of the figures. However, writers such as Vallance (1996), Sternberg (1995) and Mahoney would argue that the secret in ethical decision-making is to apply the models *in* specific business situations as they arise rather than *to* them. Nonetheless,

> The study of business ethics is not without problems of interpretation. Major ethical philosophies are sometimes in conflict with one another as to how a single issue may be resolved. (Robin and Reidenbach, 1981, p.45)

There is, however, an additional philosophy called ethical relativism which may help.

Ethical relativism

> ❝ Fire burns in Hellas and in Persia; but men's ideas of right and wrong vary from place to place. ❞
>
> (Herodotus, c. 350 BC)

Ethical relativism is the principle that ethical judgements cannot be made independently of the culture in which they are made.

Ethical relativism argues that morality depends on a particular society. There is no absolute ethical standard independent of cultural context. What is right is determined by what a culture or society says is right, so that what is right in one place may be wrong in another.

This view allows management to operate to different standards depending on the culture or country in which they are conducting business. In some countries, bribes are an expected part of business. For companies that operate internationally, ethical relativism is a convenient philosophy. It is especially so when they are competing internationally against companies based in countries with different moral codes. What might be the views of the individual managers who have their own personal ethical views, that may perhaps be more absolute than relative? What constitutes a bribe in business? This issue arises in dramatic ways when major deals for armaments or construction projects are offered to competitive tender from international companies.

Think again about some of the ethical decisions you have already looked at in this chapter. Does ethical relativism help? Would it depend on what country you were in?

It has been suggested that 'a bribe is only a bribe when it is taken as such'. Does ethical relativism help us think about the validity of corporate gift-giving? Some firms consider that it is standard industry practice to exchange gifts and therefore this creates a level playing field – so it cannot be an incentive. Others have a policy that no gift to employees from any other company is acceptable as it may affect employees' judgement.

---

n o t e b o o k   13.8

Can you be too ethical?

Imagine you are the owner of a small business dedicated to operating to the highest ethical standards. Do you still have to:

(a) *bluff* when negotiating the purchase of raw ingredients in order to get a good price for yourselves, and be able to offer a lower price to the customer,

(b) *exaggerate* the demand for your product when selling to retailers to persuade them to stock your product and make your product more easily available to your customers,

(c) *highlight* the benefits of your product when advertising to consumers in order to secure the future of your company, and your employees' jobs?

Do 'ethical' businesses still have to 'play the game' of business (Carr, 1968)? Can a business be ethical when its competitors and suppliers are not?

---

n o t e b o o k   13.9

In your job as a buyer for a multinational company, you receive a gift from one of your minor suppliers at Christmas. It is: (a) a calendar with their brand name on it, (b) a pen set with their brand name on it, (c) chocolates, (d) a bottle of wine, (e) a bottle of whisky, (f) a case of whisky.

Which offer can you accept? If any, what should you do with it? What would stop you accepting these gifts?

Should your employer have a policy which outlines solutions to such ethical problems so as to avoid the variety of approaches which may otherwise develop?

While there is often a corporate sense of right and wrong, it is suggested that business is more comfortable with the notions of accountability and responsibility. The decisions made at the corporate level are placed within the organisational culture, as well as requiring an understanding of social norms and expectations.

This consideration of the rights and wrongs of business should have shown how complex it is to apply ethical reasoning to business problems. Much of ethical decision-making is a question of trade-offs, and it is necessary to have a clear idea of who will be affected by such decision-making. While some businesses declare themselves to be ethical, it is often easier to think of the responsibilities that businesses might have, and to whom they are accountable. This can help make abstract dilemmas more real, and help the decision-making process. It is therefore to the notion of corporate social responsibility (CSR) that we now turn.

13.5 Corporate social responsibility

Social responsibility – it means something, but not always the same thing to everybody. To some it conveys the idea of legal responsibility or liability; to others it means socially responsible behaviour in an ethical sense; to others the meaning transmitted is of 'responsible for' in a causal mode; many simply take it to mean socially conscious or aware; many of those who embrace it most fervently see it as a synonym for legitimacy, in the context of belonging or being 'proper' or 'valid'; a few see it as a sort of fiduciary duty, imposing a higher standard of behaviour on business at large.

(Votaw, 1973)

Corporate social responsibility is still an ill-defined concept as the quotation below indicates. However, a way of gaining some insight is to consider to whom a company is responsible. That corporate decisions have social implications is central to the topic. In order to understand these social implications, those affected need to be identified and the problem considered from their point of view. For example, the answers that you arrived at in the notebooks were probably influenced by the point of view from which you viewed the decision. So we consider corporate responsibility by using the familiar stakeholder analysis.

Stakeholder theory

Stakeholder theory suggests that it is possible to improve decision-making by identifying and considering all individuals or groups who have some significant personal stake or interest in the organisation. This may be too narrow a definition and it may be more useful to think of those who are affected by corporate decision-making:

- Shareholders
- Customers
- Employees
- Suppliers/business associates
- Community

▶ Society
▶ Environment
▶ Future generations

Shareholders

Traditionally, management has assumed that the main concern of shareholders lies in maximising their wealth. This assumption is largely accurate, though with two qualifications. Shareholders will vary in their time-horizon. If they judge performance over the short term they will have no time for considerations of social responsibility. If they take a longer view, they may be willing to consider evidence that managing in a socially responsible way helps long-term profits. The second point is that there is clear evidence (from the growth of ethical unit trusts) that there are some 'ethical investors'. They place social priorities higher than maximising their own personal wealth and are willing to invest in companies that follow clear socially responsible policies.

Customers

Customers expect organisations to provide them with goods and services. Within the specific relationship that is established between individual customers and the organisation, there are many implicit, unstated conditions. There is often an implied assumption about quality, durability, performance, safety and other factors. The Mintel research cited earlier suggests that consumers are nowadays more aware of issues of corporate responsibility.

C A S E   Q U E S T I O N S   1 3 . 5

▶ What did customers of Ford expect of the Pinto at that time?
▶ How would customers today have different expectations?
▶ Does that affect your view of the company's actions?

Employees

As well as gaining employment from an organisation, employees also have a range of implicit work needs such as job security, safe working conditions, the creation of rewarding work, fair treatment and reward as well as esteem and personal development. The area of human resource management has developed to explore the legal as well as ethical implications of a range of issues in the workplace: equal opportunities, promotion practices, employment continuity, remuneration, trade unions, working conditions, training, job enrichment, drug/alcohol abuse, positive discrimination.

Suppliers

Suppliers have expectations of organisations with whom they trade. They expect to be paid in full by the agreed date. Many are now developing much closer long-term relationships with customers (see Chapter 19) and so the range of mutual expectations between the parties is wider and more complex.

The community

The immediate area plays a central part in the creation of the corporation, its reputation and its continued operation. It was recognised earlier that with the creation of large multinational companies the direct link between manufacturers and their local community is not so distinct as in the past. However, the communities in which corporations operate are where their customers and workers live and so remain important.

Society

Society is the broader place in which business operates. The quality of all our lives will depend on how well business accommodates the often conflicting notions of 'profit' and the 'environment'. Under the social responsibility approach, society has the right to sanction business operations, and will voice its concerns if a corporation is not recognising its global responsibilities.

The environment

The environment has, over the past fifteen years, become increasingly common within the corporate agenda, prompted by a consumer interest in the environmental impact of corporate actions, which is now apparent even in the supermarket. However, the level at which recognition and respect for the environment is demonstrated by a corporation varies considerably. The Body Shop International has led the way for many consumers in allowing them to indicate their preference for environmentally-friendly goods. Such companies recognise that at a strategic level 'the consideration of the environment of the organisation without consideration of the impact of the organisation on its environment is a nonsense' (Price, 1994).

Hoechst, the German chemicals company's guidelines on environmental protection

❝ We strive to improve our international competitiveness. Alongside the goal of profitability stand, equally, responsibility for our staff and social acceptance of our business, sparing use of our resources and care of the environment. Our company goals are at one with the ethical values of our culture and society ... At Hoechst, the demands of environmental protection lead to the following principles:

- ▶ **The environment should be polluted as little as possible by our activities.**
- ▶ **We adopt preventive measures: the research department gives due consideration to the environment in the early stages of product development.**
- ▶ **Raw materials are used economically. ❞**

(Hopfenbeck, 1993, p.72)

Migros

❝ Migros Co-operative Society, the largest Swiss retail chain, consists of [over 500] retail stores but also includes its own production works, service branches and charitable foundations. The preservation of the environment is one of the major corporate principles. Migros aims to set an example for the promotion of public health, and so no cigarettes or alcohol are sold. The Migros guidelines:

- ▶ We have enshrined environmental protection in our company goals.
- ▶ Relevant ecological factors are considered at all decision-making levels.
- ▶ The means necessary to achieve our goals are undertaken on the basis of profitability and competitiveness.
- ▶ We support environmental measures which promote general economic development.
- ▶ Our training programmes emphasise general and topical environmental themes. **"**

(Hopfenbeck, 1993, p.256)

_n o t e b o o k   13.10_

Having identified a major expectation of each of these stakeholder groups, can you see potential areas for conflict? What processes would you expect management to use in resolving those conflicts?

Management comes to pay more attention to environmental and other issues as it recognises the links between corporate action and wider implications. This stakeholder approach to business is providing a competitive advantage for companies, as it can enhance corporate reputation, customer loyalty and goodwill, as well as media coverage.

_n o t e b o o k   13.11_

Using the stakeholders listed above, try again to solve Notebook 13.6's dilemma of closing the factory. Whose 'stake' within the company should be given priority above the others? What did you decide for Ford of Europe?

Do you think that Ford, as a global company, has specific local responsibilities or a major responsibility to maintain a profitable company for the good of shareholders, customers and workers worldwide?

Having both attempted these Notebook activities and reconsidered the previous dilemma, you will be aware that the problem in such decision-making is determining not who is affected but whose interests should have

---

NOTICEBOARD Planet Earth

Planet Earth is 4,600 million years old. If we condense this to an understandable concept, the Earth is a 46 year old person.
Not until the age of 42 did the Earth begin to flower.
Dinosaurs appeared when the planet was 45.
Mammals arrived only 8 months ago.

Modern man has been around for FOUR HOURS. The Industrial Revolution began ONE MINUTE AGO
… and during those 60 seconds of biological time, man has made a rubbish tip of paradise.

Source: adapted from _Paradise Lost – Countdown to Destruction_, Greenpeace.

priority. You will probably have found that the groups are not as clearly demarcated as they may at first appear. You may have to divide them again to capture the people with the same stake in the company. Considering the community as one group quickly shows that this can constitute workers, customers, potential customers, the environment and shareholders. These groups can also be subdivided by the specific views or position that they hold, in relation to a specific problem or issue and this can add complexity to the decision-making process. Stakeholders are therefore often split into 'internal' and 'external' to the company, or those that are 'primary' (directly involved or related to the activities of business) and 'secondary', in order to help the corporation determine which group should have priority.

Johnson and Scholes (1997) identify a matrix which can help companies utilise this list of stakeholders. By further analysing them to determine their comparative levels of power and influence, and power and dynamism, it is possible to chart their relative importance to the corporation (see Figure 13.1). This requires three specific judgements to be made:

▶ How likely each stakeholder group is to impress its expectation on the company.
▶ Whether they have the means to do so.
▶ The likely impact of these expectations.

These tools can focus corporate thinking upon the impact of its decision-making and help it recognise the social fall-out from corporate activities. In this way, it can alert a corporation to potential problems and help it formulate suitable strategies to address current responsibility issues.

As the issues from which corporate responsibilities stem are driven by society, this means that they are constantly changing, just as legislation and public opinion continue to change. Social disapproval of some forms of corporate activity is prompting firms to accept a broader view of their responsibilities. This contributes to the evolving nature of corporate responsibilities. For example, while the area of equal opportunities was until recently an ethical concern, it has gained a critical mass, which has resulted in an improved legal reality for many groups who had previously suffered discrimination in the workplace.

---

n o t e b o o k   *13.12*

Brent Spar

The Brent Spar was an oil platform which Shell attempted to dispose of by sinking it in the North Sea. Having sought permission from the UK government, Shell began its operation, but had not expected the environmental activists Greenpeace to mount a campaign to stop them. The company changed its policy and agreed to store and then dismantle the platform.

How would stakeholder analysis have helped Shell to identify the groups of people with which it should have discussed its intentions? Why do you think the company so seriously underestimated the opposition?

While it has been recognised that corporate social responsibility is difficult to isolate, the stakeholder approach to corporate decision-making helps

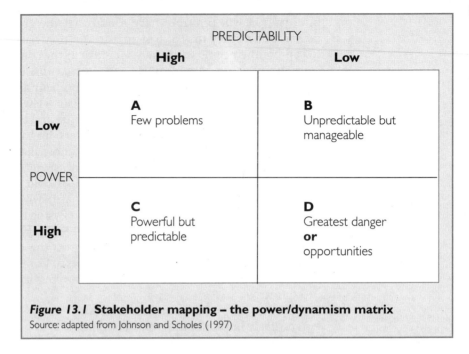

Figure 13.1 Stakeholder mapping – the power/dynamism matrix
Source: adapted from Johnson and Scholes (1997)

identify a central tenet within responsible business practice. Nonetheless, a question still remains: why would, or why should, a company respond to the recognition of its stakeholders and their concerns?

13.6 Why be socially responsible?

While there are an increasing number of high-profile responsible and ethical companies, many still believe that these concerns are outside the role of management. This 'Friedmanite' view was discussed earlier in the chapter and it remains an unresolved debate. Table 13.1 identifies three sets of arguments why companies should act in a socially responsible way and three why they should not. Price (1997) grouped these around the words – should, can and will. They are made up from many arguments within the literature.

On one side are those who argue that corporate social responsibility is good for business. It enhances the public image of the company and may avoid government intervention. For these and several other reasons this group argues that positive policies on social responsibility are in a company's long-term interests. They also point out that business has the resources to pursue such policies and in many cases the shareholders will support some action in this area.

On the opposite side are those who argue that it is not management's job to extend its role into this area. Its role is to do the best for its shareholders which will be reduced if competitiveness is lost by following wider considerations. They argue that such activities lack broad support, and that business is not democratically accountable to the wider public. Moreover, business may not have the skills to deal with these issues so that there may be more rhetoric than action.

Against that background of ideas, management today faces sources of pressure towards a more socially responsible stance. These pressures can be

Table 13.1 **Why companies should or should not act in a socially responsible way**

Should	Should not
▶ Enlightened self-interest (Mintzberg, 1983)	▶ Dilution of business's primary purpose (Davis, 1960)
▶ Sound investment theory (Bowman, 1973)	▶ Subversive (Friedman, 1970)
▶ Long-term self-interest (Davis, 1960)	▶ 'Dangerous, alien and impermissible' (Levitt, 1958)
▶ Viability of business (Davis, 1960)	▶ Hand of government (Shaw, 1991)
▶ Public image (Davis, 1971)	▶ Profit maximisers (Davis, 1971; Friedman, 1970)
▶ Avoidance of government regulation (Davis, 1960; Mintzberg, 1983)	▶ Agency argument (Stone, 1990)
▶ Prevention is better than curing (Davis, 1960)	▶ Role argument (Stone, 1990)
	▶ Weakened competitiveness (Davis, 1960)
	▶ Against the 'rules of the game' (Carr, 1968)
	▶ Imposition of 'taxes' (Friedman, 1970)
	▶ Erosion of state (Friedman, 1970)
	▶ Lack of accountability (Davis, 1960)

Can	Cannot
▶ Shareholder interest (Davis, 1960)	▶ Inept custodian (Shaw, 1991)
▶ Business has the resources (Davis, 1960)	▶ Lack of broad support (Davis, 1960)
	▶ No right to pursue social goals (Mintzberg, 1983)
	▶ Only people have responsibilities (Friedman, 1970)

Will	Will not
▶ Sociocultural norms (Davis, 1960)	▶ Cost of social involvement (Davis, 1960)
▶ Let business try (Davis, 1960)	▶ Lack of social skills (Davis, 1960)
	▶ Lack of personal capabilities (Mintzberg, 1983)
	▶ Rhetoric not action (Mintzberg, 1983)

expressed through consumer boycotts, ethical consumers and the costs of being irresponsible.

Consumer boycotts

Boycotts reflect the active disapproval of society and can generate media interest which then spreads the news of corporate misdemeanour across the globe. They register the displeasure of consumers with the corporation. In 1996 French products were (briefly) boycotted because of the decision of the French government to resume nuclear testing in the South Pacific.

There are examples of boycotts achieving their objectives (such as when Barclays Bank was persuaded during the 1980s that its involvement in South Africa supported apartheid), but they are rare. However, they are no longer the actions of extremists, and consumers are increasingly recognising new outlets for expressing their disappointment with corporate activities, for example, via street protests and road blocks.

Ethical consumers

Ethical consumers are those who take ethical issues into account in deciding what to purchase.

Until legislatory improvements match social concerns, consumer action continues to develop. With an increased access to information relating to the full range of corporate activities, consumer decision-making is altering to include ethical issues. While individual consumers feel strongly about specific issues, *The Ethical Consumer Journal* identifies ten specific areas where customers tend to require specific information:

- ▶ Operating within oppressive regimes
- ▶ Trade union relations
- ▶ Wages and conditions
- ▶ Environment
- ▶ Irresponsible marketing
- ▶ Nuclear power
- ▶ Armaments
- ▶ Animal rights
- ▶ Political donations
- ▶ Boycott calls

Such consumer action is not solely a negative response to corporate activities. There are many shoppers who use their 'ethical purchase votes' (Smith, 1990) to support the actions of companies which are conducting their business responsibly. Café Direct has been the biggest success of 'fairly traded' products. Many other companies are seeing the advantage in being responsible in areas of social concern and are responding to society's demands. For example Reebok and Nike are introducing codes of practice to eliminate child labour in the production of their products, C&A has set up an internal ethical monitoring team, and Sainsbury is developing a programme to support 'fair trade' products (Cowe and Entine, 1996).

Many organisations (Greenpeace, The New Consumer, The Ethical Consumer) are monitoring corporate actions and reporting adverse information widely. The Brent Spar, while a complex scenario, shows why business needs to recognise that society itself is constantly changing. It expects more of business. There are a multitude of stakeholders who now demand information and expect high standards of corporate behaviour. The major oil companies have realised that their contract with society has changed. For example, Shell suffered (briefly) from a consumer boycott across Europe in the summer of 1995. It also experienced some violent acts of 'eco-terrorism'. Irrespective of the merits of this debate, the media has regularly spotlighted the activities of the major oil companies. To address this increased level of negative press, many have responded to these changing social demands and are now developing ethical positions. The Shell UK chairman and chief executive, Chris Fay, accepts that 'We have to consider why trust in companies is declining' (Cowe and Entine, 1996).

n o t e b o o k   *13.13*

Have you ever made a positive or negative purchase decision?

What corporate actions or social issues would prompt you to act?

Cost of being irresponsible

The cost of being irresponsible is now counted in terms of its effect on corporate reputation. Table 13.2 summarises earlier research on the cost to corporations and society of irresponsible corporate activity. Irresponsible corporate behaviour can therefore be seen to have its costs, in terms of loss of reputation, sales and even viability as customer confidence is eroded.

Competitive advantage

There are many companies that have been successful by stating very clearly specific values and following a responsible approach to business. Their activities can prove extremely newsworthy and increase customer awareness and loyalty with little advertising. Such companies have a strategic approach to responsible business practice. Other examples of this strategic approach to responsible business practice include the Co-operative Bank, which was founded upon co-operative principles in the 1870s. It launched its present ethical policy in May 1992, under the following philosophy:

> At the Co-operative Bank, we always remember that it's your money in your account. Our role is simply to take good care of it for you – and not do things with it that you wouldn't do yourself.

Another example is Ben and Jerry's Home-made Ice-cream Company which is based on two principles: 'Business has the responsibility to give back to the community' and 'if it's not fun, why do it?'. The company credo states its intention to 'turn values into value'.

case example The Body Shop campaigns

The Body Shop has used a range of awareness-raising campaigns to spread a social message in response to its recognition of the concerns of stakeholders and the development of social issues within society. These have, over the past twenty years, included: Greenpeace – Save the Whale; Friends of the Earth – Acid Rain; Friends of the Earth – Think Globally, Act Locally; Green Consumer Week; Amnesty International; Friends of the Earth – Ozone or No Zone; Shelter; Aids; Friends of the Earth – Vanishing Countryside; Friends of the Earth – tropical rainforest; Start; Stop the Burning; Ken Saro-wiwa, The Ogoni and Shell Oil; Women's Rights are Human Rights; Domestic violence; Would they do it in Paris – nuclear testing; Against Animal Testing.

These campaigns have been issue-based and relate to the vision that The Body Shop has of its role in society. While many people feel that a company should not be so political or outspoken, such campaigns have established The Body Shop as a major player in the high street, without the need for traditional advertising.

It is possible to see the debate as simply whether a company should, or should not, accept its social and ethical responsibilities. It is clear that it can, and will, where there is an advantage in doing so. The Friedmanite/

Table 13.2 **The costs of corporate failing**

Year	Corporate failing	Cost: human/financial	Penalty/effectiveness
1970s	Production of Ford Pinto	Loss of life $250m	Loss of brand (BT)
1982 1986	Tylenol – product tamper	$50m $240m	Recall Re-establish (B)
1984	Bhopal Union Carbide	2,500 deaths $4,700m	Loss of Indian operation only (P)
1988	Exxon *Valdez* Esso	Environment $7,250m	Loss of consumer accounts (P)
1988	Piper Alpha Occidental	167 deaths $1,400m	Loss of legitimacy in UK alone (P)
1989	Kings Cross	Death $400m	No market substitution
1990	Perrier contamination	$200m	Recall Re-establish (B)
1992	The Guinness Affair	Fraud $295m	Chairman imprisoned – now runs another company
1994	Maxwell pension fraud	$1,650m	Collapse (T)
1995	Barings Bank	Financial viability	Collapse (T) and takeover

T termination   P partial impact   B impact on brand
Sources: Price (1997) derived from Cannon (1994); Harvey (1994); Hartley (1993); SAUS (1993)

corporate social responsibility debate will run, but it is clear that some companies have been able to balance responsibility and corporate success. As Freeman and Gilbert argue:

> The search for excellence and the search for ethics are the same thing ... We must learn to build corporate strategy on a foundation of ethical reasoning, rather than pretending that strategy and ethics are separate. (Freeman and Gilbert, 1988)

 n o t e b o o k   13.14

Colleges and universities also have responsibilities in this area. They are major users of paper and energy. Does your college or university have an environmental policy? Who is responsible for managing it? What environmental and other benefits has it achieved? How does it compare with the environmental policy of a commercial organisation in your area?

From this recognition of the strategic implications of corporate decision-making, and ultimately corporate practice, it has proved possible to articulate the responsibilities of business within society as:

Strategic corporate social responsibility is the awareness, acceptance and management of the implications and effects of all corporate decision-making. (Price, 1997)

Having established that some companies have benefited from their responsible approach to business, it is equally necessary to recognise that some have attempted to incorporate a high degree of ethical behaviour into their corporate actions and failed. Companies accept or incorporate notions of ethical and responsible business in a multitude of different levels. In order to represent this reality of corporate behaviour, Carroll (1991) has created a pyramid of corporate social responsibility which shows the interconnecting levels at which a business can define its responsibilities (Figure 13.2).

Ethical intent and ethical action

The gap between ethical intent and ethical action has caused many corporations problems. During the 1980s, many companies leapt onto the 'green bandwagon' and declared their products to be 'green' without specifying in what way. This encouraged consumer spend on these goods, until many were exposed as misleadingly labelled or as making exaggerated claims. This destroyed consumer confidence and has since resulted in improved legislation to prevent such false claims. The incidents raised the question of whether any improvement in corporate action is to be seen as worthwhile or whether some are ill-conceived and partial efforts. For example, does it make sense for a cosmetics company to launch an environmentally friendly shampoo in a non-biodegradable bottle. Is it sufficient that the product is (marginally) improved or must the packaging and also the manufacturing process be changed before any significant effects can be seen?

Ethical audits

The variety of the methods used to demonstrate a specific level of responsibility have been explained throughout this chapter, through the consideration of business approaches of different companies. A few ethical companies are prepared to audit their social activities, just as they do the financial aspects of the company. Vallance (1996) argues that an ethical audit contributes three things:

▶ It makes the business articulate its ethical priorities.
▶ It will make the business aware of its success and shortcomings.
▶ It will allow feedback and continuous improvement.

In this way, an ethical audit can be an effective tool in the creation of a responsible company. Ben and Jerry's and The Body Shop were two of the first companies to conduct an ethical audit of their activities. In exploring their activities against the expectations of a variety of stakeholder groups, they were able both to judge whether they really were being ethical and responsible in the operation of their businesses, and to build upon the success of their approach. Many companies now include environmental audits as part of their standard reporting procedures.

Such audit procedures can help isolate the central ethical decision-making of a company. By using a decision-making process which actually considers the ethical dimensions of business problems, a more robust ethical answer should emerge. Such processes can help a company think through

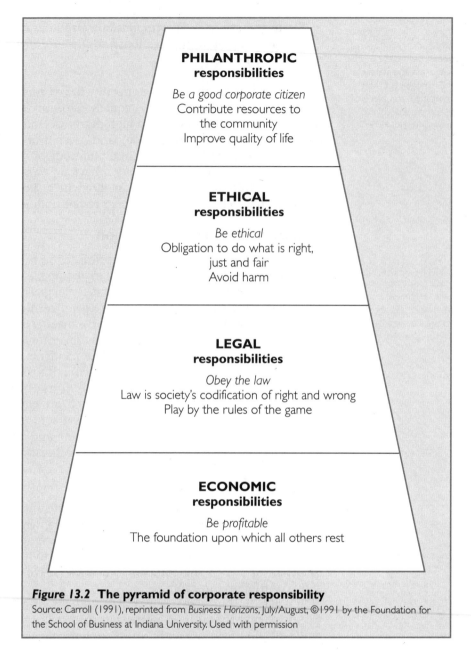

Figure 13.2 The pyramid of corporate responsibility

Source: Carroll (1991), reprinted from *Business Horizons*, July/August, ©1991 by the Foundation for the School of Business at Indiana University. Used with permission

the implications of its actions and identify potential areas of concern. An example of such a process is Elaine Sternberg's (1994) ethical decision-making model (EDM):

▶ Stage 1   Clarify the question
▶ Stage 2   Determine its relevance for this business
▶ Stage 3   Identify the circumstantial constraints
▶ Stage 4   Assess the available options

A further practical audit for checking the impact of any proposed business programme would see the company consider the following (Jones, 1996):

▶ Community health
▶ Individual health

▶ Physical health
▶ Relationship health
▶ Spiritual health
▶ Internal organisational health

As with all decision-making, it is necessary to monitor and measure the outcomes of major actions to see if they are having the effects intended. This implies an iterative approach when applying the EDM. Corporate actions have wide implications. Those with corporate power will decide how fully those implications are considered. They may choose to follow the Friedmanite philosophy, or they may choose to take account of wider interests, acknowledging the point made by Davis (1975):

> In the long run, those who do not use power in a manner which society considers responsible will tend to lose it.

13.7 Recap

Content agenda

Choices about the objectives of the organisation are ethical decisions whether or not the managers taking them think of them that way. This chapter has shown how ethical perspectives can be used in business decisions. Doing so does not lead to a triumph of ethics over business but the integration of ethical practice into business. Deciding objectives and planning how to achieve them inevitably requires trade-offs between different interests. The conventional practice is to emphasise the economic imperative. Stakeholder analysis suggests that other perspectives are equally legitimate. The difficulty is that they are less easy to measure, and so can be diminished in a culture in which powerful players choose to adopt the convention of short-term quantitative performance measures.

Some managers now recognise that their actions have widespread, often unintended, results (as indicated by the non-linear models discussed in Chapter 2). Some also recognise that they have wider social responsibilities that are not necessarily incompatible with securing an acceptable return for shareholders. A few have shown that staff can be highly motivated by association with a business that has wider aims than just delivering value to shareholders. In that way they can do both. There is potential competitive advantage to be gained from such responsible corporate behaviour, as well as penalties to pay for irresponsible corporate action (boycotts, loss of customer loyalty or corporate reputation).

Process agenda

Stakeholder theory can identify those who will be affected by corporate actions and help manage the responsibilities of corporate action. These will have different interests, and even non-corporate stakeholders will not always share environmental aims. Many traders and other local businesses have supported motorways and airport extensions against environmental protestors (possibly ignoring the long-term implications of having to live in their surrounding communities). Devising and implementing policies that are accepted as more socially responsible will reflect the use of both

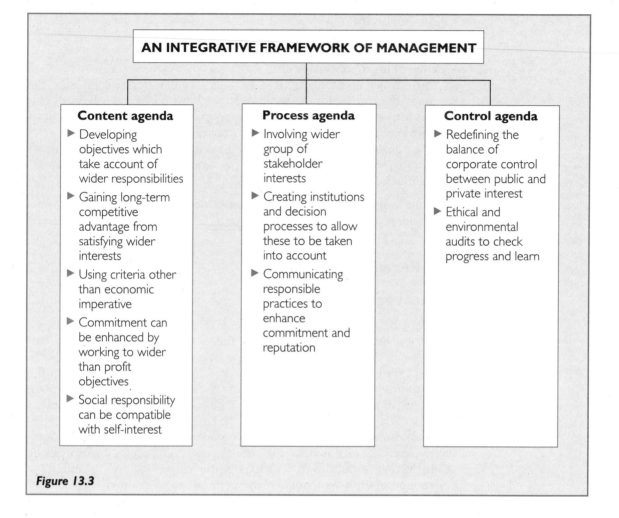

AN INTEGRATIVE FRAMEWORK OF MANAGEMENT

Content agenda
- ▶ Developing objectives which take account of wider responsibilities
- ▶ Gaining long-term competitive advantage from satisfying wider interests
- ▶ Using criteria other than economic imperative
- ▶ Commitment can be enhanced by working to wider than profit objectives
- ▶ Social responsibility can be compatible with self-interest

Process agenda
- ▶ Involving wider group of stakeholder interests
- ▶ Creating institutions and decision processes to allow these to be taken into account
- ▶ Communicating responsible practices to enhance commitment and reputation

Control agenda
- ▶ Redefining the balance of corporate control between public and private interest
- ▶ Ethical and environmental audits to check progress and learn

Figure 13.3

interpersonal and institutional sources of influence. Management will include developing decision-making processes and institutions that can take account of interests not usually part of such processes. Communications has been a powerful weapon in the hands of those presssing for more socially responsible business. It has been used equally effectively by some companies to promote their environmental education message.

Control agenda

At the macro level, the issue of corporate social responsibility is linked to the degree of control which society has over business instituions. The Friedmanite position limits this to some essential legal and financial ground-rules within which managers should be able to act as they see fit. The social responsibility position argues that these boundaries are negotiable and that society may want to protect a wider set of interests by setting more precise standards of business behaviour.

Some companies that have introduced environmental or social policies have also developed appropriate ways of auditing the results of these policies. These cannot only check the effectiveness of the policy but also make the policy open to external scrutiny. They also help organisations and the wider interest groups to learn from these experiences. Figure 13.3 summarises these points.

PART CASE QUESTIONS

▶ What was the nature of the social responsibility that Glenlight Shipping had to the remote communities that it served? How did government policy and action affect this? What arguments did the government use to withdraw the subsidy?

▶ A major issue for Glenlight was to secure government support for its operations in remote areas. What argument, from an ethical standpoint, could Glenlight have used to counter government policies?

▶ Was Glenlight a socially responsible enterprise?

13.8 Review questions

1 Identify two recent examples of corporate philanthropy. What are the benefits to the donor and the recipient?
2 List the reasons why you think 'business ethics' is important to the success of firms.
3 Summarise the Friedman and social contract positions on social responsibility with an example of each being applied.
4 List three major ethical issues facing management at the present time, and give reasons for your choices.
5 Describe in your own terms each of the four schools of ethical thought and illustrate each with an example of how it has been used to justify a decision.
6 Outline the ways in which the consumer can affect business practice, and decide whether this is effective or not.
7 List the stakeholders in the Pinto case and prioritise them in order to justify the decision to manufacture.
8 What could Ford have done to promote the communication of these difficult issues to higher management?
9 Who should determine a company's level of acceptance of social responsibilities?
10 Compare the channels of communication that can be used to explain corporate action to stakeholders.
11 Are Ben and Jerry's, The Body Shop International and the Co-operative Bank responsible companies or are they operating a form of enlightened self-interest?
12 'Ethics is obedience to the unenforceable.' Do you agree?

Further reading

Good introductions to the main issues in business ethics are provided by Chrysalides and Kale (1993) and by Hartley (1993). A European perspective can be gained in Harvey (1994). Hopfenbeck (1993) focuses on environmental issues and includes many examples and cases (though a little uncritically). The most stimulating book published recently is Vallance (1996).

W Website addresses

The Body Shop   http://www.the-body-shop.com

Co-operative Bank   http://www.co-operativebank.co.uk
The Co-operative Bank Website details the company's ethical policy, how it tries to balance profit and principles. You can also see the current mission statement and the ecology mission statement.

Marks & Spencer   http://www.marks-and-spencer.co.uk
Sainsbury   http://www.sainsburys.co.uk
The Marks & Spencer and Sainsbury sites give information on socially responsible and environmental initiatives adopted by the companies.

part four

Organising the business

4

Introduction

Part Four switches our attention to the question of how management tries to create the structure within which people work. Alongside planning the direction of the business, managers need to consider how they will achieve the direction chosen. A fundamental component of that is the form of the organisation within which people work. This is a highly uncertain area of management as there are conflicting views about the kind of structure to have and how much influence structure has on performance.

Chapter 14 describes the main elements of organisation structure and the contrasting forms they take. It also looks at the related idea of organisational culture – a less tangible but equally influential factor in organisational performance. Chapter 15 deals with one aspect of an organisation's structure: its human resource management policies. These are intended to ensure that employees work towards organisational objectives.

Management wants to know what kind of structure will best serve the organisational goals. Early studies attempted to find relatively universal solutions. This was displaced by contingency approaches which argue that the appropriate form of structure or human resource management policy depends on the particular situation. More recently still, others have argued that there is a greater political element in these choices. Such writers argue that management often does things for reasons other than the rational pursuit of organisational goals. These issues are examined in Chapter 16 which also describes some of the newer forms of organisation which are becoming possible as a result of developments in information technology. Finally, in Chapter 17 some of the practical issues that management faces in implementing change are explored. The chapter also presents some examples of the guidelines which managers can use to take them through the process.

Deciding what to do is part of the management problem. Putting those plans into effect is another matter altogether, requiring a different set of tools. Some of these are laid out.

The Part Case which is relevant to the topics introduced is an account of structure and change at Save the Children Fund, a large international charity.

Save the Children Fund

Background

Save the Children Fund (SCF) was founded in 1919 as a voluntary organisation to assist the starving and destitute in Europe. Its 1923 charter committed the organisation to the rights of the child irrespective of race, creed or colour. SCF still describes itself as a 'rights-based', value-led children's charity. SCF is a large international charity working in over fifty countries including the UK, in partnership with governments, non-governmental organisations and local communities. It provides health care, child welfare, community development and education services. It also undertakes training, consultancy, research and 'advocacy' (apolitical) activities.

In 1996, Charity Aid Foundation listed SCF sixth in a list of the top 500 fund-raising charities. In financial year 1994/95, SCF had a total income of £91.9m, expenditure of £91.8m and net assets of £46.8m. Voluntary income accounted for 45 per cent of the total; government and EEC grants for 34 per cent, and the rest came from sources such as rent and investments (Pharoah, 1996, p.114).

SCF is a mature and established organisation. It employs about 1,140 paid staff and over 20,000 volunteers. Its structure and reporting relationships are relatively clear. It is well established in its area of activity and has been described as the market leader amongst agencies working in the Third World (Bruce, 1994, p.265). Maturity has implications for an organisation. It often means increased size, more formal structures, more managerial direction and control. It is likely to have developed a strong and distinctive style.

As well as growing, SCF had also diversified during the 1980s, especially into a variety of overseas aid programmes. These were designed to meet the needs of children in particular areas. It was difficult for the centre to control these because of geographical distance and varying circumstances. Staff working on the programmes in the field needed to be able to respond to local conditions.

Until 1995, SCF was managed from London by the 'director-general' who reported to the elected council. There was a team of six functional departmental heads: Overseas, Fund-raising, UK and Europe (UKEP), Public Affairs, Personnel and Administration, and Finance.

The operations departments (Overseas, Fund-raising and UKEP) were subdivided geographically into semi-autonomous divisions which worked within a corporate policy and practice framework. They were expected to reflect organisational and departmental priorities but not be constrained by them. The service departments worked in London with some linking posts in divisional offices.

At senior management level there was considerable use of procedures, manuals, rules and memos to control steady-state activities. Staff were expected to work to the guidelines laid down. There was also a formal strategic planning process to shape the way forward for SCF.

In the field, control was looser. Project-based staff were nurtured and supported by line managers who held responsibilities for service delivery and innovation. Authority was delegated and the staff were expected to use their initiative. Management sought the views of staff in reaching decisions, in public debates and in local management committees. Staff were typically professionals who could probably earn more in other organisations but had chosen to work for SCF. Practice was controlled through regular review of agreed aims and objectives, regular meetings and fieldwork practice guidelines. Common commitment was felt towards SCF's mission and values, which helped build a common outlook among field staff and to de-emphasise conflict.

Within the UK the organisation structure can be set out as shown in Figure 1, though the pattern varied slightly within each division.

Organisational charts show four levels between director-general (CEO) and

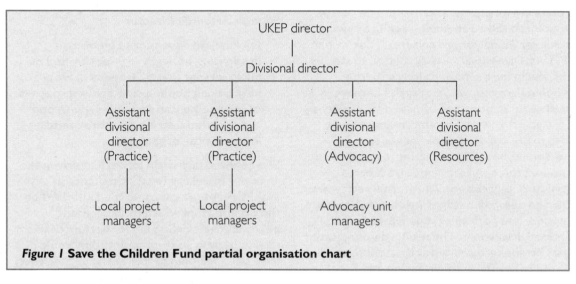

Figure 1 **Save the Children Fund partial organisation chart**

fieldworker. SCF displayed a number of problems commonly associated with this structure, and more general communication difficulties across departments, and between the centre and the divisions.

Until the late 1980s, Personnel and Administration was fairly peripheral to the day-to-day work and management of the divisions. The divisional administration officer had a closely defined set of responsibilities, policing and advising project leaders in the field on financial, personnel and administrative matters. He or she also provided technical support and advice to the divisional management team.

The onset of change

From the late 1980s, senior managers in SCF became aware that the stable professional and fund-raising environments within which the organisation had been operating were changing. There was more competition for work and finance. The solutions adopted were to try to increase efficiency, effectiveness and quality.

The early 1990s saw a number of milestones in the history of SCF. A mission statement was agreed in 1990:

> Save the Children works to achieve lasting benefits for children within the communities in which they live by influencing policy and practice based on

its experience and study in different parts of the world. In all its work Save the Children endeavours to make a reality of children's rights.

In 1992, SCF issued a statement of organisational values and characteristics, the values being that SCF needs to be:
- A developmental organisation
- An organisation which values people
- Authoritative and influential
- In control
- A learning organisation

Corporate goals were agreed in 1993. That same year, BCG Consultants were engaged to review the management structure and assist in the development of a strategic plan. SCF occupied first place in the Charities Aid Foundation league.

Thereafter the situation began to change. Within six months SCF was in a 'cutback' situation as finance became scarcer. In May 1994, the Overseas (Programmes) director replaced the previous director-general. In an internal memo to staff, he referred to 'strategic drift' and advised that senior management would now head up a corporate planning process in which all staff could expect to participate.

Between 1994 and 1996 the first and second tiers of senior managers were restructured, along with reorganisation of departments to foster the development of a corporate culture. A new post of human resources director was created. The person appointed talked about the need to develop a stronger management culture. A document, 'Future Directions', was circulated to staff as the vision for the future along with the 'Global Programme Strategy'. There were staff redundancies and programme closures.

Against this background, management also made considerable changes in the personnel, now HRM, function, ostensibly to support the new corporate strategy structure and culture. An internal review was carried out in two stages, involving a sample of users and personnel staff in a series of focused discussions. The results demonstrated that Personnel operated at the administrative level, facilitating administration and recruitment work. It focused on the day-to-day management of the organisation.

A new structure, splitting human resources from administration was agreed and implemented by SCF directors. It was intended to meet organisational needs in the areas of strategy development and forward planning, and to provide a generalist service to UK divisions/HQ departments and to maintain a cross-SCF perspective on employment practice issues. A new 'management culture' would be encouraged through the delivery of training on employment practice, and the provision of support and advice on staff management issues. The proposal was framed within the terms of 'business need' and a more 'central', 'integrated' role for Personnel within strategy formulation. Personnel staff would remain at HQ and not be decentralised to the divisions. There is an expressed commitment to management development. In 1996 these changes were consolidated by expanding what was now to be the Human Resources department headed by a human resource director.

The aftermath

In 1996 several staff were interviewed to gather their views on these and other changes. Some quotations follow.

Human Resource Director

I believe we have moved on from firefighting to begin to offer the kind of HRM service that SCF needs ... we are now talking about a strategic approach to corporate human resources – with one organisational strategy ... the overall jigsaw for the organisation.

She believed two main forces had driven the change – to ensure legal compliance in employment practice and the ambitions of the organisation which (management believed) the existing personnel function could not deliver. Implementation 'could have been handled better at the organisation level, but the change had to happen first and fast to support the rest of the change'. The new structure would be strong enough to support and develop management skills and the management of culture, driven by what is best for the organisation as a whole.

A divisional director

She believed that the new HRM function was viewed as a 'key aspect of SCF's future strategic success' as the function had increased probably sixfold in size since the early 1990s, the head of personnel had been given director status, the department had been retitled and had a new hierarchy. She believed that the main motivation for change had been 'internal' and 'reactive', perhaps for 'efficiency gains'. She wondered how much external environmental analysis there had been, although awareness of the changing competitive environment had been mentioned. She believed the drive for change had come from the directors' group and the head of personnel. She had not been involved in the design of the new Function.

Fieldwork seems to have been somewhat marginalised, which may lead to an isolationist view of human resources, and an isolationist view of organisational needs. There needs to be other perceptions on this. The management of the changes seems to have been done in rather a 'top-down' way. There is some sense of things needing to be 'driven' which is a bit contradictory to the overall ethos of the organisation. Over the last few years, gradual changes have led to a greater feeling of ambiguity, and more arm's-length contact. There is a tension between balancing the needs for flexibility and consistency, particularly if the latter means the need for rules.

The change process was not experienced as 'overt' by the field:

It would be difficult to identify the landmarks. The rise seems political, the change process 'hard', the stakeholders 'informed'. I have not been aware of much consultation.

A project leader

Policy ensures the payment of appropriate rates and equality of opportunity, but that doesn't necessarily make the manager's job any easier ... the salary structure creates problems – it costs too much now to employ certain groups of people on a sessional basis, e.g. young people. The

local rate would be more appropriate. It costs a great deal to recruit staff – local recruitment would be cheaper and more appropriate. Decisions now take a long time to turn round and the communication is sometimes difficult.

Two or three years ago the divisions were moving away from the centre and now it seems they are moving back. More control by the top tier of management. I'm only aware of a 'culture change' taking place from other people at more senior level. If there is a culture change taking place it's not impacting at local level. We work to the organisation mission, but being a partnership project makes a difference as our immediate contacts are with the social work department and the young people with whom we work.

The significance of the partnership project is that the project is partly financed by the local authority social work department and run in partnership with them. So there is a joint advisory group of the two organisations. The project must also comply with the local authority's monitoring requirements.

PART CASE QUESTIONS

There will be some questions about the case in the chapters which follow. Before starting work on them make some notes in response to these questions about the case.

▶ There is evidence in the case about different styles of management within different parts of the organisation. How would you describe them, and why did these differences arise? What problems might these different approaches raise for people in SCF?

▶ How have people in SCF been affected by (a) external events and changes, (b) actions by other people in SCF?

▶ What hints are there about the way the change process has been managed?

▶ What hints are there about the results of the change process?

Organisation structure and culture

AIM

To provide the terms and concepts that will help readers to understand and evaluate the structure and culture of an organisation.

OBJECTIVES

By the end of your work on this chapter you should be able to outline the concepts below in your own terms and:

1 Outline why structure influences performance

2 Illustrate the interaction between an organisation's main components

3 Compare alternative forms of organisation structure

4 Describe and illustrate the main forms of specialisation, and their advantages and disadvantages

5 Describe and illustrate the main forms of co-ordination

6 Compare systematically the structures of departments or organisations using ideas from the chapter

7 Describe the main dimensions of organisational culture which can be observed

8 Give examples of Charles Handy's four varieties of organisational culture

Contracting Services

The company manufactured and serviced refrigeration equipment for major supermarkets throughout the UK. Although operating throughout Europe, this case deals only with the UK contracting business which offers a maintenance and repair service.

In early 1997 there were 21 service branches and 250 service engineers. Each branch employed about 5 administrative and supervisory staff. There was overcapacity in the refrigeration industry, leading to severe competition from small suppliers, who were often able to charge less than national companies. Costs were high partly because of the branch network which did, however, provide a local point of contact with customers.

The typical process was that the manager of a supermarket called the nearest branch to report an equipment fault. The telephone operator in the branch passed the message to one of the field engineers. The engineer visited the supermarket and, if the parts were in the van, made the repair. If not, he returned to the branch or visited a wholesaler to collect the parts. When the job was complete the engineer passed the paperwork to the branch on his next visit for processing. Invoices and performance monitoring data were prepared in the branch from this paperwork.

As well as high branch costs (about £1.4m a year excluding the cost of the engineers), customer feedback indicated that customers regarded the service as inconsistent between branches, and by time of day. Branch managers varied in the performance data they provided to customers (who were usually part of national chains). After office hours, calls were passed to answering machines and then to an outside agency who contacted standby engineers. Inventory was hard to locate.

One bright spot was that the company had recently won a facilities management contract with a major supermarket group. This involved staff dealing with not only refrigeration, but also with all other mechanical facilities in 40 of the company's 200 stores. Facilities management is an attractive direction in which to go as small competitors are less likely to be able to offer a comprehensive facilities service. Management is keen to make this project work. One condition of the contract was that the company set up a call centre to handle all calls from this group of stores wherever they were located. The company had been considering introducing a call centre for its main business but had not yet reached a decision.

Call centres are based on linking computer technology and telephone switchboards. Computer telephone integration (CTI) systems allow information about the caller to appear on the screen as the agent answers the call. A single centre usually takes all calls for an organisation or service, irrespective of the location of the caller or the service staff. Call centre staff normally work within well defined procedures supported by the technology.

CASE QUESTIONS

► How much choice does management have regarding the decision to introduce a call centre?

► What issues would management need to consider if it does so?

14.1 Introduction

This chapter introduces the following ideas:
- Structure
- Formal structure
- Informal structure
- Division of tasks – vertical and horizontal
- Horizontal specialisation
- Centralisation and decentralisation
- Functional, product, geographical and matrix structures
- Co-ordination of tasks
- Organisation chart
- Span of control
- Scalar chain
- Power culture
- Role culture
- Task culture
- Person culture

When an owner-manager is running a business, he or she decides what tasks are to be done and co-ordinates them. If the enterprise grows, the need to create some form of structure usually becomes apparent. The entrepreneur divides the overall task between people, even if the division is flexible and informal. There is then a need to co-ordinate their separate activities to avoid duplication and confusion. This is done quite informally in a small operation where direct person-to-person communication is easy.

The question of how best to divide and co-ordinate tasks will regularly arise as the organisation continues to grow. Unless staff are clear about who is responsible for which tasks and how they should co-ordinate their work, there will be chaos. In some cases this may not matter much, and there are people who enjoy being surrounded by amiable muddle. But it usually obstructs the delivery of goods or services, and some degree of structure is essential if an organisation is to deliver acceptable performance.

A poor structure also damages the commitment of employees. Structures give signals to people about what others expect them to do. If these signals correctly match the needs of the business, both performance and the rewards available for staff will be good. If the structure gives confusing signals or encourages actions which are unproductive, performance and rewards will suffer. If there is confusion over who is to do what, staff will be obstructed. If communications are poor, people will duplicate or overlook work. Problems will grow if the people who need to make a decision are concentrating on other tasks. People will usually be less motivated if the structure means they have boring and repetitive jobs.

Structures also reflect and shape the distribution of power and influence. Chapter 5 described the sources of organisational power, which included access to information and resources. Such access reflects the relative power of organisational players. One tactic for those seeking to build their power base is to work on the organisation's structure. They may use existing power bases to ensure that new or existing departments report to them. They hope this will give them more information about what is going on and more resources they can use to influence others.

Managers are continually adjusting the structure of their organisations in small ways and occasionally in very big ways. There are several examples of this dynamism in the ambulance service case (Chapter 7) such as increasing the responsibility of local managers and combining the functions of separate functions. It is usually misleading to talk of the structure of a complete organisation. Large organisations have many distinct parts that often have different structural forms. This chapter introduces some ideas that help to reveal more clearly the shape of an organisation.

14.2 Models of organisation

Everybody is part of an organisation of some sort and has an interest in many others. Each has a unique history and future. To understand them and compare them, some tools are required. One tool is a definition which accurately and briefly describes what an organisation is. Another is a model that realistically represents the common components of organisations and the links between them. Definitions and models are themselves abstractions from reality. They serve a purpose if they enable real organisations to be compared and pictures of them to be gained which are more useful than if they were described without any common framework. Two early models are presented here, and then our definition and model.

The Leavitt diamond

One of the most enduring and widely used models of organisation was offered by Harold Leavitt (1965). In the early days of the academic study of organisations he proposed that, for all their unique variety, organisations in essence consisted of four elements, summed up in the Leavitt diamond (Figure 14.1).

He explained each of these in terms similar to those used below, and stressed the links between them – that a change in one would have consequences for the others. If management installs new equipment (a change in technology) this is likely to affect the people using it (a change in people). The implication was that management would need to manage these knock-on

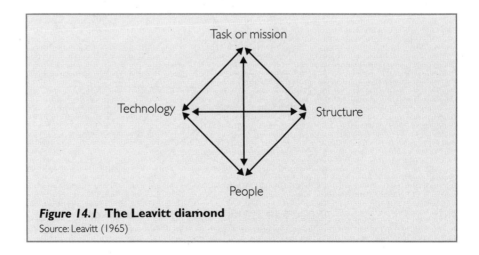

Figure 14.1 The Leavitt diamond
Source: Leavitt (1965)

effects (as well as any consequential effects on structure and mission), not just the initial change in equipment.

▶ Describe Contracting Services using Leavitt's model. Do this by noting down each of the elements, and against each writing a few words that summarise that aspect of the organisation. Then consider how a change in the technology would be likely to affect the other elements.

The McKinsey 7-S model

You are likely to meet a similar device known as the McKinsey 7-S model that Peters and Waterman (1982) introduced – see Figure 14.2.

These models remain useful. Developments in thinking about management since they were first offered, and some aspects of the approach being taken in this book, support a further version. One difference from Leavitt's model is that a distinction is made between objectives and the business processes used to achieve them (he combined mission and tasks). Another is the addition of the dimensions of culture and power as these are now much more prominent features of management discussion than they were in the 1960s. The main change from the 7-S framework is the inclusion of power as an explicit element. This book has taken a deliberately pluralist perspective.

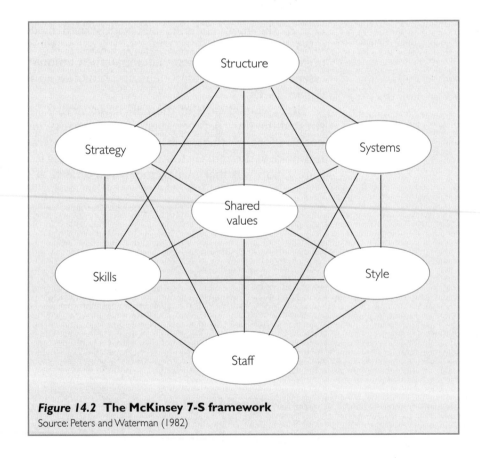

Figure 14.2 The McKinsey 7-S framework
Source: Peters and Waterman (1982)

The Peters and Waterman model gives prominence to the idea of shared values. While these can be important, this book gives greater prominence to another reality of organisational life, namely the relative power of the parties, and includes shared values within culture. On that basis, we offer our definition of organisation as consisting of people trying to influence others to achieve certain objectives that create wealth or well-being through a variety of processes, technologies, structures and cultures. Our integrative model is set out in Figure 14.3. The elements of organisation, as they inter-relate in the model, are:

> **Objectives** Symbolically at the centre of the model are the objectives that the members are seeking to achieve through their work activities. Sometimes referred to as purposes or goals, these represent some future desired state of the organisation, or a part of it.

> **Business processes** These are the groups of activities that people and technologies perform in an organisation to achieve objectives. They include processes for designing products, receiving orders, making the product, delivering, receiving payment and many more. People work together to transform raw materials and other inputs into a desired outcome.

> **Technology** This consists of all the physical facilities that people use to transform inputs into useful outputs. It includes buildings, machinery, offices, computers, telecommunication links and information systems.

> **People** This refers mainly to those who are members of the organisation in some capacity, contributing their skills, knowledge and commitment to its work. It may include people from outside the organisation as well as regular employees, if they influence performance.

> **Power** As was argued in Chapters 1 and 5, power relationships are central to understanding management. They matter when management becomes a separate activity from the task itself and so becomes institutionalised in organisation. Some writers examine the effects on management/staff relations of the balance of power between classes in the wider society. Others examine how individuals can increase their power over those above them in the hierarchy.

> **Structure** The way in which the broad work of the organisation is divided and co-ordinated. Organisation charts show this visually. There are also informal arrangements that cut across the formal chart and which can have an equally important effect on performance.

> **Culture** A less tangible idea than the others, many managers now see culture as a significant tool to help them meet their objectives. Organisational members develop particular ways of working which can in turn influence the way other members, including new staff, deal with their tasks and with each other.

Organisations consist of people trying to influence others to achieve certain objectives that create wealth or well-being through a variety of processes, technologies, structures and cultures.

CASE QUESTIONS 14.2

> Review the analysis you made of Contracting Services using Leavitt's model. Revise or add to it by using the model in Figure 14.3 as a guide for your analysis.

Definitions and frameworks of this sort help to analyse organisational situations. Given some performance problem, they suggest topics and areas

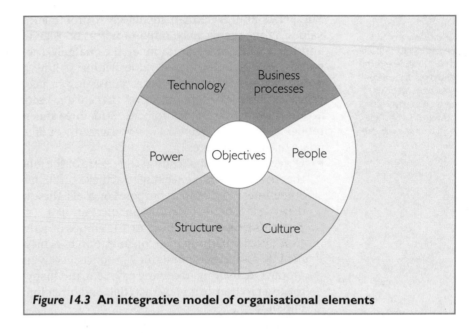

Figure 14.3 An integrative model of organisational elements

to examine. They may help in trying to understand the situation, and to diagnose possible causes. What happens to the elements will also be affected by events in the system's environment such as financial conditions, broader company policies and market changes. The elements shown in Figure 14.3 are part of a whole. The essential point is that they make up a system, so that a change in one affects the others. The elements interact, so that it is unwise to consider one without also taking account of consequential (or sometimes unrelated) changes in the others. If people anticipate these knock-on effects, they are less likely to meet unexpected consequences, and more likely to produce an acceptable solution.

Some of these elements have been dealt with elsewhere in the book – power in Chapter 5, objectives in Chapter 10, business processes and technology in Chapters 19 and 20 respectively. So here the focus is on the remaining ones – structure and culture. By setting out this framework here, the intention is to emphasise the theme of interaction between the elements. Structure and culture do not exist in isolation. They are two elements affecting, and affected by, the rest of the system. With the systems model these elements can be regarded as subsystems within the complete organisational system.

14.3 Dimensions of structure

What is structure?

Pugh and Hickson (1989) discussed structure in these terms:

> Regularities in activities such as task allocation, supervision and co-ordination are developed. Such regularities constitute an organisation's structure, and the fact that these activities can be arranged in various ways means that organisations can have differing structures. (p.4)

'The structure of an organisation [is] the sum total of the ways in which it divides its labour into distinct tasks and then achieves co-ordination among them.'
(Mintzberg, 1989)

Formal structure is the official guidelines, documents or procedures setting out how the organisation's activities are divided and co-ordinated. Informal structure is the undocumented relationships between members of the organisation that inevitably emerge as people adapt systems to new conditions and satisfy personal and group needs.

This usefully brings out the sense of structure as something that develops over time, rather than something fixed. It also alludes to the notions of allocating and then co-ordinating work. Mintzberg (1989) captures even more explicitly the parallel activities of dividing and co-ordinating work and we use his definition:

> The structure of an organisation [is] the sum total of the ways in which it divides its labour into distinct tasks and then achieves co-ordination among them.

Pugh indicates that structures are infinitely variable and this chapter will illustrate that variety. We consider both formal and informal structures.

All organisations have both formal and informal structures. In part they arise because the conditions in which they work are continually changing. However good the formal structure, situations arise where people have to ignore or adapt the rules to get things done. They learn more efficient ways of doing things that then become habitual within the team or department – and until they or someone else revises the formal system, the two will be out of line. Informal structures also arise when the formal structure does not satisfy some human needs. Friendships develop across department lines, which then provide new and unofficial communication channels. These then allow work information or exciting gossip to move rapidly around the organisation, quite apart from the formal system. The balance between formal and informal structures is a feature to remember throughout the discussion. Both exist and can either undermine or support the achievement of objectives.

A final introductory point is that the definition does *not* include only those tasks that the organisation's own employees perform. It also includes tasks done beyond the organisation which its staff nevertheless co-ordinates. Many activities traditionally done within organisations are now done by other firms, with the independent enterprises working closely together. This blurs the traditional boundaries between organisations, a theme discussed towards the end of the chapter.

Basic structure and operating mechanisms

The basic structure of an organisation describes how tasks are divided and co-ordinated. This is what we see if we look at an organisation chart. When people join a department or take on a particular job within the structure, they are being given a fairly clear signal about what they should do. The director of marketing is expected to deal with issues in marketing, not finance.

---

n o t e b o o k   1 4 . 1

How is your college or university structured? Focus on the parts most directly involved in delivering your education. How have the various parts of the task been divided up? Are all the teaching staff you see in one department or in several? Do you have a separate management library or computing suite or share a wider facility? Answers to such questions reflect how the overall task has been divided.

The operating mechanisms reinforce the signal from the basic structure. These are policies on matters such as recruitment and selection, career development, appraisal and reward. They are discussed fully in Chapter 15. They send signals to employees about what is rewarded, who is recruited and what kinds of career moves will be rewarding. The expectation is that the signals will encourage behaviour in line with objectives, but this is not always the actual result.

The organisation chart

The organisation chart shows the main departments and senior positions in an organisation and the reporting relations between them.

The usual way to start examining the structure of an organisation is to look at the organisation chart. This is a diagram showing the main departments and more senior positions within the organisation. Lines link senior executives to the other departments or people for whom they are responsible. It shows to whom each department or division reports. So the chart shows four points about an organisation's structure:

▶ **Tasks**   Taken as a whole the chart shows the major tasks or activities which the organisation undertakes.
▶ **Subdivisions**   It also shows in varying degrees of detail how those main activities have been further divided among members of the organisation.
▶ **Levels**   The management hierarchy is clearly visible, and the reporting links at each level.
▶ **Lines of authority**   The lines of authority (linking the boxes) show who has formal authority over whom.

Such charts are always changing as managers adjust the structure. They can provide a convenient summary of the current formal allocation of tasks and show who is responsible for what. The danger to be aware of is that they do not show the many informal patterns of work that are part of organisational life. However, it is becoming possible, using advanced computer software, to produce accurate pictures of these informal communication patterns to supplement the formal picture.

Managers refer to 'tall' or 'flat' organisation structures. Tall structures or hierarchies are those in which there are many layers of management between the chief executive and the operating staff. This implies that managers supervise a relatively small number of subordinates – and are therefore able to keep a close watch on what they are doing. A flat hierarchy is the opposite. Managers here have more people reporting to them, implying that subordinates will have more freedom to make decisions on their initiative. Those at the lower levels will have needed to take on more responsibilities from their managers, to allow them to supervise the larger number of subordinates. Figure 14.4 shows the two forms.

The span of control

The span of control is the number of subordinates reporting directly to the person above them in the hierarchy.

The span of control refers to the number of subordinates that any one manager can supervise. Joan Woodward's classic study of 100 firms in Essex found great variety between them in the number of subordinates supervised (Woodward, 1965). The number of people reporting directly to the chief executive ranged from 2 to 18, with the median span of control being 6. The average span of control of the first line supervisors varied from 10 to 90, with a median of 37. Woodward explained the variation by the technological

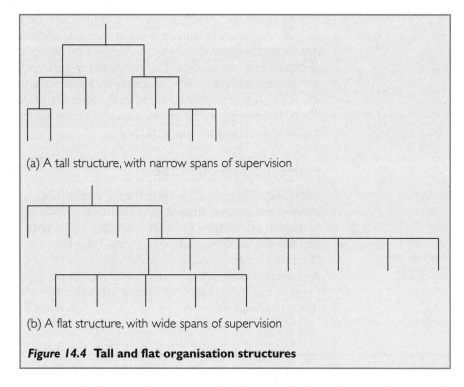

(a) A tall structure, with narrow spans of supervision

(b) A flat structure, with wide spans of supervision

Figure 14.4 **Tall and flat organisation structures**

system used (discussed more fully in Chapter 16). A trend in modern organisations is towards wider spans of control, by introducing more autonomy and teamworking.

14.4 Dividing work horizontally

One person working as an independent owner-manager has no need for an organisation structure. He or she decides what to do, and how they will plan and co-ordinate the different activities. Growth increases the problems of co-ordination, though in small businesses staff usually handle these issues quite informally by mutual give-and-take. People usually (not always) begin to experience more difficulties with informal structures if the business starts to grow. Misunderstandings become more likely, jobs are forgotten or work is wastefully duplicated. The dangers of informality begin to outweigh the benefits. So people decide to clarify who is responsible for what parts of the job, and how to link them to deliver the product or service. They are creating a structure, with both horizontal and vertical dimensions.

In making these choices, people face the dilemma of balancing external and internal diversity with uniformity. The pressure for external diversity arises as people try to arrange their structure to meet the needs of different customers, products or services, and suppliers. Some areas of the business are clearly distinct from others (such as type of customer or speed of change): should management treat them separately? There are also pressures for internal diversity. They must decide how finely to separate the tasks and functions which people need to do. For example, management may expect HRM staff to deal with recruitment, selection, training and pay. Alternatively, it may regard these as distinct activities that require specialist attention.

The dilemma is that if there is too little specialisation, staff cannot pay enough attention to different needs, or to develop their professional expertise. More diversity means more danger of overlap, complexity, duplication and administration costs. The pressure for uniformity arises from the need for the separate parts to work together. Management may want the organisation to present a unified front to the world and provide consistent treatment. It will seek to develop a uniform approach across the enterprise and create a structure that supports this.

Horizontal specialisation

Horizontal specialisation is the degree to which tasks are divided among separate people or departments.

'Job specialisation in the horizontal dimension ... is an inherent part of every organisation, indeed every human activity' (Mintzberg, 1979, p.69). Management divides work into smaller tasks, with people or departments specialising on one or more of these. They become more expert in one task than they could be in several and save time by not moving between them. By concentrating on one, they are more likely to come up with improved ideas or methods. Taken too far, specialisation leads to the negative effects noted in Chapter 6.

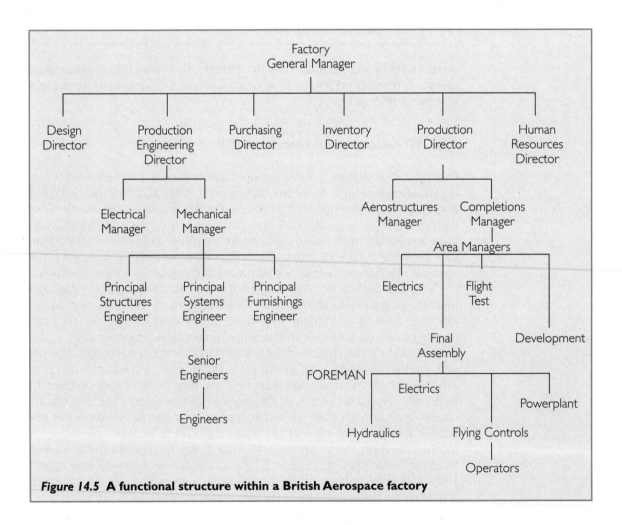

Figure 14.5 A functional structure within a British Aerospace factory

The principle applies at all levels. It shapes the work of individuals as well as of whole departments or divisions. Here we are dealing with the latter – the way managers divide the broad task of the organisation. The alternatives are easy enough to state in an abstract way, but in practice structural forms are never so neatly distinct. Designers usually base their choices on how to get information to flow most easily between those who need to share it. That can lead to different approaches in different parts of large organisations. The main forms of specialisation are by function, product or location.

Specialisation by function

This is the method in which managers group activities and employees according to the main professional or functional specialisms, such as research and development, production, finance, marketing, or information services.

Figure 14.5 shows an example of an organisation (which is part of British Aerospace, Britain's largest manufacturing company) which displays a clear functional structure.

Another example is the main structural division of a National Health Service hospital (Figure 14.6). The organisation chart at senior levels shows a clear functional division.

The functional approach is often very efficient. Management creates a separate department for each major task, and people with expertise in that task work together. They share skills and can see a possible professional career path in their department.

The problems arise when an organisation grows and diversifies into a range of different products, markets or geographical areas. Managers in charge

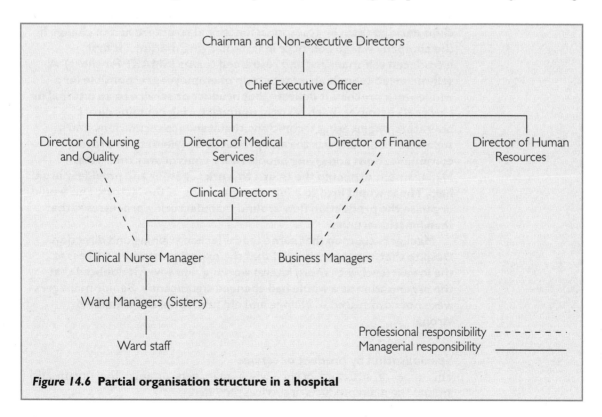

Figure 14.6 Partial organisation structure in a hospital

of delivering different products will each expect functional staff to work on their products. Conflicts over priorities or quality arise. A sales representative makes a sale – which the production department cannot meet because it has allocated capacity to another product. The focus of staff tends to be inward, towards the interests of their functional department, rather than outward towards the business as a whole.

Advantages and disadvantages of functional specialisation

Advantages

▶ Encourages specialisation in a particular skill and gives a line of career development within the function.
▶ Avoids duplicating resources as requirements are met from a common pool.
▶ Senior managers and subordinates share common expertise.
▶ Leads to focus on professional development and enhanced problem-solving.

Disadvantages

▶ Specialists become isolated from others, making communication difficult.
▶ Conflicts over which products or projects have priority.
▶ Focus on department rather than wider organisation.
▶ Managers lack organisational view.

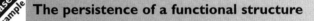

The persistence of a functional structure

The management of a leading electronics company making memory chips decided that the traditional functional structure had to change if the company was to compete in fast-changing markets. It first introduced self-managed and resourced teams (**SMART** for short). A self-managed team is an intact group of employees responsible for a whole work process. It delivers that product or service to an internal or external customer. Each team in manufacturing contains direct operators, engineering technicians, maintenance technicians, and a supervisor. The aim was to raise productivity (yield) by improving communications and giving people more control over their role. Management expected the teams to work together and provide mutual help. These would lead to a full re-engineering of the factory. This would organise the production flow around manufacturing processes rather than functional units.

Managers claimed that some teams lacked training and direction. Despite that, managers judged that the experiment was a success at the lowest level, with more lateral working. However, it doubted that the organisation as a whole had changed significantly. Senior managers were not committed to change and old functional ties remained strong.

Specialisation by product or service

This type of structure occurs when managers arrange the organisation around the main products or services provided.

Choose an organisation, and draw a chart showing the main structural divisions. If you can do this by interviewing someone you know in the organisation, ask that person which of the methods of task division (functional, product, geographical or matrix) he or she has used. What advantages and disadvantages has your interviewee experienced with that structure? Alternatively, study a copy of the company's annual report and try to establish the main structure from that. Does the report hint at any recent changes in the structure? If so, note them and the reasons given for them.

Specialisation by product or service is an attempt to overcome the difficulties which growing companies face with a functional division. The solution is to create separate units and make them responsible for all the functions necessary to deliver their service to the customer. The method is especially appropriate where groups of customers have significantly different requirements from each other. Organisations try to meet those requirements by grouping their activities so that staff specialise in a particular product or customer group. For example, the major banks have identified that wealthy private clients have different needs from other individuals – and have created separate divisions to focus solely on delivering services to those clients. Many hospitals are now introducing what they term the 'named nurse' system, in which staff allocate each patient to a single nurse. He or she is the patient's prime point of contact with the system. The nurse's job is to focus on his or her group of patients, managing as well as they can the delivery of services to the patient from other (functional) departments of the hospital. Figure 14.7 contrasts the task and named-nurse approaches.

A travel agent deals in business travel and packaged holidays, and has created separate divisions for each, in which staff concentrate on each of these areas, because of their fundamentally different requirements. It notices a growing trend towards independent holiday travel by people who have become dissatisfied with traditional packages. If it decides to try to enter this market, it will face an organisational choice: should it have staff in one of the existing divisions work on the new business, or should it create a further division?

What considerations should affect the decision?

In a product-based structure, managers give each unit the authority to design, produce and deliver the product or service, using resources under its control or bought from outside suppliers. The advantages are that they can focus all resources on the one product. Separate areas of functional expertise are more likely to co-operate as they all depend on satisfying the same set of customers. It is probably more expensive, as each product group may have a wide range of specialisms duplicating provision. The problems of co-operation

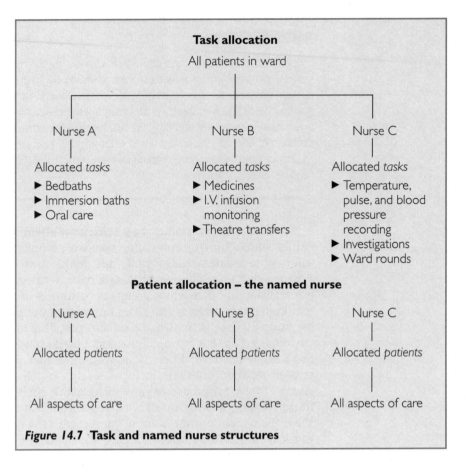

Figure 14.7 **Task and named nurse structures**

between departments that beset functional structures may still arise, though in different forms.

Advantages and disadvantages of product or service specialisation
Advantages
- ▶ Able to respond quickly to changes in demand patterns.
- ▶ Staff focused on customer needs.
- ▶ Service or product is more visible to staff in functional departments.

Disadvantages
- ▶ May still be conflict between product groups over access to some external resources.
- ▶ May develop a product focus at expense of wider company interests.
- ▶ May foster unproductive competition between lines.

Specialisation by location
Here managers divide the organisation geographically, usually according to the location of customers. They group all the tasks required under the management of that geographic region, rather than having them divided among functions at the centre. For example, large companies with many service outlets – supermarkets, hotels, breweries – often divide the business into regions. This allows management to focus on identifying and meeting

different customer requirements in the region, or on meeting different environmental conditions. A geographical management structure also makes it easier to monitor and control the many relatively small outlets. The Kwik-Fit case in the introduction to Part Five is an example of a geographically-based structure.

Advantages and disadvantages of location specialisation

Advantages
- ► Expertise develops in dealing with that distinct group of customers.
- ► All facilities required are under the control of regional management.
- ► Problems of controlling and managing dispersed units are reduced.

Disadvantages
- ► Functions duplicated in each geographical area.
- ► Locations may become too independent of centre and follow own policies.
- ► May need tighter procedures to help centre monitor strong local management.

C A S E   Q U E S T I O N S   14.3

- ► In what ways had management at Contracting Services organised the service – functional, product or geographical lines?
- ► What advantages and disadvantages does the information in the case suggest?

Matrix organisation

This refers to the arrangement where there is a combination of functional and product structures. It attempts to capture the advantages of each of these approaches, with as few as possible of the disadvantages. On one axis is a range of products or projects, with a manager responsible for each. On the other are the various functional groups, as in a functional organisation. Staff from the functional areas work on one or more projects. When a project no longer needs their expertise, they are allocated by their functional boss to work on another. Subordinates have two bosses – a long-term functional head, and a temporary head of the project currently being worked upon.

Advantages and disadvantages of matrix specialisation

Advantages
- ► Encourages co-operation between functions.
- ► By being based around novel projects and variable teams, staff gain a varied work experience.
- ► Specialised knowledge is widely shared, but developed within the functional group.

Disadvantages
- ► Costly, with possible unused resources.
- ► Requires strong interpersonal skills to manage.
- ► Employees may have difficulties in working for two bosses.
- ► Possible conflicts between product and functional managers over staff allocated to projects.

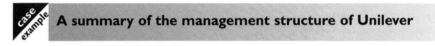

n o t e b o o k   14.4

Refer back to the Price Waterhouse case in Chapter 7. It explains how the staff in the consultancy business are organised on a matrix basis. What indications does the case give about the issues in managing a matrix structure?

Mixed forms

Especially in large organisations, practice is more complex than these simple categories suggest. Such businesses typically use a variety of methods for dividing tasks – the Body Shop example shows functional, product and geographical structures within the same company (Figure 14.8).

The structure of Unilever, the Anglo-Dutch conglomerate which produces a vast range of household brands throughout the world, is a good example of the complexity such structures can reach.

---

case example   **A summary of the management structure of Unilever**

The activities of the companies worldwide are co-ordinated by product management groups and regional management groups. These are supported by a range of functional services.

The product management groups are responsible for the overall policy of the development, production and marketing of our foods, detergents, personal products and speciality chemicals businesses respectively. The foods management group is now subdivided for reporting purposes into oil and dairy based foods and bakery, ice cream and beverages, and culinary and frozen foods, a change from 1994.

There are regional management groups for the consumer products companies in Western Europe, Central and Eastern Europe, North America, Africa and the Middle East, East Asia and Pacific, and Latin America and Central Asia. The prestige personal products and speciality chemicals operations are managed on a global basis.

The functional services are the responsibility of the Financial Director, the Research and Engineering Director and the Personnel Director.

In most countries where Unilever operates, a National Manager is responsible for contacts with local government, social policy and the provision of services. In North America, the President of Unilever United States fulfils this role.

Source: Unilever Annual Report 1995

This section has described the four alternative principles which managements can choose among when dividing tasks within the business. In practice most adopt a mixture of forms and continually adapt to changing circumstances. They seek to achieve an appropriate balance between the advantages and disadvantages of each type in their particular circumstances and in particular parts of the organisation. What is inevitably seen is a structure in transition, not a final form. These comments relate to horizontal

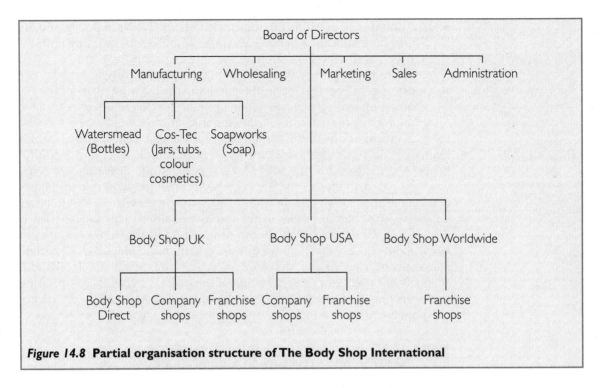

Figure 14.8 **Partial organisation structure of The Body Shop International**

specialisation that is discussed above and to the degree of vertical specialisation, which is looked at next.

14.5 Dividing work vertically

When an organisation grows beyond the smallest operation, management divides work vertically. In doing so it creates a hierarchy. Those running the business decide the key aspects of the total task that they need to recognise explicitly. They create positions that carry overall responsibility for that aspect of the work – engineering manager, customer service manager, etc. Other positions that carry responsibility for smaller parts of these tasks are created, reporting to their respective managers. If the organisation remains small, the hierarchical structure will remain small and simple. If it grows, the hierarchy will usually become more complex as management identifies additional areas of work and formally recognises them in the structure. Distinct areas of the business emerge as separate divisions, each with their hierarchy of responsibility.

The forms that have developed are infinitely variable – just compare the structures of a few major companies or public organisations. Behind the detail it is useful to distinguish between corporate, divisional and operating levels (matching Mintzberg's strategic apex, middle level and operating core – see section 14.6):

▶ **Corporate**   The most senior area, responsible for dealing with the overall direction of the organisation. This includes not only guiding and monitoring the performance of subordinate levels of the organisation, but also maintaining links with significant external institutions such as banks and political bodies.

▶ **Divisional** Responsible for implementing broad areas of policy, and for securing and allocating budgets and other resources to operating units. Managers at this level are often responsible for monitoring and controlling the performance of those at the operating level.

▶ **Operating** The level responsible for doing the technical work of the organisation – designing and making products, delivering services, arranging care for patients, or catching thieves.

In small organisations these levels will be hard to distinguish as their senior managers inevitably become involved in both middle-level and technical issues. The dangers are that lower-level managers may feel they are being over-supervised, or that senior managers neglect their primary responsibilities of taking a broad view of the business, and managing external links. In larger businesses the roles are more distinct and specialised. The danger then is that people at different levels get out of touch. Most will never see or even know about those at levels above or below them in the hierarchy. Corporate management may make decisions affecting the lower levels without adequate knowledge or understanding of the issues. Alternatively, operating managers may make decisions without being fully aware of broader corporate policy.

Vertical specialisation refers to the extent to which responsibilities at different levels are defined.

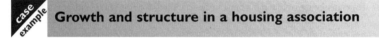

Growth and structure in a housing association

A manager in a housing association, created to provide affordable housing for those on low incomes, describes how its structure changed as it grew.

> Housing associations have to give tenants and their representatives the opportunity to influence policy. In the early days the association had few staff, no clear division of labour and few rules and procedures. It was successful in providing housing, which attracted more government funds, and the association grew. As more houses came into management this activity required an organisational structure to support it. The association no longer served a single community, but a number of separate geographical areas. Staff numbers grew significantly and specialised departments were created to provide specific and separate functions. The changes have led to concerns among both staff and committee that the organisation is no longer responsive to community needs and that it has become distant and bureaucratic.

Balance between centralisation and decentralisation

A key issue in designing the vertical hierarchy is the amount of autonomy at divisional and operating levels. Where does the right to make certain decisions lie? Organisations distribute this differently. At one extreme those at corporate level make most decisions about service production and delivery. The divisional level ensures that those at operating level follow the policy. At the other extreme, those at the operating level make decisions over large areas of the business. They can work as they think best, provided they deliver the results expected by the corporate level and keep within some broad guidelines. For example, the branch managers in a chain of retail travel agents have considerable freedom over pricing and promotional activities but are required to follow very tight financial reporting routines.

A political analogy

❛ The same issue arises in the wider political world as well. European nations vary in how they divide power between central, regional and local government. France and the UK are relatively centralised, while the Netherlands and probably Spain are more decentralised, with strong provincial or regional governments. Much of the controversy over the UK's relationship with the European Union relates to the similar question of subsidiarity: what matters should those in Brussels decide, and what should individual member states decide? As in business, pressures for changes in the current balance are always present – and the solutions reflect both rational and political influences. ❜

In practice, organisations display a mix of both. It is common to find that the centre decides some matters, while divisional or operating levels exercise considerable discretion over others. The pattern reflects management assumptions about where in the hierarchy decisions about particular issues should be made. What are the responsibilities of the respective levels, and what are the limits of their authority? These change as organisations respond to external signals. Evident delay in dealing with a local issue may lead to authority being decentralised. Alternatively, evidence that local managers have misused their authority often leads to tighter central control.

Political influence will also be at work – managers at all levels will usually be seeking more autonomy for their level. They will at the same time be resisting attempts by other managers to increase their decision-making authority and control.

Centralisation is when those at the top make most of the decisions. Other organisations favour passing more authority to lower levels of the organisation. They believe that those who are closest to the action will be in a better position to make the right decisions. They favour a greater degree of decentralisation.

Centralisation is when a relatively large number of decisions are taken by management at the top of the organisation. Decentralisation is when a relatively large number of decisions are taken lower down the organisation in particular operating units.

C A S E   Q U E S T I O N S   14.4

▶ In early 1997, is the Contracting Services organisation centralised or decentralised?

▶ How much autonomy do branch managers have?

▶ What advantages and disadvantages are there in this arrangement?

At the operating level, the vertical choices could refer to the amount of responsibility which staff have. This changes in response to views about business needs and motivation.

Several factors affect which decision areas are centralised and which are decentralised:

▶ **Costliness of decisions**   The centre is more likely to retain control over decisions that are likely to be expensive or publicly visible. So the centre often retains control over capital investment policy, even when local managers deal with most other matters. This avoids the costs of maintaining separate or incompatible systems decided upon by local managers.

► **Uniformity of policy**   The centre is likely to take decisions on matters where it is important to maintain a strong brand image, or a consistent standard of presentation. Directors often impose centralised accounting policies to allow them to compare performance across units accurately. Similarly, conformity to legislation will often lead to the imposition of centralised rules in those areas.

► **Local responsiveness**   If the business is one where customer or client needs or business conditions are significantly different between areas, then this will favour a decentralised policy over many matters.

► **Staff commitment and responsibility**   Motivation theories suggest that most staff are capable of exercising greater responsibility, and welcome more autonomy. This implies that a management that wishes to generate greater commitment amongst staff will decentralise more decisions to lower levels in the hierarchy. The Case Example on page 474 shows some links between structure and the attitudes of staff.

► **Power**   Whatever the rational arguments, will be affected by power concerns and reluctance to let go.

Centralisation – advantages and disadvantages

Advantages

► Economies of administration – common systems followed by all.
► Economies of scale in purchasing supplies and facilities.
► Less risk of local managers breaching legal requirements on, say, health and safety.
► Provides consistent image to the public – less variation in service standards.
► More productive use of scarce physical and professional resources – avoids duplication.
► Concentration of expertise at the centre makes it easier to develop new services and promote best-practice methods.

Disadvantages

► Slower response to local variations in market needs.
► Decisions may be slowed down as what is urgent locally may not be so corporately.
► Less likely to take account of local knowledge in making decisions.
► Local staff discouraged from taking responsibility – problems can be blamed on the centre.
► Centralised systems may be wasteful when applied locally – local suppliers may be cheaper and better than corporate suppliers.

14.6 Mintzberg's model

Mintzberg (1979, 1989) has described organisations in terms of five basic parts, shown in Figure 14.9. The operating core contains the people and machines doing the basic work of the organisation – receiving inputs, processing or transforming them into products or services. Some organisations deal mainly with materials, others (such as hospitals, consultancies and universities) mainly with people and information. In all cases, they then

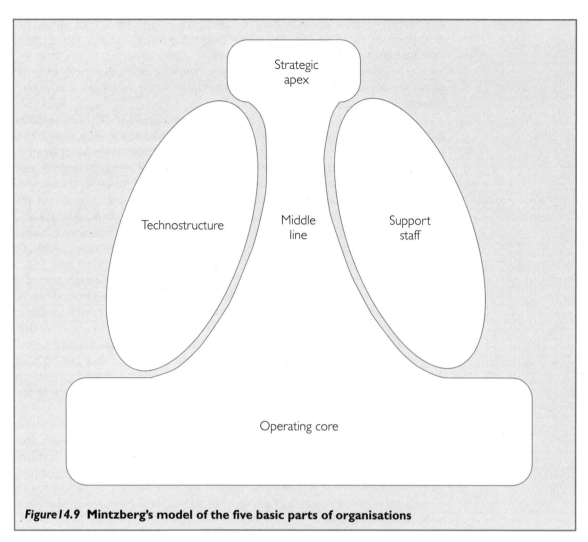

Figure 14.9 **Mintzberg's model of the five basic parts of organisations**

pass the results of the transformation processes to customers or clients. Mintzberg argues that the 'operating core is the heart of every organization, the part that produces the essential outputs that keep it alive. But except for the very smallest ones, organizations need to build administrative components ... the strategic apex, middle line, and technostructure' (1979, p.24).

At the top of the organisation are those who form the strategic apex. They are responsible for the overall direction of the business irrespective of their titles – managing director, chair, archbishop, council leader, and all the other managers with broad, organisation-wide responsibilities. Others expect them to ensure that the organisation meets the agreed or imposed objectives effectively, and that it meets the needs of influential stakeholders such as banks, shareholders and employees. They manage the boundaries of the organisation and look after the strategic links to the outside world.

Between the strategic apex and the operating core are the middle managers – linking the apex to the operators, usually connected through a single line of formal authority. Small organisations only need one manager – at the strategic apex. Additional managers supervise the work of those in the operating core as the business grows. There are practical (though highly variable) limits to the number of people any one manager can directly supervise. A supervisor is in charge of some direct operators, and a department manager is in charge of several supervisors – and so on up to the strategic apex. They pass information up and down the hierarchy, deal with internal disturbances, and manage external boundaries with suppliers, customers, journalists, etc.

Alongside this middle section and influencing it indirectly are two other parts. The technostructure refers to a range of analytical and technical activities that serve those in the operating core, but are themselves apart from it. They help by planning the work, changing it, training others to do it. Above all, in Mintzberg's model, they do most of the work required to standardise the work of the organisation – not just in the operating core but also at the middle level and the strategic apex. They do this by designing systems and procedures, redesigning processes, providing information systems or library services, analysing market information and developing new products, building financial systems, etc.

The other group in Figure 14.9 is the support structure which provides support to the organisation outside the operating workflow. It provides indirect support to the operating core, through activities like security, catering, public relations, building maintenance, counselling, mail delivery. Note that some support structures and technostructures resemble organisations themselves, with an operating core and management structure. They also exist at different levels of the hierarchy, with some, such as legal or public relations being near the top, while catering is usually rather closer to the work of the operating core.

This model provides a generalised, fairly abstract view of how organisations perform their activities. While all organisations contain these five parts, their relative size, importance and status vary greatly. The technostructure dominates some, and the operating core dominates others. Mintzberg argues that all the parts interact with each other through systems of authority, information and decision processes. In other words, the parts must be co-ordinated.

---

n o t e b o o k   14.5

Using the organisation in which you are studying (or another one to which you have access), draw a diagram like that in Figure 14.9. Show the different departments, units or groups of people who work in each of the five parts. Try to show which are the largest, or are seen to be the most significant on some other measure.

14.7 Ways to co-ordinate work

The division of work must be balanced by co-ordination if the separate activities are to support organisational goals. Without co-ordination of some kind there will be confusion and poor performance. Effective co-ordination of diverse activities becomes more essential as performance criteria tighten. They can then avoid the costs, wastes and delays that follow from poor co-ordination. At the same time, widely dispersed businesses, operating and changing at great speed, make the job of co-ordinating that much more difficult. Managers must bring facilities across the globe together. There are many mechanisms for such co-ordination, and these are described below.

Direct supervision

This is where a senior manager directly supervises the work of staff to ensure they work together in appropriate ways, and in line with company policy. The limitation lies in the idea of the span of control – the number of people whom a manager can supervise directly is fairly small.

Hierarchy

If disputes or problems arise between staff or departments, they can be reconciled by putting the arguments to their common boss in the hierarchy. It is the boss's responsibility to reach a solution. This can be slow, especially if the conditions are turbulent. Then many changes have to be dealt with, and referred up an overloaded hierarchy.

Standardisation of inputs and outputs

This involves making sure that what goes into the system, and what managers expect it to produce, are standardised. This makes co-ordination with other stages easier. If the purchaser of components specifies accurately what she requires, and the supplier meets that specification, co-ordination between those who use the parts will be easier. Similarly, if staff work to precise specifications, co-ordinating with the next stage of the process becomes easier.

Work processes

This mechanism entails providing clear guidelines on what steps to follow in doing the work.

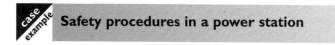

case example   Safety procedures in a power station

The following instructions govern the steps that staff must follow when they inspect control instrumentation equipment in a nuclear power station.

1.0   Before commencing work you must read and understand the relevant Permit-to-Work and/or other safety documents as appropriate.
2.0   Obtain keys for relevant cubicles.
3.0   Visually inspect the interior of each bay for dirt, water and evidence of condensation.
4.0   Visually inspect the cabling, glands, terminal blocks and components for damage.
5.0   Visually check for loose connections at all terminals.
6.0   Lock all cubicles and return the keys.
7.0   Clear the safety document and return it to the Supervisor/Senior Authorised person.

Rules and procedures

Another way to co-ordinate the activities of people or departments is to prepare rules or guidelines on how they should perform. An example is the procedure for approving capital expenditure. Senior managers usually want to be able to review all major proposals for this. Those in separate parts of the organisation are likely to propose projects at different times and in different forms, making comparison impossible. So most organisations have strict guidelines on what questions all proposals should answer, how people should prepare a case, and to whom they should submit it.

Another example is in software design projects. Companies developing new computer software have major problems in co-ordinating the work if several designers are working on different parts of the same project. People can easily duplicate work that others have done, or work on an older version, not realising that someone has produced a new version. To overcome this problem, which also arises on engineering design projects, most companies have introduced strict change control procedures. These aim to ensure that the work of different staff fits together efficiently.

Standardisation of skills

Giving the same training to staff helps to ensure that all staff in a particular activity do things in much the same way. This can reduce the need for direct supervision of people's work, if management knows that staff are applying their skills and knowledge in a consistent way.

Information systems

Information systems are required to ensure that people who need to work in a consistent way have common information about what is happening. Sharing information makes it easier to co-ordinate the different activities within a company. The Part Five case describes how Kwik-Fit invested heavily in an advanced information system early in its life. It attributes much of its success to the effects of that system.

C A S E   Q U E S T I O N S   14.5

The call centre which Contracting Services was considering early in 1997 is an example of an information system that could change the way the organisation is co-ordinated.

▶ Given what you know of the company and its processes and what you have read in this chapter, make a list of the issues that management will need to deal with if it goes ahead with that investment. This is a bigger task than it may sound, so you may want to make your own list, and then compare it with those of other students. Then produce a comprehensive list (but with priorities) of items that you think should be on the management agenda.

Direct personal contact

This is the most human form of co-ordination: people talking to each other. Mintzberg (1979) argues that people use this method in both the simplest and the most complex organisation, in the latter because it is usually the most practical way to continue. There is so much uncertainty in the complex organisation that information systems cannot cope with all eventualities. Only direct contact can co-ordinate these.

Structure and motivation in a social service organisation

The organisation cares for the elderly in a large city. Someone who had worked there for several years reflected on the structure:

Within the centre there was a manager, two deputies, an assistant manager, five senior care officers and thirty care officers. Each SCO is responsible for six care officers, allowing daily contact between the supervisor and the subordinates. While this defines job roles quite tightly, it allows a good communication structure to exist. Feedback is common as a direct result of frequent meetings of the separate groups, and of individual appraisals of the care officers by the senior care officers. This aspect of structure is valuable as the staff seem to value the opportunity for praise and comments on how they are doing.

Contact at all levels is common between supervisor and care officers during meetings to assess the needs of clients – for whom the care officers have direct responsibility. Frequent social gatherings and functions within the department also serve to enhance relations and satisfy social needs. Controls placed on behaviour of the care officers come from the highest positions in the hierarchy, especially those derived from legislation such as the Social Work Acts and the Health and Safety Executive. Performance measures also exist. For example outsiders regularly assess how the Quality of Practice code is working, along with those established in the department on absenteeism and lateness.

Structure certainly plays a major role in the effectiveness of employees at work by encouraging and motivating them. However, in a department such as this the need to improve quality of service has to come from the desire of the individual to do better for clients.

---

n o t e b o o k   1 4 . 6

What structural practices can you identify in this account?

Which theories would explain the links suggested to job satisfaction?

14.8 Organisational cultures

As well as the more visible aspects of structure, organisations also have distinctive cultures – distinctive values and beliefs about the way people should behave and work with each other. These shape many of the more visible aspects of the organisation, such as their structure and communication systems.

Schein (1980) refers to three levels of culture – artefacts, beliefs and values. Organisations develop deep-seated values and beliefs about the way that staff should run things. What degree of direction should there be? Should people have job titles? How should they dress at work? What is the expected pattern of behaviour in meetings – confrontational and challenging, or co-operative and supportive? Do bosses expect staff to defer to them, or to challenge prevailing practices and attitudes? How important is time-keeping, or meeting commitments to colleagues? Should they follow the rules or use their initiative?

You can sense and observe the distinctiveness of organisation cultures once you have been in a few different departments or organisations. They feel different; receive visitors differently; people work together differently; the pace is different – some buzz with life and activity, others seem asleep. Some feel as if rules guide behaviour, while others use procedures as little as possible. The same is true of departments and groups within organisations. Some are welcoming and look after visitors and those from outside, while others seem inward-looking. Some stick to the rules, others are entrepreneurial and risk-taking. Some have regular social occasions while in others staff rarely meet except at work.

Interest in organisation cultures has grown rapidly in recent years, as academics and managers have realised that culture exerts a significant influence on behaviour. Several writers have argued that a strong and distinct culture helps to integrate individuals into the team or organisation (Peters and Waterman, 1982; Deal and Kennedy, 1982). They claim that creating the right culture is a key element in high-performing organisations – provided the culture is the right one for the situation. Not all cultures are right for all conditions, and what works at one stage of an organisation's growth may not be appropriate later. Others have gone further in questioning the link between a strong culture and economic performance. Kotter and Heskett (1992) studied 207 companies, and attempted to relate the strength of their culture to economic performance. Although the two variables were positively correlated, the relationship was much weaker than the advocates of organisational culture as a variable to influence have predicted.

> 'Corporate culture is the pattern of basic assumptions that a given group has invented, discovered or developed in learning to cope with its problems of external adaptation and internal integration. [These] have worked well enough to be considered valid, and [are] therefore taught to new members as the correct way to perceive, think and feel in relation to those problems.' (Schein, 1985)

Components of organisational cultures

While the idea of culture appears vague and hard to measure or compare, several models suggest ways of identifying distinct components. Schein's model of the components of culture was described in Chapter 8. More recently Hall (1995) has suggested the ABC of culture:

▶ **A – Artefacts and etiquette (surface level)**   These are the visible, concrete elements of culture such as language, form of greeting, clothing, the physical layout (open-plan or closed offices).

▶ **B – Behaviours and actions (deeper level)**   These are the consistent patterns of behaviour that make up this aspect of cultural style. They include the way that people make decisions, how teams work together and styles of problem-solving. These behaviours are less visible than the artefacts of culture.

▶ **C – Core morals, beliefs, values (deepest level)**   The judgements that members hold about what is right or wrong, fair or unfair. Organisational members can develop different collective or shared views on ethical issues to do with their business. Examples include whether to take or offer bribes, and the significance or otherwise of shareholders, which can have a marked effect on the way people work.

Types of organisational culture

Charles Handy, developing an idea of Roger Harrison, has distinguished four distinct types of culture: power, role, task and person.

Power culture

A power culture is one in which people's activities are strongly influenced by a dominant central figure.

In the power culture a dominant central figure holds power. Others follow the policies expressed at the centre, and interpret new situations in the way the leader would. Many entrepreneurial firms operate in this way, with the founder visibly in charge and others working in the way he or she would expect. There are few rules, but these will be well-understood, implicit codes on how to behave and work. The firm relies on the individual rather than on seeking consensus through discussion. Such organisations can respond quickly and experimentally. Once the centre approves, staff implement ideas. The main problem with this culture is size. As it grows, it becomes harder for the person at the centre to maintain the required degree of close control. He or she may be unwilling to let go and remain involved in detail. This overloads the decision-making system and delays response to new situations.

Role culture

A role culture is one in which people's activities are strongly influenced by clear and detailed job descriptions and other formal signals as to what is expected of them.

Typical characteristics of the role culture are the job description or the procedure. Managers define what they expect in clear, detailed job descriptions. They select people for a job if they meet the specified requirements. Procedures guide the way that people or departments interact with each other. If all the parts follow the rules, co-ordination is a straightforward matter, with few exceptions. So the hierarchy is able to co-ordinate the activities of those lower down with little difficulty. People's position in the hierarchy determines their power and so the authority to influence others to do what they require.

A role culture works well in a stable environment, where things are predictable. What has worked before and been refined by experience, will continue in which the external world requires few changes. Local authorities and public organisations used to operate in this way – at least in part to ensure that they treated everyone equally. Some large companies operate in this way too. Problems arise when things change. Then it becomes hard for the role culture to adapt, with problems as expectations mount.

Task culture

A task culture is one in which the focus of activity is towards completing a task or project using whatever means are appropriate.

The task culture focuses on getting the task or project completed, rather than the formal roles that people occupy. People value each other for what they can contribute to the task in hand, and expect everyone to help each other as needed. The emphasis is on getting the resources and people for the job and then relying on their commitment and enthusiasm to see it through to completion. People will typically work in teams, as a further way of combining diverse skills into a common purpose. Expertise is typically the source of power – the person with the evident knowledge taking the lead for that part of the task.

Because groups can reform quickly around new tasks this form of organisation is highly adaptable. It works well for volatile or high-technology businesses such as research laboratories and entrepreneurial financial and consultancy services. Task cultures are hard to control and may waste resources. Staff may develop less professional or technical knowledge than they would in a role culture, as they are moving between different projects too quickly for full specialisation.

Person culture

Here, Handy argues, the individual is at the centre of the culture, and any structure or system is there to serve the individual. The form is unusual – places such as small professional or artistic organisations are probably closest to it. These organisations exist to meet the interests of the professional stars, rather than some larger organisational goal. Various forms of experiment in communal or co-operative living may also take this form. They do things to satisfy the needs of the members rather than an external market.

Handy also points out that while the full form of personal culture is rare, many technically specialised individuals in conventional organisations aspire towards that form of environment. Their primary loyalty is to their interests or their profession's. The formal organisation is merely a convenient vehicle for satisfying these deeper interests.

A person culture is one in which activity is strongly influenced by the wishes of the individuals who are part of the organisation.

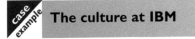

The culture at IBM

As IBM prepared for the much more complicated business environment in which it is now working, the chief executive articulated a new set of beliefs and norms to guide the actions of the company's staff.

The three basic norms were to pursue excellence, provide the best customer service, and show respect for each employee. The eight beliefs or principles of the new culture are the following:

1 The marketplace is the driving force behind everything we do.
2 At our core, we are a technology company with an overriding commitment to quality.
3 Our primary measures are customer satisfaction and shareholder value.
4 We operate as an entrepreneurial organisation with a minimum of bureaucracy and a never-ending focus on productivity.
5 We never lose sight of our strategic vision.
6 We think and act with a sense of urgency.
7 Outstanding, dedicated people make it all happen, particularly when they work together as a team.
8 We are sensitive to the needs of all employees and to the communities in which we operate.

Source: extract from Egan (1994, pp.110–11)

14.9 Recap

Creating an organisation structure is essentially what Hales (1993) has referred to as institutionalising the management activity. Some aspects of management are performed directly and personally by the people involved. Others are supported and reinforced by arrangements that are institutionalised in what we call an organisation's structure. A further, less tangible but equally pervasive tool is the culture of the organisation.

Content agenda

Management creates a structure to help it achieve organisational objectives. Resources are acquired and are then arranged in some more or less stable pattern to encourage attitudes and behaviour in line with the current objectives. Two models of this were presented: Mintzberg's view of organisational typologies, and another that developed Leavitt's classic model of the elements of organisation. Management divides work on both a vertical and a horizontal dimension. The first creates a hierarchy of authority and influence, and so shapes the (unequal) distribution of power through defining access to organisational resources. The second creates a degree of functional or other specialisation – and again influences the distribution of influence around the organisation. The pattern of vertical and horizontal specialisation may be guided by management's concern for control, and as such affects the problem of gaining the motivation and commitment of the managed. As was seen in Chapter 6 some structures appear to have a more positive effect on human motivation than others. The chapter examined a variety of structures that managements have evolved. Similarly, several different kinds of culture were observed. Although culture is a much more recent topic of study in management, many believe that it has significant effects on organisational performance.

Process agenda

The form of structure adopted affects the position of stakeholders in the organisation. It determines such things as their status, their experience of work, their power, and their ability to be involved in or to influence decisions. Structures affect many of the processes of management such as decision-making and communicating. Some make it possible to involve the appropriate people in decisions. Others obstruct that and can severely hinder the ability of the organisation to react to changing circumstances. Some forms of structure encourage horizontal communication among a wide network of people. Others have the effect of limiting communication within narrowly defined functions or departments. Structures also shape and influence the flow of information into and out of the organisation.

Control agenda

Structures fundamentally affect the ability of management to control other organisational members. Centralised structures tend to work in favour of those at the top, while decentralised structures enhance in some degree the positions of those lower in the hierarchy. So the design of structure is not a technical matter. Different groups will try to influence structure to maintain or increase their access to institutional sources of power, such as knowledge and economic resources. Mintzberg sets out a range of control methods which augment direct supervision. Information technology is greatly increasing the ability of managers to monitor what is happening around the organisation, even if they are not personally present. Appropriate structures are also needed to support the learning opportunities identified in the control processes.

The integrative framework is set out in Figure 14.10.

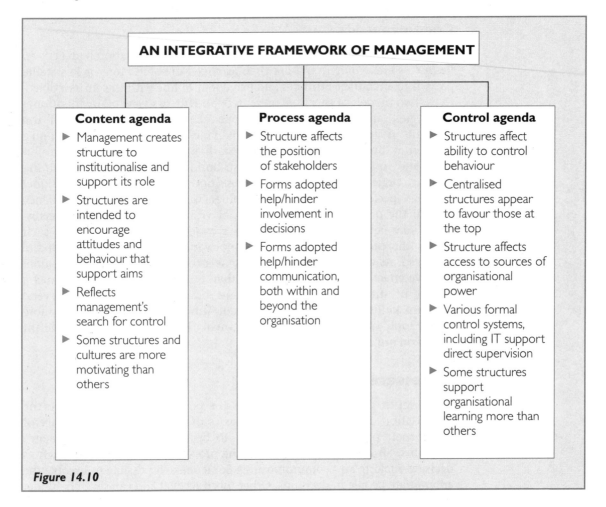

AN INTEGRATIVE FRAMEWORK OF MANAGEMENT

Content agenda
- Management creates structure to institutionalise and support its role
- Structures are intended to encourage attitudes and behaviour that support aims
- Reflects management's search for control
- Some structures and cultures are more motivating than others

Process agenda
- Structure affects the position of stakeholders
- Forms adopted help/hinder involvement in decisions
- Forms adopted help/hinder communication, both within and beyond the organisation

Control agenda
- Structures affect ability to control behaviour
- Centralised structures appear to favour those at the top
- Structure affects access to sources of organisational power
- Various formal control systems, including IT support direct supervision
- Some structures support organisational learning more than others

Figure 14.10

PART CASE QUESTIONS

- What is the balance between centralisation and decentralisation in Save the Children?
- Both Save the Children Fund and Contracting Services are geographically dispersed organisations. Compare the methods of co-ordination used by each.
- How would you describe Save the Children's culture in terms of Handy's four types?

14.10 Review questions

1 Describe what is meant by a model of an organisation, and compare two organisations using any model from the chapter.
2 Analyse an organisation that you know, showing how a change in one element of the Leavitt diagram has had some effects on one or more of the other elements.

3 Draw the organisation chart of an organisation or department that you know. From discussing it with people in one or more of the positions shown, compare their account of the structure with that shown on the chart.

4 Summarise the advantages and disadvantages of the various forms of horizontal specialisation outlined.

5 What business and political factors shape the balance between centralisation and decentralisation?

6 Several forms of co-ordination are described. Select two of these which you have seen in operation and describe in detail how they work – and how well they work.

7 Explain the elements in Mintzberg's model of organisation structures. Which part is dominant in (a) the place in which you are studying, (b) the place in which you have a part-time job?

8 Describe, using Handy's cultural types, an educational or commercial organisation that you know.

Further reading

A clear and comprehensive discussion of organisational structure is provided in Mintzberg (1979). Hall (1995) gives a very clear and practical introduction to the difficult topic of culture, based on extensive empirical work within major European companies. Handy (1993) offers a brief overview of both areas. A recent book by Burnes (1996), while mainly on change, includes chapters on basic elements of organisational structure and culture.

15

Human resource management

CONTENTS

AIM

To introduce the topic of human resource management and to examine some of the major practices.

OBJECTIVES

By the end of your work on this chapter you should be able to outline the concepts below in your own terms and:

1 Understand the reasons for the increased interest in human resource management

2 Recognise the potential importance of the relationship between organisational performance and the management of people

3 Describe and evaluate some of the controversies surrounding the role and influence of human resource management

4 Understand the importance of organisations adopting a strategic approach in relation to the management of people

5 Discuss how the nature of the wider organisational structure and operating environment shapes the ability to change human resource management

6 Understand some of the difficulties in being able to introduce a longer-term planning orientation into human resource management

7 Describe and analyse the changing nature of job requirements in contemporary organisations

8 As a potential job seeker, recognise some of the important issues that will face you at the recruitment/selection stage

9 Understand the skills that are involved in a successful performance appraisal interview

10 Recognise that change in one area of human resource management will almost invariably trigger the need for change in other areas

This case study describes some of the recent human resource management (HRM) changes which have been introduced in BMW's German operations as part of its strategic response to competitive pressures in the German car industry.

BMW was established in 1916. By 1964 output was 144,788 cars, with a turnover of DM1.4 billion; the company grew substantially in subsequent years. Following the establishment of the EU, subsidiaries were set up in member countries and in the United States, and a car plant established in Austria. By the late 1980s, BMW had a workforce of some 54,000, was the seventh largest automobile manufacturing company in the world, and had subsidiaries in many European countries, New Zealand, South Africa, the United States, Canada and Japan. Its presence outside Germany has increased in recent years. In 1995, BMW had a worldwide workforce of 101,000 employees, including the Rover Group and a new BMW car plant in the United States; its workforce in Germany was 58,000. The combined BMW/Rover group sold over 1 million cars in 1995, with BMW selling 592,000. Western Europe is the major market for the group, accounting for 761,000 units which represents a 6.3 per cent market share. It also manufactures motorcycles and has a joint venture with Rolls-Royce to produce aircraft jet engines.

BMW needs to be placed in the larger context of growing concerns about the loss of competitiveness in the German motor industry. A 1996 report by the German Motor Industry Association identified increased wage costs, higher non-wage labour costs, shorter agreed working time than many competitor countries and the continuing strength of the Deutschmark as being major sources of concern in this regard. These concerns have lowered employment in the industry, stimulated investments abroad and resulted in a high priority being given to initiatives to improve productivity.

Diversification has been central to BMW's competitive strategy, while the recent HRM changes (to be detailed in this chapter) derive from, and are highly consistent with, the company's 'six inner values': communication, ethical behaviour to its staff, achievement and remuneration, independence, self-fulfilment and the pursuit of new goals. This value-oriented policy dates back to the early 1980s, arising out of a scenario-planning exercise among senior managers. This underlying philosophy is particularly important in shaping the design of any new BMW plant ('an open design' which advances the visual management of the process) and the process of introducing any new or reformed HRM practices in existing facilities. In the latter case much emphasis is placed on extensive consultation, information-sharing and seeking to establish positive interrelationships between individual changes.

CASE QUESTIONS

- ▶ What issues concerning the management of people are likely to be raised in a group like BMW that has rapidly expanded its production and distribution facilities?

- ▶ How have these issues been affected by domestic developments in Germany?

- ▶ How is the increased competition likely to affect the people who work for BMW?

15.1 Introduction

This chapter introduces the following ideas:
- ▶ Human resource management
- ▶ External fit
- ▶ Internal fit
- ▶ Succession planning
- ▶ Job analysis
- ▶ Competences
- ▶ Selection tests
- ▶ Assessment centres
- ▶ Performance-related pay
- ▶ Performance appraisal

---

n o t e b o o k   15.1

Before reading on, note down how you would define human resource management. What topics and issues do you think it deals with, and how does it relate to management as a whole? Keep your notes by you and compare them with the topics covered in the chapter as you work through it.

Human resource management is the effective use of human resources in order to enhance organisational performance.

Management influences other people through both personal and institutionalised practices. This chapter focuses on some institutionalised practices intended to influence the attitudes and behaviour of employees. These practices are commonly referred to as those of human resource management (HRM).

The discussion concentrates on the basic purpose and objectives of HRM, and the reasons for its greater prominence in management discussions. Some of the important debates surrounding the topic are also highlighted. The influential Harvard Business School (Beer and Spector, 1985) approach identifies four areas of HRM:
- ▶ Employee influence (i.e. employee involvement in decision-making).
- ▶ Human resource flow (i.e. recruitment, selection, training, development and deployment).
- ▶ Work systems (i.e. word design, supervisory style).
- ▶ Reward systems (i.e. pay and other benefits).

Employee influence and work systems have been discussed elsewhere, particularly in Chapters 5, 6, and 9. Here, the focus is on policies and arrangements under human resource flow, which concerns the flow of individuals into and through the organisation: human resource planning, job analysis, employee recruitment and selection, and performance appraisal. Management designs these practices to help ensure that the organisation has the right people available to help it achieve its larger strategic objectives. Aspects of reward systems, particularly that of performance-related pay, are also examined.

These issues illuminate some of the more general issues concerning HRM, especially the concepts of external and internal fit. They also constitute areas where some of the most notable contemporary changes are occurring in the way that organisations are seeking to manage people.

15.2 Emergence and meaning of human resource management

The term 'human resource management' (HRM) is relatively new, gaining prominence in American companies and business schools since about 1980. It is now widely used in the business world, though in some countries such as the Netherlands the term is often consciously avoided because of the potentially negative connotations of viewing people or employees as a 'resource' which can be manipulated or controlled by management. Such connotations are to some extent offset by the fact that trade unions and the government commonly play more important roles in HRM in Europe than is the case in the United States (Brewster, 1994).

Guest (1987) attributes the wider use of the term 'human resource management' to the following factors:

▶ The emergence of more globally integrated markets in which competition is more extensive and severe. Product lifecycles are shorter, with innovation, flexibility and quality often replacing price as the basis of competitive advantage.

▶ The economic success during the 1980s of countries which had given employee management a relatively high priority, such as Japan and (West) Germany.

▶ The highly publicised 'companies of excellence' literature (Peters and Waterman, 1982) which suggested that high-performance organisations were characterised by a strong commitment to human resource management.

▶ Changes in the composition of the workforce, particularly the growth of a more educated staff.

▶ The decline in trade union membership and collective bargaining in many advanced industrialised economies.

Traditionally, mangagement had tried to institutionalise the way staff were managed by creating separate personnel departments. Partly stimulated by the human relations model of management (see Chapter 2), management believed that effective management of people could be achieved by paying attention to employee grievances and looking after their general welfare. Growing trade union power also led management to create departments that specialised in conducting negotiations and monitoring the agreements reached.

Such 'old style' personnel management departments typically had limited power, at least in American and UK organisations. The function has always found it difficult to show that it contributed to financial or any other measures of organisational performance (Legge, 1978; Tyson and Fell, 1985). Personnel was seen as reactive, self-contained and obsessed with procedures. It was overwhelmingly concerned with managing employee grievances, discipline and the relationship with trade unions. The main aim was to minimise costs and the disruptive effects of strikes and other industrial action on production. The consequence was that specialised personnel management functions typically had little influence on the strategic decisions of organisations.

Greater competition, and changes in the nature of that competition, led to a change. Writers on HRM have argued that the more effective management of people will lead to improved organisational effectiveness and

Table 15.1 **A human resource management model**

HRM policies	HRM outcomes	Organisational outcomes
Organisation/job design		High job performance
Management of change	Strategic integration	High problem-solving, change and innovation
Recruitment, selection and socialisation	Commitment	
Appraisal, training, development	Flexibility/adaptability	High cost-effectiveness
Reward systems	Quality	Low turnover, absence, grievances
Communications		

Source: Guest (1988)

performance. Table 15.1 shows the HRM policies that are likely to affect HRM outcomes and wider organisational outcomes.

The view that the better management of people can contribute to improved organisational performance is based in theories of sustained competitive advantage which emphasise the importance of firm-specific, valuable resources which are difficult to imitate (Pfeffer, 1994).

CASE QUESTIONS 15.1

▶ When did HRM policies begin to be seriously developed at BMW?

▶ What led management to take this initiative?

Management began to take the view that the topic of human resource management was too important to be left exclusively to personnel specialists with that image. In essence, the new approach put forward in the HRM literature argues that *line* management needs to become much more fully and actively involved in people management. Only if it does can it ensure that the matter receives more attention and priority in the senior management decision-making circles of individual organisations (Fombrun *et al.*, 1984). In particular, the early advocates of HRM argued that the approach involved something very new and distinctive compared with personnel management: the key themes or watchwords of HRM were 'integration', 'planning', a 'long-run' orientation, 'proactive' and 'strategic'.

Many managers and academics advocate raising the emphasis that organisations give to managing people. They stress the advantages of adopting what has been variously labelled a 'high commitment', 'best practice' or 'mutual gains' human resource management model. The Noticeboard shows the key features of this model.

Proponents of the model typically argue that it will be a source of benefit to both employees and management, involving high performance in the marketplace, favourable terms and conditions of employment and relatively high levels of job satisfaction. In short, what is advocated here is a high-quality competitive strategy, underpinned by a high wage/high productivity employment relationship. BMW is very much an example along these lines.

NOTICEBOARD **Features of an organisation with a strong commitment to HRM**

▶ The firm competes on the basis of product quality and differentiation as well as price.

▶ Human resource considerations weigh heavily in corporate strategic decision-making and governance processes. Employee interests are represented through the voice of human resource staff professionals and/or employee representatives consult and participate with senior executives in decisions that affect human resource policies and employee interests. In either case, employees are treated as legitimate stakeholders in the organisation.

▶ Investments in new hardware or physical technology are combined with the investments in human resources and changes in organisational practices required to realise the full potential benefits of these investments.

▶ The firm sustains a high level of investment in training, skill development and education, and

personnel practices are designed to capture and utilise these skills fully.

▶ Compensation and reward systems are internally equitable, competitive and linked to the long-term performance of the firm.

▶ Employment continuity and security are important priorities and values to be considered in all corporate decisions and policies.

▶ Workplace relations encourage flexibility in the organisation of work, empowerment of employees to solve problems, and high levels of trust among workers, supervisors and managers.

▶ Workers' rights to representation are acknowledged and respected. Union or other employee representatives are treated as joint partners in designing and overseeing innovations in labour and human resource practices.

Source: Kochan (1992)

---

n o t e b o o k   15.2

An organisation has decided to pursue a quality-enhancement strategy in which teamworking arrangements will be a central feature. It recognises the need to enhance its level of workforce training and to replace its individual performance-related pay arrangements. Are there any other changes in the HRM area that it needs to consider? (Use Table 15.1 to assist your answer.)

Within the broad HRM approach some commentators draw attention to differing emphases. One particularly popular distinction here is between the 'hard' and 'soft' emphases of human resource management (Storey, 1992, pp.26–8; Legge, 1995, pp.66–7). The former emphasises the resource notion, rational planning activities and a strategic, business-led perspective. The latter puts more weight on people as valuable assets whose motivation, involvement and development should receive a relatively high priority.

However, the literature emphasises that, for HRM to have the desired effect on performance, management needs to balance two key themes: external and internal fit (Beer and Spector, 1985).

External fit

External fit refers to the link between wider stratgey and HRM strategy. Ideally management tries to establish a close and consistent link between

External fit is when there is a close and consistent relationship between an organisation's competitive strategy and its HRM strategy.

the two so that HRM activities encourage people to act in ways that support the wider competitive strategy. There are various ways in which an organisation can compete in the product market (see Chapter 12). It may pursue a low-cost competitive strategy or it may offer a better product that can sell for a higher price. These differing strategies require differing employee attitudes and behaviours, encouraged by appropriate HRM policies. Extensive training, teamworking and shopfloor problem-solving arrangements are likely in an organisation committed to high quality. Such HRM practices are less likely in an organisation that competes by paying low wages to a casual labour force.

C A S E   Q U E S T I O N S   15.2

- ▶ What is your image of BMW cars? What words would you use to describe them?
- ▶ In order to meet these expectations, what kind of behaviour would you expect of employees?
- ▶ What management practices will encourage/discourage that behaviour?

n o t e b o o k   15.3

List the major differences in HRM policies that you would expect to observe between two organisations, one pursuing a low cost strategy and the other a quality enhancement strategy. (Use the contents of the Noticeboard on page 493 to assist your answer.)

Internal fit

Internal fit is when the various components of the HRM strategy support each other and consistently encourage certain attitudes and behaviour.

Organisations need to have HRM policies that are internally consistent. The individual components need to encourage a single pattern of employee attitudes and role behaviour. The individual measures in the full set of policies need to complement and reinforce each other by sending a *consistent* set of signals to the workforce. For instance, an organisation seeking to encourage teamworking can support this through the payment system. It is likely to fail if this rewards people mainly for their individual contribution, encouraging people to compete rather than co-operate.

The ability of the HRM policies to contribute depends on the power and status of the HRM function within the organisation. Currently the personnel or HRM function appears to have more of a planning, strategic orientation in national systems (see Table 15.2) where the functional area has historically been relatively powerful and influential. However, in other systems, such as the UK and the United States, there are increased calls for the function to assume a more strategic role.

The important question is how should this be brought about? To many personnel or HRM specialists the answer is to play more of a partnership role with senior line management. However, as a Towers Perrin/IBM study noted:

> Representing the views of line management will not maximise the value added HR managers can bring to business partnerships. The value added

Table 15.2 **Personnel specialists' involvement, from the outset, in the development of corporate strategy (percentage of organisations in each country, 1991)**

Country	%
Switzerland	48
Germany	55
Denmark	42
Spain	46
France	50
Italy	32
Norway	54
Netherlands	48
Sweden	59
UK	43

Source: Brewster (1994, p.72)

comes from an independent viewpoint backed by distinctive capabilities. In an environment where employee involvement and participation are growing in importance and qualified job applicants are becoming scarcer, the successful HR function will have to balance the views of both senior management and employees. (1992, p.23)

In short, there is substantial agreement on the need for the HRM function to be more strategic in nature, but considerable disagreement over how to achieve this.

Another view is that the responsibility for developing a strategically-focused set of HRM practices should not be the responsibility of a separate functional group, but of line management. This in turn may lead to a devolution of HRM policies from the central function often found in large organisations to a more devolved and decentralised approach. The following quote is an example of such a recommendation from a public sector organisation.

The personnel function in the Irish civil service
❢ **Two issues arise in relation to the personnel function. First, personnel management, as currently practised, needs to be more broadly defined since it tends to be mainly administrative in nature, with insufficient attention being given to resource planning, career management, staff development, workload distribution and, especially, performance management. In short, the more developmental and strategic aspects of Human Resource Management as now widely practised have not had a significant impact on public service management to date.**

Secondly, the degree of central regulation and control of the human resource function has increasingly been called into question, particularly in the context of the more effective operation of the Administrative Budget system. In this regard, the Group accept the increasing need to devolve greater autonomy and responsibility for the control and management of personnel resources from the centre to Departmental managements, consistent with overall budgetary requirements and policy. ❢

(Stationery Office, 1996, p.34)

In view of the above, it is important to ask whether line managers are in practice becoming increasingly involved in HRM issues. In general, the answer seems to be yes, although there is considerable variation in this matter between countries. For example, the first Cranfield/Price Waterhouse survey conducted in 1991 and reported in Brewster (1994) found that devolvement to line managers was much more common in Switzerland, Denmark, Sweden and the Netherlands than in other European countries: Italy was characterised by the least devolution. The latest version of this survey (1995) indicates that line management responsibilities for HRM issues have continued to grow, especially for training and development (Price Waterhouse/Cranfield Project, 1997).

15.3 Human resource planning

There is a considerable literature on human resource planning or what used to be known as manpower planning. The latter literature, prominent in the 1960s and 1970s, tried to develop appropriate *techniques* for forecasting both the demand and supply of labour in individual organisations. In essence, the demand for labour was viewed as deriving from the content of an organisation's business plan (i.e. its future financial objectives, product mix, technology, etc.). This then required an estimate of the numbers and types of employees to meet these financial and output objectives. There are various techniques for making these estimates. At one extreme, current staffing levels are simply extrapolated into the future. At the other, sophisticated statistical techniques are employed based on forecasts of workload indicators (e.g. productivity levels, production levels, budgets) or on personnel ratios. Here are some examples:

▶ **Forecasting human resource demands**   Two technique are used here: judgemental forecasts or statistical projections. An example of the former is the *Delphi technique*. This approach involves obtaining independent estimates of future staffing needs by means of the successive distribution of questionnaires to various levels of management. The expectation is that some four or five iterations should produce a convergence in the estimates. An example of the latter is *simple linear regression* in which projected future demand is based on a past relationship between the organisation's employment level and a variable such as the level of sales.

Succession planning is the use of a deliberate process to ensure that staff are developed who are able to replace senior management as required.

▶ **Forecasting human resource supplies**   Again, techniques fall into two groups: judgemental and statistical. An example of the former is *replacement or succession planning* which involves the development of charts indicating the names of present job incumbents and the names of possible replacements. An example of the latter is *Markov matrix analysis* which can model or simulate human resource flows by examining the rates of movement between job categories over time.

The ability to meet forecast staffing needs (in terms of overall numbers and types of workers) depends on existing staffing levels in the various job categories at the beginning of the planning period, adjusted for (a) the outflow of staff over the planning period (e.g. retirements, dismissal, resignations), (b) the inflow of staff during the planning period (i.e. new recruits), and (c) the internal movement of staff between job categories (e.g. promotions).

The older manpower planning approach developed various techniques to estimate these changes in the supply of available labour. In some cases, statistical forecasting techniques (e.g. simulation, Markov chain analysis) were used and in others more subjective judgements made.

One of the major concerns of human resource planning has been to ensure an adequate replacement of senior management personnel, known as succession planning.

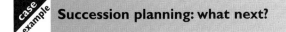

case example Succession planning: what next?

An organisation recently acquired two separate plants. The general manager responsible for both plants is due to retire in three years' time. The board believes that it is important to appoint a potential successor who can act as an 'understudy' to the retiring general manager for much of this three-year period. It initiates two search processes. First, the company contracts with an executive recruitment agency to search (within, but also outside the relevant industry) for a suitable candidate. Secondly, the notice of an opening for an understudy is circulated to the management teams of both plants. Five internal candidates indicate they intend to apply. The HRM director discusses these internal candidates with the present general manager who provides the following information/judgements:

▶ **Two of the candidates have performed well in their present positions, but 'lack larger vision' due to their limited experience outside the company and industry.**

▶ **Two other candidates are good performers, but are not seriously seeking the general manager's position, although they are clearly interested in receiving promotion.**

▶ **The fifth applicant is a good performer, but has long been critical of the performance of existing senior management; the impression is that he wants to use the interview to air some of his concerns and criticisms.**

---

n o t e b o o k   15.4

Has the company made a mistake in searching both inside and outside the organisation?

What should it do next: interview all of the internal candidates, or only some of them? If it interviews only some, which ones? Should it suspend the external recruitment process, or intensify it?

More broadly, the major difference between the older manpower planning and the newer human resource planning approaches has been a movement beyond the individual techniques of planning. The latter approach has argued for a close external fit between business strategy and human resource planning. Yet the evidence of such a fit is hard to find despite a

NOTICEBOARD **The gap between theory and practice in HRM**

If one takes policymaking as part of the planning process, then certain data from Marginson *et al.* (1988) illustrate the size of the gap [between theory and practice]. They found 84 per cent of UK managers claiming they had an overall employee policy; 50 per cent had a written policy; and 23 per cent said they gave a copy to employees. However, most could not describe the strategy in any detail. The Cranfield/Price Waterhouse comparative European study found that the proportion of all managers claiming to have a written human resource strategy ranged from 74 per cent in Norway to 20 per cent in

Denmark (and 45 per cent in the UK). Even fewer were likely to translate them into operational programmes, but were more likely to do so in relation to management development. US researchers found similar results. For example, a 1981 survey found 54 per cent of a sample of Fortune 500 companies did some human resource planning, but only 15 per cent did so in the comprehensive way suggested in the literature.

Source: Rothwell (1995, pp.175–6)

great deal of research in the HRM area particularly in the UK and the United States. Some of the relevant evidence cited in a recent review article is in the Noticeboard.

There are two main explanations for the gap between the theory and practice of human resource planning. One emphasises uncertainty, the other politics. Uncertainty may, paradoxically, make comprehensive planning a waste of time. This view is that management balances the *incentive* for, and *ability* to produce, a comprehensive human resource planning approach. Operating in a highly competitive, changeable environment provides a strong incentive to engage in human resource planning. At the same time, these same circumstances make sophisticated planning extremely difficult. The forecasts are likely to be of limited accuracy and value because of rapidly changing circumstances.

 Uncertainty and human resource planning

This computer manufacturing plant operates in a very competitive product market, characterised by short product lifecycles (i.e. six months) and strong, unpredictable shifts in product demand. It forecasts future sales and estimates a corresponding demand for labour on an annual basis. These figures (which are invariably 'wildly wrong') are 'fine-tuned' on both a quarterly and monthly basis. However, it solely 'produces to order' (i.e. holds virtually no stock) and has found that sales, output and hence its demand for labour vary a great deal even on a weekly basis. As a consequence, it has established a pool of some forty people in the local area (generally unemployed), which it can draw on to meet sharp upswings in demand. At the same time, it has utilised more and more temporary workers to deal with sharp downturns in demand. Currently, some 15–20 per cent of its workforce are temporaries, with many of these being on contracts of only one month's duration.

The other explanation for the gap is a political one. This is that the personnel or human resources function is simply not a sufficiently powerful enough player in senior management decision-making circles to ensure that HRM matters receive priority. Evidence to this effect includes the facts that senior managers rarely label human resource matters as strategic decisions, the presence of personnel directors on company boards is limited, and the functional area is frequently involved only in implementing, rather than in designing new policies or operating systems. There are, however, notable national variations in the apparent role and strength of the functional area, as indicated by Table 15.2.

In general, the problem of personnel management obtaining full and ready access to the corridors of power is particularly severe in organisations driven by a concern to meet short-run, financial performance measures. In contrast, HRM developments appear to have enhanced the role and influence of the personnel function in national systems (e.g. Germany) where the functional area has traditionally been important.

15.4 Job analysis

Job analysis is the process of determining the characteristics of an area of work according to a prescribed set of dimensions.

Job analysis typically leads to a written job description which has important implications for employee selection, training and performance appraisal. The Case Example presents an example of a job description recently given to a recruitment agency.

case example   A job description

The appointment
Title: **Assistant General Manager, Mills**
Reports to: **General Manager, Mills**

Main functional role
To provide a strategic focus and overview of production optimisation issues, constraints and development opportunities equally for both mills.

Responsibilities
To work with established mill management teams to proactively address matters of plant future developability and resolution of current problems through line management.

To improve the overall performance of the mill management teams through example and leadership.

To liaise with UK and International Sales in order to ensure the needs of the customer are met by anticipating and overcoming production challenges through research and comprehension of key issues.

To assist with all administrative tasks of the General Manager, in particular ensuring that all reports to Head Office of mill performance are completed accurately, on time and with such elaboration as required on trend deviations from budget, and plans to overcome.

To deputise for the General Manager in his absence and to attend Senior Managers' and other meetings as necessary on mills' performance.

The candidate
Experience and Qualifications: **A graduate of chemical/mechanical engineering or paper science or chemistry, with subsequent experience in paper science. 8–10 years' experience in the paper (ideally, but not exclusively) or other process industry as a production line manager or engineer. Strong production orientation focus and proven capability in sorting out production problems which have a technical origin.**

Skills
▶ **Clear conception of an overview with the initiative and judgement to identify the optimum route for implementation.**
▶ **Ability to maintain a number of ongoing activities without losing perspective or priority.**
▶ **Ability to identify with and champion corporate focus and direction for the mills.**
▶ **Strong interpersonal and leadership skills in influencing mill management teams.**
▶ **Presentation skills.**

Future prospects
Candidates must possess potential for further career development with the Group to General Manager or equivalent.

The literature on job analysis is largely concerned with the following steps:
▶ What are the methods of collecting job description data or information? There are various possibilities here such as interviews with the job incumbent, observation of people doing the job, the distribution and completion of questionnaires.
▶ Who should collect this information or data? Should it be the job incumbent, the supervisor or a specialist from inside or outside the organisation?
▶ How should the job information collected be structured and put into a standardised format?

NOTICEBOARD **Some key terms concerning job analysis**

Job analysis The process of describing and recording many aspects of jobs.

Job title Refers to a group of positions that are identical with regard to their significant duties.

Position description Refers to a collection of duties performed by a single person.

Work performed Identifies the duties and underlying tasks that make up a job.

Job requirements The experience, education, training, knowledge, skills and abilities needed to perform a job.

Job context The environment that surrounds the job.

Job elements The smallest identifiable components of a job.

Job descriptions Are generated from the information gathered through job analysis. On the basis of job descriptions, performance appraisal forms can be developed, and job classification systems established for job evaluation purposes.

Source: based on Schuler and Huber (1990, pp.74–80)

These three steps seek to describe the purpose of a job, its major duties and activities, the conditions under which it is performed and the necessary knowledge, skills and abilities involved. That is, individual jobs are broken down into job *elements*, such as information input, mental processes, work output, relationship with other people, and job context. Under the third step such elements can be rated along various dimensions, such as extent of use, importance to the job, amount of time involved, possibility of occurrence, etc. The Noticeboard outlines some of the key terms involved.

case example — Job analysis in an electronics plant

This example outlines how management in a wafer fabrication facility produced a job analysis. In this plant, teamworking operations (eventually without any supervisory personnel) are all-important. A new job was created, that of manufacturing team member. To help identify the key competences involved, a work profiling questionnaire was completed by certain key people in the plant, including the production manager, engineering manager, production supervisors and HR manager. The questionnaire produced a number of key tasks for the position, which were ranked in order of importance by the participants at a follow-up meeting. The skills identified were as follows:

▶ **Hard skills: visual checking, technical understanding, fault-finding skills, and mechanical comprehension.**
▶ **Soft skills: attention to detail, data rational, practical, and sociable/ supportive in a team environment.**

There are some important changes and issues to consider about job analysis. For instance, many organisations have deliberately reduced the number of people they employ. This has often reduced the number of individual job categories and broadened the job descriptions of the remaining employees. There has also been a move towards teamworking in many organisations, as discussed in Chapter 9. This has major implications for the approach to job analysis:

❝ Essentially, job analysis consists of methods and procedures that accurately describe the set of tasks that represent jobs. Inherent in the traditional approach to job analysis is the assumption that the work activities of individual employees can be objectively described … [In] a team situation individual tasks may be quite fluid. Further, team effectiveness often asks for team members to develop a wide variety of skills so that they are capable of providing an assortment of inputs. Thus cross-training is becoming more common and narrow job descriptions are giving way to individual contributions being driven by dynamic relationships within the team. The fluidity of tasks and the flux of individual inputs as a function of interdependency on the inputs of other team members means that a snapshot of the work activities for individual employees may be difficult to take and would likely soon be limiting and out of date in a team environment. Thus, the traditional job analysis assumption of continuing tasks for individuals appears to be incorrect when in team situations. **?**

(Academy of Management, 1996, p.11)

The continuation of the BMW Case Study below shows the teamworking arrangements recently introduced among production employees in the German operations of the group. The aim is to enhance productivity via these new work structures as a response to the increased competitive difficulties of the industry in Germany.

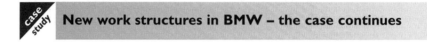

New work structures in BMW – the case continues

In response to increased competiton, market overcapacity and substantial reductions in collectively agreed working hours in Germany (i.e. a 35-hour week in the metal/electrical industries from October 1995), BMW has sought greater efficiency through cost reduction and increased individual employee performance. Following a 1991 agreement on a 'pilot phase for future work structures' and with the agreement of the works council, the company introduced in 1995 new forms of work organisation known as **NAS**. Employees are to be arranged into self-managing organisational groups (each involving 8–15 workers), with a high degree of autonomy but with clearly defined tasks. Members of the group decide upon each individual's responsibility and the rotation of jobs, as well as making on-the-spot suggestions and decisions concerning product improvement. Each group elects a spokesperson as an activity co-ordinator and representative of the group, although they have no power to give orders or take disciplinary action. Supervisors remain as the group's immediate superior in technical and disciplinary matters, but are to play more of an advisory/facilitating role. The supervisor is to be responsible for proposing and agreeing objectives, presenting progress figures, helping progress continuous improvements and ensuring the improvement of qualifications of group members. The company has to ensure that adequate training is available, goals are agreed upon and results circulated. Improved product quality and increased job satisfaction are the sought after objectives as a means of enhancing productivity. **BMW** is looking for a 4 per cent longer-term productivity figure from **NAS**, compared with 2 per cent under the previous arrangements.

Source: *European Industrial Relations Review*, issue 271 (1996), pp.23–4

CASE QUESTIONS 15.3

▶ How will the introduction of teamworking help to improve the external fit between HRM and broader strategy?

▶ To achieve internal fit, what other changes will BMW need to make to support teamworking?

▶ What comparisons and contrasts can you see between the BMW and Opel (Chapter 9) approaches?

Competences are those behaviours required for satisfactory ('threshold competence') or excellent ('superior competence') performance in a job.

Finally, some mention needs to be made of the development of the 'competences' theme. The aim here has been to identify and develop the behavioural competences required for the satisfactory and/or high performance of individual jobs. Competences, which derive from individual attributes such as personality traits, skills and abilities, are frequently grouped under two headings: threshold management competences (i.e. minimally acceptable level of behavioural performance), and superior management competences, defined as the level achieved by high performers. An interview-based study examined pan-European management competences and produced the following listing (Barham and Antal, 1994):

'Doing competences' (i.e. four main roles)
► Championing international strategy
► Operating as cross-border coach and co-ordinator
► Acting as intercultural mediator and change agent
► Managing personal effectiveness for international business

'Being competences' (i.e. concerned with values, beliefs and thinking, reasoning)
► Cognitive complexity
► Emotional energy
► Psychological maturity

---

n o t e b o o k   15.5

Identify the five leading competences which you would expect an ideal international manager to have. This is an individual who performs his or her job well in different national or cultural settings. Following your discussion, use your library resources to compare your list with that reported in the *Financial Times*, 9 April 1991.

Competence frameworks are being increasingly used by organisations for job analysis purposes, which has, in turn, resulted in changes in job descriptions, job evaluation exercises and training/development programmes. The Case Example below illustrates the approach used by a consultancy firm involved in a recent exercise along these lines.

 Competence framework used by a consultancy firm

The consultancy firm asked a representative cross-section of the organisation's employees to self-assess the nature of their job according to various behavioural competences. As an example of their approach the employees were asked: how much do your decisions or actions typically impact on the internal operation of the company? The respondents were asked to select a statement from A–E below which best describes the internal impact of their decisions or actions:
A Is limited to your own work and affects the performance of immediate colleagues.

B Decisions or actions may impact on the effectiveness of your own department or work area and occasionally on the efficiency of other departments.

C Decisions or actions have a continuing impact on the effectiveness of your own team/department's work and also impact on the effectiveness of other areas.

D Decisions or actions have a substantial impact on the direction and/or achievement of departmental objectives.

E Decisions or actions impact on the direction and/or achievement of corporate objectives.

Responses were scored as A=1, B=2, C=3, D=4 and E=5. The company repeated this approach to produce overall job scores in relation to a list of behavioural competences that were originally identified by a focus group.

15.5 Employee recruitment and selection

A job analysis exercise is intended to produce a comprehensive and accurate job description. The next part of the HRM process is that of recruitment and selection. The aim here is to produce a good pool of applicants and select the best of these to fit the job. Firms appear to be attaching more time, resources and priority to the selection process, even if the example below is extreme.

case example **Selecting a part-time packer**

A student recently applied for a job as a part-time packer in a supermarket. He was asked to attend a selection day based in a local hotel. There were about forty applicants there and six members of the management of the organisation. The session lasted from 10 am to 4 pm It involved: (1) an introduction to the company (i.e. videos and management presentations) which covered history, performance and 'values'; the latter stressed the importance of first-name terms, a happy family atmosphere and the customer is king; (2) aptitude tests (e.g. numerical calculations, examples of lateral thinking); (3) exercises and verbal presentations concerning customer needs and priorities; and (4) a final face-to-face interview.

Firms in different countries favour different selection techniques. Those in Finland place a great deal of emphasis on employee testing, while those in France make considerable use of graphology (i.e. handwriting analysis). Whatever the methods, the traditional purpose of the selection process remains the same, namely:

▶ to minimise *false positive errors*, whereby the selection process predicts success in the job for an applicant, who is therefore hired, but who fails, and

▶ to minimise *false negative errors*, whereby an applicant who would have succeeded in the job is rejected because the process predicted failure.

As the costs of the latter are not directly experienced by the organisation, it is in essence the problems, costs and consequences of the former that are of major concern to organisations.

The traditional, central concern in the employee selection literature has been the concept of *validity* which is concerned to see whether a statistically significant relationship exists between a predictor (e.g. a selection test score) and subsequent measures of on-the-job performance. Additional considerations, concerns and criteria in the selection process include equity and fairness (i.e. non-discrimination) and cost.

Interviews

Management traditionally relies on application forms, references and interviews for selecting employees. The interview remains popular (because of low direct costs and applicability to a wide range of jobs) despite research that has long demonstrated that the validity of the method is extremely low (Robertson, 1996). That is, interviewer ratings correlate poorly with measures of the subsequent on-the-job performance of the candidates hired (i.e. it generates far too many false positive errors). The reason for this is that many interviewers are not good at seeking, receiving and processing the amount and quality of information that is necessary to make an informed hiring decision. Some of the problems with the interview as a selection device are:

▶ Decisions are made too quickly.
▶ Information in the early stage of the interview disproportionately shapes the decision reached.
▶ Individual applicants are compared with an idealised stereotype.
▶ Appearance and non-verbal behaviour can strongly shape decisions.
▶ Interviewers are poorly prepared and ask too many questions of limited value.
▶ 'Good' responses to certain questions are overly generalised.

---

n o t e b o o k *15.6*

Interviewing interviewees

Arrange to talk to some friends or colleagues who have recently been interviewed for jobs. Ask them to describe the overall process and to identify any features or aspects of the experience which they particularly liked or disliked. Ideally you should talk to at least one person who was offered the job and to one who was not.

As background work for this exercise, compile a checklist of the key features of 'good practice' interviews which should help inform the way you ask questions. A useful reference here is Jack Gratus, *Successful Interviewing* (Penguin, 1988, pp.91–3). As well as practising your own interviewing skills, you should compare the experience of the interviewees with best-practice techniques.

Aware of these difficulties, more organisations are systematically training people in good interview techniques. Others make use of standard interview schedules in which all applicants are asked the same set of questions in roughly the same order. The membership of interview panels is also changing. Organisations using teamworking arrangements often include existing team members in the selection process as well as personnel staff and line management.

Selection tests

Selection tests are formal, often psychologically-based methods of assessing candidates' likely suitability for a job.

The weaknesses of the interview method and the changing nature of jobs has encouraged more managements to use formal testing methods in the selection process. A recent survey (*People Management*, August 1996, p.22) reported the following figures for 350 of The Times 1000 companies:
- The use of ability tests rose from under 30 per cent in 1985 to around 64 per cent in 1995.
- The use of personality questionnaires rose from around 35 per cent in 1985 to around 75 per cent in 1995.

Psychometric tests appear to be even more popular in Sweden and Portugal than in the UK, although they are less used in France, Switzerland and the Netherlands (Sparrow and Hiltrop, 1994, p.341). They can occasionally be more trouble than they are worth, as this Case Example illustrates.

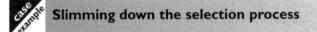

case example Slimming down the selection process

This computer manufacturing plant opened in 1994, and in 1997 employed about 800 people. Initially the selection process for operator grades involved reference checks, two interviews (by HR department and team leader) and abilities tests. This meant that a job applicant had to visit the site three or four times before a final hiring decision was made. In 1996, management decided that the process took too long and cost too much. It also concluded that the abilities test was adding little value as nine out of ten people passed. The extensive process also raised unreasonably high expectations among employees about the nature of the job as many were only temporary positions. The company therefore eliminated the abilities test and one of the interviews.

There are many long-established tests available, both for abilities and personality. In recent years it has been the growing use of personality tests which has been particularly noticeable, and at the same time controversial. The Case Example on pages 500–1 described a wafer fabrication facility. Management had identified a set of key skills for the new position of manufacturing team member. It then established the following selection process for candidates for this position:
- Three or four aptitude tests concerned with technical understanding, fault diagnosis, mechanical comprehension and/or visual checking.
- One personality test concerned with tolerance, attention to detail, data rational, initiative, sociable, supportive, willingness to take responsibility and critical. This test would only be scored for candidates who reach second interview.
- First interview covering work experience, health, suitability for shift working, and an eyesight test.
- Second interview – structured, using the results of the personality test.

Organisational psychologists hold varying opinions about the accuracy and value of personality tests. Some of the concerns and criticisms of this form of testing are:

▶ They should only be used and interpreted by qualified and approved experts.

▶ Candidates can fake the answers to some questions, to give the answers they think the organisation is looking for.

▶ An individual's personality may vary according to the particular circumstances they find themselves in.

▶ Good performers in the same job may have rather different personalities.

The Case Example below is the personality test score of a director's secretary in one company; it is based on the 16 PF test, one of the most commonly used.

---

case example **A personality profile (16 PF test)**

	(1 2 3 4 5 6 7 8 9 10)	
Reserved	8	Outgoing
Concrete thinking	8	Abstract thinking
Affected by feelings	7	Calm, unruffled
Not assertive	8	Assertive, dominant
Serious, reflective	6	Happy-go-lucky
Expedient	6	Conscientious
Shy	5	Venturesome
Tough-minded	7	Tender-minded
Trusting	6	Suspicious
Practical	6	Imaginative
Forthright	5	Shrewd
Self-assured	10	Apprehensive
Conservative	6	Experimenting
Group-oriented	8	Self-sufficient
Undisciplined	8	Self-disciplined
Relaxed	8	Tense

There is also a growing concern that the use, or misuse, of tests may run foul of equal opportunities legislation and regulations. A final point is the potential problem of managing employee expectations. One long-standing criticism of the employee selection process is that the organisation is 'over-sold' to those hired. If employees' expectations are then not met on the job they are likely to leave. There is a danger of creating a sense of an elite labour force that will be well looked after when 2,000 applicants are reduced to less than 300 who are offered a job. Extensive testing risks adding to the traditional 'over-sell' problem at the recruitment/selection stage.

Assessment centres

Another method that is growing in popularity is the assessment centre. For example, among 350 of The Times 1000 companies, assessment centre usage was up from 20 per cent in 1985 to just under 50 per cent in 1995 (*People*

Assessment centres are multi-exercise programmes designed to identify the recruitment and promotion potential of key personnel.

Management, 8 August 1996, p.22). Some evidence for European countries suggests that assessment centre usage is relatively high in the Netherlands, but much less common in Portugal, Switzerland and France (Sparrow and Hiltrop, 1994, p.341). Assessment centres, with their multiple tests and multiple assessors, have long been used for certain highly specialist positions (e.g. army officers). Their use for selection and development purposes has become more widespread in recent years.

They appear to have much higher levels of validity for selection purposes than interviews and employee tests. To some this is a positive finding. That is, the package approach of assessment centres (with their multiple tests and multiple assessors) comes closest to being a reasonable simulation of what the actual job will involve. Other commentators offer a more critical explanation for the relatively high validity of the results from assessment centres – they involve a self-fulfilling prophecy. Knowing that someone has succeeded in an assessment centre, their managers and colleagues act in ways that ensure that the person subsequently does well. Other concerns about assessment centres include:

▶ Their relatively high cost.
▶ Their tendency to become a 'paper factory' with a huge amount of documentation being generated and analysed.
▶ The ethical and practical problems of providing feedback to individuals whose performance was not impressive.
▶ The possibility of producing 'clones' who are very similar to the present job incumbents, which may not be appropriate in rapidly changing circumstances.

n o t e b o o k   15.7

Eight trainee managers join the company on the basis of their assessment centre performance. All eight stay with the company for five years. Gillian, who received the highest ranking in the initial assessment centre, receives more promotion in those years than any of the others. Form into two groups to provide a list of the possible reasons for Gillian's performance. One group is to provide a positive list for this performance, the other a more critical one.

Evaluation

This essentially narrow, technical task of achieving an 'individual employee/ individual job fit' has been called into question in recent years by some of the strategic human resource management literature. For instance, some of the literature on cultural change programmes (see Chapter 16) has emphasised the need to recruit and select employees who fit well with the larger direction of change in the organisation. A specific instance of change along these lines is the attempt to identify individuals who will be at home with teamworking arrangements. Such an orientation will have important implications for job analysis. It is also likely to result in important changes in selection methods, and the individuals involved in selection processes. Indeed, there is now a growing body of literature which argues that individuals should be hired for the organisation, not the job. As Bowen *et al.*(1996) write:

NOTICEBOARD Hiring for the organisation rather than the job

Potential benefits
- ▶ More favourable employee attitudes (e.g. greater organisational commitment).
- ▶ More desirable individual behaviours (e.g. lower absence and turnover).
- ▶ Reinforcement of organisational design (e.g. support for desired organisational culture).

Potential problems
- ▶ Greater investment of resources in the hiring process.

- ▶ Relatively undeveloped and unproven supporting selection technology.
- ▶ Individual stress.
- ▶ May be difficult to use the full model where pay-offs are greatest.
- ▶ Lack of organisational adaptation.

Source: Bowen et al. (1996, p.146)

> Diverse firms … are using the approach to build cultures that rely heavily on self-motivated, committed people for corporate success. New, often expensive, hiring practices are changing the traditional selection model. An organisational analysis supplements a job analysis, and personality attributes are screened in addition to skills, knowledge and abilities. (p.139)

The *organisational* analysis mentioned here is concerned with the leading components of the larger work *context*, such as the longer-term goals and values of the organisation, rather than simply the content of the individual job. The Noticeboard outlines the various potential benefits and costs of adopting a hire-for-the-organisation, as opposed to individual job approach.

C A S E   Q U E S T I O N S   1 5 . 4

- ▶ In what ways are developments in BMW already rated as encouraging a 'hire for the organisation, not for the job' approach?
- ▶ What implications will that have for achieving internal fit in the company's HRM policies?

15.6 Performance appraisal

Performance appraisal is a systematic review of a person's work and achievements over a recent period, usually leading to plans for the future.

The prime purpose of performance appraisal is to try to help improve an individual's current on-the-job performance, although the process may also be important for pay purposes ('performance-related pay') and for longer-term training/development purposes.

Performance appraisal, at least on a formal basis, is not a widespread feature of all national systems. For instance, it is not a characteristic of even relatively large organisations in Finland, while in many well known Japanese companies it is a much more informal, ongoing process than is the case in UK and American organisations. In the UK, performance appraisal has changed in a number of ways in recent years. First, from its early concentration on middle managers in large, private-sector manufacturing organisations, performance appraisal has spread to different organisations and

NOTICEBOARD **A survey of performance appraisal in the UK: key findings from 306 organisations**

- ▶ Eighteen per cent had no formal appraisal schemes.
- ▶ A substantial growth in systems for appraising non-management employees.
- ▶ Emphasis on current rather than future performance.
- ▶ Appraisal linked to pay in 40 per cent of the schemes, although only 15 per cent of organisations carried out a salary review at the same time as the performance review.

- ▶ Some 78 per cent of the sample organisations provided appraisal skills training.
- ▶ The immediate supervisor almost universally (98 per cent) acts as the appraiser.
- ▶ Growth in the extent to which appraisees see all or parts of the completed appraisal forms.

Source: Long (1986)

different groups of employees. Performance appraisal is now more of a feature of the public sector, while in some organisations manual employees are being appraised for the first time. The Noticeboard lists the findings of a survey on performance appraisal in the UK. Personnel and human resource managers frequently cite performance appraisal arrangements as the area of their responsibilities that they would most like to improve. Few are satisfied, and in consequence performance appraisal arrangements are frequently changing.

case example — Appraising the appraisal system

In this organisation, the human resource director carried out interviews with forty employees about their experience with performance appraisal. Their comments were highly critical of the process, with the particular concerns being that it only occurred once a year, was rushed, the only input was from the appraiser, and there was much cynicism about individual ratings (and those across departments). Many of his senior management colleagues agreed with his view that the present arrangements needed to be changed. However, they overwhelmingly favoured changing the nature and content of the written appraisal form. In contrast he advocated shorter, more frequent appraisal interviews (once a quarter) and training appraisers in coaching skills.

Attempts to improve the appraisal process usually concentrate on four issues: the criteria used to appraise performance, the face-to-face appraisal interview, who does the appraisal and what happens afterwards.

The criteria

The criteria used in appraisal systems have changed in recent years. Early arrangements concentrated on employee traits, such as leadership or loyalty. These have generally given way to criteria that focus on the employee's *on-the-job behaviour*. More recently still, the emphasis has been on job *outcomes* –

Table 15.3 **Use of merit/performance-related pay for managerial staff (percentage of organisations, 1991)**

Country	%
Switzerland	65
Germany	24
Denmark	14
Spain	48
France	70
Italy	85
Norway	18
Netherlands	27
Sweden	13
UK	68

Source: Brewster *et al.* (1994, p.117)

what the person has achieved. As part of the general increase in performance management, contemporary appraisal systems frequently consider whether employees have achieved their specified job performance goals over the appraisal period. There are, of course, important differences here in the length of the appraisal period and the extent to which the performance goals were jointly set.

Another change has been the increased use of performance appraisal for some element of pay determination purposes. Table 15.3 contains some comparative information.

Review and change are regular features of performance appraisal systems, often including the criteria of the system. For example, in one plant which introduced a total quality management (TQM) system involving team-working arrangements, the traditional 1–5 rating scale has been removed. This was deemed to 'set employees against each other in a competitive scramble'. Now the emphasis is solely on identifying an individual's training or development needs.

The interview

For many appraisers and appraisees, the interview is a particularly awkward moment. It brings to the surface various tensions, conflicts and contradictions. Beer (1985) summarised the essence of these difficulties:

> The most significant conflict is between the individual and the organisation. The individual desires to confirm a positive self-image and to obtain organisational rewards of promotion or pay. The organisation wants individuals to be open to negative information about themselves so they can improve their performance. It also wants individuals to be helpful in supplying this information. The conflict is over the exchange of valid information. As long as individuals see the appraisal process as having an important influence on their rewards (pay, recognition), their career (promotions and reputation), and their self-image, they will be reluctant to engage in the kind of open dialogue required for valid evaluation and personal development. (p.316)

NOTICEBOARD **Common appraisal interview problems**

The halo effect The appraiser gives a favourable rating to overall job performance in essence because the person being appraised has performed well in the particular aspect of the job which the appraiser considers all-important.

The pitchfork effect This is the exact opposite of the halo effect, whereby the appraiser gives an unfavourable rating to overall job performance in essence because the appraisee has performed poorly in the particular aspect of the job which the appraiser considers all-important.

Central tendency The appraiser deliberately avoids using the end-points of the rating scale and rates all employees as average in virtually all aspects of job performance.

The recency error In rating an employee's job performance over, for example, a twelve-month period, the appraiser makes disproportionate use of instances of performance which are relatively recent (i.e. close to the interview in time) to make an assessment.

Length of service bias The appraiser assumes that an experienced employee who has been rated well in the past has absorbed and responded well to any new aspects of his or her job, and hence does not closely monitor performance in this regard.

The loose rater In order to avoid any conflict with a subordinate, an appraiser does not discuss any weak areas of an individual's job performance.

The tight rater An appraiser has unrealistically high expectations for all subordinates which means that no one receives an excellent or outstanding rating.

The competitive rater An appraiser links his or her own rating with that of subordinates so that no one receives a rating higher than the appraiser's.

Source: adapted from Lowe (1986, pp.60–2)

There are numerous ways that individual appraisers can adjust to the potential dilemma of being both a judge and a helper. In some organisations the formally scheduled appraisals do not actually take place. The human resource (HR) director in the example above says that one manager in three is still not actively carrying out the quarterly appraisals he introduced. In other cases, the appraiser seeks to avoid disrupting working relationships by giving the appraisee an easy time. The Noticeboard lists the main problems encountered in appraisal interviews.

Aware of these problems, management in other organisations have tried to improve the quality of the face-to-face appraisal interviews. They have provided training to eliminate the problems listed by Lowe in the Noticeboard. They try to develop a process with the following features:

▶ Regular informal monitoring of and feedback to the appraisee takes place prior to the appraisal interview. There are then no surprises (e.g. unexpected information) during the formal interview.
▶ A completed self-appraisal form provides the basis for the interview.
▶ The content of the interview is largely shaped by the person being appraised. They do most of the talking, and are encouraged/coached to identify weaknesses, discuss these and suggest solutions.
▶ The appraiser should use open questions to encourage dialogue.
▶ Criticism must be constructive in nature, with positive comments substantially outweighing negative ones.
▶ Comments must be factually based and focused on specific job activities.

Different approaches to appraisal

An appraisal interview training video (with a recommended approach along the above lines) was shown to an audience which included managers from UK and French companies. Comments by the French managers indicated many similarities in approach. They also highlighted the following differences:

- ▶ The appraisal interview lasted much longer in France (three hours compared with an hour or so in the UK).
- ▶ The interview involved three people (i.e. the appraisee, the boss and their boss), rather than two.
- ▶ The very detailed self-appraisal form (8–10 pages) was much more significant in the French than in the UK organisations represented.

The appraiser

Traditionally, appraisals have involved an individual being appraised by his or her immediate superior. However, Fletcher (1996) has observed:

> With fewer management layers and more direct reports to each manager, increased use of matrix or project management and greater geographical spread of staff, the old principle of the immediate boss carrying out the appraisal becomes unworkable in many instances. A manager may have too many appraisees to deal with, or see them too infrequently to know how they are doing. An appraisee may work for several bosses throughout the year. Who, then, should be the appraiser? (pp.235–6)

This question is the subject of active discussion in many organisations. There seems considerable emphasis on encouraging more self-appraisal while, in some team-based organisations, peer group appraisals have been introduced. Some organisations have gone even further in this regard, using full-circle appraisal arrangements. These involve self-assessment, appraisals by superiors, subordinates, peers and in some cases outside customers. An HR manager made these comments about such arrangements:

- ▶ In theory, such arrangements have a great deal to recommend them.
- ▶ In practice they are extremely time-consuming.
- ▶ Only a small, self-contained part of his organisation uses them. They appear to have been most successful at the top of the organisation where numbers are small.
- ▶ Such arrangements are probably most suitable for smaller organisations characterised by close 'high trust' working relationships.
- ▶ It is difficult to maintain the momentum of such arrangements over time, particularly in the face of more immediate business pressures.

The aftermath

What happens when the appraisal has been conducted and training needs identified? The issues here can be illustrated by the case of an organisation which annually appraised all its white collar and professional staff to assess development needs. At the company's request, a senior academic conducted focus group meetings with 40–50 of the staff to gain their perceptions of the value of the process. The major points made were:

▶ The overwhelming majority of the staff rated the interpersonal skills of the appraisers very highly. The interviews were well conducted.

▶ The development needs of individuals that were identified were rarely followed through. Training courses were promised but never delivered.

This arose from policy in the training section of the HR department. The content of the annual training plan was driven by budgetary concerns and the programmes offered by local training consultants. The results of the appraisals did not enter the plan in any significant way. One unexpected outcome of this exercise was the departure of the training manager.

The weak link demonstrated here between the appraisal system and the development/training programme is by no means unique. Indeed, this finding is highly consistent with the general view that training/development activities in many organisations are determined in a very piecemeal manner. In order to ensure a much better follow-up process to appraisal interviews it will be essential for organisations to involve the HR department more fully in the appraisal process. They will need to recognise that at least three parties, and not just two (the appraisee and appraiser) are involved. An example of this is the organisation that has recently changed its performance appraisal system with a view to encouraging more regular self-appraisal for personal development purposes. Its new documentation sets out the following areas of responsibility:

▶ Appraiser: sets the direction, coaches on a day-to-day basis, provides timely reviews on request, conducts final assessment of results.

▶ Job-holder: interprets manager's direction, develops plans, arranges meetings and leads the system, tracks own development progress.

▶ HR department: issues the documentation, provides training where appropriate, audits the system, approves the outcome.

15.7 Performance-related pay

Performance-related pay refers to payment systems in which a percentage of pay depends on the assessed performance of individuals, groups or the organisation as a whole.

The use of performance-related pay arrangements for managerial staff has already been noted in Table 15.3. The Case Study below shows the new bonus payment arrangements for production employees in the German operations of BMW. These team- or group-based payment arrangements were associated with the new work structures outlined earlier.

case study **New work structures in BMW – the case continues**

The new work structures (NAS), with their emphasis on multiskilled workers, quality objectives, and the individual's contribution to group performance, have been accompanied by new payment arrangements. A bonus system applies to all 36,000 production employees who operate with defined performance targets. *Basic remuneration* consists of the minimum pay rate agreed in the metalworking industry collective agreement, plus a 10 per cent BMW supplement. The previous six wage groups have been expanded to nine. This allows for finer gradations determined by the demands placed on the employee. These reflect the

criteria of function, difficulty and variety of activities, and scope for decision-making. If a worker regularly performs a higher-value activity, then movement up the groups is possible. In order to assign an employee to one of the nine pay groups, the job is calculated on the basis of the activities that are performed regularly during normal working.

On top of the basic remuneration, a fixed 25 per cent *additional bonus* is paid to all employees for meeting prearranged quotas. This quota involves producing a set number of units to the company's quality standards by a workforce of an agreed size. To determine work quotas and the number of personnel needed, the tasks involved in a field of work are combined and assessed, and the time needed to carry out each task is determined. Under the new system, employees in each group are consulted and they are able to put forward their own estimates as to whether the quotas are realistic and achievable.

Employees can also earn extra pay through a *personal supplement*, which is payable if an individual contributes to the group results. The supplement is paid monthly at three levels, with the basic amount fixed at DM98. An individual's contribution is assessed at one of four levels: the initial level (carrying no supplement) applies to an employee who meets the agreed quantities to the agreed quality standards; the target level (which carries the basic supplement of DM98) applies when an employee fulfils the expectations for co-operation, overall quality, flexibility and initiative; a Stage 1 increment (worth DM196) applies when the employee has made a particular positive contribution; a Stage 2 increment (the highest level, worth DM294) is attained when an employee has a significant influence upon the group result. Expectations and specific goals are discussed and agreed in talks between the employee and the supervisor. An individual's contribution to the group is discussed every year and this assessment determines the personal supplement received.

This system came into effect in July 1996. A further component of the pay system is a one-off payment in the form of a bonus – payable to the individual or the group – which is awarded for a *specific contribution to improved productivity* as part of the process of continuous improvement. In 1995, BMW paid out some DM14 million on this account.

Source: *European Industrial Relations Review*, issue 271 (1996), p.24

CASE QUESTIONS 15.5

▶ What external business factors have prompted this review of the payment system at BMW?

▶ How will it affect the management of the appraisal system?

▶ How will it affect the demands on the management information system (see Chapter 20)?

Performance-related pay arrangements involve a linkage between a human resource flow activity (i.e. performance appraisal) and reward systems, which are two separate subsets of activities in the Harvard Business School approach to HRM. To some observers this is an unfortunate linkage to make because it risks 'overloading' the appraisal process. That is, it is asking the appraisal process to achieve too many objectives, risks making awkward interviews even more difficult and will ultimately cause the training/development objectives of appraisal to take second place to money considerations.

That said, there are some positive points to be made about performance-related pay arrangements, namely:

▶ Such arrangements do have some theoretical or conceptual underpinnings in expectancy theory (see Chapter 6).

▶ Some organisations have used such arrangements for many years and report positive effects on both individual and organisational performance.

However, there are many other organisations where the track record of performance-related pay has been much less impressive. Either there has been little positive impact on organisational performance or the arrangements have been counterproductive for other reasons. In short, the record of performance-related pay arrangements has been highly variable. There are various possible reasons for this:

▶ The expectancy theory of employee motivation that underpins such arrangements does not apply universally or at all times.

▶ Performance-related pay arrangements have not been well received by employees because of inadequate prior discussion, consultation and explanation. (The Case Example below suggests an organisation that may well experience some problems in this regard in the future.)

▶ Performance-related pay fits the circumstances of some organisations much better than others. For instance, introducing performance-related pay arrangements into an organisation characterised by 'low trust' relationships between employees and management is almost a certain recipe for creating further problems.

▶ Performance-related pay arrangements have multiple goals or objectives, but not all of these can be achieved by the one set of arrangements. For instance, individual-based performance-related pay is most successful in seeking to instil in employees a belief that a genuine pay–performance linkage exists in the organisation. However, relative to performance-related pay arrangements based on a group or organisation-wide basis, it is much more likely to inhibit co-operation within the workforce.

 Performance-related pay in a not-for-profit organisation

This not-for-profit organisation has 23 separate grades of employees, with annual salary increases being related to changes in the cost of living, and incremental payments occurring (within grades) every three years. In 1995, a new chairman (with a private sector background) was appointed, with some other individuals (also from the private sector) being appointed to the finance committee. The chairman and other new appointees were highly critical of the existing salary/grading arrangements. They were viewed as 'very old-fashioned, with little capacity to motivate staff'. In particular, the absence of performance-related pay was viewed as highly undesirable. Although the personnel manager could point to no employee dissatisfaction with the existing arrangements or give examples of tangible organisational difficulties,

a senior working party was established to 'move things along' and a consultancy firm engaged to help introduce some changes.

---

n o t e b o o k   1 5 . 8

Identify some of the key features of an organisation where performance-related pay arrangements are likely to be appropriate.

One of the major growth areas of performance-related pay in recent years has been in the public sector of many advanced industrialised economies. The Noticeboard indicates some of the early problems encountered with such arrangements.

15.8 Critical perspectives on HRM

Although the philosophy and terminology of HRM has spread widely in the management literature, there are questions about how widely management has applied it, whether it can show reults when it has been applied, and its effects on power relations within organisations, involving a set of techniques and practices that are potentially contradictory (Blyton and Turnbull, 1994).

More rhetoric than reality?

One argument is that while many managements talk about human resource management a much smaller number use it in the fullest sense of the term. It may not suit the circumstances of all countries. For example, an economy which typically follows a low-wage strategy, has a limited tradition of planning and works to short-run financial measures will not provide a suitable place in which to develop advanced HRM policies. Even within a more benign national system, HRM is likely to be confined to a relatively small

---

NOTICEBOARD **Common problems with performance-related pay in the public sector**

▶ A lack of differentiation in performance ratings.
▶ A clustering of managers at the top of the salary range in merit pay schemes where they are no longer eligible for merit increments.
▶ Dissatisfaction among staff who are rated fully satisfactory but who, under quotas and other restrictive guidelines for some schemes, either receive a smaller pay award than their colleagues or no award at all in a given year.

▶ Relatively low levels of funding which make schemes highly competitive and, in some countries, cut-backs in funds during times of economic restraint.
▶ A narrowing of the range and a reduction in the average size of bonuses paid.

Source: OECD (1993)

and atypical group of organisations. Foreign-owned, non-union, greenfield site operations have often been identified as the most natural homes for such an employment approach (Guest, 1987). Another point is that, while organisations may adopt certain HRM practices, few will do so in a comprehensive, strategic manner. In other words, there will be little evidence of internal fit; rather, a more *ad hoc*, reactive, piecemeal approach will be apparent (Storey, 1992).

Does it work?

The second line of questioning in relation to HRM is the limited evidence that the use of the approach has enhanced organisational effectiveness and performance. That is, the quantity and quality of evidence supporting a strong, positive relationship between HRM and organisational performance is far from impressive (Legge, 1995). Certainly there are some individual studies which have demonstrated such a relationship. For example, an important study in the United States involving some one thousand firms, reported a strong relationship between a set of high performance work practices and certain measures of firm performance, such as employee turnover, productivity and financial performance (Huselick, 1995). Clearly, more studies of this type and quality are needed. Furthermore, it has been argued that a bottom-line pay-off will only come about if a more strategic orientation is adopted towards the introduction and operation of HRM, i.e. the notions of external and internal fit are more strenuously observed. The need for more convincing evidence of a positive impact is growing as alternative approaches and themes in management (e.g. business process re-engineering) are being increasingly urged.

Does it shift the power balance?

Finally there is a line of criticism that HRM can have negative effects on employees and unions. The underlying contention here is that HRM embodies a unitary view of organisations. This view (see Chapter 2) rejects the legitimacy of employees/management conflict in the employment relationship and seeks to align the aims and objectives of individual employees with those of owners and their agents (i.e. senior management). To some commentators, HRM is simply the latest in a long line of attempts to shift the terms of the wage/effort bargain in favour of management. Others stress that HRM practices are designed to help organisations to be run on a non-union basis, or at least that they will have the effect of reducing the role, strength and presence of unions. However, in the UK, HRM practices seem to be more a feature of the union rather than non-union sector, probably because there are more small firms in the non-union sector (Beaumont, 1996). This being said, the relevance of HRM practices to small firms should not be ignored, as one UK survey indicates:

> ❝ the larger the organisation, the more chance there was that each of the new employment initiatives had been launched. The reasons are fairly obvious: the larger organizations had more expertise at their disposal, and the relevance of some of the initiatives was clearly tied to size. However, there was an interesting and important new

finding. When we looked at the degree to which certain initiatives
had been sustained, we found that smaller organizations had
enjoyed the greater success. The reason for this is presumably that
once the head of a small enterprise decides to introduce a new
approach, it is more likely to be followed through. **'**

(Storey, 1995, p.20)

15.9 Recap

Organisations in countries such as Japan and (West) Germany have tended
to give people management a relatively high priority. In others, including
the United States and the UK, employment management has been secondary
to financial management factors. In recent years many managements in the
latter countries have attempted to change this and to raise the prominence
of HRM issues in their organisations. These need to be evaluated in terms of
their external and internal fit. Unless there is a good degree of fit they are
unlikely to have any lasting effect on business performance.

Content agenda

HRM practices represent an attempt to institutionalise those aspects of
management concerned with employees. The approach is an attempt to
support the achievement of broader business objectives and strategy. It does
this by organising activities such as HR planning and job analysis to ensure
that available resources fit the requirements of the external world. Organising
and planning the approach also aims to ensure a degree of internal fit
between the several components of HRM. It also seeks a fit with other organisational policies such as teamwork or the creation of autonomous business
units. An underlying principle is that employees can be motivated to appropriate behaviours by HRM practices which accurately reflect their pattern of
human needs. The approach is also criticised by some commentators for
having other, more covert objectives. It may be followed for primarily cost-
cutting reasons or as a way of weakening the power of representative bodies
such as trade unions.

Process agenda

HRM initiatives are affected by the interests of other stakeholders around
the organisation. They may or may not see their interests served by HRM.
Other senior managers may be more powerful than the HRM specialists, and
have other priorities. An organisational commitment to HRM initiatives is
inevitably competing with other possible innovations such as business
process re-engineering. HRM may also be opposed by trade unions if the
latter see it as an attempt to shift the power balance against them or to
remove some of the functions they have performed on behalf of their
members. There is a discussion within management as to whether HRM
policies are decided and managed by a central department or delegated to
the line managers responsible for particular business units. The acceptance
of the approach is likely to vary between countries, depending on wider
institutional arrangements.

Control agenda

HRM can be seen as one of the ways in which management seeks to exercise control over employees. Some accuse those promoting the approach of adopting a fundamentally unitary approach to management and seeking to displace or weaken trade unions. It can also contribute to both individual and organisational learning. Practices such as performance appraisal attempt this at the individual level. However, commentators have noted that few companies regularly appraise the appraisal process to see if it is meeting whatever objectives were held for it. Not doing so prevents learning about the benefits or otherwise of the monitoring, correction and learning cycles embodied in appraisal systems. Similarly there are few studies showing convincingly whether HRM really does contribute to the achievement of wider organisational objectives in the way intended.

The integrative framework is set out in Figure 15.1.

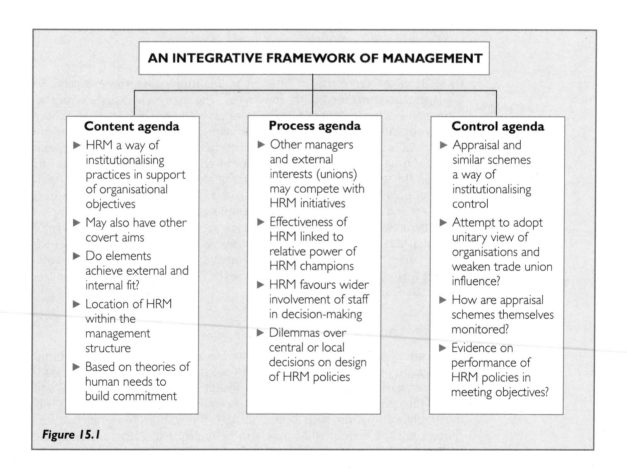

AN INTEGRATIVE FRAMEWORK OF MANAGEMENT

Content agenda
- ▶ HRM a way of institutionalising practices in support of organisational objectives
- ▶ May also have other covert aims
- ▶ Do elements achieve external and internal fit?
- ▶ Location of HRM within the management structure
- ▶ Based on theories of human needs to build commitment

Process agenda
- ▶ Other managers and external interests (unions) may compete with HRM initiatives
- ▶ Effectiveness of HRM linked to relative power of HRM champions
- ▶ HRM favours wider involvement of staff in decision-making
- ▶ Dilemmas over central or local decisions on design of HRM policies

Control agenda
- ▶ Appraisal and similar schemes a way of institutionalising control
- ▶ Attempt to adopt unitary view of organisations and weaken trade union influence?
- ▶ How are appraisal schemes themselves monitored?
- ▶ Evidence on performance of HRM policies in meeting objectives?

Figure 15.1

▶ What are the main elements of the human resource strategy in Save the Children Fund described in the case?

▶ From your understanding of the material in the chapter, what aspects of HRM should Save the Children Fund be focusing its efforts upon?

▶ What similarities and differences are there between teamwork at Save the Children and at BMW?

▶ What implementation issues are raised in the Save the Children case?

15.10 Review questions

1 What do the terms internal and external fit mean in an HRM context?
2 What are the arguments put forward in favour of an organisation adopting a deliberate HRM strategy?
3 Summarise the criticism of HRM that it is based on a unitary perspective of organisations? You could refer to the discussion in Chapter 1 of critical perspectives on management.
4 Another criticism of HRM is that there is not much evidence that it has achieved the business objectives claimed for it. What evidence would you look for, and how would you show the link between cause and effect?
5 How would the concept of organisational analysis support the employee recruitment process?
6 What are the main criticisms of personality testing?
7 Why is the practice of performance appraisal controversial? Consider both technical and underlying explanations.
8 What lessons can you draw from the way BMW has used the payment system to support other aspects of the HRM policy? More generally, summarise the lessons you would draw from the BMW case?

Further reading

Two early and influential articles should be mentioned. Guest (1987) provides an outline of the essence of HRM and its implications for existing industrial relations arrangements. Similarly, Hendry and Pettigrew (1990) examine the origins of the concept and practice of HRM, with an outline of research needs in the area. A comprehensive collection of readings covering strategic issues, key practice areas and an international perspective is available in Storey (1995). A critical, non-prescriptive perspective underlies both texts. Legge (1995) provides a highly critical examination of many of the leading, individual themes in HRM. She emphasises the difference (gap?) between the theory and practice of HRM. An explicitly European perspective on the topic is available in Sparrow and Hiltrop (1994). This is a comprehensive, well written textbook which has a genuine European focus in the material presented.

16

The developing organisation

CONTENTS

AIM

To review the development of organisations in response to external change, and the role of management in shaping their evolution.

OBJECTIVES

By the end of your work on this chapter you should be able to outline the concepts below in your own terms and:

1 Explain why organisational structure is deliberately shaped by management

2 Summarise the main elements of Joan Woodward's research and explain why it was significant

3 Compare the features of mechanistic and organic structures

4 Outline the perspective that links the appropriate form of structure to the nature of the external environment

5 Distinguish between and explain the significance of the determinist and structural choice approaches

6 List the main factors which are prompting change in organisations, and give original examples of each

7 Describe how developments in information technology offer new organisational possibilities

8 Outline a model of organisational change and the stages through which an organisation passes in its development

Oticon

This Danish company is one of the world's five largest producers of hearing aids, with about 1,200 staff. It has its own basic research and production facilities and stresses the high engineering and design quality of its products. Competition intensified during the 1980s and the company began to lose market share. Lars Kolind was appointed chief executive in 1988. In 1990 he concluded that a new approach was needed to counter the threats from larger competitors who were becoming stronger. Oticon's only hope for survival and prosperity was to be radical in all aspects of the business. The changes were intended to turn Oticon from an *industrial* organisation producing hearing aids into a *service* organisation with a physical product.

Work is organised around projects. The project leader is appointed by management and has to recruit a team. Employees choose whether or not to join – and can only do so if their current project leader agrees. Previously, most people had a single skill; now all have several. Chip designers have skills in customer support, for example. Employees can work on several projects at once. These arrangements allow the company to respond quickly to unexpected events and to use skills fully. Different backgrounds mean more insights.

Previously, Oticon had a conventional structure, now it has no departments, and no hierarchy. There is no formal structure, just teams. Kolind refers to this as 'managed chaos'. The company tries to overcome the dangers of this by developing a very strong and clear purpose and mission 'to help people with X problem to live better with X'; and a common set of written values. Examples include: 'an assumption that we only employ adults (who can be expected to act responsibly)', and 'an assumption that staff want to know what and why they are doing it', so all information is available to everyone (with a couple of legally excepted areas). There are no titles – people do whatever they think is right at the time. Again the potential for chaos is averted by building underneath the flexible organisation a set of clearly defined business processes, setting out how they are to be carried out. 'The better your processes are defined, the more flexible you can be.' The absence of departments avoids people protecting local interests and makes it easier to cope with fluctuations in workload.

Oticon has redesigned the workplace to maximise disturbance. It refers to this as the mobile office, in which each workstation consists of a desk without drawers (nowhere to file paper). There is no installed telephone – but everyone has a mobile. The workstations are equipped with very powerful PCs through which all work is done. Staff have a small personal trolley, really for personal belongings only, which they wheel to wherever they are working that day.

Source: based on Bjorn-Andersen and Turner (1994)

CASE QUESTIONS

▶ **What are the most striking things in this account?**

▶ **How would you have expected staff to react to changes of this sort?**

▶ **Can you see any parallels with the W.L. Gore case in Part Two?**

16.1 Introduction

This chapter introduces the following ideas:
▶ Mechanistic structure
▶ Organic structure
▶ Differentiation
▶ Integration
▶ Contingency approaches
▶ Determinism
▶ Structural choice
▶ Virtual organisation
▶ Organisational development

Chapter 14 showed the variety of organisational structures. This chapter examines why structures take the form they do, and how external changes encourage new approaches.

Managers face countless choices over how they should shape their organisation, or their part of it. The incentive to change is the belief that structure affects performance. As Figure 14.3 implied, whether managers' objectives are achieved does not depend only on a single factor, such as people, or on using the latest technological gadgets. It depends also on the other factors in that diagram, and the interaction between them. Here we focus on structure, starting with those theories which try to explain when one type of structure works better than another.

In designing their department or organisation, managers decide how to shape the variables listed in Chapter 14. How much horizontal specialisation should there be? Which decisions should those at the centre (or strategic apex) take? Which should the middle line take? And which should those in the operating core take? Should managers rely on the hierarchy or on rules and procedures to co-ordinate activities? Or should they encourage more direct lateral contact and mutual adjustment? The main issues which research suggests they should consider in shaping these choices are:
▶ What is the nature of the external business environment in which they are operating?
▶ How is the available technology opening up new design possibilities?
▶ What theories or models are there about how organisations develop?

16.2 Structure and the business environment

The study of structure

As long as entrepreneurs and managers have been creating organisations, they have been choosing how to divide and co-ordinate work. Comparative discussion of the options is much more recent. It began when Taylor and the Gilbreths in the United States, Fayol in France and Urwick in the UK began to publish their observations and theories. The topic is now widely discussed by consultants, academics and managers themselves, many of whom offer prescriptions to managers on how to redesign their organisations. Some are based on reasonably sound evidence, and you can save time by concentrating on them. Ignore the speculative or unsupported.

Joan Woodward

Joan Woodward's classic study of organisations and their structure (Woodward, 1965) is notable for the careful research on which she based her conclusions. In themselves these are inevitably only a partial contribution to understanding why structures take the form they do. Her theory nevertheless remains an essential entry to a study of organisational structure because of the way it was produced, and its influence on later ideas.

At the time of the study, Woodward was teaching courses on management. The dominant view at the time was that there were certain principles (see, for example, Brech, 1957) which managers should apply, irrespective of the business they were in. These principles were based on the work of writers in the scientific management tradition, and on the work of Elton Mayo and the human relations approach, discussed in Chapter 2. In either case, the emphasis was on identifying the 'one best way', which would apply universally. However, 'Woodward was uncomfortable in propagating such definite principles of management without putting them to some sort of empirical test ... so she decided to test the current theories of organization which lay behind these prevailing principles' (Dawson and Wedderburn, 1980, p.xiv). Her conclusions had a profound effect on practitioners and theorists alike: 'in demonstrating the importance of systematic comparative studies as a basis for management thinking, Woodward was charting new territory in a world where most study had previously been highly prescriptive' (p.xvi). That is, she based her conclusions on substantial empirical research into current practice in real organisations.

Questionnaires returned by one hundred firms demonstrated that there was no single pattern of organisation. The main dependent variables were the span of control of chief executives and of first line supervisors, and the number of levels in the hierarchy between them. The measures showed a wide variation. The research team tried to explain this by repeatedly reviewing and sorting the data, but without success. The results appeared to be without pattern or explanation, until they began to analyse a range of technical variables – the methods and processes of manufacture. Although there were so many variations that every firm was in some respects unique, they nevertheless found that they could group firms into eleven categories, of three broad types. These formed a scale of increasing technical complexity: 'the production of unit articles to customers' individual requirements being the oldest and simplest form of manufacture, and the continuous-flow production of dimensional products, the most advanced and complicated' (p.40). They were then able to observe a relationship between these technical variables and the structural arrangements in the company. The companies were arranged on a scale of the technical complexity of their production process – small batch and unit, large batch and mass, and process. The results are shown in Figures 16.1(a) and (b).

n o t e b o o k   1 6 . 1

In your own words, describe the patterns shown in Figures 16.1(a) and (b). What differences do the diagrams show between the structures most commonly found in the different types of production system?

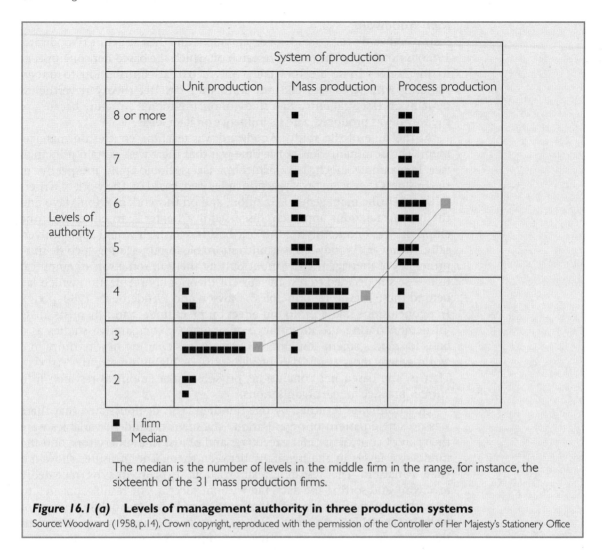

	System of production		
	Unit production	Mass production	Process production
8 or more		■	■■ ■■■
7		■ ■	■■ ■■■
6		■ ■■	■■■■ ▨ ■■■
5		■■■ ■■■■	■■■ ■■■
4	■ ■■	■■■■■■■■ ▨ ■■■■■■■■	■ ■
3	■■■■■■■■■ ■■■■■■■■ ▨	■ ■	
2	■■ ■		

Levels of authority

■ I firm
▨ Median

The median is the number of levels in the middle firm in the range, for instance, the sixteenth of the 31 mass production firms.

Figure 16.1 (a)   Levels of management authority in three production systems
Source: Woodward (1958, p.14), Crown copyright, reproduced with the permission of the Controller of Her Majesty's Stationery Office

Woodward's research team was not only interested in what kinds of structure were used, it also wanted to know if a particular kind of structure ensured business success. Assessing 'success' caused many difficulties. Having collected a range of indicators of both financial and other measures, each firm was classified as being either 'average', 'below average' or 'above average' in success. The earlier results on structure and technical complexity were then compared with data on success.

The conclusion was that firms which conformed to the median organisational structure for their 'technology group' were more successful financially than those which deviated from it. Firms which had adopted the classic management principles, such as an emphasis on clear formal definitions of responsibility, were not always financially successful. The classic principles seemed to be appropriate in large batch and mass production. They did not work so well in unit or process production systems.

Woodward argued that different manufacturing techniques impose different kinds of demands on people and organisations. These demands had to be met by an appropriate structure, and the commercially successful

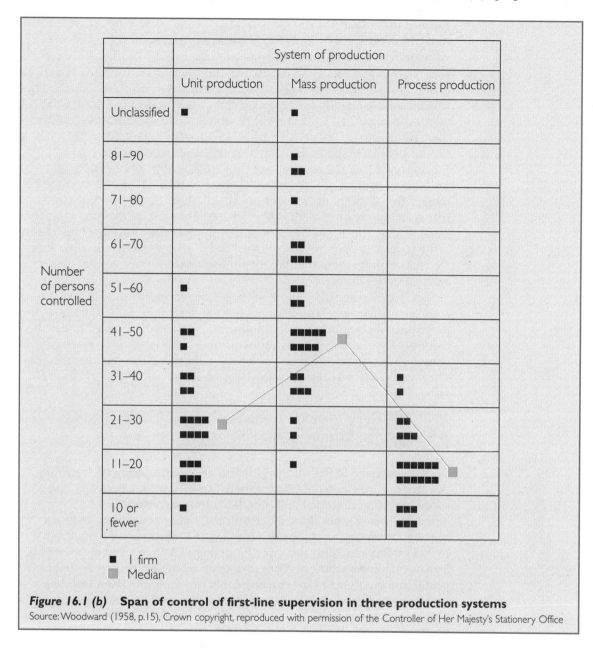

Figure 16.1 (b) **Span of control of first-line supervision in three production systems**
Source: Woodward (1958, p.15), Crown copyright, reproduced with permission of the Controller of Her Majesty's Stationery Office

firms were those where the structure provided the right kind of support to the work of employees. For example, unit production firms were more successful if they had short lines of command, as this permitted interpersonal and direct communications between managers of different functions. This allowed them to cope with the many uncertainties and changes involved in designing and producing 'one-off' items. Firms with large batch or mass production systems faced less uncertainty, and more of the necessary knowledge had been incorporated into the design of the plant itself, its machinery, its procedures. So there was less need for close communication between people in the respective departments.

Burns and Stalker

Also in the early 1960s, Tom Burns and G.M. Stalker from the University of Edinburgh were conducting research amongst two distinct groups of companies. Their conclusions strengthened the view that the form which an organisation takes should reflect the environment in which it operates. They studied a long-established rayon plant in Manchester, and contrasted the way it was organised with the way in which the new electronics companies then being created in the east of Scotland were organised. Both types of organisation were successful – but were organised in very different ways.

The rayon plant had clearly set out rules, tight job descriptions, clear procedures, and co-ordination was primarily through the hierarchy. They termed this a mechanistic form of organisation. In this kind of structure, management creates a high degree of specialisation by dividing tasks into small parts. The boundaries of responsibility and authority are clearly defined, and people are discouraged from acting outside of their remit. Decision-making is centralised, with information flowing up the hierarchy, and instructions down.

The small companies in the newly created electronics industry were completely different. They had very few job descriptions and their rules and procedures were ambiguous and imprecise. Staff were expected to use their own initiative in deciding priorities. They worked together to solve problems. Communication was largely lateral, rather than through the hierarchy. They termed this an organic form of organisation.

Oticon – the case continues
Communication and technology

Staff are allowed to file anything they want, except paper. All incoming documents are electronically scanned into the system, read in a special room, and then shredded and recycled. However, important communication is not done electronically. The management believes that if you want to be competitive, dialogue is better than e-mail, and therefore has a building designed for dialogue. When it has an issue (e.g. a customer complaint), staff are forbidden to write a memo. Instead the problem-owner gets two or three people together and has a stand-up meeting. Decisions are noted in the computer (accessible by everyone). This saves a great deal of time, with a direct focus on getting work done. Staff turnover is very low (many doubters nevertheless stayed), and a Copenhagen Business School study showed staff to be more satisfied than before.

The transformation from a traditional organisation has been enabled by advanced and expensive IT systems. Oticon has cut product development time in half while doing 250 per cent more business. It employs only half the 1990 administrative staff, but double the number on product development. The company estimates that the percentage of time which its professional staff spends on R&D work has risen from 25 per cent to 80 per cent. The financial numbers and company valuation have improved dramatically, with the goodwill element now valued by the banks at Kr400m rather than Kr10m, while fixed assets have only doubled.

Hardware companies have organisations that look like machines: a company that produces knowledge needs an organisation that looks like a brain, i.e. which looks chaotic and is unhierarchical. (Lars Kolind)

Source: based on Bjorn-Andersen and Turner (1994)

C A S E   Q U E S T I O N S   16.1

▶ Oticon has had both mechanistic and organic structures: what prompted the change?

▶ What are the specific features of the present form? In what ways does it correspond to the organic model?

▶ What effects is the new structure having on performance?

In a mechanistic organisation, there is a high degree of task specialisation, people's responsibility and authority are closely defined and decision-making is centralised. In an organic organisation, people are expected to work together and to use their initiative to solve problems; job descriptions and rules are few and imprecise.

Burns and Stalker concluded that both organisational forms were appropriate for their particular circumstances. The rayon plant was operating in a very stable environment. It was the production unit of a larger business, and its sole purpose was to supply a steady flow of the single product to the company's spinning factories. The schedule for these deliveries was set well in advance and rarely changed. The technology of rayon manufacture was well known, as rayon was one of the the first commercially produced artificial fibres. The process had gradually been refined in the light of experience, and the methods clearly documented in printed manuals. These also set out in detail how operators should deal with any faults which arose.

The electronics companies worked in completely different circumstances. They were in direct contact with their customers, the largest of which was the Ministry of Defence. The demand for both commercial and military products was highly volatile, so forward-planning of the production schedule was tentative. The technology was new and relatively unknown, often being an early commercial application of a new scientific discovery in a research laboratory. Contracts were often taken on in which neither the customer nor the electronics company would know what the solution would be – it would be created during the course of the work. Table 16.1 summarises the contrasts between the two systems.

Burns and Stalker concluded that neither mechanistic nor organic structures were appropriate in all situations. Stable, predictable environments

Table 16.1 **Some characteristics of mechanistic and organic systems**

Mechanistic	Organic
Specialised tasks	Contribute experience to common tasks
Hierarchical structure of control	Network structure of contacts
Knowledge located at top of hierarchy	Knowledge widely spread
Vertical communication	Lateral communication
Loyalty and obedience stressed	Commitment to goals more important

were likely to be best served by a mechanistic structure. The most efficient way of working could be codified into a standard way of operating. Volatile, unpredictable environments were likely to be best served by an organic structure. The inherent uncertainties could be tackled by enabling individuals to share ideas and create solutions in the way they thought best. Burns wrote that:

> the effective organisation of industrial resources ... does not approximate to one ideal type of management system, but alters in important aspects in conformity with change in extrinsic factors ...

and:

> We have endeavoured to stress the appropriateness of each system to its own specific set of conditions. Equally, we desire to avoid the suggestion that either system is superior under all circumstances to the other. In particular, nothing in our experience justifies the assumption that mechanistic systems should be superseded by organic in conditions of stability.

Burns and Stalker showed that differences in environmental conditions place different demands upon organisations. This was a major step forward in understanding why companies adopted such widely different structures.

---

n o t e b o o k   16.2

Is your college or university a mechanistic or an organic organisation? What about the department in which you study? Look for evidence of the characteristics in Table 16.1 to help you assess whether it is closer to one form than the other.

Interview someone who works in an organisation to find out if his or her organisation is, on balance, mechanistic or organic. See if you can establish why it has developed the form it has. Compare your conclusions with those of other students and see if you can identify any common themes emerging from the data you have collected.

Lawrence and Lorsch

Burns and Stalker's work was developed by two American scholars, Paul Lawrence and Jay Lorsch. They observed that organisations operated not in one but in several environments. Typically, organisations contain distinct and specialised subunits as a result of the way the overall task has been divided. If these subunits are doing different tasks, each will face a separate segment of the total environment. These will place different demands on each subunit – some being relatively stable, others relatively unstable. Lawrence and Lorsch predicted that in order to cope with this demand, the subunits will develop different structures and ways of working, appropriate to their respective environments. Those in volatile or uncertain environments would move towards organic forms, while those in a stable setting would move towards mechanistic forms. How would that diversity affect the task of co-ordinating their efforts? These issues were examined by studies in six organisations, in different industries facing stable, moderately stable

Differentiation is the state of segmentation of the organisation into subsystems, each of which tends to develop particular attributes in response to the particular demands posed by its relevant external environment.
Integration is the process of achieving unity of effort among the various subsystems in the accomplishment of the organisation's task.

and unstable environments respectively. One firm in each was chosen as a successful operation, the other as an unsuccessful one.

The research team wanted to know how organisations functioned internally as they coped with the demands made upon them by their environment. Two concepts which they used to help understand this were those of differentiation and integration. Lawrence and Lorsch stressed that this is different from the traditional idea of the division of labour. The act of dividing tasks into subunits means that the members of those subunits concentrate on meeting the demands of their particular segment of the environment. They therefore develop their own ways of thinking and working, so that they become progressively more differentiated from each other. This increases the problem of getting them to work well together.

As discussed in Chapter 14, integration takes many forms. One of Lawrence and Lorsch's contributions was to show how the form of integration used varied with the environment faced by the units which needed to work together. The four measures which they used to measure differentiation were:

▶ Reliance on formal structures
▶ Whether staff emphasised people or tasks in their discussions
▶ Time orientation – short-term or long-term
▶ Goal orientation – the primary goals pursued by the unit.

The subunits studied were:

▶ Production
▶ Sales
▶ Applied research
▶ Fundamental research

---

n o t e b o o k   16.3

Given what you can imagine about the nature of the work of these departments and the environmental demands upon them, how would you expect them to differ on the four measures?

C A S E   Q U E S T I O N S   16.2

▶ How does Oticon co-ordinate its activities?
▶ What evidence is there that the company has both mechanistic and organic elements?

Lawrence and Lorsch concluded that the subunits did indeed differ from each other, and in ways that were predicted by a knowledge of their respective environments. Those facing more uncertain environments (research and development) had less formal structures than those facing relatively certain ones (production). The greater the differences between departments, the more effort that needed to be put into integrating them. Successful firms were much better at bringing about this degree of integration than the unsuccessful ones. They used a variety of integrating devices such as taskforces and project managers with the required interpersonal skills.

The less effective companies in the uncertain environment used rules and procedures.

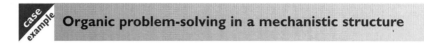

Organic problem-solving in a mechanistic structure

'The organisation I work for has just come through a short-term cash-flow crisis. The problem arose because, while expenditures on contracts are relatively predictable and even, the income flow was disrupted by a series of contractual disputes.

The role culture permeates the head office, and at first the problem was pushed ever upwards. But faced with this crisis, all departments were asked for ideas on how to improve performance. Some have been turned into new methods of working, and others are still being considered by the 'ideas team', drawn from all grades of personnel and departments. This was a totally new perspective, of a task culture operating within a role culture – that is, we developed an organic approach. What could be more simple than asking people who do the job how they could be more efficient?

To maintain the change in the long run is difficult, and some parts have now started to drift back to the role culture.'

The topic has also been examined by Rosabeth Moss Kanter, as shown in the Noticeboard. She is identifying what form of structure is best suited to firms in turbulent business environments.

NOTICEBOARD Rosabeth Moss Kanter on segmentalist and integrative structures

Rosabeth Moss Kanter distinguishes between 'segmentalist' (mechanistic) and 'integrative' (organic) management structures:

I found that the entrepreneurial spirit producing innovation is associated with a particular way of approaching problems that I call 'integrative': the willingness to move beyond received wisdom, to combine ideas from unconnected sources, to embrace change as an opportunity to test limits. To see problems integratively is to see them as wholes, related to larger wholes, and thus challenging established practices – rather than walling off a piece of experience and preventing it from being touched or affected by any new experiences ...

Such organisations reduce rancorous conflict and isolation between organisational units; create mechanisms for exchange of information and new ideas across organisational boundaries; ensure that multiple perspectives will be taken into account in decisions; and provide coherence and direction to the whole organisation. In these team-oriented co-operative environments, innovation flourishes ...

The contrasting style of thought is anti-change-oriented and prevents innovation. I call it 'segmentalism' because it is concerned with compartmentalising actions, events and problems and keeping each piece isolated from the others ... Companies where segmentalist approaches dominate find it difficult to innovate or to handle change.

Source: Kanter (1983, pp.27–8)

16.3 Contingency and management choice approaches

The ideas discussed in section 16.2 are collectively referred to as the contingency approach to organisation structure. This says that the most effective structure will depend (be contingent) upon the situation in which the organisation is operating:

> The organization is seen as existing in an environment that shapes its strategy, technology, size and inovation rate. These contingent factors in turn determine the required structure; that is, the structure that the organization needs to adopt if it is to operate effectively. The effectiveness of the organization is affected by the fit between the organizational structure and the contingencies. This leads the organization to adapt its organization structure so that it moves into fit with the contingency factors. In this way organizational structure is determined by the contingencies. (Donaldson, 1996, p.2)

Donaldson goes on to argue that the main contingencies which research in this tradition has identified are those of task uncertainty, size and strategy.

Contingency approaches to organisational structure are those which are based on the idea that the performance of an organisation depends on having a structure that is appropriate to its environment.

Task uncertainty

Classical organisation theories specified, broadly, that management should exercise control over employees through practices such as tight job descriptions, clear rules and a defined hierarchy. As the studies described in section 16.2 have shown, these methods work well when conditions in the environment are certain. They also show that they are not likely to work in uncertain conditions. Burns and Stalker showed that an organisation trying to innovate in either its products or its processes faces a high degree of uncertainty which can only be managed by structures which enable staff to share information freely, move flexibly between areas of work, and which generally encourage creativity and commitment towards a solution. Hage and Aiken (1967) similarly showed that innovation in health and welfare programmes was negatively related to formalisation and positively related to participation. A review by Gerwin (1979) reached a similar conclusion. Tasks that are non-routine, complex and hard to manage are best served by structures which allow participation, rather than by those which emphasise formalisation.

Size

Size refers to the effect which the scale of the organisation, especially the number of people to be managed, has on the structure. Weber (1947) argued that larger organisations tended to have more formal, bureaucratic structures. The famous studies by the Aston group (Pugh and Hickson, 1976) showed that size of organisation was positively related to increasingly formal structures. Blau (1970) argued that size leads to greater differentiation, in both the vertical and horizontal directions (more levels in the hierarchy, and more separate specialised units). In small organisations, the necessary co-ordination between the parts can be achieved informally by face-to-face contact, direct supervision and so on. As a growing business is divided into more separate units, perhaps over a wide geographical area, management puts in more formal controls. These include writing more detailed job descriptions, establishing formal reporting relationships and building routine control systems.

Strategy

Other studies have shown how changes in the broad strategies of organisations have affected their structure. The strategies which an organisation is pursuing (focus, diversification, geographical spread) have implications for the work that people need to do. That must be supported by an appropriate structure. Chandler (1962) argued that different kinds of strategy lead to different kinds of structure. A study by Hill and Pickering (1986) of companies with the divisionalised form of structure showed wide variations in performance. Those which had passed more decision-making authority to business units performed more successfully than those which had not. This was explained in terms of the decentralised business units being a more appropriate structure in volatile conditions.

Hence contingency theorists take the view that successful organisations adopt a structure which is right for their strategy and for the environment in which they are working. Effective management involves formulating an appropriate strategy. It also involves developing a form of organisation which supports that strategy. It does so by encouraging behaviour which is appropriate for the strategy in that particular environment. The emphasis is determinist (the form is determined by the environment) and functionalist (the form is intended to serve organisational effectiveness) (Donaldson, 1995).

> Determinism is the view that an organisation's structure is determined by its environment.

C A S E   Q U E S T I O N S   16.3

▶ How have these variables of task uncertainty, size and strategy affected Oticon's evolving structure?

The appropriate form develops incrementally as management observes some misfit in its present arrangements. It makes what it hopes will be appropriate adjustments in aspects of the structure. For example, it may alter the pattern of specialisation by rearranging the work of groups or departments; it may change the degree of formalisation by introducing or eliminating some procedures or rules; or it may alter the degree of centralisation to give more or less influence to local management.

A counterview: structural choice

The contingency approach has become the mainstream theory attempting to explain the shape of organisations, and it has obvious practical implications. However, it has been criticised on several grounds by writers such as John Child (1972, 1984). He argues that the determinism of contingency theory has been overstated. It ignores the scope which managers have for choice in the form of structure which they adopt. The process of organisational choice and design is not only a technical, rational matter, but one shaped by political processes. These political considerations (reflecting the values and interests of influential groups) are able to influence the structure which emerges for the following reasons:

> Structural choice approaches emphasise the scope which management has for deciding the form of structure, irrespective of external conditions.

▶ The standards of performance against which organisational performance is assessed are not always rigorous. Some degree of underperformance caused by an inappropriate stucture may be tolerated if there is sufficient 'slack' within the system.

▶ There is evidence that a degree of choice is available between different modes of organisation without serious diseconomies being incurred. So managers can choose from the available range, in view of their own or their staff's preferences, rather than be required to adopt the form implied by contingency theory for their environment.

▶ To the extent that political interests are pursued in organisational life, structures will reflect the interests of politically powerful groups within the organisation. They will try to secure organisational structures which protect or advance their positions. This approach rejects the functionalism of contingency approaches.

Overall, writers of this view argue that contingency theory reduces managers almost to automatons, or puppets, able to exercise little influence on their own actions. In practice, they argue, managers do have choice over the structure they design.

Those favouring a contingency approach reject these criticisms. They concede that managers exercise choice, but argue that this choice is constrained by the need to adapt the structure to ensure acceptable performance:

> As an organization grows it must bureaucratize and structurally differentiate. Similarly as an organisation diversifies it must adopt a more decentralized structure, shifting from functional to multi-divisional. Organizations are under pressure to perform from several sources: from competitors, from stakeholders such as owners and employees, and from the aspirations of their own managers. Therefore organizations will seek to avoid the performance loss that comes from retaining structures that are in misfit with the contingencies. [They] will move from misfit into fit by adopting the structure which fits. There will typically be one particular structure, or a narrow band of structural alternatives, out of all the various conceivable types of structure. Hence the discretion exercised will be severely limited. (Donaldson, 1996, p.51)

This implies that while managers go through the motions of choosing, the direction they can follow is substantially set. Nevertheless their role remains significant. It includes, for example, interpreting the contingencies correctly, selecting a form of structure appropriate for those contingencies, implementing it and continuing to adapt it. They add value by choosing and implementing a struture which will be effective in those circumstances.

n o t e b o o k   16.4

Arrange an interview with someone who works in an organisation. Ask him or her to describe how his or her organisation or department is structured and to comment on whether that structure is right for the environment the business is working in.

Would you describe the organisation or department as relatively mechanistic or relatively organic? Does this fit the environment it is in?

Have there been major changes in structure recently? If so, what prompted management to make them?

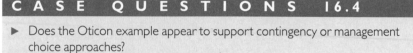

▶ Does the Oticon example appear to support contingency or management choice approaches?

▶ Does the role of management in the company support either of these approaches?

16.4 Political and governmental sources of change

One of the biggest sources of organisation change is government policy. Four examples illustrate the phenomenon: trade liberalisation, deregulation, privatisation and public sector efficiency.

Trade liberalisation

Membership of the European Union, and support for other moves towards the liberalisation of world trade through the World Trade Organisation, has meant that many companies now compete internationally. As legislation removes protective barriers, companies experience new competition and new opportunities. In some instances this has led to specific structural changes to ensure proper attention is given to new market sectors. More generally, it has added a further set of market demands to be met, and a pressure for greater responsiveness. The airline industry is a good example of a sector greatly affected by government policies of this sort.

Deregulation

Policies to deregulate protected industries have made a difference. This is most obvious in financial services. Traditionally there were sharp distinctions between banks, building societies and insurance companies. Companies operated in one or other of these sectors and could not compete in others. The Financial Services Act 1986 ended that protected position, freeing the participants to seek business in any of these areas. It also made it possible for non-financial companies to offer financial services. The effects of this can be seen in the way that banks now offer mortgages, building societies offer banking services, and many companies now offer insurance services.

Privatisation

Selling publicly-owned trading companies has led to huge changes in the way these organisations are structured. Most had developed a style of operating suited to a relatively secure monoploy position. They now have to compete (in some cases) with other businesses, and all have to meet shareholders' profit expectations. This has led to dramatic internal changes of structure for efficiency reasons. Some have used their privatised status to enter new business areas – such as when power companies take over water companies. The Case Example illustrates how one of the privatised electricity companies has changed its form.

Changes at ScottishPower

case example

ScottishPower is a vertically integrated utility established to generate, transmit and sell electricity to consumers. The company was formed in 1992 when the government privatised the former South of Scotland Electricity Board. The former organisation had a bureaucratic structure, with clear lines of authority and rigid procedures. It was said to focus mainly on achieving excellence in engineering terms, and paid little attention to customer needs. Training and development was unstructured, driven only by an inividual's persistence.

A manager within the company noted that:

Changes in the past four years have been nothing short of dramatic, such as:

▶ The company broken up into individual business units, namely Generation, Transmission, Retail, and Telecoms, which all produce their own accounts and are given profit targets to achieve.

▶ Company administered from a central corporate offce with fewer than forty staff.

▶ All previous central services such as typing, finance, purchasing and contracts have been dispersed to the individual business units to ensure full accountability.

▶ Benchmarking (systematically comparing performance and methods) against 'best-in-class' American utilities, giving targets for performance and staff numbers.

▶ Workforce numbers reduced substantially, mainly through voluntary severance.

▶ Management layers reduced to give a flatter management structure.

▶ Union pay bargaining moved from national to company and then to divisional level.

▶ Company profit-sharing and divsional gain-sharing schemes negotiated.

▶ Open learning centres established at all locations, open to staff and family members.

▶ Various culture change initiatives intended to create an environment in which change is accepted more readily and cost accountability is paramount.

▶ Pay progression linked to competence in the workplace as measured by VQ [vocational qualification] assessment.

Clearly the organisation (which now owns electricity and water companies in England) is seen by insiders as being dramatically different. Similar changes have occurred at other formerly nationalised industries.

Public sector efficiency

Pressures to improve performance in the remaining parts of the public sector, especially the civil service and local government, has also affected structures. Governments throughout Europe are trying to improve the efficiency and effectiveness of organisations in the public sector. In the UK the government has since the early 1980s been trying to change radically the established culture of the civil service. The main route towards this has been to decentralise the delivery of services. Major departments have been divided into smaller units or cost centres, each with their own budget for running costs. Financial responsibilities have been delegated, with units much more accountable for the way money is spent than was traditionally the case. More radically, some departments have been converted into semi-autonomous agencies, with a chief executive responsible for operating the agency (such as the Prison Service or the Benefits Agency) within the frame-work of policy direction and resource allocations made by the minister.

Whatever the merits or otherwise of the policy, it has led to significant changes in the structure of many parts of the service, and a much greater interest in the kinds of management issue previously of concern mainly to the private sector. Similar practices are evident in local government, where many services have to be subjected to regular competitive tendering with private contractors, rather than being a permanent monopoly supplied by the existing staff.

Similarly, there have been dramatic changes in the National Health Service. The 'purchaser/provider split' means that responsibility for providing health care is split between those who purchase health care on behalf of a community (health boards), and those who provide it (hospital trusts). The former operate within tight budgets and rising demand for care, while the latter compete with other trusts to provide the services required by the health boards. Management has proposed many changes in the struc-ture and culture of the health boards and trusts to allow staff to meet the new requirements. The Case Example indicates what these changes have meant, and the difficulties one board has experienced in making them work.

case example ▸ Developing the organisation of the National Health Service

'The National Health Service was traditionally bureaucratic and hierarchical, discouraging individual initiative or responsibility. People worked within their discipline and had little interaction with others. Under the new pattern, a member of one board commented that 'the health board recognised the need to shift to a culture of multidisciplinary teamworking and to encourage leadership and decision-making within the organisation. A national strategy to support management development in the service has seven key elements: shifting the culture, new vertical relationships, organisational leadership, managing horizontally, professionals in management, acquiring skills and improving information.

The health board has endorsed the basic ideas by identifying a strategy, and has addressed the internal arrangements of structure and process necessary to support the strategy. But we are still struggling to make it work. Although we have espoused the principles of performance management, leadership, teamwork, openness and trust, we have still retained a hierarchical dominance. Although we have talked about the principles of change set out in the national guidelines, the core management team is operating just as it did before.'

16.5 Technological sources of change

Advances in information and communications technologies are changing the goods and services which organisations offer, and how they organise to deliver them.

Developments in information and communication technologies

We are all familiar with the advances in computing technology which have made personal computers such a widespread feature of organisational life. The ability of machines to gather, store, process and distribute information is greater than ever before. Since organisations depend on information, they are deeply affected by applications of new information technologies (which are discussed more fully in Chapter 20).

Equally dramatic changes are taking place in communications technology. The cost of transmitting information and materials is falling steadily, and in some cases dramatically. Lower freight and air transport costs have had significant effects in changing our diet and creating the package holiday industry – but spread over many years. Changes in satellite and telephone charges have been much more rapid, as technical developments and the introduction of fibre optic cables increase capacity. The marginal cost of making long-distance calls will continue to decline. Prices charged will continue to fall as previously protected telephone companies are privatised and exposed to competition.

n o t e b o o k   1 6 . 5

Before reading on, note down what you think might be some of the effects of national and international call charges being as low as local charges are now – in the sense that you pay little attention to cost in deciding whether or not to make the call. Think about questions like: where will you order goods from? Where will people providing a service work? Where will they be managed from?

Some of the factors which will constrain or prevent developments of the kind you have envisaged in the Notebook activity are listed below.

▶ **Global 0800 numbers**   Many organisations now offer these numbers (in which the customer calls free, and the company pays for the call) to potential customers within a country as a way of attracting business. If costs fall low enough, it will pay some organisations to have a single worldwide number, which customers can call from anywhere in the world. Companies producing goods or services which are easily distributed will find it much easier to reach a global market – as will their competitors.

▶ **Home service delivery**   As telecommunications costs fall, more households will be permanently linked to the wider world via their domestic computer. The arrangements which companies in the financial services area have already introduced (see Case Example below) will become much more widespread. These links will become the delivery method for many services. Possibilities include: ordering and receiving software; managing the whole range of activities involved in charging, billing and paying for gas, electricity and water supplies; some forms of medical diagnostics; and taking part in tutorials or examinations.

The Internet and financial services

The huge growth in the use of the Internet over the past few years has presented an entirely new set of opportunities (and threats) to providers of financial services. Banks in particular have taken to this new means of addressing their customers in a wide variety of ways. A presence on the Internet allows them to generate contacts with new customers, and also provides a basis for managing accounts by linking their own internal networks to the Internet. The Internet is an attractive medium for companies wishing to provide financial services as it is widely available across the globe at low cost. People using the Internet are also younger and richer, on average, than the population as a whole – attractive targets for companies offering financial services.

---

n o t e b o o k   16.6

Look at some of the financial services Websites such as:

Barclays Bank (http://www.barclays.com/)
Security First National Bank (http://www.sfnb.com/)
First Chicago NBD (http://www.fcnbd.com/index.html)
National Westminster (http://www.botf.natwest.co.uk/)
Quicken (http://www.qfn.com/)
or one or more of your own choice

Describe some of the ways in which banks have addressed the use of the Internet. How does the use of the Internet differ between US and UK banks?

What new means of providing financial services have been born on the Internet?

Why is the Internet an attractive medium for the provision of financial services? What problems do banks face in providing services over the Internet?

Why is the Internet particularly attractive to new entrants to the financial services markets?

You could divide the banks among your fellow students and compare your answers.

Jobs and customers

Traditionally, people have moved to where the jobs were. When most economic activity was to make goods, and transport costs were relatively high, producers and customers were physically close. Most things were made locally. As costs changed in favour of larger units, people moved to where these jobs were being created, leading to the concentrations of economic activity and wealth seen today. This applies both nationally and globally. Screen-based financial, educational or information services can be made anywhere, and delivered cheaply to consumers anywhere. So the jobs are likely to go to wherever the best-value workers can be found in terms of cost and appropriate skills level. It is not uncommon for manufacturing operations to be moved around the world in search of lower costs. The same mobility is now becoming possible in the provision of services. In 1996, British Airways announced that as part of a drive to cut costs it would soon relocate most of the company's routine accounting functions from London to India. The cost of employing well educated English-speaking staff in India was estimated to be about one-quarter of that in London. The country also had good telecommunication links, which were essential to link the accounting computer systems with BA operations around the world.

The advantages of size?

Cheap telecommunications mean that size and location become less import-ant factors in the competitive position of organisations. Especially in services, small companies with access to the worldwide telecommunications network will be just as able to trade nationally and perhaps internationally as large ones. Large companies will retain advantages where factors like development costs, production economies or brand names are important, but in many areas, the flexibility of the small company will be greatly enhanced by the new communication technologies.

 Organisations in the network age

Boddy and Gunson conducted a long-term study of six organisations (a travel agent, a retail business, an ambulance service, a library co-operative, a transport business and an insurance company), each of which had introduced some form of networked computer system. Here are some of their conclusions about the issues which management had to deal with.

They involved risk – but so did doing nothing
Network systems offered the chance to gain a significant lead, and to improve dramatically the organisation's public image or competitive performance. But technical and organisational risks came with the technology. Some of the applications which were at the limits of the underlying technology were late, or failed – though other risks paid off. Applications which linked parts of the organisation where people were not used to IT or where they had previously worked independently also carried risks. These potential human or managerial obstacles were not as great as expected. In nearly all cases, if nothing had been done the organisation would not have been able to cope efficiently with a growing administrative burden.

The networks were used on primary business activities
IT is not the 'back office' technology it once was. In all the companies it changed the way routine administrative operations were conducted. In

some there was little choice but to use advanced technologies if major customers were to be retained. Effective networks were a matter of survival when customers required suppliers to process orders, invoices and payments electronically. They provided significant support to companies operating internationally by linking their sites. They offered managers opportunities to enter new areas of business. IT changed how the companies worked and the kind of work they did.

Networks affected the customer relationship
The systems also had direct effects on customers' image of the business. Cash dispensers, point-of-sale terminals and reservation systems are just a few of the instances where the perceptions of an organisation's service quality depended on the quality of the IT system. Staff who had up-to-date information on-screen about the customer were able to smooth and personalise the relationship. When they had easy access to information about the customer or the product during the transaction, they felt more professional. Networks also enabled prices or other policies to be communicated consistently all round the business, supporting a coherent corporate image. IT had ofen become an essential part of the customer relationship.

Networks helped to manage current operations –
if the structure was right
Systems which captured data at the time of the transaction gave management rapid, accurate information about the business, even when this was on many sites. This supported managers' decisions about stocks, staff levels, overtime, capacity and so on. Some organisations were able to use such information to monitor quickly the effects of price or other changes, and decide tactics accordingly. Managers were keen to gain access to this valuable information, especially on-line. Delays, constraints or development priorities sometimes prevented that. In other cases, the information available to middle managers was late, hard to use and irrelevant. In two cases, information went first to those at head office, and much later to managers in the field who could have acted on it had it been made available sooner.

Likely benefits were hard to predict
Most systems were so novel that management could not be sure in advance how valuable they would be. Some expected benefits did not appear. Conversely, some managers reported benefits they had not expected. Networked systems installed to make administrative savings by eliminating data entry and other routine tasks usually achieved them. Staff then saw how the management information now available could be used to change the way the business operated. Business success, as distinct from technical success, depended on organisational as well as technical changes.

Assessing the likely costs was also difficult
Hardware and software usually costs more than expected (cables, building alterations, upgrades, maintenance). Human and organisational costs (training, support, project management, disruption) also add to the

bill. Promoters naturally underestimated costs and other difficulties to get approval.

Source: adapted from Boddy and Gunson (1996)

McBride (1997) takes a cautious view of the effects of the Internet on business. He suggests ways in which they can use it:

▶ **E-mail** 'For many businesses the principal benefit of Internet access will lie in the use of e-mail' (p.59), which combines the speed of the telephone with the permanence and accuracy of the written record.
▶ **Cheap marketing** While a good home page can benefit a company's image, that image can also be damaged very easily. The page may be accessed by customers who are unlikely to use the services, or the page itself may be unattractive.
▶ **Selling** This will become easier as security improves, although services will vary in their suitability for Internet selling.
▶ **Database access** Databases provide opportunities to gather market intelligence or information on the activities of competitors. The Internet provides access to a global library of information which, if linked to the company's internal system, can be especially useful in marketing and product development.

16.6 Globalisation as a source of change

A third major trend affecting the structure of organisations is the trend towards globalisation. In consumer goods there are many global brands – Pepsi and Coke, Marlborough, Christian Dior, to name but a few. Similarly, in the area of industrial products many companies have built their product or service to a position where they are referred to as global players – Sun Microsystems, British Airways, Philips, News International and so on. Companies such as these compete to deliver products or services to customers across the world. They compete with other global players and with local suppliers.

---

n o t e b o o k   16.7

Identify a business which operates globally – one of those listed above, or one of your own choice. Gather as much information as you can about it, by consulting financial databases, newspapers or *The Economist*, or see if it has a Web site which you can visit. In particular, try to find out how it has structured its operations. How does it balance the needs of the whole business with the needs of the different areas of the world in which it operates?

The development of the global business economy is not accidental. It has been aided by political developments at international level. One source of this has been the pressure from already major companies to expand their markets. They have sucessfully lobbied international bodies to negotiate agreements (such as the General Agreement on Tariffs and Trade, GATT) which reduce or eliminate various import restrictions. These are erected by many countries to protect local producers against foreign competition. Greater international business has also been made easier by technological developments. Communicatons technology and air travel have meant that previously protected organisations and industries are now subject to new competition. Equally, other companies have benefited from access to new sources of supply and to new markets. Whatever the reasons for the growth in global businesses, such businesses require different structures from those operating more locally.

Some of the problems of operating globally are those of any organisation, but made more complex by the physical distances involved. In an age of improving communications these may seem less important, but are easily underestimated. Physical distance makes direct contact between managers difficult. At the most basic level, working in different time zones reduces the chance of holding a conversation at a time which is convenient to all the participants. There are differences in holiday and working week arrangements. People in different countries have different patterns during the working day. In the United States, lunch is typically a quick snack; in Spain it can be a three-hour break.

Structural options for the international business

How important the global dimension is obviously varies amongst organisations. For some it is a marginal issue which can be dealt with by an existing domestic structure. As the scale of international involvement grows, it becomes more important to make deliberate structural adjustments. Don Hellriegel and John Slocum (1988) have proposed a model with six degrees of involvement which a company may experience (see Noticeboard).

Industrial convergence

A final change which is occurring is the breaking down of traditional barriers between industries. For example, industries such as entertainment, publishing, computing and telecommunications traditionally operated in distinct markets. They had different ways of delivering services to customers, and fundamentally different ways of operating. Each of these sectors now offers examples of companies beginning to work in other sectors as well, either through joint ventures with established players, or by increasing their own capabilities.

16.7 New organisational forms

The stimuli for change presented in Chapter 14 are not independent, and emerging organisational forms reflect combinations of these and other pressures.

Technology-centred forms

Information technology is now so significant that writers such as Peter Drucker (1995) and Henry Lucas (1996) have suggested that it is becoming

NOTICEBOARD Six degrees of international involvement

▶ **Commission agent**   If a company receives occasional enquiries from overseas for its products, it may choose to appoint a local agent to handle the business, in return for a commission on any sales made.

▶ **Export manager**   As business or opportunities increase, the firm may decide on a more active overseas involvement. This could be reflected in the appointment of an export manager charged with actively seeking and promoting opportunities in a range of markets.

▶ **Export department**   If the overseas business continues to grow, the export manager will need to build his or her support staff to service the growing number and variety of overseas customers. It becomes increasingly important to ensure that documentation and payment arrangements are handled accurately and on time. The risks and delays inherent in overseas trade need to be professionally managed.

▶ **International division**   With the growth in business it becomes impractical to supply it all from the home manufacturing base, so as well as all the functions of an export department, an international division will be able to set up and manage manufacturing facilities in other countries.

▶ **International corporation**   Here the focus of the business is no longer that of supplying other countries from a domestically controlled business, even if some manufacturing is done locally. The company operates in a variety of countries, manufacutring in several and conducting trade between them. The business now cuts across national boundaries.

▶ **Multinational corporation**   The distinctive features are that managers take a worldwide view in assessing opportunities, subsidiaries operate in several countries, and top management is willing to consider locations throughout the world. Such companies may follow a multidomestic or a global strategy, and create the organisation necessary. A multidomestic strategy is one in which the company modifies products and practices to suit the conditions of each of the local markets in which it works. The focus is on the particular geography, and marketing and production are planned accordingly. Management stresses the uniqueness of each locality. A global strategy is one where the emphasis is on consistency of policy across the world. While products may be adapted for particular countries, they are planned as part of a worldwide product strategy which is then implemented by managers responsible for particular regions or countries.

Source: Hellriegel and Slocum (1988)

central to decisions about the design of organisations. As has been shown, the shape of an organisation reflects the choices made about the alternative form of the design variables in dividing and co-ordinating work. For example, if management believes that staff in the design department should work more closely with those in production, various linking mechanisms are available:

▶ Put a production engineer in the design group to act as a link.
▶ Set up a design–production co-ordinating committee to meet as required.
▶ Set up electronic links between the departments and encourage staff to co-ordinate by e-mail, perhaps using a common electronic database.

Lucas argues that while, in the past, one of the first two options would have been chosen, companies can now consider basing much more of their organisation on electronic means. More radically, rather than start with the structure and ask how technology can support this, they may consider how objectives can best be served by electronic means, and then build a structure to support that. This is a radically different alternative.

The 'electronic design variables', as he calls them, include networked computing and telecommunications systems, video-conferencing, artificial intelligence, virtual reality, facsimile and so on. These design solutions can either be used in place of conventional design variables or as extensions of them. These can be applied to the design activities as follows. Work can be restructured by dividing it into subunits, using IT to replace internally owned activities by 'virtual' components or 'virtual' staff. These are physically and legally separate from the organisation but readily available as required through electronic systems. Automating some of the information processing activities between work processes eliminates some structural divisions. Automating some of the information processes in the vertical hierarchy removes layers of management and gives wider spans of control – what Lucas calls 'technological levelling'. Co-ordination of work can be improved by using electronic links of various kinds to ensure smoother flow within and between organisations.

The boundaryless organisation?

Ashkenas and his colleagues (1995) explore how many organisational boundaries are becoming more permeable, to allow greater fluidity and movement of people, energy, ideas and information. They argue that in order to be able to respond to external changes, organisations should confront and reshape four types of boundary: vertical, horizontal, geographical and external.

▶ **Vertical**   Expressed in the formal hierarchy, and measured by the spans of control, the number of levels and the pattern of reporting relationships, vertical boundaries emphasise authority and rank. In 'boundaryless' organisations, rank matters less than competence. Ideas are sought and respected wherever they arise, in an effort to respond quickly and maintain the commitment of staff.

▶ **Horizontal**   These exist between the functions or product lines of the organisation, emphasising particular areas of specialisation. Conflicts of interest and priority can arise as people look after the interests of their corner rather than those of the organisation as a whole. These diminish if people begin to think in terms of the processes which move across those areas, rather than on the areas themselves.

▶ **External**   Organisations typically have a distinct legal identity, which serves to separate them from other entities. There are also well developed psychological and commercial processes which help to construct boundaries, or barriers, to the flow of ideas and information between them. Typically, organisations have had an arm's-length relationship with suppliers and customers, with minimal information and exchange, and an attitude towards each other which was fundamentally adversarial. An alternative view is that a more effective way of doing business may be to work closely with suppliers and customers. Suppliers and customers may be able to offer ideas and resources to help one another to work more effectively than they could in isolation. Ideas about developing such closer working relationships with other companies are developed more fully in Chapter 19.

▶ **Geographical**   Companies are usually identified with a single country, which contains their head office and most of their operations. Easier communications of all kinds mean that some kinds of goods and services are designed and delivered on a global basis. Mobile consumers informed by international television systems identify with products which are marketed globally, even when they have local variations within the overall brand. Others companies operate globally to secure the most economic supplies of people or components, while others do so in order to project an image of a company and management that are players on the global business stage. This leads to a breaking down of this fourth form of barrier, that between units in different geographical areas.

Emerging forms

Warren Bennis implied three decades ago that most organisations may no longer have the luxury of such choice: most organisations now face turbulent environments, and Bennis predicted the death of mechanistic, bureaucratic structures as a result.

> The social structure of organisations of the future will have some unique characteristics. The byword will be 'temporary'. There will be adaptive, rapidly changing temporary systems. There will be taskforces organised around problems to be solved by groups of relative strangers with diverse professional skills. The group will be arranged on an organic rather than mechanical model; it will evolve in response to a problem rather than to programmed role expectations. The executive thus becomes co-ordinator or 'linking pin' between various taskforces. People will be evaluated not according to rank but according to skill and professional training.
>
> Adaptive, problem-solving, temporary systems of diverse specialists, linked together by co-ordinating and task evaluating executive specialists in an organic flux – this is the organisational form that will gradually replace bureaucracy as we know it. As no catchy phrase comes to mind, I call these new style organisations adaptive structures. (Bennis, 1969, p.34)

Research conducted by Ashridge Management Centre (1988), based on a study of ten leading European companies, offers some support for Bennis's claim that organisation structures are tending to become more organic and adaptable. The Ashridge study asked what the sample companies 'are doing to stay successful in the global markets of the 1990s'. One common concern in the companies covered in this study was, 'how to equip managers to function in a more complex international environment'. Changes in organisation structure, the research revealed, had led to decentralisation of decision-making and to flatter hierarchies, and had increased the ambiguity facing managers. Internationalisation had also tended to obscure organisational boundaries. The report argued for the development of the 'flexible manager', which involved:

▶ awareness of and ability to relate to the economic, social and political environment,
ability to manage in a turbulent environment,
▶ ability to manage with complex organisation structures,
▶ to be innovative and initiate change – to be 'animateurs',
▶ to manage and utilise increasingly sophisticated information systems,
▶ to manage people with widely different and changing values and
▶ expectations.

Organisational and personal development in the organisations studied were, in addition, seen to depend on corporate cultures which encouraged openness, trust, involvement, and which encouraged initiative and continuous learning, even from failures. Asea Brown Boveri (ABB) is a global company which has created a unique form, as described in the Case Example.

Asea Brown Boveri – a global business

ABB was formed in 1987 by the merger of two established companies, to create a powerful world business in the market for electrical systems and equipment. It has continued to expand by internal growth and by acquiring other companies. It employs more than 200,000 people around the world. Europe accounts for about 60 per cent of revenues, with a growing presence in Eastern Europe where there is a huge capital investment programme.

The company has no geographical centre, and is seen by its chairman as a federation of national companies with a global co-ordination centre. The headquarters are in Zurich, but only one hundred professionals work there. The chairman is Swedish, but only two of the eight members of the board of directors are Swedes. They report their financial results in US dollars, and English is ABB's official language.

The organising logic of ABB
While the company is a diverse global organisation, it has an apparently simple organising principle. Along one dimension, the company is grouped by products. Managers decide on product strategy and performance irrespective of national borders. On a second dimension there is a collection of traditionally organised national companies, serving their respective markets as well as they can.

The executive committee, made up of the chairman, Percy Barnevik, and twelve colleagues, is at the top of the company. This group meets every three weeks to plan and monitor ABB's global strategy and performance. The executive committee consists of Swedes, Swiss, Germans and Americans. Several members of the executive committee are based outside Zurich, and their meetings are held around the world.

The managing directors of the (approximately) fifty business areas into which the company's products and services are divided report to the executive committee. The business areas are grouped into eight business segments, each the responsibility of a member of the executive committee. For example, the industry segment, which sells components, systems and software to automate industrial processes, has five business areas, including metallurgy, drives and process engineering.

Source: based on Taylor (1991)

Another view of the organisation of the future
    ❛Twisted into a new shape by fierce global competition, changing markets, and technological breakthroughs, the business organisation of the future is merging with distinct characteristics. It will be:
- ▶ information-based

- ▶ decentralized, yet densely linked through technology
- ▶ rapidly adaptable and extremely agile
- ▶ creative and collaborative, with a team-based structure
- ▶ staffed by a wide ariety of knowledge workers, and
- ▶ self-controlling, which is possible only in an environment of clear, strong, and shared operating principles and of real trust **?**

(Champy and Nohria, 1996)

Virtual organisations

Virtual organisations are organisations which deliver goods and services, but they have few of the physical features of conventional organisations. They are typically an amalgamation of independent agents who are linked together in delivering a service. The agents usually work from home, thus eliminating the need for a physical office. They co-ordinate their activities by intensive telephone and electronic communication via linked computer systems. Researchco is an example of a new company which is modelled on the concept of the virtual organisation.

Virtual organisations are those which deliver goods and services but have few, if any, of the physical features of conventional businesses.

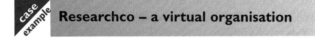

Researchco – a virtual organisation

Researchco was founded in 1995 and conducts research and analysis for major IT companies. The work supports the product positioning, pricing and marketing decisions of its customers. Researchco uses advanced data monitoring and modelling techniques to offer market research and consultancy services. It is in a high-tech and rapidly changing market.

To the shareholders, directors, contractors and clients, Researchco is an organisation. It has a name, a legal status (as a limited liability company), VAT registration, trading addresses, bank accounts and so on. However, it neither owns nor rents any premises, and there are no employees. The company subcontracts almost all activity to a pool of geographically dispersed contractors using telephone and Internet technology. All the directors and contractors are self-employed and work from their homes throughout the UK. They work on a variety of projects for clients. Contractors routinely come together in different roles to fit the needs of the client and then disband once the project or task is complete. No one in the company draws a salary and all remuneration is on the basis of invoices for work done. Researchco secures work from clients and passes the activity to subcontractors. They in turn submit invoices to the company for their part of the project. Some contractors work for other companies, others exclusively for Researchco. Overheads are very low.

The directors want their company to be structured for the twenty-first century. They believe that the virtual structure will allow the company to compete effectively and react flexibly to clients' needs throughout Europe. Titles and labels are not important within the company, although they are retained to reassure clients by conveying a more traditional notion of the company – clients may not understand the concept of the virtual company, and this would be a drawback. The company also hopes to develop flexible relations with its clients which

mirror those with its contractors. This implies that all those in the company need to work out their roles and relationships within this novel structure.

16.8 Organisational development

Organisational development is the activity of deliberately changing major aspects of an organisation to improve its effectiveness.

The external forces described above mean that change of some sort is an everyday feature of organisations. Some change is trivial and of no concern. Some just happens, as when the organisation is taken over, or a co-ordinating link disappears when someone leaves and is not replaced, or when a new manager imposes a new procedure. Other changes are planned deliberately to improve the organisation's effectiveness. The name usually given to this form of planned change is 'organisational development'. The process is typically started by managers who want to bring aspects of the organisation more closely into line with the demands of customers or other influential stakeholders.

Leavitt (1965) distinguished between different aspects of the content of change when he identified the entry points of change programmes, which he labelled task, technology, people or structure. His argument was that, faced with a business problem, those seeking to solve it could take as their point of entry one or other of these elements – though the systemic nature of organisations would mean that the others would need to be dealt with as well. Similarly, Tichy (1982) proposed that change involves three interacting elements: technology, politics and culture. He refers to these as representing three fundamental problems that require continuous attention, and moreover that: 'Not only does each area require attention on its own, but problems of all three are interdependent, so problem-solving must be co-ordinated among them' (p.62).

Building on these approaches, we suggest that major organisational development activities can be viewed from the perspective of the organisational elements model presented earlier and repeated here as Figure 16.2.

In order to meet the organisation's objectives, management decides that some change is needed in one or more of the areas shown in the figure. This

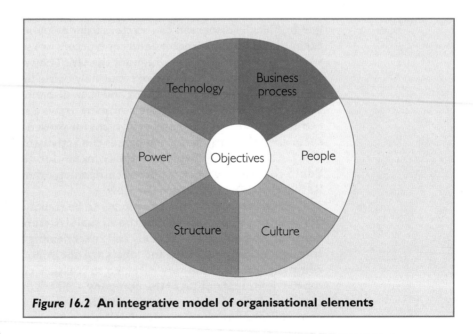

Figure 16.2 An integrative model of organisational elements

is then the focus of the organisational development activity. The diagram also implies that, whatever the entry point, there are likely to be significant ripple effects on other elements. These also need to be dealt with as part of the overall planned change activity.

What knock-on effects will need to be managed?

Putting in a major IT system sets off ripples which touch many other aspects of the organisation – the objectives or mission itself, together with human and organisational matters. A study of a technological change in public and private sector organisations showed the extent of the changes which had to be managed.

As well as difficult choices concerning the basic new system, there were *technical interdependencies* to handle. The new systems had to fit with existing physical facilities such as space and buildings, and with existing IT systems.

There were also *human* and *organisational* effects to manage. In most of the cases the new systems allowed significant reductions in administrative staff, which had to be carefully planned. Training had to be arranged at the right time, often alongside the continuing performance of regular tasks. In some cases the opportunity was taken to combine or rearrange jobs as the technology was introduced, which again needed to be thought out in advance. If sales staff were expected to enter transaction details while they dealt with a customer, would that disrupt the flow and cause delay? A common effect was that many staff were expected to work to a much tighter specification than before. More generally, how would the new arrangements affect the intrinsic quality of jobs?

The availability of more information about current performance was immediately attractive to those at the top of the organisations studied, and in most cases the centre was able to exercise much tighter control over what junior managers did. While this was usually consistent with the values of the organisation, it was recognised by some that there were dangers here. In other cases, senior managers found that existing structural arrangements prevented them using the information to full effect. In one case, managers became too zealous in analysing the computer-generated data in their offices, instead of getting out to visit the depots in person. This ran counter to a strongly held value in the organisation, and action was quickly taken to stop this practice. Other middle managers complained that the information available to them from the system was not good enough to allow them to carry out their roles properly – roles which assumed they would have adequate information available.

Source: Boddy and Gunson (1996)

People approaches

The earliest organisation development work often concentrated on people, in attempts to increase the self-awareness of individual managers or staff members, and to improve their awareness of the processes taking place within a group. Other objectives include team-building, improving leadership styles, decision-making and problem-solving skills, communications and relations between groups.

Structural approaches

Another group of development activities is that which aims to change the structure of the organisation in a planned way. Usually this arises for the reasons indicated earlier in the chapter, when the organisation is perceived to have a structure which does not match the current environment. The interventions may be designed to clarify roles and reporting relationships – commonly to shorten the hierarchy so as to give greater responsibilities to those lower down. They may also include efforts to redesign jobs, or to introduce empowerment or semi-autonomous teams as part of a restructuring activity.

Organisation and environment relationships

Finally, some organisational development programmes are directed at improving the links between the organisation and its external environment. The aim, following the arguments earlier in this chapter, is to help the organisation achieve a better fit between its internal arrangements and its external environment. Interventions are therefore designed to help the organisation get a better understanding of that environment and devise appropriate responses. This may lead to the introduction of mechanisms to scan the environment more closely, and to ensure that the organisation responds proactivley to new threats and opportunities arising in the external world.

16.9 The nature of planned change

Managements trying to develop their organisation implicitly or explicitly use some theory about planned change. These theories describe how change takes place – the stages which it goes through, and the actions which help or hinder the process. Four such models are briefly presented.

Pettigrew's context and process model

Change cannot be understood or managed apart from its context. Andrew Pettigrew (1987) has placed particular emphasis on the need to understand this aspect. He sees major change as a historical process interacting with both an internal and an external environment. The former refers to a range of structural, cultural and political arrangements within the organisation itself which shape the world of those trying to implement change, and which can help or hinder implementation. Decision-making structures are given particular attention by many writers on change. Pettigrew (1985), for example, showed how the availability or otherwise of appropriate discussion fora affected the implementation of strategic change at ICI. Hinings *et al.* (1991) showed how the prevailing authority structure obstructed change in an autonomous professional organisation. This implies that a key step in the change process is the creation, if necessary, of an appropriate structure within which the change can be debated and managed.

The external environment refers to the familiar range of political, economic and other factors outside of the firm. Pettigrew emphasises the scope for interaction between the two. The external setting clearly exerts an influence, but management can amplify or play down the signals which are coming fom the outside world. Equally, it may in some ways be able to influence the outside world – managers are not passive recipients of whatever is going on around them. So the external context both shapes and is itself shaped by management activities.

Lewin's change model

The American psychologist Kurt Lewin offered a model of change which is still widely used today. He argued that, to understand change we should start by understanding stability. What are the forces which establish and maintain the current equilibrium? They are those forces which are pushing for change, and those which are trying to maintain things as they are. He called these 'driving' and 'restraining' forces, respectively. If both are roughly balancing each other, the situation will be stable.

For change to happen, either the forces pushing for change must increase or those maintaining the current state must decrease – or some combination. The example in Figure 16.3 shows the forces maintaing the equilibrium in an organisation which has recently undergone major change.

Lewin suggested that someone trying to move the situation would find the task easier by trying to reduce the restraining forces. This would produce less tension. Increasing the forces for change may only increase resistance.

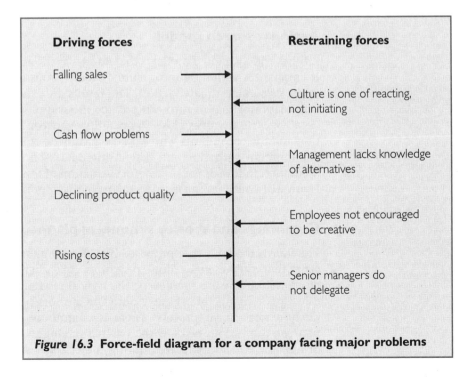

Figure 16.3 **Force-field diagram for a company facing major problems**

Lewin's other contribution to understanding change was to present change as consisting of three steps:

▶ **Unfreezing**   Something needs to be done to break away from existing practice. Most organisations are very set in their ways, and are adept at brushing aside attempts at change. To overcome this, dramatic moves may be needed. The aim is to confront organisational members with information about the present state of affairs which they may have ignored or discounted. The idea is that until this is done, people will be resistant to change, not realising or accepting that it is needed. The difficulty is to get the right balance: if the future seems too alarming, then people may become more resistant than ever. The solution seems to be to present disconcerting evidence of the need to change, coupled by some reassuring messages that a viable way forward can be developed.

▶ **Moving**   In this step, things are done which are intended to move the behaviour of people or departments into a new pattern. It can involve any or all of the activities outlined in the previous section: people-centred, structure-centred and so on.

▶ **Refreezing**   Here things are done to embed new practices into the organisation. Lewin's theory was that, unless this happened, people would soon revert to their old ways of working. They could be pursuaded to stay with the new by such things as support, praise and hard information that the new system was bringing benfits.

Lewin's model provides a broad framework for thinking about the stages in developing organisations. It leaves the detail to those making the change. In the current climate, some would question the concept of 'refreezing'. This seems rooted in times when major change was unusual, interspersed with periods of stability. In times of constant change, management would usually want to emphasise that the new pattern was itself temporary, and likely to be replaced before long.

Action research model

A third, widely quoted model is that known as the action research approach. It emphasises gathering information widely about the state of the organis-ation, as a guide to later action. The results are assessed to provide further information which in turn can provide the stimulus to further action. This iterative cycle involves close co-operation between people in the organisa-tion and the consultants who would typically do this work. There is a heavy commitment gathering and diagnosing data. Action planning and imple-mentation follow, as well as careful evaluation of results after action is taken. Figure 16. 4 outlines the main elements of the approach.

Cummings and Worley's model of planned change

The fourth model is that proposed by Cummings and Worley (1993). They claim that it represents a modern synthesis of earlier approaches. The model describes four basic activities, or the typical sequence of events, that those directing a change effort carry out. The authors point out that change is rarely a neat linear process. There is commonly overlap and confusion between the various tasks, with activities having to be restarted in the light of new information gathered during the change, an alteration in external

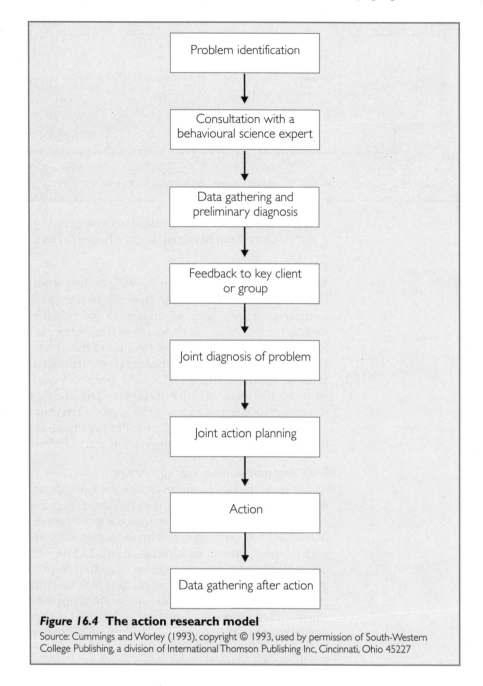

Figure 16.4 The action research model
Source: Cummings and Worley (1993), copyright © 1993, used by permission of South-Western College Publishing, a division of International Thomson Publishing Inc, Cincinnati, Ohio 45227

conditions, or some other change elsewhere in the same organisation. The process is set out in Figure 16.5

Entering and contracting
Planned change starts with processes of entering and contracting. These help managers to decide whether to start a planned change and whether to commit resources to it. Entering involves gathering initial data to try to understand the issues facing the organisation. Potential problems and ways

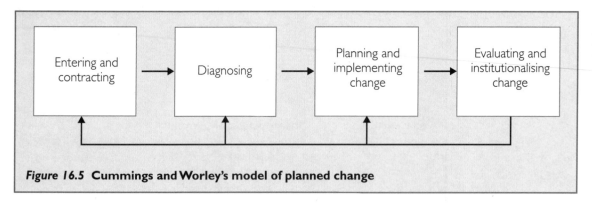

Figure 16.5 **Cummings and Worley's model of planned change**

of approaching them are presented to managers. They are debated to develop a mutual agreement to engage in the change project.

Diagnosing

This stage of development involves gathering a wide range of information about the organisation and the problems relevant to the change process. This a central part of the process, which aims to understand both internal and external factors. Information and conclusions drawn from it are regularly fed back to managers to assist the change (including the unfreezing of established attitudes and behaviours). Since organisations are seen as systems, the diagnostic phase is further complicated by the need to look for possible interactions amongst the elements identified. The data are typically gathered through interviews or questionnaires, or by direct observation of meetings and work activities. They are often given back to organisation members in a processed form, to engage them in interpretation and in helping to design solutions.

Planning and implementing change

At this stage the details of the change are worked out, with varying degrees of involvement by the organisation members. Typically it will involve one or more of the types of change mentioned above – people, structural, technological or business process. It may also involve examining the organisation's relations with its environment. In addition, it will include efforts to gain the commitment of people to the changes envisaged. If the changes are controversial, the strategies may also include ideas on how to develop and maintain political support and how to sustain momentum once the initial enthusiasm has worn off. In this stage, organisation members and practitioners jointly plan and implement organisational development interventions.

Evaluating and institutionalising change

In Cummings and Worley's model the development process concludes with some attempt to evaluate the impact of the intervention. It also includes activities to reinforce the change as part of the normal way of working (Lewin's refreezing stage). Successful change needs to be institutionalised by reinforcing new behaviours through feedback, rewards and training.

Two concluding points can be made. The first is that major change is political. It is quite likely to raise anxieties amongst those who feel they will suffer in some way or be exposed to closer scrutiny, or have greater (or less) responsibility. This leads to negative or critical reactions as people protect their own or their department's interests. Major information technology projects have experienced this, where the greater availability of information has altered the power balance in a variety of ways (especially by increasing the centre's knowledge of local performance). Those planning such systems need to take account of how this may affect managers' reaction to the change and their willingness to accept it.

The other point not explicitly mentioned in Cummings and Worley's model is that change usually comes in a cluster of changes. The business and political environments are such that an organisational development project is likely to be only one of many changes going on at the same time. Organisations are also likely to be having to cope with takeovers or mergers, new product launches, organisational changes for other reasons, competitive tendering, privatisation, new competitive expectations, and many other events. These introduce new uncertainties about the business and its future, and add to the difficulties of making change successful.

16.10 Recap

Content agenda

External changes in the business or political environment can lead to changes in the objectives that management is following. Such a change in strategy often prompts management to change other organisational elements so that they match the new strategy. A rational view of change management suggests that planning how to deal with the change involves paying attention to the relevant parts of the content agenda, and the interactions between them. Contingency approaches stress limited management choice in adapting structure to external events. Other views suggest that management has more scope to decide on structure with limited penalties.

Process agenda

Many organisations are characterised by inertia and a reluctance to change, despite considerable management efforts. Stakeholder interests will affect change: change champions may stimulate change to enhance their position, or out of concern for corporate performance. Change can be seen from several perspectives, each with different implications for how the change is managed. Lewin's force-field model can indicate where opposition and support may be found. Outcomes of change will be affected by the form of decision processes that management creates and which of the parties it involves. Signals about performance and external change compete for management attention. Information has to be accurately received before someone can attend to it, so communication skills also affect this aspect of management. Communication can also be used by stakeholders to deliberately distort the situation by amplifying or suppressing information.

Control agenda

If change is seen as threatening to alter the pattern of control, some may resist these attempts to control them. Those pushing such change will need to build their power to overcome resistance, especially by creating

AN INTEGRATIVE FRAMEWORK OF MANAGEMENT

Content agenda

▶ External or internal change can lead management to review objectives and strategy

▶ New objectives can be supported by change in other aspects of organisation

▶ Contingency view that environment affects internal form

▶ Implies little scope for management choice

▶ Strategic choice view proposes management has wider discretion

▶ Generating action supported by perceived legitimacy of change to staff

Process agenda

▶ Stakeholder interests drive or resist change

▶ Change promoters may have private as well as corporate objectives

▶ Force-field model analyses drivers or restrainers of change

▶ Change management needs right decision processes or mechanisms

▶ Communication affects direction of change

Control agenda

▶ Change that is seen to extend control is likely to be resisted

▶ Promoters need power to move forward

▶ Organisational change can be prompted by signals from control system

▶ Change process itself needs monitoring

Figure 16.6

institutional support mechanisms. Organisational development often begins as a result of signals from the organisational control systems that corrective action is needed. However, the perception and interpretation of these external signals are not technical but human processes, and the interpretations are not unique. The change process itself can also be monitored to compare results with stated plans.

The integrative framework is set out in Figure 16.6

PART CASE QUESTIONS

▶ In what ways does the structure of different parts of Save the Children Fund reflect their respective environments?

▶ What wider governmental, technological or globalisational changes are affecting Save the Children Fund and prompting further changes in structure?

▶ Which steps in the change process at Save the Children Fund can you recognise in the organisational development model presented above?

16.11 Review questions

1 What is the main criticism of the contingency approaches to organisation structure?
2 If contingency approaches stress the influence of external factors on organisational structures, what is the role of management in designing organisational structures?
3 What are the main sources of external change affecting organisations? For each one, can you find a specific recent example of an external change which has prompted change within an organisation?
4 How are external changes affecting educational organisations? What examples can you find of ways in which they are adapting to those changes?
5 What are the four types of organisational boundary which are being eroded by current technological and other developments?
6 What do you understand by the term 'virtual organisation'? Find an original example of this type, and find out how it works.
7 What are the three stages in Lewin's model of change? Which of them do you think are most and least appropriate to those managing change now?

Further reading

The research reports by Woodward (1965), Burns and Stalker (1961) and Lawrence and Lorsch (1967) which initiated the contingency approaches to organisation were published over thirty years ago. They are short and accessible accounts of the research process, and it would add to your understanding to read at least one of them in the original. The second edition of Woodward's book (1980) is even more useful, as it includes a commentary on her work by two later scholars. This chapter has been quite brief in its presentation of the various organisational development models, and you may want to read more about these. The frequently cited work is that by French and Bell (1995), though Cummings and Worley (1993) is also good. For a European perspective, see Mastenbroek (1993). An earlier classic is the account by Andrew Pettigrew of the way John Harvey Jones went about creating great change at ICI (Pettigrew, 1985). The book is dauntingly long, but it does give an accurate sense of the complexities behind major change.

CHAPTER 17

Managing change

AIM

To outline different forms of change in organisations and how management attempts to introduce it.

OBJECTIVES

By the end of your work on this chapter you should be able to outline the concepts below in your own terms and:

1 Explain how external events and pressures can stimulate efforts to make changes within organisations

2 Give examples of changes that were misguided or served sectional rather than organisational interests

3 Identify and illustrate the different types of change that managements introduce

4 Explain the meaning of internal and external contexts, and show how they can help or hinder change

5 Compare alternative models which management uses to implement change and indicate when they are likely to work

6 Know how to recognise these alternative approaches when being used in practice and evaluate the methods

7 Outline the skills needed to apply the alternative approaches

8 Recognise the different forms of resistance to change, including the practices of counterimplementation

9 Evaluate management proposals to implement change by using these models and perspectives

The travel agency

The company is a successful and growing travel agency, with about 300 retail branches. The main function of a branch is to sell package holidays to customers, together with other services like car hire and foreign currency. A typical branch has a manager, an assistant manager, a cashier, and between four and six sales staff. The company has four divisions, with each divisional director responsible for the performance of about seventy branches.

The branch network had built up rapidly through growth and acquisition. Although there were standard company procedures, staff used the manual systems in a variety of different ways depending on the history and circumstances of the branch. They refer to the holidays available through an industry-wide computer network which enables them to bring a range of holidays onto a screen. When the customer has chosen a holiday, the sales staff make the reservation directly with the tour operator through the computer terminal.

Each reservation generates a large administrative load for the agency. This includes taking payment, issuing receipts, calculating commissions to be claimed, balancing income with tours sold, ensuring tickets and travel plans are issued, and monitoring the financial performance of each branch. This administrative work used to be carried out by the sales staff and branch managers. It caused much delay, error and stress, especially as the company continued to expand. Margins in the business are small, and a slight change in the pattern of business rapidly affects profitability. A particular problem was the lack of timely management information about branch and business performance.

Senior management decided to create a computer-based branch accounting system. As a sale was completed, the details would be entered onto a PC which would hold the data in the branch and then send it overnight to head office. This would reduce paperwork, errors and administrative costs in the branches and at head office. It would also provide information the following morning about many critical aspects of the business, including sales, turnover and cash received.

A project group comprising people from head office, the branches and the system supplier was set up to oversee implementation. The group undertook a survey in six branches to find out what was required of the new system. The group also considered the social and organisational problems the project would raise. Its recommendations to the board included communicating the plan to all staff early in the project; involving branch managers in the detailed plans for automating their branch; appointing a project manager whose job would be to concentrate on implementation; and having a pilot study to test the system in a few branches before finalising the design.

Source: based on a case in Boddy and Gunson (1996)

CASE QUESTIONS

- ▶ What has prompted management to go ahead with this project?
- ▶ From the information in the case, what management (rather than technical) issues may arise during design and implementation?

17.1 Introduction

This chapter introduces the following ideas:
- ▶ Project management models
- ▶ Rational-linear models
- ▶ Participative models
- ▶ Political models
- ▶ Inner context
- ▶ Outer context
- ▶ Counterimplementation
- ▶ Competence

Earlier chapters have shown the forces for change affecting organisations of all kinds. Managers attempt to know what is happening within the wider environment and to the internal resources available to them. These sources of information help them shape the future strategies of their organisation. Moving from the present to those futures is only achieved by some more-or-less deliberate attempt at change. That is more easily said than done. Many attempts by management to introduce change end in failure.

The broad trends in the business world described in Chapter 16 clearly show the scale of change which management has to contend with. A survey by the Institute of Management (1995a) showed that 70 per cent of respondents had experienced one or more corporate restructurings in the past two years. A similar study carried out by the University of Manchester Institute of Science and Technology also found that while most mangers accepted the need for change, many were anxious about the outcome of change in their organisation and the way it had been carried out. Organisations still experience great difficulty in managing change successfully.

Many changes today stem from the introduction of new computer technologies into organisations. There is abundant evidence that significant technical innovation generates organisational change. More than thirty years of research have shown that applying computer technology to work triggers change in tasks and jobs, in the organisation of work, in the organisation structures and in organisational mission or strategy (see McLoughlin and Clark, 1994, for a review of research). It does not follow that managements introduce the organisational changes that would support their financial investment in hardware and software. Wider organisational changes are often neglected, or those that are made are inappropriate. Projects are consequently less successful than they might have been. We also know, despite the wide publicity given to the achievements of information technology (IT) in business, much of which is being transformed by it, that there is a high failure rate of applications. The acceptability of and pay-off from some systems has been poor. The reasons for these failures are well documented. It is clear that the main problems are organisational and managerial rather than technical.

For example, a survey of 400 British and Irish companies revealed that only 11 per cent had been successful in their applications of information technology. The criteria included the breadth of applications, the benefits achieved, completion on time and return on investment (Kearney, 1990). The report concluded that this rate 'must be judged unacceptably low', and also indicated that the reality may be bleaker since this was a self-selected set

NOTICEBOARD TQM and BPR

'Though Total Quality Management [TQM] appears to be central to the success of Japanese companies, the experience of Western companies has been that it is difficult to introduce and sustain. Indeed, one of the founders of the TQM movement, Philip Crosby (1979), claimed that over 90 per cent of TQM initiatives fail. Though a 90 per cent failure rate seems incredibly high, studies of the adoption of TQM by companies in the UK and other European countries shows that they too have experienced a similarly high failure rate – perhaps as much as 80 per cent or more.' (Kearney, 1992; Economist Intelligence Unit, 1992).

Business Process Re-engineering [BPR] has been hailed as 'the biggest business innovation in the 1990s' (Mill, 1994, p.26). Wastell *et al.* (1994, p.23) … concluded from the available evidence that 'BPR initiatives have typically achieved much less than promised'. Other studies have come to similar conclusions (Coombs and Hull, 1994).

Therefore even well-established change initiatives, for which a great deal of information, advice and assistance is available, are no guarantee of success.

Source: Burnes (1996, pp.172–3)

of respondents to a mail questionnaire which was presumably returned by the more competent and, in their own estimation, effective companies.

Part of the reason for the failure of many IT projects lies in the advanced nature of the technology. However, this is not the main reason. The explanation lies in the way change is managed rather than in the novelty of the change itself. Boddy and Buchanan's (1992) research into project management skills deliberately included managers who were implementing IT and non-IT projects. The management issues that arose were broadly common to all types of change. As the Noticeboard above shows, organisational innovation of any kind is a challenging management task. Major change attempts often end in failure. To begin to understand this we need some tools. One is to distinguish different types of change, in terms of their content, systemic nature, critical dimensions and vulnerability.

n o t e b o o k   1 7 . 1

From discussion with colleagues or managers, identify a major attempt at change in an organisation. Make notes on the following questions and use your case as a point of reference throughout the chapter.

What was the change – what was the specific topic of the change? Why was it introduced? What were the specific objectives? How did management try to plan and implement it? How far did it meet the objectives? What lessons have those involved learned from the experience?

17.2 Types of change

Content

Content refers to the particular elements of the organisation that management is trying to change. It may be a strategic reorientation, a technical

---

NOTICEBOARD **Some areas of change in organisations**

Objectives
▶ Developing a new product or service.
▶ Changing the overall mission or direction.
▶ Changing the emphasis given to a particular market.

Business processes
▶ Introducing a new process for dealing with customer orders.
▶ Improving the way maintenance and repair services are delivered.
▶ Redesigning systems to handle the flow of cash and funds.

Structure
▶ Reallocating functions and responsibilities between departments.

▶ Redesigning work to increase empowerment.
▶ Centralising or decentralising decisions.

Technology
▶ Installing new computer hardware or software.
▶ Building a new factory.
▶ Creating a Website on the Internet.

People
▶ Designing a training programme to enhance skills.
▶ Changing the tasks of staff to offer a new service.
▶ Deliberately encouraging staff to be more friendly to customers.

---

change, the launch of a new product or an attempt to introduce closer relations with suppliers or customers. Change can begin with any element of the organisation – the Noticeboard gives some examples.

Some of the elements listed in the Noticeboard are easier to change than others. Hardy and Redivo (1994) distinguish between behavioural, attitudinal and cultural change in the following terms:

▶ **Behavioural** Changes that are directed at how specific tasks and procedures are performed. Success is judged by changes in established measures such as productivity or waste.

▶ **Attitudinal** These are directed at changing people's awareness or understanding of a situation. The intention is to improve performance in some way as a result of new attitudes leading to new behaviour.

▶ **Cultural** Describes attempts to bring about system-wide change in assumptions, norms and values. These in turn are expected to lead to attitudinal and behavioural change, and to radical changes in performance.

Hardy and Redivo's studies show that attempts to introduce attitudinal and cultural change encounter greater resistance than behavioural ones. They conclude that managers introducing these forms of change need to draw on different sources of power and skills. Similarly, Hinings *et al.* (1991) distinguish between different types of change:

▶ **Substantive** Based on a product or visible technical system.

▶ **Structural** Which is more difficult to explain and justify.

▶ **Process** Which has a more problematic relationship with eventual success.

Like Hardy and Redivo, Hinings *et al.* argue that changes involving structure and process are more difficult to achieve than those involving tangible, substantive matters.

Systemic nature

The systemic nature of organisations means that a change that starts in any of the five broad areas listed in the Noticeboard is likely to have implications for the others. Introducing a networked computer system will affect not only technology but also some aspects of structure, people and business processes. It might also affect some aspects of the objectives – if, for example, it allows the organisation to enter a new market. These ripple effects have to be managed too. Ignoring them is a major reason why change programmes fail to do what was expected.

Similarly, Tichy (1982) proposed that change involves three interacting elements: technology, politics and culture. He refers to these as representing three fundamental problems that require continuous attention, and moreover that, 'Not only does each area require attention on its own, but problems of all three are interdependent, so problem-solving must be co-ordinated among them' (p.62). Hinings *et al.* (1991) studied an attempt at change in a professional organisation, and also concluded that the content of a change, together with the ideas and rationales underlying it, significantly affected the kind of planning and implementation process which was needed to secure acceptance.

CASE QUESTIONS 17.1

► Identify the possible ripple effects that may need to be managed in the travel agency. Do this by drawing five circles on a sheet of paper. Label them: technology, business processes, structure, people and objectives, respectively. Start by entering the branch automation system in the technology area. Then think of the possible implications that introducing this will have for the other elements of the organisation. These begin to form the management agenda for this project. Compare your lists with those of colleagues to see if there are any important ideas you have missed.

Critical dimensions

Changes vary in their perceived significance to the organisation and their status on management's agenda. Boddy and Buchanan (1992) worked closely with the project managers of a wide range of changes. Analysis of these changes suggested that two dimensions distinguished projects in a significant way. The first is how central the change is to the primary task of the organisation (core or marginal) and the second its novelty in that context (ranging from novel to familiar). This gives four quadrants – and they predict that changes of the core/novel character are more likely to encounter barriers, and be more difficult to implement, than those which are marginal and familiar.

In quadrant 1 of Figure 17.1 the change is novel, but marginal to the main task of the organisation. The personal vulnerability of the change agent is therefore low. A change to outsource an organisation's catering arrangement would probably be of this type. Quadrant 2 change is that which is seen as marginal to the main task and is also a familiar change to existing practices. A change to the organisation's system for paying pensions to retired employees is an example. Quadrant 3 change is a familiar change to adapt from existing activities but affects the core of the organisation's activity. It will be a more challenging change to manage as it can damage the business if it fails. The new command and control systems introduced by the

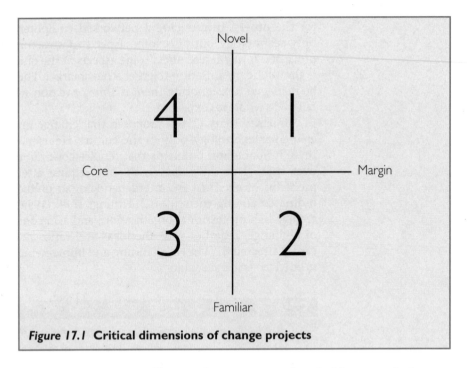

Figure 17.1 Critical dimensions of change projects

ambulance service in Chapter 7 is an example of this sort of change. Quadrant 4 changes are those that affect the core activity and are also a novel departure from existing arrangements. These are the most difficult of all changes. They present those managing them with major implementation problems, both organisational and technical. Penalties for failure and the vulnerability of the change agent will be high.

Change projects can also move between quadrants as staff gain experience. Managers and staff often only begin to see the strategic potential of networked computer systems during and after implementation. For example, Boddy and Gunson (1996) quote several examples of IT projects that began as quadrant 1 or quadrant 3 changes. As the importance of the information systems to future business developments became clear, the projects moved into quadrant 4.

Other characteristics of change projects affect the task of those who are managing them:

▶ **Pace** At one extreme, management chooses (or is obliged) to make a change at great speed with little time for investigation, consultation or testing. Others are able to make the change at a more leisurely pace, perhaps with pilot schemes or extensive testing before full implementation.

▶ **Controversy** Some changes are vigorously opposed from the start by one or more parties, who seek to undermine the project by overt or covert means. Others are seen as desirable by all concerned who work together to make the change happen.

▶ **Shifting goals** The goals of change projects often continue to evolve as the project itself is planned and implemented. Sometimes these changes reflect poor initial planning. More often they reflect the fact that the business world has changed since the project began. Management then needs to change the change itself to keep it relevant.

- ▶ **Senior stance** The attitude of top management towards the change is critical. Senior managers cannot give detailed guidelines to change managers, and may not even set a clear blueprint for change, but they can affect the project by the scale and consistency of their support. Where difficulties or resource problems arise, someone managing a change needs to have, or obtain, adequate and consistent support from senior managers if they are to have a chance of making the change.
- ▶ **Outside links** Many projects depend on either physical or organisational changes in areas beyond the immediate focus of the project: they need the co-operation of people in other departments or organisations, who are not necessarily as committed to the change as those directly promoting it. Managers dealing with a change of this sort clearly need to exert influence over those responsible for these other links. If the latter have different priorities, this task will not be easy. Figure 17.2 illustrates the additional complexities that linkages bring to the change manager.
- ▶ **Variable ownership** Change projects need sustained commitment and support and a sense of ownership from powerful backers. These may be higher in the hierarchy, or in other areas of the organisation. Other managers may be willing to express generalised support, but rather less willing to put effort and resources in when a project is in difficulty.

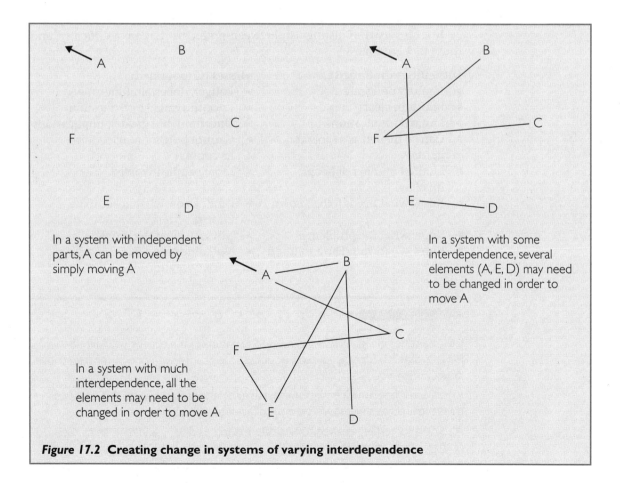

Figure 17.2 **Creating change in systems of varying interdependence**

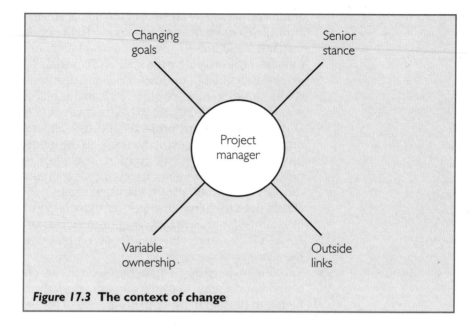

Figure 17.3 The context of change

These factors are summarised in Figure 17.3. This shows that many projects are not isolated events but part of a wider business system. Other things happen in that system that may help or hinder change.

It is also used to distinguish between problems that are a difficulty, and those that are a mess:

Difficulties (bounded)	Messes (unbounded)
▶ Limited timescale	▶ Longer, uncertain timescale
▶ Priorities clear	▶ Priorities called into question
▶ Limited implications	▶ Uncertain, but greater, implications
▶ Can be treated as a separate matter	▶ Cannot be disentangled from its context
▶ Limited number of people involved	▶ More people involved
▶ Know what needs to be known	▶ Don't know what needs to be known
▶ Know what the problem is	▶ Not sure what the problem is
▶ Know what would be a solution	▶ No 'solutions'

n o t e b o o k   17.2

Use the scales in Figure 17.4 to analyse the nature of the change you identified in Notebook 17.1. Do this yourself, or discuss the change with one or more of those directly involved.

What does the pattern imply for the management of the change? Which issues does the analysis suggest will be most difficult to manage?

Also do a force-field analysis to illustrate the forces driving and restraining the change (see Chapter 16).

Significant change?	Margin	1	2	3	4	5	Core
Solution	Familiar	1	2	3	4	5	Novel
Shifting goals	Rare/minor	1	2	3	4	5	Often/major
Senior stance	Supportive	1	2	3	4	5	Unsupportive
Outside links?	Few	1	2	3	4	5	Many
Sense of ownership	High	1	2	3	4	5	Low
Will there be a fight?	Uncontroversial	1	2	3	4	5	Controversial
Is it a . . .	Difficulty	1	2	3	4	5	Mess

Figure 17.4 **Scoring change – a high score indicates likely trouble**

The points made so far are summed up in the dimensions shown in Figure 17.4. Managers faced with a project can analyse the characteristics by circling the number on each line which best describes it.

NOTICEBOARD The Tropics test

Another approach is suggested by McCalman and Paton (1992) who distinguish between hard and soft problems. Pure scientific, engineering or technological problems tend towards the hard end of the spectrum. In cases where the project demands a technological or functional expertise then mechanistic solution methodologies will suffice. These problems are rare as most systems involve human beings at some stage. They recommend assessing the magnitude and the nature of a change event by using the Tropics test. This is an early warning device to give a quick and understandable view of the nature of a change.

Tropics factor	A Hard	B Soft
Timescales	Clearly defined, short to medium term	Not clearly defined, medium to long term
Resources	Clearly defined and committed	Unclear and variable
Objectives	Objective and quantifiable	Subjective and visionary
Perceptions	Shared by those affected	Creates conflict of interest
Interest	Limited and well defined	Widespread and ill defined
Control	Within the managing group	Shared beyond the managing group
Source	Originates internally	Originates externally

McCalman and Paton recommend reviewing each factor and deciding which of the statements in the columns best describes the situation in the current project. The more factors judged to be in column A, the more likely it is that the change can be handled by a relatively mechanistic approach. The more that are in column B, the more likely that the change will require more organic, intuitive approaches. Most change is a combination of hard and soft elements, so managing it requires a blend of methods.

17.3 The context of change

Change cannot be understood or managed apart from its context. Pettigrew has placed particular emphasis on the need to understand this aspect, and in so doing distinguishes between the outer and inner contexts of the organisation (Pettigrew, 1987). The former refers to the political, environmental, economic and other factors outside the firm which both shape and are shaped by management activities. The latter refers to a range of structural, cultural and political arrangements within the organisation itself which shape the world of those trying to implement change, and which can help or hinder implementation.

External context

Chapter 11 has described at length the substantive nature of the external environment of business, and the way that management needs to analyse this. However, the information in the outside world is not automatically available to or understood by all those within the organisation. Some may be quite unaware of trends or developments that seem critical to others. Some may see and interpret information about a competitor as threatening the survival of a business; others may not accept the information or may play down its significance.

The point of this to managing change is that whatever information is available about the external environment has to be transmitted in some way to people and institutions within the organisation. They then decide whether or not to respond to it, and if so how. Managers wanting to influence change can affect that process by managing external information. They can, for example, magnify and exaggerate customer complaints, competitor actions or industry trends in order to shape the views of their colleagues in favour of the change they are proposing. Or they can play down the information and suggest that others are exaggerating it, if they wish to avoid change.

Managers promoting or facing change can use external support to help them introduce or counter it. Being able to quote the support or otherwise of influential industry or competitor players or the views of valuable customers or suppliers can help win internal arguments.

CASE QUESTIONS 17.2

▶ What changes in the external context are affecting the travel agency?

▶ What effects are they likely to have for management and staff?

Internal context

Structure

Change can be helped or hindered by wider structural aspects of the organisation. These refer to the way tasks are divided up – whether in a tightly specified and detailed way, or rather loosely, with significant local discretion – and to the way they are co-ordinated, so that the separate parts work together in a reasonably co-ordinated manner. It also refers to the pattern of authority, such as the structures and processes through which resource allocation decisions are made. Kanter (1983) and Pettigrew (1985) have both shown how segmented functional divisions impede the flow of information and decisions necessary for major change. For example, many organisations are trying to implement a change in the relationship they have with suppliers. They want to move from an adversarial towards a more collaborative, partnering approach. This involves many changes, both external and internal. Narrowly functional organisations would, for example, need to reconsider the roles of the groups involved with suppliers and customers, to ensure that the basis of their specialisation and their relationships with others reflect the requirements of a partnering approach and not some earlier priority.

The vertical hierarchy of the two organisations will also be relevant, particularly with respect to decision-making structures and processes. These are the mechanisms which should link the external world and the organisation's strategies to cope with it (Galbraith, 1977). Management needs a forum in which it can try to achieve a coherence and consistency among the organisation's activities. Such mechanisms determine whose interests matter and establish what actions are taken on goals, priorities, roles, communication systems and so on. They are the result of past organisational choices, which shape the choices members can make in the present.

Culture

The prevailing organisational culture is expected to be a powerful influence on the success or failure of innovation. Culture may need to change in line with new requirements, but is itself a possible constraint on making that change. As discussed in Chapter 14, culture represents the pattern of assumptions that a group considers a valid way 'to perceive, think and feel in relation to ... problems' (Schein, 1985, p.9).

Egan (1994) suggests that culture has both a 'doing' side – the observable patterns of behaviour – and a 'thinking' side – the shared beliefs, values and norms which drive the behaviour. He goes on to argue that culture permeates all aspects of an organisation, expressed in observable patterns of behaviour, such as how strategy is handled, how structure is shaped, what personnel systems are in place and so on. These can often be described in terms of a culture which sums up particular features of the organisation, as in 'a culture of tradition' or a 'culture of change'.

The following comments come from employees of one of the most successful companies in the electronics industry and give an insight into its culture and attitudes to change. Given the business it is in, and the research-based origins of the company, the culture was often expressed in terms of flexibility, constant change, proactive, individual responsibility:

> ❝ A very dynamic organisation, it's incredibly fast and the change thing is just a constant that you live with. They really promote flexibility and adaptability in their employees. Change is just a constant, there's change happening all of the time and people have become very acclimatised to that, it's part of the job. The attitude to change, certainly within the organisation is very positive at the moment. ❞

> ❝ A lot of people come and leave – almost a transitory career move. They say that themselves: 'don't plan to retire from here'. That whole attitude generates a different working environment. You get individual responsibility quickly. ❞

❝ very quick to change, and you're expected to work until you get the job finished. You're definitely expected to do whatever is needed to get the job done. Quite hard driving, under the surface. ❞

The significance of the concept to change is that culture, especially the deeper values and beliefs, has a force and momentum which is difficult to change, as it reflects fundamental assumptions about the nature of people, the organisation and the environment. It is therefore a crucial factor in determining an organisation's receptiveness to innovation, such as who will innovate, in what areas and with what results? Lorsch (1986) argues that the culture (in his definition, 'the shared beliefs top managers in a company have about how they should manage themselves and other employees, and how they should conduct their business' (p.95)) can be a significant barrier to coping with new conditions. This is mainly because these beliefs have been developed through many years of successful operation: 'Managers learn to be guided by these beliefs because they have worked successfully in the past' (p.97). Beliefs can be about many things – the nature of market expectations, competitors, or about internal organisation.

Schein (1985) argues that cultures are created as groups and their leaders solve the problems of coping simultaneously with the problems of the outside world and of their internal functioning. Changing cultures which are deeply embedded sounds daunting, but there are examples of companies which appear to have made significant transformations. Lorsch (1986) argues that a key step is to make beliefs explicit, since they are usually only implicit and taken for granted. This can be done by asking questions of managers and others about the problems, opportunities and challenges the business is facing in chosen areas. This process helps to identify the underlying assumptions which guide behaviour (Egan, 1994).

Power

Pfeffer (1992) argues that power is essential in order to get most things done in organisations. Decisions in themselves change nothing: it is only when they are implemented that anyone notices a difference. When managers make a decision they cannot know if they have made a good or bad one. What they do know is that they will spend more time living with the consequences of the decision than they did in making it. Pfeffer therefore argues that they should spend more time learning how to implement decisions and to deal with the consequences and ramifications. They should work to improve decisions and to make sure they achieve what was expected. They

---

NOTICEBOARD Why change programmes fail

A critical point to raise is whether management's enquiry into the business's problems and opportunities is directed at changing the culture or at changing behaviour. Beer et al. (1990) have argued convincingly that change programmes which are centrally directed, and which focus initially on attitudes or cultural change, usually fail. Instead, they propose that change efforts should focus explicitly on creating new roles, responsibilities and relationships, which in turn lead to new attitudes and behaviour, which can then be reinforced by the rewards system and so on. But the starting point is the joint diagnosis of business problems, leading to explicit vision and action.

may need to work to alter the situation to their benefit as the change unfolds, by being creative and opportunistic.

In an earlier book, Pfeffer (1981) proposed that change and innovation require more than an ability to solve technical or analytical problems. They frequently threaten the status quo, and so are likely to be resisted by stakeholders who benefit from the prevailing arrangements. If organisations are fundamentally political entities, successful innovation depends on those behind the change developing political will and expertise. Promoters need to build their power. This implies that an influential aspect of the context of change is the prevailing pattern of power within the relevant part(s) of the organisation. Furthermore, it is through the exercise of power that that pattern can be changed. Especially when change involves several departments, where performance is difficult to assess, or where there is uncertainty and disagreement, the exercise of power is likely to be essential to implementation.

---

n o t e b o o k   1 7 . 3

Identify a major change being introduced into a public company or agency. Gather information from the media, the organisation and other interested groups. Use that to test the validity of the ideas being presented here.

C A S E   Q U E S T I O N S   1 7 . 3

▶ What clues are there in the case about these factors within the travel agency?

▶ How may they affect the way that management has to manage the change?

17.4 Project management, participative and political models

Buchanan and Boddy (1992) argued that significant change can be viewed from three alternative, but complementary, perspectives, each with different implications for those managing the process of change. First, they outline the project management perspective, which argues that success in managing a project depends on the clear definition and statement of four dimensions: objectives, responsibilities, deadlines and budgets. This implies that the project manager needs to be skilled in the substance or content of the change, and in techniques of monitoring and control.

Secondly, the participative perspective emphasises the benefits of establishing a sense of ownership of the change amongst those whose support will be needed, or who will have to live with the change when it is implemented. Typically this would include involving those affected by the change in the design of solutions, consulting widely about possible options, ensuring that information is widely communicated, providing training and support, and ensuring that conflicts or disagreements are openly and skilfully dealt with.

Thirdly, the political perspective starts from the assumption that there are likely to be many different interests involved in change. These interests will pull in different directions, and will usually be pursuing personal as well as organisational goals, as the Case Example illustrates. The project manager would need to exercise not only problem-solving skills and to encourage participation, but also political skills to overcome opposition and build credibility.

Eastern Electronics Company

case example

Eastern Electronics has 150 employees engaged in designing, manufacturing and selling air conditioning, refrigeration and various kinds of electronic equipment. It is part of the Khan Industrial Group, a major industrial company in India. Khan had had increasing problems in gathering financial data from units within the group as each company had adopted its own methods. Head office wanted to control the financial system more closely in order to reduce its workload and give more insight into group performance. It decided to introduce a computer-aided production management system (CAPM).

Head office decided to establish the CAPM system without consulting the group companies, which resulted in little response from them. The implementation has run into several problems:

▶ CAPM is an integrated system which cannot simply replace the existing manual system. Other organisational changes are needed. These include changes in the way Eastern staff handle and process information and the way departments co-operate.

▶ Eastern felt no ownership of the system because the investment and selection decision had been imposed by the parent company.

▶ Company managers often argued that Eastern was not big enough for such a sophisticated system.

▶ Eastern had an organic management structure, with little definition of responsibilities, unclear tasks and a belief that change occurs at its own pace.

▶ Departments within Eastern were divided in their view of CAPM. The purchasing department disagreed strongly with the system. The purchasing manager had created the current manual system and believed that CAPM was created for group needs, rather than to benefit the companies. The engineering department did not at first see the value of the system, but when it saw some of the functions it could provide, it rapidly became a supporter. The production department was strongly in favour. Both the director and manager had previously worked in a computerised environment and could see the advantages.

After two years of work the system was still not implemented, though considerable work had been done.

 *n o t e b o o k   17.4*

What are the lessons that you would draw from this case? What do they imply about the problem of managing change?

Project management models of change

Most of the published advice and commercial training available for project managers responsible for implementing change reflects the idea of the phased project lifecycle. This approach recommends defining objectives clearly, setting out responsibilities, fixing deadlines and setting budgets. In this model, successful change management depends on specifying these elements at the start and then monitoring them tightly to ensure that the project stays on target. Ineffective implementation is due to managers failing to do this. Change managers in this approach are thus expected to be skilled on two primary dimensions: first, with respect to the substance or content of changes introduced (whether this is a computerised management information system, a new factory building or a revised payment system), and secondly, with respect to project control – they have to define outcomes and the necessary activities to reach them, must monitor progress and must take remedial action to minimise deviations from the plan.

The structures of project management texts and manuals are typically based on a version of the project lifecycle, identifying and elaborating the tools and techniques relevant to each stage. Darnell and Dale (1985), however, advocate a 'total approach' to project management. This is based on a four-phase project cycle and related control disciplines involving planning, construction, commissioning and post-commissioning stages. Dinsmore (1990) labels the four main phases of project development as conceptualisation, planning, execution and termination. Dinsmore's definitions of project and project management are:

> A project is a unique venture with a beginning and an end, conducted by people to meet established goals within parameters of cost, schedule and quality.
>
> Project management is the combination of people, systems, and techniques required to co-ordinate the resources needed to complete projects within established goals. (Dinsmore, 1990, p.17)

Also reinforcing the goal-driven, resource-bound nature of project management. Robert Graham (for whom the four phases of a project are creation, planning, execution and ending) offers the following definition:

> A project is a set of people and other resources temporarily assembled to reach a specified objective, normally with a fixed budget and with a fixed time period. Projects are generally associated with products or procedures that are being done for the first time or with known procedures that are being altered. (Graham, 1985, pp.1–2)

Fred Harrison (1985) describes the role of the project manager in terms of planning, control, cost estimating, planning tools, work breakdown techniques, performance analysis and procurement. In a discussion of human behaviour he criticises the lack of training for engineers in 'human relations skills' such as team-building, conflict resolution and interpersonal behaviour.

The emphasis in these accounts is consistently with planning and control. Skills in dealing with 'human factors' or 'behavioural issues' are seen as important but tend to be just another item (often the last) on the list. They appear to be subordinate to the much broader range of issues concerned with project planning and control tools and techniques. However,

Dinsmore (1990) does argue that, from his experience, at least half of the typical problems faced by project managers are behavioural rather than technical. He elaborates many of the issues mentioned by Harrison (1985), such as team-building, time management, handling conflict, negotiating, communicating, decision-making and problem-solving. Dinsmore's treatment is unusual in the emphasis he gives to human factors, concentrating on the interpersonal, group and structural issues, rather than wider organisational and political issues:

> The consulting firm PA specifies the implementation cycle for change projects thus:
> 1 Develop a strategy.
> 2 Confirm top level support.
> 3 Use a project management approach:
>   (a) identify tasks
>   (b) assign responsibilities
>   (c) agree deadlines
>   (d) initiate actions
>   (e) monitor
>   (f) act on problems
>   (g) close down.
> 4 Communicate results.

---

n o t e b o o k **17.5**

Apply Dinsmore's or a similar model of project management to a domestic, study or leisure task that you are planning to undertake. How does it affect the way you go about it? What issues does it neglect, if any?

In the same way, Gunton (1990) describes the conventional system development life cycle used in information technology projects:

> In the conventional approach to systems development, the development lifecycle is seen as a linear process divided into a number of consecutive phases. The first phase is a feasibility study or requirements analysis, designed to establish whether computer development is worthwhile and what objectives should be set for a subsequent project. This is followed successively by systems analysis, system design and programming, each of which works out the design in more detail and expresses it in terms appropriate for the computer equipment that will be used. Next follows testing and installation, and the process concludes with an enhancement and maintenance phase. (Gunton, 1990, p.222)

Gunton argues that this linear process worked well with 'the hard and specific requirements of applications such as financial accounting and stock control', but that it is less relevant where requirements are 'soft' and in organisational environments of constant change. He points out that more volatile environments mean that changes may have to be introduced during the project lifecycle. These disrupt timescales and damage the morale of the project team – with the alternative of delivering an application that no longer meets requirements. Where the context of the change is itself subject to change, Gunton argues: 'The inevitable result is that too many development projects develop into a guerrilla war between developers and users, with each fighting to gain territory jealously guarded by the other' (1990, p.222). Gunton's portrayal of the conventional model is shown in Figure 17.5: it can be used to guide the management of any kind of organisational change.

These and other models of the project management approach to change share two common features. First, they depend on the assumption that planned change in organisations unfolds in a logically sequenced manner. Solutions are not identified until the problem has been clearly defined. An effective solution is not selected until the various options have been systematically compared. Implementation does not begin until there is agreement on the solution. The key actors in the implementation process each have clearly specified tasks and responsibilities. The progress of implementation is systematically monitored and deviations from plan are corrected. The implementation process is bounded in terms both of resources (people and money) and time, with a clear termination or close-down date. The 'logical unfolding' property of these accounts has led to their being labelled 'rational-linear' models of change.

Secondly, they rely on the assumption that the participation or involvement of those affected by the change is but one important step in the overall implementation process. Other writers have argued that participation is more central to effective change management. Their views are outlined next.

Rational-linear models of change are those that view change as an activity that follows a logical, orderly sequence of activities that can be planned in advance.

Participative models of change

The participative approach to managing change has become a well established aspect of the management literature. Few would now openly argue that participative management (however defined), except in extreme circumstances, is not an effective approach to the implementation of organisational change. It is expected to help overcome resistance and win commitment to new ideas. Pettigrew (1985) described this as the 'truth, trust, love and collaboration approach' to change. This is a key feature of the North American organisational development literature, and has also become an integral component of European and Scandinavian management thought and practice. The concept of establishing 'ownership' of change became central to this argument in the late 1980s. The term is generally used in a vague and imprecise manner to indicate feelings of personal involvement in and contribution to events and outcomes. The underlying, and wholly reasonable, assumption is that if people are able to say 'I helped to build this', they will be more willing to live and work with it, whatever it is.

Participative models of change are those that recommend change managers to consult widely and deeply with those affected and to secure their willing consent to the changes proposed.

Many texts offer advice on how to involve employees in implementing change effectively. This applies to the 'quality of working life' movement of the 1960s and 1970s (Buchanan, 1979), to the 'quality circle' movement of the 1970s and 1980s and to 'high involvement management' practices in general (Lawler, 1986). As an example, the Australian academic Dexter Dunphy (1981) argued that successful change programmes in organisations tend to have most of the following fifteen features:

▶ Clear objectives
▶ Realistic scope, planned, simple
▶ Informed awareness around the organisation

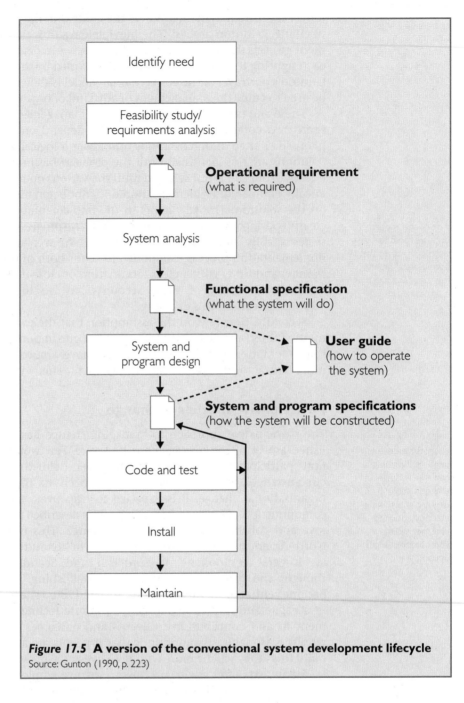

Figure 17.5 A version of the conventional system development lifecycle
Source: Gunton (1990, p. 223)

- ▶ Selection of appropriate intervention strategies
- ▶ Good timing
- ▶ Genuine participation
- ▶ Support from key power groups
- ▶ Use of existing power structure and experience
- ▶ Open assessment before implementation
- ▶ Majority support for perceived benefits
- ▶ Competent staff support to offer temporary resources

- ▶ Integration of new methods into routine operations
- ▶ Transfer and diffusion of successful innovations
- ▶ Continuing review and modification
- ▶ Adequate rewards for implementers and those affected

This appears to be a straightforward blend of project management and participative management advice, with four of the fifteen items (informed awareness, genuine participation, open assessment, majority support) related directly to establishing ownership of change amongst those affected. These look uncontentious. The difficulties arise when one seeks to identify the day-to-day implications of the fifteen recommendations. On the surface it looks like an easy prescription, but to follow this guidance fully shows that the change management task has many layers and aspects. It would, above all, be enormously time consuming for those leading the process.

Kotter and Schlesinger (1979) also offer some prescriptions from a participative management perspective. They suggested a more parsimonious and often-quoted list of six specific methods for change implementation to overcome resistance:

- ▶ **Education and counselling**   Management should share knowledge, perceptions and objectives with those to be affected by change. This may involve a major training programme, face-to-face counselling, group meetings, and the distribution of reports.
- ▶ **Participation and involvement**   Those who might resist should be involved in planning and implementing change in order to reduce opposition and enhance commitment. This also reduces anxieties that individuals may have about the unknown consequences of change, and also makes effective use of existing skill and knowledge.
- ▶ **Facilitation and support**   People may need to be provided with counselling and therapy to help overcome fears and anxieties about change.
- ▶ **Negotiation and agreement**   It may be necessary to establish a mutually agreeable compromise through trading and exchange. The content of change may have to be adjusted to meet the needs and interests of potential resistors.
- ▶ **Manipulation and co-optation**   This involves covert attempts to sidestep potential resistance and can be achieved through emotional appeal to sensitive groups, and through the selective dissemination of potentially distorted information to highlight benefits and ignore disadvantages. Key resistors can be co-opted by giving them privileged access to the decision-making process.
- ▶ **Explicit and implicit coercion**   Management here abandons attempts to reach consensus and resorts to the use of force or threats, offering to transfer or threatening to fire or demote individuals or to stifle their promotion and career prospects.

CASE QUESTIONS 17.4

- ▶ Which of the techniques mentioned so far were used by management in the travel agency as it developed and introduced the branch accounting system?
- ▶ What other ideas from Kotter and Schlesinger's list would you suggest that management should try to apply?

Kotter and Schlesinger argue that the six techniques they identify can be used in any combination, depending on circumstances. Unilateral, directed, autocratic change management, however, is still likely to be less effective than participation in some form, they argue.

The field of systems design and of human/computer interaction is now driven by participative approaches. A well known example of participative systems design methodology is Enid Mumford's (1983) Ethics approach. Here the key ingredients include user involvement in system development, recognising the social issues in implementation and using sociotechnical principles to redesign work. Several other methodologies are available for involving users in the system design process, for understanding users' needs more effectively, and for giving them wider influence in design decisions that will affect their work. The work of Ken Eason (1988) has been particularly influential in this area.

However, despite the otherwise convincing evidence in the general management literature on change concerning participative approaches, Ives and Olson (1984), from a review of twenty-two studies, conclude that the evidence to support user involvement in information system design is weak, and that the benefits of such approaches remain to be demonstrated. Child (1984) explores the circumstances in which participation may be inappropriate or unworkable. While supporting the view that the involvement of those to be affected by change is ethically desirable, Child argues that where there is full agreement on how to proceed, or where management is powerful enough to force changes through, participation may be seen simply as a waste of time. Similarly, where there is fundamental disagreement and inflexible opposition to change, participation may be used to obstruct implementation. Child also cites American research suggesting that it is wholly unrealistic to think of moving to consensus through participation in large public sector bureaucracies with rigid hierarchies pervaded by competing political interest groups. Some large private sector companies have these bureaucratic and political characteristics too.

Political models of change

Project management and participative models work in certain circumstances. Where the change is relatively straightforward and uncontentious they provide a valuable guide to management responsible for implementing such change programmes. However, it is clear from the many examples of failed attempts to change that the two approaches are inadequate in some circumstances. For example, Whipp et al. (1988) argue that change often involves a number of actors, representing different levels and sections of the organisation, pulling in different directions, in the pursuit of personal as well as organisational goals:

> Strategic processes of change are now more widely accepted as multi-level activities and not just as the province of a few, or even a single, general manager. Outcomes of decisions are no longer assumed to be a product of rational ... debates but are also shaped by the interests and commitments of individuals and groups, forces of bureaucratic momentum, and the manipulation of the structural context around decisions and changes.

Strategy in this perspective is 'emergent' in that it derives from a series of smaller-scale and incremental changes, rather than the conventional view of strategy as a rationally intended grand master plan set out in advance (see Chapter 10). This view of change as *logical incrementalism* was originally identified by Quinn (1980). He saw the development of strategy as both a political and an analytical process characterised by 'muddling through with purpose'. Change is an accumulation of small steps. It is an evolutionary process of trial, error, experimentation and learning, rather than one of early commitment to a radical longer-term fixed plan.

There have been a number of analyses of change implementation which criticise both the lack of attention to the process and context of change, and the rational-linear view of that process. These analyses emphasise the political and cultural nature of the change process (Quinn, 1980; Pettigrew, 1985, 1987; Pfeffer, 1992) and seek to demonstrate how the rational and political dimensions are interwined. Pettigrew (1985, 1987) and Kanter (1983) have been particularly influential, as has the more recent work of Kotter (1996) – see Noticeboard.

Pettigrew (1985) advocates a perspective on strategic change implementation that recognises the combination of rational, cultural and political factors in decision making, and that also takes into account the influence of historical and contextual factors in relation to the continuous process of change. This perspective again takes issue with rational-linear models of change which are dismissed as inadequate ways of theorising events and as oversimplified guides to appropriate management action. The managerial process in Pettigrew's view is a complex and untidy cocktail of ostensibly rational assessment mixed with differential perceptions, quests for power, visionary leadership, and the 'subtle processes' of marshalling support for ideas.

Political models of change emphasise that change is likely to affect the interests of stakeholders unevenly and that those who see themselves losing will resist the change despite the rationality of the arguments or invitations to participate.

Pettigrew has been concerned with the management of strategic change, which he defines as follows:

strategic changes are viewed as streams of activity involving at various times the differential attention of individuals and groups, which occur mainly but not solely as a consequence of environmental change, and which can lead to alterations in the product market focus, structure, technology, and culture of the host organisation. Strategic is just a

---

NOTICEBOARD Kotter's eight-stage process of creating major change

John Kotter (1996) has proposed an eight-stage process for creating major change. Each step matches one of what he sees as the fundamental errors in managing change. The first four steps aim to get change moving, by tackling in-built resistance and inertia. Steps 5–7 combine participative and political practices to secure and maintain support. The final stage matches Lewin's (1947) emphasis on embedding the change in the continuing culture of the organisation:

1 Establishing a sense of urgency
2 Creating the guiding coalition
3 Developing a vision and strategy
4 Communicating the change vision
5 Empowering broad-based action
6 Generating short-term wins
7 Consolidating gains and producing more change
8 Anchoring new approaches in the culture

Source: Kotter (1996, p.21)

description of magnitude of change in, for example, structure and organisational culture, recognising the second-order effects, or multiple consequences of any such changes. (1985, p.438)

Central to Pettigrew's analysis of 'the processual dynamics of changing' is a concern with 'management of meaning' and with the processes through which change – which may be strategic or operational – is legitimised. This analysis is a clear challenge to the participative approach to change. Pettigrew also highlights the influential and potentially legitimating role of the context into which changes is introduced, and to the way in which those managing change can use that context to support their approach.

Turning to the practical implication of this view, Pettigrew highlights the need for skills in intervening in an organisation's political and cultural systems. These skills include building adequate support for proposals, and the simultaneous management of the content, context and process of change and the relationships between these three sets of factors. He also distinguishes between inner and outer context. The inner context of change relates to the history of the organisation, its structure, its culture and its political system. The outer context of change relates to environmental factors, such as competitor behaviour or customer demands, the sources 'from which much of the legitimacy for change is derived' (Pettigrew, 1987, p.650). All of which implies that an optimistic participative approach is unlikely to be enough to overcome apathy and win support.

> The inner context of change relates to the history of the organisation, its structure, its culture and its political system – including the form of its decision-making structures.
> The outer context of change relates to environmental factors, such as competitor behaviour, customer demands or other factors in the external environment

---

C A S E   Q U E S T I O N S   1 7 . 5

▶ Where might opposition to the computer system come from in the travel agency?

▶ Why might some people be unhappy with the changes proposed?

▶ What skills may management then need to exercise?

Kanter (1983) argues that the change agent in the modern corporation requires a portfolio of 'power skills' to overcome resistance and apathy to new ideas. She identifies a number of techniques for blocking interference from those who would impede change, similar to those indicated by Pettigrew. Kanter also offers broadly similar advice on what she calls the 'power skills' of the change agent, under the heading of 'techniques for blocking interference'. These techniques include:

▶ **Wait them out**   In time they should go away if you persist.

▶ **Wear them down**   Keep pushing, keep arguing, and again your persistence should eventually prevail.

▶ **Appeal to higher authority**   Which can either be senior management (you had better agree because the boss does), or to a set of values or standards (such as standards of health care in a hospital which have to be maintained).

▶ **Invite them in**   Have them join the party, co-opt them onto the steering group.

▶ **Send emissaries**   Ask friends, in whom you know your resistors believe, to talk to them and convince them.

▶ **Display support**   Make sure that your people are present and vocal at key meetings.

▶ **Reduce the stakes**   Make changes, where possible, in areas that are not particularly damaging to key individuals and groups.

▶ **Warn them off**   Let them know that senior management, and perhaps other key actors, will challenge their dissent.

Kanter argues that power skills, team skills and 'change architect' skills are required to hold together what she describes as a three-stage change process involving problem definition, coalition building, and mobilisation and completion respectively.

These three views – project management, participative and political – are not necessarily competing with each other. Rather they are complementary, in that successful large-scale change is likely to require elements of each. Each perspective can be linked to a series of management practices, which can help or hinder the implementation of change.

NOTICEBOARD   **Tom Burns on politics and language**

Following the contention that the change process is rarely rational and linear, a number of commentators have offered practical advice on the management conduct required to operate in the political domain of the organisation. Tom Burns (1961), in his discussion of the micropolitics of institutional change, clearly establishes the concepts of organisations as political systems, and of politics as a mode of behaviour concerned with the pursuit of individual and group self-interests. A point of particular interest to the management of change is the way in which political behaviour in the organisation is invariably concealed or made acceptable by subtle shifts in the language that people use:

> Normally, either side in any conflict called political by observers claims to speak in the interests of the corporation as a whole. In fact, the only recognised, indeed feasible, way of advancing political interests is to present them in terms of improved welfare or efficiency, as contributing to the organisation's capacity to meet its task and to prosper. In managerial and academic, as in other legislatures, both sides to any debate claim to speak in the interests of the community as a whole; this is the only permissible mode of expression.
>
> It is backstage, so to speak, that the imputations of empire-building, caucus log-rolling, squaring, and obstructionism occur. The linguistic division, which is also a moral one, is

particularly marked in universities, where mutually exclusive sets of expressions exist for discussion in faculty meetings or committees, and in bars, common rooms, or parties. (p.260)

The change agent is thus advised to pay attention to language and setting. Can I speak in this way to this group in this situation? It is legitimate, for example, to seek to damage perceptions of the competence and credibility of other individuals and groups in what Burns labels 'gossip sessions'. In formal meetings, such discussion is proscribed because the author of such statements will attract public suspicion of being in pursuit of personal gain. The change agent is thus advised to pay attention to what will be regarded as 'acceptable argument' in a given setting.

Burns also points out that personal motives are acknowledged in organisational action, and are indeed recognised as valuable expressions of drive, ambition, enterprise and initiative. Personal motives contribute to career success and are thus legitimately pursued. So, 'while there is a dual linguistic and moral code attached to the co-operative and competitive aspects of society and its constituent systems, there is also a sense in which we recognise both kinds of value, incompatible as they may appear to be in the discussion of immediate issues concerning the distribution of rewards and resources.' (p.262)

Source: extracts from Burns (1961)

17.5 Resistance to change

Many writers have considered the forms of and resistance to change. Much of the management literature presents resistance in pejorative terms as something to be overcome by those promoting change. This discussion takes a more neutral stance. Some changes are clearly of general benefit to the organisation and all or most of its members. There is a great deal of anecdotal evidence that some changes are introduced to further sectional interests – to build a personal reputation or extend the influence of a department. Since organisations are made up of political and career systems as well as working systems (see Chapter 14), some innovations will be intended to support career or political interests rather than to support the better working of the organisation. It is also the case that even when people intend to support organisational interests they may misread or misinterpret signals from the outside world and propose changes that are misconceived.

For all these reasons, people at all levels in an organisation will sometimes resist change. They may see it as a threat to their interests or status. Or they may believe that the change proposed will damage rather than benefit the organisation.

Forms of resistance

As Keen (1981) has pointed out, overt and public resistance is rare and often unnecessary. There are many other ways in which those opposed to a change can begin to slow it down. Symptoms of reluctant acceptance include:

▶ Refusing to use new systems or procedures
▶ Making no effort to learn
▶ Using older systems whenever possible
▶ Not attending meetings to discuss the project
▶ Excessive fault-finding and criticism
▶ Deliberate misuse
▶ Saying it has been tried before and did not work
▶ Protracted discussion and requests for more information
▶ Linking the issue with pay or other industrial relations matters
▶ Not releasing staff for training

Sources of resistance

Johnston *et al.* (1967), in one of the earlier papers on the topic, make the distinction between change that one can choose to accept or reject and change over which one has little influence or control. They propose that only the latter sort of change is resisted, for reasons such as a threat to economic security or job status (including symbolic factors), uncertainty and increased complexities. As well as the individual reaction in isolation, they also suggest that resistance may stem from changes in group relations, especially if the importance of these informal social relationships in the workplace is underestimated. A change may also disrupt superior/subordinate relationships: if change means that the superior exercises closer control over the subordinate, then change is likely to be resisted by the subordinate.

Discuss with someone who has tried to introduce change in an organisation what evidence there was of resistance. Which of the forms listed by Keen (above) were in evidence? Can they identify any other forms?

Have you ever resisted a proposed change? What form did your resistance take?

Kotter and Schlesinger (1979) also identify some individual sources of resistance, such as self-interest, when people think they will lose something valuable, as well as misunderstanding and lack of trust: 'people will resist change when they do not understand its full implications and they perceive it will cost them much more than they will gain'. They also point out that employees assess the situation differently from their managers and see more costs than benefits resulting from the change not only for themselves but also for the company as well. Similar points were made by Recardo (1991), based on a study of the implementation of new manufacturing systems. Change requires learning and exposure to uncertainty and insecurity, alterations in social interactions, and is often marked by poor communication and management of the change process. Additional factors which he identified as engendering resistance were reward systems that did not reward the desired behaviour, and a poor fit between the change and the existing corporate culture.

A substantial body of the organisational literature points to the relative durability of existing arrangements – even in the face of significant external pressure. Hannan and Freeman (1989) maintain that inertia depends on internal and external constraints:

▶ **Internal**   Investment in equipment and people which are not readily transferable; insufficient information being received by decision-makers; internal politics, in particular self-interest; organisational histories and precedent.

▶ **External**   Legal and economic barriers to entry into new areas of activity; lack of external information; lack of awareness of the need for the change to meet expectations.

Markus (1983) shows how threats to status and political influence can encourage people to resist change. The two major problem areas which could constrain change and maintain the status quo are related to information and internal politics and self-interest. There will be winners and losers, and Hannan and Freeman (1989) maintain that change can be affected by the strong inertial tendencies generated by individuals who stand to lose from a change. They propose that losers will oppose change with more determination than winners will support it. Keen (1981) discusses the many overt and covert tactics of what he calls counterimplementation, which can be used by those wishing to subvert a change.

The main sources of resistance identified in earlier work can be summarised as follows:

▶ **People**   Resistance is explained by individuals' characteristics, such as their personalities, attitudes, values, preferences, skills and interests.

▶ **Design**   Resistance is attributed to the design of the change – such as whether new systems or procedures will be easy to use, whether they

Counterimplementation refers to attempts to block change without displaying overt opposition.

NOTICEBOARD **Peter Keen on counterimplementation**

Keen (1981) suggested that overt resistance to change is often risky, and may not in practice be necessary. He identified several ways in which those wanting to block a change can do so – even while appearing to support it. They include such tactics as:

▶ **Divert resources** Split the budget across other projects; have key staff given other priorities and allocate them to other assignments; arrange for equipment to be moved or shared.

▶ **Exploit inertia** Suggest that everyone wait until a key player has taken action or read the report or made an appropriate response; suggest that the results from some other project should be monitored and assessed first.

▶ **Keep goals vague and complex** It is harder to initiate appropriate action in pursuit of aims that are multidimensional and that are specified in generalised, grandiose or abstract terms.

▶ **Encourage and exploit lack of organisational awareness** Insist that 'we can deal with the people issues later', knowing that these will delay or kill the project.

▶ **'Great idea – let's do it properly'** And let's bring in representatives from this function and that section, until we have so many different views and conflicting interests that it will take for ever to sort them out.

▶ **Dissipate energies** Have people conduct surveys, collect data, prepare analyses, write reports, make overseas trips, hold special meetings ...

▶ **Reduce the champion's influence and credibility** Spread damaging rumours, particularly amongst the champion's friends and supporters.

▶ **Keep a low profile** It is not effective openly to declare resistance to change because that gives those driving change a clear target.

Source: based on Keen (1981)

are right for the job, and whether the benefits to them will be worth the effort.

▶ **Organisation** Resistance is explained by the interaction between the change and the organisational context. The key factor is the distribution of responsibilities. Change often means new patterns of working which may cut across traditional ways.

▶ **Process** This refers to the way the change is managed, irrespective of the specific change being made. Change is disturbing, and people are likely to resist if they do not feel they have been able to participate in discussion about the form it should take.

▶ **Power** Here resistance is explained by the interaction between the change and context, but the emphasis is on the distribution of power. Changes often makes it possible to alter the ownership of information, access to information and the exercise of autonomy.

Ways to manage resistance

If management has a reasonably clear view of the causes of resistance then it is better placed to act on the right problem. For example, if it thinks that the reason for resistance to automated equipment is that the system is not working properly, a reasonable response would be to spend time and money in redesigning the system. This would be wasted if the resistance was owing to the fact that no one had asked staff for their views.

In planning a project, managers use ideas such as those below to help avoid resistance and to try to ensure committed and enthusiastic acceptance.

People

▶ **Market the change** Take time to 'market' the change, rather than merely to 'sell' it. Find out what benefits it can offer people, and how it can meet their needs, as well as those originally envisaged.

▶ **Publicise benefits** Ensure that the benefits obtained, especially the unquantifiable ones, are documented and made known.

▶ **Allay fears** Take care to allay, if possible, fears over jobs, status and career prospects. These can usually be phased over a long period to avoid some individual hardship.

Design

▶ **Specification** Ensure that enough time and resources are spent at an early stage to understand the situation and what the new system needs to do.

▶ **Pilot systems** Set up tests or pilots of the change, and take the lessons into account. Take care to ensure a pilot study is representative.

▶ **Check it works** Double-check that the system proposed is really able to do the job. People may be quite right to resist a bad system that will do the organisation more harm than good. Ensure adequate time is allowed for the changeover, and for training.

Organisation

▶ **Complement skills** Design work so that it provides quality jobs, where people's skills and experience are complemented, not replaced.

▶ **Create working groups** Ensure that workgroups are arranged so that staff are able to move between jobs and have a reasonable degree of communication within the group.

▶ **Enhance flow of information** Use technology to give people more information so they can make better decisions, rather than removing their scope for intervention.

Process

▶ **Involve users** Involve users as fully as is practical in system design and implementation, to develop a sense of ownership. This will encourage people to make 'their' system work.

▶ **Communication** Rumours travel fast and bad news even faster. Set up deliberate communication systems to ensure that people learn from a reliable source.

▶ **Plan implementation** Ensure that the detail is there in terms of how the changeover will be handled. Think about timing and avoid busy times or holiday periods.

▶ **Create a need** Ensure that people understand and accept the need to change, by showing that the old ways no longer work.

Power

▶ **Be alert to losers** Ensure that people whose authority may be eroded are isolated, or that they are given new things to do if necessary.

▶ **Identify leaders** Identify the 'opinion leaders' in a group, and pay special attention to gaining their acceptance and support.

> ► **Manage power changes**   Consider whether changes in autonomy and decision-making really are intended and are not just accidental.

17.6 Managing front-stage and backstage

The development and implementation of any kind of major change is a complex and uncertain process. There is a series of paradoxes between the logic of establishing 'ownership' and the logic of establishing the rational legitimacy of the system. There is often dissonance between the available skills of the change agents and the differing project agendas they have to manage. The vulnerability and visibility of the change agent is increased still further if the nature of change is in quadrant 4 of Figure 17.1 (core/novel). This should encourage the change agent to combine overt strategies aimed at generating feelings of ownership and involvement, with more devious political activities to muster support, manipulate opinion and threaten dissenters.

Two types of strategy are necessary to implement large-scale changes in vulnerable contexts. Those promoting the change have to produce a 'public/front-stage performance' (Buchanan and Boddy, 1992) of logical and rationally planned change linked to widespread and convincing participative mechanisms. They also have to pursue 'backstage activity'. They have to exercise power skills, influencing, negotiating, selling, searching out and neutralising resistance. Kotter and Schlesinger (1979) identify a series of 'front-stage' strategies – education, participation, facilitation, negotiation – combined with 'backstage' manipulation and co-optation and explicit and implicit coercion.

Front-stage performances

Change processes within organisations have to conform to organisational 'theatre' to be successful. People affected have to be convinced that they are genuinely involved in the change and have some influence over its outcome. Top management and expert staff have to be convinced that the change is technically rational, logical and also congruent with the strategic direction of the organisation. Established project management techniques such as network planning and control techniques, cost/benefit analysis and technological appraisals are useful in themselves (see, for example, Locke, 1996). So are bar and Gantt charts, cumulative spending curves and scheduling tools. Such techniques are widely recognised as appropriate tools for managing change projects. They are also valuable in sustaining the image of the project manager. They reassure senior managers that the right things are being done in their name.

There may also be an element of theatre in user-involvement. Management aims to convince people that genuine user-involvement, as well as technical elegance, is part of the change process. Many involvement mechanisms may be symbolic acts or rituals which contribute towards a general feeling of participation in the unfreezing, moving and refreezing processes. They may affect the attitudes of people throughout the organisation without getting to the root of real worries and anxieties. Hirscheim (1985) describes the commonly used participation strategies as inherently manipulative. In any case, their effect on commitment or system performance is uncertain. Attempts to evaluate the benefits of user-participation in terms of satisfaction with the system and its use are often inconclusive (Franz and Robey, 1986). Participation does not necessarily lead to satisfied users.

Backstage activities

The literature on participative management, 'ethically the correct procedure' (Child, 1984), consistently advises that manipulation and threats as project management techniques are counterproductive. Nevertheless, in large, complex projects, management resorts to them owing to lack of time, resources and expertise as well as to the scale and complexity of the project. It is also necessary to confront the political realities of managing complex projects in quadrant 4 of Figure 17.1.

Keen's solution to this paradox is a political approach, a 'counter-counter-implementation' strategy which establishes who can damage the project, co-opts likely opposition early on, provides clear incentives and benefits from the new system and tries to create a bandwagon effect. This is a 'backstage' political strategy that technical staff are unlikely to have the skill to operate. The method depends heavily on the presence of a 'fixer' with prestige, visibility and legitimacy. Boddy and Gunson (1996) cite several examples of such moves based on negotiation mobilising coalitions. Some led from the front and put strong political pressure on sometimes reluctant managers to push a project through. For example, the travel agency in the Case Study set up a users' forum to exert peer pressure on more resistant branch managers.

It is widely recognised that the role of the change agent is inherently manipulative and political (Burns, 1961; Keen, 1981; Pettigrew, 1985; Morgan, 1997), and that while the front-stage activities of technical and strategic logic and user-participation strategies are important to provide organisational credibility at all levels, the backstage activity is key to success or failure.

Backstage activity at Girobank

case example

Morley (1993) offers some advice to the data processing (DP) manager seeking to convince a board of directors of the value of proposed investments in new systems. As the board is usually impressed only by demonstrations of cost-effectiveness, skills in 'selling up' are required, in order to manipulate board members' perceptions and decisions: 'Today's DP manager must plot the presentation to the board with as much cunning as he or she would devote to bargaining with IT suppliers.' Morley describes new systems development at Girobank, arguing not only that quantitative and qualitative cost/benefit analysis is important, but also for the necessity of 'an arsenal of points', and:

> Planning for the sell to the board also entailed putting the personality of individual directors under scrutiny. We gained a view of the personality, disposition and potential hostility of various directors and

decided that it would be in our best interests to keep the presentation as short as possible. (p.21)

If backstage techniques are to be successfully employed it is important that the change agent has access to the backstage politics of the organisation. A change agent who has little insight into internal power politics will be unable to operate this type of strategy successfully.

Individual traits and skills

Are there any personal attributes which might be associated with the successful management of change? Kanter (1989) suggests that, to manage change, people need the following traits:

▶ Able to work independently, without the power and sanction of the management hierarchy.
▶ An effective collaborator, able to compete in ways that enhance rather than destroy co-operation.
▶ Able to develop high trust relations, with high ethical standards.
▶ Possessing self-confidence tempered with humility.
▶ Respectful of the process of change as well as the substance.
▶ Able to work across business functions and units – 'multifaceted and multidextrous'.
▶ Willing to take rewards on results and gains satisfaction from success.

Buchanan and Boddy's (1992) detailed diary and related research into the way that a group of change managers handled the task led them to identify five broad competences and fifteen specific attributes as relevant to the effective management of change:

Competence concerns the actions and behaviours identified by change agents as contributing in their experience to the perceived effectiveness of change implementation.

Goals

▶ Sensitivity to senior and external changes, and their effect on the project
▶ Clarity in defining achievable goals
▶ Flexibility in adapting goals to changes beyond their control

Roles

▶ Team-building skills to bring key stakeholders into an effective team
▶ Networking skills to build and use internal and external contacts
▶ Tolerance of ambiguity, able to function in an uncertain setting

Communication

▶ To transmit to colleagues the need for change and ways to do it
▶ Interpersonal skills such as listening, identifying concerns, managing meetings;
▶ Personal enthusiasm in expressing ideas
▶ Stimulating motivation and commitment in others

Negotiating

▶ Selling plan and ideas to others
▶ Negotiating with key players for resources, changes to plans and to resolve conflict

Managing up

▶ Political awareness in identifying coalitions
▶ Influencing skills to gain support from sceptics and resistors
▶ Ability to stand back and see the broader picture

Institutional support

Boddy *et al.* (1998) suggest that interpersonal skills may not in themselves be sufficient to manage major change. The team conducted a survey which gathered information from 100 companies which had introduced a specific organisational change (moving to closer relationships with their suppliers or customers). The results showed that 46 per cent had been successful in this while 54 per cent had been unsuccessful. Respondents were asked questions about their use or otherwise of a range of change management techniques which the literature suggests will assist the implementation of change in general. The data were analysed using a variety of techniques to identify those factors which had a statistically significant influence. One of the clearest results was that, in organisations which had been successful in implementing partnering, senior management had created clear structures within which to manage the change. This was consistent with the view that expressions of support from top management are not enough – these need to be backed by clear structures.

The result was also consistent with responses to another question, which indicated that successful companies had created specific lines of authority linking the senior team to the operational team. This is perhaps a warning against over-reliance on interpersonal relations. The change literature has regularly stressed the importance to change of a strong promoter or champion, and of various forms of participative management. The survey suggests that the strong champion is a necessary but not a sufficient condition for success. While 74 per cent of the successful companies agreed with the statement, so did 51 per cent of the unsuccessful ones.

The inference that may be drawn from this research is that when the change is complex it is a mistake to rely on personal contact and relationships to make it happen. Given the pressures on those involved, unless the change is backed and monitored by a formal structure, it is likely to fail.

External advice

Many managers seek the advice and support of external consultants to manage change. Schein (1969) cited seven reasons why they do so:

▶ Managers often do not know what is wrong and require assistance to fully diagnose the problem – 'they are simply too close to the problem to think objectively'.

▶ Clients may be unaware of the nature and sources of external expertise and knowledge – 'a professional networker will provide additional input'.

▶ Clients generally have the will to seek constructive improvements but fail to act – 'an outsider offers an additional resource dedicated to the task at hand'.

▶ Organisations must learn from past experiences and capitalise upon them in the future – 'a consultant helps structure and deliver the lessons'.

▶ Organisations can benefit form an extra, non-partisan pair of eyes to clarify situations and crystallise attention – 'two heads are better than one'.

▶ Clients, owing to the pressure of work, often require assistance in ensuring involvement and therefore ownership – 'the outsider may assist in orchestrating the process'.

▶ Clients often fail to capitalise on the lessons learned in a sustainable manner – 'consultants may bring the skills required to assist in institutionalising the change and ensure the transfer of change management skills and knowledge'.

The role envisaged for the external change agent is thus complementary to that of the internal problem-owner. It is the latter's responsibility to establish the need for an outsider and to ensure that the skills are as far as possible transferred into those who have to live with the change in the long term.

17.7 Recap

Content agenda

Management spends a great deal of time managing change. Its aim is usually to ensure that the organisation continues to add value to resources as the external world changes. Change can start in any of the elements of the organisation and will usually have indirect effects on other aspects of the organisation. Although change is widespread, the evidence suggests that it is often poorly managed. This affects business performance and staff commitment, and may be particularly damaging when the change is at the core of the business and has novel features – the quadrant 4 projects. A technique was described which those managing change can use to assess where particular planning and implementation problems are likely to arise. Since change will usually require some significant modifications in behaviour, generating action in new directions may be more difficult than maintaining present levels. Those expected to change do not necessarily understand or accept the change promoter's reasoning. The benefits of change may not seem greater than the individual costs.

Process agenda

Change may challenge the interests of some stakeholders. While those promoting the change clearly see advantages, others have different goals – especially that of protecting their own or their department's interests. Three alternative and complementary models were presented of how management typically tries to generate the action it requires in change – project management, participative and political. The first two will be adequate in some combination if the change is uncontroversial and does not threaten valued interests. However, careful planning and involving people in decision-making will not ensure they accept the outcome if they are going to be worse off. They will be inclined to resist the change (perhaps wisely), and management may need to use a range of political approaches to get things done. Change may require managers to combine their public performance with backstage activity. Interpersonal skills and activities also need to be supported by appropriate institutions through which the change agents can exercise their skills.

Control agenda

Some changes are introduced as an attempt by one group or department to gain more control over another. In that event, change is not a neutral activity for the benefit of the organisation but a reflection of sectional inter-

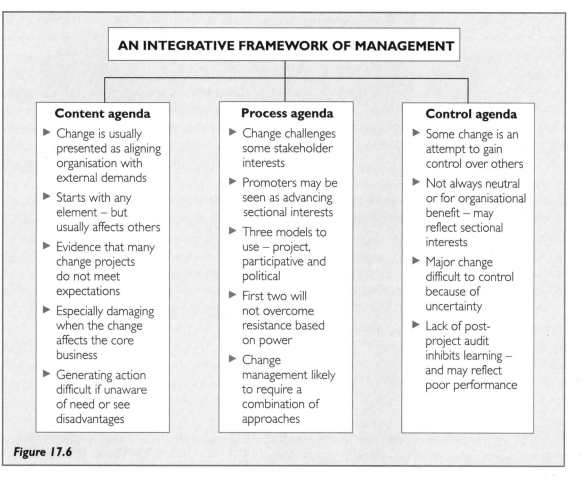

Figure 17.6

ests. As such, it may be contested by those who themselves want to retain or extend their control.

Major change projects are especially difficult to control – which may be one of the reasons why so many do not meet expectations. Measures need to be established for both the content and the process aspects of the change. When the change occurs in a volatile and uncertain environment, monitoring and control are uniquely difficult. Post-project audits appear to be rare, and the opportunities of learning lessons on how to handle future change are thereby lost.

The integrative framework is set out in Figure 17.6.

PART CASE QUESTIONS

▶ Which model(s) of change did Save the Children Fund management use to implement its new policies? What evidence is there to support this conclusion?

▶ What are the differences and similarities between Save the Children Fund and the travel agency in terms of (a) the causes of change, and (b) the methods used to manage it?

▶ What aspects of the inner context at Save the Children Fund helped or hindered change?

17.8 Review questions

1   What types of change are likely to be the most difficult to introduce?
2   What are the implications for management of the systemic nature of major change?
3   Review the change that you identified in Notebook 17.1 and compare its critical dimensions with those at Save the Children Fund.
4   Explain what is meant by the inner context of change, and compare at least two organisations in these terms.
5   How does the culture of an organisation affect change? Compare two examples, one where the prevailing culture helped change and one where it hindered it.
6   Outline the project management model of change and explain when it is most likely to be useful.
7   What are the distinctive characteristics of a participative approach?
8   What, if any, are the similarities between the project and participative approaches?
9   What skills are used by those employing a political model?
10 Is resistance to change necessarily something to be overcome? How would you advise someone to resist a change to which he or she was opposed?
11 Evaluate an example of change management in view of the models in this chapter.

Further reading

You can gain valuable insights into the management of change by reading accounts of specific cases of change. Pettigrew's (1985) account of change at ICI gives, at great length, many illuminating illustrations of the process. A much shorter and more recent study in a similar mode is Jon Clark's (1996) study of change at Pirelli, the multinational tyres and cables group. By examining a major change in one division over several years it emphasises the long-term, evolutionary nature of change. Each chapter begins with a review of relevant theory which is then used to guide the analysis of events in the company. A valuable overview of the area is offered by Bernard Burnes (1996) – the second edition has long case studies which supplement an up-to-date treatment of theory in the area. Mabey and Mayon-White (1993) is a useful collection of readings, including some of the classic articles in the area of change management. A good source of information on conventional project management techniques is Locke (1996).

part five

Controlling the business

Introduction

Any purposeful human activity needs some degree of control if it is to achieve what is intended. From time to time you check where you are in relation to your destination. The sooner you do this, the more confident you are that you are on track. Frequent checks ensure you take corrective action quickly to avoid wasting effort and resources.

An owner-manager can often exercise control by personal observation, reference to limited paper and then a decision about corrective action. As the organisation grows so does the complexity. It becomes increasingly difficult to know the current position as work goes on in many separate places at the same time. People in those separate places may differ about their precise objectives and targets.

To help them exercise control, management is able to use a range of systems and techniques. Financial control is clearly of major interest – how does management try to keep the financial score while all around it everything is changing? Chapter 18 introduces the main issues in this area. Financial measures reflect what has been happening in the actual operations of the organisation. The more information management has about actual progress compared with intended performance, the easier it is to adjust,

so Chapter 19 reviews the main concepts in operations management. Control depends on information. Developments in information technology are revolutionising this aspect of management. Technical developments make it possible to have much more information, much more quickly than ever before. These possibilities and the mangement issues raised in making effective use of new information systems are examined in Chapter 20.

Finally, control is about power. The design of control systems inevitably alters the power of different groups within the organisation. This applies both horizontally between departments and vertically between levels of the management hierarchy. So the ideas in this part provide an opportunity to bring into consideration ideas about influence, power and motivation and structure that were examined earlier.

The case is Kwik-Fit Holdings. A nationwide UK company with a small presence in some other European countries, Kwik-Fit has grown rapidly since it was created in 1971. It operates in a competitive industry with low margins. Tight control of operating systems and costs have been central to its success. This has been greatly helped by the management decision to install innovative information systems in 1980 which have supported its rapid growth since then.

Kwik-Fit Holdings

In 1997, Kwik-Fit was Europe's largest independent tyre and exhaust retailer. Tom Farmer had created the business in 1971, using the proceeds from the sale of an earlier company. Although now much bigger, the core business in 1997 was still the drive-in, 'while you wait', fitting of replacement tyres, exhausts, batteries, brakes and shock absorbers. The company also offered engine oil and filter change services and supplied and fitted child safety seats. In 1995 it had begun to sell motor insurance. The company had also entered the fleet market, offering the Kwik-Fit service to, for example, contract hire firms and large fleet operators.

Services were delivered to customers through roadside centres, each staffed by a manager and a team of fitters. A customer arriving at a centre was met by the manager or a fitter and stated his or her requirement. The fitter checked the fault, and that the parts were in stock. The fitter then gave the customer a written quotation of the cost and, if accepted, did the work immediately. The customer then paid and left.

The growing market

In 1991, the company estimated that it had 30 per cent of the market for replacement car exhausts, and 12 per cent of that for replacement tyres. The aftercare market was rising long-term, with growth in the number of cars. It was also competitive. Two groups owned by tyre companies each had over four hundred depots and there were many local competitors. To build a dominant national position, the company had to provide a standard of service that would, in the words of the Kwik-Fit slogan, achieve '100% delighted customers'. Factors thought to be valued by customers included convenience of location, cleanliness of premises, speed and quality of workmanship, price and availability of the parts required.

A critical and costly aspect of the business was to have enough spare parts on hand to cope with the range of cars requiring service.

Each depot's stock reflected as accurately as possible the types of car likely to be driven in.

The administrative burden

Transactions generated administration – notably to account for the day's revenue, and to replenish stocks. In the early years, the company used a manual administrative system. Records of transactions, receipts and stocks were kept on paper in boxes and files. There was a very small central management team, based in Edinburgh, and led by Tom Farmer. Kwik-Fit's structure was described by one insider as: 'a very flat structure, in as much as if we wanted to change something tomorrow we could do it – we haven't got a hierarchy that has to be gone through.' Farmer believed firmly in keeping the number of administrative staff as low as possible. With over four hundred and fifty UK depots, it employed only about ninety staff at head office.

Organisation and style

The main operating company, Kwik-Fit (GB), was organised into five geographical divisions. Day-to-day management was in the hands of a management board between the main board and the divisional management. Management throughout the company was expected to be in direct contact with market conditions facing the depot managers and staff. They were expected to support the depots, not to dominate them: 'We're not a big organisation – we're a collection of small businesses ... in our company culture, head office is seen as a support operation.'

Depots were grouped in partnerships, made up of three nearby outlets. A more senior manager, or partner, supervised two other depots as well as their own, and received a share of the profits each generated. This reflected the philosophy that staff should share in the success of the business.

These aspects of the structure were relevant to the operation of the computer network, and the scope it gave for central monitoring of the depots: 'The whole computer system is based around the depot manager as king. It doesn't restrict the manager in what he does, but he has to account for it.'

Farmer's philosophy was that, since continued success depended on the loyalty of customers, a high level of staff training was essential. All staff were trained to adhere to the Kwik-Fit Code of Practice, designed to ensure that every customer's vehicle received a high standard of service. Training also covered technical and product knowledge, depot management, sales methods and communications skills. In 1990, the company received a National Training Award in recognition of its commitment to training.

The network system

The first computer network system at Kwik-Fit was installed in 1982. It consisted of electronic point-of-sale (EPOS) terminals in each depot, linked to a mainframe computer at head office. A specially designed point-of-sale microcomputer, known as a Management Action Terminal (MAT), was installed in each depot. These were robustly designed for use by the managers and fitters.

The keyboard was clear and easy to use, each key being marked with a system function, such as 'cash sale' or 'stock delivery'. Pressing a key led the user through the process to be followed. Details of the stock held by the depot were stored in the MAT, and automatically updated as each transaction was processed.

During the day, the MAT performed administrative tasks within the centre, such as issuing quotations in response to customer enquiries and producing invoices. For a few minutes each night, the MAT became a terminal attached to the mainframe computer at head office. That computer automatically called each depot in turn. Each MAT responded by sending data about all transactions made during the day to the mainframe, such as on sales, payments, stock received and transferred and hours worked by staff.

These raw data were processed into management reports for internal use, and into instructions to suppliers and banks. The reports for head office use were printed out early the following day. The telephone link which brought the data in from each depot was also used to send information back, on such matters as price changes.

Stock levels were a critical feature of the business. These had to be sufficient for staff to meet service requests on demand, without the costs of excessive stocks making the operation uncompetitive. Stock control was previously done manually, with depots physically checking their stock and placing orders directly with suppliers. This was very time consuming, and a major aim of the system was to get better stock control:

> It's critical to the whole business that every depot has the right stock. You can't put the same stock in every garage, because the pattern is different between areas, depending on the cars people have. We needed to computerise because the information wasn't available sufficiently quickly. There was no method whereby any one person in head office, or at a given depot, could know what stock was in that depot.

Previously, stock had been controlled manually, with depots raising their own orders, and placing them with suppliers.

Outcomes

The EPOS system achieved the expected benefits – and many more as well. The system allowed automatic replenishment of stock. Sales were converted into orders which were automatically transmitted to four of the biggest suppliers overnight, giving a forty-eight hour cycle of delivery. By 1991, 50 per cent of sales were being automatically reordered from suppliers through the computer, and 75 per cent of invoices were received and paid electronically.

> We run a very simple business. The only complexity in our business is size. MAT reinforces procedures in an easy way

without being overburdensome. It removes from the equation a lot of the complexity which our size and geographical dispersal could create.

The system also provided benefits which were not envisaged when the original specification was set. This was particularly true in the area of management information. The system had been designed to convert the existing (and effective) manual administration into an equally effective computerised one. Once that was implemented, managers rapidly realised that they now had a great deal of information about the business which had previously been unavailable. The IT director responsible for implementing the system commented:

> We totally underestimated the potential for management information. When you switch an EPOS network on, you get flooded with mountains of data. It's live, current, happened yesterday – and you don't know what to do with it all. We totally underestimated that, and didn't realise just how useful the data would be in controlling the company.
>
> We were producing tables and statistics that surprised a lot of people. 'I didn't know that about the company' – but all of a sudden they had a tool that would let them find out.

More generally, managers at head office now had much more information available to them about performance across the whole of the growing company. For example, the sales director could review the following day how any depot had performed, in as much or as little detail as required:

> It gives us prices, margin control, and all the necessary monitoring elements. All this information goes to the managers as well, because they need to know how they are doing as well. So if I call a depot, and ask the manager how he is doing, he could press the key on the machine and would be able to say what he sold today, and what he sold yesterday. And that information is important because their earnings depend on how well they are doing.

The system also provided daily forecasts of sales and margins against budget for the current month. This allowed managers to see whether they were likely to be ahead of target or behind, and to take remedial action quickly.

Before the introduction of the system, depot managers had a lot of autonomy. Although there were company pricelists, head office did not know what prices the depots actually charged. The information took weeks to reach them. Managers were also responsible for ordering their own stocks of parts, using their judgement about what was needed. The supplier delivered an order to the depot and was later paid by head office.

The area managers had to monitor what was going on in his depots – which in some cases was extremely difficult:

> With a manual system, some depots needed a lot of hand-holding. You couldn't leave them alone, because you always had to go back and do lots of checks on them – count the cash, make sure the stocks were there. Discounts were very difficult to monitor – we didn't have a clue what was going on.
>
> Before computerisation it was uncontrollable. There was a pricelist, but we never knew if the depot was selling at that price, or at half of it. There was no method of looking at sales and controlling sales of specific items, and particularly of controlling discounts, because there was no way to record them.

The computer system significantly reduced the autonomy of the depot manager:

> Now there is a lot more control at head office. The depot can still do whatever it wants … the theory is that the point-of-sale system doesn't restrict the manager in what he does, but he has to account for it. The whole system is based around giving the depot manager freedom in running his business.

The system enabled senior management to monitor what was going on in each depot – in effect a small business – and at the same time to provide them with support, by way of marketing, administration and a constantly balanced stock.

> I think it has enabled us to get the benefit of decentralised management, but with uniform procedures applied. And to be seen to be applied, and to be committed at the centre to intervene if there's a deviation.

Senior managers were able to monitor compliance with depot procedures. If things were not being done in the correct way, such as unusual discounts or late banking, that would be visible at head office the following day. Depot managers came to realise that someone would be in touch with them very quickly and they did not repeat a mistake.

The system thus brought a sharper focus to the work of the depot manager:

> We have taken all of the essential elements of the Code of Practice over management procedures which were previously summarised on two sides of a plastic covered A4 sheet [known as the Management Summary] and we have encapsulated all of that within the MAT software. So now the MAT focuses the managers' attention on doing things exactly the way Kwik-Fit requires them to be done. That really was the breakthrough. It still allows a degree of discretion on the part of management, but any discretion has to be accompanied by a reason, and these reasons are carried forward into our central systems.

Tom Farmer expressed the same point:

> Before we were computerised, to find out things that were wrong we had to check so much stuff – and we were always 8–10 weeks behind: and by then it wasn't much use speaking to the guy – it was too late to do anything about it. Whereas, now we've got the information and can talk about things that happened yesterday.

Similar views were expressed by another manager who saw it as bringing much tighter control:

> I would say there is less branch autonomy – it is more uniform. The guy will act to the same guidelines, wherever he is in the country – which again probably makes the company look a lot more professional – rather than each guy doing his own thing. It makes them more uniform. Head office have a greater command of the sales picture. They don't need to be in a depot to know how profitable it is – they can just tell from the information day by day.

Tom Farmer commented on the process of striking the right balance of control in the business:

> We have gone through periods of centralising and decentralising. But with certain things like stock control, for example, we would never decentralise that. Whereas before it was left to every depot to look after their own stock, nowadays they have nothing to do with stock: that's entirely centralised, with automatic replenishment.
>
> But there are other things, so we are not running a completely centralised operation. And one of the reasons is that you can't just run a centralised business – because you must make sure you don't lose the human element.

PART CASE QUESTIONS

▶ What are the main problems of control in a company of this sort?

▶ What information does management at different levels need in order to do its job well?

▶ How is the information system helping management to exercise control?

18

Finance and budgetary control

CONTENTS

AIM

To show why organisations need finance, where it comes from, how its use should be controlled and why financial measures are critical indicators of performance.

OBJECTIVES

By the end of your work on this chapter you should be able to outline the concepts below in your own terms and:

1 Understand the role of the finance function in management

2 Be able to interpret basic financial reports

3 Know the difference between profit and cash

4 Know what a simple financial plan contains and its purpose

5 Understand the importance of financial results to evaluate performance

6 Know the basic steps in calculating the financial consequences of a management decision

7 Be able to explain how budgets aim to ensure internal activities are directed at meeting external financial requirements

case study

Siemens AG

Siemens began as a German company. Its corporate centre is in Munich, but it is now best described as an international company with various business activities spread across the world. Its main businesses are in electrical and electronic activities.

The rapidly changing nature of its products, processes and markets requires that the company should have a strong commitment to research and development. In 1996, approximately 8 per cent of its sales revenue was spent on research and development (DM 7,300 million) and 74 per cent of its sales were derived from products and services which were less than five years old (48 per cent in 1980). To accomplish greater flexibility and responsiveness to changes in technology and markets, the company has had to change its organisation and culture. The 1996 company report comments on the growing need to develop long-term partnerships, working closely with customers to discover how Siemens can help to solve their problems. This help extends to financial support through direct investment in power generation projects, and the application of expertise to facilitate financing arrangements for major infrastructure projects. Flexibility and responsiveness have required changes in organisation and working arrangements for employees. Fostering personal initiative, encouraging enterprise, more open management style, international experience as a requirement for appointments to key positions, commitment to training, flexible working hours and location such as teleworking from home are examples of changes taking place. Increased empowerment and encouragement of initiative also require a high degree of trust.

A summary of the Siemens AG financial report for year ended 30 September 1996 follows:

CASE QUESTIONS

▶ **What was the company's profit in the year to 30 September 1996?**

▶ **What proportion of its sales revenue was spent on research and development?**

▶ **What questions does the information in the profit statement raise for you?**

		DM millions
Sales		94,180
Less Cost of sales		66,710
		27,470
Research and development	7,296	
Marketing and selling	14,170	
General administration	3,039	
Other items	658	
		25,163
		2,307
Income from investments in other companies		314
Interest and financial gains		637
		3,258
Less Taxation		767
Income after tax from continuing operations		2,491
Add Extraordinary gains		496
Net income		2,987

18.1 Introduction

This chapter introduces the following ideas:

- ▶ Capital market
- ▶ Limited liability company
- ▶ Shareholder
- ▶ Cash flow statement
- ▶ Profit statement
- ▶ Balance sheet
- ▶ Assets
- ▶ Liabilities
- ▶ Fixed assets
- ▶ Current assets
- ▶ Shareholders' funds

Chapter 1 described organisations as aiming to add value to the resources they used. It is crucial to the success of an organisation that it has the appropriate resources and that these are managed to achieve the results that stakeholders expect. Whatever the nature of the organisation or its line of business, it will need financial resources to operate. It needs to manage these well if it is to prosper.

The Part One Case presented information about The Body Shop. This is an interesting company which has a strong sense of social responsibility. It can only promote its social objectives if it remains in business. This is what the chairman said in the 1996 annual report:

> ❛ Questions are often raised as to whether taking a socially responsible approach is consistent with delivering shareholder value. We have no doubt that it is. We are committed to continuing to build this business for the long-term benefit of all of our stakeholders … ❜

Financing your retirement

Many people reading this book will be expecting to start a career which they hope will provide an income to support an attractive lifestyle. Few will be thinking about retirement or the need to support themselves after their working lives have ended. This may be a sombre subject to introduce, but it is fundamentally important to understanding the financial environment in which organisations operate. Governments are increasingly concerned about the ability of traditional public pension schemes to support people in old age. They expect individuals to take more responsibility for their retirement.

---

n o t e b o o k   *18.1*

Find a copy of the Annual Report and Accounts 1996 for Storehouse plc (trading as BHS and Mothercare) or Allied Domeq (brands include Teachers whisky and Dunkin Donuts). What can you discover about the shareholders in the company?

Pension funds and life assurance companies undertake to pay their investors an acceptable income when they retire. The funds can only do this if they invest contributions successfully, and investors naturally expect their premiums to be invested profitably by pension fund managers. Much can change, and it does not follow that a fund which has performed well in the past will necessarily continue to do so, but it is probably the best indication available.

Another aspect of this discussion is the competitive nature of the pension fund and life assurance business. These companies would like to maximise the contributions they receive. As they grow bigger, the rewards for their managers increase and the funds become more influential.

---

n o t e b o o k   *18.2*

In relation to a recent company takeover or merger, use some recent financial or business newspapers to see if you can discover how influential the fund managers were in deciding the outcome of the merger.

There is pressure on the fund managers to perform well, and the rewards are high. This pressure to perform by identifying good investment opportunities is also in the investors' best interests as eventual pensioners. The fund managers will be looking for good investment opportunities in companies that are profitable and well managed.

Pressures on companies to perform

This is where the discussion comes full circle back to the investor. In order to attract money into its business to enable it to expand, management needs to demonstrate to the capital market that it is a profitable and successful business.

The fund managers in the capital market expect managements to operate their businesses profitably. So this pressure from the external capital market directly affects the organisation and all employees. There may be bad years or periods of low or negative profitability (losses) and the capital markets know that. But continual losses will eventually lead to failure. The business will simply run out of money and not be able to meet its financial obligations. So the pressures to perform that managers and employees feel originate outside the company or organisation. However, as future pensioners, dependent on the performance of fund managers, those pressures serve their long-term interests (Coggan, 1995).

Within an organisation it is unlikely that managers, apart from those at the top of an organisation, will feel the direct pressure from outside. Even if they did, what power would they have to influence the share price, for example? Very little in fact. This matter is returned to later.

18.2 The world outside the organisation

Raising capital

If you have looked at the annual report of a major company it is likely that the pension funds and life assurance companies will be major shareholders, although it is not always possible to identify them. They are just one of the many sources from which large organisations raise capital.

The capital market comprises all the individuals and institutions which have money to invest, including banks, life assurance companies and pension funds, and as users of capital, business organisations individuals and governments.

A limited liability company has an identity and existence in its own right as distinct from its owners (shareholders in Europe, stockholders in North America). A shareholder has an ownership right in the company in which the shares are held.

A large public company can raise money by issuing shares to people and institutions which respond to a share issue. This enables companies to raise money to finance activity on a large scale. The shareholders appoint the directors who are responsible for managing the company. A shareholder is entitled to vote at general meetings in accordance with the number of shares owned. Once the shareholders have paid for their shares in full, they cannot generally be required to pay more money into the company, even if it fails.

The great benefit of the limited company is its opportunity to raise capital from the public and financial institutions. The affairs of companies are governed by company law and by the body governing the share market, such as the Stock Exchange in the UK and the Bourse in France. Before a company can invite the public to subscribe for shares it has to be registered with the national financial regulators and to fulfil a number of requirements. The first step after registration in order to raise money is to issue a prospectus. Again there are many rules and legal matters that have to be satisfied. In essence, the prospectus explains the history of the company, what it plans to do generally and what it plans to do with the money raised.

If the business is small, it will not invite the public to buy shares. The promoters will contribute their own money, most likely in sufficient amount to ensure that they have control (more than 50 per cent of the shares). The amount of capital available to the company in these circumstances will be limited by the money the founders can afford to contribute. They may go to a bank to seek finance, but the willingness of a bank to lend will also depend on the amount subscribed by the shareholders.

Banks, fund managers and investors at large will contribute only if they believe that there is a good, sound, well managed business which is likely to make a profit. The investors have many investment opportunities. They will not invest in a company that will not reward them, as by investing they are taking a risk. The amount of return they expect will be related to the risk – the greater the risk, the greater the required return.

---

notebook   18.3

Find out the interest rate at which you could borrow money to buy (a) a car, (b) a house. Can you explain what you discover?

A limited liability company gives a business access to large amounts of capital, but at the same time allows some protection to the shareholders, as they cannot be held liable for the debts of the business in the event of its financial failure. This is known as limited liability, and it means that investors can contribute capital knowing that their private and personal assets are not at risk. Of course, they could lose all their investment in the shares. This is the risk they take, which is why they expect a higher return than they would receive if they put their money in a bank or in government securities, where the risk of default is virtually zero.

Because a company has access to capital in this form, there has to be regulation. The Companies Act is the principal instrument of control, with the addition of the Stock Exchange for those which are listed as public companies within the UK. A most important requirement is to provide information about the performance of the business from time to time (Arnold *et al.*, 1994; Elliott and Elliott, 1996).

The most comprehensive information about the current affairs of a business is found in its annual report. Amongst other things it includes detailed financial information of three distinct types. There is a cash flow statement, a profit and loss statement and a balance sheet.

n o t e b o o k   18.4

Obtain a copy of a company annual report and list the kinds of information that you find in it, for example, financial, product, management.

Cash flow statement

The easiest to understand of the three types of statement is the cash flow as it states just that. It shows where cash has come from and how it has been spent. The following is a simplified summary of the cash flow statement for The Body Shop for the year ended 2 March 1996:

> A cash flow statement shows the sources from which cash has been generated and how it has been spent during a period of time.

		£m
Net cash inflow from operating activities		45.1
Interest paid on loans, and dividends to shareholders		(5.9)
Payment of taxation		(11.8)
Investments (including property and equipment)		(18.9)
Net cash inflow		8.5
Financing: new share capital	0.2	
repayment of loans	(6.7)	(6.5)
Increase in cash for the year		2.0

> The assets are the property, plant and equipment, vehicles, stocks of goods for trading, money owed by customers and cash: in other words, the physical resources of the business.

In the ordinary course of successful business it might be expected that the cash received from trading (selling products or services) should be greater than the cash spent to purchase components, supplies, labour, energy and all the other resources combined to make, promote, distribute and secure the sales. The cash surplus could then be reinvested to help finance expansion and some of it paid to the shareholders by way of dividend to recompense them for their investment. The original contribution remains in the company, however, as part of the continuing capital base. In the case of The Body Shop, there was a cash surplus of £2 million after repaying some loans, paying dividends and investing in some new assets.

The idea of a cash surplus as being the essential requirement from operations is appealing but unfortunately too simplistic. Taking as an example a motor vehicle manufacturer, a car has to be designed, tested, components sourced from suppliers, production line prepared, cars distributed to dealers, and motoring journalists and publicity agents organised in preparation for a major launch promotion. All of this, before any of the cars can be sold – so there will be very heavy cash outflows before cash starts to come in. This process may take a couple of years. In the pharmaceutical industry there is a large investment in continuing research and development that may take ten years or longer before cash begins to flow back, and then only if the research is successful. The heavy investment in product development in the electronics industry has to be made before any products emerge. It would be highly unlikely in these conditions for the business to show a cash surplus in periods when it is making such heavy investment. Indeed it may be necessary to raise additional capital from shareholders or banks to finance the investment in plant and in training the people who will operate it.

---

n o t e b o o k   18.5

Look at the annual report for Siemens, Philips or any large manufacturing business and find out what it tells you about research and development. List the projects that the report mentions. What does the report say about the length of time before the projects will be profitable?

It would be impossible to draw sensible conclusions about the company's financial performance on the basis of cash flow alone. Not only is the annual surplus or deficit influenced by major investment, but other infrequent events, such as a major asset replacement programme during the life of a product, could also distort the impression.

Profit and loss statement

A profit statement reflects the benefits derived from the trading activities of the business during a period of time.

The profit and loss statement is designed to overcome the limitations of a cash flow statement although cash has the important characteristic of complete objectivity. Cash flows can be observed, measured and verified. Subjectivity enters into the measurement of profit.

Here is a simplified summary of the profit statement for The Body Shop for the year ended 2 March 1996:

	£m
Sales of products	256.5
Cost of goods sold	(107.6)
Gross profit (or gross margin)	148.9
Operating expenses (shops, administration and distribution)	(115.2)
Operating profit	33.7
Payment of interest on loans	(1.0)
Taxation on profit	(14.1)
Profit after taxation	18.6
Dividends to shareholders	(6.5)
Profit retained in the business	12.1

The profit after taxation and the profit retained in the business are quite different from the cash surplus reported in the cash flow statement. This is because the profit statement is not based on cash but on transactions which may result in cash transactions in the future or reflect cash transactions from previous periods. Sales may be credit sales which approved customers may pay later. Cost of goods sold may include the purchase of goods which will be paid for in the next financial year. Operating expenses will include depreciation which, with other terms, is explained below.

C A S E   Q U E S T I O N S   18.1

Refer to the summary profit statement of Siemens AG.

▶ Calculate the gross profit as a percentage of sales.

▶ Calculate the profit before tax as a percentage of sales.

---

n o t e b o o k   18.6

Look at the annual report of a company that interests you, probably in a similar line of business to Siemens. Calculate the gross profit of the company in a recent year as a percentage of sales. Calculate the profit before tax as a percentage of sales.

How does the company compare with these measures for Siemens AG?

Is there a major difference in the items in the profit statements of the two companies?

Depreciation

Depreciation is a major difference between cash flow and profit. Think about the investments mentioned in relation to motor vehicle production. Apart from occasional modifications, the same basic model may be produced and sold for several years, perhaps as many as ten for a small-volume producer. So the initial investment to develop the design and make the cars should be spread over the life of the investment and will be subtracted from sales revenue in each year. This process is called depreciation. The idea is simple, but there are several estimates required before the annual amount can be measured. Depreciation is based on the original cost of the investment, including set-up and training, less the expected scrap value at the end of its life. It may also be necessary to add the expected cost of decommissioning. Think about a nuclear power generator in this respect. Hence an estimation must be made of the life of the investment, the residual value and the initial cost, which itself is open to conjecture. To make matters worse, there are at least four methods of spreading the cost over the lifespan. The simplest is to allocate an equal amount each year.

Credit

Most products are not sold for cash but on credit. In some cases the credit arrangement can spread over a long time. A retail store might offer generous credit terms in order to promote sales – 'nothing to pay for 6 months' or 'easy terms over 9 months' are familiar promotional devices. Before the salesperson, or more likely the credit controller, will give credit, the customer's creditworthiness will be checked. However, even the most careful checkers cannot ensure that the customer may not become redundant or fall ill and not be able to work. As an example, suppose that the company's financial year ends on 31 December and that a customer is buying a personal computer at the end of October on nine months' credit of equal monthly payments. Should the company report the full value of the sale, the three instalments that the customer has paid, or nothing until the PC has been paid for in full? It is usual practice to report the full amount, as the business has a legal contract to force the customer to pay. The idea is fine, but experience shows that not all customers will pay in full. There will be bad debts. An estimate of doubtful debts has to be made before arriving at profit.

Warranty claims

If a problem arises with a good sold under warranty, it will be fixed, but at a cost to the manufacturer. The cost of repairing under warranty has to be estimated because warranty claims may not be made within the same financial year as the sale.

These are simple examples of subjectivity in profit measurement. There are many more, but these suffice to illustrate the point that the measure of profit cannot be said to be accurate. It is an approximation. Nevertheless, it is the main indication of trading performance measured in financial terms. The question remains, how much does profit reflect good performance? To evaluate this, profit needs to be related to the amount of investment in the business.

18.3 Measuring periodic performance

Both the cash flow and the profit statements relate to a period of time – conventionally to a financial or fiscal year, although the reports may also be produced for shorter periods. It is usual for large organisations to produce brief reports on their performance quarterly or half yearly, not just annually.

Just how much profit is desirable has to be considered in relation to the investment in a business. Therefore a measure of investment is needed with which to compare periodic profit. When you think that an investor (fund manager) could invest in risk-free government securities for a guaranteed minimum return known in advance, an investment in a risky company which did not offer at least the same expectation of reward, would not be contemplated. So the return, or ratio of profit to investment, would be expected to be higher for a risky investment than for a risk-free opportunity. The rate of return required for a particular investment has to be assessed by comparing alternative investment opportunities and their rates of return.

Measuring the investment base

How can the investment base be measured? The obvious base is the amount of the initial investment. If you deposit money in a bank deposit account it will attract interest. At the end of the year you can measure the rate of return by expressing the interest earned for the year as a percentage of the initial investment. If you leave the interest in the account, the following year you would need to base your calculation of the rate of return on the initial investment plus the interest you earned in the first year which now becomes a part of the capital base as you chose not to withdraw it. The investment base can grow over time. Much the same happens in a business. Profit is generated, some is distributed as a cash dividend, and the balance, usually the larger proportion, is retained in the business to finance expansion.

An alternative course of action would be for the directors to pay out all the profit and then ask the shareholders to contribute more share capital. The effect would be the same except that there may be adverse taxation implications in some tax regimes. There would certainly be costs associated with the share issue that are avoided by simply retaining some profit.

A simple measure of the capital base with which to compare profit appears to be the amount of capital originally contributed, plus profit which is retained and added each year to the base. This measure is inadequate.

A successful business will grow and develop a good reputation and image which will reflect the result of good, professional management and reliable, high quality products and service. If you own shares in such a company you would expect the value of those shares to increase to reflect the success of the business. The price of the shares quoted in the stock market will be the price at which buyers and sellers are prepared to trade and it will reflect expectations about the profitable future of the business. It will not be the same value as the total of contributed capital, plus retained earnings, divided by the number of shares on issue (that is the net tangible asset value per share). As a business grows profitably, it will generate goodwill, particularly reflected by, for example, customer loyalty, brand reputation and reliability, loyal relationships with suppliers of components and services and good design. The question of share value is revisited later.

18.4 The balance sheet

A balance sheet shows the financial position of a company at a particular time. It shows the physical resources (assets) of the business and, to match that, the sources from which finance has been raised both from shareholders and from borrowing.

The report which shows the capital base of a business is the balance sheet. The Body Shop balance sheet as at 2 March 1996 showed the following information:

	£m	£m
Property, plant and equipment (fixed assets)		79.4
Stocks of goods for resale	37.6	
Money owing from customers		
(debtors – UK or accounts receivable)	44.0	
Cash and bank accounts (current assets)	30.1	111.7
		£191.1
These resources were financed by shareholders		
(including retained profit)	122.6	
Money owing to suppliers, banks and tax	68.5	£191.1

The balance sheet reveals two separate but related aspects of the business. First it shows the total assets of the business. These include the physical resources such as property, buildings, machinery, computers, stocks (or inventories) of raw materials, work in progress and completed products, money owed by customers, and cash. The other dimension is the sources of the finance which has enabled the business to acquire these assets. Finance (or capital) comes from shareholders by way of contributions for shares when they are first issued together with retained profits from successful operations as previously explained. This is the shareholders' capital (or shareholders' funds). In addition, there will usually be money borrowed from a bank and possibly from other sources as well. These are the liabilities of the organisation. The sum total of the shareholders' funds and liabilities will be equal in aggregate to the amount of assets. The former represents the source from which the finance has been raised. The latter shows the destination or the physical resources in which the capital has been invested.

The balance sheet of Siemens AG is presented as another example.

Siemens AG – the case continues
Group balance sheet as at 30 September 1996

Assets		DM millions
Intangible (patents, licences, goodwill)		1,382
Property, plant and equipment at cost	53,828	
Less Accumulated depreciation	33,880	19,948
Investments		19,278
		40,608
Current assets		
Inventories	8,084	
Accounts receivable from customers and others	31,024	
Liquid assets (including cash)	7,785	46,893
		87,501
Shareholders' equity		
Issued shares	2,800	
Additional paid in capital	8,617	
Retained earnings (net)	13,781	25,198
Liabilities		
Pension fund and other commitments	38,489	
Loans	6,179	
Accounts payable and other short-term obligations	17,635	62,303
		87,501

CASE QUESTIONS 18.2

▶ In the balance sheet for Siemens AG, calculate the proportion of shareholders' funds represented by retained earnings (profit).

The shareholders are the main risk-takers and the profit is attributable to them, so the measure of the rate of return is profit after tax divided by shareholders' funds, commonly known as the *return on equity*. However, there are many imperfections in the measure, one of which is the fact that goodwill will not usually be included as an asset unless it appears following the purchase of another business. Brand names such as the title of a newspaper or the name of a consumer product may be valued by the directors and included as assets. This apparent inconsistency may be surprising. Accountants argue that newspaper mastheads, or brand names, could be sold separately from the business, whereas goodwill can only be sold with the business as a whole. Many companies only include brands if they have purchased them from another company, or in the case of goodwill, taken over another company for a price greater than the value of the tangible assets minus the liabilities (net worth). Further difficulties in measuring a rate of return arise from problems in measuring depreciation and, consequently, asset values, changes in price levels over time, and share values.

CASE   QUESTIONS   18.3

▶ Refer to the summary financial information for Siemens AG. Calculate the rate of return (after tax) on equity (shareholders' funds).

Depreciation

The discussion of the profit statement explained that depreciation in particular was an expense item that was difficult to measure. It represents an attempt to estimate the proportion of the cost of using long-term assets that is attributable to a particular accounting period. Any of the cost that has not already been subtracted in the profit statements remains to be subtracted in the future. In The Body Shop annual report for 1996 the assets, plant and equipment were shown in the notes as having cost £55.2m. The depreciation for the year that was included in the profit statement as an item of expense (within the figure of £115.2m) amounted to £6.0m. When added to depreciation charged in earlier years, and allowing for the sale of some assets, the book value in the balance sheet as at 2 March 1996 was £30.8m. This means that of the amount of £55.2m, there remains an amount of £30.8m to be charged against sales revenue in future years. This remaining balance is the value which appears in the balance sheet for long-term assets (fixed or non-current assets).

A fixed or non-current asset is expected to be of benefit to the business for a period exceeding one year and in the normal course of business will not be a trading asset. A current asset can be expected to be cash or to be converted to cash within a year.

---

notebook   18.7

Look at the annual reports for two or three companies in the same (or similar) industry and read the section called accounting policies. Make a list of practices that seem to be different.

If the value in the market – either buying price or selling price – is similar to this book value, that is purely coincidental. It is not a main task of accountants to value assets. The balance sheet figure is simply original cost minus the proportion so far depreciated. The estimate of doubtful debts subtracted from customers' outstanding accounts (debtors or accounts receivable), estimated warranty claim costs, estimated pension fund liabilities, the value of goodwill, brands or other intangible assets are all highly subjective measures. Furthermore, the accounting policies may well differ between companies even though they are in the same industry. So the aggregate amount shown in the balance sheet for assets is not necessarily a reflection of market values.

Price level differences

There is a further complication to measuring performance, especially in periods of unstable prices. An asset is recorded at its original cost less depreciation. Suppose there are two companies involved in much the same business with similar assets, but one company purchased its equipment when prices were much lower than was the case for the second company. Although they may have similar physical assets, the costs showing for one may be quite different from those for the other. Traditionally, accountants do not make allowances for differences in price levels through time. Money amounts at different times are added together as though they represented the same values, which is clearly nonsense. Consequently, during a period of changing prices it is difficult to compare the rate of return on equity between companies based on the profit statement and balance sheet.

Share values

There is another way of approaching the question of performance measurement. If you were thinking of buying shares in the market through the stock exchange you would consider the likely future returns in relation to the price you would have to pay for the shares. You will therefore be comparing different investment opportunities and will attempt to buy one that offers the best return for whatever degree of risk you are prepared to accept. Nevertheless, the return you expect would only be an estimate of future dividends plus the likely growth in the share price. You would be relating this to the price you would have to pay to buy the shares. If you were a shareholder in a different company from the one you are thinking of investing in, you would review the selling price of your existing shares in relation to the expected returns. If the potential investment, involving the same degree of risk, offered a greater potential return, not only would you be inclined to buy the new shares, you would also be inclined to sell your existing shares to buy more new ones to increase your return. Leaving aside the question of a narrowed portfolio as a result of this action, it would be rational for all investors in this position to behave in the same way. The consequence of this action should be clear. Selling pressure for the shares of one company would drive the price down to the point at which investors would be indifferent as to which company's shares they purchased. In a well organised and efficient market this represents likely behaviour and is the process known as arbitraging (Ross *et al.*, 1995).

Hence the measure of performance that shareholders are likely to adopt will not be directly related to the company's financial reports, but more to the financial markets. They will be comparing expected returns with the prices of securities (shares) in the market. This does not mean that financial reports from companies do not serve any useful purpose. They do, because they provide some of the information that helps the traders in shares to assess the likely returns from these companies in the future, and above all, provides information about past performance and recent financial position. Whilst share prices in the market are directly influenced by buying and selling pressure, the expectations which give rise to those pressures come in part from the financial reports.

Returns to shareholders are in the form of dividends and growth in the share price. A firm can only sustain these returns to its shareholders if it is profitable in the long term. Shareholders (and potential shareholders) will be watching the share price and making judgements about buying and selling shares. A company whose shares do not offer returns consistent with competitors' are likely to become takeover targets with bids from stronger, more efficient performers.

Figure 18.1 shows the comparative changes in the share price for two companies in the hotel business – Granada and Forte. Granada successfully launched a takeover bid for Forte towards the end of 1995. The graph shows clearly how the share price for Granada increased over a five-year period compared with Forte. The shareholders in Granada (and those buying and selling) believed that Granada was performing better than Forte.

Company directors have to watch share price movements. Unexpected movements might signal activity in the market that they ought to know about. For example, if a company is actively buying shares in the market and so pushing the price up, this might indicate that a takeover bid is coming. If a shareholder is dumping shares, thus pushing the price down, has performance in the company fallen short of expectations? In both circumstances the directors need to find out what they can about the market activities in order to take defensive action.

---

n o t e b o o k   18.8

Look at the requirement for Case Question 18.4. Compute the same measure for The Body Shop plc. What strikes you about these measures? What do they tell you about these companies? Would it make a difference to your decision to buy shares in one and not the other? Can you explain?

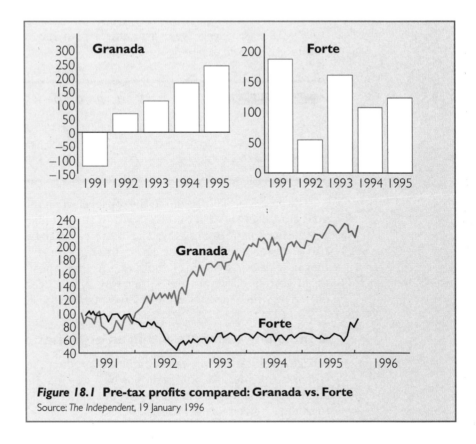

Figure 18.1 Pre-tax profits compared: Granada vs. Forte
Source: *The Independent,* 19 January 1996

The directors and senior managers of a company cannot ignore what is going on in the markets outside their business. They operate in markets, some specific to their own activities, and some general – the capital and labour markets. Their performance is being evaluated all the time and they need to know what the markets (buyers and sellers) are thinking. Financial managers will be watching the share price. The external pressures which the market imposes have to be translated or converted into pressure for internal action. This is what financial management is about.

18.5 Internal control

Most managers and employees can do little themselves to influence the share price directly. Nevertheless, much of what they do has financial implications and eventually will affect the price. So management needs systems and procedures to ensure that the financial consequences of decisions are understood and that the action proposed is acceptable. An organisation cannot wait until the accountant prepares a financial report at the end of the year to see if the operation has been profitable or not. It is too late to do anything. Profit does not just happen. It has to be planned (Horngren *et al.*, 1997). At least once a year a financial plan has to be prepared. This is commonly known as a budget.

n o t e b o o k   1 8 . 9

Prepare a simple cash budget for your own finances for next month. You will need to consider the cash you have available from savings in the past, how much cash you expect to receive during the month and what you plan to spend.

The process usually begins at the top level when the directors set a target or goal most likely related to the growth in shareholder value required to keep the business performing as well as, if not better than, its competitors. From this assessment will be derived a profit target for the whole organisation. It may be expressed as a rate of return on invested capital (shareholders' funds) or as an absolute amount, but either way it will need to be translated into objectives which have meaning at lower operating levels within the business.

Controlling elements within an organisation

A large organisation will have a variety of products, markets and locations in which it operates. An international business may have virtually complete and independent operating divisions in a variety of locations, each expected to achieve a given rate of return.

In contrast, a smaller business may have just one location, but within it a range of functions such as purchasing, design, production, assembly, inspection, dispatch and accounts receivable. Each may be independently managed yet co-ordinated to ensure that they are all operating to achieve the required corporate objective. None of these divisions could be set a required rate of return or even a profit target because none of them has independent control over its activities. The volume of production will depend on sales, purchases will depend on production and accounts receivable on sales. However, each has control over certain aspects of the business. Purchasing must negotiate prices and specifications for supplies of material or components, but it has little control over volume. Based on the sales and production plan, it will have a reasonable idea of volume, but it will be subject to change as the year progresses in light of actual sales and production. Similarly, the performance of the dispatch and shipping operation will depend on sales and customers' delivery requirements. They can base plans on the sales projections but, like all plans in business, the actual activities will inevitably be different.

All parts of the organisation, then, have to be flexible and adaptable in response to market opportunities and customers' requirements. It is not unusual in smaller organisations to hear managers complain that the process of planning and budgeting is a waste of time because events always turn out differently. They certainly do, but this is no reason not to plan. As circumstances change, plans should also change. Since the mechanics of budget preparation can be readily developed on fairly cheap desk-top computers, the tedium of budget revision involving numerous computations can easily be avoided by the use of suitable technology. So budgets should always be up-to-date and reflect contemporary operating and market conditions.

The earnings per share (profit after tax divided by the number of shares issued) for The Body Shop declined from 11.5 pence in 1995 to 9.8 pence in 1996. It cannot be known what plans the directors have. The annual report does not include forecasts or plans. However, it can be seen from the operating and financial review that the deterioration in the rate of profit was possibly attributable to increased administrative costs. If so, management can be expected to focus attention here when it is developing the budget for 1996/97. It is possible that, as a basis for developing the budget, the directors may have decided that an appropriate objective would be to raise earnings per share, possibly not to the 1995 level in one year, but towards that target. This is only one of a number of possible objectives.

Without a plan there is no sense of direction or clarity of purpose at operating levels. The process of budget preparation in itself is a useful exercise: not only does it enable the various parts of an organisation to relate their activities to others, but also it is a valuable co-ordination device to help ensure that the various parts of the organisation are focused on the same objective. The starting point for planning at operational level is generally the sales plan in a profit-oriented organisation. In not-for-profit organisations it may be the desired level of service to its constituency, for example the number of units of blood to be collected by the transfusion service.

In all cases, the capacity to achieve the desired volume will depend on the resources available – especially people, equipment and finance. If added resources are needed, management can anticipate both what is required and when. For example, if more people are required, they have to be recruited and trained so that they will be ready to contribute to productive activity at the appropriate time. If more cash is needed to pay for added supplies of raw materials, it is important to have a financial plan to present to the bank manager well in advance of the time that a cash crisis begins to occur. Crises often arise because there has been insufficient care and attention with planning – and failure to update plans as circumstances change. Plans need to be changed as activity grows for the simple reason that growth requires added finance. Labour, supplies of materials and services will have to be paid for before cash begins to flow back from customers.

Planning growth and improved performance

The length of the planning cycle depends on the kind of product or service. It may be no more than a couple of months or it could be much longer. Companies can fail as they grow simply because the rate of growth outpaces the ability to generate cash or because they have not anticipated the need for cash and made the necessary plans. Co-ordination of the various aspects has to be supervised centrally in the organisation to ensure that the overall objectives are achievable in the plan.

Much of the detail has to come from the operating units, especially performance targets related to work activity. It is here that there is likely to be a process of negotiation with central co-ordinators. Their activity is to improve productivity, whereas the objectives at the lower level may be to ensure that the performance targets do not put excessive pressures on employees. A process of genuine negotiation and co-operation may well lead to a budget which is acceptable both to operating divisions and to the central organisation. However, a budget cast in conditions of fear and apprehension can lead to attempts to create budget slack. This is exemplified by the readiness or otherwise of employees to introduce improved working methods. It is conceivable that more efficient working methods can be discovered through experience. Staff and management may choose not to disclose or introduce them at the earliest opportunity. Instead they may keep them in reserve to cushion the effects of a tight budget at some future time. Such behaviour is not in the best interests of the business as a whole, but it shows the way that budget preparation can lead to conflicts. The subject of participation in the process of budget preparation has been a topic for extensive research in recent years (Emmanuel *et al.*, 1991; Drury, 1996).

Once the budget is negotiated and agreed it becomes an operating plan which reflects expectations about the conditions in which the organisation is operating. Sometimes, alternative budgets are prepared for different purposes. For example, the performance targets incorporated for operating divisions may have been negotiated at a tighter level than past achievements with the objective of improving productivity. Although these targets may be achieved during the period of the budget, the process may take some months. If the cash or profit forecast given to the bank is based on these targets, it is likely that the cash or profit projections will not be achieved. So the cash budget may be based on looser performance. Similarly, a sales budget might reflect a higher sales level than that incorporated in the profit plan. The risk of having different budgets is the possibility that they will lose credibility within the organisation.

Performance measurement

Another favourite research topic has been the way in which budgets are used to judge performance. The behaviour of managers can be seriously influenced by the budget style in an organisation. If this is authoritarian and unthinking in manner, in which achieving the budget is the primary objective of management, it may lead to suboptimal performance. The pressure may be translated into action which is against long-term interests. For example, a salesperson might threaten customers with a price increase in the coming month to boost current sales and achieve a sales target.

The immediate reaction to employees who fail to achieve budget is to presume that they are to blame. Any idea that the budget itself may be inappropriate or unachievable is not entertained. If this style is carried forward to performance evaluation it can be equally destructive. In contrast, a budget can be prepared after discussion with those who know the area. It can then be used as a guide for judging performance after allowing for changing circumstances. This approach is more likely to achieve employee support.

Consistent failure to achieve budget should first lead to a review of the budget to ensure that the targets are fair and achievable. Only then should there be an attempt to take remedial action to improve an activity. The successful use of budgets depends on those affected, managers and staff alike, developing a sense of ownership towards them. As conditions change, the budget should be revised so that it continues to be credible.

A budget is, in essence, short-term. Usually it is for no more than one year. Nevertheless, it has to be set in a longer-term context and be consistent with the strategy for the future development of the organisation. Long-term investments in research and development, product and market development, new plant and equipment or even the acquisition of other businesses have to be included in the short-term budget and cash requirements in the cash budget.

If, in the longer term, a product is going to be phased out, it would be senseless to mount a major promotion campaign to strengthen its market position. It may make sense to promote it at a discount in stores in order to clear inventories. This further illustrates co-ordination, but, in particular, it shows a link between short-term action and longer-term strategy.

18.6 Decision-making

The one certainty in any organisation is that conditions will change. The budget cannot be revised every time minor changes occur or fresh opportunities arise. An organisation has to be flexible and responsive. Frequently, opportunities arise that require prompt action – for example, a special order for a normal product or service, but to be sold at a low promotional price into a new market. In these circumstances the normal measurement of the average cost of producing and delivering the service may well be an inappropriate starting point for computing potential profit. Many of the costs will not change as a result of accepting this opportunity: there will be no further research and development, no requirement to increase productive capacity (assuming that capacity is available) and, possibly, no added labour cost. In these conditions, consideration need only be given to the costs that will increase directly as a result of choosing to accept this order: delivery, materials or additional resources consumed which will have to be paid for. Depreciation can be ignored and, in the very short term, so too can the labour cost since the employees will already have been paid for their time.

Let us suppose that Philips has an opportunity to make and sell electric light bulbs to a retailer. The bulbs will be packaged especially for the retailer and not identified with Philips. How will the costs be estimated?

▶ Is there enough manufacturing capacity without having to reduce normal production? If so, there is no need to take account of any additional capital costs.

▶ Are additional employees required or will existing employees have to work longer? If so, the extra costs will be attributable to this order; otherwise there are no added labour costs.

▶ Materials will be required according to the retailer's specification.

▶ Are there packaging costs? In this case there may be design and printing costs, as well as packaging material. The set-up costs will have to be included.

▶ Will the retailer collect the bulbs, or do they need to be delivered? Will there be added costs, or will existing transport arrangements be adequate?

The important issue is to identify costs which are directly traceable and attributable to this opportunity. The normal average cost of producing light bulbs may be irrelevant since that includes research and development, capital equipment costs and administrative overheads which will not necessarily increase with this order.

Undoubtedly the retailer is looking for a special price, lower than that which Philips might normally charge. If this price exceeds the identified cost, it may be an attractive opportunity. The critical issue for Philips to decide is whether or not this might damage its own long-term market position. Against this is the threat that the retailer will probably also be negotiating with a competitor to supply the light bulbs.

Suppose that the normal selling price is 80 pence and that the usual cost is made up (per unit):

	pence
Labour	10
Materials	20
Packaging	5
Delivery	3
Overheads	25
	63
Contribution to profit	17
	80

The retailer wants to buy lamps at a price of 60 pence. If we establish that Philips's overheads will not increase, that labour costs will be 8 pence, materials 20 pence and packaging 10 pence, then the appropriate cost per unit will be 38 pence. If additional delivery is £100 per journey for up to 10,000 light bulbs and the design and set-up costs for printing the packaging is £10,000 and the order is for 100,000 bulbs, is it acceptable to sell at 60 pence?

		pence
Unit costs:	labour	8
	material	20
	packaging	10
		38

	£
Cost for 100,000	38,000
Delivery cost	1,000
Design, set-up	10,000
Relevant cost	49,000
Revenue	60,000
Contribution to profit	11,000

This appears to be an acceptable sales opportunity as long as it does not erode Philips's normal market and as long as the existing customers do not expect the normal price to be lowered.

It is the job of the cost or management accountant to process financial information quickly in order to assist managers to take decisions of the kind described above. It is not usual for the information to be directly available from the financial records. The accountant will have to find out the alternative courses of action, extract the appropriate financial data from the system, process it and report in a coherent and understandable way to those responsible for taking the decision. Accountants are more likely to be useful if they understand the processes of service or product delivery. They also need to appreciate that they are providing a service to other managers.

Routine information for managers

Another aspect of internal financial measurement is more routine. Unlike the system of financial reporting for the organisation as a whole, which is geared to the needs of the capital market, internal information has to be related to the needs of the managers. They will be interested in financial measurements related to their own area of responsibility. For example, a marketing manager will need information about groups of products, brands, customers, regions or marketing areas. In research and development, costs accumulating for each project might be compared with research progress to date. This approach runs right through the value chain, recognising that value can be added from research, development, design, through to distribution and customer service. It is not just the manufacturing process or service delivery process that adds value and requires to be measured.

As organisations develop stronger alliances and co-operative arrangements, at both the strategic and operational levels, the role of the accountant is expanded beyond the limits of the organisation within which he or she works. Co-operation in the supply chain can result in improved performance for both organisations involved. To achieve benefits of cost reduction and/or improved profitability through quality improvement there has to be an open relationship and trust between the organisations. Accountants play a role in this co-operation by advising on the financial consequences for both organisations (Atkinson *et al.*, 1995).

18.7 International aspects of financial reporting

Internal financial analysis and control processes are generally designed to meet the needs of management and are not constrained by legal requirements. The principles and methods are universally applicable, although in some locations cultural factors and custom may mean that accountants go about their tasks in a different manner.

External financial reporting is rather different. In the English-speaking world, financial reports appear to be similar, terminology aside. Nonetheless, across the western world the system of double-entry book-keeping is at the foundation of all financial record-keeping systems. Within the UK, the limits to acceptable methods of reporting are governed by the Companies Acts 1985 and 1989, and the Accounting Standards Board which produces accounting standards.

Different legal systems, industry financing, taxation systems, structure of the accounting profession, language and traditions mean that financial reporting varies from one country to another. France, Germany, Portugal, Spain and Japan have historically required compliance with a rigid framework for financial reporting (Alexander and Nobes, 1994).

C A S E   Q U E S T I O N S   1 8 . 5

▶ Look at the summary of significant accounting policies in the 1996 annual report for Siemens AG. How have different standards impinged upon the reporting process?

In Eastern Europe, accountants were regarded merely as book-keepers. There was no need to produce financial statements for public consumption since the system was centrally controlled. Political changes accompanied by privatisation have created a need for a different system more akin to those in the English-speaking world.

Not surprisingly, the system in the United States has much in common with the UK system, but there are also important fundamental differences. The US system has been much more regulated through the Securities and Exchange Commission, at least in so far as large public companies are concerned. Accounting standards are established by the Financial Accounting Standards Board (FASB). Its requirements have tended towards a more conservative approach than in many countries. For example, it generally requires all research and development costs to be subtracted from revenue as incurred and not carried forward in the balance sheet to be offset against future gains.

The differences in detail make it difficult to compare the financial performance of companies in different countries. Given the increasing integration of business and the international nature of capital markets, these differences are not helpful for investors or anyone else who is interested in evaluating the performance of companies in financial terms. This was why, in 1973, the International Accounting Standards Committee was formed with the purpose of developing accounting standards which could be applied worldwide. By 1994, eighty countries were represented on the IASC. Some countries have adopted the international accounting standards directly (e.g. Malaysia), some adapt to suit local conditions (e.g. Singapore) and others develop their own standards independently, but adapt them to conform to the IASC requirements (e.g. UK). The international standards are somewhat bland because they have to reflect a consensus, and therefore a variety of accounting treatments may be possible. As time passes, it is to be expected that the standards will be revised and improved to promote international conformity. Within the European Union, aspects of company law have been, and continue to be harmonised. This helps to promote compatibility, but cultural differences persist.

_n o t e b o o k_ _18.10_

Look at Philips Electronics NV 1996 annual report, page 62. To what extent was the trading result different under US standards?

18.8 Recap

Managing the financial resources of an organisation is fundamental to its success, but no more so than other aspects of management. Without a good product and a receptive market the best financial management in the world cannot create a profitable company. Conversely, an otherwise successful company can soon fail without proper financial information to assist decision-making and control.

Content agenda

Management needs funds, along with other resources, to help achieve the objectives of the business. It also needs to decide which of many opportunities facing the business it should invest in. Shareholders expect management to invest in projects and gradually develop a strategy that add to shareholder value. To do this, management depends on adequate financial information if it is to make the right strategic choices. The budgeting process can help to give focus and direction to the plans that management makes to achieve objectives. It also helps to co-ordinate the activities of different functions and departments by giving them a common framework and plan within which to work. The finance function offers a system for assessing the financial consequences of decisions in a relatively objective way – though there are also many uncertainties in financial information. The levels at which budgets are set have effects on motivation – impossible budgets or very slack ones have little beneficial effect. Those that are challenging but achievable have a positive effect on commitment.

Process agenda

Organisations normally have a regular cycle of budgeting activity, conducted between those at the centre and those in the operating units. This is to ensure that the separate parts work towards the overall objectives. This process may challenge local interests and may be contentious. Hence budgets are typically set through a process of negotiation, with varying degrees of participation by line managers in the process. In some companies, line managers

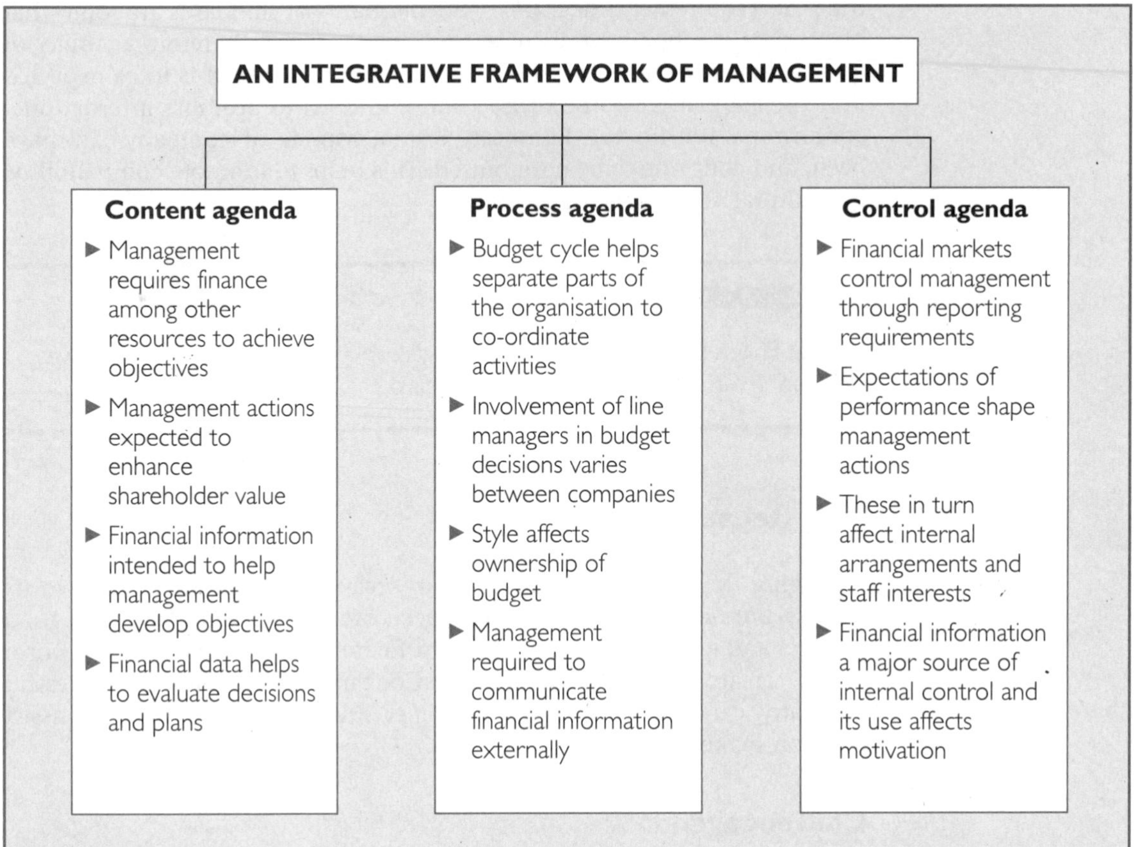
AN INTEGRATIVE FRAMEWORK OF MANAGEMENT
Content agenda
▶ Management requires finance among other resources to achieve objectives
▶ Management actions expected to enhance shareholder value
▶ Financial information intended to help management develop objectives
▶ Financial data helps to evaluate decisions and plans
Process agenda
▶ Budget cycle helps separate parts of the organisation to co-ordinate activities
▶ Involvement of line managers in budget decisions varies between companies
▶ Style affects ownership of budget
▶ Management required to communicate financial information externally
Control agenda
▶ Financial markets control management through reporting requirements
▶ Expectations of performance shape management actions
▶ These in turn affect internal arrangements and staff interests
▶ Financial information a major source of internal control and its use affects motivation

Figure 18.2

are heavily involved in decisions about budgets, in others the budgets are imposed from the centre in an authoritarian way. These alternative styles affect the degree to which employees and managers accept ownership of the budgets. Management is also required to communicate financial information about the company to actual and prospective shareholders.

Control agenda

Owners and shareholders, and the capital market generally exercise significant control over managers. This is institutionalised in legislation such as the Companies Acts and by the *Regulations of the Stock Exchange*. The capital markets' reaction to reports of financial performance affect the ability of the company to raise capital. Management will experience this pressure from outside. As it begins to change policy and practice to satisfy these external interests, internal arrangements will also be affected. Financial information also helps to measure management performance internally – as when actual expenditure can be compared with the budget. Routine financial information is also used to help control the management of projects, to ensure that what is spent corresponds to what has been agreed.

The integrative framework is set out in Figure 18.2.

18.9 Review questions

1 Why do companies have to make a profit?
2 How is profit measured?
3 Explain why profit is different from cash.
4 What does a balance sheet tell us about an organisation?
5 Can you explain how the external pressures on a company to generate a profit are translated into internal planning systems?
6 What is the purpose of a budget?
7 How does a budget operate as a control mechanism?
8 Explain why the financial information prepared for external purposes is not necessarily appropriate for managers.
9 Explain the notion of contribution to the profit of a business.
10 What are international standards of accounting? Explain how they differ from requirements in your country.

PART CASE QUESTIONS

▶ How do you expect that Kwik-Fit's investment in IT systems will have affected specific items in (a) the profit and loss statement, and (b) the balance sheet?

▶ How will the systems have helped the internal control of decision-making? With what financial consequences, explicitly?

▶ What can you discover from the financial press about the movement in the company's share price over the past year and the reasons for this? Is there any evidence of it affecting internal management policy and practice?

Further reading

A useful introduction to the mechanisms that management can use to raise capital (and the expectations they have to satisfy) is provided by Coggan (1995). A standard text that covers all areas in great detail is Horngren *et al.* (1997), while a European perspective is offered by Alexander and Nobes (1994). You should also write to one or two prominent companies which interest you and obtain a copy of their annual reports for the last two years. As well as illustrating the financial issues covered in this chapter, they usually provide a lot of information which relates to other chapters.

W Website addresses

Many major companies now provide five-year financial information on their Websites, together with a recent annual report and statements to the financial markets. Those cited in the text include:

Marks & Spencer http://www.marks-and-spencer.co.uk
Granada http://www.granada.co.uk
Siemens http://www.siemens.de
You can update the information in the Case Study by visiting Siemen's site, which includes an overview of the company, the major business segments it operates and the comments of management in the latest annual report.

Managing operations and quality

AIM

To set the operations function in its historical context and show how it supports other aspects of manufacturing and service organisations.

OBJECTIVES

At the end of your work on this chapter you should be able to outline the concepts below in your own terms and:

1 Understand the position and role of the operations function in the wider organisational context

2 Analyse an operations system and recognise the key management challenges it faces in delivering customer satisfaction

3 Select appropriate operations management approaches to suit the context of a particular organisation through recognising the strengths and weaknesses of each

4 Recognise the need to develop an integrated approach to the organisation and its extended supply chain in which the operations function will contribute both strategically and operationally to the desired goals

Benetton

There are many aspects to the success of Benetton. One of these is undoubtedly its unusual operations management system.

With a radical approach to knitted goods, the Benettons in effect created a knitted pullover as a seasonal fashion good rather than a garment for comfort intended for years of service. Their bold colours brought a youthful image and created a need for dedicated retail outlets working to a closely defined and controlled specification. As a two-person business there was little need for systems. Giuliano designed and produced while Luciano sold. Their early success encouraged them to buy new machines and recruit local staff to produce a small range of goods in greater volume.

Where production was in Benetton factories, employees' suggestions for improvement were encouraged and acted upon while, early on, the company used subcontractors as producers. Initially these were outworkers to whom part-made garments would be delivered in their homes for completion and later collected. Larger groups of such workers formed a subcontractor network around the main Benetton factories. These grew up at a time when Benetton could not raise its own capital to build capacity internally. Instead, Luciano devised a partnership agreement with them such that, in return for providing a steady stream of work, the suppliers would invest in fixed assets. They had to promise to work only for Benetton, however.

The nature of the relationship with the retailers also impacts on Benetton's operations systems. The retail outlets are separate businesses (or franchises but which do not pay royalties to their parent company) which are expected to pay cash on delivery to earn a 10 per cent discount.

The product line has increased each year with new garments and materials being used, but the essence of the Benetton system remains in operation terms dependent on a large number of independent entrepreneur suppliers working very closely in partnership with Benetton, growing and developing with them.

Benetton thus demonstrates many of the characteristics of the Japanese auto companies in their supply system relationships: tiers of subcontractors collaborate to make their supply chains effective against Benetton's competitors. All of this is done without compromising the core of the Benetton belief system that customers deserve choice, variety, value for money and a guaranteed level of quality and service.

Source: based on *Building the Benetton System*, European Case Clearing House, No. 390-042-1

CASE QUESTIONS

▶ What business practices has Benetton introduced that seem unusual to you?

▶ What particular issues do you think may arise in managing an organisation with so many independent suppliers and franchise owners?

▶ What contrasts and similarities are there between Benetton and The Body Shop from a management point of view?

19.1 Introduction

This chapter introduces the following ideas:
- Craft production
- Factory production
- Scientific management
- Inventory
- Economic order quantity (EOQ)
- Material requirements planning (MRP)
- Systems approach
- Input and output
- Transformation
- Feedback
- Line layout
- Cell layout
- Functional layout
- Concentric layout
- Innovation
- Cost reduction
- Total quality management (TQM)
- Business process
- Demand and supply leadtime
- Supply chain
- Just-in-time (JIT)
- Partnering relationship
- Order winners
- Order qualifiers

This chapter sets the operations function in its historical context and shows how this function supports other manufacturing or service activities. It then considers the current state of development of the management approaches inside the function and the increasingly cross-boundary aspects being demonstrated in the best organisations. The boundaries being crossed include those between departments of the same organisation. The role of the operations function often incorporates the management of the whole integrated supply chain. This begins with the supplier of raw material and ends with the delivery of the product or service to the customer. Thus the function has a major strategic dimension where it can hinder or help the achievement of corporate goals.

The first section outlines the main historical events, people and techniques. These have shaped our understanding of what we mean by operations and quality and how they support business activities.

19.2 Historical development

Craft production

The operations activity has existed for as long as there have been intelligent beings working with tools to transform base material into something different and desirable. In this regard, management created the specialism earlier than marketing, information systems and human resources. These latter depend more on size and complexity to justify separate status. Nevertheless, in some European cultures, management saw the purpose of operations as being to provide whatever the rest of the business wanted. They often did (in some fashion), but often this was due mainly to the abilities of the people in the function, not to a coherent approach.

This chapter looks at how the evolutionary process has changed the nature of the need that the operations function has to fill. It also examines how some organisations are paying more attention to designing and operating this transformation function. Their intention is to benefit customers and providers alike.

---

n o t e b o o k   19.1

Craft production

Visit a craft fair and talk to one or two of the craftworkers about the way they work, how they sell, if they design to order or according only to their ideas, and how they organise the production of goods and the supply of materials.

Craft production refers to a system in which the craft producers do everything. With or without customer involvement, they design, source materials, make, display, sell, perhaps service and do the accounts.

From the beginnings of trade, craft producers have embodied their ideas and skills in a product or service, and usually some elements of both. Craft producers do everything themselves. With or without actual customer involvement they design, source materials, make, display, sell, perhaps service and do the accounts. Once they generate income, they reinvest and often train apprentices to continue the skills.

Craft producers conduct each stage of the complete product lifecycle. Their output is unique and very variable. Sometimes batch production is possible – for example, the limited edition of five hundred prints from an original piece of artwork, each signed by its creator.

The range of skills employed by a craftworker are a microcosm of the operations function. The variations are to some extent forced by a need to produce repetitively in high volumes. Yet the flexibility that craft producers can achieve and their ability to modify their ideas to suit customer requirements are increasingly being sought by large producers. In addition, the personal satisfaction that craft producers get from completing the whole complex set of tasks should not be overlooked.

Factory production

Factory production broke down the integrated nature of the craftworker's approach and made it possible to increase the supply of goods by dividing tasks into simple and repetitive sequences.

Factory production made it possible to increase the supply of goods to rapidly growing populations. It broke down the integrated nature of the craftworker's approach. Management realised that dividing work into smaller units allowed workers to concentrate on developing a narrow range of specialised skills. The division of labour was between different tasks and between the thinking and doing tasks of manager and worker. This division began the evolution towards narrow, functionally defined boundaries with jealously guarded 'patches of turf'. These would become the focus of territorial wars across the organisation.

Many large manufacturers offer visiting facilities. Try to visit several to see if you can understand the way that they work.

Dividing tasks into simple and repetitive sequences allowed managers to employ a wider range of people in the factory and so enabled them to increase production.

Managers found that two other complementary features were also necessary to enable high-volume production. These were the notions of standardisation and interchangeability. If several people are producing sets of parts that must fit together at some stage, they must work to a standard specification. Moreover, each similar part must be completely interchangeable with its equivalent produced by someone else. This was not an issue for the craftworker as he or she could only work on one product at a time. In any case, they had the skill to shape the parts so that they fitted together. Managements in the developing factory system wanted to avoid this 'fitting' effort, so they designed both processes and machines to be more regular and repeatable. This also influenced the nature of capital investment. At first, factory owners used this mainly to provide motive power for essentially human-based machines. In this regard the investment was largely to supplement human muscle power not, initially, brain power. By removing variable human effort and providing increased power the machines themselves worked more precisely, so it became easier to make interchangeable parts.

C A S E   Q U E S T I O N S   19.1

▶ Is Benetton a craft or a factory system?

▶ Review the information about the system Benetton uses and list the advantages and disadvantages.

Twentieth-century developments

The school of management called 'scientific' attempted to create a science of factory production.

The school of management called 'scientific' attempted to create a science of factory production. The aim of Taylor and the Gilbreths (see Chapter 2) was to move away from methods that were very variable and dependent on individual abilities and motivation (Gilbreth, 1911). Some western commentators have devalued Taylor's approaches to work measurement in recent years. Yet people who are performing a sequence of related activities need to know how long to allow for each stage and what resources they need. The method study approaches that the Gilbreths pioneered as they searched for the 'one best way of working' have a great deal to offer. What has changed now is that management often expects operating staff themselves to look for improved ways of working. This is part of the continuous improvement effort.

A distinct downside to the scientific school was that the concentration was on finely subdivided tasks that a worker would repeat thousands of times in a working life. This process was in essence deskilling and dehumanising and permitted no variation or individuality.

This reached its peak with Henry Ford's automobile assembly plants. Ford brought high levels of interchangeability to moving production lines, highly 'scientific' management and vertical integration along the lines of supply (Ford, 1922). That is to say, Ford owned all the stages of production from raw materials through to final distribution to customers. In the 1920s his system was capable of going from raw iron ore to finished car in 81 hours, of which only about 5 hours were manufacturing and assembly. It was economically very efficient and progressively reduced the real cost of car production over the years of continuous output and improvement. In fact, over an eighteen year period the retail price of the Model T Ford decreased from just over $3,000 to less than $900. Ford's was a single model system, but General Motors later put product variety, different organisational principles and distribution systems together to create severe competition to Ford.

At the height of Ford's capability, one of the many visitors was Taichi Ohno who was the production engineer at the fledgling Toyota car company in Japan. While some of the Ford system impressed Ohno, he learned more from American supermarkets. He noted in particular how stores satisfied the needs of customers with minimal shelf space in the store. As customers took products away, staff restocked the shelves. This is the logic behind what many observers regard as the world's best manufacturing company. It was also an early example of the two-way technology transfer (of managerial technologies) between West and East.

It was around this time that a method was developed which applied a statistical approach to the control of quality. The method used control charts and sampling plans. Control charts tried to prevent people creating defects. Sampling plans ensured that any defects did not pass beyond the sampling stage. This statistical process control (SPC) was instrumental in supporting the war production effort in the Second World War. It was also during that war that a different applied mathematical approach began its development. Operational research, or management science, attempted to create mathematical models of management situations. Staff could then manipulate these models to develop optimum results which managements could use to inform their actual decisions. The assumptions needed to make some problems feasible for mathematical models were sometimes too great for managers to regard them as suitable surrogates for the real world. Nevertheless some of the approaches still offer utility to practising managers who use them widely. A prime example (developed during the 1950s and 1960s) is critical path analysis. The technique helps to manage complex projects of any description.

It was also during the 1960s that computing power began its dramatic surge in availability and increase in power-to-cost ratio. The availability of relatively cheap computers allowed the development of systems to manage production and inventory, known as material requirements planning systems (Orlicky, 1975). These aimed to manage the production activity by controlling every part at every process stage, and seemed to offer the prospect of complete computer integration of the whole business process. The reality was often less than ideal. Nevertheless this caused the western world to divert towards a goal where computers would solve the increasingly complex problems of managing production systems that were beginning to spread their supply chains across the globe.

Meanwhile management in resource-starved Japan followed a different approach. Ford's model of mass production had not made sense to Toyota.

Inventory consists of materials and part or finished goods which are held in anticipation of need by customers along a chain of supply from raw materials through to final consumption (and recycling?).

Ohno began to build a system that modelled the supermarket in its ideas of simplicity and customer-driven operations. This simple approach did not need computers but did need dedicated and capable people working together.

n o t e b o o k   19.3

Visit a Burger King or similar fast-food outlet and try to discover the material inventories that are used. What non-material inventories will there be?

Consider a hospital accident and emergency unit. What inventories are normally stored in such units?

Systems thinking and models

At this point it is necessary to consolidate a number of things hinted at in the earlier discussion.

The systems approach looks at the different parts of an interacting set of activities as a whole and considers the best way for the whole to function.

Any operation can be represented as a system that takes inputs of various kinds and transforms them into some kind of desired output. Inputs may include materials, equipment, finance and people. Outputs include products, services, reputation and waste. The aim of systems thinking is to use an abstract view of the total system and then to operate each subsystem according to the defined 'best way' for the complete system. This can be drawn as a simple systems diagram. A control mechanism is included to ensure that the outputs expected are delivered and that they meet customers' needs. Thus a feedback control loop is introduced to measure, analyse and modify the inputs, as shown in Figure 19.1.

The transformation stage can take many forms, only one of which is production. Service-oriented types are more numerous although the history of the subject concentrates on production.

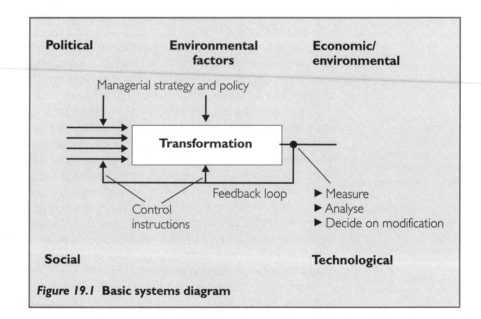

Figure 19.1 **Basic systems diagram**

▶ Draw a systems diagram that represents the Benetton production system.

▶ What are the main sources of feedback?

▶ How critical are they to input activities?

Table 19.1 lists the transformation types. Note that there are two major distinguishing factors for operations systems. The first is whether there is a tangible 'product' that can be stored. If not, either someone consumes the output immediately or the system has wasted the capability to produce it then. If a hotel does not have someone to occupy a room, it creates no output. It cannot store it and has lost for ever the opportunity to sell that night's occupancy of the room. A car, on the other hand, embodies its value in a less time-dependent form.

The second distinguishing factor links with the first. In a pure service transformation (for example, a visit to the hairdresser) the customer must be present throughout the transformation and largely defines the details of the transformation. In the production of goods there can be a separation of customer from transformation. In product production, both design and transformation can, in theory, be done away from and before contact with the customer. In service businesses the people with whom the customer interacts *are* the service. This raises the old questions of variability and motivation that the trends in factory production were trying to manage more effectively. In this sense, some service businesses try to become more factory-like, especially in back-office areas without contact with customers (such as cheque processing in banks). Conversely, many factories are trying to make more effective contact with their customers to satisfy needs more precisely.

The objectives of operations managers are to select and manage the best mix of resources and transformation process to meet customer requirements. They must also do this in a way that permits the organisation to make an acceptable financial return on its investments. The customer

Table 19.1 Transformation types

Transformation	System	Variations
Physical	Production	Additive, e.g. automobile assembly Subtractive, e.g. oil refining
Locational	Transportation	Goods People
Attitudinal	Education Entertainment	Statutory or voluntary Escapist or informative
Physiological	Health care Fitness	Remedial/preventive
Presentational	Fashion	Clothes Hair Cosmetics

requirements will cover aspects of product or service design, delivery, reliability, speed and quality. All must be at an acceptable cost.

There have been various attempts to clarify generic forms of operational system. The characteristics that differentiate them relate to:

- output volume,
- nature of processing (continuous or intermittent),
- whether the outputs are continuous or discrete (e.g. electricity or cars),
- the degree to which the output and the flexibility of the system's response is specific to or specified by the customer,
- the physical layout of transformation equipment.

Volume ranges from unique items, such as a dam or fine art picture, through multiple copies or batches of similar items through to mass production. The latter can be continuous (cement) or discrete (video recorders).

Figure 19.2 shows a rough arrangement of these systems with examples of each. It lists across the top the different physical layouts that tend to match each type.

Line layout is completely specified by the sequence of activities needed to perform a given transformation. It is relatively fixed but may have similar processes scattered through the line as and when needed. It will tend to have specially designed process equipment and use people with a limited range of skills.

Cell layout permits more variety by creating multiple cells (which look like small line layouts) dedicated to producing families of output types. Within the cell, people have several skills and move between jobs as required to keep the flow of transformation steady. The people are also likely to have a wider range of decision-making authority to complement their wider range of skills.

Line layout is completely specified by the sequence of activities needed to perform a given transformation.

A cell layout creates multiple cells dedicated to producing families of output types.

		Line	Cell	**Layout** Functional	Concentric	*Examples*
High		MASS (Rigid)				Ford model T (discrete) Cement (continuous) General Motors
						Electricity supply
Volume			MASS (Flexible)			Toyota
				BATCH		90 per cent of organisations
Low					UNIQUE	Civil engineering Bespoke tailor
		Low		**Flexibility**	*High*	

Figure 19.2 Forms of operations system

In both of these types the focus is on the transformed materials or customer. The aim is to keep them flowing through the system without delay. If necessary, operators use parts of the transformation system at less than the theoretical capacity to keep the process moving.

In the *functional* layout the thinking is different. Here the system tries to keep the elements of the transformation process fully used and able to produce the required variety of output. Each of the similar physical processes is co-located and the materials and/or customers then have to visit these areas as demanded by the product or service design. This produces a very tangled flow path round these different locations, often involving extensive queuing time between the different processing stages which, since they are being used 'efficiently', are operating at non-synchronised rates. This kind of system needs high levels of inventory while the operating staff perform highly specialised tasks. This system is common in factories, hospitals, insurance companies, restaurants and many other places.

The *concentric* layout may not appear as uniform as the name suggests, but the idea is of a target or focus on an area where an assembly is taking place. Examples of shipbuilding or building a dam capture the nature of this. The process is one of bringing together all the resources needed, in the required sequence and time, to create a unique output. Skill ranges are extensive. The integration is also complex, so staff often use the critical path analysis technique referred to earlier.

It is important to realise that these stereotypes are simply that. They are labels that bring certain assumptions with them so that using the label paints a mental picture as a form of shorthand in discussions. In practice, organisations can often display a number of these stereotypes under one roof. For example, a restaurant might have a functionally organised kitchen producing batches of meals for parties of diners. The waiter is a pure service person interacting to create a uniquely specified meal for a single diner. If there is a buffet or carvery area, this may be in a line with customers moving along and being part of the transformation process.

> A functional layout groups similar physical processes together and brings materials and/or customers to these areas.

◄▬▬▬▬ *n o t e b o o k   1 9 . 4*

Define the transformation type and possible layout form of the following:
(a) university matriculation or enrolment process, (b) a motorway fast-food servery, (c) a hospital accident and emergency unit, (d) a Benetton customer sales and service area.

One of the dangers of diagrams like Figure 19.2 is that they may imply that there are limited choices. Certainly there is a tendency to fit these categories together. The idea of the trade-off suggests that people can design systems to do certain things well – but they will then do other things less well (Skinner, 1969). When this is true, that original decision is very important, especially since the investment cost and the time and cost to make major changes of system structure will be significant. Nevertheless, it may be possible to reduce these trade-offs in some way. If customer satisfaction is improved, then this improvement will be an important aspect of competitive advantage. This is what the best organisations try to do. They challenge the assumptions underlying the trade-offs and continually strive to do more with less while ensuring continuing and expanding customer support.

19.3 The operations function and its contribution

The operations function has been set in its historical context and some models have been provided of the balance between market need and supply capability. The chapter now examines how the operations function can support the rest of the business.

In what follows it is assumed that management has made decisions on product or service design. Ideally, it will have discussed the options with the operations function – but the marketing and design staff play the major role in that. The operations function can help ensure that people implement design decisions in a way that adds value to the business. The main contributions are in the areas of innovation, quality, delivery and cost.

Innovation

Innovation covers incremental and/or step change (breakthrough) changes in products and/or processes which change function, form, performance or resource use in an advantageous way.

In products, the impetus for a change can come from two sources. Market pull occurs when either customers make new demands on suppliers or when competitors try to change the strategic balance in some way. In some ways such developments are low-risk. It is likely that there will be a demand for the new product. It is also likely the product will be based on what is already known and understood, so the costs may be fairly easy to estimate. The danger is that such innovations are too incremental. That is to say that, while safe, they do not advance quickly enough to create a real advantage over the competition.

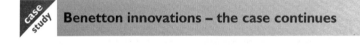

case study   **Benetton innovations – the case continues**

One famous innovation took place in 1972, at a time when the colours were still simple, i.e. one colour per garment and no complicated patterns. Traditionally, wool is dyed its final colour when it is still a yarn, i.e. a long time before being used in a garment and a long time ahead of actual customer demand. By designing a process to dye the completed garment, Benetton incurred some increased production costs but greatly reduced the cost of carrying the inventory of coloured garments formerly needed to react to customers' demands. Instead, the decision about colour was moved much closer to customers' buying decision thus removing much risk and complexity. It also meant that stocks that were selling well could be replenished, while stocks of less popular goods could be minimised.

As the company grew, it continued to rely on a network of subcontractors – often created by internal groups being encouraged to become independent contractors to Benetton. By 1987, only 5 per cent of final garment sewing assembly was done internally by Benetton.

Source: based on *Building the Benetton System*, European Case Clearing House, No. 390-042-1

Technology push is the other main force. Here an expert with an idea about what is possible proposes a new and often dramatic innovation. The danger is that no customer has yet requested this item, and many will not be able to express a need for it. Such innovations are inherently high-risk. There are no forecasts of market demand and no historical data for cost estimates. Many innovations of this type fail. Those that succeed, however, can change companies, industries and societies, as the Benetton case demonstrates. Only think of the photocopier, jet engine, scanning electron microscope to realise the importance of major breakthrough innovations. In reality, management needs to consider both possibilities. It can seek incremental innovation continuously while the essentially intermittent nature of a breakthrough needs different management approaches.

Technology is more likely to stimulate process innovation. Even here, multiple small changes can create wide competitive gaps if continued over a long period.

Organisations need innovation in products but, especially, in all processes, not just those in the production area. Many office systems and most service businesses repay a serious effort to redesign them in more effective ways. Telephone-based insurance companies have dramatically increased their market share by innovations in the way they deliver the service. Banking is going in the same direction.

Quality

In craft production the quality of output is crucial, for without it customers may not pay and will certainly not return. Craftspeople also tend to have pride in their work and continuously strive to improve their mastery of the craft. During the evolution of the factory system this ideal suffered as management subdivided the work process. Management separated quality approval from production. Even quality control charts were tools for quality inspectors not production workers.

During the 1950s the Americans sent a number of their statisticians to Japan to help rebuild their productive capability. The Japanese learned from W.E. Deming (Deming, 1988), Joseph Juran (Juran, 1974), Armand Feigenbaum (Feigenbaum, 1993) and others and applied the lessons well, conscientiously and extensively. They did, however, recognise the fundamental truth of craft production – that the person who performs the transformation is the best person to ensure quality is correct at the moment of its performance. History has thus come full circle, with individuals taking pride in doing quality work and striving to make regular improvements.

Another realisation is that quality and customer satisfaction are responsibilities for all in the business and not simply the producer at the end of the chain. Each customer throughout the chain must receive top quality performance. This is a message top management must believe in and then act on accordingly.

The Noticeboard brings together the main features of total quality management. The underpinning philosophy is the recognition that not having perfect quality wastes resources. Some of these wastes are obvious – scrapped material through equipment failure – but other wastes come through bad systems or poor communications and may be more difficult to find and measure. The other aspect of this philosophy is that a constant effort to

Quality of a product or service is the (often imprecise) perception of a customer that what has been provided is at least what was expected for the price he or she paid.

NOTICEBOARD **Principles of total quality management**

- **Philosophy** Waste reduction through continuous improvement
- **Leadership** Committed and visible from top to bottom of the organisation
- **Measurement** Costs involved in quality failures – the cost of quality
- **Scope** Everyone, everywhere across whole supply chain
- **Methods** Use of simple control and improvement techniques implemented by teams

remove these wastes pays dividends. Progressive, small improvements repay mightily from both customer satisfaction and revenue viewpoints. They also reduce costs as the system uses resources more effectively. Leadership of a visible and tangible type is needed to keep the efforts going. It also avoids a tendency to consider delivery of any product as more important than the delivery of the correct product. Philip Crosby introduced the idea that 'quality is free': it is getting it wrong which costs money (Crosby, 1979). Costs are incurred for quality in four areas:

- Prevention (getting the systems right)
- Appraisal (measuring how the systems are performing)
- Internal failure (faults found during checks inside the operation)
- External failure (faults found by users – the worst kind)

Quality will never be completely free because of the investment in prevention. It is clear, however, that switching proportionately more resources into prevention cuts other costs such that the total reduces.

To make this happen, management cannot allow a division of labour. Everyone has to take responsibility for his or her proportion of the quality effort. This includes those people outside the organisation who nevertheless contribute towards the total quality of the supply chain. Thus the whole supply chain must function as a total quality system. Methods used include simple descriptive statistics, brainstorming techniques and simple statistical process controls (Oakland, 1994). The people performing the transformation are the ones trained and encouraged to use these tools and they will often display the results in their work area to spur further improvement. In this they will work as a team, calling on different people to support them as required.

At company levels, the team can try for a number of awards. The Deming prize in Japan set the tone, with high prestige enjoyed by the winners. In America, the Baldrige Quality Award has set a pattern of very wide-ranging definitions of quality, and this has been influential on the equivalent European Quality Awards. At a more local level, various national standards for quality are often demanded of organisations to qualify as approved providers of goods or services. The key is not the award but the thought processes of all the people in the organisation and their commitment to the total quality ideals.

An important consideration is the leverage effect of thinking about quality at the design stage. This stage can create or avoid problems later. It is best that choices here incorporate ideas and information from as many insiders, customers and suppliers as is sensible. Such processes capture the prevention and right-first-time ideals and create cost- and time-saving opportunities.

Waste minimisation is the goal. Waste is any use of resources that does not contribute to the sum of value-adding activity as evaluated by the customer. Note, however, that customers are not the only stakeholders. It may be that an activity is justified for reasons other than those directly related to the requirements of a direct customer. Environmental considerations fall into this category, as do those based on legislation. If an activity is justified then we still need to ask the following questions:

▶ Who is doing it?

▶ How is it being done?

▶ Where and at what time is it done?

We also need to investigate alternative ways of meeting requirements. These questions form the basic approach of method study suggested by the Gilbreths many decades ago.

Many western organisations have been trying to catch up with best Japanese experience and practice in understanding and applying the lessons of quality control. They will have active measurement and improvement programmes in place, but many will not yet be paying the same attention to delivery.

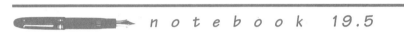

n o t e b o o k   19.5

Define what quality means in the following: (a) a fast-food hamburger restaurant, (b) a five star hotel, (c) an executive automobile, (d) a travel agency, (e) the products sold by Benetton, (f) the service provided by Benetton sales staff.

Delivery

A point made before is worth repeating here. Each link in the chain of supply from raw material to final consumer is formed between an individual or group acting as a customer to a supplier. The customer is in turn the supplier to another. Thus the next customer along the chain immediately feels any failure in quality, unless large amounts of inventory hide the failure. This is a direct benefit of reducing inventory: it exposes quality problems so that people can deal with them permanently.

Benetton innovations – the case continues

The fashion cycle for the important spring/summer season begins in February with selection of around 500 items. During May–July, small samples are produced to allow retailers a chance to place orders for the season seven months ahead. As the first orders roll in, production plans are made and subcontractors informed. The shop owners are then obliged to buy the goods produced as Benetton does not accept any returned goods unsold at the end of the season. Most of the shop orders are delivered between November and the following May as the Basic collection in readiness for the new season. The balance of the orders fall into two categories: 'Flash' consists of reactions to new trends or competitor offerings while 'Reassortment' allows for individual choice of produce mix in a particular store, and possibly for those late-dyed popular colours.

Thus the operations system has to cope with fairly stable production runs of the 'standard order' for 80–90 per cent and 'specials' on a much faster response time for the late variations.

Source: based on *Building the Benetton System*, European Case Clearing House, No. 390-042-1

d Delivery relates to the achievement of all promises made by any supplier to a customer.

As with quality, so with delivery. Any failure to supply the customer when expected causes the wastes of delay, remedial action and wasted effort. There is therefore a priority of need for delivery performance. The first is total reliability. Every downstream customer is dependent on every upstream supplier fulfilling his or her delivery promise, otherwise – more waste. Every chain needs reliability, but sometimes it also needs speedy delivery. Speed is crucial when a company is bringing a new product to the market. It wants to make sales to early adopters before competitors can produce alternatives which will drive the price down. In competitive situations, speed of response may be the distinguishing factor that wins the order. Figure 19.3 captures the relative timescales on the supply and demand side.

d Demand leadtime is the elapsed time that a customer is prepared to allow between placing an order for a product or service and actually receiving it; in certain situations this time is effectively zero.
Supply leadtime is the total elapsed time between first decision to obtain the basic input resources to the final delivery of the product or service to the customer.

Figure 19.3 considers the case of a manufactured product that has a customer prepared to wait some time between placing and receiving the order – the demand leadtime. Note that in some markets, for example retail, this time is zero. That is, supply has to be instantaneous (off the shelf) or the buyer goes elsewhere or selects another product. In most manufacturing situations the addition of all the supply-side activities that constitute the supply leadtime far exceeds the demand leadtime. The critical fact is that all of the investment tied up in decisions to the left of the order placement point are at risk. In these areas there is no guarantee that a customer will place an order. So there is continual pressure to reduce the time needed on the supply side of the balance. Ideally, the supply total would be less than the demand total. That would guarantee sales success, but only markets producing customised products to order are like this.

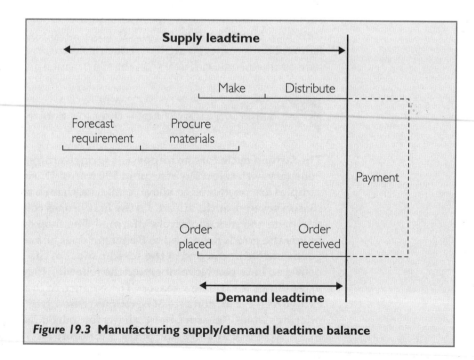

Figure 19.3 **Manufacturing supply/demand leadtime balance**

Demand leadtime is the elapsed time that a customer is prepared to allow between placing an order for a product or service and actually receiving it; in certain situations this time is effectively zero.

Supply leadtime is the total elapsed time between first decision to obtain the basic input resources to the final delivery of the product or service to the customer.

In service businesses the situation is different since the customer must be present during the service (see Figure 19.4). The service processing time will extend through the need to provide capacity (people and equipment) plus any consumable materials needed for the service. Generally there is likely to be a closer balance. Here, however, the customer perception of what is an acceptable service time can produce difficulties for the supply system if the system cannot match expectations effectively.

One of the most effective ways to reduce the supply leadtime in any linked supply chain is to consider the flow of materials through to the final customer as the real challenge. The task then is to synchronise all of the tributary flows into the main stream to maximise the main flow and minimise waste. Such synchronisation calls for co-ordinated effort in scheduling deliveries from internal and external suppliers according to an integrated master plan and reinforces the need for absolute control of quality and delivery performance.

n o t e b o o k   19.6

Consider the total supply leadtime for a bridal dress made from Chinese silk. List and guess the timescales for the different stages of production and supply up to the final garment being made for the bride.

Cost

There is no disputing the need for the real cost of a transformation process to reduce with time. If organisations continually innovate to improve their systems and remove waste, and given that the learning effect of operating

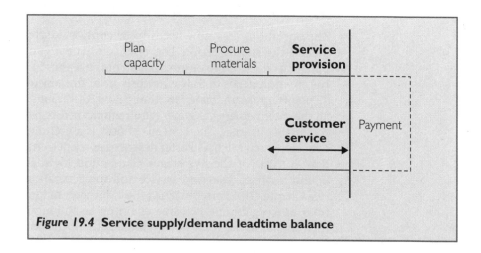

Figure 19.4 Service supply/demand leadtime balance

Cost expresses in money units the effect of activating or consuming resources. It is an internal control process of the producing organisation and is not visible to outside parties.

the systems also reduces waste and time taken, then cost should decrease. There is, however, a preferred sequence. An organisation must first build a solid base of quality performance and reinforce it with careful control over delivery. Doing these things correctly will lead to lower cost. If, on the other hand, the organisation tries to reduce costs and simply take resources away, this is likely to lower overall quality and delivery performance.

Cost is also an internal factor which customers do not always need to know. What they need to understand is what pricing possibilities the organisation can offer as a result of its performance on cost reduction.

It is also important that an organisation does not concentrate solely on the direct money aspect of the business transaction since many of the factors which go towards creating a satisfied customer will not necessarily be reflected in the unit price quoted for the good or service. The total acquisition cost of a supplied good or service tries to capture all of the direct and less tangible costs to make properly informed decisions. Traditional methods of allocating overheads used in cost accounting do not help this judgement (Kaplan and Norton, 1996). Such approaches base the calculations on hours worked by direct labour. In many businesses these are among the least significant costs. In manufacturing, materials costs will be 60–70 per cent and direct labour around 5–10 per cent of the total. Inappropriate costing information makes decisions about whether to make items in-house or to buy them from an outside supplier difficult and prone to error. In similar fashion, getting meaningful data to establish a true cost of quality is difficult. Typical numbers are 30 per cent of sales turnover as cost of unquality, reducing to around 10 per cent for the best performers; but most organisations do not and cannot know the correct answer to this question.

Cost information is, however, crucial to sensible decision-making. Cost accounting professionals are developing alternative systems known as activity-based cost management. These try to tie the numbers into the real world of activities that consume resources and thereby incur cost. The world of business keeps score by means of money, but the reality is in the activity of the business which adds the value for which customers are happy to pay.

The operations function has an important role to play as part of the supply chain team which delivers the goods and/or services in the most effective manner.

Synchronisation and flow

The operations area now needs to be considered as part of the much wider idea of the supply chain. The essence of the argument about delivery reliability is the need to ensure that all of the wastes in the chain are removed. Information needs to flow efficiently from the consumer to the producers at all points upstream. Materials should flow continuously downstream to satisfy all the intermediate customer requirements before passing from the chain to the final consumer. The concept of flow is a useful one. It is implied in the concept which Michael Porter describes as a value chain. Here the horizontal flow consists of the five stages of inbound logistics, transformation, outbound logistics, sales and service and the generation of a financial margin (see Chapter 10). Porter extends the value system idea to include the output from one organisation's value chain being the input to another one. It is then similar to the supply chain model described above (Porter, 1980b).

The key part of this concept is that final consumers want to receive their chosen goods as they require them without hindrance or problem. So organisations need to make the flow as smooth, speedy and consistent as possible. Anything interfering with this smooth flow is a waste, causing customer dissatisfaction. Speed of flow also brings financial benefits: the quicker the flow becomes a sale, the quicker the company can recover the investment incurred in supply. Inventory or material turnover rates become a measure of effective use of resources and a measure of the speed and fluency of the flow. The definition of this measure is the ratio of sales turnover to the value of inventory held in stock in the system. Depending on the sector, this number can range from low single digits in capital goods production to many hundreds in food retail.

CASE QUESTIONS 19.3

▶ Consider the supply leadtime for the Benetton Basic collection and for the Flash or Reassignment goods. What is the demand leadtime for each of these categories?

The earlier discussion about forms of physical layout associated with different transformations described the functional layout. The objective was not to aim at efficient flow of materials or people but to maximise the efficient use of the functional equipment. This is contrary to the concepts of flow described here and demonstrates why such an approach is inherently costly. However, it still demonstrates another aspect of this approach. In the functional form, inventory buffers between process stages separate the stages and allows them to operate at their most efficient rate. The corollary is that, to enable flow processes it is necessary to couple the processing rates such that they produce at the same rate even if this means at the rate of the slowest. This is called synchronised flow and is essential to remove the inventory buffers. The choice being made is that the business benefit of flow outweighs the occasionally inefficient processing speeds of some parts of the linked chain. In other words, the emphasis is on designing the system to satisfy the end customer effectively rather than having individual sections run efficiently.

This concept lies behind the just-in-time (JIT) system of production where the total quality management (TQM) and synchronised flow approaches are coupled with a cross-trained and committed workforce to produce very effectively (Schonberger, 1983). The synchronisation is not internal to just one organisation, and so managements try to establish a complete supply chain working collaboratively on this basis.

To make synchronisation possible, management has to attack the problem that led to a functional focus. This is the traditional view that the best way to make a financial return on a piece of equipment is to keep it producing. The new thinking is that the equipment has to support the flow and no more. Thus, if the output is already sufficient then the process should stop and not build inventory for which there is no immediate demand. Management also needs to attack the thought that if it is expensive to change over from one production run to another then it should do this less often, in other words it should produce large quantities before changing.

This builds those costly inventories again. A better approach is to reduce the costs of changing, so that the pressure for large production runs is no longer there. Management can then approach the just-in-time ideal of making a little of everything every day. When this is achieved, the system can produce to customer order with no delays and no inventory.

Cost reduction

Price is external to organisations and determined by conditions and perceptions in the marketplace. Cost, on the other hand, is a wholly internal measure which is meant to capture the consumption of resources to create the opportunity to sell. Cost is therefore an outcome of doing other things, those other things necessarily being the ones that use the resources which have to be paid for from cash flow or other finance.

The market price arises from a negotiation between buyer and seller. Reducing the internal costs of production or service increases the room within which the seller can negotiate. If the seller does not need this space to reduce the selling price, then the profit margin rises. Management encourages any change in supply conditions which reduce costs.

Management should approach such cost reduction possibilities with care. The preferred sequence of ensuring quality at source and managing the delivery performance to enable cost reductions was discussed earlier. It is very easy to think of apparent cost reduction actions that could adversely affect the ability of a system to satisfy customers – even though they reduce costs.

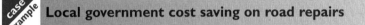 **Local government cost saving on road repairs**

Following a budget reduction, a local authority reduced the number of staff working on road repairs. Vehicle repair bills increased as road conditions became worse. This shows the difficulties in discussing cost reduction. First, the cost reduction happened quickly and was very visible in one system's performance indicators (i.e. the local government group). The negative impact of the change took longer to become evident and did not appear inside the target group's indicators. Someone else paid for the extra repair costs. The road user customers are less than satisfied.

The Case Example also demonstrates that the impact of a decision does not fall in only one organisation. There is no mechanism by which all the interested parties can come together to decide a more sensible course of action. Instead each tries to maximise its performance at the expense of an effective solution for all.

This form of system awareness is important when possible cost reductions in the supply system are considered. Each organisation or unit has an interest in supporting both the immediate and the final customer. Each also has to look good in terms of its own current performance. The difficulty is that sometimes the best supply chain solution means that one part operates less efficiently (from a local perspective) to improve overall chain performance.

The classic description of this relates to the ideal specifications for the production area and the sales area. The manufacturing stereotype is a preference for long runs of a standard product. The sales stereotype is a preference for providing unique products which meet particular customer requirements. There has to be a balance. It is possible for an organisation to become bankrupt satisfying customer requirements that it is not designed to satisfy, so the maxim cannot be 'customer satisfaction at all costs' since some costs are unacceptable.

Thus cost reduction is a continuing necessity but needs to be done with care. Suppliers can reduce some costs without any impact on the customer simply by doing things more smartly. It is well established that, by repeated application to a task, skill levels increase and actions become automatic and more rapid. This learning curve effect allows staff to estimate the reduced time needed to produce in future. Continuous improvement enhances skill in this sense. If an improvement involves a radical redesign of the work pattern then old rhythms may inhibit this new knowledge. They become barriers to change.

Other cost reduction areas internal to organisations involve the time to change over production or service from one type to another. Management can initiate much of this at little capital cost. Staff can apply some basic industrial engineering principles to analyse where value is added. They can then redesign the process to eliminate waste caused by bad planning, organisation, equipment and inefficient motion.

One waste worth challenging is the amount of material held in the various categories of stock. By re-examining where to hold protection stocks and eliminating all others, a supplier can make large savings at no risk to customer service.

C A S E   Q U E S T I O N S   1 9 . 4

▶ Examine the points in the Benetton supply chain where inventory is stored and identify why it is likely to be held there.

The major leverage point for cost reduction is, however, at the initial design stage. Staff make decisions here that incur costs later. Thus by thinking through both quality and operational logistics issues at this stage it is possible to avoid creating unnecessary costs at the source.

19.4 Business process view

The concept of flow as horizontal through the organisation is opposed to the vertical orientation of traditional organisational principles based around functions. This is in accord with a greater focus on customers and their satisfaction. Customers have little interest in their suppliers' internal organisation except when they come into contact with it. Then they would be satisfied if the contact person could truly act on behalf of the whole organisation. The functional structure reflects the same thought patterns which lead to the functional layout discussed earlier. Both optimise internally regardless of the effect on the customer.

To escape from this mindset, organisations are trying to restructure their activities around basic business processes that all organisations will use to

The business process view puts satisfying customers' requirements at the heart of a design process to develop a supply system which will operate without waste. The orientation is towards speed of response and two-way flow of information and other resources.

meet their customers' requirements. By defining these in as generic and general terms as possible they hope to create new insights. The essence of flow also means removing the waste from the interfaces between the traditional functional silos. Since organisations are unique, there are no universally accepted definitions of these core processes. They will vary between organisations. Some common major processes are outlined here and the main points of consideration indicated.

Create and capture customers' intent to buy the product or service

This process recognises the two sources of innovation – technology push or market pull – and uses either or both to define new product or service packages to bring to the customer market. Defined as a business process this will cover activities often associated in the past with marketing, product design, prototype production, trial marketing, and product advertising and launch. The creative process is intended to bring together all of the interests associated with a forward look at customers. The aim is to fully define their requirements. In the case of truly innovative ideas, the intention is to specify the product or service in a way that determines what the operations systems have to do to support these new market requirements.

Customer order fulfilment

Having created the intention to buy, this process does everything necessary to deliver the product or service to the customer. It aims to do this in such a way that the transaction satisfies both the customer and the supply system.

The process starts with capturing a customer order or with planned production against a demand forecast. If the latter is the case, it will also encompass the forecasting process. From here it will cover all of the planning stages that allocate resources to produce and deliver the order. It also recognises the need to source resources from other suppliers in the chain. Thus the traditional functions of sales processing and forecasting, production planning and control, manufacture or service provision and resource procurement (buying) can all be included. So too can those concerned with the physical movement of materials and ensuring people are available to do the work. The flows in this process are clearly two-way: from customers to supply system about demand, and from supply system to customers with the order. The flow returns again with money to pay for the exchange. There are many interfaces between activities in this business process often acting in very short timescales, and clearly this is one of the major (direct) value-adding sets of activities in the organisation.

Depending on the nature of the demand (a forecast or a firm customer order) the planning process can be aimed either at building inventory or at meeting the customer order. Speed is not always necessary, although delivery reliability is. In building for inventory, management strikes a balance between the costs of making a large and economical batch now and the costs of holding stocks of finished goods. If it produces too much for immediate requirements it has to store and care for the product until sold. The *economic order quantity* (EOQ) can be calculated by making assumptions about actual cost patterns. Management can then establish and manage stockholding policies.

Computerised planning approaches are appropriate when demand is known or can be calculated. If demand for a higher level of product assembly is available, companies use the simple arithmetical logic of material requirements planning (MRP). This calculates the quantities of lower-level components that the assembly area will need. This logic takes the demand for the higher-level assemblies of parts and explodes this into the demand for the components. Every order for a family car will generate an order for five wheels. Planners then add to this how long they believe it will take to produce or purchase the wheels. They can then decide when they need to place an order for the earlier parts of the supply system. They can also take into account the number of items already in stock or due for delivery based on earlier orders. They then use an arithmetic calculation to decide whether they need to ask for additional production and when they require it.

The just-in-time approach omits the computer calculations. It replaces them with a simple 'pull' signal sent when a customer removes some material from the end of the previous stage of the supply chain. This action sends a replenishment signal (a *kanban*) upstream telling the supplier to produce replacement parts. The signal can then ripple its way upstream and, ideally, the supply chain then operates quickly and with a much reduced level of inventory compared with both of the other ways described.

In a pure service operation where storage of the service is not an option, the order fulfilment process is different. It concentrates on planning and scheduling service staff to ensure that they are available to deal with the customers as they arrive.

Cash handling and reporting

Transactions to transfer the ownership of goods or to pay for services must be properly accounted for. It is also necessary to create an audit trail to establish that the activities have been done legally. This process also provides the funds with which the organisation pays its own bills. More businesses fail through mismanaging their cash flow than fail for lack of customers. This is another reason to look for speed through the business processes in order to convert customer interest into cash. The problem with the traditional ways of accounting are that they do not recognise the speed of transactions in an efficient supply chain. The final customers may have had the goods for weeks. Suppliers in the chain may still be waiting for payment. Supermarkets are prime examples of this – they receive cash or credit transfers almost instantaneously but only pay their suppliers on terms that might be thirty days from the date of the invoice. They therefore have the opportunity to earn interest on both sets of money in the short-term financial marketplace. It is perhaps not surprising that the larger retail chains are providing their own banking opportunities for their customers. In some ways they have been behaving as banks for years. At the same time they have been highly efficient at converting shelf space to sales with minimum in-store inventory.

In previous days, each movement of material or service delivery required paper to record the transaction. There were many copies, signatures, checks for accuracy and cross-checks to other documents. This employed many people who added little of value to the customer. New ways of working eliminate much of this in favour of simplified techniques and place greater responsibility on the suppliers to do what they have contracted to do without the customer doing all the checking. For example, in the car wheel example, all cars leaving the assembler's premises must have five wheels. Rather than arrange a transaction for each delivery of wheels, common practice now is to record the number of cars leaving the system (which is done anyway). The system multiplies that number by five and regularly pays the supplier for that number of wheels. As an alternative, for low-value items all purchasers can be issued with the equivalent of a plastic bank card so that orders can be sent in, deliveries made and a fully detailed statement sent to the purchasing organisation at the end of the month for one payment.

Much of traditional financial accounting is more about external reporting to shareholders, tax authorities and other interested parties and this requirement does not diminish. Accountants recognise the need to provide more timely and targeted data to support the internal decision-makers. They are working to link actual activity to the resources used in the activity in a more realistic way. Such activity-based cost management would be a significant forward step to support the supply chain since so many of the costs are not easily visible to managers in the chain.

Maintaining service

In different forms of product market, the ongoing commitment to support the product in use is increasingly a factor to be considered. In some cases, an attempt to limit the responsibility is made, for example a limited duration warranty, but in others the time can be extended – it can be over twenty years for defence-related equipment. In some markets the life of the product is in effect extended indefinitely under a 'design, build and maintain' contract for hospitals or roads. Current UK government initiatives in construction are aimed at sharing the immediate risk and future maintenance cash flow in a partnership between the public and private sectors.

In other product areas, management has come to realise the cost of retaining a customer as against finding a new one (usually assumed to be a ratio of one-to-ten). This has caused them to re-examine the nature of the customer relationship and to support valued customers well beyond any contractual or warranty requirement.

In service areas, the degree of direct involvement with the client or customer changes the nature of the considerations again. The arguments about customer retention are even more important in this environment and often there will be a need to keep in regular contact (special newsletters, magazines, offers) to try to keep the relationship going.

In all cases, current customers have great value in evaluating new product or service ideas at the trial market stage. They also help secure new customers through recommendations and contact names. This will be the case particularly where the price for a single transaction is not the most important factor in the buying decision.

Resource development

Organisations employ very many resources to enable their success and there is a requirement to both maintain and enhance that capability. The range includes equipment, people and systems.

The role of equipment varies in significance. Some equipment is central to the business, some fairly marginal as far as the customer is concerned. Equipment has to be appropriate for current requirement while not providing problems in terms of future needs. The rate of technological changes brings the danger of not having recovered the capital investment in the equipment before having to upgrade to the next generation. Often the changes in the equipment happen faster than the supply system can respond. The system is then continually trying to catch up or trying to jump ahead in a risky venture with unproved technology.

People are the only factor of production that competitors cannot replicate. All others can be purchased, given time and money. An organisation's staff and the way they work are the most important differentiators in competitive markets. Many organisations repeat these words in annual reports, but often the reality of how they treat this resource is well short of the rhetoric they employ. In most organisations the trend away from muscle power to brain power is well established. In a changing world, only the better organisations clearly recognise the continual need to re-educate and develop. Part of the problem is that the costs are in the short term. People in training are not meeting immediate customer requirements. Such activities are investments for the future: without them the company may not be able to meet the needs of future customers. The form of training and development also changes. It moves from a focus on current operating skills to those of analysis and improvement. It also stresses team-based processes and the ability to work with new technologies.

The third major area of resource development is in systems development. This covers the ways in which people choose to work as well as hardware- and software-based systems, and this change in working practice is an example of systems development in practice. Organisations perceived a problem of customer dissatisfaction with existing methods of organising and created new systems to meet these needs with the horizontal flow based approach discussed earlier. At one level, this is simply a reorganisation of people into new groupings, but it often means redesigning the information systems that gather, analyse and support decision processes. Thus some of the gurus of the business re-engineering approach stress the role of IT. New systems make possible the radical changes in organising people that allow for major break-throughs in operating performance (Champy and Hammer, 1993).

n o t e b o o k   1 9 . 7

Describe the organisations or groups of people who constitute the supply chains delivering: (a) double glazing windows to domestic customers, (b) home banking services, (c) clothes to Benetton, (d) fresh food produce to Marks and Spencer's.

While there is great merit in appropriate command and control systems, a further dimension of systems thinking is also coming to the fore. Viewing the supply chain as interdependent and co-ordinated raises awareness and the field of vision to outside the boundary of a single organisation. This requires a form of systems thinking to recognise the interactions and their implications as well as to challenge existing solutions and recipes.

Organisations can thus move from single-loop learning to double-loop (Argyris and Schon, 1978) and build a future-oriented capability to further enhance their supply system's competitiveness.

19.5 Interfaces with other functions – partnering in the supply chain

In traditionally structured organisations, the operations function has many interfaces as it contributes to nearly all crucial decisions relating to business performance. In some of these, the operations function will be in a distinctly subordinate position, in others more to the fore. The aim should be to meet business requirements by satisfying the customer at the end of the chain. To do this, all parts of the organisation need to understand each other's strengths and weaknesses. They then need to build a system that recognises the first and improves on the second. The new way of looking at the needs of the business in terms of the business processes recognises explicitly the need to manage across boundaries. Most commonly, change teams focus on processes that cross department functions. Some also review processes that cross the boundaries between organisations into (upstream) suppliers or (downstream) to the customers.

The argument here is that certain parts of the chain are experts at their portion of the total task. Those at other stages should allow them to perform those tasks without interference from arrogant customers telling them what to do. Those in the chain need to manage the relationships so that the chain as a whole meets the needs of the final customer. So the tasks are now about influence, information and co-ordination between independent but co-operating organisations. This is a different form of management from that which exercises command and control within an isolated business. It is also about encouraging, recognising and implementing innovation from all in the chain to the chain's competitive advantage and the ultimate customers' delight.

When separate organisations use this approach they often refer to it as partnering (Macbeth and Ferguson, 1994). The logic applies to all management activities that cross boundaries, not only those with different ownership. The essence is to recognise complementary capabilities, look for ways to co-ordinate informational and logistical flows and to invest for the long term in a jointly planned way.

Partnering describes a business relationship based on taking a long-term view that the partners wish to work together according to a mutually acceptable vision in ways which enhance all customers' satisfaction levels. The partners also seek to develop the relationship so that each will benefit in recognised business performance areas.

> ## CASE QUESTIONS 19.5
>
> ▶ What would a partnering approach imply for Benetton's management?
> ▶ What benefits might the company obtain from such a practice?
> ▶ What benefits might its suppliers and franchisees obtain?
> ▶ What could be the obstacles?

This recognises that internal competition is no longer the only way to demonstrate value for money. Rather it is about demonstrating that by removing the wastes from the chain the whole chain becomes more competitive than other chains. Working together increases the chances of success and of obtaining the rewards of success. It is not a comfortable or easy option since the pressures to stay expert in each area are intense. The need to innovate constantly to reduce waste further and to enhance the offer to the final consumers is unrelenting. In addition, the need to fully support the partner organisation creates its own dynamic pressure.

In order to make this a reality, partners must be chosen carefully. The parties then need to create joint teams to address, in a planned manner, areas where improvements can be made that benefit both sides. They also need to measure and reward joint performance in new and creative ways (Supply Chain Management Group, 1995). In all of this they aim to apply the essential operations management practices that have been described across all aspects of the joint organisations. Companies have to be best in class in three areas: inside each of the partner organisations and in the areas of explicitly joint responsibility.

The future orientation of the partnering process means that each has a responsibility to scan its field of expertise and interest. The customer organisation has to keep sight of developments in its own marketplace. It has to get close to its customers and watch its competitors' movements. It must also watch for new entrants with developments that threaten the whole chain. The supplier should scan its environment in a similar way. In particular, it should look for new technologies that might improve service to the immediate and ultimate customer. In this view, organisations, departments and individual people are both customers of and suppliers to others. While the roles may take a different importance at different times, the responsibility to manage proactively in both directions is not diminished.

19.6 Strategic position of operations

Section 19.5 has demonstrated a new realisation of the importance of the operations function in an integrated approach to managing the supply system in support of the customer. The key questions relate to the capabilities that the system needs currently and which should be developed for future requirements. A related issue is the selection of those complementary suppliers who can provide the other aspects of the product or service, and finally the choice of market segments in which to compete. This latter decision might still be more influenced by factors associated with financial returns and market positioning. The broad nature of the operations activity means that making these decisions without reference to the ability of the system to respond and change will in turn make it difficult to achieve the objectives.

Customer demands in the markets usually change faster than production systems. These latter are made up of investments in hardware, software and people – not all of which can be changed rapidly. There needs to be an iterative process involving all interested parties deciding what the company must do well in order to succeed in the market. The concepts of order winners and order qualifiers can help to frame the discussion and bridge the language gap between the marketing and the operations staff (Hill, 1993).

An *order winner* is some feature or combination of features of the product and service that positively differentiates it from those of competitors and makes customers want to buy it in preference to those others. Ideally it is

An order winner is some feature or combination of features of the product or service that positively differentiates it from those of competitors and makes customers want to buy it in preference to those others.

An order qualifier is a necessary but not sufficient requirement to be considered by a customer.

something that is unique which competitors cannot replicate. An *order quali-fier* is the ticket to the game. It is a feature that is a necessary but not a sufficient requirement for purchase. Customers will not consider you without it. Qualifiers get the seller into the race but do not guarantee that it will win the prize. Some qualifiers are so critical that any deviation from the expected standard means instant disqualification. Customers will ignore otherwise attractive features if the seller does not meet this basic requirement.

These concepts are useful in opening up the debate between marketing and operations personnel since they can be defined in terms that both can understand. The operations staff can convert them into system specifications for process design once the parties agree them. It is also possible to rein in the wilder flights of fancy from marketers who see a new opportunity that the operations system has no prospect of satisfying in a sensible time. It is better to recognise this and to modify the target market than to risk everything to make a total change of operating system.

Of course, such order winners and qualifiers are dynamic. They change as customers become more demanding and as competitors become more proficient.

case example Japanese colour television production

When the Japanese producers of colour televisions first entered the European market they created the order winner of quality and produced at such an improved level that they captured a large market share. The European producers took up this competitive challenge and attempted to match the quality standards. Quality then became a qualifier and the Japanese moved the order winner to price. In doing so they further improved their competitive position. The Europeans had failed to understand and implement cost-efficient ways of ensuring quality, so they were unable to compete as they were spending more than the Japanese merely to reach the qualifying levels of quality. They were certainly not able to reduce their production costs enough to compete on price as well.

Thus the discussion of order winners and qualifiers needs to be a regular part of the chain process. Often it is a service-related feature that distinguishes qualified products. It is these aspects that are most likely to occur at the boundaries between traditional organisations. An integrated view of the whole supply chain helps management to improve them.

If all can produce at the qualifying level, the factors that will distinguish one competitor chain from another are various. They include the rate at which it can innovate in products, operational processes, service delivery and support, financing arrangements, recycling support or some other feature of value to customers. It is here, at the basic design stage, that management needs to harness all the expertise and creativity from wherever it originates. Thus the choice of partners in the chain becomes of great significance. Unless a customer organisation is prepared to be the sole customer of a sole supplier (and this is not usual), then suppliers have to supply a customer's competitors as well as themselves. The challenge is then to become a preferred customer to that preferred supplier in order to capture their innovative ideas for an agreed amount of time before the new knowledge is opened up to others. The way to do this is to build a business relationship as partners in a joint approach to future competitiveness. This means sharing the future vision and commitment in an integrative and collaborative venture delivering benefits to all in the chain and satisfaction to the final customers.

n o t e b o o k   19.8

Define the order winners and qualifiers for the following: (a) music, food and drink club catering for students, (b) a personal computer. Highlight those features most likely to change and comment on the implications for the operations system design needed to support them.

How might new communication technologies (for example, the Internet) affect the supply chain for food shopping?

19.7 Recap

Content agenda

Having set objectives and strategies, management is able to use ideas from the operations area in planning how to achieve them. Operations exists to develop systems that satisfy customers. Operations managers try to select the best mix of resources and types of transformation process to meet customer needs. Their particular contribution is in the areas of innovation, quality, delivery and cost. They also aim to secure a smooth flow through successive processes and to contribute towards worthwhile cost reductions. The current emphasis is to challenge conventional functional structures in favour of structures based on business processes. The perspective also emphasises the possibilities of working closely across organisational boundaries with partners. These may be at earlier and later points in the value chain.

Process agenda

There are stakeholders in functional areas and attempts to reorganise around business processes may threaten their interests. Operations stresses that management cannot divide responsibility for functions such as customer satisfaction and quality. Those at all stages in the supply chain are responsible and so should take part in decisions on those matters that affect them. Operations seeks to understand the links in the supply chain and to manage them in a more integrated way. To do this it creates mechanisms to bring the parties together to agree a solution that is most effective for all. It promotes system awareness, rather than narrow functional concentration.

Control agenda

Reducing waste in manufacturing or service processes depends on control. Systems theory emphasises the significance of feedback loops to measure,

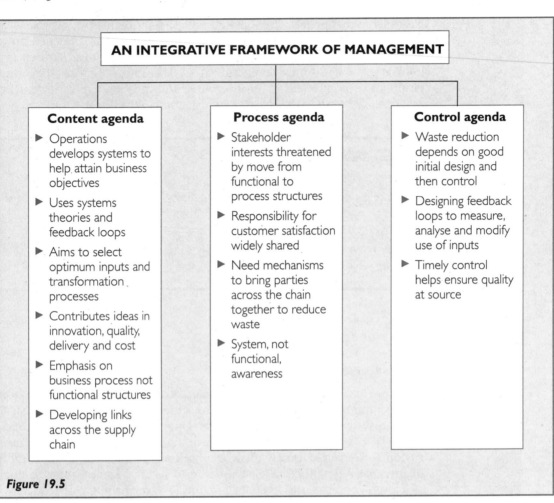

AN INTEGRATIVE FRAMEWORK OF MANAGEMENT

Content agenda
- Operations develops systems to help attain business objectives
- Uses systems theories and feedback loops
- Aims to select optimum inputs and transformation processes
- Contributes ideas in innovation, quality, delivery and cost
- Emphasis on business process not functional structures
- Developing links across the supply chain

Process agenda
- Stakeholder interests threatened by move from functional to process structures
- Responsibility for customer satisfaction widely shared
- Need mechanisms to bring parties across the chain together to reduce waste
- System, not functional, awareness

Control agenda
- Waste reduction depends on good initial design and then control
- Designing feedback loops to measure, analyse and modify use of inputs
- Timely control helps ensure quality at source

Figure 19.5

analyse and modify inputs. The earlier someone exercises control the cheaper it is to find and rectify problem areas. The discipline offers many techniques of control, such as critical path analysis and statistical process control. Control systems indicated the failures of functional organisations and led to the current emphasis on business processes.

The integrative framework is set out in Figure 19.5.

PART CASE QUESTIONS

- What were the main operational problems which Kwik-Fit management had to deal with as the company grew?
- What similarities and differences are there between Kwik-Fit's retail operation and that of Benetton?
- What are the major business processes in Kwik-Fit which are crucial to satisfying customer requirements?

19.8 Review questions

1 Describe systems concepts as they apply to an operating system.
2 What are the major categories of operations system and their associated physical layout types?
3 Why is control over quality at source so important?
4 Why is delivery reliability more important than delivery speed?
5 Describe and discuss the importance of the demand/supply balance.
6 In what ways is the business processes approach different from traditional approaches?
7 List and discuss the main features of a partnering approach to business relationships.
8 Discuss the concepts of order winners and order qualifiers.

Further reading

Brown (1996) provides much detail about operations management in a product environment and offers extra material about many of the concepts covered in this chapter. Womack and Jones (1996) develops the theme established in *The Machine that Changed the World* by Womack *et al.* (1990) which first comprehensively described the Toyota production system as clearly superior to other car assemblers' systems by means of a benchmarking study. It sets JIT, TQM and supply chain thinking in an integrated framework. The latest book uses a number of case examples.

Kay (1993) is a highly rated text on strategy but, interestingly, emphasises a number of key capabilities which are related to operations and the supply chain view as described here.

W Website addresses

Benetton   http://www.benetton.com
Benetton's Website gives a detailed account of the company's approach to its business processes and is worth visiting.

Severn Trent Water   http://www.severn-trentco-uk
Much of this chapter has been about managing quality. The Severn Trent Water site is unusual in giving much information on how the company measures water quality.

CONTENTS

AIM

To examine why managers need information and how they can use technology to make the most of this resource.

OBJECTIVES

By the end of your work on this chapter you should be able to outline the concepts below in your own terms and:

1   Explain the difference between data and information

2   Indicate the information which managers need to perform their tasks and responsibilities

3   Understand criteria which indicate the value of information

4   Explain the role of information systems in organisations

5   Describe different forms of information system

6   Summarise three ways of developing information systems and compare their suitability for particular situations

7   Compare alternative structures for the information systems function

8   Understand how information systems affect people in organisations

9   Explain how management can use information policy to support wider strategies

10   Discuss the potential impact of information systems on an organisation's strategy

St Antonius Hospital

Saint Antonius is a children's hospital linked to the medical faculty of a Dutch university. There are 500 beds and 12 separate medical departments. The hospital employs 700 people. There are 70 doctors, 100 medical assistants, 350 nurses and almost 200 non-medical staff.

Information Services (IS) is part of the finance department, simply because that was the first area to use computers. There are 30 employees in IS. Most have a technical background. Their main responsibility is to manage the systems and to maintain existing computer applications. These include: a system which stores data about patients, including treatments and their cost; the financial system which handles the financial settlement of treatments, calculating and sending out invoices and recording payments; and the personnel system that supports the payment of salaries and management information derived from these payments. These three applications run on a minicomputer networked to 200 terminals around the hospital. Both software and hardware are old and need a lot of maintenance. This takes up most of the time of the IS staff. They have neither capacity nor expertise to meet requests for new and improved applications. The head of the finance department is willing to improve this situation, but he will require a significantly higher budget.

The three directors clearly need more management information to help them with certain decisions. Financial reports are often out of date, which makes financial planning difficult. Simple questions about numbers of patients, costs of treatments and costs per patient are difficult to answer, as are questions from government bodies and insurance companies.

The directors feel insecure in the field of IT and depend on the information which the finance department provides. Improving the situation will be expensive, and they can only do so if they cut the budgets for other services.

There are also problems at the operational level. For example, parents sometimes complain that tests are being repeated on their children by different doctors because the doctors do not have each other's data. It is not always clear what medicines doctors have given and it is hard to get information on the comparative success of treatments. The medical departments criticise the support they receive from IS. Doctors complain that the central patient's file is unreliable: some refuse to co-operate with central systems, preferring to use their own computer or paper-based files. Several now use their budgets to buy personal computers (sometimes connected in small local networks) for administrative tasks within their department. Others use computers to support their medical work, for example in diagnosis or to record treatments given. As doctors have taken these initiatives independently, the hospital now has many incompatible software packages for these functions.

CASE QUESTIONS

- Make a list of the computer-based information systems mentioned in this case.
- What do you believe are the main objectives of each of these systems?
- What are the main problems that the organisation faces with its information systems? Distinguish between technological and human problems.

20.1 Introduction

This chapter introduces the following ideas:
- ► Information
- ► Information system
- ► Information system manager
- ► Operational system
- ► Electronic data interchange
- ► Monitoring system
- ► Decision support system
- ► Knowledge system
- ► Electronic mail
- ► Top-down system development
- ► Bottom-up system development
- ► Sociotechnical approach
- ► Information vision
- ► Information system plan

Managers can only carry out their role effectively if they receive accurate and timely information. Information systems make internal processes more efficient (for example by helping the accounts department to pay bills more easily). They also help to control the business functions in an integrated manner (for example by helping to relate sales orders to production and distribution plans). They often link an organisation with suppliers and customers (for example by passing production schedules easily from a customer to the suppliers). Managers need to be aware of this dependence and to ensure that their organisation has information systems to collect and use the necessary data. This information is now critically important to the strategy and competitiveness of many organisations. So while the design of information systems depends on the skills of information systems (IS) experts, management rarely leaves the whole design to them. It is a management task to ensure that the IS staff focus their skills on developing systems that serve the needs of the business. This responsibility has become much more widely spread in recent years as information technology (IT) itself has moved from the background to the foreground of organisations.

Between 1965 and 1975, organisations concentrated on automating those functions where they could make large efficiency gains. Typical targets were those which processed many routine transactions, such as payrolls, stock controls and invoices. Department managers often delegated responsibility for information management to an emerging IS department. These became skilled at running large, routine and usually centralised systems. This function became influential, and during this period, department managers were rarely involved. The technologies did not yet affect many smaller organisations. The objective of most applications was to process routine transactions more efficiently.

In the following decade, automated systems spread widely. In large organisations, more departments discovered the possibilities of IT and manufacturers developed systems that were suitable for smaller organisations. Technical developments made smaller systems possible and more attractive to managers in other parts of the organisation. The spread of technology in organisations allowed departmental managers to become more familiar with issues of budgeting for hardware, requesting support, defining requirements and prioritisation.

Since the mid 1980s, the IT environment in many organisations has changed significantly. Technical developments have brought information systems to the foreground of corporate policy. Systems that have supported for decades the core business functions of finance, manufacture and distribution continue to develop and employ more modern technology, but other business functions have also begun to receive attention. Suppliers of IT have expanded product lines to include more specific, even diverse, business functions of production forecasting, supplier rating and project management. IT is still expensive but the payback justifies the investment. Information technology often supports managers and professional staff directly. Non-technical staff or small business owners can access computer-based information.

Examples of such new developments are:

- the emergence of powerful and relatively cheap PCs,
- the ability to link these into networks (local and in a wider environment),
- the ability to link computer systems with those in other organisations to create interorganisational networks (also called electronic data interchange, EDI),
- using the Internet for electronic commerce,
- using information technologies for communication, for example e-mail, video-conferencing and desk-top conferencing systems,
- creating integrated databases that can be used in different applications at many levels throughout the organisation,
- increasing possibilities to support core processes with technology such as knowledge-based or process-automation systems; this may lead to a fundamental reconsideration of work processes.

These developments require departmental and other senior management to take an active role in the information systems of the organisation. The functionality, possibilities and value of information are greater than ever before. However, implementing systems effectively is not easy, as the Case Study shows. The hospital has inherited systems that have been rejected by the target users, who have adopted their own decentralised systems without integration – posing a problem for management.

---

n o t e b o o k   20.1

The media frequently report new software applications. Collect examples over the next week of new systems which seem likely to have implications for how people manage their organisations. Compare notes with other students and decide which of the systems you have found is likely to be of the greatest organisational significance over the next two years.

This chapter begins with a discussion of the role and value of information in organisations and describes different kinds of system. Section 20.2 examines the role of information in organisations, while section 20.3 outlines the different forms of information system that are used. Later sections focus on computer-based information systems, especially their function, scope and implementation. The final section considers how management can use IT for the strategic benefit of the organisation.

20.2 Role of information in organisations

What is information?

Organisations store and process large amounts of data, which they may or may not convert into useful information. This depends on the organisation's ability to collect data that provides useful information to departmental managers.

Figure 20.1 shows the relation between data, information and information systems.

Historically, people recorded data on paper, transformed it into information and presented it on paper. Now, information systems are more likely to use electronic means to record, transform, store and often present information. Figure 20.2 shows the elements of a computerised information system.

Each element in Figure 20.2 is present in, for example, a computerised student record system in a university. This system requires people (for example, clerical staff) to enter data (name and other information about students and their results) according to certain procedures. For example, there is a rule that only employees may enter data on student results. Students are not permitted to do this. Another rule is that a student cannot graduate unless the system confirms that the student has paid his or her fees and library fines.

The hardware consists of the computers and peripherals such as printers, monitors and keyboards. This runs the student record system (the software) to print out the results for each student. Another procedure sends results to each student. For the students, this periodical statement is information. The management of the department might want to know the pass rates of all the courses – so this then becomes an element of the university's management information.

Value of information

The quality of information depends on four main criteria:

▶ **Reliability (accuracy)** If a railway timetable changes by only 10 per cent, most people will see the old timetable as highly unreliable. If only a small part of the information provided in a document is inaccurate, people will see the quality of the whole source as low and treat it with suspicion.

▶ **Timeliness** Information is only useful if it is available in time. A manager who needs to keep expenditure within a set budget requires cost

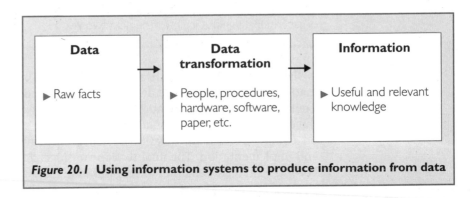

Figure 20.1 **Using information systems to produce information from data**

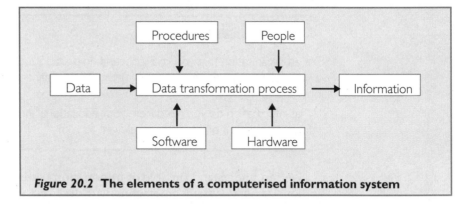

Figure 20.2 **The elements of a computerised information system**

information frequently enough to be able to act on any unfavourable trends – getting the information three months later will be too late.
▶ **Right quantity**   Many managers suffer information overload, in the sense that they are not able to digest and use all the information they receive as a basis for action – there is simply too much of it. This may suggest that the data have not been processed to a format or level of detail suitable for managerial action.
▶ **Relevance**   This depends on the tasks and responsibilities a person has. A manager who has a daily responsibility for production wants a daily report about production numbers, waste percentages, etc. A senior manager, however, may prefer more aggregated data about production and future plans. A student only perceives a schedule of lectures within his or her field of study as relevant information.

C A S E   Q U E S T I O N S   20.1

▶ Does the hospital have problems with any of these four value criteria?
▶ Make a list showing systems that fail to meet at least one criterion.

To illustrate the criterion of relevance, Figure 20.3 indicates the difference in information needs of senior managers and operational managers who are responsible for the daily work of the organisation (Gorry and Scott-Morton, 1971).

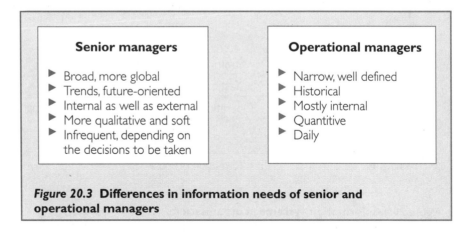

Figure 20.3 **Differences in information needs of senior and operational managers**

For an organisation that you know or can find out about, give a specific example of a piece of information that is useful (a) for a senior manager, and (b) for an operational manager.

What information do you need from your educational institution? What information does it provide that is relevant to you?

We can understand the role of information better by thinking of organisations as open systems interacting with their environment. Refer back to Figure 19.1 in the previous chapter which shows this model. To manage this system adequately, managers need information, and Figure 20.4 shows an open systems model with the information flows emphasised. The information systems which provide this information (represented by double lines) can be of many kinds. They could be the manager's own informal system or a company-wide system that collects internal and external data. Examples of internal data are productivity numbers, quality rates of products, inventory levels and staff turnover. External data could be about suppliers, customer preferences, market share and economic trends.

Apply the open system model to a business that you know, for instance to a school or a university. What are the outputs? What are the inputs? Describe the transformation process. What information do managers at various levels need to manage the business?

Applying this approach to the Case Study, the output of the hospital is (usually) healthy patients. Inputs are sick patients, but also medicines, equip-

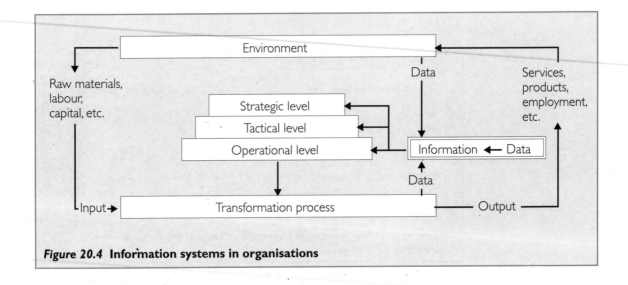

Figure 20.4 Information systems in organisations

ment, personnel, a building, etc. The transformation process combines these factors to treat patients. Managers want information about this process. What resources did staff use on different treatments? How successful were they? They also need information about environmental factors such as other hospitals and the expectations of patients and their relatives.

20.3 Forms of information system

Information systems take different forms, ranging from very informal, to paper-based, to highly automated computer-based systems.

Human information systems

These are informal information systems. Everyone uses sense organs to receive impulses from the environment; the brain interprets these impulses that lead to decisions on how to respond. From this perspective, everyone is an information system. For managers, this means observing events in the organisation and in the environment and using this information to help manage their area of responsibility. The style of 'managing by walking around' suggests that direct communication between managers and subordinates and direct observations by managers are effective ways of collecting information.

Studying is also a human information process. All available study material is data, but the student has to remember relevant information and use it in tutorials and written examinations. A person may use it again in his or her professional life.

Paper-based information systems

Paper-based systems are just as formal as any other system. Companies often use them to define their procedures. They are cheap to implement, easily understood and suitable for interdepartmental data flows. Staff are confident with information on paper. Paper systems have some virtues and the genuinely paperless office is still rare. Staff can file a hard (paper) copy and use it easily for audit purposes. Staff often use paper systems when traceability is important and responsibility is high. Consider an insurance company in which senior directors must still write and sign cheques of high value. The format of paper information systems is often a piece of A4 paper with printed instructions or boxes to complete. It may be a label attached to a part being routed through a shopfloor with instructions on what work to do. A manual, paper-based attendance list kept by a lecturer is another example, as is an address book or diary.

***

n o t e b o o k   *20.4*

Identify two formal but paper-based information systems that you use, or which affect you. What are the advantages and disadvantages of a paper-based system?

Computerised information systems

Most information systems beyond the smallest now use electronic means to collect data and to provide information. Electronic devices often now collect the initial data, such as the barcodes and scanners that capture product details in shops. Thereafter, electronic systems process, manipulate, distribute and record the data. The systems can provide paper output if required at various stages. Examples are the till receipt for the customer, or a summary report on the pattern of sales for managers. The Noticeboard lists some examples of electronic systems.

n o t e b o o k   20.5

List three computerised information systems you use or that affect you. What are the objectives of these systems? Could you process that information without using computers?

What advantages and disadvantages have you experienced with these systems? Are computerised systems always better?

20.4 Functions of computerised information systems

Markus (1984) distinguished five functions that information systems can perform: operational, monitoring, decision support, knowledge (or expert) and communication.

Operational systems

An operational system is a computer application that processes transactions in an orderly and efficient way to provide a desired output.

Early computer systems were operational ones. Management introduced them to process routine transactions and this is still a major function. The systems rationalise and standardise transactions in an efficient, reliable and uniform way. Common examples in businesses of such systems are payroll and order entry systems. When a student informs administration of a new

---

NOTICEBOARD Some examples from different business areas

Retail Point-of-sale terminals provide faster customer checkout, identify customer preferences, and improve inventory control. This control is linked with the computer systems of the suppliers.

Financial services Automated teller machines support 24-hour a day banking services. Telephone banking is used by many customers to make banking transactions directly from their home. On-line and Internet banking is now available.

Travel Computerised reservation systems provide up-to-date information to agents, enabling them to give better advice to travellers and to alter prices depending on the precise circumstances.

Manufacturing Linking computer-aided design and computer-aided manufacturing improves the time to market significantly. Better logistics by computerised material requirements planning. Electronic data interchange (EDI) with suppliers and customers.

address, he or she expects the change to apply quickly and all the files of the university to be updated. The university would use a transaction processing system. Banks and other financial institutions also rely on operational systems to process millions of transactions (such as cheques and other payment instructions) daily in an efficient, reliable and uniform way.

Such an operational system (or transaction processing system) can also exchange data between organisations, such as a customer or a supplier. Connections between the transaction processing systems of separate organisations is called electronic data interchange (EDI).

In retailing, EDI systems help retailers to control the amount of stock and manage the whole supply chain much better:

> ❢ **The attraction of EPOS [electronic point-of-sale] systems is that they instantly record each sale, using a laser scanner which reads the barcode on the product, so retailers no longer have to wait for a periodic stock-take to find out what they need to re-order. Through a system called EDI the shops are hooked up with the computers of the firm's main suppliers.** ❢
>
> (*The Economist*, 4 March 1995)

Barcoding has also been used in surgery to 'check in' and 'check out' all the equipment used during an operation to prevent any tools being left inside the patient.

Electronic data interchange (EDI) is a set of standards, hardware and software technology that permits computers in separate organisations to transfer documents electronically.

---

n o t e b o o k   20.6

Identify an example of an operational system in an organisation with which you have contact, such as a hospital, a fast-food chain or a supermarket. Could EDI be useful there, or not? Explain your answer.

Can you give an example of a useful application of EDI in schools or universities? Explain your answer.

Monitoring systems

Monitoring systems check the performance of a system at regular intervals. The factor being monitored can be financial, quality, departmental output or personal performance. Being attentive to changes or trends gives the business an advantage: it can act promptly, even before problems occur, to change investment, and it can improve quality, reduce output, or train or discipline employees.

A monitoring system is a computer-based system that processes data to provide information about the performance of a business process.

---

n o t e b o o k   20.7

Identify a monitoring system you have experienced, and consider its effect on motivation. How might it improve the motivation of people? Can you give an example of a monitoring system that has reduced motivation, and thus become counterproductive?

Note the pros and cons of monitoring systems generally.

Universities in the Netherlands use student trail systems that monitor the academic progress of students. These systems link to the national institution that provides scholarships, and the information enables this institution to stop or reduce the scholarship when results are below the required standard.

Decision support systems

A decision support system is a computer-based system, almost interactive, designed to assist managers in making decisions.

Another way of using information systems is as decision support systems (DSSs). These can help managers to calculate the consequences of different alternatives in order to make better decisions. This happens, for instance, by simulation and what-if analysis. A DSS incorporates both data and models to help a decision-maker solve a problem. The data would often originate in the operational systems.

Some examples of DSSs are:

▶ Businesses make use of decision support systems to calculate the expected financial consequences of alternative investments.
▶ Schools and universities use decision support systems to optimise room allocation and lecturer time to produce the schedules for students.
▶ Some ambulance services use a command and control system to assist staff to make decisions about which ambulance to send to an emergency, such as a road accident or a critically ill patient. The Case Study at the start of Chapter 7 describes one such system.

Knowledge systems

A knowledge system is a system that incorporates the decision-making logic of a human expert.

Certain information systems are designed to support people in making decisions by incorporating human knowledge into the computer system. To design such a system, a knowledge engineer works with one or more experts in the domain under study to try to learn how experts make decisions. This knowledge is then put into a part of the software application (called the knowledge base).

Examples of knowledge functions are:

▶ Some banks use knowledge systems to analyse proposed bank loans. Such systems incorporate the experience of experts in this field which enables banks to allow less experienced employees to assign loans.
▶ The AMC, a large Dutch hospital, uses an expert system to enable people with relatively little experience to deal with emergency calls. The system proposes the questions to be asked and, having dealt with these questions, proposes a plan of action.
▶ Insurance companies use a knowledge system to treat applications for insurance. Aegon, a Dutch insurer, uses such a system to enable insurance agents to make insurance contracts with clients without the intervention of the insurer.

In the 1980s, developers aimed to develop real 'expert systems' which would replace human experts (Leith, 1986). In the 1990s, organisations are often more realistic in their expectations. It is very hard (and often unrealistic) to comprehend all the knowledge and experience of human experts and to reach the same quality of decision-making. An additional problem is that systems are less able than people to interpret and adapt new knowledge and experience. Because of this, many people nowadays prefer to speak about *knowledge systems* rather than about *expert systems* (McCauly and Ala, 1992).

Some knowledge systems are really able to replace the experts to some extent (see also the examples), but many others intend to support experts in their decision-making. The system makes suggestions to the human expert that help him or her to improve the quality of the decisions rather than trying to take over the expert's job. In this context, Hirschheim and Klein (1989) make the distinction between 'systems for experts' (these are supportive to the human experts) and 'expert systems' (which replace people who are expert in a certain field).

Communication systems

Electronic mail is a system whereby users send and receive messages electronically, permitting communication between people who are not present at the time.

Management designs communication systems to overcome geographical and time barriers, making it easier to pass information around and between organisations. A common example of a communication system is electronic mail (e-mail) which can be used within and between organisations. Another example is the World Wide Web, which many companies use as a marketing tool to support communication with customers.

A relatively new phenomenon in this field is Groupware (Turoff *et al.*, 1993). Groupware systems, also known as workflow systems, support co-operation among people who are working in teams. The systems provide e-mail services, diary management and record historical information about employees, customers and documents. Components of groupware systems can be:

- ▶ Electronic communication and messaging
- ▶ Information-sharing
- ▶ Collaborative writing, authoring and design
- ▶ Workflow management and co-ordination
- ▶ Decision support and meeting systems
- ▶ Scheduling systems, calendars and diaries
- ▶ Conference systems
- ▶ Administration of documents

n o t e b o o k   20.8

Do you think that communication systems or groupware are, or could be, helpful in an educational setting? Explain your answer.

The distinction between the five types of system described above is not always distinct. Some companies use these systems in an integrated manner. Their decision support systems are linked with the operational systems to use the most current data. Communications systems link both to other employees and to other organisations.

20.5 Scope of computerised information systems

Computerised information systems vary in the scope of their operation, and this affects their influence on the organisation.

Individual systems

Many people use word processing (WP) systems, spreadsheet programs and database systems to manage their work. It is also possible to download data from company-wide systems for use on individual tasks. The main advantage of such systems is that the user is deciding what to use the system for and is able to control the way they work. The disadvantage is that the quality of the software varies greatly. The data extracted from the corporate database are no longer current and the systems may not link easily with the systems of other users. As examples, secretaries or professional staff may use their own WP and office systems on an individual basis. Schedulers may use standalone scheduling systems.

Local or departmental systems

If separate units or departments in companies have a distinct task to perform, it may be worth their having their own information systems. Management often creates these as separate systems, though many are now being integrated into the systems network of the whole company. For example, a department of a university uses a system that provides information about courses and assessments on the local departmental network which students can access.

Company-wide systems

These systems integrate departments and are used by people throughout the organisation. In hospitals, many units use centralised patient data to retrieve or update information about a patient. Such systems make it much easier for staff from various departments to treat a patient in a consistent way. If the hospital is to implement a company-wide system successfully it must discourage the continued use of standalone systems. This may typically, with today's technology, be a list of one doctor's patients held on a spreadsheet that he or she considers to be the definitive list. Copies of patient data can be made but the copy is not current.

case example A company-wide system at GEC Marconi

GEC Marconi is implementing a common suite of software packages throughout its forty companies. Implementing such a system will standardise systems among its component companies that previously ran a variety of accounting and manufacturing systems yielding a massive saving on the cost of ownership. Each of the companies uses a computer to manage its business locally, and periodically submits results to headquarters where management takes a complete and current view. This is possible through servers (communicating through a corporate wide area network), standardised software and an agreed structure of accounts.

Interorganisational systems

Many systems now link organisations electronically to each other. For example, the car-maker Lancia delivers its newest model in 122 colours and delivery takes place within four weeks. A direct electronic link between the dealer, the importer and the manufacturer makes this possible.

Stages in using information systems

The people in organisations have to learn how to use and manage information systems. Thus they must pass along a learning curve made up of different stages (Figure 20.5).

The model suggests that any new technology follows these stages. *Initiation* is when the innovators within a firm start using the technology in an experimental way. These experiments are not often very efficient but some people become experienced and enthusiastic. This enthusiasm moves to other parts of the organisation where others start to imitate the initiators, leading to the *diffusion* of the technology. This leads again to organisational learning but threatens failure and results in centralised corporate control being lost. Managers may feel that the new technology is useful but has to be managed to make it efficient for the organisation – this is the *consolidation* stage. Finally, *integration* takes place when the new technology is accepted as a normal tool for people to use to do their work and becomes part of the way the organisation works. This is a continuous process as new technologies are constantly emerging and being adopted by enthusiastic innovators.

C A S E   Q U E S T I O N S   20.2

▶ What stage do you think St Antonius Hospital has reached on the learning curve?

▶ What evidence have you based your conclusion upon?

▶ What management challenges does this imply?

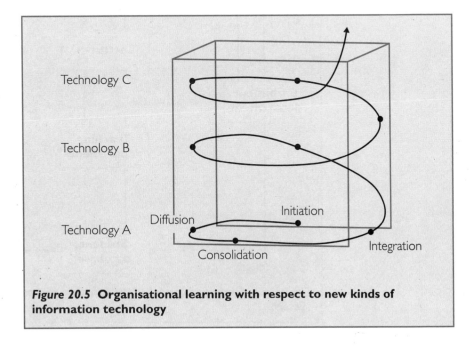

Figure 20.5 **Organisational learning with respect to new kinds of information technology**

20.6 Implementing information systems

Acquiring information systems

Logically, the first step in installing or enhancing an information system is for the provider – the development team or salesperson – to understand the user's information needs. There are two approaches:

▶ By asking people what information they need to make proper decisions and to do their job well. Typical questions are: What are your tasks? What do you need to know to perform those tasks? Which decisions do you have to make? What do you need to know to make those decisions?

▶ By analysing what tasks people have and what information they need in order to do them properly. Design staff observe people, review their job descriptions and then compare and analyse the data.

Having analysed the information needs, designers use the conclusions to create a diagram showing the system in the organisational setting. Such a scheme shows which data the system will capture and the relationships between different organisational units. Figure 20.6 shows a simplified example of such an analysis done for a university record system.

This model shows how the system could store student data. The enrolment department is responsible for making available to the student database basic information about students. Other departments access this for their own purposes. The teaching departments need it to organise their classes and to enter the students' results. At the end of the process the graduation office uses the student records to ensure that students have met the requirements for their qualification.

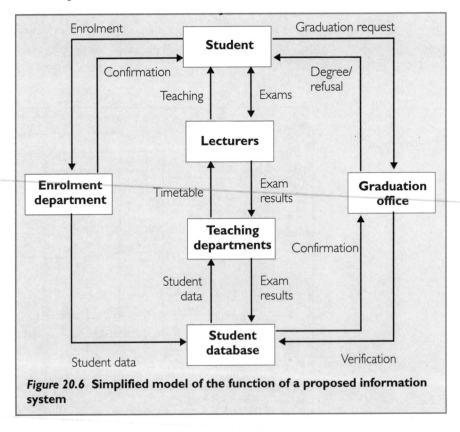

Figure 20.6 **Simplified model of the function of a proposed information system**

When those responsible have a clear picture of what information users need, they decide how to acquire the system to provide it. A basic choice is whether to buy a ready-made application package or to develop a purpose-built system. There are advantages and disadvantages in both approaches.

Buying an application package

There are software packages for many information needs. Martin *et al.* (1994) suggest several reasons for the popularity of application packages:
► They require fewer in-house development resources.
► They speed up development significantly.
► They provide more sophisticated applications than many companies can create in-house.

IS staff can adapt many such application packages to specific organisational needs. In relation to the Case Study, many hospitals use application packages which are developed as well as maintained by a vendor. The vendor adapts these systems according the latest legal requirements, while the users can adapt the system to their specific desires.

While ready-made packages are attractive, experience shows that this route carries risks. These risks include:
► **Functionality** The off-the-shelf solution may not meet the information needs of the organisation. A package may offer more functions than the organisation needs while possibly missing some other requirements.
► **Supplier ability** How long has the supplier been in the market? Many software companies are very new, and if they collapse, the purchaser may be without technical support for a package it has bought.
► **Service level** Consider what help and technical support the supplier provides. What are the upgrade terms, when will it fix bugs and what is the cost and availability of on-site consultants? The decision to rely on a system supplier involves making a significant commitment.

Developing a customised system

Another option is to develop the package in a tailor-made way. The in-house systems department of the company or an external software provider can do this. There are three ways of developing information systems: the waterfall, the evolutionary and the incremental approaches.

Waterfall approach

The waterfall approach divides the process of systems development into stages, usually as listed below. The model suggests that each phase follows the previous one in strict sequence though this is not usually typical or even ideal in the real world.
► **Planning** In this stage, the system developers plan the whole design process and perform a feasibility study. This means that they describe the technical, financial, social and organisational consequences of the system.
► **Analysis** System analysis describes the next phase. IS staff interview staff in the user department to establish their responsibilities, the departmental input and output, and their information needs. This can be an opportunity for users to identify and appeal for new best practices.

▶ **Design**   System design means that the developers describe in detail how the system will work, what the outputs will be and what inputs are needed. Similarly, procedures are described and hardware requirements defined. Figure 20.6 shows a simplified system design.

▶ **Realisation**   Using the design report, programmers develop the system as they have defined it following the interviews. They also acquire the hardware needed at this phase.

▶ **Implementation**   Users receive training and the hardware and software is installed. Developers test the system and users begin to use it. They will often do this in parallel with the old until they are completely confident.

In recent years, users have criticised this waterfall approach to developing systems. It has the following disadvantages.

▶ **User expectations**   It is difficult to know and express explicitly in advance what they expect from the system. When people work with a system they often adjust their needs and wishes.

▶ **Time**   The waterfall approach often takes a great deal of time. Users needs and their circumstances change during this period.

▶ **Division of task**   This approach supposes a clear and somewhat rigid division of tasks between analysts, designers and programmers. A fresh approach by management and new technologies such as graphical development tools (for example, Visual Basic and Visual C++) have made programming more accessible. Enthusiastic and technically minded users can do more themselves.

Evolutionary approach

The evolutionary approach tries to develop a working system as soon as possible. As users comment on it, the system is changed in a continuous, evolutionary way. This method depends on close co-operation between users and designers.

Incremental approach

When organisations follow the incremental approach to systems development they try to split a development into various subtasks. IS staff develop and build the different subtasks as soon as possible. The saying, 'if you do

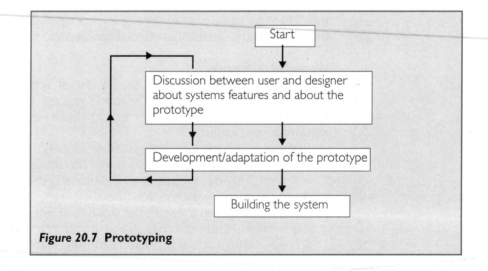

Figure 20.7 Prototyping

not know what you are doing, do not do it on a large scale' is a good summary of this method of systems development.

Developers who use this approach often use prototyping techniques. A prototype appears as a working model, a mock-up of the application. This will include the users' interface (the screen layout and paper reports). At this stage it would tend not to have validation, security and detailed functionality. Figure 20.7 shows the prototyping technique of systems development.

If the system described in Figure 20.6 were developed incrementally, the three subsystems (enrolment, departmental use and graduation) would be developed sequentially. If the developers used prototyping, they would sketch the final system quickly and ask users to comment. These comments help them to develop the system further, as shown in Figure 20.7.

Another strategy to adopt would be that of facilities management (FM) of IT requirements whereby a company takes over an IT department. This reduces the indirect overheads of the company and allows it to concentrate on its core businesses.

In summary, management faces an important decision when choosing to implement software. The choice will depend on trends, corporate policy, availability of software and the requirements of the organisation. Should management buy an off-the-shelf package, develop the system in-house or use a facilities management company?

A commercial off-the-shelf solution can be relatively cheap but is not likely to be specific to the organisation and implies a long-term relationship with the supplier. In-house development requires an IT department so the overhead is high, but the software will meet very specific requirements. Facilities management (often called outsourcing) is a current trend that reduces overheads and the cost is static over the long term.

20.7 Human aspects of implementing systems

Implementing information systems is not just a technical activity of developing or buying a package that provides the information needed. Systems

---

NOTICEBOARD Reasons for failed systems

An article in *Forbes Magazine* described a number of failed systems development projects. The main reasons for these failures were:

▶ User needs were not fully understood.

▶ User requirements were made secondary or even disregarded in favour of technical enthusiasm for the latest or most exciting, but inappropriate, method.

▶ Business changes during the development period were not reflected in the system by the implementation date.

▶ The time and money needed to develop and implement systems were underestimated. This caused overspending, partial implementation and dissatisfied users.

▶ During implementation, politics and conflicts emerged as departments protected old systems.

Source: *Forbes Magazine*, 29 August 1994

affect people in their work. The tasks of people may change (working with the system) and their relation to managers may change. New systems implementation has social, technical, organisational, economical and political dimensions. Research by Boddy and Gunson (1996) as well as experiences from practice suggest that managers who consider these factors will deliver more successful projects. It is also clear that many managers do not consider these aspects. Users are then often reluctant to use new systems so the benefit to the organisation is forgotten or lost.

Most computer-based information systems have significant effects on the organisation. They can change the tasks and the skill levels required for them. In a hospital, the emergency room receives telephone calls that require some action. This room could be staffed by a two-person team of a nurse and a doctor. Alternatively an operator with less medical knowledge can use an expert system which prompts the operator to ask questions. The operator enters the responses and the system suggests the most appropriate action. This allows medical staff to be employed in other areas.

Computer-based systems can remove functions that had to be conducted on a routine basis. Many supermarket chains have installed electronic data interchange (EDI) systems to connect them to their suppliers. Their buying departments now perform quite different tasks from before. They are less involved with placing orders, as that is done automatically. Instead they spend more time with suppliers on forward planning and jointly finding ways to improve efficiency. Even small retailers do not tend to shut down for a day to stocktake as they used to.

Computer-based systems allow organisations to decentralise some functions and centralise others. Mobile salesforces are more informed because they can connect to corporate databases and query trends, popular products and advise customers accordingly. Telephone sales can be centralised to single call centres. This is currently proving massively successful with banks and other services. This centralisation reduces the cost of sales and allows the companies to compete with new entrants.

These systems allow management at head office to control subsidiaries or branch offices much more tightly. Head office can gather information much more frequently and measure branch performance almost as it happens rather than by weekly or monthly reports. Whether it is a good idea to do so is another matter: the Case Example contains an example of a company that decided not to use this technological possibility.

Knowing where to draw the line

A multinational with manufacturing plants around the world decided to install an office automation system at its head office in Europe. When equipment and software suppliers were asked to submit proposals, they all emphasised that their system would allow management to obtain financial and other performance information from their operating units much more rapidly than before. At the time, the information was provided monthly in a very summary form, and quarterly in more detail.

Senior management considered that one of the reasons for the company's success was that subsidiaries had been allowed to operate

with considerable autonomy. It believed that if local managers knew that their performance was being monitored on a weekly or monthly basis, they would be more concerned about ensuring that the most recent figures looked good than about developing the business in the way they believed best. Consequently, senior management declined to include tighter subsidiary monitoring systems in its automation plans.

Making an information systems plan

Traditionally, information planning implied the technical aspects, such as hardware delivery, software development and preparation for training and implementing new systems. With the growing awareness of the impact of information systems on business, planning now focuses more on the links between information systems and the overall business planning of the organisation. It therefore ideally uses the mission of the organisation itself based on management's view of the environment in which it is operating.

For a certain planning period, management will have objectives to be achieved by delivering products and services. A range of business processes are needed to make these. Management both needs and produces information. Figure 20.8 shows this line of thinking.

The approach in Figure 20.8 represents a rational perspective on decision-making. It is a top-down approach.

A top-down approach develops the IS plan by identifying those applications that senior management believes would be most helpful to the organisation.

A disadvantage is that it can lead to unrealistic expectations. Research showed that just 24 per cent of the defined projects led to new working systems; 38 per cent of the implemented systems were not part of the original plan (Lederer and Sethi, 1988). It seems that planners (consultants and executives) regularly ignore the cultural characteristics of the organisation,

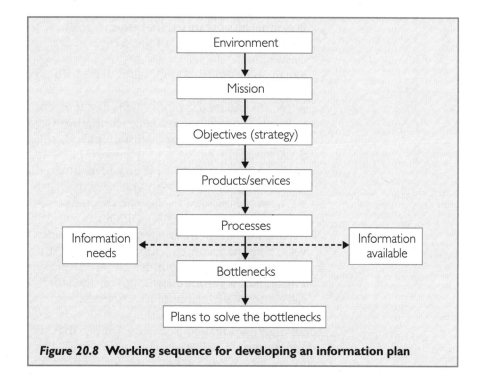

Figure 20.8 **Working sequence for developing an information plan**

possible resistance, traditional working habits and interest groups with a particular view on system proposals. When the senior management of St Antonius Hospital decides to implement an organisation-wide system to capture patient data, it threatened the existence of the current local departmental systems organisation. If the users do not believe in the benefits of the systems they may feel threatened.

Various authors suggested that organisational culture, interest groups, the user community and the structure have a major influence on systems development (Keen, 1981; Markus, 1983; Markus and Robey, 1983; Noble and Newman, 1993). This is a plea for a bottom-up approach of IS planning and implementation. Markus and Robey (1983) call this the organisational (in)validity of information systems.

Staff following such an approach will seek gradual improvements to existing systems. They will want them to support existing working procedures and working relations. Management often proposes such an approach in order to improve job satisfaction (see Chapter 6).

A bottom-up approach develops the IS plan by concentrating on the current and expected problems and ideas for change at the operating level of the organisation.

Broader agendas of information systems plans

The information system plans of a company can cover a variety of subjects. Themes that are common in such plans are:

- The relation between the information policy and the company policy.
- Priorities of systems and software.
- The pace of implementation.
- Technical aspects such as networks and telecommunications, operating systems and hardware facilities that are currently in place. What current technology can the organisation justify and use?
- Financial projections for budgets and costs against the benefits of modern, cheap to maintain systems that improve quality and service.
- Personnel and organisational aspects: position, responsibilities and role of user departments and of the IS experts; organisational design use of consultants.
- The fit and validity of proposed systems with existing organisational arrangements.
- Approach and methods of systems development. What development methods and tools are available within the organisation? This might now include the broad user base with simple PC skills. What skills does the IT department currently have? What level of interdepartmental integration is desirable and affordable. Who will maintain the systems in the long term – internally or through a facilities management contract that will allow for the business to concentrate on its core business?
- Systems and data protection. Different applications and business environments require different levels of security. Public systems must be very robust and, consequently, the cost of testing is high.
- It is also important to consider the technical aspirations of competitors. Consider how the industry is moving towards either contracting external call centres with legions of telephonists or investing in Internet sales and advertising.

These organisational consequences imply that the process of introducing information systems is especially important. Mumford (1983) argued that in many system development projects there is an overemphasis on the technical side, leading to neglect of the human side. This means that the change and attractiveness of jobs when the system has been implemented are given little attention by system developers. To balance this, she developed the Ethics method. Ethics is an acronym for Effective Technical and Human Implementation of Computer-based Systems. The assumptions of this method are:

▶ Many kinds of computer technology are sufficiently flexible to allow for the design of systems that take into account the need of employees for satisfying work. Therefore designers should work on both the technical and the human parts of a system with this objective in view.

▶ That even in situations where designers have produced a technical system it is still possible to redesign jobs in a way that will make them more satisfying.

The dimensions of job satisfaction used in her model are:

▶ **Knowledge fit** Job allows skills and knowledge to be used and developed.

• **Psychological fit** Job allows furtherance of private interests for achievement, recognition, advancement or status.

• **Efficiency fit** Job offers financial rewards and supervisory controls that are acceptable to the employee.

• **Task structure fit** Job meets the employee's requirements for variety, interest, feedback and autonomy.

• **Ethical fit** The degree to which the values and philosophy of the employer are compatible with those of the employee.

The method follows two tracks: the technical track and the human track. Each side is worked on independently and brought together in a later stage. This method is intended to ensure that developers give enough time and

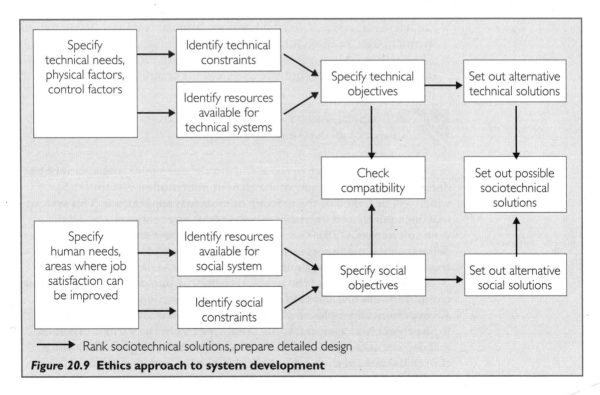

Figure 20.9 **Ethics approach to system development**

The sociotechnical approach is a systems development strategy that attempts to improve simultaneously the performance of the organisation and the quality of the working life of the workers.

attention to both dimensions. Figure 20.9 shows the Ethics approach in schema.

The approach leads not only to working systems (from a technical perspective) but also to more attractive systems from a human point of view, enhancing motivation and job satisfaction. It develops the idea of organisations' sociotechnical systems that were discussed in Chapter 2.

Two factors are very important and determine in many cases the success or failure of systems implementation: user involvement and senior management support (Markus and Keil, 1994).

User involvement

When prospective users take part in the design of information systems it is likely that the outcome will be close to their expectations and to what they need in order to do their job. They are likely also to develop a sense of ownership towards the system, which will in turn make adoption easier. User involvement takes different forms, each of which is likely to help both quality and implementation (Morley, 1993):

▶ **Participation** Users are able to contribute to the development process (McKeen *et al.*, 1994).

▶ **Communication** Regular face-to-face contact between developers and users improves understanding between both sides: not only are requirements understood but also technical possibilities are communicated

▶ **Education** Education ensures that users receive clear instructions, training and enough technical information on the system to accept it confidently into their working environment.

▶ **Information** Keeping users informed of progress, changes and compromises avoids surprises and disappointment and so maintains a high level of service. This could be done through corporate newsletters or frequent user meetings for smaller projects.

▶ **Conviction** Managers explain why they are implementing the system and the benefits it will bring to users and the organisation.

---

case example

A hospital invests in a new management information system

In a large hospital with five thousand employees senior management has decided to purchase a new management information system (MIS) which will be linked to the existing operational applications. This system had been purchased from an overseas supplier as commercial off-the-shelf software (COTS). The main aim is to support divisional and departmental managers by giving them a picture of their budgets, treatment patterns, expenditures and aggregated patient data.

The supplier advised the hospital to put the package onto the existing computer network and feed data from the operational systems into it. An experienced employee of the IS department was appointed as full-time project manager, and some employees from the various divisions and departments were also invited to work on the project. They were chosen because of their interest in automation and were made responsible for promoting and selling the use of the package in their unit.

Once every two months a steering group consisting of a member of the board of directors and other senior staff had a meeting to discuss progress. The project manager attended with the project team, and would describe project activities, divide tasks and oversee the change. He has a year to implement the system, by which time it is expected that managers will be using the system to control their unit and to report performance to senior management.

The licence for the package costs £1 million per year, but the top management believes that this investment will be paid back by a better informed and more effective management.

---

notebook 20.9

Describe the decision-making process for acquiring this package.

What do you think about the project organisation?

What evidence is there about different forms of user involvement?

What evidence is there about top management support?

Senior management support

Another key factor of the successful implementation of information systems is the clear and unequivocal support of the senior management. Users and developers need to know that the senior management supports the new system with various means: attention, budget and commitment. In this light, it is ideal when a senior manager is chairman of the steering group of the various system development initiatives. This is especially true where information systems are becoming of ever-greater strategic importance.

20.8 Information systems and corporate strategy

Information systems planning and policy

Before developing and implementing information systems, many companies develop a vision of how they will use IT and information systems. Such a vision may lead to a concrete plan to realise the vision in practice.

An information systems plan can have the character of a blueprint that sets out in detail how the organisation will develop its use of information systems in the medium term. Other organisations have found that such a blueprint can be a constraint rather than a stimulus for effective use of systems. They set out a broader framework with plenty of scope to change direction if this seems necessary because of changing market conditions, changes in the organisation itself, or unforeseen technical developments. There are several reasons for developing such visions and plans.

An information vision is an expression of the desired future for information use and management in the organisation (based on Martin et al., 1994).
An information systems plan is a document that describes how the company will realise the information vision by allocating time and resources to it.

▶ **Strategic importance** Many organisations now rely entirely on their information systems to do their business. Therefore it becomes increasingly important to use them effectively. Implementing systems on an *ad hoc* basis leads to a fragmented, incompatible and ineffective use.

▶ **High costs** The cost of developing and using systems is high. This is a strong incentive to formulate various alternative ways of using information systems and to prioritise these alternatives in terms of costs and benefits.

▶ **Ripple effects** The organisational implications of systems use are significant. They affect many people both inside (managers and users) and outside the organisation (suppliers and customers). This is also a reason to formulate a balanced and well considered vision on systems use.

The IT strategy of a company can be offensive or defensive. An offensive strategy strives to make positive moves to apply technology in order to improve the business. They may launch new products, improve services and realise gains in quality and flexibility to meet the market. Davenport (1993) provides many examples of where IT can enable innovation. These are shown in the Noticeboard.

NOTICEBOARD IT as the enabler of innovation

Sales and order management
▶ Portable salesforce automation systems
▶ Customer site workstations for order entry and status-checking
▶ Electronic data interchange between firms
▶ Expert systems for configuration, shipping and pricing
▶ Integration of voice and data (e.g. automated number identification)
▶ Empowerment of frontline workers

Marketing
▶ Customer relationship databases/frequent buyer programs
▶ Point-of-sale systems tied to individual customer purchases
▶ Expert systems for data and trend analysis
▶ Statistical modelling of dynamic market environments

Research
▶ Computer-based laboratory modelling and analysis
▶ Computer-based field trials and communication of results
▶ Wide dissemination of information on project status

Engineering and design
▶ Computer-aided design and physical modelling
▶ Integrated design databases
▶ Design-for-manufacturability expert systems
▶ Conferencing systems across design and other functions

▶ Cross-functional teams

Manufacturing
▶ Linkages to sales systems for build to order
▶ Real-time systems for custom configuration and delivery commitment
▶ Materials and inventory management systems
▶ Quality and performance information

Logistics
▶ Electronic data interchange and payment systems
▶ Configuration systems
▶ Third party shipment and location tracking systems
▶ Close partnerships with customers and suppliers
▶ Rich and accurate information exchange with suppliers and customers

Management
▶ Executive information systems that provide real-time information
▶ Electronic linkages to external partners in strategic processes
▶ Standard technology infrastructure from communication and group work
▶ Standard reporting structures and information
▶ Acknowledgment and understanding of current management behaviour as a process
▶ Accountability for management process measurement and performance

The Case Study shows how the hospital makes use of many different systems that staff had developed over many years, without any shared vision on systems use. Suppose management has decided that it should start to deal with its information problems by developing a vision on systems use and a plan on how to realise that vision.

▶ What are that questions with which you think that vision should deal?

▶ Use the discussion in the last few pages to prompt questions.

An offensive strategy strives to make positive moves to apply technology in order to improve the business. A defensive strategy describes the situation where there is a risk of failure due to disparate systems being used within an inconsistent system.

A defensive strategy describes the situation where there is a risk of failure due to disparate systems being used within an inconsistent structure. Staff on development groups implement projects partially and so fail to satisfy user needs. Users may be unable to define or even decide their requirements. The hardware and software may be unplanned. There may be isolated inflexible systems that require data to be duplicated or re-entered. There may be insufficient investment in networking, disk space or processor speeds confounded by a lack of continuity and standards. Systems that rely on older technology that did not include an ability to deal with the millennium threaten to disrupt the organisations using them. The cost of owning multiple disparate systems is very high. The need for specialists becomes more pressing just as skills become difficult to find. Software interfaces cause problems and hardware maintenance increases.

▶ Is the hospital an example of an organisation using a defensive approach? Explain your conclusion.

▶ What elements could it include in an offensive strategy?

Accepting the limitations of COTS software

A risk of buying commercial off-the-shelf software is that it can stifle innovative strategies. An exercise was carried out on a large scale by an organisation. Months were spent defining its current systems. Expert business users were then invited to define their 'blue skies' (ideal) systems by applying all their knowledge of textbook idealism, global corporate standardisation and the possibilities of leading-edge technology. This proved to be wasteful, as the purchased application was only able to provide a very standard level of functionality. COTS applications will never provide the most current and functionally rich solution. They have conflicting agreements with other customers to honour, the leadtime of development and version compatibility to consider.

The Noticeboard above describes ways in which organisations have been able to use information systems for competitive advantage. This, and its significance for organisations, is discussed more broadly below.

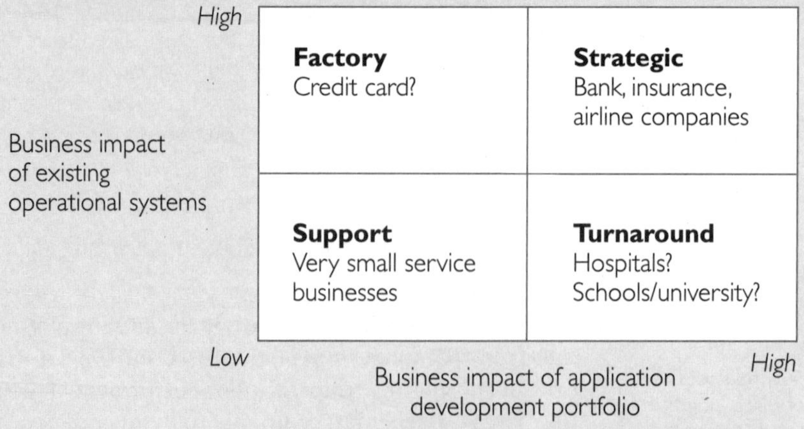

Figure 20.10 shows a 2×2 grid. Vertical axis labelled "Business impact of existing operational systems" ranging from Low to High. Horizontal axis labelled "Business impact of application development portfolio" ranging from Low to High.

	High business impact of application development	
Factory Credit card?	**Strategic** Bank, insurance, airline companies
Support Very small service businesses	**Turnaround** Hospitals? Schools/university?

Support	IT is not critical to the business, either now or in the future
Factory	IT is crucial to current business operations but not at the heart of the organisation's strategic development
Turnaround	IT is not critical at present, but is vital if the organisation is to achieve its strategic objectives
Strategic	IT has been critical to business success for some time and will remain so in the future.

Figure 20.10 The IT strategic grid

Strategic uses of information systems

Information technology is now offering many new ways of creating business opportunities and significantly changing the competitive position of organisations. This strategic use of IT is a development of great significance to the future of organisations and their management (Earl, 1989; Daniels, 1994; Mata *et al.*, 1995).

McFarlan and McKenney (1983) have developed a framework which helps to position a firm when deciding the system's criticality and the possibility of strategic use (Figure 20.10).

The *support* position means that IT is not critical to the business, either now or in the future. IT constraints are not critical to corporate success, so general management involvement can be relatively low. The *factory* position means that IT is crucial to current business operations, but not at the heart of the organisation's strategic development. The *turnaround* position means that IT is not critical at present, but is vital if the organisation is to achieve its strategic objectives. IT vision has to be closely linked to the firm's overall strategic plan and needs much general management attendance. The *strategic* position means that IT has been critical to business success for some time, and will remain so in the future. Such firms require much attention to IT matters from senior management and a well considered IT plan.

Many firms in the banking, insurance, retailing and travel business see themselves as being in the turnaround or strategic box. They believe the effective use of information systems is already of strategic importance and that their reliance on such systems will increase. A strategic information system is one which uses information, information processing and/or information systems as a vehicle for implementing a business strategy. It will often enable change in the products, services and competitive advantage of an organisation. Some examples of such a strategic use are given below.

Changing the pattern of information flow

▶ A consultancy firm installs a groupware system to link its staff more closely to each other and to the company's knowledge base in order to improve its service to clients.

▶ A car manufacturer has an information system which links importers and dealers. When a customer buys a car, the specifications can be put immediately into the system of the manufacturer. All kinds of information, such as delivery time can be given to the customer. (See also Mukhopadhyay *et al.* (1995) who explain the business impact of EDI at the Chrysler Corporation.)

Reducing inventory costs

▶ Rover Cars is only invoiced for components when the completed assembly leaves the factory. It is known that two headlamps have been used; Lucas (the component supplier) is informed of this consumption, it then invoices and replenishes supply. Inventory levels are then kept to a minimum. This is a tactic known as *backflushing* and is only possible by the use of detailed on-line inventory control systems but turns the traditional manufacturing supply system upside-down (see Chapter 19).

Closer management control

▶ A travel agent's branch accounting system can now provide detailed patterns of business to managers, enabling them to monitor trends more closely, and to take better-informed pricing and promotional decisions. Management information systems can expand the span of control of individual managers, which can support the flattening of organisations.

Creating completely new businesses

▶ Telephone banking, doing business in information (direct marketing) are relatively new phenomena which have become possible with advanced information systems.

Caterpillar Tractors

case example

Imagine the following scenario. A part on a Caterpillar machine operating at a copper mine in Chile begins to deteriorate. A district centre that continuously monitors the health of all the Caterpillar machines in its area by remotely reading the sensors on each machine automatically spots a problem in the making and sends an electronic alert to the local dealer's field technician through this portable computer. The message tells him the identity and location of the machine and sends his computer the data that sparked the alert and its diagnosis. Then, with the aid of the computer, the technician validates the diagnosis and determines the service or repair required, the cost of labour and parts, and the risks of not performing the work.

The technician's computer also tells him exactly which parts and tools he will need to make the repair. Then, with a touch of a key, the technician ties into Caterpillar's worldwide information system, which links dealers, Caterpillar's parts distribution facilities, its suppliers' factories and large customers' inventory systems. He instantly determines the best sources of the parts and the times when each source can deliver them to the dealer's drop-off point. Next, the technician sends a proposal to the customer by computer or telephone, and the customer tells him the best time to carry out the repair. With a few more keystrokes, the technician orders the parts. The electronic order instantly goes to the factories or warehouses that can supply the parts in time. At the factories and warehouses, the message triggers the printing of an order ticket and automatically sets into motion an automated crane that retrieves the parts from a storage rack. Soon the parts are on their way to the dealer's pick-up site. Within hours of the initial alert, the technician is repairing the machine. An interactive manual on his computer guides him, providing him with the latest best-practice procedures for carrying out the repair. The repair completed, the technician closes the work order, prints out an invoice, collects by credit card and electronically updates the machine's history. That information is added to Caterpillar's databases, which helps the company to spot any common problems that a particular model might have and thereby continually improve its machines' designs.

Source: *Harvard Business Review*, March/April 1996

---

notebook *20.10*

This is an example of a vision, articulated in terms of customer/supplier relations. Make a sketch to show how the described situation works.

Which strategic objectives did Caterpillar have with its IS vision? Which information systems and IT means are needed to realise this vision? Which order of systems development would you recommend to realise this vision?

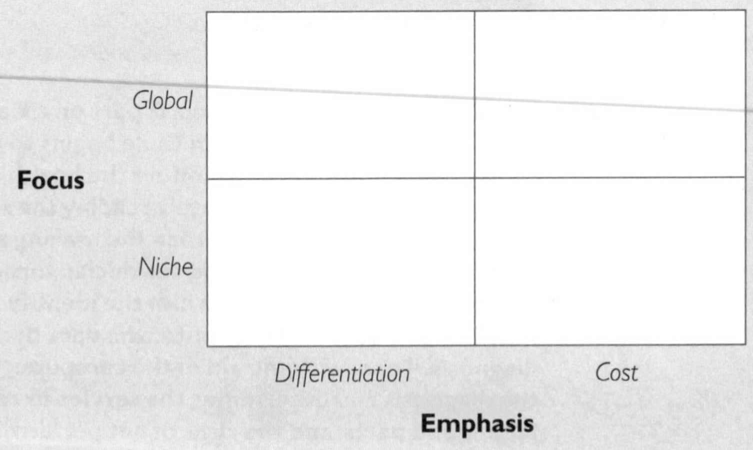

Figure 20.11 **IT and the characteristics of the firm and the business: the Porter model**

Traditionally, IT is used to improve existing positions by improving effectiveness and efficiency. However, IT can also be used to enable new positions. As Figure 20.11 shows, these positions can relate either to the focus of a business (global or niche) or to the emphasis within them (differentiation or cost). Cost leadership can often be enhanced or made feasible by IT. Examples of such an enhancement are the substitution of robotics for labour, driving down inventory costs with stock control systems or advanced logistic systems, reducing order processing costs by on-line order entry systems and reducing downtime and scrap by machine sensing. Differentiation is usually concerned with creating uniqueness in the eyes of the customer, this can be supplied using the flexibility of computer manufacturing and detailed inventory control – customers value uniqueness. Often, IT systems can create or support such competitive edges. Examples of such a use of IT are on-line ordering, dealer networks, expert system advice, computerised quotation or retrieval systems and communications-based customer hotlines.

These examples show that IT and information systems may become mechanisms for creating, supporting or changing generic strategies. The Ford Case Example shows how companies can use IT to fulfil their strategy.

 Ford

At the beginning of the 1980s Ford was examining the requirements for a viable automobile manufacturing business for the next twenty years. The Japanese attack on export markets, predicted zero or low growth in European companies and overcapacity in the industry combined to paint a difficult scenario. Ford reasoned that survival depended on driving down costs rather than either raising prices or aiming for volume growth. However, market share had to be maintained, which demanded good and responsive product design, good and reliable product quality and customer satisfaction and loyalty.

The Ford Europe systems office began to plan its IT investment on these assumptions. It developed business visions of CAD/CAM bringing quality products to the market faster, computer-integrated manufacturing driving down costs and raising quality, and telecommunications enabling the company to get closer to the customer. By 1990, 90 per cent of its design work was computer aided, manufacture was planned and controlled by systems built on the just-in-time philosophy – including links to suppliers and between factories – and dealers were using stock control systems, customer query and vehicle locator facilities and point-of-sale and finance contract routines based on terminals connected into the Ford network. IT had become the foundation of survival in improving productivity and performance.

Source: Earl (1989)

n o t e b o o k   *20.11*

Which strategic objectives did Ford follow? How did these objectives affect its information systems plan?

Changing face of organisations

Whilst systems development is big business, it can be still very much a craft industry, in that every system and each new program is unique in the same sense that the crafted products of artisans prior to industrialisation were individual. Programs are not produced on a production line, process flow environment or in batches of multiple units. This is significant because it explains in part the difficulty of estimating the time it will take to develop them. The skill and ability of those developing are critical to success. It is widely understood that an expert's output, once testing and rework are considered, is more than ten times greater than average. Estimating the time that it will take to develop a new system is a skill for such a unique product and many methods have been developed to help.

The paperless office has not been realised yet and is not likely ever to be. The concept is one in which automation pervades every corner of every system and so eradicates the need for paper. When predicting the level of automation on a strategic scale it is usual to apply a ratio that occurs throughout business life – the Pareto ratio (the 80/20 rule). That is to say, approximately 80 per cent of the business can be automated by concentrating and applying technology to only 20 per cent of its systems. It becomes increasingly expensive, with progressively less payback to automate peripheral, seldom used systems – the remaining 20 per cent. There is a perception of security and trust in paper, it cannot be altered remotely, it is robust. The increase in information available, desire for detail, and knowledge that information can be extracted easily all contribute to the persistence of hard copy. The new technology even produces more paper, as copies can be produced and old habits persist, such as when individuals print an e-mail before reading it. The paperless office is not likely to be realised – it is important to recognise the practical limitations of the technology.

Virtual organisations have no physical location, individuals work from home, on the road or at client sites. They are characterised by mobile communications including pagers, mobile faxes and powerful lap-tops (employees can even claim to be working as they answer a mobile in the pub). Forms of virtual organisation are most applicable to small, leading-edge service companies that are familiar with technology. Certain organisational functions have been doing this for years but many more can now see the possibilities.

Hot-desking is a new term that describes the sharing of workspace. A desk with a terminal can be used by different employees, even with different roles (see the Price Waterhouse case in Chapter 7). The organisation provides the working space for only a fraction of its total employees, the understanding being that holiday, sickness, local meetings and field visits typically leave real estate and hardware investment idle. The benefit to the company is the reduced overheads of maintaining space, heating and facilities; for the employee it allows marginally more flexibility: all the data required to carry out a certain function can be retrieved from any workstation. This might include telephone help desks, customer accounts, insurance policy processing or computer programming. Security is applied via user passwords rather than physical walls. Personal files and memos can be stored centrally and accessed remotely. Physical location is less significant. Whilst working from home is practised, it has not yet become the revolution on a scale once prophesied. Hot-desking could be viewed as similar to the introduction of flexitime which was successfully adopted by many companies in the 1980s and can only be practical if the data systems are truly centralised with appropriate technology to access organisation-wide systems. Whether companies choose to exploit this opportunity remains to be seen and may be more easily implemented at new office sites where change is already in progress.

20.9 Recap

Content agenda

Management depends on accurate and timely information about internal and external events to perform its role effectively. Such information is essential to developing objectives that reflect customer needs and competitors' action. Information helps ensure that organisations add value to the resources they use. Technological developments are enabling these traditional information functions to be performed more rapidly and extensively than ever before, so IT is itself becoming a source of competitive advantage. Management can use computing and IT to offer new products and to radically reshape the organisation that delivers current goods and services. Information technology enables management to introduce completely new organisational forms. Staff motivation is affected by the way technological developments and human aspects interact. Management choices – for example about the use of complementary, sociotechnical models – affect these outcomes.

Process agenda

The extensive effects of modern computing and communications technologies mean that introducing the technologies affects many of an organisation's stakeholders. These stakeholders can be widely dispersed in the innovating organisation and in other organisations with which it does business. Wider flows of information enable more people and interests to be involved in decision-making, especially through particular technologies such as groupware and video-conferencing. Other factors can constrain what is technologically possible. The introduction of these new technologies also raises major process issues, reflecting their potential effects on stakeholders. Effective introduction is supported if management combines project, participative and political models of change. Transmission of data and information has become technically easier with computing and communications technologies. The ability of the receiver to understand the sender's meaning can still be problematic.

Control agenda

Information technologies can significantly increase the ability of those in power to control others. Systems design is not a neutral activity but is shaped by those providing the resources, who will tend to preserve rather than disrupt existing power relations. The performance of subsidiaries,

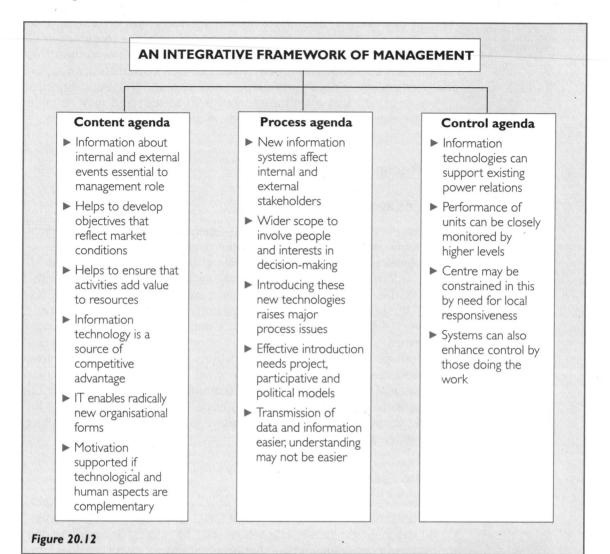

Figure 20.12

- ► What information is most important to managers at different levels within Kwik-Fit, and how does the MAT system provide this?
- ► What are the main differences between the state of the information system at Kwik-Fit and that described at St Antonius Hospital?
- ► How has Kwik-Fit been able to use the MAT system to support the strategic development of the business?
- ► How has the system changed the role of the depot managers?

divisions, branches and individuals can be much more closely monitored with modern information systems. However, action on this information by those at the centre can be constrained by other considerations. These include awareness of the benefits of local autonomy and responsiveness that would be damaged by heavy-handed control from the centre. The systems can also be designed in a way that enables people to enhance their control over operations. They can be designed to feed more useful performance information to operators and teams so that they are better able to use their skills to manage the situation responsibly.

An integrative framework is set out in Figure 20.12.

20.10 Review questions

1 Give some examples of data and of information which you have at this moment. What information do you lack which harms your work or study performance? How should this information be generated?

2 Mention examples of the use of information systems in a business you know. How are they helping or hindering the managers in performing their tasks? Compare the needs of senior and lower-level managers if possible.

3 Give an example of the strategic use of IT in a business you know. To what extent has the business become more competitive?

4 (a) Describe an information vision for your own working environment.
   (b) What would the realisation of this vision imply in terms of the information technology and the information systems which you would need?
   (c) What steps would you recommend between the vision and the acquisition of the systems?

5 A governmental agency with more than five hundred employees, working in three different buildings, gets e-mail as an additional means of communication. This is a first step. The management intends to implement modules for information sharing, work-flow management and electronic conferencing during the next three years. At present, telephone, paper-based mail, fax, etc. are the most common ways of communication. A year after implementation, just 10 per cent of the employees use this new technology fully.

   What do you think could be the reasons of this result? What action would you recommend?

6 A European country is considering the possibility of a nationwide information system which helps to collect traffic fines. At the moment this takes place on a regional basis. Identify and discuss system development and implementation aspects, focusing particularly on the managerial aspects.

7 Compare the advantages and disadvantages of two alternative ways of developing information systems, based, if possible, on discussion with someone who has experienced them.

Further reading

Applegate *et al.* (1996) provide a broad perspective on the management implications of the rise of information systems. The book is organised around a management audit of the information services activity. Another useful background text written from a management perspective is by Martin *et al.* (1994). This focuses on the opportunities and pitfalls of computer and communications technologies. A useful non-technical book which looks at ways of exploiting IT from a European and managerial perspective is that by Earl (1989). It emphasises strongly the relation between corporate strategy and IS strategy. A good article on the human aspects of systems implementation is by Markus and Keil (1994). The authors discuss, with the aid of a case study, the reasons behind resistance towards new information systems and argue that companies should approach system-building as a process where implementability is built in.

On information systems planning, the article by Galliers *et al.* (1994) is recommended. This discusses the way that systems planning can take place in organisations and how senior managers can become involved. The three cases combine successful and unsuccessful styles of IS planning. An alternative is Iivari and Hirschheim (1996).

W Website addresses

Royal Bank of Scotland   http://www.royalbankscot.co.uk/)
Tesco   http://www.tesco.co.uk
The text refers to the way in which some organisations are using developments in IT to offer new ways of providing services. To see examples of these, you could visit the Royal Bank of Scotland site (regarded as one of the best financial services sites) and the Tesco site for information about its Internet Superstore.

Glossary

Activities   Activities are the physical or mental tasks that people undertake.

Administrative management   Administrative management is the use of institutions and order rather than relying on personal qualities to get things done.

Applied ethics   Applied ethics is the application of moral philosophy to actual problems, including those in management.

Assessment centre   Assessment centres are multi-exercise programmes designed to identify the recruitment and promotion potential of key personnel.

Assets   The assets are the property, plant and equipment, vehicles, stocks of goods for trading, money owed by customers and cash: in other words, the physical resources of the business.

Balance sheet   A balance sheet shows the financial position of a company at a particular time. It shows the physical resources (assets) of the business and, to match that, the sources from which finance has been raised both from share-holders and from borrowing.

Behaviour modification   Behaviour modification is a general label for attempts to change behaviour by using appropriate and timely reinforcement.

Bottom-up approach   A bottom-up approach develops the IS plan by concentrating on the current and expected problems and ideas for change at the operating level of the organisation.

Bureaucracy   Bureaucracy is a system in which people are expected to follow precisely defined rules and procedures rather than to use personal judgement.

Business process view   The business process view puts satisfying customers' requirements at the heart of a design process to develop a supply system which will operate without waste. The orientation is towards speed of response and two-way flow of information and other resources.

Capital market   The capital market comprises all the individuals and institutions which have money to invest, including banks, life assurance companies and pension funds, and as users of capital, business organisations individuals and governments.

Cash flow statement   A cash flow statement shows the sources from which cash has been generated and how it has been spent during a period of time.

Cell layout   A cell layout creates multiple cells dedicated to producing families of output types.

Centralisation   Centralisation is when a relatively large number of decisions are taken by management at the top of the organisation.

Channel   A channel is the medium of communication between a sender and a receiver.

Collectivism   Collectivism pertains to societies in which people, from birth onwards, are integrated into strong, cohesive groups.

Communication   Communication is the exchange of ideas, opinions and information through written or spoken words, symbols or actions.

Competence   1. Competence concerns the actions and behaviours identified by change agents as contributing in their experience to the perceived effectiveness of change implementation. 2. Competences are those behaviours required for satisfactory ('threshold competence') or excellent ('superior competence') performance in a job.

Competitive advantage 'Competitive advantage arises from discovering and implementing ways of competing that are unique and distinctive from those of rivals, and that can be sustained over time.' (Porter, 1994)

Competitive strategy Competitive or business strategy 'is concerned with the firm's position relative to its competitors in the markets which it has chosen.' (Kay, 1996)

Concertive control Concertive control occurs when team members create a system of values and norms which members submit to.

Consumer-centred organisation A consumer-centred organisation is focused upon and structured around the identification and satisfaction of the demands of its consumers.

Consumers Consumers are individuals, households, organisations, institutions, resellers and governments which purchase the products offered by other organisations.

Content Content is the specific substantive task that the group is undertaking.

Contingency approaches Contingency approaches to organisational structure are those which are based on the idea that the performance of an organisation depends on having a structure that is appropriate to its environment.

Corporate culture 'Corporate culture is the pattern of basic assumptions that a given group has invented, discovered or developed in learning to cope with its problems of external adaptation and internal integration. [These] have worked well enough to be considered valid, and [are] therefore taught to new members as the correct way to perceive, think and feel in relation to those problems.' (Schein, 1985)

Corporate strategy Corporate strategy 'is concerned with the firm's choice of business, markets and activities' (Kay, 1996), and thus it defines the overall scope and direction of the business.

Cost Cost expresses in money units the effect of activating or consuming resources. It is an internal control process of the producing organisation and is not visible to outside parties.

Counterimplementation Counterimplementation refers to attempts to block change without displaying overt opposition.

Craft production Craft production refers to a system in which the craft producers do everything. With or without customer involvement, they design, source materials, make, display, sell, perhaps service and do the accounts.

Critical success factors 'Critical success factors are those aspects of strategy in which an organisation must excel to outperform competition.' (Johnson and Scholes, 1997)

Critical perspective A critical perspective is one which evaluates an institution or practice in terms of its contribution to human autonomy, responsibility, democracy and ecologically sustainable activity.

Culture Culture is the pattern of basic assumptions developed by a group as the correct way to perceive, think and feel in doing a task.

Current asset A current asset can be expected to be cash or to be converted to cash within a year.

Data Data are raw, unanalysed facts, figures and events.

Decentralisation Decentralisation is when a relatively large number of decisions are taken lower down the organisation in particular operating units.

Decision support system A decision support system is a computer-based system, almost interactive, designed to assist managers in making decisions.

Decoding Decoding is the interpretation of a message into a form with meaning.

Defensive strategy A defensive strategy describes the situation where there is a risk of failure due to disparate systems being used within an inconsistent system.

Delegation Delegation occurs when one person gives another the authority to undertake specific activities or decisions.

Delivery Delivery relates to the achievement of all promises made by any supplier to a customer.

Demand leadtime Demand leadtime is the elapsed time that a customer is prepared to allow between placing an order for a product or service and actually receiving it; in certain situations this time is effectively zero.

Deontology Deontology is the application of established general rules or moral laws to a decision.

Determinism Determinism is the view that an organisation's structure is determined by its environment.

Differentiation Differentiation is the state of segmentation of the organisation into subsystems, each of which tends to develop particular attributes in response to the particular demands posed by its relevant external environment.

Distant teams Distant teams are those that meet the definition of teams but work with little, if any, face-to-face interaction because members are widely spread geographically.

Effectiveness Effectiveness is a measure of the degree to which an organisation meets its objectives and the expectations of stakeholders.

Efficiency Efficiency is a measure of the output produced with each unit of input.

Egoism Egoism is the practice of evaluating a decision against the criterion of whether it serves a person's self-interest.

Electronic data interchange (EDI) Electronic data interchange is a set of standards, hardware and software technology that permits computers in separate organisations to transfer documents electronically.

Electronic mail Electronic mail is a system whereby users send and receive messages electronically, permitting communication between people who are not present at the time.

Encoding Encoding is translating information into symbols for communication.

Ethical audits Ethical audits are the practice of systematically reviewing the extent to which an organisation's actions are consistent with its stated ethical intentions.

Ethical consumers Ethical consumers are those who take ethical issues into account in deciding what to purchase.

Ethical investors Ethical investors are people who only invest in businesses that meet specified criteria of ethical behaviour.

Ethical relativism Ethical relativism is the principle that ethical judgements cannot be made independently of the culture in which they are made.

Ethnocentrism Ethnocentrism is the tendency to regard one's own group as the standard and all other different groups as strange and usually inferior.

External fit External fit is when there is a close and consistent relationship between an organisation's competitive strategy and its HRM strategy.

Factory production Factory production broke down the integrated nature of the craftworker's approach and made it possible to increase the supply of goods by dividing tasks into simple and repetitive sequences.

Feedback Feedback occurs as the receiver expresses his or her reaction to the sender's message.

Femininity Femininity pertains to societies in which social gender roles overlap.

Fixed asset   A fixed or non-current asset is expected to be of benefit to the business for a period exceeding one year and in the normal course of business will not be a trading asset.

Formal group   A formal group is one that management has deliberately created to perform specific tasks to help meet organisational goals.

Formal structure   Formal structure is the official guidelines, documents or procedures setting out how the organisation's activities are divided and co-ordinated.

Functional layout   A functional layout groups similar physical processes together and brings materials and/or customers to these areas.

Functional managers   Functional managers are responsible for the performance of a common area of technical or professional work.

General managers   General managers are responsible for the performance of a distinct unit of the organisation.

Globalisation   'Globalisation is a more advanced form of internationalisation which implies a degree of functional integration between internationally dispersed economic activities.' (Dicken, 1992)

Group   A group or team consists of two or more people with some shared purpose who assume different responsibilities, depend on each other, co-ordinate their activities, and see themselves as part of the unit.

Groupthink   '[Groupthink is] a mode of thinking that people engage in when they are deeply involved in a cohesive in-group, when the members' striving for unanimity overrides their motivation to realistically appraise alternative courses of action.' (Janis, 1977)

High-context culture   High-context cultures are those in which information is implicit and can only be fully understood by those with shared experiences in the culture.

High-performance team   A high-performance team is a team which meets all the requirements of a real team, but in addition shows commitment to the personal growth of members and performs beyond expectations.

Horizontal specialisation   Horizontal specialisation is the degree to which tasks are divided among separate people or departments.

Human resource management   Human resource management is the effective use of human resources in order to enhance organisational performance.

Individualism   Individualism pertains to societies in which the ties between individuals are loose.

Influence   Influence is the process by which one party attempts to modify the behaviour of others by mobilising power resources.

Informal group   An informal group is one that emerges when people come together and interact regularly.

Informal structure   Informal structure is the undocumented relationships between members of the organisation that inevitably emerge as people adapt systems to new conditions and satisfy personal and group needs.

Information   Information is useful knowledge derived from data.

Information system   An information system is a set of people, procedures and resources that collects and transforms data into information and disseminates this information.

Information systems management   Information systems management is the planning, acquisition, development and use of these systems.

Information systems plan   An information systems plan is a document that describes how the company will realise the information vision by allocating time and resources to it.

Information vision   An information vision is an expression of the desired future for information use and management in the organisation (based on Martin *et al.*, 1994).

Inner context of change   The inner context of change relates to the history of the organisation, its structure, its culture and its political system – including the form of its decision-making structures.

Innovation   Innovation covers incremental and/or step change (breakthrough) changes in products and/or processes which change function, form, performance or resource use in an advantageous way.

Institutional advantage   'Institutional advantage is when a not-for-profit body performs its tasks more effectively than other comparable organisations.' (Goold, 1997)

Integration   Integration is the process of achieving unity of effort among the various subsystems in the accomplishment of the organisation's task.

Interaction   Interactions are the communications that people have with each other in any way.

Internal fit   Internal fit is when the various components of the HRM strategy support each other and consistently encourage certain attitudes and behaviour.

Internationalisation   'Internationalisation is the increasing geographical dispersion of economic activities across national borders.' (Dicken, 1992)

Inventory   Inventory consists of materials and part or finished goods which are held in anticipation of need by customers along a chain of supply from raw materials through to final consumption (and recycling?).

Job analysis   Job analysis is the process of determining the characteristics of an area of work according to a prescribed set of dimensions.

Knowledge system   A knowledge system is a system that incorporates the decision-making logic of a human expert.

Leadership   'Leadership involves a social influence process whereby intentional influence is exerted by one person over other people to structure the activities and relationships in a group or organization.' (Yukl, 1994)

Liabilities   The liabilities of a business as reported in the balance sheet are the debts and financial obligations of the business to all those people and institutions who are not shareholders, e.g. a bank, suppliers.

Limited liability company   A limited liability company has an identity and existence in its own right as distinct from its owners (shareholders in Europe, stockholders in North America). A shareholder has an ownership right in the company in which the shares are held.

Line layout   Line layout is completely specified by the sequence of activities needed to perform a given transformation.

Line managers   Line managers are responsible for the performance of activities which are directly involved in meeting customers' needs.

Low-context culture   Low-context cultures are those where people are more psychologically distant so that information needs to be explicit if members are to understand it.

Management as a general human activity   Management as a general human activity occurs whenever people take responsibility for an activity and consciously try to shape its progress and outcome.

Management as a specialist occupation   Management as a specialist occupation develops when activities previously embedded in the work itself become the responsibility not of the employee but of owners or their agents.

Manager   A manager is someone who gets things done with the aid of other people.

Market segmentation   Market segmentation is the process of dividing markets comprising the heterogeneous needs of many consumers into smaller parts or segments comprising the homogeneous needs of smaller groups of consumers.

Marketing environment   The marketing environment consists of all those forces which impact upon the marketing activities of an organisation. It includes both micro and macro components.

Marketing information system   A marketing information system is the systematic processes and systems for the effective and efficient collection, analysis and distribution of marketing information.

Marketing mix   Marketing mix is the mix of decisions about product features, prices, communications and distribution of products used by the marketing manager to position products competitively within the minds of consumers.

Marketing philosophy   Marketing philosophy is an organisational philosophy which believes that organisational success is most effectively achieved by the organisation's satisfaction of consumer demands.

Masculinity   Masculinity pertains to societies in which social gender roles are clearly distinct.

Mechanistic organisation   In a mechanistic organisation, there is a high degree of task specialisation, people's responsibility and authority are closely defined and decision-making is centralised.

Metaphor   A metaphor is an image used to signify the essential characteristics of a phenomenon.

Model   A model represents a complex phenomenon by identifying the major elements and relationships.

Monitoring system   A monitoring system is a computer-based system that processes data to provide information about the performance of a business process.

Noise   Noise is anything that confuses, diminishes or interferes with communication.

Non-current asset   *See* Fixed asset.

Norms   Norms are the informal rules that express beliefs about how people should behave.

Objectively rational   An action is objectively rational when the connection between the actions and the results can be shown to hold objectively.

Observing   Observing is the activity of concentrating on how a team works rather than taking part in the activity itself.

Offensive strategy   An offensive strategy strives to make positive moves to apply technology in order to improve the business.

Open system   An open system is one which interacts with its environment.

Operational strategies   Operational strategies are those deployed by the different functions of the organisation, such as manufacturing, marketing, finance and human resource management, and which contribute to the achievement of corporate strategy.

Operational system   An operational system is a computer application that processes transactions in an orderly and efficient way to provide a desired output.

Order qualifier   An order qualifier is a necessary but not sufficient requirement to be considered by a customer.

Order winner   An order winner is some feature or combination of features of the product or service that positively differentiates it from those of competitors and makes customers want to buy it in preference to those others.

Organic organisation   In an organic organisation people are expected to work together and to use their initiative to solve problems; job descriptions and rules are few and imprecise.

Organisation   Organisations consist of people trying to influence others to achieve certain objectives that create wealth or well-being through a variety of processes, technologies, structures and cultures.

Organisation chart   The organisation chart shows the main departments and senior positions in an organisation and the reporting relations between them.

Organisational development   Organisational development is the activity of deliberately changing major aspects of an organisation to improve its effectiveness.

Organisational philosophy   Organisational philosophy is a set of principles, values and beliefs which guide the approach which organisations adopt towards their activities.

Organisational structure   'The structure of an organisation [is] the sum total of the ways in which it divides its labour into distinct tasks and then achieves co-ordination among them.' (Mintzberg, 1989)

Outer context of change   The outer context of change relates to environmental factors, such as competitor behaviour, customer demands or other factors in the external environment.

Participative models of change   Participative models of change are those that recommend change managers to consult widely and deeply with those affected and to secure their willing consent to the changes proposed.

Partnering   Partnering describes a business relationship based on taking a long-term view that the partners wish to work together according to a mutually acceptable vision in ways which enhance all customers' satisfaction levels. The partners also seek to develop the relationship so that each will benefit in recognised business performance areas.

Perception   Perception is the active psychological process in which stimuli are selected and organised into meaningful patterns.

Performance appraisal   Performance appraisal is a systematic review of a person's work and achievements over a recent period, usually leading to plans for the future.

Performance-related pay   Performance-related pay refers to payment systems in which a percentage of pay depends on the assessed performance of individuals, groups or the organisation as a whole.

Person culture   A person culture is one in which activity is strongly influenced by the wishes of the individuals who are part of the organisation.

Political models of change   Political models of change emphasise that change is likely to affect the interests of stakeholders unevenly and that those who see themselves losing will resist the change despite the rationality of the arguments or invitations to participate.

Potential team   A potential team is a collection of individuals who could perform more effectively and are putting effort into developing the necessary skills and methods.

Power culture   A power culture is one in which people's activities are strongly influenced by a dominant central figure.

Power distance   Power distance is the extent to which the less powerful members of organisations within a country expect and accept that power is distributed unevenly.

Preferred team role   Preferred team roles are the types of behaviour that people display relatively frequently when they are part of a team.

Process   Process is the way the members interact with each other in performing the substantive task, such as how they make decisions.

Product   Product is a generic term used to identify both tangible goods and intangible services.

Product position   Product position is the position in which consumers place a product relative to that of an alternative supplier.

Profit statement   A profit statement reflects the benefits derived from the trading activities of the business during a period of time.

Project   'A project is a unique venture with a beginning and an end, conducted by people to meet established goals within parameters of cost, schedule and quality.' (Dinsmore, 1990)

Project management 'Project management is the combination of people, systems, and techniques required to co-ordinate the resources needed to complete projects within established goals.' (Dinsmore, 1990)

Pseudo-team A pseudo-team is a collection of individuals who could perform more effectively but have shown no interest in developing the necessary skills and methods.

Psychological contract The psychological contract is the set of understandings people have regarding the commitments made between themselves and their organisation.

Quality Quality of a product or service is the (often imprecise) perception of a customer that what has been provided is at least what was expected for the price he or she paid.

Rational-linear models of change Rational-linear models of change are those that view change as an activity that follows a logical, orderly sequence of activities that can be planned in advance.

Real team A real team is a collection of individuals with complementary skills who have become committed to common purposes, goals and working methods.

Receiver The receiver is the person whose senses perceive the sender's message.

Relationship marketing Relationship marketing is an approach which focuses on developing a series of transactions with consumers.

Role Role is the sum of the expectations that other people have of a person occupying a position.

Role culture A role culture is one in which people's activities are strongly influenced by clear and detailed job descriptions and other formal signals as to what is expected of them.

Role set Role set is those people or institutions that have expectations of a person.

Scientific School of Management The school of management called 'scientific' attempted to create a science of factory production.

Selection test Selection tests are formal, often psychologically-based methods of assessing candidates' likely suitability for a job.

Sentiments Sentiments are the feelings, emotions and attitudes that people have towards each other.

Skill Skill refers to a person's ability to perform various types of cognitive or behavioural activity effectively.

Social contract The social contract consists of the mutual obligations that society and business recognise they have to each other.

Sociotechnical approach The sociotechnical approach is a systems development strategy that attempts to improve simultaneously the performance of the organisation and the quality of the working life of the workers.

Sociotechnical system A sociotechnical system is one in which outcomes depend on the interaction of both the technical and social subsystems.

Span of control The span of control is the number of subordinates reporting directly to the person above them in the hierarchy.

Staff managers Staff managers are responsible for the performance of functions which provide support to line managers.

Stakeholders Stakeholders are those people, groups, or institutions that have an interest in, or are affected by, an organisation.

Strategic corporate social responsibility 'Strategic corporate social responsibility is the awareness, acceptance and management of the implications and effects of all corporate decision-making.' (Price, 1997)

Strategic management Strategic management is an organisation-wide task involving both the development and implementation of strategy. It demands the ability to steer the organisation as a whole through strategic change under conditions of complexity and uncertainty.

Strategy   Strategy is concerned with deciding what business an organisation should be in, where it wants to be, and how it is going to get there.

Structural choice   Structural choice approaches emphasise the scope which management has for deciding the form of structure, irrespective of external conditions.

Structure   Structure is the regularity in the way the group is organised, such as the roles that are specified.

Subjectively rational   An action is subjectively rational when it is based on a set of beliefs about how means are related to ends.

Subsystem   Subsystems are the separate but related parts which make up the total system.

Succession planning   Succession planning is the use of a deliberate process to ensure that staff are developed who are able to replace senior management as required.

Supply leadtime   Supply leadtime is the total elapsed time between first decision to obtain the basic input resources to the final delivery of the product or service to the customer.

Supportive relationships, system of   A system of supportive relationships refers to the interactions and experiences that build a person's sense of personal worth.

System   A system is a set of interrelated parts designed to achieve a purpose.

System boundary   A system boundary separates the system from its environment.

Systems approach   The systems approach looks at the different parts of an interacting set of activities as a whole and considers the best way for the whole to function.

Target market   Target market is the segment of the market selected by the organisation as the focus of its activities.

Task culture   A task culture is one in which the focus of activity is towards completing a task or project using whatever means are appropriate.

Team   A group or team consists of two or more people with some shared purpose who assume different responsibilities, depend on each other, co-ordinate their activities, and see themselves as part of the unit.

Team-based reward   'Team-based rewards are payments or non-financial incentives provided to members of a formally established team and linked to the performance of the group.' (IPD, 1996)

Teleology   Teleology is the practice of evaluating a decision against the criterion of whether the outcome achieves the original goal.

Top-down approach   A top-down approach develops the IS plan by identifying those applications that senior management believes would be most helpful to the organisation.

Traits   Traits are a variety of individual attributes, including aspects of personality, temperament, needs, motives and values.

Transactional marketing   Transactional marketing is an approach which focuses upon one-off exchanges with consumers.

Uncertainty avoidance   Uncertainty avoidance is the extent to which members of a culture feel threatened by uncertain or unknown situations.

Utilitarianism   Utilitarianism is the practice of evaluating a decision against the criterion of its consequences for the majority of people.

Value   Value is added to resources when they are transformed into goods or services that are worth more than their original cost plus the cost of transformation.

Value chain   'The value chain divides a firm into the discrete activities it performs in designing, producing, marketing and distributing its product. It is the basic tool for diagnosing competitive advantage and finding ways to enhance it.' (Porter, 1985)

Value for money service   A service that represents value for money is one that is provided economically, efficiently and effectively.

Vertical specialisation   Vertical specialisation refers to the extent to which responsibilities at different levels are defined.

Virtual organisations   Virtual organisations are those which deliver goods and services but have few, if any, of the physical features of conventional businesses.

Working group   A working group is a collection of individuals who work mainly on their own but interact socially and share information and best practices.

References

Academy of Management (1996), Human Resources Division, *News*, Summer.

Ackenhusen, M., Muzyka, D. and Churchill, N. (1996), 'Restructuring 3M for an integrated Europe', *European Management Journal*, Vol. 14, No. 1, pp.21–36.

Acker, J. and Van Houton, D.R. (1992), 'Differential recruitment and control: the sex structuring of organizations', in A.J. Mills, and P. Tancred (eds), *Gendering Organizational Analysis*, Sage, London.

Adair, J. (1986), *Effective Team Building*, Gower, Aldershot.

Adair, J. (1989), *Action Centred Leaders*, Industrial Society, London.

Adams, K. (1996), 'Respecting the difference: international competences for managers', *Competency*, Vol. 4, No.1, pp.24–30.

Alderfer, C. (1972), *Existence, Relatedness and Growth: Human Needs in Organizational Settings*, Free Press, New York.

Alexander, D. and Nobes, C. (1994), *A European Introduction to Financial Accounting*, Prentice Hall International, Hemel Hempstead.

Al-Faleh, M. (1987), 'Cultural influences on Arab management development', *Journal of Management Development*, Vol. 6, No. 3, pp.19–33.

Alvesson, M. and Wilmott, H. (1996), *Making Sense of Management*, Sage, London.

Ansoff, H.I. (1965), *Corporate Strategy*, Penguin, London.

Ansoff, H.I. (1987), *Corporate Strategy* (rev. edn), Penguin, London.

Ansoff, H.I. (1994), Comment on Henry Mintzberg's 'Rethinking strategic planning', *Long Range Planning*, Vol. 27, No. 3, pp.31–2.

Applegate, L.M., McFarlan, F.W. and McKenney, J.L. (1996), *Corporate Information Systems Management: Text and Cases* (4th edn), Irwin, Chicago.

Argenti, J. (1997), 'Stakeholders: the case against', *Long Range Planning*, Vol. 30, No. 3.

Argyris, C. and Schon, D. (1978), *Organizational Learning: A Theory of Action Perspective*, Addison-Wesley, Wokingham.

Arkin, A. (1996), 'Pulling ahead of the pub crawlers', *People Management*, 18 April.

Arnold, J., Hope, T., Southworth, A. and Kirkham, L. (1994), *Financial Accounting*, Prentice Hall International, Hemel Hempstead.

Arthur Andersen/Cardiff Business School (1995), *World Class*, Arthur Andersen, London.

Ashkenas, R., Ulrich, D., Jick, T. and Kerr, S. (1995), *The Boundaryless Organization*, Jossey-Bass, San Francisco.

Ashridge Management Research (1988), *Management for the Future*, Ashridge Management Research Group, Berkhamsted.

Atkinson, A.A., Banker, R.D., Kaplan, R.S. and Young, S.M. (1995), *Management Accounting*, Prentice Hall, Englewood Cliffs, NJ.

Avison, D., Kendall, J.E. and DeGross, J.I. (eds) (1993), *Human, Organizational, and Social Dimensions of Information Systems Development* (A-24), North-Holland, Amsterdam.

Babbage, C. (1835), *On the Economy of Machinery and Manufactures*, Charles Knight, London. Reprinted in 1986 by Augustus Kelly, New Jersey.

Baier, V.E., March, J.G. and Saetren, H. (1994), 'Implementation and ambiguity' in D. McKevitt and A. Lawton (eds), *Public Sector Management*, Sage, London.

Baker, M. (1991), *The Marketing Book*, Butterworth/Heinemann.

Ballé, L. and Gottschalk, A. (1994), 'Negotiating with other Europeans', *Management Extra*, Association of MBAs, London.

Barham, K. and Antal, A.B. (1994), 'Competences for the pan-European manager' in P.S. Kirkbride (ed.), *Human Resource Management in Europe*, Routledge, London.

Barham, K. and Wills, S. (1992), *Management Across Frontiers: The Competences of Successful International Managers*, Ashridge Management Research Group/ Foundation for Management Education, Berkhamsted.

Barker, J.R. (1993), 'Tightening the iron cage: concertive control in self-managing teams', *Administrative Science Quarterly*, Vol. 38, pp.408–37.

Barnard, C. (1938), *The Functions of the Executive*, Harvard University Press, Cambridge, Mass.

Baron, R.A. and Greenberg, J. (1990), *Behavior in Organizations: Understanding Managing* (3rd edn), Allyn & Bacon, New York.

Bartlett, C.A., Doz,Y. and Hedlund, G. (eds) (1990) *Managing the Global Firm*, Routledge, London.

Bass, B.M. (1985), *Leadership and Performance Beyond Expectations*, Free Press, New York.

Bass, B.M. (1990), *Handbook of Leadership: A Survey of Theory and Research*, Free Press, New York.

Beaumont, P. B. (1996), 'Trade unions and HRM' in B. Towers (ed.), *A Handbook of Human Resource Management* (2nd edn), Blackwell, Oxford.

Beer, M. (1985), 'Note on performance appraisal' in M. Beer and B. Spector (eds), *Readings in Human Resource Management*, Free Press, New York.

Beer, M. and Spector, B. (eds) (1985), *Readings in Human Resource Management*, Free Press, New York.

Beer, M., Eisenstat, R.A. and Spector, B. (1990), 'Why change programs don't produce change', *Harvard Business Review*, Nov./Dec., pp.158–66.

Belbin, R.M. (1981), *Management Teams: Why They Succeed or Fail*, Butterworth/ Heinemann, Oxford.

Belbin, R.M. (1993), *Team Roles at Work*, Butterworth/Heinemann, Oxford.

Bendell, T., Boulter, L. and Kelly, J. (1993), *Benchmarking for Competitive Advantage*, Pitman, London.

Bennett, R. (1997), *European Business*, Pitman, London.

Bennis, W.G. (1969), *Organization Development: Its Nature, Origins and Prospects*, Addison-Wesley, Reading, Mass.

Biggs, L. (1996), *The Rational Factory*, The Johns Hopkins University Press, Baltimore.

Birsh, D. and Fielder, J.H. (eds) (1994), *The Ford Pinto Case: A Study in Applied Ethics, Business and Technology*, Albany State University of New York Press.

Bjorn-Andersen, N. and Turner, J. (1994), 'Creating the twenty-first century organization: the metamorphosis of Oticon' in R. Baskerville *et al.*, *Transforming Organizations with Information Technology*, Elsevier Science/North-Holland, Amsterdam.

Blake, R.R. and Mouton, J.S. (1964), *The Managerial Grid*, Gulf Publishing, Houston.

Blau, P.M. (1970), 'A formal theory of differentiation in organizations', *American Sociological Review*, Vol. 35, No.2, pp. 201–18.

Bloom, H., Calori, R. and Woot, P. de (1994), *Euromanagement: A New Style for the Global Market*, Kogan Page, London.

Blyton, P. and Turnbull, P. (1994), *Reassessing Human Resource Management*, Sage, London.

Boddy, D. and Buchanan D.A. (1992), *Take the Lead: Interpersonal Skills for Project Managers*, Prentice Hall International, Hemel Hempstead.

Boddy, D. and Gunson, N. (1996), *Organizations in the Network Age*, Routledge, London.

Boddy, D., Macbeth, D.K., Charles, M. and Fraser-Kraus, H. (1998), 'Success and failure in implementing partnering', *European Jounal of Purchasing and Supply* (forthcoming).

Bounds, G.M. and Dobbins, G.H. (1993), 'Changing the managerial agenda', *Journal of General Management*, Vol. 18, No. 3, pp.77–93.

Bowen, D.E. and Lawler, E.E. (1992), 'The empowerment of service workers: what, why, how and when?', *Sloan Management Review*, Spring, pp.31–9.

Bowen, D.E., Ledford, G.E. and Nathan B.R. (1996), 'Hiring for the organization, not the job' in J. Billsberry (ed.), *The Effective Manager: Perspectives and Illustrations*, Sage, London.

Bowman, E.H. (1973), 'Corporate social responsibility and the investor', *Journal of Contemporary Business*, Winter, pp.21–43.

Boyatzis, R.E. (1982), *The Competent Manager*, Wiley, New York.

Brech, E.F.L. (1957), *Organization: The Framework of Management*, Longmans Green, London.

Brewster, C. (1994), 'European HRM: reflection of, or challenge to, the American concept?' in P. Kirkbride (ed.), *Human Resource Management in Europe*, Routledge, London.

Brewster, C., Hegewisch, A. and Mayne, L. (1994), 'Trends in European HRM: signs of convergence?' in P. Kirkbride (ed.), *Human Resource Management in Europe*, Routledge, London.

Brookfield, S. (1987), *Developing Critical Thinkers*, Open University Press, Milton Keynes.

Brown, R. (ed.) (1997), *The Changing Shape of Work*, Macmillan, London.

Brown, S. (1996), *Strategic Manufacturing for Competitive Advantage*, Prentice Hall International, Hemel Hempstead.

Bruce, I. (1994), *Meeting Need*, ICSA Publishing, London.

Bryson, J.M. (1995), *Strategic Planning for Public and Nonprofit Organizations*, Prentice Hall International, Hemel Hempstead

Buchanan, D.A. (1979), *The Development of Job Design Theories and Techniques*, Saxon House, Aldershot.

Buchanan, D.A. (1987), 'Job enrichment is dead: long live high performance work design', *Personnel Management*, May, pp.40–3.

Buchanan, D.A. and Boddy, D. (1992), *The Expertise of the Change Agent*, Prentice Hall International, Hemel Hempstead.

Buchanan, D. A. and Huczynski, A.A. (1997), *Organizational Behaviour* (3rd edn), Prentice Hall International, Hemel Hempstead.

Burgoyne, J. (1993), 'The competence movement: issues, stakeholders and prospects', *Personnel Review*, Vol. 22, No. 6, pp.6–13.

Burnes, B. (1996), *Managing Change*, Pitman, London.

Burns, J.M. (1978), *Leadership*, Harper & Row, New York.

Burns, T. (1961), 'Micropolitics: mechanisms of organizational change', *Administrative Science Quarterly*, Vol. 6, pp.257–81.

Burns, T. and Stalker, G.M. (1961), *The Management of Innovation*, Tavistock, London.

Butt, J. (ed.) (1971), *Robert Owen: Prince of Cotton Spinners*, David & Charles, Newton Abbott.

Campbell, A. (1997), 'Stakeholders: the case in favour', *Long Range Planning*, Vol. 30, No. 3.

Cannon, T. (1994), *Corporate Social Responsibility*, Pitman, London.

Cannon, T., (1996), *Basic Marketing: Principles and Practice* (4th edn), Cassell, London.

Carlson, S. (1951), *Executive Behaviour*, Stromberg Aktiebolag, Stockholm.

Carr, A.Z. (1968), 'Is business bluffing ethical?', *Harvard Business Review*, Jan./Feb. pp.143–53.

Carroll, A. (1991), 'The pyramid of corporate social responsibility: toward the moral management of organisational stakeholders', *Business Horizons*, July/Aug.

Carroll, S.J. and Gillen, D.J. (1987), 'Are the classical management functions useful in describing work?', *Academy of Management Review*, Vol. 12, No.1, pp.38–51.

Carson, D., Cromie, S., McGowan, P. and Hill, J. (1995), *Marketing and Entrepreneurship in SMEs: An Innovative Approach*, Prentice Hall International, Hemel Hempstead.

Carter, P. and Jackson, N. (1993), 'Modernism, postmodernism and motivation, or why expectancy theory failed to come up to expectation' in J. Hassard and M. Parker (eds), *Postmodernism and Organizations*, Sage, London

Catterick, P. (1995), *Business Planning for Housing*, Chartered Institute of Housing, Coventry.

Caulfield, I. and Schultz, J. (1989), *Planning for Change: Strategic Planning in Local Government*, Longman, Harlow.

Champy, J. and Hammer, M. (1993), *Re-engineering the Corporation*, Nicholas Brealey, London.

Champy, J. and Nohria, N. (1996), *Fast Forward*, Harvard Business School Press, Cambridge, Mass.

Chandler, A.D. (1962), *Strategy and Structure*, MIT Press, Cambridge, Mass.

Cherns, A. (1987), 'The principles of sociotechnical design revisited', *Human Relations*, Vol. 40, No. 3, pp.153–62.

Child, J. (1972), 'Organizational structure, environment and performance: the role of strategic choice', *Sociology*, Vol. 6, pp.1–22.

Child, J. (1984), *Organisation: A Guide to Problems and Practice* (2nd edn), Harper & Row, London.

Chrysalides, G.A.D. and Kale, J.H. (1993), *An Introduction to Business Ethics*, Chapman & Hall, London.

Clark, J. (1996), *Managing Innovation and Change*, Sage, London.

Clegg, S.R. and Dunkerley, D. (1980), *Organization, Class and Control*, Routledge & Kegan Paul, London.

Clutterbuck, D. (1994), *The Power of Empowerment*, Kogan Page, London.

Clutterbuck, D. and Dearlove, D. (1996), *The Charity as a Business*, Directory of Social Change, London.

Coggan, P.C. (1995), *The Money Machine: How the City Works*, Penguin, London.

Constabile, M., Ostillio, M.C. and Valdani, E. (1994), 'Nescafé Italy: global brand, local culture' in J. Montana (ed.), *Marketing in Europe: Case Studies*, Sage, London.

Constable, J. and McCormick, R. (1987), *The Making of British Managers*, BIM/CBI, London.

Coombs, R. and Hull, R. (1994), 'The best or the worst of both worlds: BPR, cost reduction, and the strategic management of IT', paper presented to the OASIG Seminar on Organizational Change, London, September.

Cowe, R. and Entine, J. (1996), 'Fair enough?' *The Guardian Weekend*, 14 December, pp.30–7.

Cravens, D.W. (1991), *Strategic Marketing* (3rd edn), Irwin, Chicago.

Critchley, W. and Casey, D. (1984), 'Second thoughts on team building', *Management Education and Development*, Vol.15, No. 2, pp.163–75.

Crosby, P. (1979), *Quality is Free*, McGraw-Hill, New York.

Cummings, T.G. and Worley, C.G. (1993), *Organizational Development and Change* (5th edn), West Publishing, Minneapolis.

Daniels, N.C. (1994), *Information Technology: The Management Challenge*, Addison-Wesley, Wokingham.

Darnell, H. and Dale, M.W. (1985), *Total Project Management*, British Institute of Management, London.

Davenport, T.H. (1993), *Process Innovation: Reengineering Work through Information Technology*, Harvard Business School Press, Boston, Mass.

Davis, K. (1960), 'Can business afford to ignore social repsonsibilities?', *California Management Review*, Vol. 2, No. 3, pp.70–6.

Davis, K. (1971), *Business, Society and Environment: Social Power and Social Response*, McGraw-Hill, New York.

Davis, K. (1975), 'Five propositions for social responsibility', *Business Horizons*, June, pp.19–24.

Dawson, S. (1992), *Analysing Organisations*, Macmillan, Basingstoke.

Dawson, S. and Wedderburn, D. (1980), 'Joan Woodward and the development of organization theory' in J. Woodward, *Industrial Organization* (2nd edn), Oxford University Press, Oxford.

Deal, T.E. and Kennedy, A.A. (1982), *Corporate Culture: The Rites and Rituals of Corporate Life*, Addison-Wesley, Reading, Mass.

Deming, W.E. (1988), *Out of the Crisis*, Cambridge University Press, Cambridge.

Dent, C.M. (1997), *The European Economy: The Global Context*, Routledge, London.

Dibb, S., Simkin, L., Pride, W.M. and Ferrell, O.C. (1997), *Marketing: Concepts and Strategies* (4th edn), Houghton-Mifflin, New York.

Dicken, P. (1992), *Global Shift: The Internationalisation of Economic Activity*, PCP, London.

Dinsmore, P.C. (1990), *Human Factors in Project Management* (2nd edn), American Management Association, New York.

Donaldson, L. (1995), *Contingency Theory*, Dartmouth, Aldershot.

Donaldson, L. (1996), *For Positive Organization Theory*, Sage, London.

Dopson, S. and Stewart, R. (1993), 'Information technology, organizational restructuring and the future of middle management', *New Technology, Work and Employment*, Vol. 8, No. 1, pp.10–20.

Doyle, P. (1994), *Marketing Management and Strategy*, Prentice Hall, Englewood Cliffs, NJ.

Drabek, Z. and Greenaway, D. (1984), 'Economic integration and intra-industry trade: the CMEA and the EEC compared', *Kyklos*, Vol. 38, pp.489–504.

Drucker, P.F. (1955), *The Practice of Management*, Pan, London

Drucker, P.F. (1967), *The Effective Executive*, Harper & Row, New York.

Drucker, P. (1973), *Management: Tasks, Responsibilities, Practices*, Heinemann, London.

Drucker, P.F. (1974), *Management: Tasks, Responsibilities, Practices*, Harper & Row, New York.

Drucker, P. (1981), 'What is business ethics?', *The Public Interest*, Spring, pp. 18–36.

Drucker, P.F. (1985), *Innovation and Entrepreneurship*, Heinemann, London

Drucker, P.F. (1995), *Managing in a Time of Great Change*, Butterworth/Heinemann, Oxford.

Drummond, D. (1989), ' "Specifically designed?" Employers' labour strategies and worker responses in British railway workshops, 1838–1914', *Business History*, Vol. 31, No. 2, pp.8–31.

Drury, C. (1996), *Management and Cost Accounting*, VNR, London.

Dunphy, D. (1981), *Organizational Change by Choice*, McGraw-Hill, Sydney.

Dyer, W.G. (1985), 'The cycle of cultural evolution in organizations' in Kilmann and Associates (eds), *Gaining Control of the Corporate Culture*, Jossey-Bass, San Francisco.

Earl, M.J. (1989), *Management Strategies for Information Technology*, Prentice Hall International, Hemel Hempstead.

Earth Limited (1991), *50 Simple Things Your Business Can Do to Save the Planet*, Greenleaf Publishing, Sheffield.

Eason, K.D. (1988), *Information Technology and Organizational Change*, Taylor & Francis, London.

Easterby-Smith, M., Thorpe, R. and Lowe, A. (1991), *Management Research: An Introduction*, Sage, London.

Economist Intelligence Unit (1992), *Making Quality Work: Lessons from Europe's Leading Companies*, Economist Intelligence Unit, London.

Egan, G. (1993), *Adding Value*, Jossey-Bass, San Francisco.

Egan, G. (1994), *Working The Shadow Side: A Guide to Positive Behind the Scenes Management*, Jossey-Bass, San Francisco.

Elliott, B. and Elliott, J. (1996), *Financial Accounting and Reporting*, Prentice Hall International, Hemel Hempstead.

Emmanuel, L., Otley, D. and Merchant, K. (1991), *Accounting for Management Control*, Chapman & Hall, London.

Engel, J., Kollatt, D. and Blackwell, R. (1978), *Consumer Behaviour,* Dryden Press, Boston, Mass.

Equal Opportunities Commission (1992), *Women and Men in Britain*, HMSO, London.

Ezzamel, M., Lilley, S. and Wilmott, H. (1994), 'The "new organization" and the "new managerial work"', *European Management Journal*, Vol. 12, No. 4, pp.454–61.

Fayol, H. (1949), *General and Industrial Management*, Pitman, London.

Feigenbaum, A.V. (1993), *Total Quality Control,* McGraw-Hill, New York.

Fiedler, F.E. and House, R.J. (1994), 'Leadership theory and research: a report of progress' in C.L. Cooper and I.T. Robertson (eds), *Key Reviews of Managerial Psychology,* Wiley, Chichester.

Fleishman E.A. and Harris, E.F. (1962), 'Patterns of leadership behavior related to employee grievance and turnover', *Personnel Psychology*, Vol. 15, pp.43–56.

Fletcher, C. (1996), 'Appraisal: an idea whose time has gone?' in J. Billsberry (ed.), *The Effective Manager: Perspectives and Illustrations*, Sage, London.

Fletcher, K. (1990), *Marketing Management and Information Technology*, Prentice Hall International, Hemel Hempstead.

Flynn, N. (1997), *Public Sector Management* (3rd edn), Prentice Hall International, Hemel Hempstead.

Follett, M.P. (1920), *The New State: Group Organization, The Solution of Popular Government,* Longmans Green, London.

Fombrun, C., Tichy, N.M. and Devanna, M.A. (1984), *Strategic Human Resource Management*, Wiley, New York.

Fondas, N. and Stewart, R. (1992), 'Understanding differences in general management jobs', *Journal of General Management*, Vol. 17, No. 4, pp.1–12.

Fondas, N. and Stewart, R. (1994), 'Enactment in managerial jobs: a role analysis', *Journal of Management Studies*, Vol. 31, No. 1, pp.83–103.

Ford, H. (1922), *My Life and Work,* Heinemann, London.

Franz, C.R. and Robey, D. (1986), 'Organizational context, user-involvement and the usefulness of information systems', *Decision Sciences*, Vol. 17, pp.329–59.

Frederick, W.C., Post, J.E. and Davis, K. (1992), *Business and Society*, McGraw-Hill, New York.

Freeman, R.E. and Gilbert, D.R. (1988), *Corporate Strategy and the Search for Ethics*, Prentice Hall, Englewood Cliffs, NJ.

French, W.L. and Bell, C.H. (1995), *Organization Development*, Prentice Hall, Englewood Cliffs, NJ.

French, J. and Raven, B. (1959), 'The bases of social power' in D. Cartwright (ed.), *Studies in Social Power*, Institute for Social Research, Ann Arbor, MI.

Frey, R. (1993), 'Empowerment or else', *Harvard Business Review*, Sept./Oct., pp.80–94.

Friedman, M. (1970), 'The social responsibility of business is to increase its profits', *New York Times*, 14 September.

Gabrial, Y. (1988), *Working Lives in Catering*, Routledge, London.

Galbraith, J. (1977), *Designing Complex Organizations*, Addison-Wesley, Reading, Mass.

Gallagher, M. (1992), *Women and Men in Broadcasting: Prospects for Equality,* Commission of the European Communities, Brussels.

Galliers, R.D., Pattison, E.M. and Reponen, T. (1994), 'Strategic information systems planning workshops: lessons from three cases', *International Journal of Information Management,* February, pp.51–66.

Gardner *et al.* (1996), 'Lufthansa: the challenge of global competition', London Business School, case reference LBS-CS96-050.

German, C. (1995), 'It all comes out in the wash', *The Independent,* 21 January.

Gerwin, D. (1979), 'Relationships between stucture and technology at the organizational and job levels', *Journal of Management Studies*, Vol. 16, No. 1, pp.70–9.

Ghauri, P.N. and Prasad, S.B. (eds) (1995), *International Management: A Reader*, Dryden Press, London.

Gilbreth, F. B. (1911), *Motion Study,* Van Nostrand, New York.

Gillespie, R. (1991), *Manufacturing Knowledge: A History of the Hawthorne Experiments*, Cambridge University Press, Cambridge.

Glaister, K.W. (1991), 'Virgin Atlantic Airways' in C. Clark-Hill and K. Glaister, *Cases in Strategic Management,* Pitman, London.

Glass, N. (1996), 'Chaos, non-linear systems and day-to-day management', *European Management Journal*, Vol. 14, No. 1, pp.98–106.

Goffee, R. and Jones, G. (1995), 'Developing managers for Europe: a re-examination of cross cultural differences', *European Management Journal*, Vol. 13, No. 3, pp.245–50.

Goffman, E. (1959), *The Presentation of Self in Everyday Life,* Doubleday, New York.

Goffman, E. (1961), *Encounters. Two Studies in the Sociology of Interaction*, Bobbs–Merrill, New York.

Goldratt, E. and Cox, J. (1989), *The Goal*, Gower, Aldershot.

Goold, M. (1997) 'Institutional advantage: a way into strategic management in not-for-profit organizations', *Long Range Planning*, Vol. 30, No. 2, pp.291–3.

Gordon, C. (1996), *Business Culture in France*, Butterworth/Heinemann, Oxford.

Gorry, G.A. and Scott Morton, M.S. (1971), 'A framework for management information systems', *Sloan Management Review*, Vol. 13, No. 1.

Gorz, A. (1989), *Critique of Economic Reason*, Verso, London.

Gough, J.W. (1957), *The Social Contract,* Clarendon Press, Oxford.

Graen, G.B. and Scandura, T.A. (1987), 'Towards a psychology of dyadic organizing', *Research in Organizational Behavior*, Vol. 9, pp.175–208.

Graham, P. (1994), *Mary Parker Follett: Prophet of Management*, Harvard Business School Press, Boston, Mass.

Grundy, F. (1996), *Women and Computers*, Intellect Books, Exeter.

Guest, D. E. (1987), 'Human resource management and industrial relations', *Journal of Management Studies*, Vol. 24, No. 5, pp.502–21.

Guest, D. (1988), 'Human resource management: a new opportunity for psychologists or another passing fad?', *The Occupational Psychologist*, February.

Guirdham, M. (1995), *Interpersonal Skills at Work*, Prentice Hall International, Hemel Hempstead.

Gunton, T. (1990), *Inside Information Technology: A Practical Guide to Management Issues*, Prentice Hall, Englewood Cliffs, NJ.

Guzzo, R.A. and Shea, G.P. (1992), 'Group performance and intergroup relations in organizations' in M.D. Dunnette and L.M. Hough, (eds), *Handbook of Workgroup Psychology*, Vol. 3, pp.269–313, Consulting Psychologists Press, Palo Alto, Ca.

Haasen, A. (1996), 'Opel Eisenach GmbH: creating a high-productivity workplace', *Organizational Dynamics*, Spring, pp.80–5.

Habermas, J. (1972), *Knowledge and Human Interests*, Heinemann, London.

Hackman, J. R. (1990), *Groups that Work (and Those That Don't)*, Jossey-Bass, San Francisco.

Hackman, J.R. and Oldham, G.R. (1980), *Work Redesign*, Addison-Wesley, Reading, Mass.

Hage, J. and Aiken, M. (1967), Program change and organizational properties: a comparative analysis', *American Journal of Sociology*, Vol. 72, pp.503–19.

Hales, C.P. (1986), 'What do managers do? A critical review of the evidence', *Journal of Management Studies*, Vol. 23, No.1 , pp.88–115.

Hales, C. (1993), *Managing Through Organization*, Routledge, London.

Hall, W. (1995), *Managing Cultures*, Wiley, Chichester.

Hamel, G. and Prahalad, C.K. (1994), *Competing for the Future*, Harvard Business School Press, Boston, Mass.

Hamel, G. and Prahalad, C.K. (1996), 'Competing in the new economy', *Strategic Management Journal*, Vol. 17, pp. 237–42.

Handy, C. (1987), *The Making of Managers*, MSC/NEDC/BIM, London.

Handy, C. (1988), *Understanding Voluntary Organizations*, Penguin, Harmondsworth.

Handy, C. (1993), *Understanding Organizations* (4th edn), Penguin, Harmondsworth.

Handy, C. (1994), *The Empty Raincoat: Making Sense of the Future*, Hutchinson, London.

Hannan, M.T., and Freeman, J. (1989), *Organizational Ecology*, Harvard University Press, Cambridge, Mass.

Hardy, C. and Redivo, F. (1994), 'Power and organizational development: a framework for organizational change', *Journal of General Management*, Vol. 20, No. 2.

Harris, P.R. and Moran, R. (1991), *Managing Cultural Differences*, Gulf Publishing, Houston.

Harrison, F. (1985), *Advanced Project Management*, Gower, Aldershot.

Harrison, J., Holloway, M., Jenkins, T., Martin, F. and Mills, G. (1995), *Management and Strategy*, Certified Accountants Educational Projects Ltd, A.T. Foulks Lynch, Feltham.

Hartley, R. F. (1993), *Business Ethics: Violations of the Public Trust*, Wiley, New York.

Harvey, B. (ed.) (1994), *Business Ethics: A European Approach*, Prentice Hall International, Hemel Hempstead.

Hassard, J. and Parker, M. (1993), *Postmodernism and Organizations*, Sage, London.

Hastings, C., Bixby, P. and Chaudry-Lawton, R. (1986), *Superteams*, Fontana, London.

Haveman, H.A. (1992), 'Between a rock and a hard place: organizational change and performance under conditions of fundamental environmental transformation', *Administrative Science Quarterly*, Vol. 37, pp.48–75.

Hayes, N. (1997), *Successful Team Development*, International Thompson Business Press, London.

Hellriegel, D. and Slocum, J.W. (1988), *Management* (5th edn), Addison-Wesley, Reading, Mass.

Hendry, C. and Pettigrew, A. (1990), 'Human resource management: an agenda for the 1990s', *International Journal of Human Resource Management*, Vol. 1, pp.17–43.

Herzberg, F. (1959), *The Motivation to Work*, Wiley, New York.

Herzberg, F. (1987), 'One more time: how do you motivate employees?' *Harvard Business Review*, Vol. 65, Sept./Oct.

Hill, C.W.L. and Pickering, J.F. (1986), 'Divisionalization, decentralization and performance of large United Kingdom companies', *Journal of Management Studies*, Vol. 23, No. 1, pp.26–50.

Hill, T. (1993), *Manufacturing Strategy*, Macmillan, Basingstoke.

Hiltrop, J-M. (1995), 'The changing psychological contract: the human resources challenge of the 1990s', *European Management Journal*, Vol. 13, No. 3, pp.288–94.

Hinings, C.R., Brown, J.L. and Greenwood, R. (1991), 'Change in an autonomous professional organization', *Journal of Management Studies*, Vol. 28, No. 4, pp.375–93.

Hirscheim, R.A. (1985), 'User experience, work and assessment of participative systems design', *MIS Quarterly*, December, pp.295–303.

Hirschheim, R. and Klein, H.K. (1989), 'Four paradigms of information systems development', *Communications of the ACM*, Vol. 32, No. 10, pp.1199–214.

HMSO (1989), *Working for Patients*, HMSO, London.

Hofstede, G. (1980), *Culture's Consequences: International Differences in Work-Related Values*, Sage, Beverley Hills, Calif.

Hofstede, G. (1989), 'Organizing for cultural diversity', *European Management Journal*, Vol. 7, No. 4, pp.390–7.

Hofstede, G. (1991), *Cultures and Organizations: Software of the Mind*, McGraw-Hill, London.

Hofstede, G. (1994), 'Management scientists are human', *Management Science*, Vol. 40, No. 1, pp.4–13.

Hogwood, B.W. and Gunn, L.A. (1984), *Policy Analysis for the Real World*, Oxford University Press, Oxford.

Homans, G. (1950), *The Human Group*, Harcourt, New York.

Honerich, T. (ed.) (1995), *Ethical Reasoning*, Oxford University Press, Oxford,

Hopfenbeck, W. (1993), *The Green Management Revolution*, Prentice Hall International, Hemel Hempstead.

Horngren, C.T., Foster, G. and Datar, S.M. (1997) *Cost Accounting: A Managerial Emphasis*, Prentice Hall, Englewood Cliffs, NJ.

House, R.J. and Mitchell, T.R. (1974), 'Path–goal theory of leadership', *Contemporary Business*, Vol. 3, No. 2, pp.81–98.

Howard, J.A. and Sheth, J. N. (1969), *The Theory of Buyer Behaviour*, Wiley, New York.

Huselick, M. A. (1995), 'The impact of human resource management practices on turnover, productivity and corporate financial performance', *Academy of Management Journal*, Vol. 38, No. 3.

Huseman, R.C. and Alexander, E.R. (1979), 'Communication and the managerial function: a contingency approach' in R.C. Huseman, and A.B. Carroll (eds), *Readings in Organization Behaviour*, Allyn & Bacon, Boston.

Iivari, J. and Hirschheim, R. (1996), 'Analyzing information systems development: a comparison and analysis of eight development approaches', *Information Systems*, Vol. 21, No. 7, pp.551–75.

Incomes Data Services (1993), *A Changing Workforce: Labour Market Analysis*, IDS Report No. 640.

Indvik, J. (1986), 'Path–goal theory of leadership: a meta-analysis', *Proceedings of the American Academy of Management Meeting*, pp.189–92.

Institute of Management (1995a), *Report of the Taylor Working Party*, Institute of Management, Corby.

Institute of Management (1995b), *Finding the Time: A Survey of Managers' Attitudes to Using and Managing Time*, Institute of Management, London.

IPD (1996), *The IPD Guide on Team Rewards*, Institute of Personnel Development, London.

Ives, B. and Olson, M.H. (1984), 'User involvement and MIS success: a review of research', *Management Science*, Vol. 30, No. 5, pp.586–603.

Jackson, T. (1993), *Organizational Behaviour in International Management*, Butterworth/Heinemann, Oxford.

Jackson, T. (1997), '"Dare to be different", The management interview with Michael Porter', *Financial Times*, 19 June.

Janis, I. (1977), *Groupthink: Psychological Studies of Policy Decisions*, Houghton Mifflin, Boston, Mass.

Johnson, G. (1990), 'Managing strategic change: the role of symbolic action', *British Journal of Management*, Vol. 1, No. 4, pp.183–200.

Johnson, G. and Scholes, K. (1993) *Exploring Corporate Strategy* (3rd edn), Prentice Hall International, Hemel Hempstead.

Johnson, G. and Scholes, K. (1997), *Exploring Corporate Strategy* (4th edn), Prentice Hall International, Hemel Hempstead.

Johnston, R.A., Kast, F.E. and Rosenweig, J.E. (eds) (1967), 'People and systems' in *The Theory and Management of Systems*, McGraw-Hill, New York.

Jones, I. (1996), paper delivered at a conference on ethical marketing, Ridley Hall, Cambridge, February.

Juran, J. (1974), *Quality Control Handbook,* McGraw-Hill, New York.

Kakabadse, A. (1993), 'The success levers for Europe: the Cranfield executive competences survey', *Journal of Management Development*, Vol. 12, No. 8, pp.12–17.

Kanter, R.M. (1979), 'Power failure in management circuits', *Harvard Business Review*, Vol. 57, July/Aug. pp.65–75.

Kanter, R.M. (1983), *The Change Masters*, Unwin, London.

Kanter, R.M. (1985), 'Managing the human side of change', *Management Review,* April, pp.52–6.

Kanter, R.M. (1989a), *When Giants Learn to Dance*, Simon & Schuster, London.

Kanter, R.M. (1989b), 'Becoming PALs: pooling, allying and linking across companies', *Academy of Management Executive*, Vol. 3, No. 3, pp.183–93.

Kanter, R.M. (1995), *World Class: Thriving Locally in the Global Economy*, Simon & Schuster, New York.

Kaplan, R.S. and Norton, D.P. (1992), 'The balanced scorecard: measures that drive performance', *Harvard Business Review*, No. 1, Jan./Feb.

Kaplan, R.S. and Norton, D.P. (1993), 'Putting the balanced scorecard to work', *Harvard Business Review*, No. 5, Sept./Oct., pp.134–47.

Kaplan, R. S. and Norton, D. P. (1996), *The Balanced Scorecard*, Harvard Business School Press, Harvard, Mass.

Kast, F.E. and Rosenzweig, J.E. (1973), *Contingency Views of Organizations and Management*, Science Research Associates, Chicago.

Katz, D. and Kahn, R.L. (1978), *The Social Psychology of Organizations* (2nd edn), Wiley, New York.

Katzenbach, J.R. and Smith, D.K. (1993a), 'The discipline of teams', *Harvard Business Review*, Mar./Apr., pp.111–20.

Katzenbach, J.R. and Smith, D.K. (1993b), *The Wisdom of Teams*, Harvard Business School Press, Boston, Mass.

Kay, J. (1993), *Foundations for Corporate Success: How Business Strategies Add Value*, Oxford University Press, Oxford.

Kay, J. (1996), *The Business of Economics*, Oxford University Press, Oxford.

Kearney, A.T. (1990), *Barriers to the Successful Application of Information Technology*, Department of Trade and Industry/CIMA, London.

Kearney, A.T. (1992), *Total Quality: Time to Take Off the Rose-tinted Spectacles*, IFS, Kempstown.

Keen, P. (1981), 'Information systems and organization change' in E. Rhodes and D. Weild (eds), *Implementing New Technologies*, Blackwell/Open University Press, Oxford.

Kirkbride, P.S. (ed.) (1994), *Human Resource Management in Europe,* Routledge, London.

Knights, D. and Murray, F. (1994), *Managers Divided: Organizational Politics and Information Technology Management,* Wiley, London.

Kochan, T.A. (1992), *Principles for a Post-New Deal Employment Policy,* Sloan School of Management, MIT, Working Paper 5.

Kolb, D., Rubin, E. and McIntyre, J. (1991), *Organizational Psychology,* Prentice Hall International, Hemel Hempstead.

Kotler, P. (1997), *Marketing Management: Analysis, Planning, Implementation, and Control* (9th edn), Prentice Hall International, Hemel Hempstead.

Kotler, P. and Armstrong, G. (1997), *Marketing: An Introduction* (4th edn), Prentice Hall International, Hemel Hempstead.

Kotler, P. and Levy, S.J. (1969), 'Broadening the concept of marketing', *Journal of Marketing,* January.

Kotler, P., Armstrong, G., Saunders, J. and Wong, V. (1996), *Principles of Marketing;* (European edition), Prentice Hall International, Hemel Hempstead.

Kotter, J. (1982), *The General Managers,* Free Press, New York.

Kotter, J.P. (1996), *Leading Change,* Harvard Business School Press, Boston, Mass.

Kotter, J. and Heskett, J. (1992), *Corporate Culture and Performance,* Free Press, New York.

Kotter, J.P. and Schlesinger, L.A. (1979), 'Choosing strategies for change', *Harvard Business Review,* March/April.

Krackhardt, D. and Hanson, J.R. (1993), 'Informal networks: the company behind the chart', *Harvard Business Review,* July/Aug., pp.104–11.

Kristensen, P.H., *The Changing European Firm,* Routledge, London.

Lambin, J-J. and Hiller, T.B. (1994), 'Volvo Trucks Europe' in J. Montana, *Marketing in Europe: Case Studies,* Sage, London.

Lancaster, G. and Messingham, L. (1993), *Essentials of Marketing* (2nd edn), McGraw-Hill, New York.

Larson, C.E. and LaFasto, F.M.J. (1989), *Teamwork: What Must Go Right, What Can Go Wrong,* Sage, New York.

Laurent, A. (1983), 'The cultural diversity of western conceptions of management', *International Studies of Management and Organization,* Vol. 13, Nos 1/2, pp.75–96.

Lawler, E.E. (1986), *High Involvement Management: Participative Strategies for Improving Organizational Performance,* Jossey-Bass, San Francisco.

Lawrence, P. and Lorsch, J.W. (1967), *Organization and Environment,* Harvard Business School Press, Boston, Mass.

Leach, S. (1996), *Mission Statements and Strategic Visions: Symbol or Substance,* Local Government Management Board, London.

Leavitt, H. J. (1965), 'Applied organizational change in industry: structural, technological and humanistic approaches' in J.G. March (ed.), *Handbook of Organizations,* Rand McNally, Chicago,

Lederer, A.L. and Sethi, V. (1988), 'The implementation of strategic information systems planning methodologies', *MIS Quarterly,* Vol. 12, No. 3, pp.445–61.

Legge, K. (1978), *Power, Innovation and Problem Solving in Personnel Management,* McGraw-Hill, London.

Legge, K. (1995), *Human Resource Management: Rhetorics and Realities,* Macmillan, London.

Leith, P. (1986), 'Legal expert systems: misunderstanding the legal process', *Computers and Law,* Vol. 49, September.

Lengel, R.H. and Daft, R.L. (1988), 'The selection of communication media as an executive skill', *Academy of Management Executive,* Vol. 11, No. 3, pp.225–32.

Levitt, T. (1958), 'The dangers of social responsibility', *Harvard Business Rev* Sept./Oct., pp.27–36.

Levitt, T. (1960), 'Marketing myopia', *Harvard Business Review*, July/Aug., pp.45–56.

Lewin, K. (1947), 'Frontiers in group dynamics', *Human Relations*, Vol. 1, pp.5–41.

Lieberson, S. and O'Connor, J.F. (1977), 'Leadership and organizational performance: a study of large corporations', *American Sociological Review*, Vol. 37, pp.117–30.

Likert, R. (1961), *New Patterns of Management*, McGraw-Hill, New York.

Likert, R. (1967), *The Human Organization: Its Management and Value*, McGraw-Hill, New York.

Lindblom, C.E. (1959), 'The science of muddling through', *Public Administration Review*, Vol. 19, No. 2, pp.79–88.

Locke, D. (1996), *Project Management* (6th edn), Gower, Aldershot.

Lodge, D. (1989), *Nice Work*, Penguin, London.

Long, P. (1986), *Performance Appraisal Revisited*, Institute of Personnel Management, London.

Lorsch, J.W. (1986), 'Managing culture: the invisible barrier to strategic change', *California Management Review*, Vol. 28, No. 2.

Lorsch, J. and Morse, J. (1970), 'Beyond Theory Y', *Harvard Business Review*, Vol. 48, May/June, pp.61–8.

Lovelock, C.H. (1991), *Services Marketing*, Prentice Hall, Englewood Cliffs, NJ.

Lowe, T.R. (1986), 'Eight ways to ruin a performance review', *Personnel Journal*, January.

Lucas, H.C. (1996), *The T-form Organization: Using Technology to Design Organizations for the 21st Century*, Jossey-Bass, San Francisco.

Luthans, F. (1988), 'Successful vs effective real managers', *Academy of Management Executive*, Vol. 11, No. 2, pp.127–32.

Mabey, C. and Mayon-White, B. (eds) (1993), *Managing Change* (2nd edn), The Open University/Paul Chapman Publishing, London.

Mabey, C. and Salaman, G. (1995), *Strategic Human Resource Management*, Blackwell, Oxford.

Macbeth, D.K. and Ferguson, N. (1994), *Partnership Sourcing: An Integrated Supply Chain Approach*, Financial Times/Pitman, London.

Maccoby, M. (1988), *Why Work: Motivating and Leading the New Generation*, Simon & Schuster, New York.

Mangham, I. and Silver, M. (1986), *Management Training, Context and Practice*, ESRC, London.

Manz, C.C. and Sims, H.P. (1987), 'Leading workers to lead themselves: the external leadership of self-managed teams', *Administrative Science Quarterly*, Vol. 32, pp.106–28.

Markus, M.L. (1983). 'Power, politics and MIS implementation', *Communications of the ACM*, Vol. 26, No. 6, pp.430–44.

Markus, M.L. (1984), *Systems in Organizations*, Pitman, London.

Markus, M.L. and Keil, M. (1994), 'If we build it, they will come: designing information systems that people want to use', *Sloan Management Review*, Summer, pp.11–25.

Markus, M.L. and Robey, D. (1983), 'The organizational validity of management information systems', *Human Relations*, Vol. 36, No. 3, pp.203–26.

Marshall, J. (1984), *Women Managers – Travellers in a Male World*, Wiley, Chichester.

Martin, E.W., Hoffer, J.A., DeHayes, D.W. and Perkins, W.C. (1994), *Managing Information Technology: What Managers Need to Know*, Macmillan, New York.

Martinko, M.J. and Gardner, W.L. (1990), 'Structured observation of managerial work: a replication and synthesis', *Journal of Management Studies*, Vol. 27, No. 3, pp.329–57.

Maslow, A. (1970), *Motivation and Personality* (2nd edn), Harper & Row, New York.

Mastenbroek, W.F.G. (1993), *Conflict Management and Organization Development*, Wiley, Chichester.

Mata, F.J., Fuerst, W.L. and Barney, J.B. (1995), 'Information technology and sustained competitive advantage', *MIS Quarterly*, Vol. 19, No. 4, pp.487–505.

Mayer, M. and Whittington, R. (1996), 'The survival of the European holding company: institutional choice and contingency' in R. Whitley and P.H. Kristensen (eds), *The Changing European Firm*, Routledge, London.

Mayo, E. (1949), *The Social Problems of an Industrial Civilization*, London.

McBride, N. (1997), 'Business use of the Internet', *European Management Journal*, Vol. 15, No.1, pp.58–67.

McCalman, J. and Paton, R. (1992), *Managing Change*, Paul Chapman Publishing, London.

McCauly, N. and Ala, M. (1992), 'The use of expert systems in the health care industry', *Information and Management*, Vol. 22, pp.227–35.

McClelland, D. (1961), *The Achieving Society*, Van Nostrand Reinhold, Princeton, NJ.

McFarlan, E.W. and McKenney, J.L. (1983), *Corporate Information Systems Management:* The *Issues Facing Senior Executives*. Dow Jones/Irwin, Chicago.

McGregor, D. (1960), *The Human Side of Enterprise*, McGraw-Hill, New York.

MCI (1991), *Crediting Competence,* Management Charter Initiative, London.

MCI (1997), *Occupational Standards for Managers*, Management Charter Initiative, London.

McKeen, J.D., Guimaraes, T. and Wetherbe, J.C. (1994), 'The relationship between user participation and user satisfaction: an investigation of four contingency Factors', *MIS Quarterly*, Vol. 18, No. 4, pp.427–51.

McLoughlin, I. and Clark, J. (1994), *Technological Change at Work* (2nd edn), The Open University Press, Milton Keynes.

Meidan, A. and Moutinho, L. (1993), *Cases in Marketing of Services, An International Collection*, Addison-Wesley, Wokingham.

Meidan, A. Lewis, B. and Moutinho, L. (1997), *Financial Services Marketing: A Reader,* Dryden Press, Mass.

Michaels, E.G. (1982), 'Marketing muscle', *Business Horizons* May/June, pp.63–74.

Mill, J. (1994), 'No pain, no gain', *Computing*, 3 February, pp.26–7.

Miller, D. and Ming-Jer Chen (1994), 'Sources and consequences of competitive inertia: a study of the US airline industry', *Administrative Science Quarterly*, Vol. 39, pp.1–23.

Miller, P., Pons, J.M. and Naude, P. (1996), 'Global teams', *Financial Times*, 14 June.

Mintel (1995), *The Green Consumer Report*, Mintel Publications, London.

Mintzberg, H. (1973), *The Nature of Managerial Work*, Harper & Row, New York.

Mintzberg, H. (1979), *The Structuring of Organizations*, Prentice Hall, Englewood Cliffs, NJ.

Mintzberg, H. (1983), 'The case for corporate social responsibility', *Journal of Business Strategy*, Vol. 4, No. 2, pp.3–15.

Mintzberg, H. (1989), *Mintzberg on Management*, Free Press, New York.

Mintzberg, H. (1994a), *The Rise and Fall of Strategic Planning*, Prentice Hall International, Hemel Hempstead.

Mintzberg, H. (1994b), 'Rethinking strategic planning. Part I: Pitfalls and fallacies', *Long Range Planning*, Vol. 27, No. 3, pp.12–21.

Mintzberg, H. (1994c), 'Rethinking strategic planning Part II: New roles for planners', *Long Range Planning*, Vol. 27, No. 3, pp.22–30.

Misumi, J. (1985), *The Behavioral Science of Leadership: An Interdisciplinary Japanese Research Programme*, University of Michigan Press, Ann Arbor.

Moncrieff, J. and Smallwood, J. (1996), 'Strategic management: ideas for the new millennium', *Financial Times*, 19 July.

Montana, J. (ed.) (1994), *Marketing in Europe: Case Studies*, Sage, London.

Montanari, J.R. and Bracker, J.S. (1986), 'The strategic management process at the public planning unit level', *Strategic Management Journal*, Vol. 7, No. 3.

Morgan, G. (1997), *Images of Organization*, Sage, London.

Morley, C. (1993), 'Information systems development methods and user participation: a contingency approach' in D. Avison, J.E. Kendall and J.I. DeGross (eds), *Human, Organizational, and Social Dimensions of Information Systems Development* (A-24), North-Holland, Amsterdam.

Morley, L. (1990), 'Expense account', *Computing*, 2 May, pp.18–19.

Morse, J.W. and Lorsch, J. J. (1970), 'Beyond Theory Y', *Harvard Business Review*, May/June, pp.61–8.

Moutinho, L. (1995), *Cases in Marketing Management*, Addison-Wesley, Wokingham.

Mukhopadhyay, T., Kekre, S. and Kalathur, S. (1995), 'Business value of information technology: a study of electronic data interchange', *MIS Quarterly*, Vol. 19, pp.137–54.

Mumford, E. (1983), *Designing Human Systems: Ethics – Effective Technical and Human Implementation of Computer-based Systems*, Manchester Business School, Manchester.

Mumford, E. and Weir, M. (1979), *Computer Systems in Work Design: The Ethics Method*, Associated Business Press, London.

Murray, F. (1991), 'Technical rationality and the IS specialist: power, discourse and identity', *Critical Perspectives of Accounting*, Vol. 2, pp.59–81.

Nash, L. (1990), *Good Intentions Aside*, Harvard Business School Press, Boston, Mass.

Noble, F. and Newman, M. (1993), 'Integrated system, autonomous departments: organizational invalidity and stem change in a university', *Journal of Management Studies*, Vol. 30, No. 2, pp.195–219.

Nugent, N. and O'Donnell, R. (1994), *The European Business Environment*, Macmillan, Basingstoke.

Oakland, J. (1994), *Total Quality Management,* Butterworth/Heinemann, Oxford.

OECD (1993), *Private Pay for Public Work: Performance Related Pay for Public Sector Managers*, OECD, Paris.

Orlicky, J. (1975), *Material Requirements Planning*, McGraw-Hill, New York.

Parker, D. and Stacey, R. (1994), *Chaos, Management and Economics: The Implications of Non-linear Thinking*, Hobart Paper 125, Institute of Economic Affairs, London.

Pascale, R. (1990), *Managing on the Edge*, Penguin, London.

Pearce, J.A. and Robinson, R. (1991), *Strategic Management: Formulation, Implementation and Control*, Irwin, Homewood, Ill.

Peattie, K. (1992), *Green Marketing,* M&E Handbooks, London.

Peters, T. J. (1987), *Thriving on Chaos: Handbook for a Management Revolution*, Alfred A. Knopf, New York.

Peters, T.J. and Waterman, D.H. (1982), *In Search of Excellence*, Harper & Row, London.

Pettigrew, A. (1985), *The Awakening Giant: Continuity and Change in Imperial Chemical Industries*, Blackwell, Oxford.

Pettigrew, A. (1987), 'Context and action in the transformation of the firm', *Journal of Management Studies*, Vol. 24, No. 6, pp.649–70.

Pfeffer, J. (1981), *Power in Organizations*, Ballinger, Cambridge, Mass.

Pfeffer, J. (1992), *Managing with Power*, Harvard Business School Press, Boston, Mass.

Pfeffer, J. (1994), *Competitive Advantage Through People*, Harvard Business School Press, Cambridge, Mass.

Pharoah, C. (ed.) (1996), *Dimensions of the Voluntary Sector*, Charities Aid Foundation, West Malling.

Podmore, D. and Spencer, A. (1986), 'Gender in the labour process: the case of women and men lawyers' in D. Knights and H. Willmott (eds), *Gender and the Labour Process*, Gower, Aldershot.

Porter, L.W. and Roberts, K.H. (1983), 'Communication in organizations' in Dunnette, M. (ed.), *Handbook of Industrial and Organizational Psychology*, Wiley, New York.

Porter, M.E. (1980a), *Competitive Strategy*, Free Press, New York.

Porter, M. (1980b), *Competitive Advantage,* Free Press, New York.

Porter, M.E. (1985), *Competitive Advantage: Creating and Sustaining Superior Performance*, Free Press, New York.

Porter, M.E. (1990), *The Competitive Advantage of Nations*, Free Press, New York.

Porter, M.E. (1994), 'Competitive strategy revisited: a view from the 1990s' in P. Barker Duffy (ed.), *The Relevance of a Decade*, Harvard Business School Press, Boston.

Price, A. (1994), 'A practical approach to corporate ethical decision making', unpublished conference paper.

Price, A. (1997), Phd thesis (forthcoming).

Price Waterhouse/Cranfield Project (1995), *International Strategic Human Resource Management*, University of Limerick, Limerick.

Pugh, D.S. and Hickson, D.J. (1976), *Organization Structure in its Context: The Aston Programme I*, Gower, Aldershot.

Pugh, D.S. and Hickson D.J. (1989), *Writers on Organisations* (4th edn), Penguin, London.

Quinn, J.B. (1980), *Strategies for Change: Logical Incrementalism*, Irwin, Homewood, Ill.

Quinn, R.E., Faerman, S.R., Thompson, M.P. and McGrath, M.R. (1996), *Becoming a Master Manager* (2nd edn), Wiley, New York.

Recardo, R. (1991), 'The what, why and how of change management', *Manufacturing Systems,* May, pp.52–8.

Ritzer, G. (1993), *The McDonaldization of Society*, Pine Forge Press, London.

Robertson, I. (1996), 'Personnel selection and assessment' in P. Warr (ed.), *Psychology at Work* (4th edn), Penguin, Harmondsworth.

Robin, D.P. and Reidenbach, R.E. (1981), *Business Ethics: Where Profits Meet Value Systems*, Prentice Hall, Englewood Cliffs, NJ.

Robin, D.P. and Reidenbach, R.E. (1987), 'Social responsibility, ethics and marketing strategy: closing the gap between concept and application', *Journal of Marketing*, Vol. 51, Jan., pp.44–58.

Robson, M. (1993), *Problem Solving in Groups* (2nd edn), Gower, Aldershot.

Roddick, A. (1991), *Body and Soul*, Ebury Press, London.

Roethlisberger, F.J. and Dickson, W.J. (1939), *Management and the Worker*, Harvard University Press, Cambridge, Mass.

Ross, S.A., Westerfield, R.W. and Jordan, B.D. (1995), *Fundamentals of Corporate Finance,* Irwin, Chicago.

Rothwell, S. (1995), 'Human resource planning' in J. Storey (ed.), *Human Resource Management*: *A Critical Text*, Routledge, London.

Rousseau, D.H. (1995), *Psychological Contracts in Organisation*, Sage, London.

Sandberg, A. (ed.) (1995), *Enriching Production*, Avebury, Aldershot.

SAUS (1993), *Good Business: Cases in Corporate Social Responsibility,* New Consumer/SAUS, Bristol.

Schein, E.J. (1969), *Process Consultation: Its Role in Organization Development.* Addison-Wesley, Reading, Mass.

Schein, E.H. (1980), *Organizational Psychology* (3rd edn), Prentice Hall, Englewood Cliffs, NJ.

Schein, E.H. (1985), *Organizational Culture and Leadership*, Jossey-Bass, San Francisco.

Schonberger, (1983), *Japanese Manufacturing Techniques*, Free Press, New York.

Schuler R.S. and Huber, V.L. (1990), *Personnel and Human Resource Management* (4th edn), West Publishing, St Paul, Minneapolis.

Selznick, P. (1957), *Leadership in Administration: A Sociological Interpretation*, Harper & Row, London.

Sengenberger, W. (1992), 'Lean production: the way of working and producing in the future?' in F. Pyke, and W. Sengenberger (eds), *Industrial Districts and Local Economic Regeneration*, International Institute for Labour Studies, Geneva.

Shamir, B. (1991), 'Meaning, self and motivation in organization', *Organization Studies*, Vol. 12, No. 3, pp.405–24.

Shaw, M.E. (1978), 'Comunication networks fourteen years later' in L. Berkowitz (ed.), *Group Processes*, Academic Press, New York.

Shaw, W.H. (1991), *Business Ethics*, Wadsworth, California.

Silver, J. (1987), 'The ideology of excellence: management and neo-conservatism', *Studies in Political Economy*, Vol. 24, pp.105–29.

Simon, H.A. (1947), *Administrative Behaviour*, Macmillan, London.

Simon, H.A. (1957), *Administrative Behaviour* (2nd edn), Macmillan, London.

Simons, R. (1995), 'Control in an age of empowerment', *Harvard Business Review*, Mar./Apr., pp.80–8.

Skinner, B.F. (1971), *Contingencies of Reinforcement*, Appleton-Century-Crofts, East Norwalk, Conn.

Skinner, W. (1969), 'Manufacturing – the missing link in corporate strategy', *Harvard Business Review*, May/June.

Smith, A. (1776), *The Wealth of Nations*, edited with an introduction by Andrew Skinner (1974), Penguin, Harmondsworth.

Smith, N.C. (1990), *Morality and the Market*, Routledge, London.

Smith, P.B. (1992), 'Organizational behaviour and national cultures', *British Journal of Management*, Vol. 3, pp.39–51.

Smith, R.J. (1994), *Strategic Management and Planning in the Public Sector*, Longman/Civil Service College, Harlow.

Sonnentag, S. (1994), 'Team leading in software development: a comparison between women and men' in A. Adams, J. Emms, E. Green and J. Owen (eds), *Women, Work and Computerisation* (A-57), Elsevier/North-Holland, Amsterdam.

Soothill, K., Mackay, L. and Webb, C. (eds) (1995), *Interprofessional Relations in Health Care*, Edward Arnold, London.

Sparrow, P. and Hiltrop, J. (1994), *European Human Resource Management in Transition*, Prentice Hall International, Hemel Hempstead.

Spriegel, W.R. and Myers, C.E. (eds) (1953), *The Writings of the Gilbreths*, Irwin, Homewood, Ill.

Stamp, P. and Robarts, S. (1986), *Positive Action: Changing the Workplace for Women*, National Council for Civil Liberties, London.

Stark, A. (1993), 'What's the matter with the business ethics?', *Harvard Business Review*, May/June, pp.36–48.

Stationery Office (1996), *A Programme of Change for the Irish Civil Service*, The Stationery Office, Dublin.

Steiger, T. and Reskin, B.F. (1990), 'Baking and baking off: deskilling and the changing sex makeup of bakers' in B.F. Reskin and P.A. Roos (eds), *Job Queues, Gender Queues*, Temple University Press, Philadelphia, Pa.

Sternberg, E. (1995), *Just Business: Business Ethics in Action*, Warner Books, New York.

Stewart, J. and Walsh, K. (1994), 'Performance measurement: when performance can never be fully defined', *Public Money and Management*, Apr./June, pp.45–49.

Stewart, R. (1967), *Managers and their Jobs*, Macmillan, London.

Stewart, R. (1991), *Managers Today and Tomorrow*, Macmillan, London.

Stewart, R., Barsoux, J-L., Kieser, A., Ganter, H-D. and Walgenbach, P. (1994), *Managing in Britain and Germany*, Macmillan, Basingstoke.

Stogdill, R.M. (1974), *Handbook of Leadership: A Survey of the Literature*, Free Press, New York.

Stone, C. (1990), 'Why shouldn't corporations be socially responsible?' in W.M. Hoffman, and J.M. Moore (eds), *Business Ethics: Readings and Cases in Corporate Morality*, McGraw-Hill, New York.

Stonham, P. (1996), 'Whatever happened at Barings?' *European Management Journal*, Vol. 14, No. 2, pp.167–75 and No. 3, pp.269–78.

Storey, J. (1992), *Developments in the Management of Human Resources*, Blackwell, Oxford.

Storey, J. (ed.) (1995), *Human Resource Management: A Critical Text*, Routledge, London.

Supply Chain Management Group (1995), *The Supply Chain Improvement Process and the Relationship Positioning Tool*, SCMG Ltd, University of Glasgow, Glasgow.

Suutari, V. (1996), 'Leadership ideologies among European managers: a comparative study in a multinational company', *Scandinavian Journal of Management*, Vol. 12, No. 4, pp.389–409.

Tayeb, M.H. (1996), *The Management of a Multicultural Workforce*, Wiley, Chichester.

Taylor, B. (1997), 'The return of strategic planning – once more with feeling', *Long Range Planning*, Vol. 30, No. 3, pp.334–44.

Taylor, F.W. (1917), *The Principles of Scientific Management*, Harper, New York.

Taylor, W. (1991), 'The logic of global business: an interview with ABB's Percy Barnevik', *Harvard Business Review*, Mar./Apr., pp.90–105.

Thomas, A.B. (1993), *Controversies in Management*, Routledge, London.

Thompson, J.D. (1967), *Organizations in Action*, McGraw-Hill, New York.

Thompson, P. and McHugh, D. (1995), *Work Organisations*: *A Critical Introduction* Macmillan, Basingstoke.

Thomson, A., Storey, J., Mabey, C., Gray, C., Farmer, E. and Thomson, R. (1997), *A Portrait of Management Development*, Institute of Management, London.

Thurley, K. and Wirdenius, H. (1989), *Towards European Management*, Pitman, London.

Tichy, N.M. (1982), 'Managing change strategically: the technical, political, and cultural keys', *Organizational Dynamics*, Autumn.

Towers Perrin/IBM (1992), *Priorities for Competitive Advantage*, Towers Perrin, London.

Tuckman, B. and Jensen, N. (1977), 'Stages of small group development revisited', *Group and Organizational Studies*, Vol. 2, pp.419–27.

Turner, A.N. (1961), 'A conceptual scheme for describing work group behavior', Case No. 461-001, Harvard Business School, Boston, Mass. Reprinted in P.R. Lawrence and J.A. Seiler (1965), *Organizational Behavior and Administration* (rev. edn), Irwin, Homewood, Ill.

Turoff, M., Hiltz, S.R., Bahgat, A.N.F. and Rana, A.R. (1993), 'Distributed group support systems', *MIS Quarterly*, Vol. 17, No. 4, pp.399–417.

Tyson, S. and Fell, A. (1985), *Evaluating the Personnel Function*, Hutchinson, London.

Vallance, E. (1996), *Business Ethics at Work*, Cambridge University Press, Cambridge.

Vecchio, R.P. (1984), 'Models of psychological inequity', *Organizational Behavior and Human Performance*, Vol. 34, pp.266–82.

Votaw, D. (1973), 'The nature of social responsibility' in D. Votaw and S.P. Sethi (eds), *The Corporate Dilemma: Traditional Values and Contemporary Problems*, Prentice Hall, Englewood Cliffs, NJ.

Vroom, V. (1964), *Work and Motivation*, Wiley, New York.

Vroom, V.H. and Yetton, P.W. (1973), *Leadership and Decision-making*, University of Pittsburgh Press, Pittsburgh.

Wastell, D.G., White, P. and Kawalek, P. (1994), 'A methodology for business process redesign: experience and issues', *Journal of Strategic Information Systems*, Vol. 3, No. 1, pp.23–40.

Watson, T.J. (1994), *In Search of Management*, Routledge, London.

Weber, M. (1947), *The Theory of Social and Economic Organization*, Free Press, Glencoe.

Weiner, N. and Mahoney, T.A. (1981), 'A model of corporate performance as a function of environmental, organizational and leadership influences', *Academy of Management Journal*, Vol. 24, pp. 453–70.

Weinstein, K. (1995), *Action Learning*, Harper Collins, London.

Wells, P. (1995), 'Premier Teas', New Consumer Research Working Paper.

West, M.A. and Anderson, N.R. (1996), 'Innovation in top management teams', *Journal of Applied Psychology*, Vol. 81, No. 6, pp.680–93.

Whipp, R., Rosenfeld, R. and Pettigrew, A. (1988), 'Understanding strategic change processes: some preliminary British findings' in A. Pettigrew (ed.), *The Management of Strategic Change*, Blackwell, Oxford.

Whitley, R. (1996), 'The social construction of economic actors' in R. Whitley and P.H. Kristensen (eds), *The Changing European Firm*, Routledge, London.

Wickens, P.D. (1995), *The Ascendant Organisation*, Macmillan, Basingstoke.

Wilkins, A.L. and Dyer, W.G., Jr (1988), 'Toward culturally sensitive thoeries of culture change', *Academy of Management Review*, Vol. 13, No. 4, pp.522–33.

Williams, K., Haslam, C. and Williams, J. (1992), 'Ford vs Fordism: the beginnings of mass production?', *Work, Employment and Society*, Vol. 6, No. 4, pp.517–55.

Wilmott, H. (1984), 'Images and ideals of managerial work', *Journal of Management Studies*, Vol. 21, pp.349–68.

Wilmott, H. (1987), 'Studying managerial work: a critique and proposal', *Journal of Management Studies*, Vol. 24, pp.248–70.

Wilson, F. (1995), *Organizational Behaviour and Gender*, McGraw-Hill, London.

Wilson, F. (1996), 'Research note. Organizational theory: blind and deaf to gender?', *Organization Studies*, Vol. 17, No. 5, pp.825–42.

Womack, J.P. and Jones, D.P. (1996), *Lean Thinking*, Simon & Schuster, New York.

Womack, J.P., Jones, D.P. and Roos, J. (1990), *The Machine that Changed the World*, Macmillan, Basingstoke.

Woodward, J. (1958), *Management and Technology*, HMSO, London.

Woodward, J. (1965), *Industrial Organization: Theory and Practice*, Oxford University Press, Oxford. Second edition 1980.

Yukl, G. (1994), *Leadership in Organizations*, Prentice Hall, Englewood Cliffs, NJ.

Index